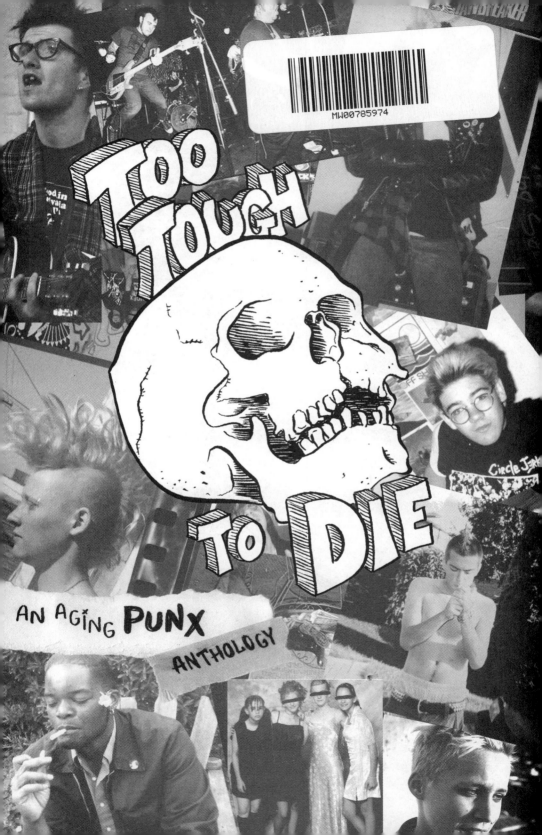

TOO TOUGH TO DIE

AN AGING PUNX ANTHOLOGY

TOO TOUGH TO DIE: An Aging Punx Anthology

published by Birdcage Bottom Books
324-A West 71st Street
New York, NY 10023
U.S. of A.

co-edited by Haleigh Buck & J.T. Yost

Cover art by Haleigh Buck with coloring by J.T. Yost

book design & layout by J.T. Yost

Birdcage Bottom Books logo designed by D.I.Y. guru Michael Lassiter
mlassiter.com

Printed in the U.S. of A.!

first edition: September 2021
ISBN: 978-1-7331509-4-1
LCCN: 2021937123

"Wanna Fight?" by Gideon Kendall originally appeared in "Wait...It Gets Worse #4"

"Family" by CN 'Pinky' Frankenstein originally appeared in "Tears of the Leather-bound Saints" (published by Fantagraphics Books)

"Young and Dumb Inside" by Emily Flake originally appeared in The New Yorker's December 4, 2017 issue

excerpt from "The HIGH DESERT" by James Spooner is from a graphic memoir to be published by Houghton Mifflin Harcourt in Spring 2022.

"Spooner's No Fun" by James Spooner originally appeared in issues of RazorCake fanzine

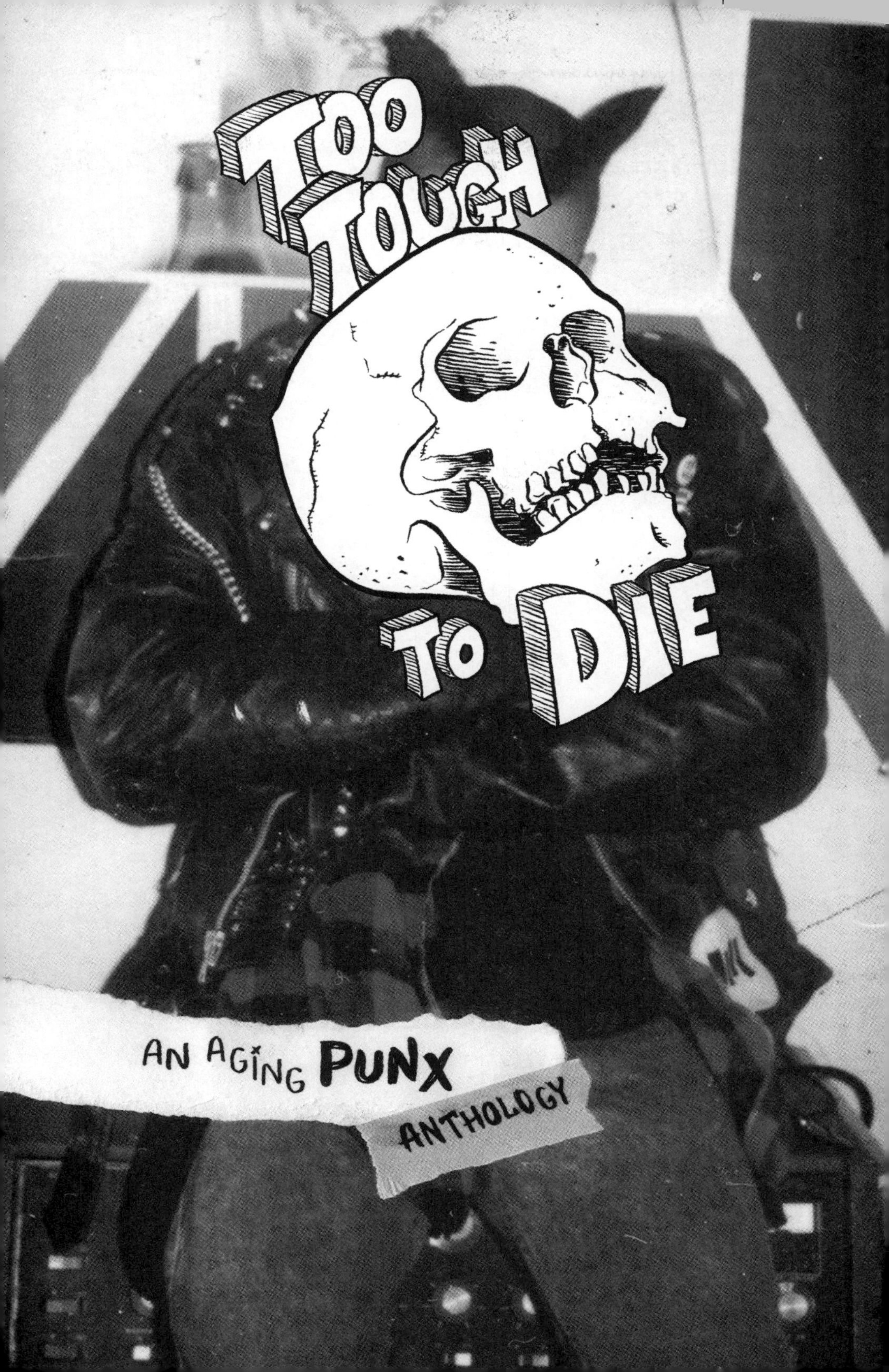
TOO TOUGH
TO DIE
AN AGING PUNX
ANTHOLOGY

A MESSAGE FROM THE EDITORS!

BACK IN SEPTEMBER 2018 AT SPX, I WAS TABLING WITH THE MASTER OF MATINEE, JORDAN JEFFRIES. WHILE SETTING UP FOR THE FIRST MORNING OF THE SHOW, YOU COULD HEAR THE SUBTLE CLICKS, POPS, AND CRACKS ECHOING THROUGHOUT THE CONVENTION HALL, LIKE CRICKETS IN A FEILD. AS I WHIPPED OUT ONE OF MY PRECIOUS PRESCRIPTION LIDOCAINE PATCHES TO PUT ON MY SHOULDER, JORDAN NOTICED HOW MANY OF US NOW WORE CARPAL TUNNEL WRIST BRACES OR HAD THE BEGINNING STAGES OF "ARTIST HUMPS" FROM OUR TWISTED SPINES AND POOR POSTURE. HE COMMENTED ON HOW OLD PUNX NEVER SEEM TO DIE, THEY JUST SLOWLY DETERIORATE. WE COMPARED OUR FAVORITE STRETCHING TECHNIQUES AND THE TRIALS OF BALANCING OVER-THE-COUNTER OR "HIPPY" TREATMENTS. SWAPPING STORIES ABOUT OLD SCARS AND WISHING WE DIDN'T GROW UP ACTING LIKE WE WERE "TOO TOUGH TO DIE" SO WE WOULD HAVE TAKEN BETTER CARE OF OURSELVES WHEN WE WERE YOUNGER. I REMARKED ON HOW RAD IT WOULD BE IF SOMEONE WOULD MAKE A LIDOCAINE BAND PATCH SO I COULD "LOOK COOLER" WHEN I'M IN PAIN. JORDAN KEPT COMING UP WITH HILARIOUS VERSIONS LIKE 4 PATCHES IN THE SHAPE OF BLACK FLAG BARS OR THE LOGO SCREENPRINTED ON IT. CUSTOM WALKING STICKS OR WALKERS, ORTHOPEDIC FAUX-LEATHER BOOTS, SPIKES FOR A JACKET BUT THEY ARE CAPSULES FOR MEDICATIONS, SKATEBOARD WHEELCHAIRS, SHIT LIKE THAT. WE BOUNCED BACK AND FORTH FOR MOST OF THE DAY EVENTUALLY PULLING J.T. YOST INTO OUR NEW COMBINED COMEDY ROUTINE.

— HALEIGH

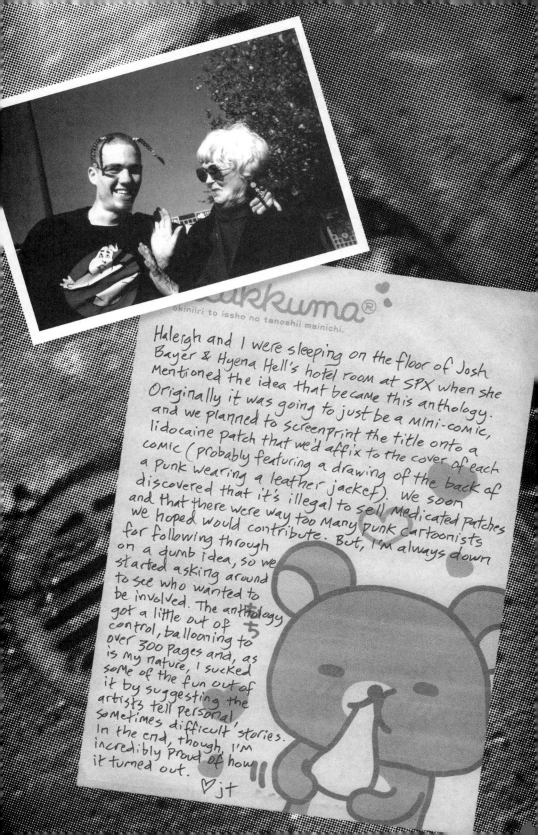

Haleigh and I were sleeping on the floor of Josh Bayer & Hyena Hell's hotel room at SPX when she mentioned the idea that became this anthology. Originally it was going to just be a mini-comic, and we planned to screenprint the title onto a lidocaine patch that we'd affix to the cover of each comic (probably featuring a drawing of the back of a punk wearing a leather jacket). We soon discovered that it's illegal to sell medicated patches and that there were way too many punk cartoonists we hoped would contribute. But, I'm always down for following through on a dumb idea, so we started asking around to see who wanted to be involved. The anthology got a little out of control, ballooning to over 300 pages and, as is my nature, I sucked some of the fun out of it by suggesting the artists tell personal, sometimes difficult, stories. In the end, though, I'm incredibly proud of how it turned out.

♡jt

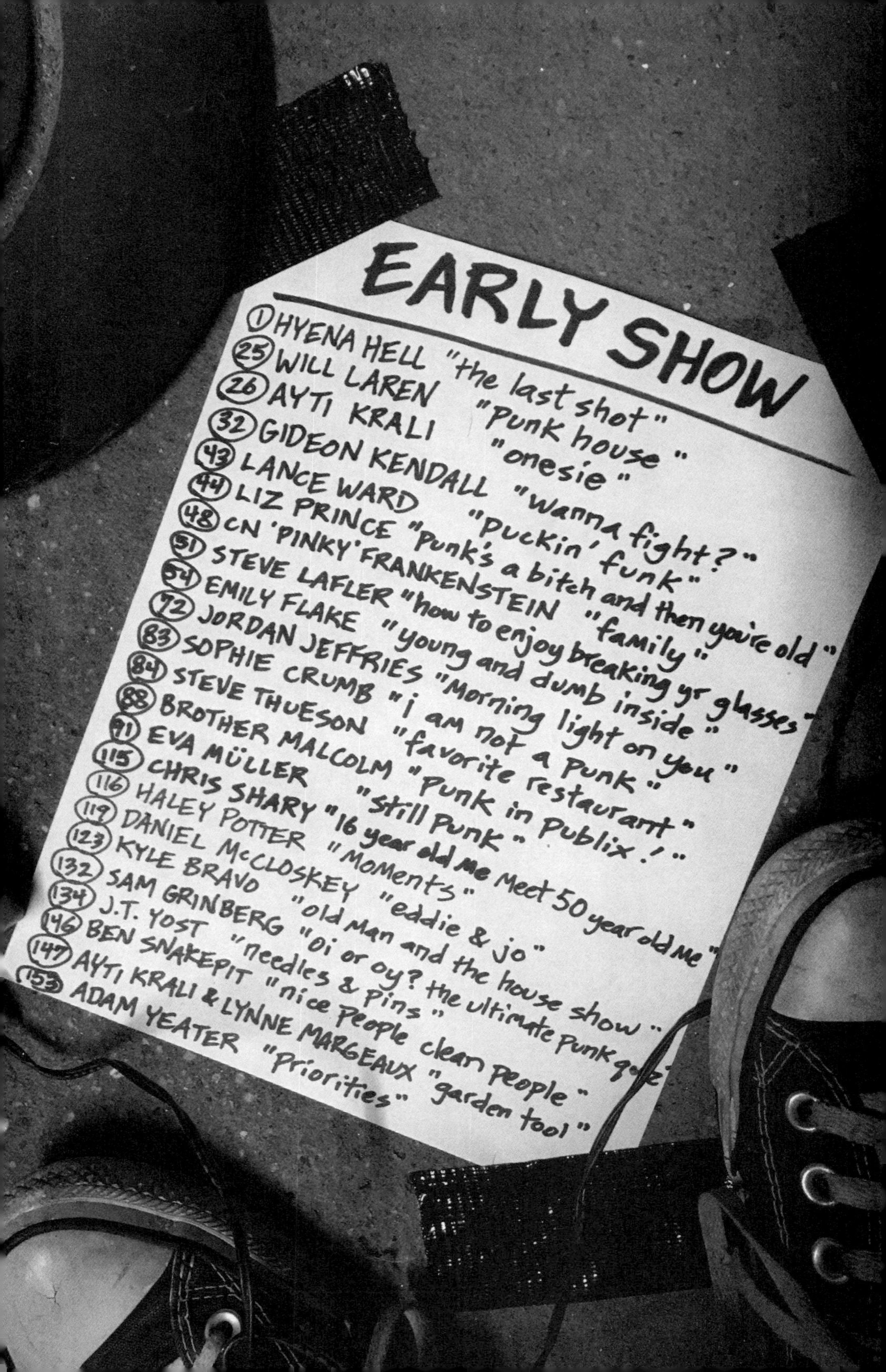
EARLY SHOW
1 HYENA HELL "the last shot"
25 WILL LAREN "Punk house"
26 AYTI KRALI "onesie"
32 GIDEON KENDALL "wanna fight?"
43 LANCE WARD "puckin' funk"
44 LIZ PRINCE "punk's a bitch and then you're old"
48 CN 'PINKY' FRANKENSTEIN "family"
51 STEVE LAFLER "how to enjoy breaking yr glasses"
54 EMILY FLAKE "young and dumb inside"
72 JORDAN JEFFRIES "Morning light on you"
83 SOPHIE CRUMB "i am not a punk"
84 STEVE THUESON "favorite restaurant"
88 BROTHER MALCOLM "Punk in Publix!"
91 EVA MÜLLER "still punk"
115 CHRIS SHARY "16 year old me meet 50 year old me"
116 HALEY POTTER "Moments"
119 DANIEL McCLOSKEY "eddie & jo"
123 KYLE BRAVO "old man and the house show"
132 SAM GRINBERG "oi or oy? the ultimate punk
134 J.T. YOST "needles & pins"
146 BEN SNAKEPIT "nice people clean people"
147 AYTI KRALI & LYNNE MARGEAUX "garden tool"
153 ADAM YEATER "Priorities"

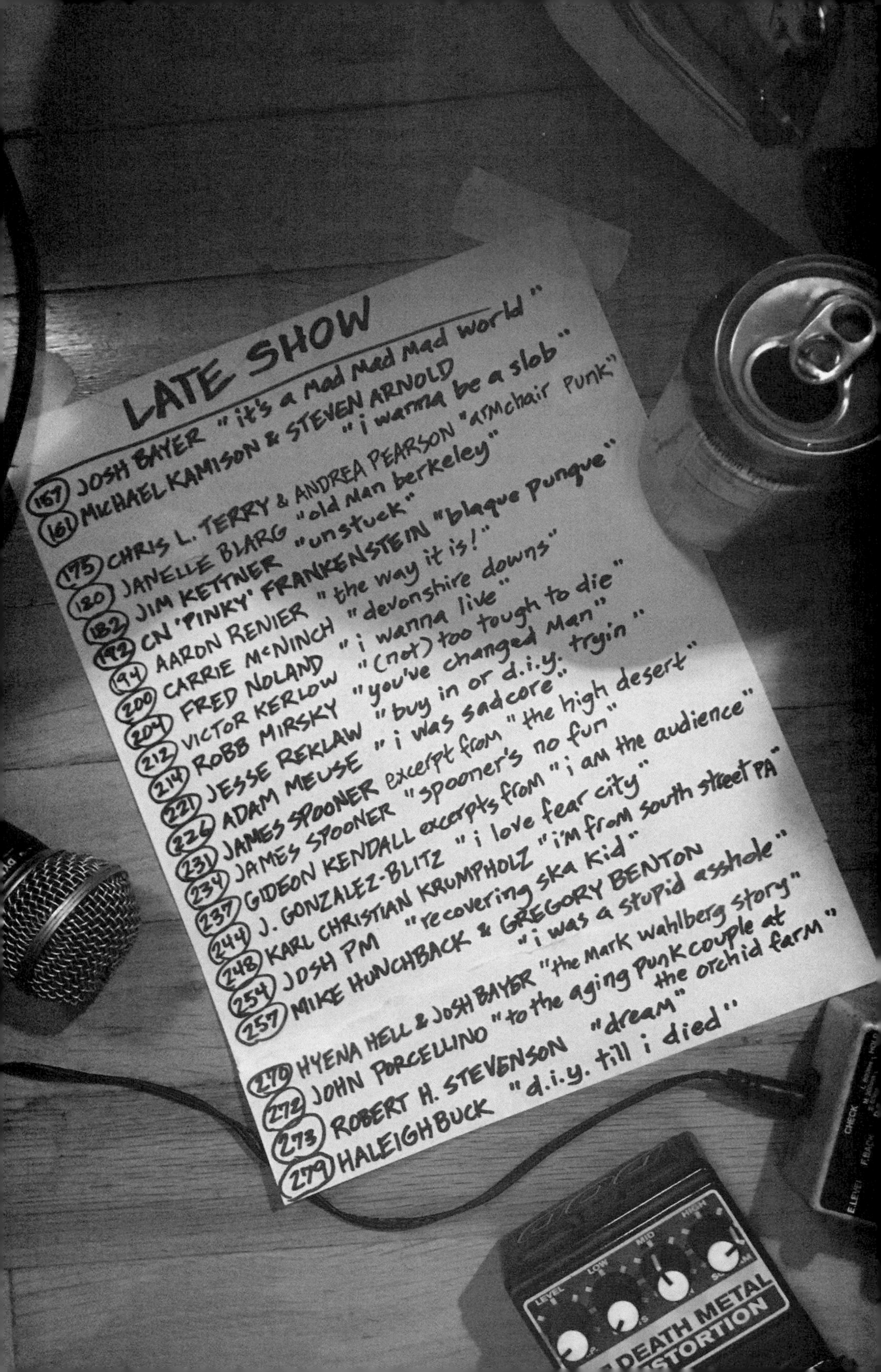
LATE SHOW
157 JOSH BAYER "it's a mad mad mad world"
161 MICHAEL KAMISON & STEVEN ARNOLD "i wanna be a slob"
175 CHRIS L. TERRY & ANDREA PEARSON "armchair punk"
180 JANELLE BLARG "old man berkeley"
182 JIM KETTNER "unstuck"
192 CN 'PINKY' FRANKENSTEIN "blaque punque"
194 AARON RENIER "the way it is!"
200 CARRIE McNINCH "devonshire downs"
204 FRED NOLAND "i wanna live"
212 VICTOR KERLOW "(not) too tough to die"
214 ROBB MIRSKY "you've changed man"
221 JESSE REKLAW "buy in or d.i.y. tryin"
226 ADAM MEUSE "i was sadcore"
231 JAMES SPOONER excerpt from "the high desert"
234 JAMES SPOONER "spooner's no fun"
237 GIDEON KENDALL excerpts from "i am the audience"
244 J. GONZALEZ-BLITZ "i love fear city"
248 KARL CHRISTIAN KRUMPHOLZ "i'm from south street PA"
254 JOSH PM "recovering ska kid"
257 MIKE HUNCHBACK & GREGORY BENTON "i was a stupid asshole"
270 HYENA HELL & JOSH BAYER "the mark wahlberg story"
272 JOHN PORCELLINO "to the aging punk couple at the orchid farm"
273 ROBERT H. STEVENSON "dream"
279 HALEIGHBUCK "d.i.y. till i died"
LEVEL
LOW
MID
HIGH
DEATH METAL
CHECK

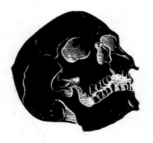

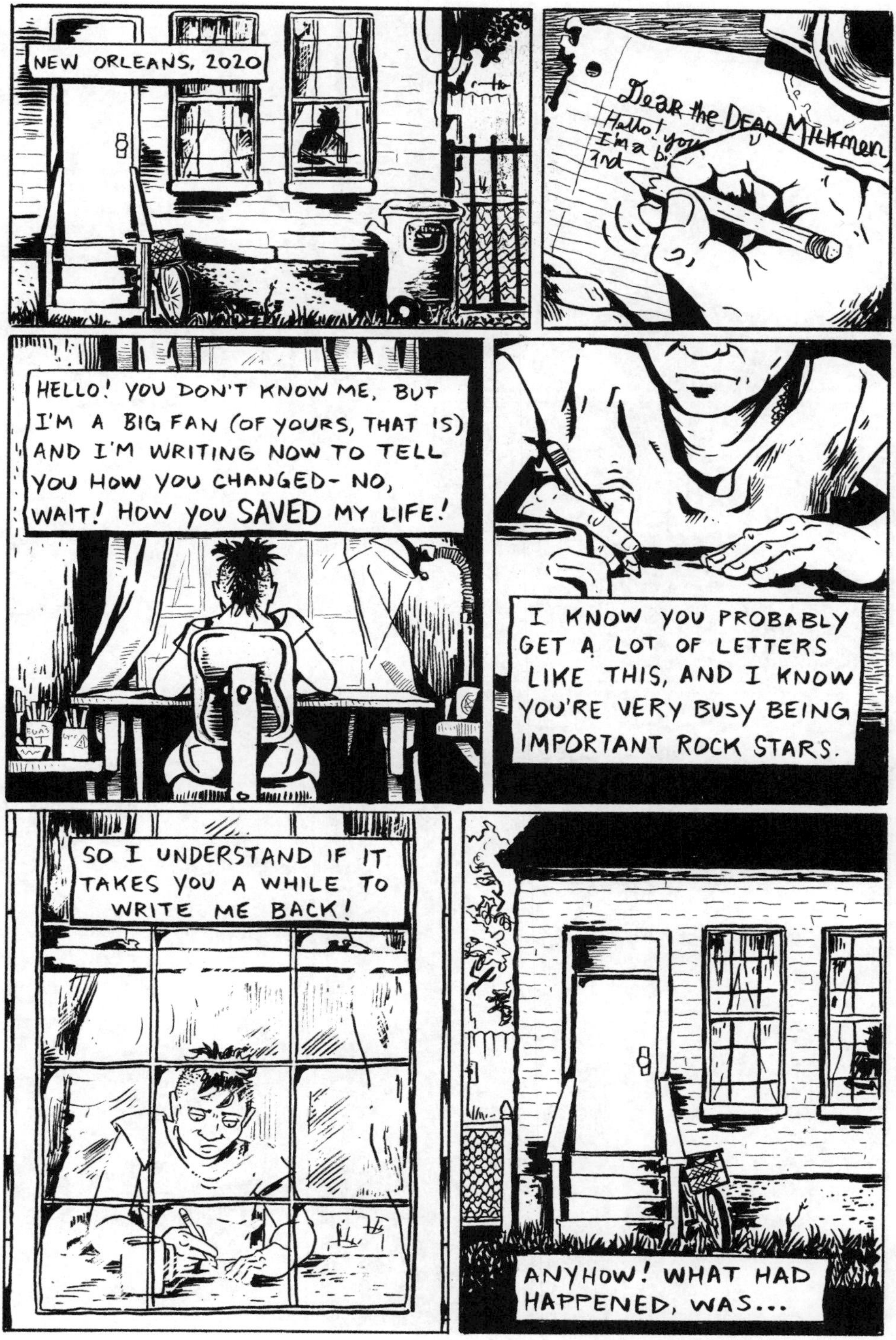
NEW ORLEANS, 2020
Dear the Dead Milkmen
Hello! you
I'm a b
and
HELLO! YOU DON'T KNOW ME, BUT I'M A BIG FAN (OF YOURS, THAT IS) AND I'M WRITING NOW TO TELL YOU HOW YOU CHANGED- NO, WAIT! HOW YOU SAVED MY LIFE!
I KNOW YOU PROBABLY GET A LOT OF LETTERS LIKE THIS, AND I KNOW YOU'RE VERY BUSY BEING IMPORTANT ROCK STARS.
SO I UNDERSTAND IF IT TAKES YOU A WHILE TO WRITE ME BACK!
ANYHOW! WHAT HAD HAPPENED, WAS...

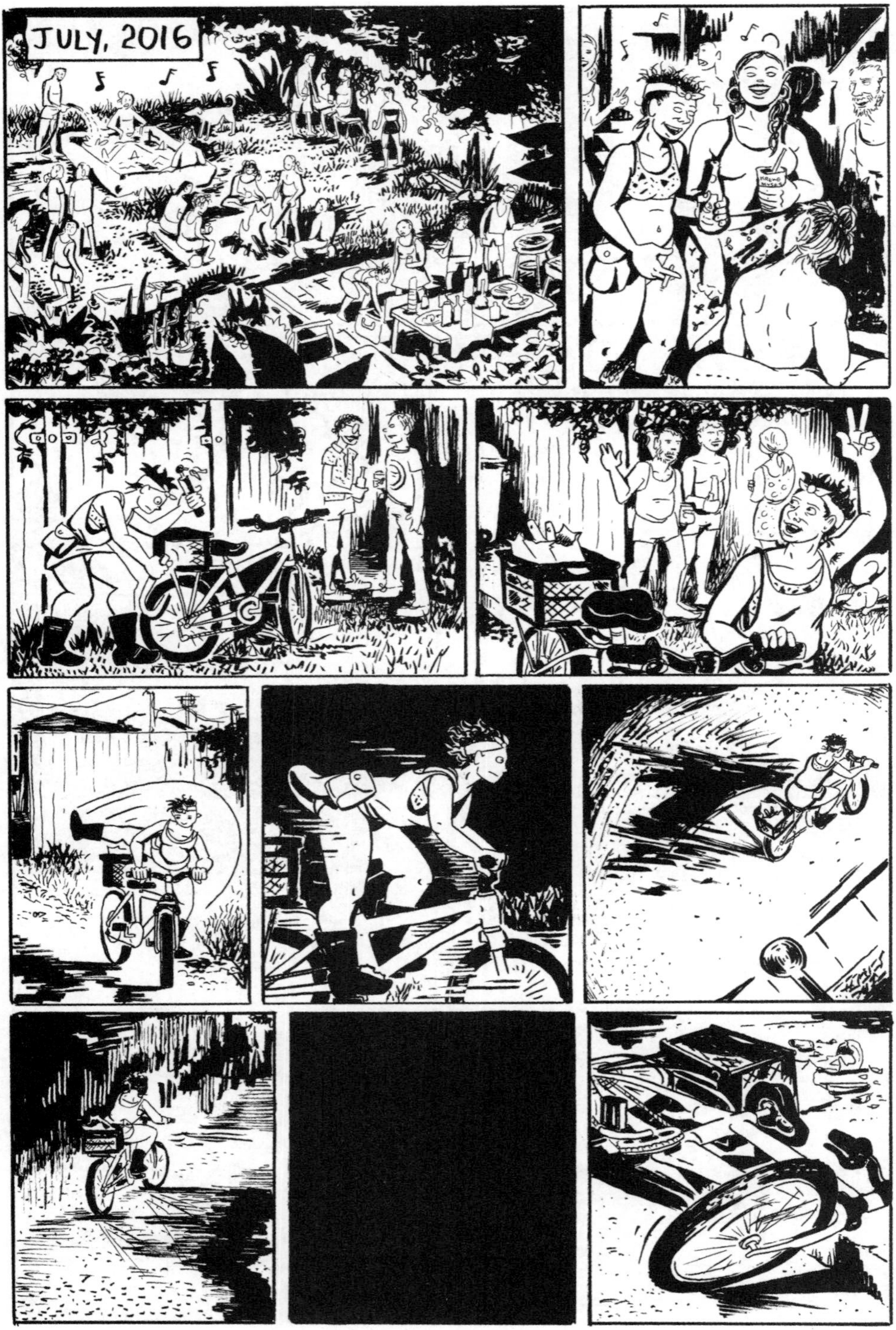
JULY, 2016

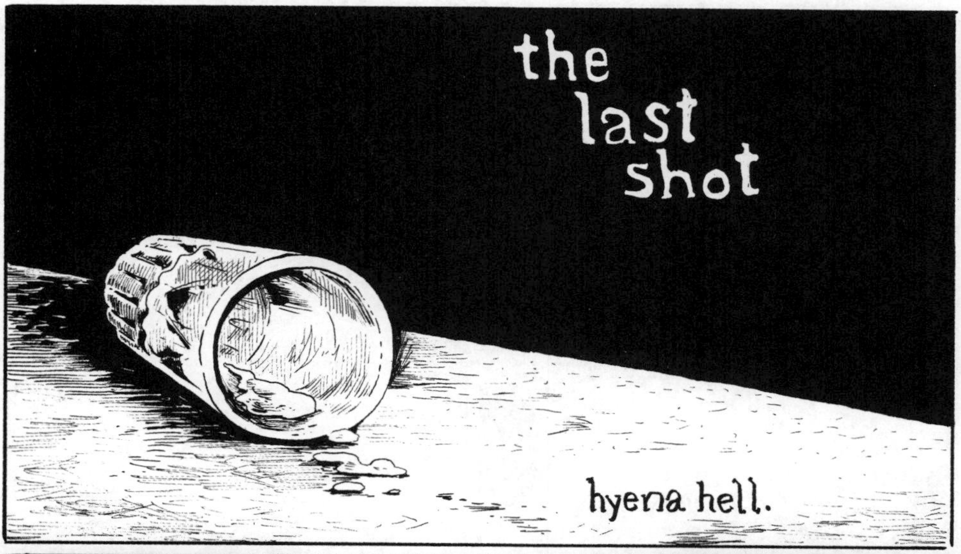
the last shot
hyena hell.

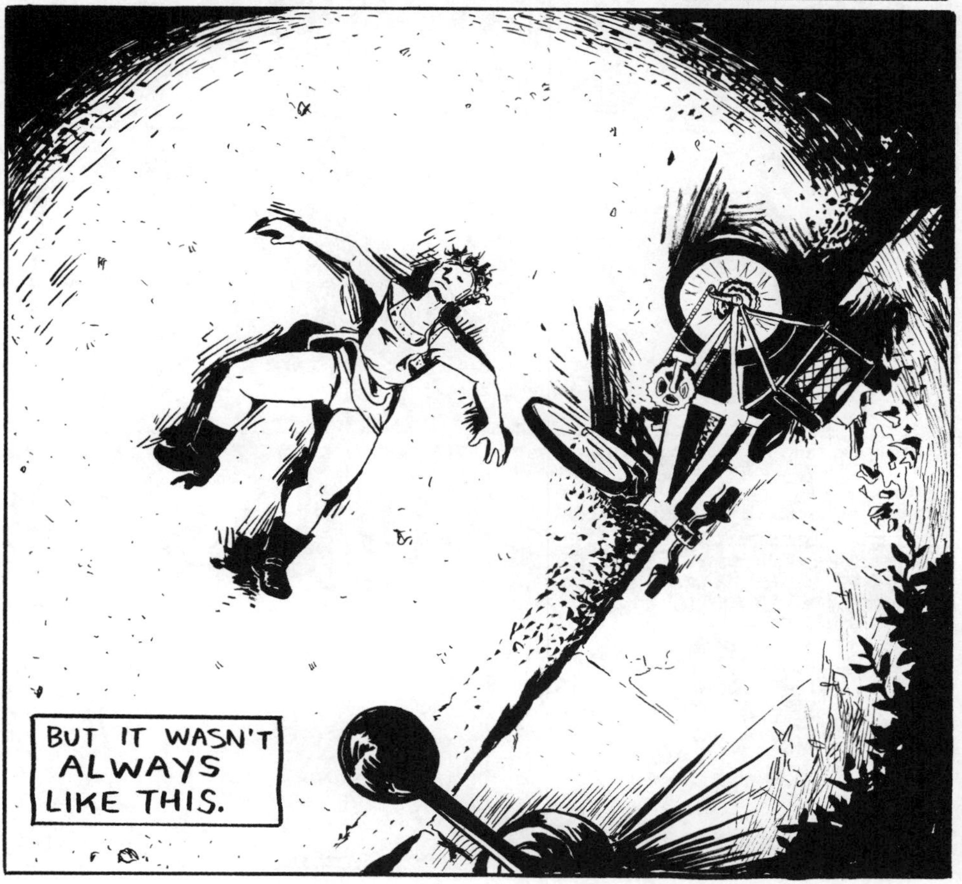
BUT IT WASN'T ALWAYS LIKE THIS.

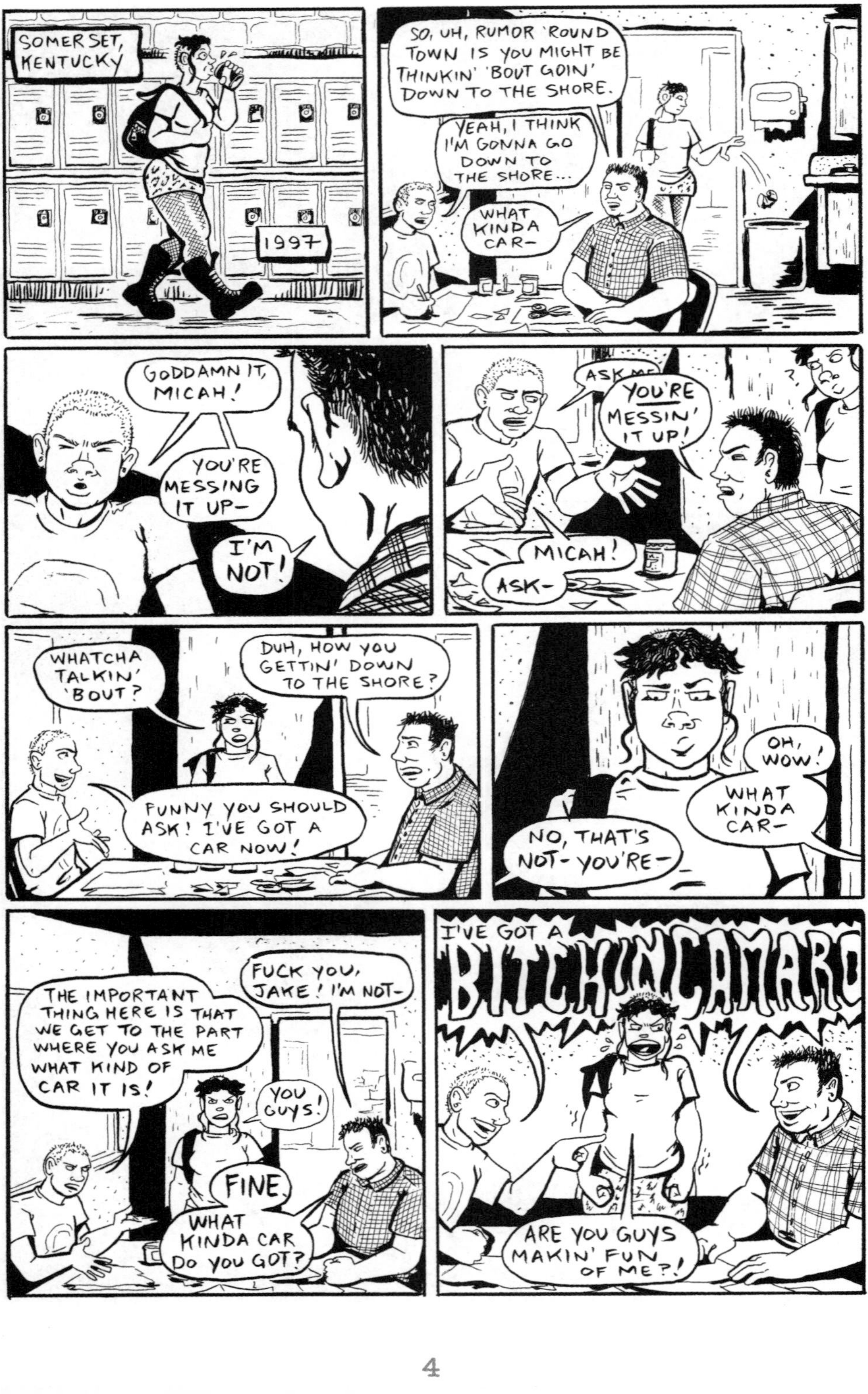
SOMERSET, KENTUCKY
1997
SO, UH, RUMOR 'ROUND TOWN IS YOU MIGHT BE THINKIN' 'BOUT GOIN' DOWN TO THE SHORE.
YEAH, I THINK I'M GONNA GO DOWN TO THE SHORE...
WHAT KINDA CAR-
GODDAMN IT, MICAH!
YOU'RE MESSING IT UP-
I'M NOT!
ASK ME
YOU'RE MESSIN' IT UP!
?
MICAH!
ASK-
WHATCHA TALKIN' 'BOUT?
DUH, HOW YOU GETTIN' DOWN TO THE SHORE?
FUNNY YOU SHOULD ASK! I'VE GOT A CAR NOW!
OH, WOW!
WHAT KINDA CAR-
NO, THAT'S NOT- YOU'RE-
THE IMPORTANT THING HERE IS THAT WE GET TO THE PART WHERE YOU ASK ME WHAT KIND OF CAR IT IS!
FUCK YOU, JAKE! I'M NOT-
YOU GUYS!
FINE.
WHAT KINDA CAR DO YOU GOT?
I'VE GOT A
BITCHIN CAMARO
ARE YOU GUYS MAKIN' FUN OF ME?!

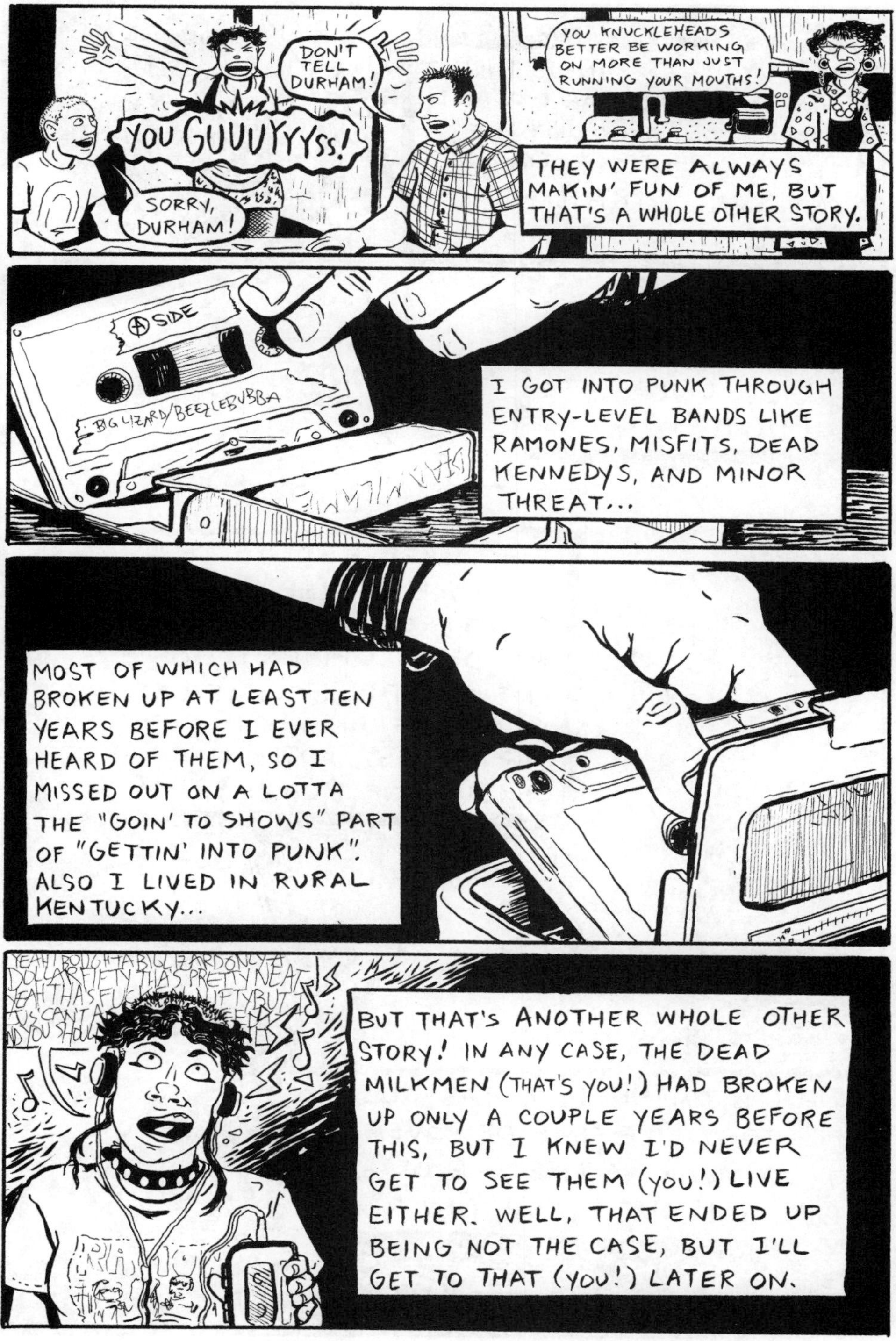
DON'T TELL DURHAM!
YOU GUUUYYYSS!
SORRY, DURHAM!
YOU KNUCKLEHEADS BETTER BE WORKING ON MORE THAN JUST RUNNING YOUR MOUTHS!
THEY WERE ALWAYS MAKIN' FUN OF ME, BUT THAT'S A WHOLE OTHER STORY.
Ⓐ SIDE
BIG LIZARD/BEEZLEBUBBA
I GOT INTO PUNK THROUGH ENTRY-LEVEL BANDS LIKE RAMONES, MISFITS, DEAD KENNEDYS, AND MINOR THREAT...
MOST OF WHICH HAD BROKEN UP AT LEAST TEN YEARS BEFORE I EVER HEARD OF THEM, SO I MISSED OUT ON A LOTTA THE "GOIN' TO SHOWS" PART OF "GETTIN' INTO PUNK". ALSO I LIVED IN RURAL KENTUCKY...
BUT THAT'S ANOTHER WHOLE OTHER STORY! IN ANY CASE, THE DEAD MILKMEN (THAT'S YOU!) HAD BROKEN UP ONLY A COUPLE YEARS BEFORE THIS, BUT I KNEW I'D NEVER GET TO SEE THEM (YOU!) LIVE EITHER. WELL, THAT ENDED UP BEING NOT THE CASE, BUT I'LL GET TO THAT (YOU!) LATER ON.

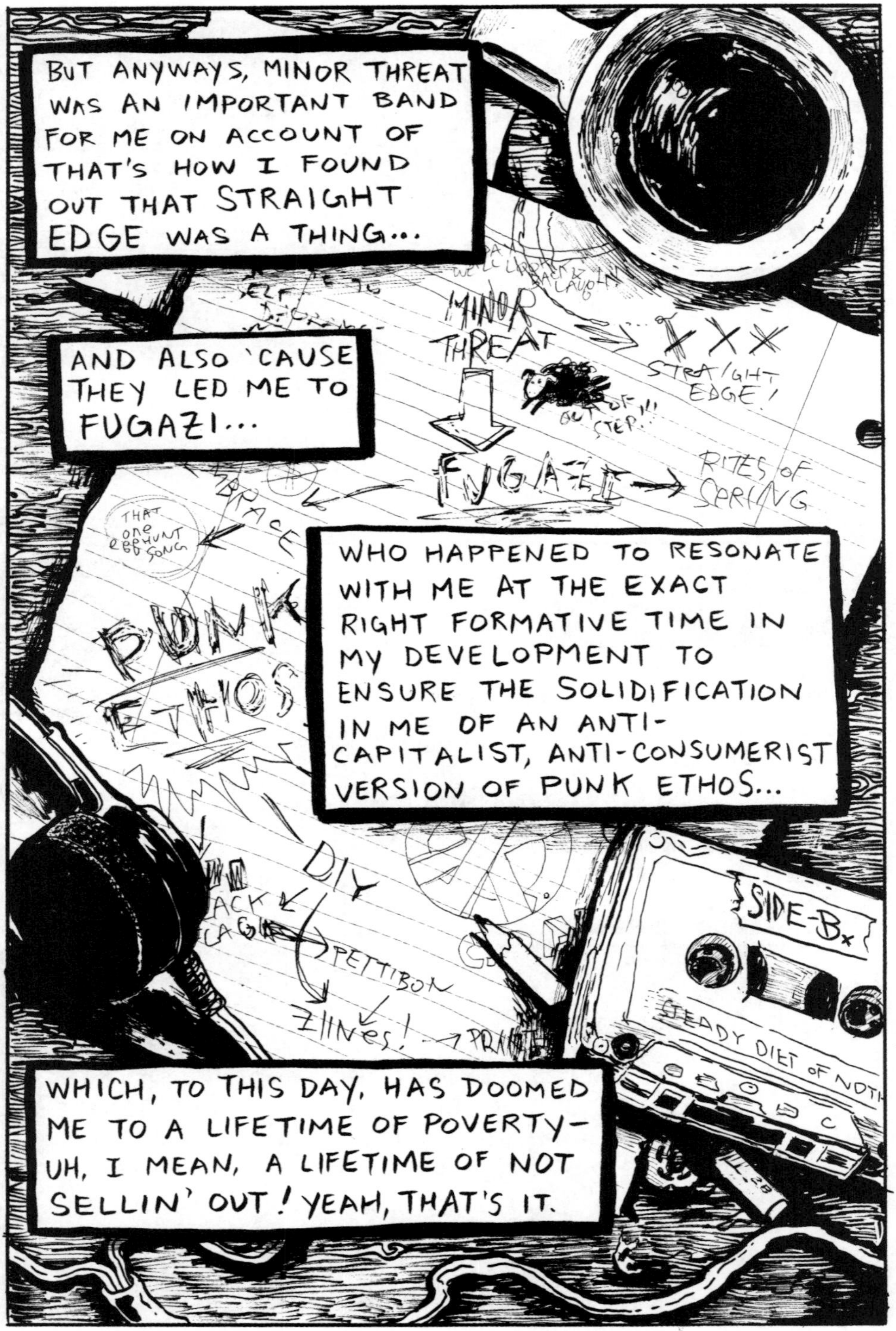
BUT ANYWAYS, MINOR THREAT WAS AN IMPORTANT BAND FOR ME ON ACCOUNT OF THAT'S HOW I FOUND OUT THAT STRAIGHT EDGE WAS A THING...
MINOR THREAT
XXX
STRAIGHT EDGE!
OUT OF STEP!!
AND ALSO 'CAUSE THEY LED ME TO FUGAZI...
FUGAZI
RITES OF SPRING
WHO HAPPENED TO RESONATE WITH ME AT THE EXACT RIGHT FORMATIVE TIME IN MY DEVELOPMENT TO ENSURE THE SOLIDIFICATION IN ME OF AN ANTI-CAPITALIST, ANTI-CONSUMERIST VERSION OF PUNK ETHOS...
PUNK ETHOS
DIY
PETTIBON
ZINES!
SIDE-B
STEADY DIET OF NOTH
WHICH, TO THIS DAY, HAS DOOMED ME TO A LIFETIME OF POVERTY— UH, I MEAN, A LIFETIME OF NOT SELLIN' OUT! YEAH, THAT'S IT.

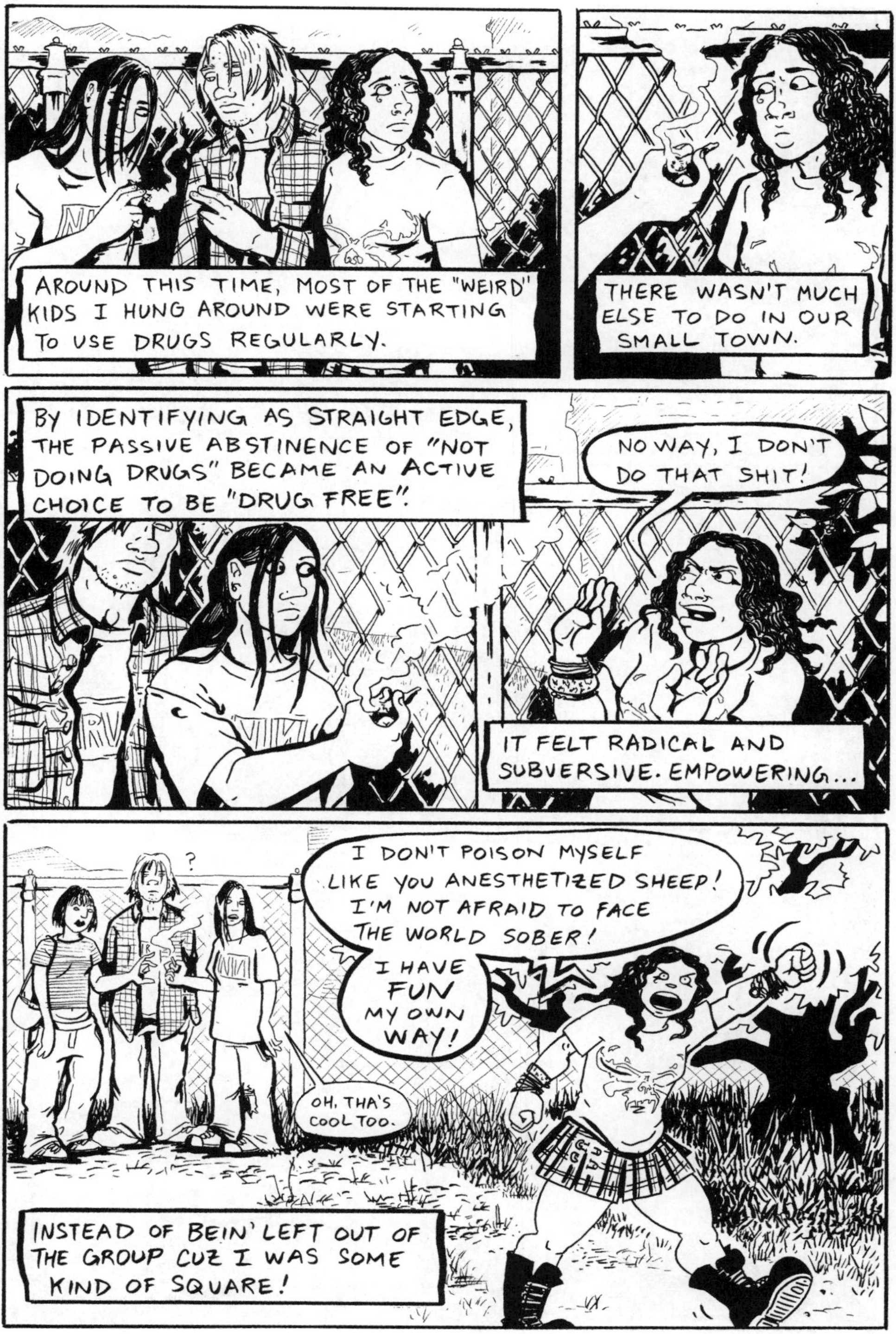
AROUND THIS TIME, MOST OF THE "WEIRD" KIDS I HUNG AROUND WERE STARTING TO USE DRUGS REGULARLY.
THERE WASN'T MUCH ELSE TO DO IN OUR SMALL TOWN.
BY IDENTIFYING AS STRAIGHT EDGE, THE PASSIVE ABSTINENCE OF "NOT DOING DRUGS" BECAME AN ACTIVE CHOICE TO BE "DRUG FREE".
NO WAY, I DON'T DO THAT SHIT!
IT FELT RADICAL AND SUBVERSIVE. EMPOWERING...
?
I DON'T POISON MYSELF LIKE YOU ANESTHETIZED SHEEP! I'M NOT AFRAID TO FACE THE WORLD SOBER!
I HAVE FUN MY OWN WAY!
OH, THA'S COOL TOO.
INSTEAD OF BEIN' LEFT OUT OF THE GROUP CUZ I WAS SOME KIND OF SQUARE!

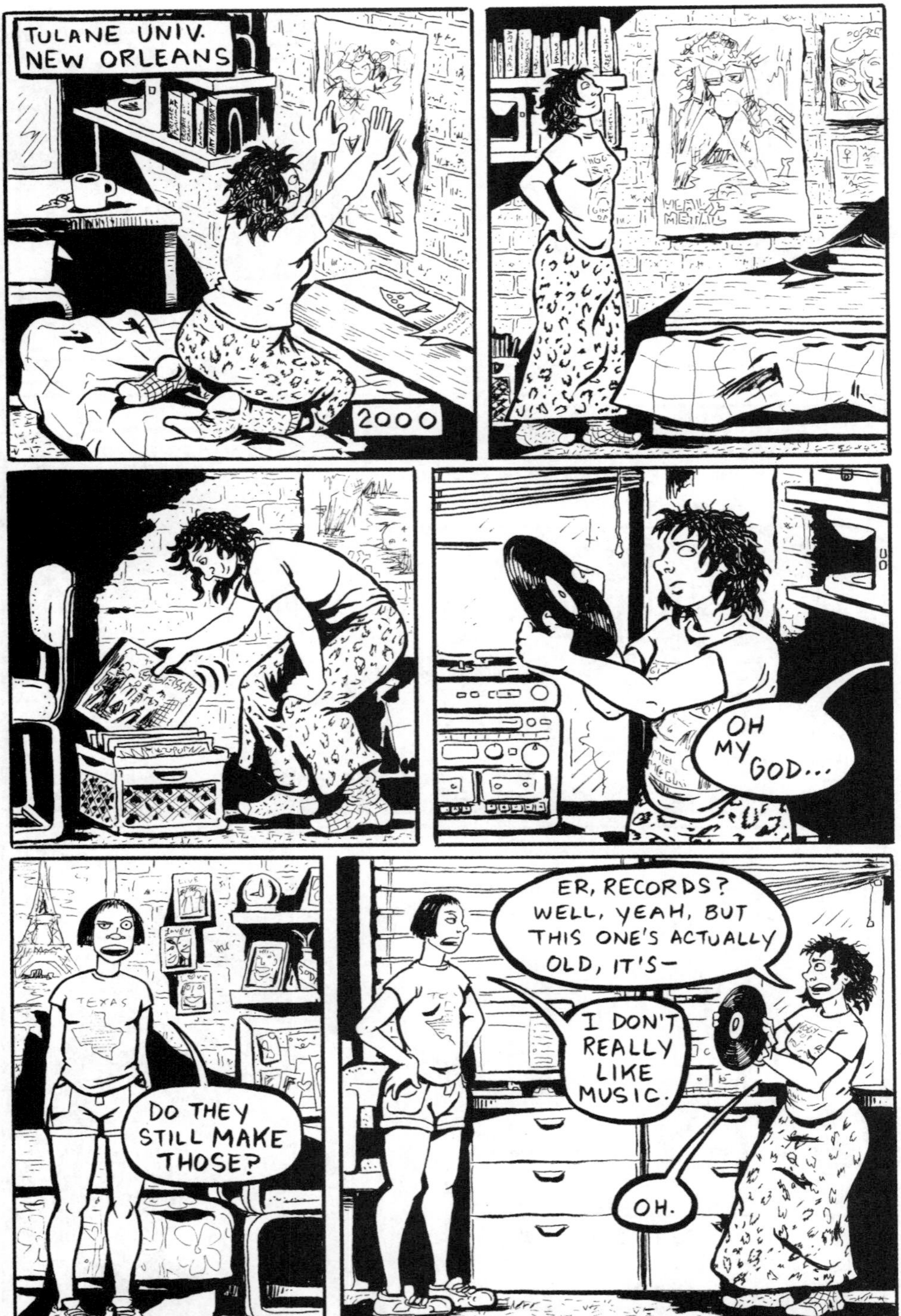
TULANE UNIV.
NEW ORLEANS
2000
OH MY GOD...
DO THEY STILL MAKE THOSE?
ER, RECORDS? WELL, YEAH, BUT THIS ONE'S ACTUALLY OLD, IT'S—
I DON'T REALLY LIKE MUSIC.
OH.

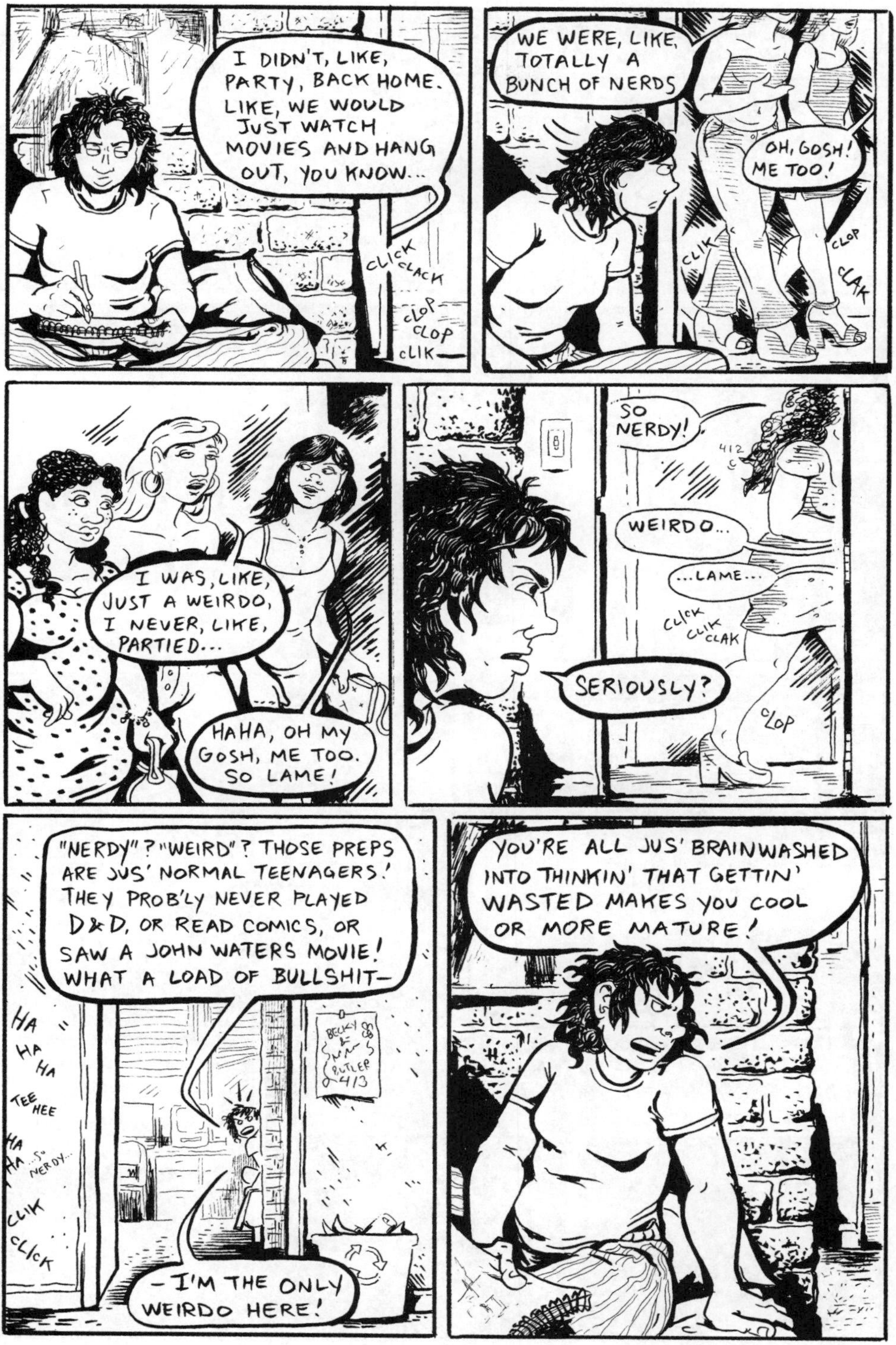
I DIDN'T, LIKE, PARTY, BACK HOME. LIKE, WE WOULD JUST WATCH MOVIES AND HANG OUT, YOU KNOW...
CLICK CLACK
CLOP CLOP CLIK
WE WERE, LIKE, TOTALLY A BUNCH OF NERDS
OH, GOSH! ME TOO!
CLIK
CLOP CLAK
I WAS, LIKE, JUST A WEIRDO, I NEVER, LIKE, PARTIED...
HAHA, OH MY GOSH, ME TOO. SO LAME!
SO NERDY!
WEIRDO...
...LAME...
CLICK CLIK CLAK
SERIOUSLY?
CLOP
"NERDY"? "WEIRD"? THOSE PREPS ARE JUS' NORMAL TEENAGERS! THEY PROB'LY NEVER PLAYED D&D, OR READ COMICS, OR SAW A JOHN WATERS MOVIE! WHAT A LOAD OF BULLSHIT—
HA HA HA
TEE HEE
HA HA ...SO NERDY...
CLIK CLICK
—I'M THE ONLY WEIRDO HERE!
YOU'RE ALL JUS' BRAINWASHED INTO THINKIN' THAT GETTIN' WASTED MAKES YOU COOL OR MORE MATURE!

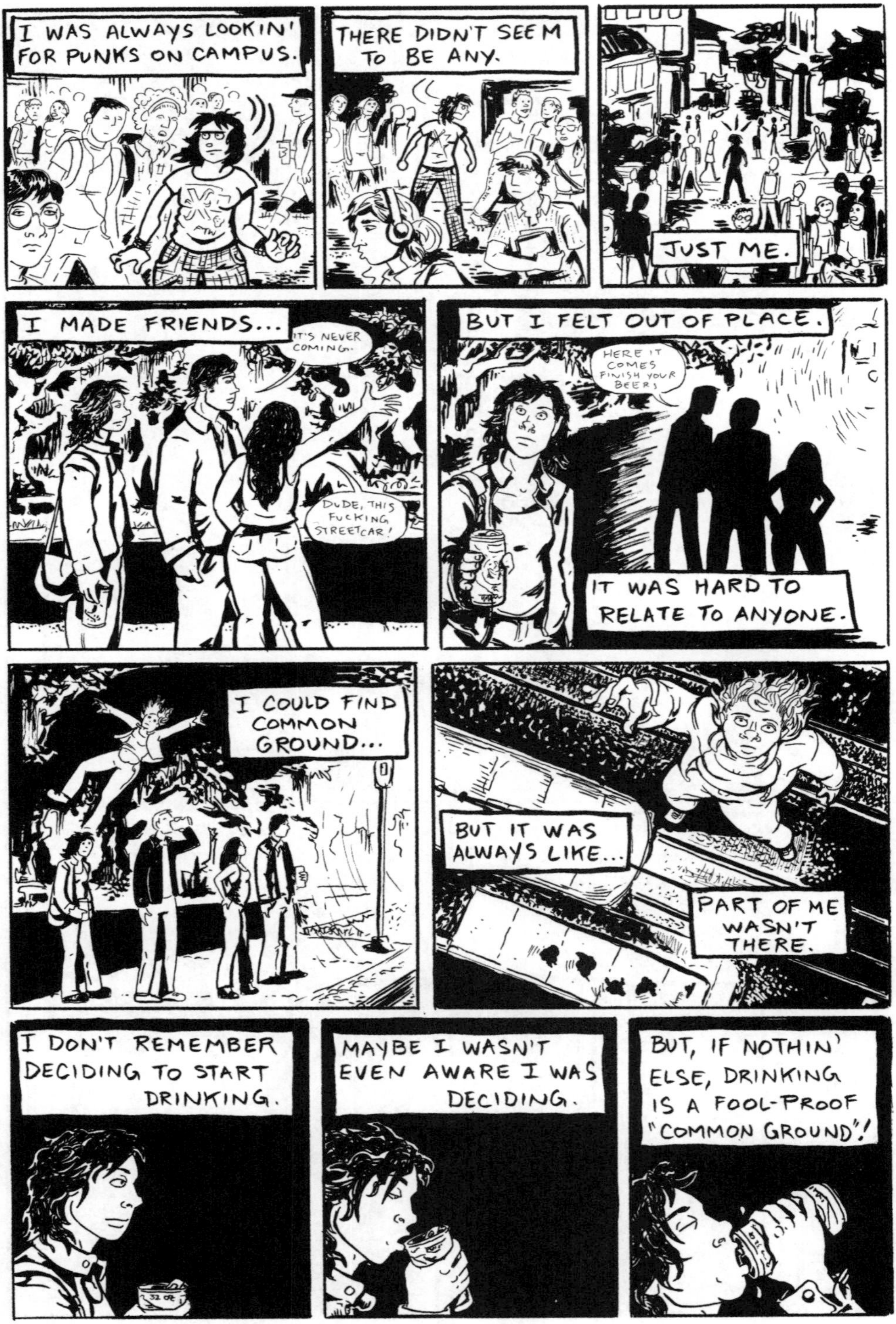
I WAS ALWAYS LOOKIN' FOR PUNKS ON CAMPUS.
THERE DIDN'T SEEM TO BE ANY.
JUST ME.
I MADE FRIENDS...
IT'S NEVER COMING.
DUDE, THIS FUCKING STREETCAR!
BUT I FELT OUT OF PLACE.
HERE IT COMES FINISH YOUR BEERS
IT WAS HARD TO RELATE TO ANYONE.
I COULD FIND COMMON GROUND...
BUT IT WAS ALWAYS LIKE...
PART OF ME WASN'T THERE.
I DON'T REMEMBER DECIDING TO START DRINKING.
MAYBE I WASN'T EVEN AWARE I WAS DECIDING.
BUT, IF NOTHIN' ELSE, DRINKING IS A FOOL-PROOF "COMMON GROUND"!

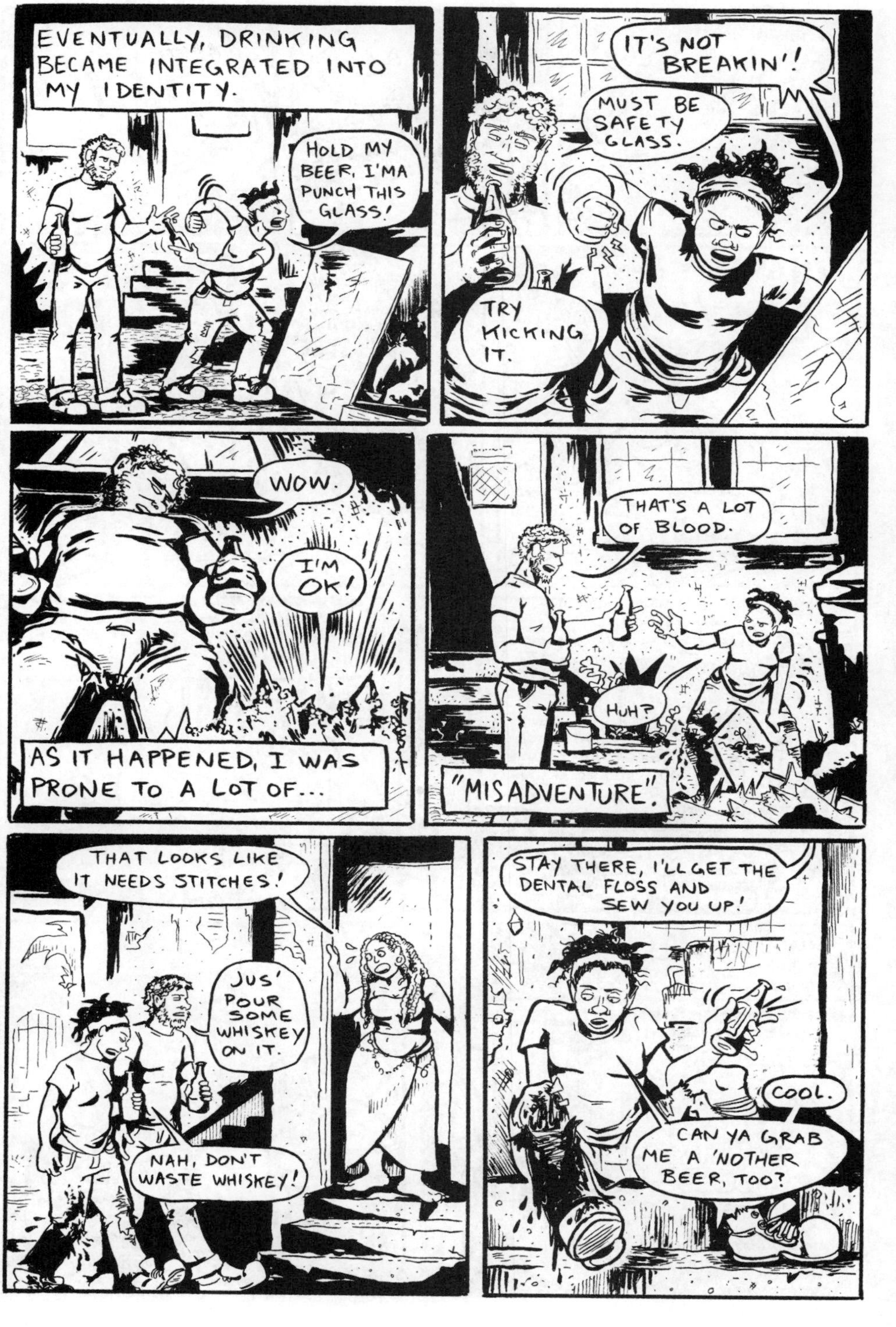
EVENTUALLY, DRINKING BECAME INTEGRATED INTO MY IDENTITY.
HOLD MY BEER, I'MA PUNCH THIS GLASS!
IT'S NOT BREAKIN'!
MUST BE SAFETY GLASS.
TRY KICKING IT.
WOW.
I'M OK!
AS IT HAPPENED, I WAS PRONE TO A LOT OF...
THAT'S A LOT OF BLOOD.
HUH?
"MISADVENTURE".
THAT LOOKS LIKE IT NEEDS STITCHES!
JUS' POUR SOME WHISKEY ON IT.
NAH, DON'T WASTE WHISKEY!
STAY THERE, I'LL GET THE DENTAL FLOSS AND SEW YOU UP!
COOL.
CAN YA GRAB ME A 'NOTHER BEER, TOO?

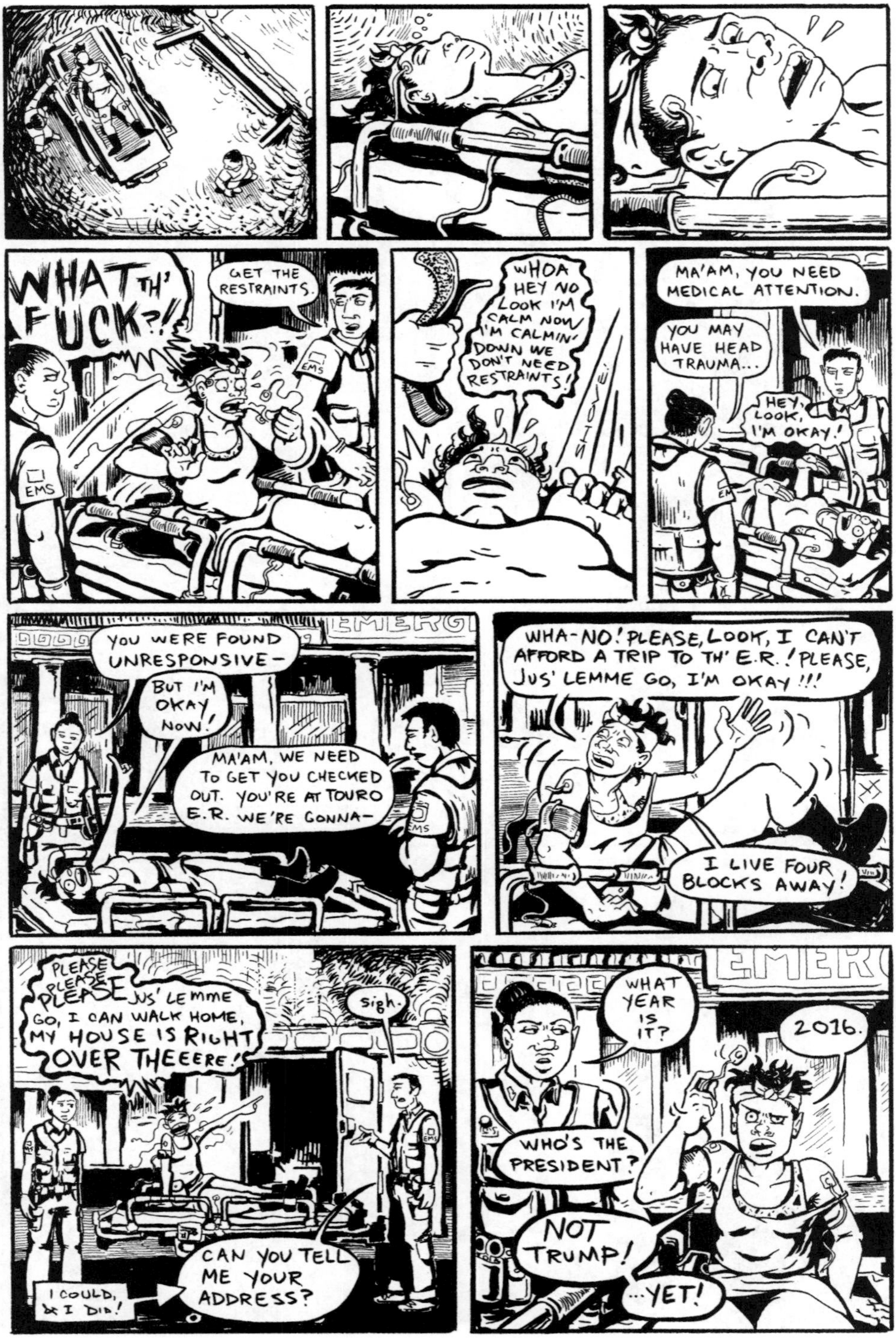
WHAT TH' FUCK?!
GET THE RESTRAINTS.
WHOA HEY NO LOOK I'M CALM NOW I'M CALMIN' DOWN WE DON'T NEED RESTRAINTS!
SHOVE!
MA'AM, YOU NEED MEDICAL ATTENTION.
YOU MAY HAVE HEAD TRAUMA...
HEY, LOOK, I'M OKAY!
EMERG
YOU WERE FOUND UNRESPONSIVE–
BUT I'M OKAY NOW!
MA'AM, WE NEED TO GET YOU CHECKED OUT. YOU'RE AT TOURO E.R. WE'RE GONNA–
WHA-NO! PLEASE, LOOK, I CAN'T AFFORD A TRIP TO TH' E.R.! PLEASE, JUS' LEMME GO, I'M OKAY!!!
I LIVE FOUR BLOCKS AWAY!
PLEASE PLEASE PLEASE JUS' LEMME GO, I CAN WALK HOME, MY HOUSE IS RIGHT OVER THEEERE!
Sigh.
CAN YOU TELL ME YOUR ADDRESS?
I COULD, & I DID!
EMER
WHAT YEAR IS IT?
2016.
WHO'S THE PRESIDENT?
NOT TRUMP!
...YET!

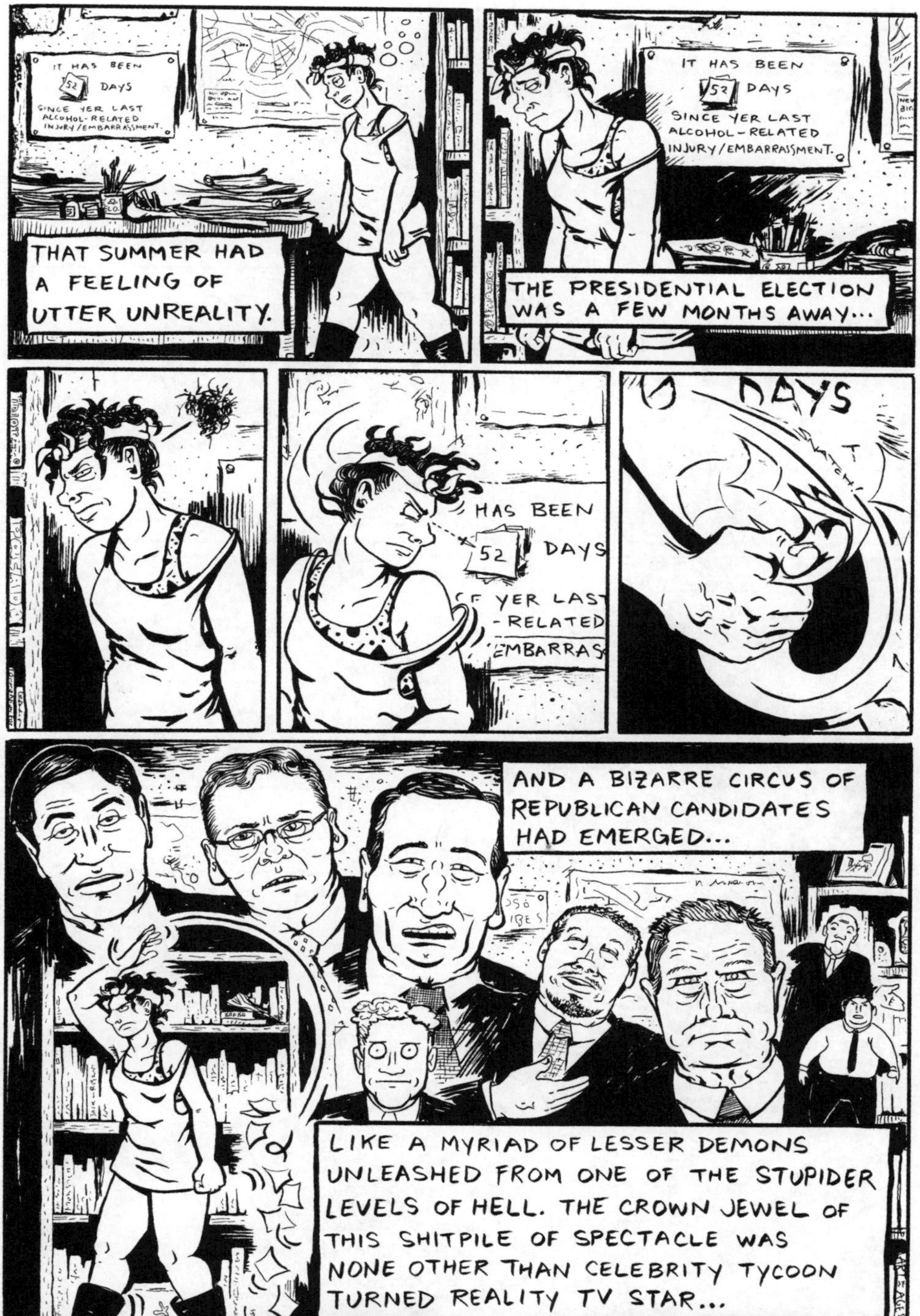
IT HAS BEEN
52
DAYS
SINCE YER LAST
ALCOHOL-RELATED
INJURY/EMBARRASSMENT.
THAT SUMMER HAD A FEELING OF UTTER UNREALITY.
IT HAS BEEN
52
DAYS
SINCE YER LAST
ALCOHOL-RELATED
INJURY/EMBARRASSMENT.
THE PRESIDENTIAL ELECTION WAS A FEW MONTHS AWAY...
HAS BEEN
52
DAYS
YER LAST
-RELATED
EMBARRAS
DAYS
AND A BIZARRE CIRCUS OF REPUBLICAN CANDIDATES HAD EMERGED...
LIKE A MYRIAD OF LESSER DEMONS UNLEASHED FROM ONE OF THE STUPIDER LEVELS OF HELL. THE CROWN JEWEL OF THIS SHITPILE OF SPECTACLE WAS NONE OTHER THAN CELEBRITY TYCOON TURNED REALITY TV STAR...

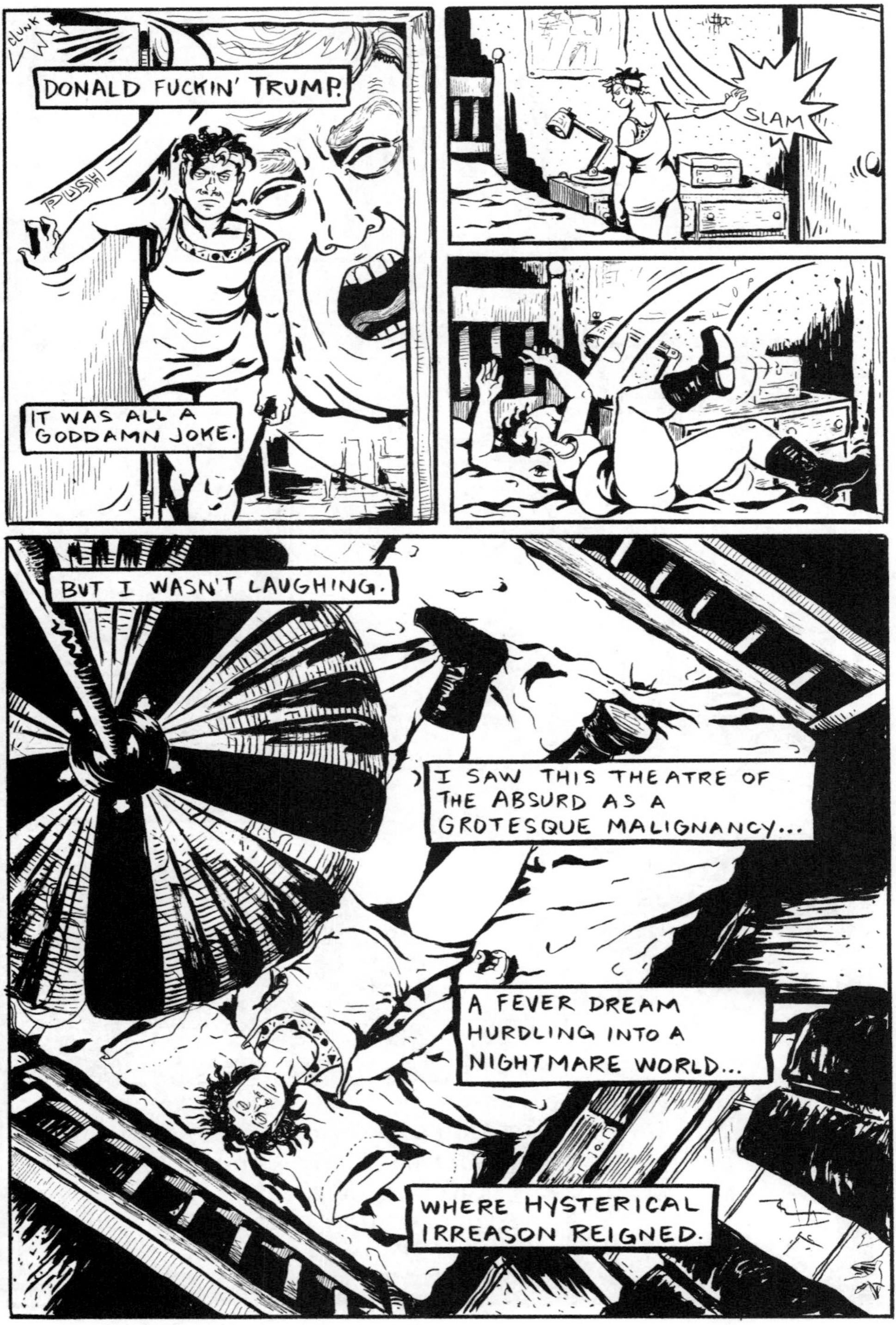
CLUNK
DONALD FUCKIN' TRUMP.
PUSH
IT WAS ALL A GODDAMN JOKE.
SLAM
FLOP
BUT I WASN'T LAUGHING.
I SAW THIS THEATRE OF THE ABSURD AS A GROTESQUE MALIGNANCY...
A FEVER DREAM HURDLING INTO A NIGHTMARE WORLD...
WHERE HYSTERICAL IRREASON REIGNED.

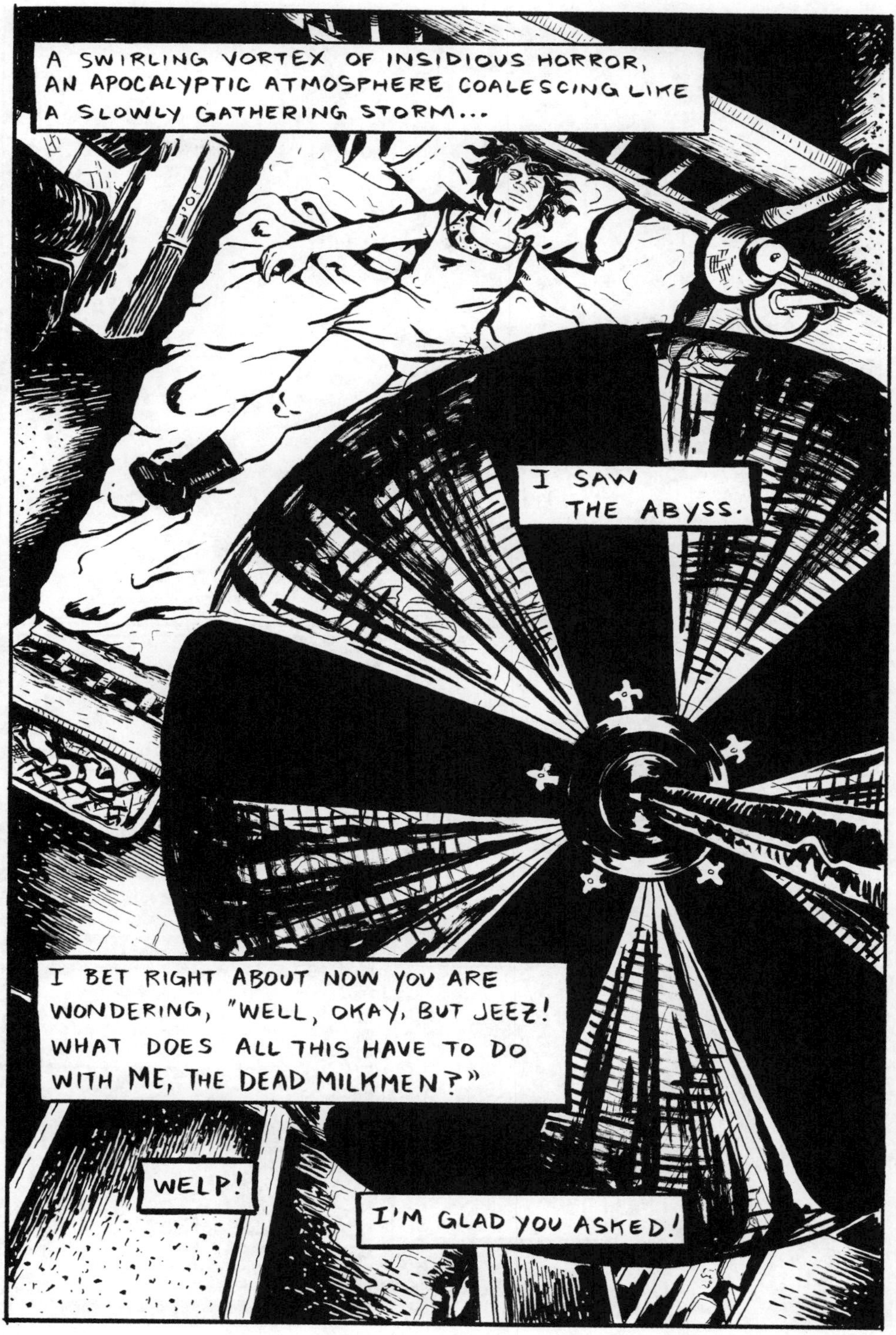
A SWIRLING VORTEX OF INSIDIOUS HORROR, AN APOCALYPTIC ATMOSPHERE COALESCING LIKE A SLOWLY GATHERING STORM...
I SAW THE ABYSS.
I BET RIGHT ABOUT NOW YOU ARE WONDERING, "WELL, OKAY, BUT JEEZ! WHAT DOES ALL THIS HAVE TO DO WITH ME, THE DEAD MILKMEN?"
WELP!
I'M GLAD YOU ASKED!

NOVEMBER 6TH

HOLY SHIT DUDE

FUCK FUCK FUCK FUUUCCK FUCK fuck

DUDE!!!

FUCK DUDE TH' DEAD MILKMEN ARE PLAYIN' TIPITINA'S TONIGHT

SLAP

TONIGHT!

ARE... YOU... OK?

SOMEHOW, AFTER 20 YEARS OF GOIN' TO SHOWS, I STILL THINK I NEED TO BE THERE AT THE EXACT TIME THAT THE POSTER SAYS IT STARTS...

RIGHT... NOW WHAT?

SO, YOU KNOW— LIKE FOUR HOURS EARLY.

THIS IS HOW IT'S ALWAYS BEEN.

THIS IS HOW IT'S ALWAYS GONNA BE.

WELL, GUESS AS LONG AS I'LL BE WAITIN' A WHILE, I MIGHT AS WELL HAVE A BEER OR TWO OR FIVE... YEAH, I'LL KEEP IT OPEN.

IT'S ALMOST LIKE VENUES DO IT ON PURPOSE, FOR SOME REASON!

16

ANOTHER PRE-SHOW TRAP I ALWAYS FALL INTO: A VAGUE ACQUAINTANCE WILL WAYLAY ME, INVITING ME TO JOIN THEIR ENTOURAGE...

WHA'S THEIR NAME...?

ARE YOU HERE BY YOURSELF?! COME STAND WITH US!

ONLY TO IMMEDIATELY BAIL AND LEAVE ME TO CONTEND WITH THE DREGS OF SAID ENTOURAGE.

OH, I SEE MY FRIEND—

—BETTER GO SAY HI!

SO, UM, YEAH. I'M PRETTY STOKED FOR THIS SHOW.

I FUCKIN' LOVE THIS BAND.

I DON'T REALLY LIKE MUSIC.

OH.

HEEY, I SEE MY FRIEND— BETTER GO SAY HI!

AND I'M STUCK MAKIN' SMALL TALK WITH SOME STRANGER UNTIL I CAN BAIL ON THEM TO GO BACK TO STANDING ALONE BY THAT ONE ILL-PLACED AND SEEMINGLY PURPOSELESS POST THAT EXISTS IN EVERY CLUB.

THIS PARTICULAR CLUB WAS BETTER KNOWN FOR **FUNK** THAN **PUNK**...

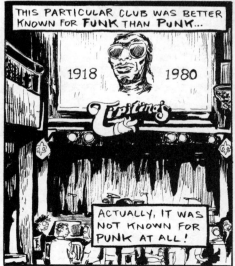

1918   1980

Tipitina's

ACTUALLY, IT WAS NOT KNOWN FOR PUNK AT ALL!

WHICH WAS PROBABLY WHY, BY ALL EVIDENCE, THEY'D TAKEN EVERY PRECAUTION TO ENSURE THE MOSTLY MIDDLE-AGED CROWD WAS KEPT UNDER CONTROL!

SHOOT! ARE YOU GONNA STAND THERE THE WHOLE SHOW?

SECURITY

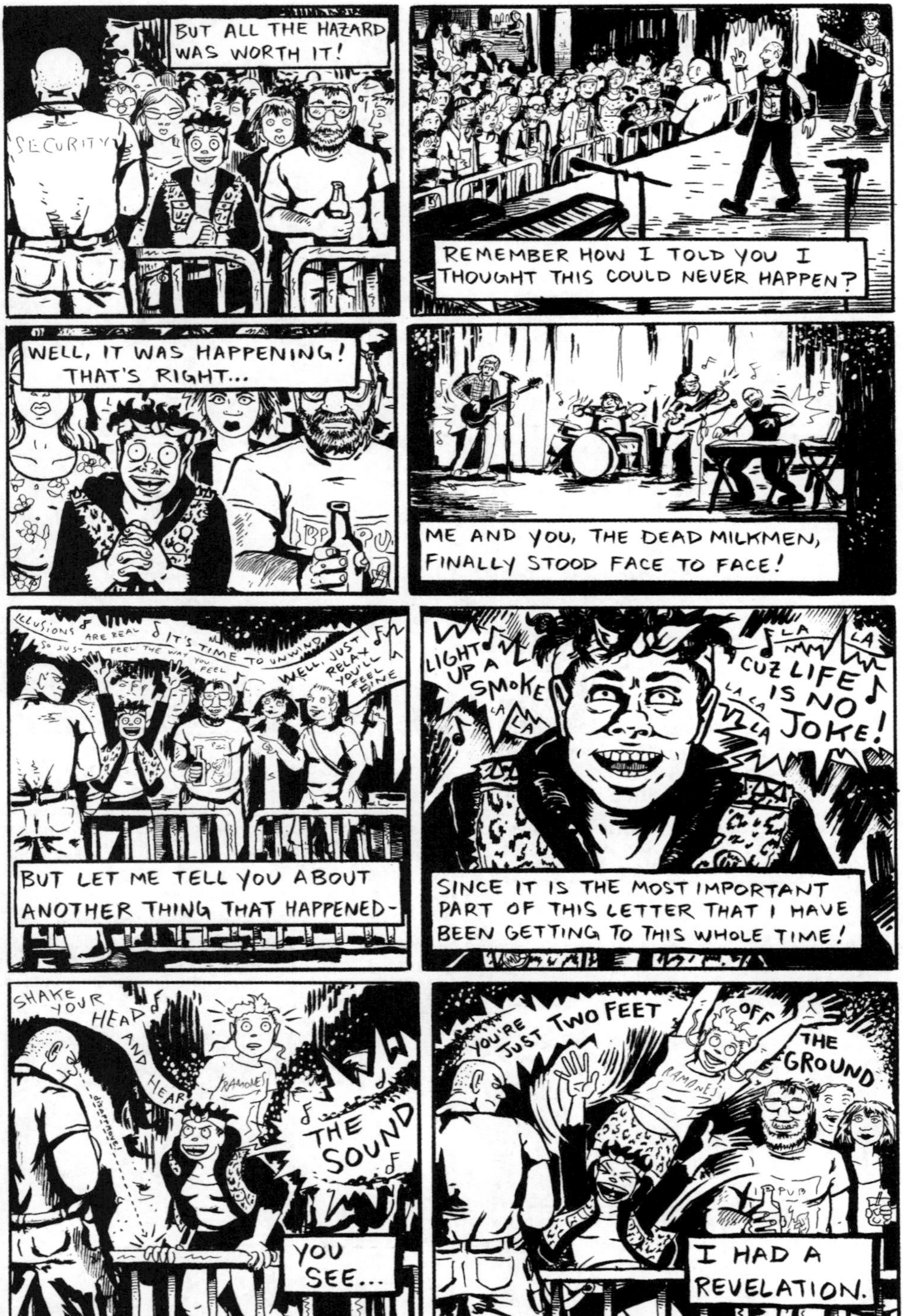
BUT ALL THE HAZARD WAS WORTH IT!
SECURITY
REMEMBER HOW I TOLD YOU I THOUGHT THIS COULD NEVER HAPPEN?
WELL, IT WAS HAPPENING! THAT'S RIGHT...
ME AND YOU, THE DEAD MILKMEN, FINALLY STOOD FACE TO FACE!
ILLUSIONS ARE REAL
IT'S TIME TO UNWIND
SO JUST FEEL THE WAY YOU FEEL
WELL, JUST RELAX YOU'LL FEEL FINE
BUT LET ME TELL YOU ABOUT ANOTHER THING THAT HAPPENED-
LIGHT UP A SMOKE
LA LA
LA LA
CUZ LIFE IS NO JOKE!
LA LA LA
SINCE IT IS THE MOST IMPORTANT PART OF THIS LETTER THAT I HAVE BEEN GETTING TO THIS WHOLE TIME!
SHAKE YOUR HEAD AND HEAR
RAMONES
THE SOUND
YOU SEE...
YOU'RE JUST TWO FEET OFF THE GROUND
RAMONES
I HAD A REVELATION.

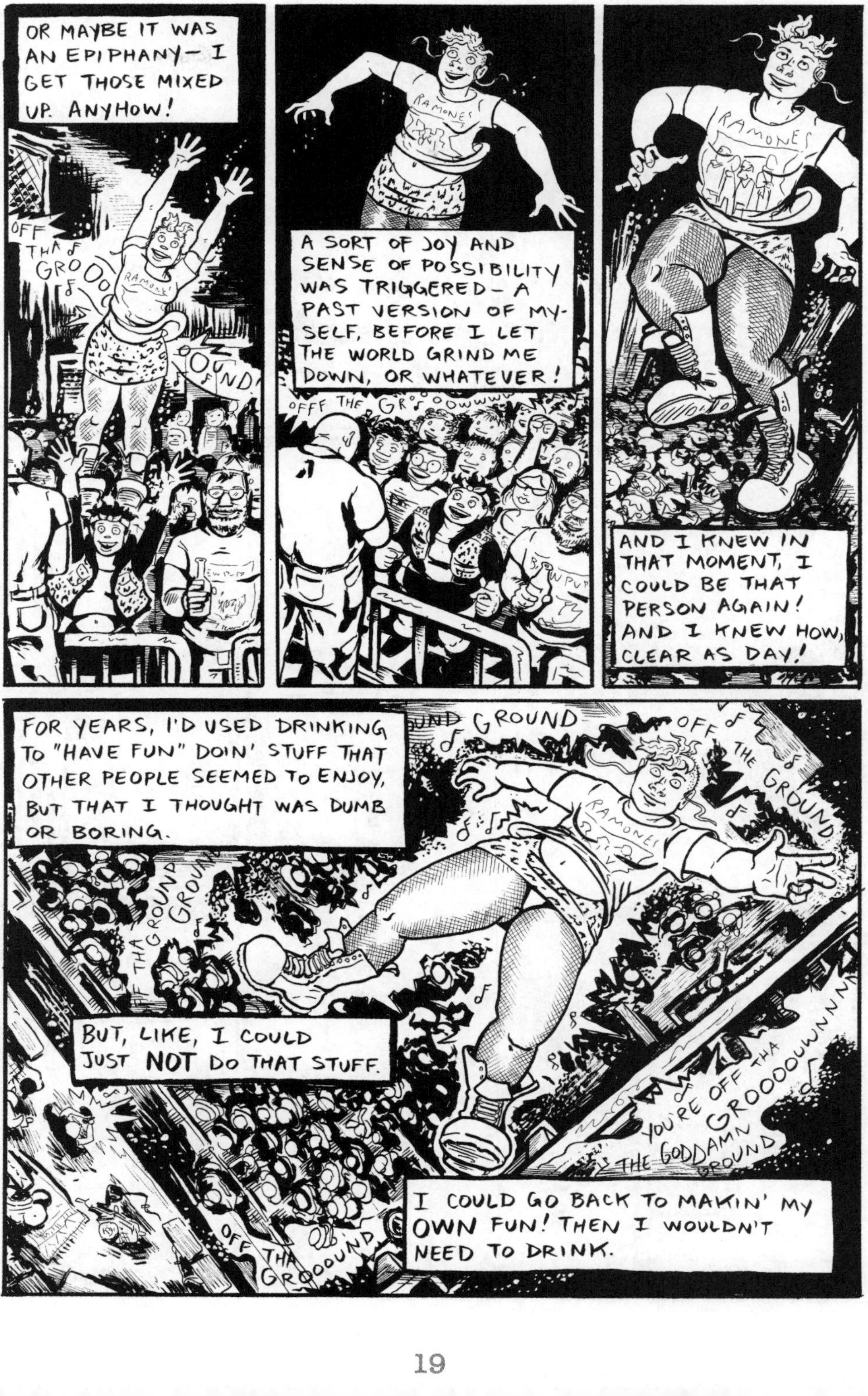
OR MAYBE IT WAS AN EPIPHANY— I GET THOSE MIXED UP. ANYHOW!
OFF THA GROOO
GROUND!
RAMONES
A SORT OF JOY AND SENSE OF POSSIBILITY WAS TRIGGERED— A PAST VERSION OF MYSELF, BEFORE I LET THE WORLD GRIND ME DOWN, OR WHATEVER!
OFFF THE GROOOWWW
RAMONES
AND I KNEW IN THAT MOMENT, I COULD BE THAT PERSON AGAIN! AND I KNEW HOW, CLEAR AS DAY!
FOR YEARS, I'D USED DRINKING TO "HAVE FUN" DOIN' STUFF THAT OTHER PEOPLE SEEMED TO ENJOY, BUT THAT I THOUGHT WAS DUMB OR BORING.
GROUND
OFF THE GROUND
RAMONES
THA GROUND GROUND
BUT, LIKE, I COULD JUST **NOT** DO THAT STUFF.
YOU'RE OFF THA GROOOOWNNN
THE GODDAMN GROUND
I COULD GO BACK TO MAKIN' MY OWN FUN! THEN I WOULDN'T NEED TO DRINK.
OFF THA GROOOUND

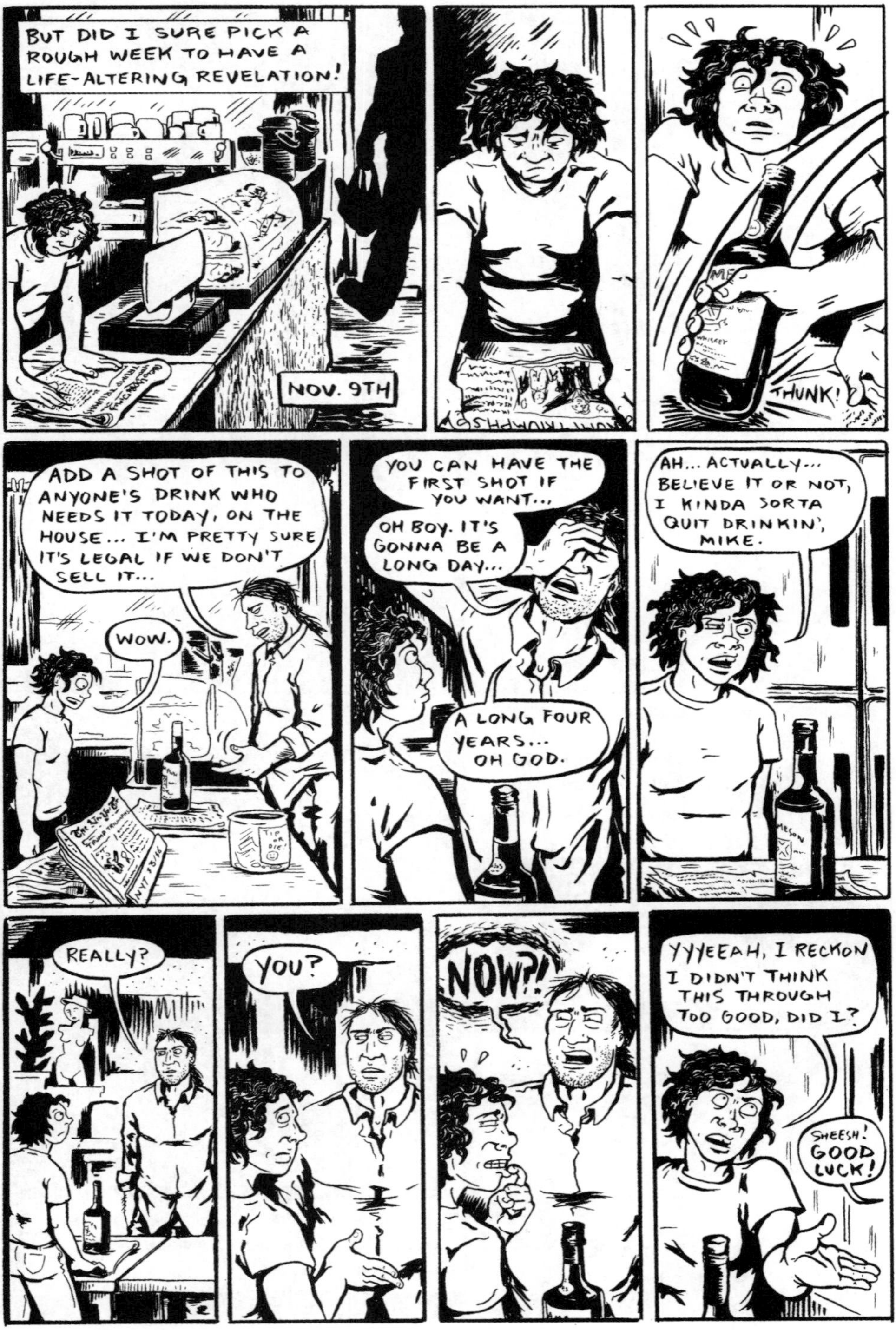
BUT DID I SURE PICK A ROUGH WEEK TO HAVE A LIFE-ALTERING REVELATION!
NOV. 9TH
THUNK!
ADD A SHOT OF THIS TO ANYONE'S DRINK WHO NEEDS IT TODAY, ON THE HOUSE... I'M PRETTY SURE IT'S LEGAL IF WE DON'T SELL IT...
WOW.
YOU CAN HAVE THE FIRST SHOT IF YOU WANT...
OH BOY. IT'S GONNA BE A LONG DAY...
A LONG FOUR YEARS... OH GOD.
AH... ACTUALLY... BELIEVE IT OR NOT, I KINDA SORTA QUIT DRINKIN', MIKE.
REALLY?
YOU?
NOW?!
YYYEEAH, I RECKON I DIDN'T THINK THIS THROUGH TOO GOOD, DID I?
SHEESH! GOOD LUCK!

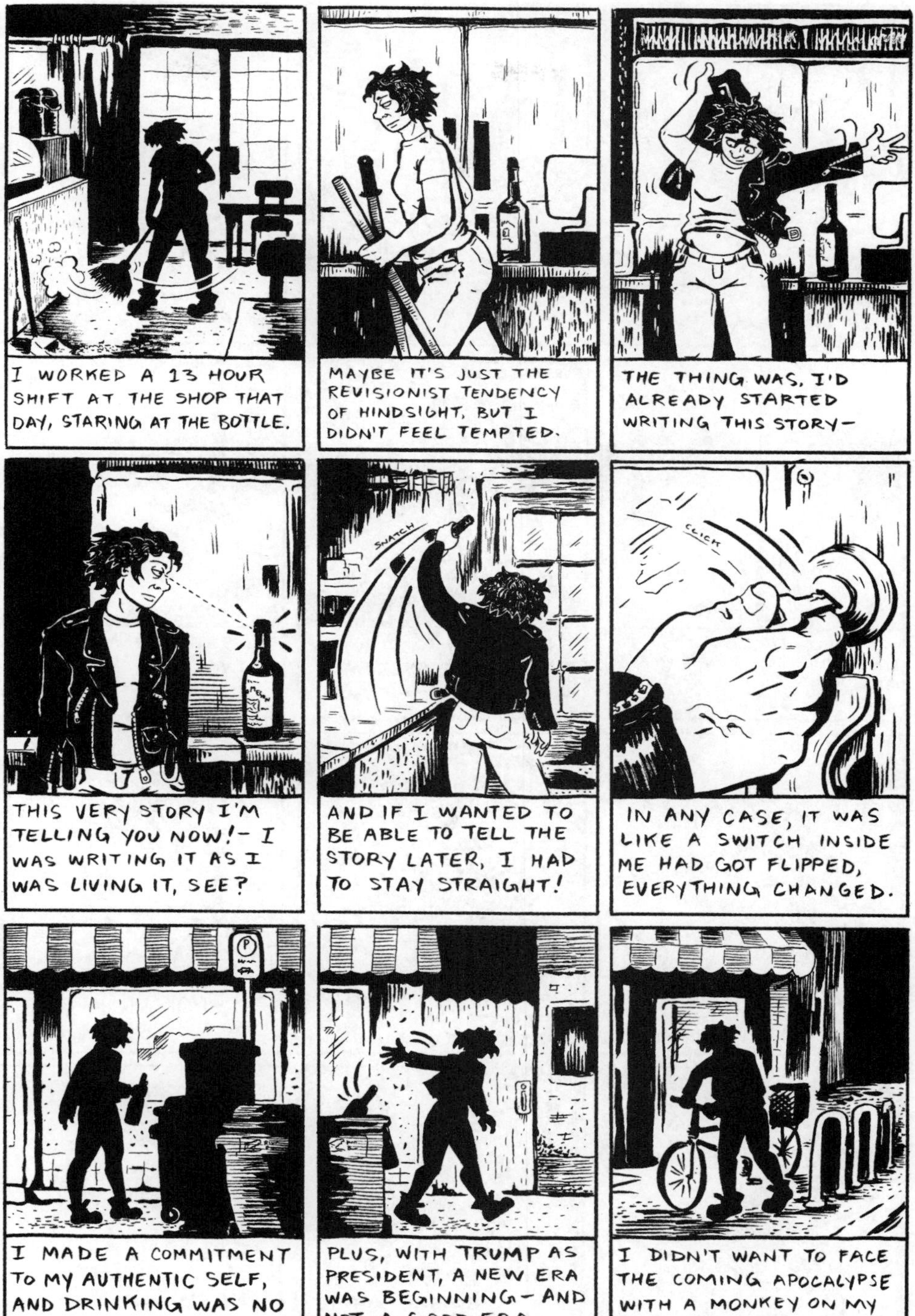
I WORKED A 13 HOUR SHIFT AT THE SHOP THAT DAY, STARING AT THE BOTTLE.
MAYBE IT'S JUST THE REVISIONIST TENDENCY OF HINDSIGHT, BUT I DIDN'T FEEL TEMPTED.
THE THING WAS, I'D ALREADY STARTED WRITING THIS STORY—
THIS VERY STORY I'M TELLING YOU NOW!— I WAS WRITING IT AS I WAS LIVING IT, SEE?
SNATCH
AND IF I WANTED TO BE ABLE TO TELL THE STORY LATER, I HAD TO STAY STRAIGHT!
CLICK
IN ANY CASE, IT WAS LIKE A SWITCH INSIDE ME HAD GOT FLIPPED, EVERYTHING CHANGED.
I MADE A COMMITMENT TO MY AUTHENTIC SELF, AND DRINKING WAS NO LONGER A THING I DID.
PLUS, WITH TRUMP AS PRESIDENT, A NEW ERA WAS BEGINNING— AND NOT A GOOD ERA, EITHER, I WAS SURE!
I DIDN'T WANT TO FACE THE COMING APOCALYPSE WITH A MONKEY ON MY BACK, IF NOTHING ELSE!

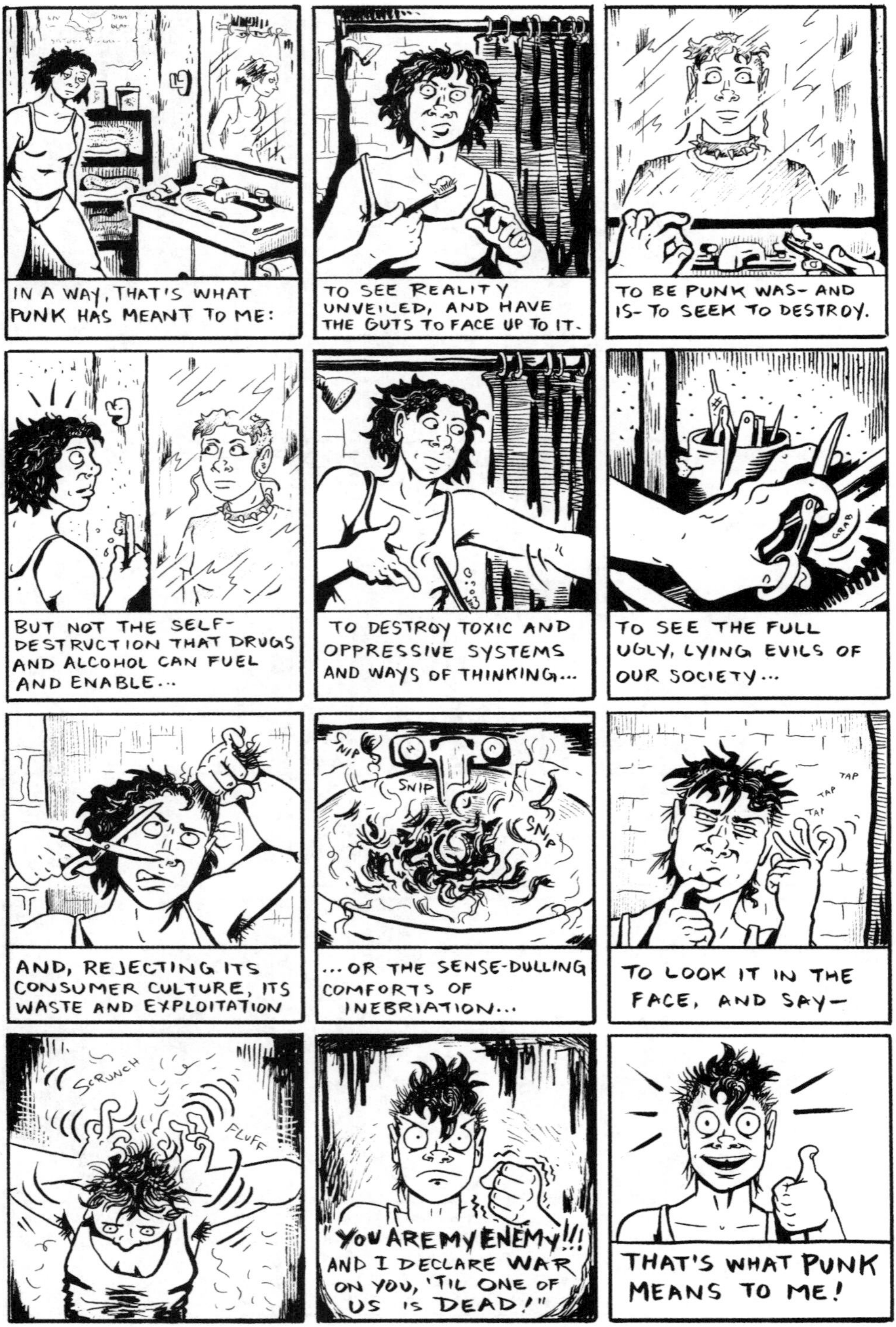
IN A WAY, THAT'S WHAT PUNK HAS MEANT TO ME:
TO SEE REALITY UNVEILED, AND HAVE THE GUTS TO FACE UP TO IT.
TO BE PUNK WAS- AND IS- TO SEEK TO DESTROY.
BUT NOT THE SELF-DESTRUCTION THAT DRUGS AND ALCOHOL CAN FUEL AND ENABLE...
TO DESTROY TOXIC AND OPPRESSIVE SYSTEMS AND WAYS OF THINKING...
GRAB
TO SEE THE FULL UGLY, LYING EVILS OF OUR SOCIETY...
AND, REJECTING ITS CONSUMER CULTURE, ITS WASTE AND EXPLOITATION
SNIP
SNIP
SNIP
...OR THE SENSE-DULLING COMFORTS OF INEBRIATION...
TAP
TAP
TAP
TO LOOK IT IN THE FACE, AND SAY—
SCRUNCH
FLUFF
"YOU ARE MY ENEMY!!! AND I DECLARE WAR ON YOU, 'TIL ONE OF US IS DEAD!"
THAT'S WHAT PUNK MEANS TO ME!

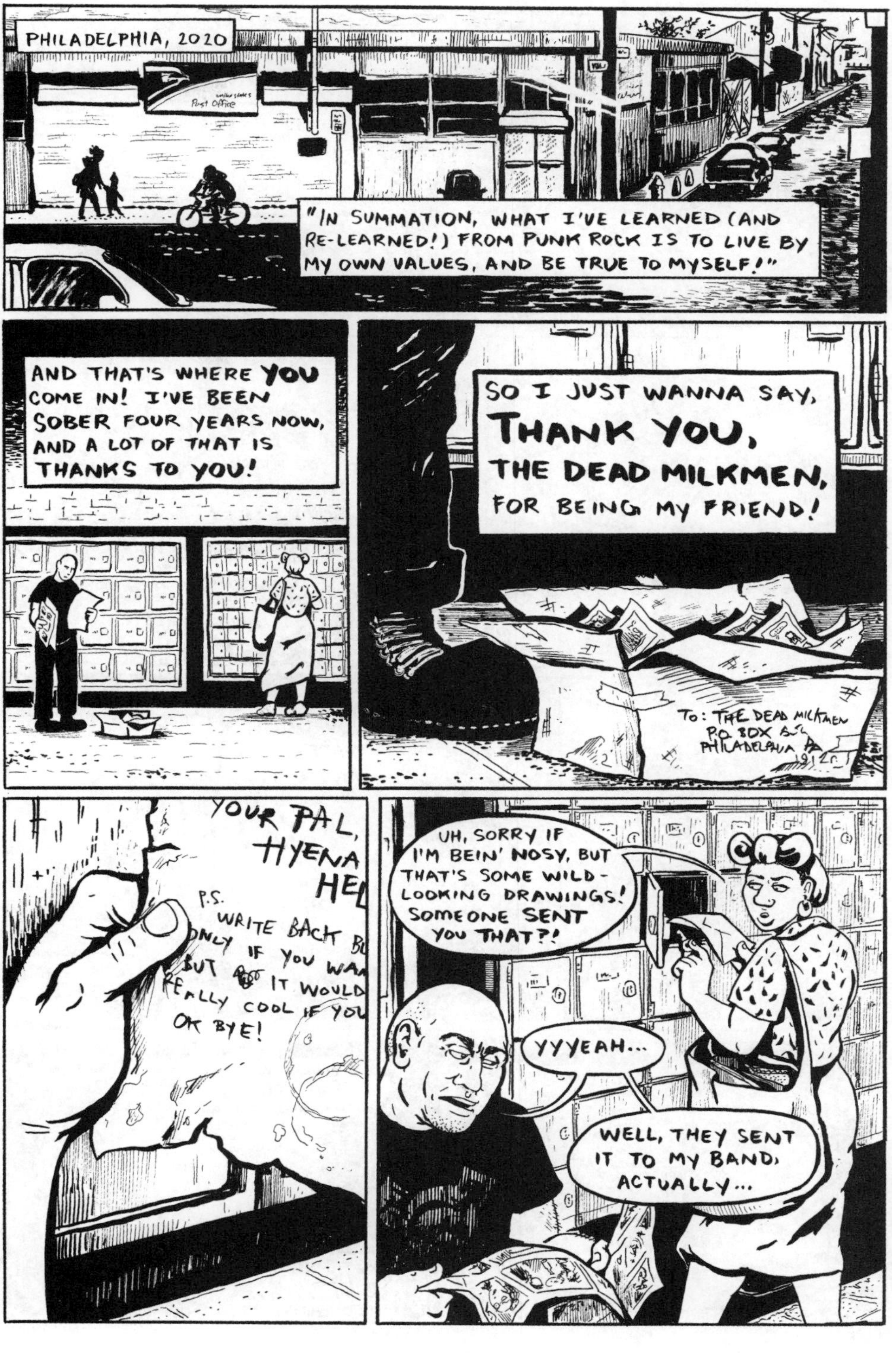
PHILADELPHIA, 2020
United States Post Office
"IN SUMMATION, WHAT I'VE LEARNED (AND RE-LEARNED!) FROM PUNK ROCK IS TO LIVE BY MY OWN VALUES, AND BE TRUE TO MYSELF!"
AND THAT'S WHERE YOU COME IN! I'VE BEEN SOBER FOUR YEARS NOW, AND A LOT OF THAT IS THANKS TO YOU!
SO I JUST WANNA SAY, THANK YOU, THE DEAD MILKMEN, FOR BEING MY FRIEND!
To: THE DEAD MILKMEN P.O. BOX PHILADELPHIA PA
YOUR PAL, HYENA
P.S. WRITE BACK ONLY IF YOU WA BUT IT WOULD REALLY COOL IF YOU OK BYE!
UH, SORRY IF I'M BEIN' NOSY, BUT THAT'S SOME WILD-LOOKING DRAWINGS! SOMEONE SENT YOU THAT?!
YYYEAH...
WELL, THEY SENT IT TO MY BAND, ACTUALLY...

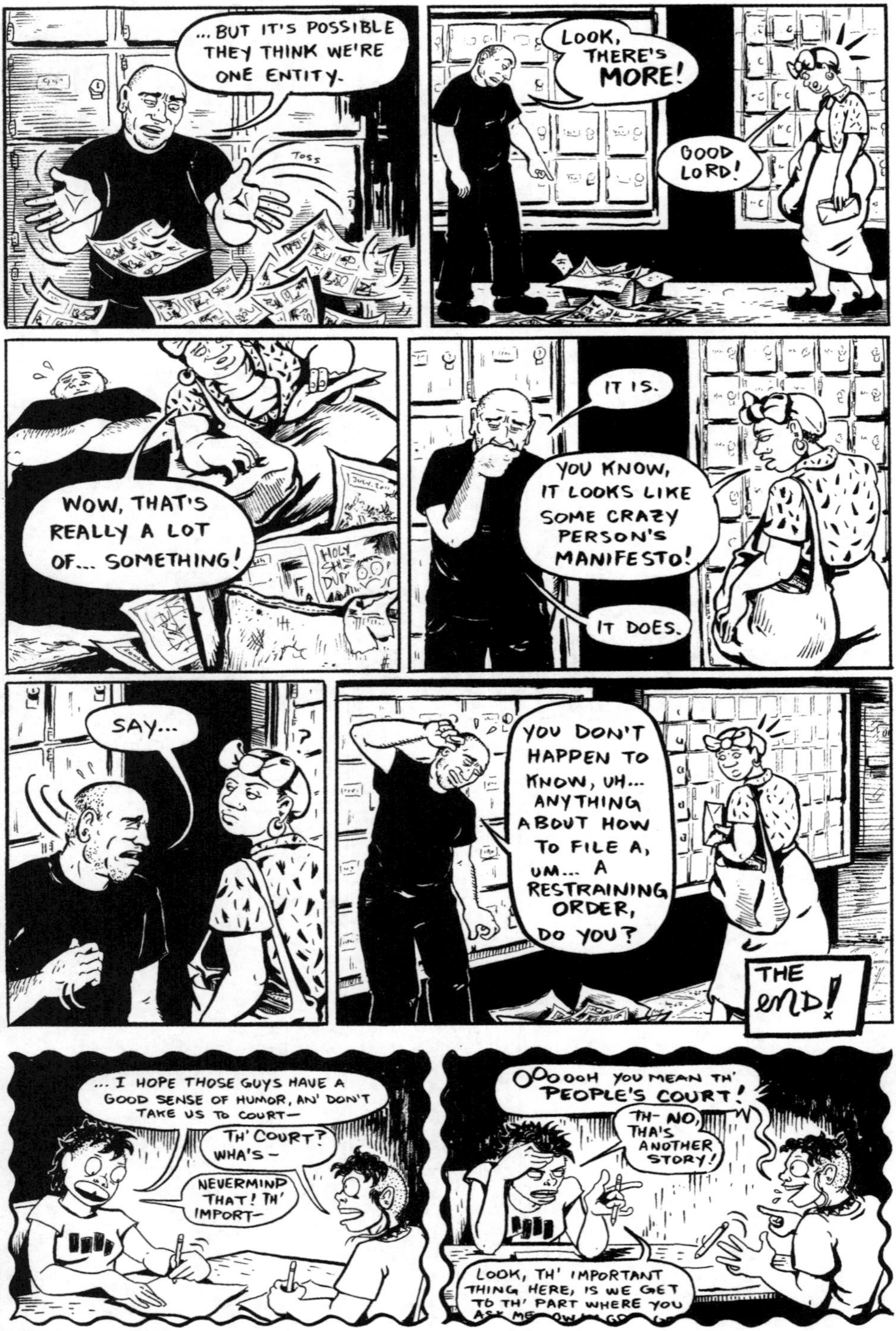

...BUT IT'S POSSIBLE THEY THINK WE'RE ONE ENTITY.
TOSS
LOOK, THERE'S MORE!
GOOD LORD!
WOW, THAT'S REALLY A LOT OF... SOMETHING!
IT IS.
YOU KNOW, IT LOOKS LIKE SOME CRAZY PERSON'S MANIFESTO!
IT DOES.
SAY...
?
YOU DON'T HAPPEN TO KNOW, UH... ANYTHING ABOUT HOW TO FILE A, UM... A RESTRAINING ORDER, DO YOU?
THE END!
...I HOPE THOSE GUYS HAVE A GOOD SENSE OF HUMOR, AN' DON'T TAKE US TO COURT—
TH' COURT? WHA'S—
NEVERMIND THAT! TH' IMPORT—
OOOOOH YOU MEAN TH' PEOPLE'S COURT!
TH- NO, THA'S ANOTHER STORY!
LOOK, TH' IMPORTANT THING HERE, IS WE GET TO TH' PART WHERE YOU

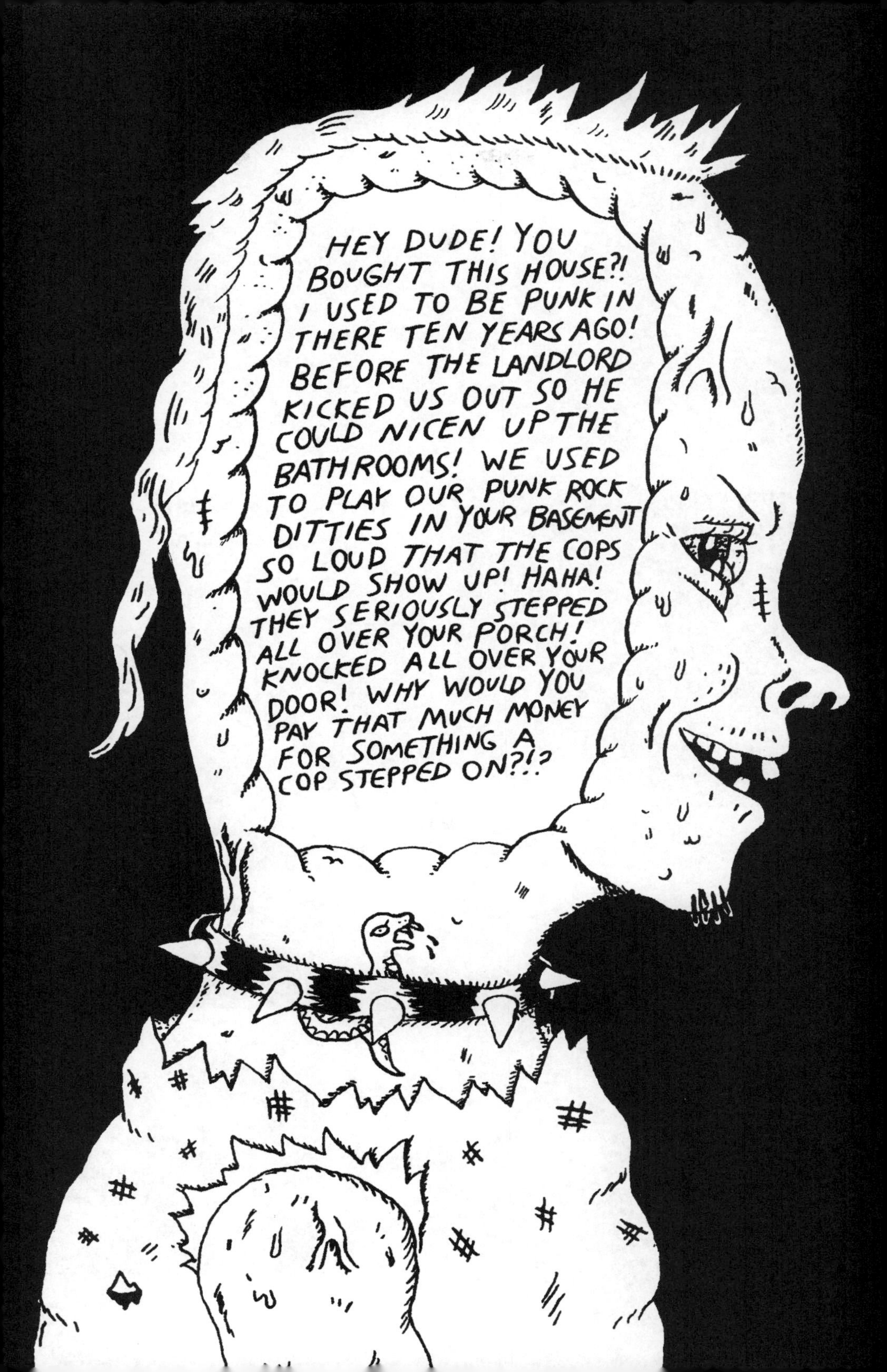
HEY DUDE! YOU BOUGHT THIS HOUSE?! I USED TO BE PUNK IN THERE TEN YEARS AGO! BEFORE THE LANDLORD KICKED US OUT SO HE COULD NICEN UP THE BATHROOMS! WE USED TO PLAY OUR PUNK ROCK DITTIES IN YOUR BASEMENT SO LOUD THAT THE COPS WOULD SHOW UP! HAHA! THEY SERIOUSLY STEPPED ALL OVER YOUR PORCH! KNOCKED ALL OVER YOUR DOOR! WHY WOULD YOU PAY THAT MUCH MONEY FOR SOMETHING A COP STEPPED ON?!?

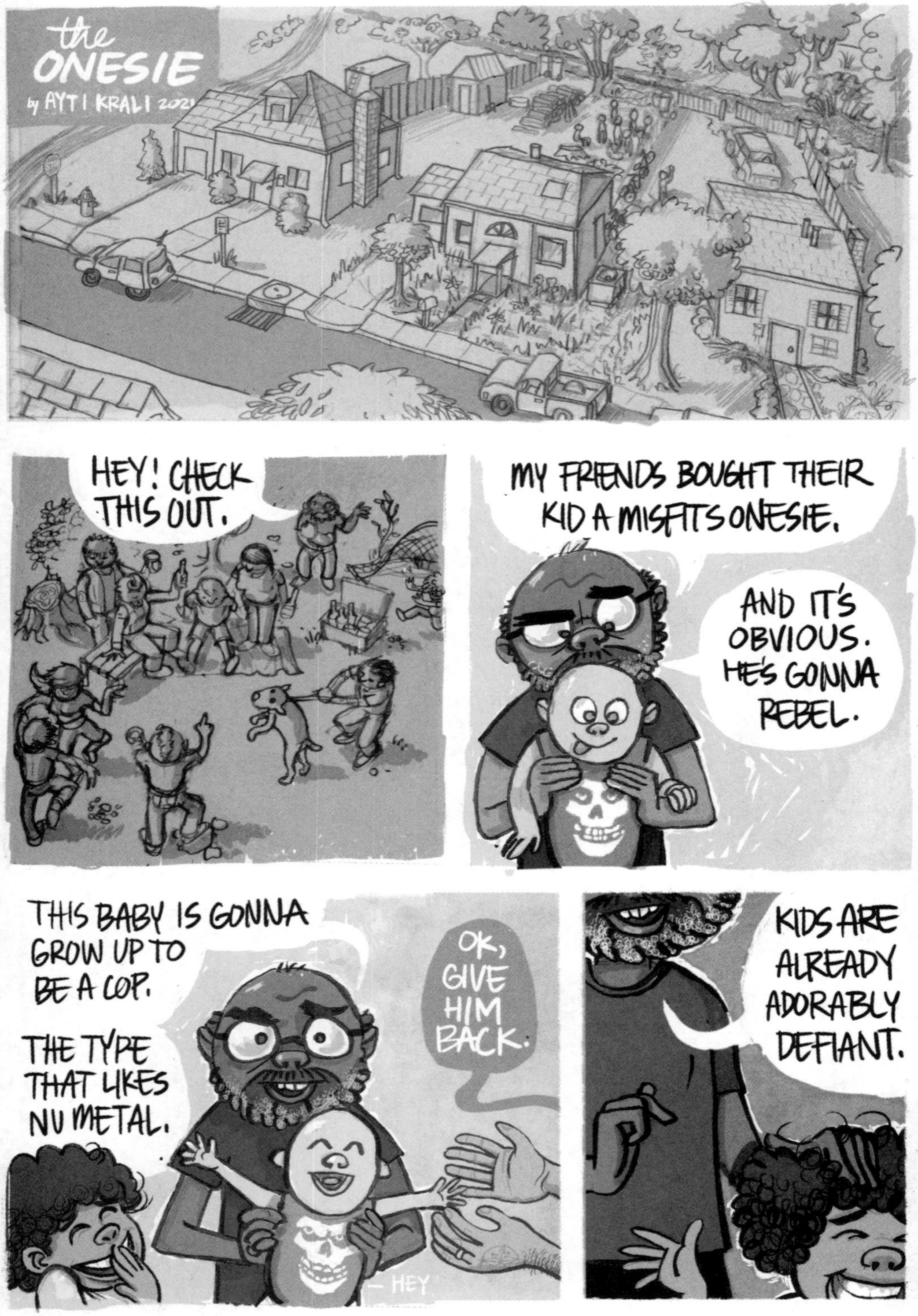
the ONESIE
by AYTI KRALI 2021
HEY! CHECK THIS OUT.
MY FRIENDS BOUGHT THEIR KID A MISFITS ONESIE.
AND IT'S OBVIOUS. HE'S GONNA REBEL.
THIS BABY IS GONNA GROW UP TO BE A COP.
THE TYPE THAT LIKES NU METAL.
OK, GIVE HIM BACK.
- HEY
KIDS ARE ALREADY ADORABLY DEFIANT.

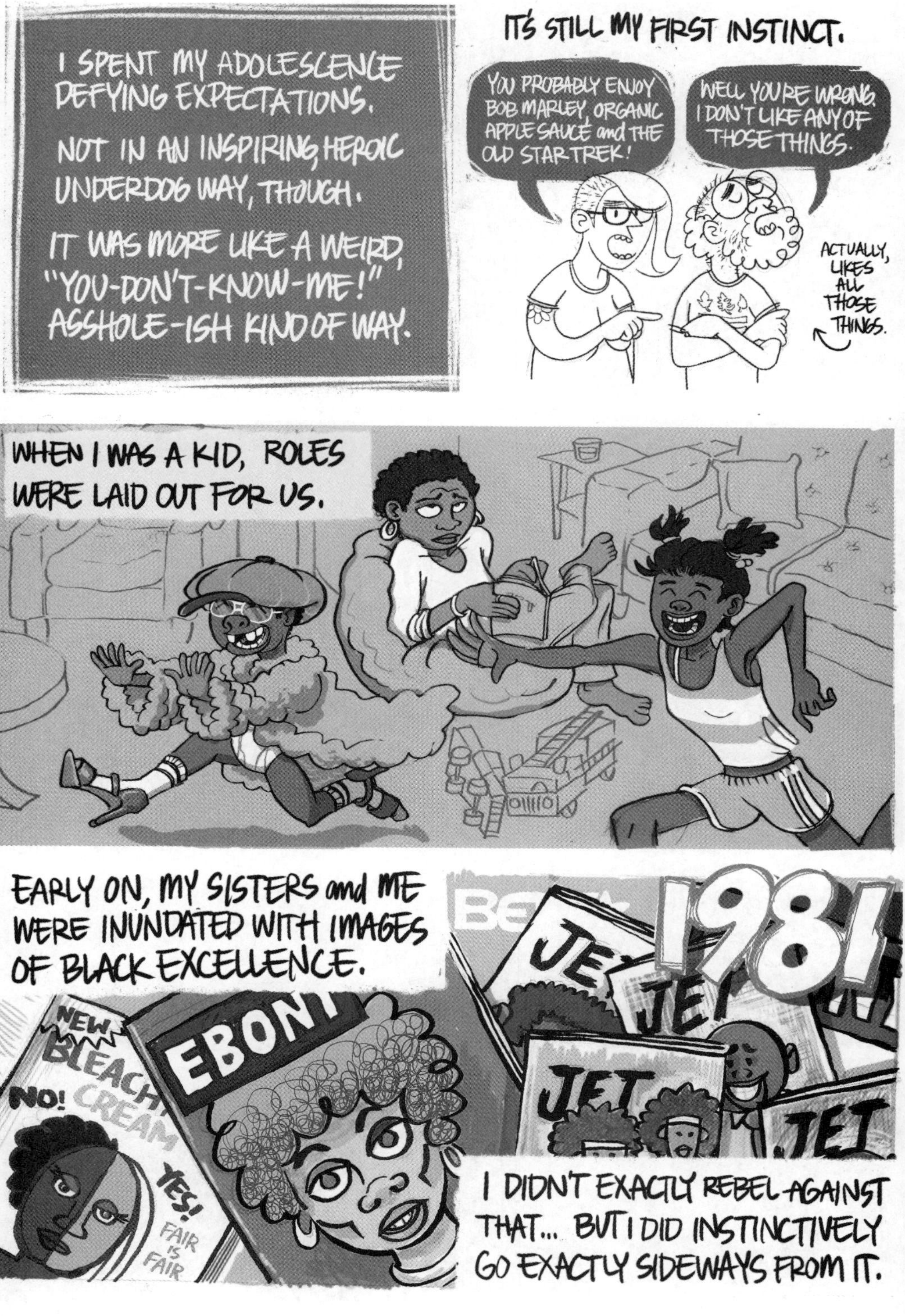
I SPENT MY ADOLESCENCE DEFYING EXPECTATIONS.
NOT IN AN INSPIRING, HEROIC UNDERDOG WAY, THOUGH.
IT WAS MORE LIKE A WEIRD, "YOU-DON'T-KNOW-ME!" ASSHOLE-ISH KIND OF WAY.
IT'S STILL MY FIRST INSTINCT.
YOU PROBABLY ENJOY BOB MARLEY, ORGANIC APPLE SAUCE and THE OLD STAR TREK!
WELL YOU'RE WRONG. I DON'T LIKE ANY OF THOSE THINGS.
ACTUALLY, LIKES ALL THOSE THINGS.
WHEN I WAS A KID, ROLES WERE LAID OUT FOR US.
EARLY ON, MY SISTERS and ME WERE INUNDATED WITH IMAGES OF BLACK EXCELLENCE.
1981
JET
EBONY
NEW BLEACH CREAM
NO!
YES!
FAIR IS FAIR
I DIDN'T EXACTLY REBEL AGAINST THAT... BUT I DID INSTINCTIVELY GO EXACTLY SIDEWAYS FROM IT.

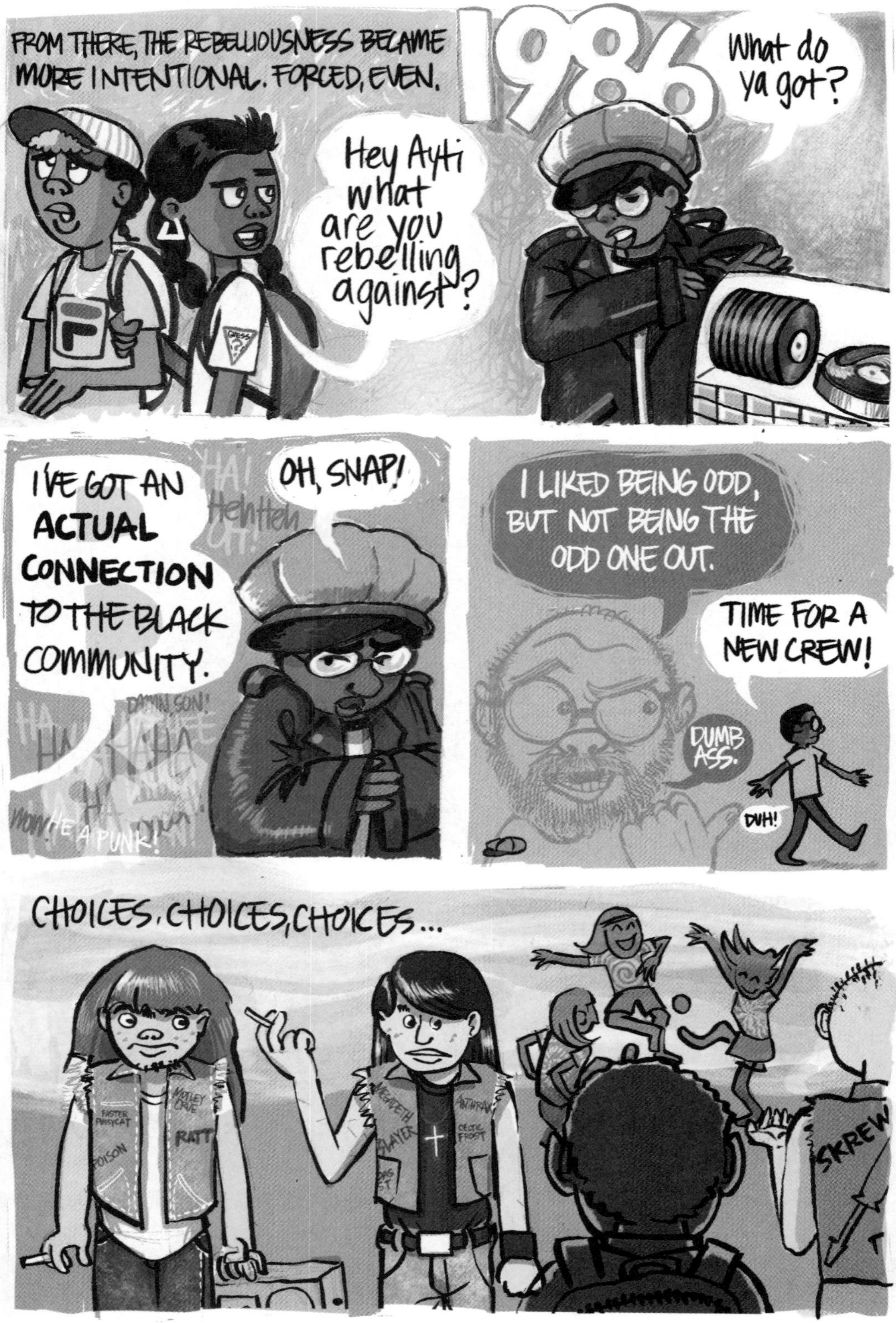

FROM THERE, THE REBELLIOUSNESS BECAME MORE INTENTIONAL. FORCED, EVEN.
1986
Hey Ayti what are you rebelling against?
What do ya got?
I'VE GOT AN **ACTUAL CONNECTION** TO THE BLACK COMMUNITY.
OH, SNAP!
DAMN, SON!
WOW! HE A PUNK!
I LIKED BEING ODD, BUT NOT BEING THE ODD ONE OUT.
TIME FOR A NEW CREW!
DUMB ASS.
DUH!
CHOICES, CHOICES, CHOICES...
MOTLEY CRUE
FASTER PUSSYCAT
RATT
POISON
MEGADETH
SLAYER
ANTHRAX
CELTIC FROST
SKREW

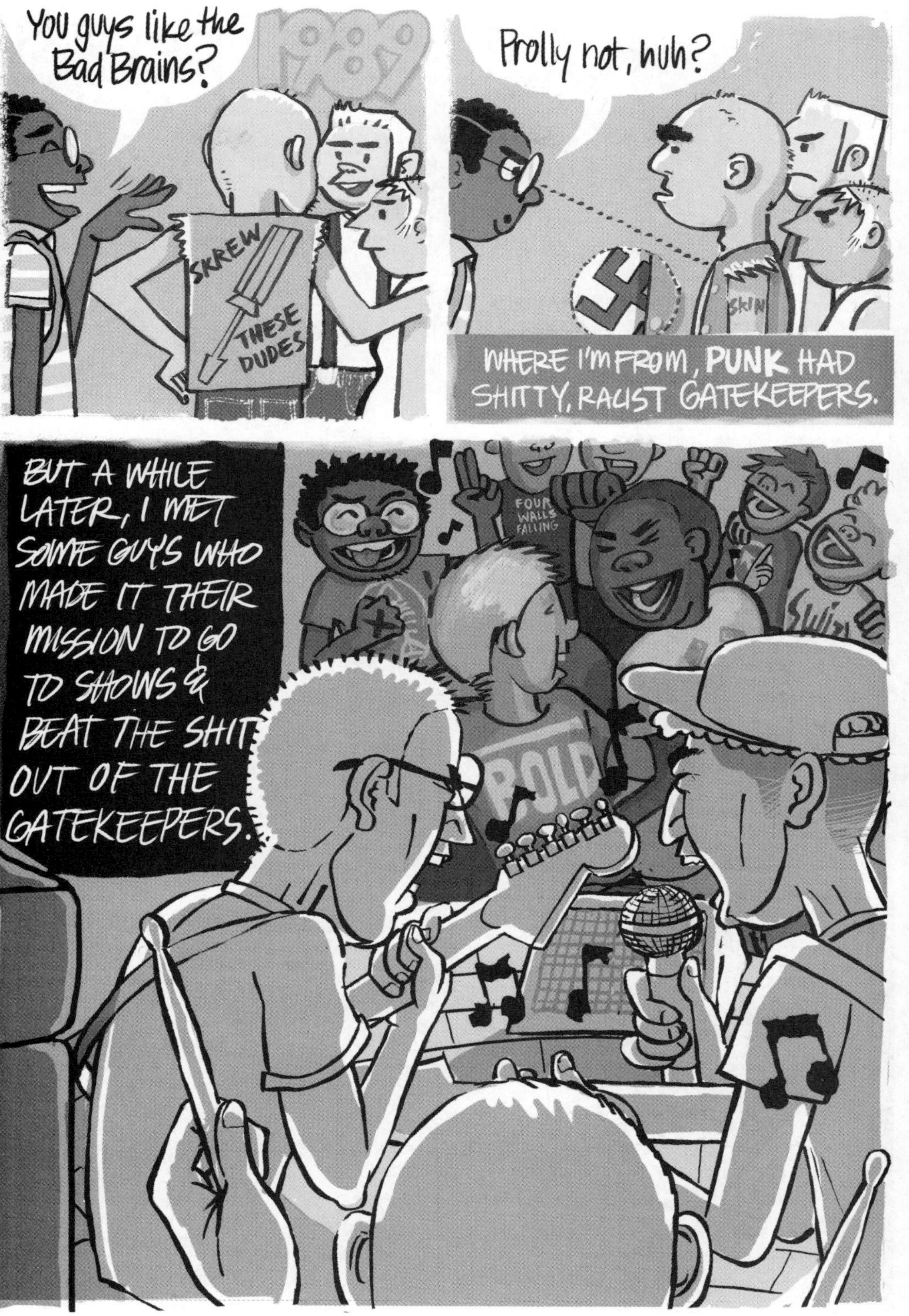
You guys like the Bad Brains?
1989
SKREW THESE DUDES
Prolly not, huh?
SKIN
WHERE I'M FROM, PUNK HAD SHITTY, RACIST GATEKEEPERS.
BUT A WHILE LATER, I MET SOME GUYS WHO MADE IT THEIR MISSION TO GO TO SHOWS & BEAT THE SHIT OUT OF THE GATEKEEPERS.
FOUR WALLS FALLING
BOLD

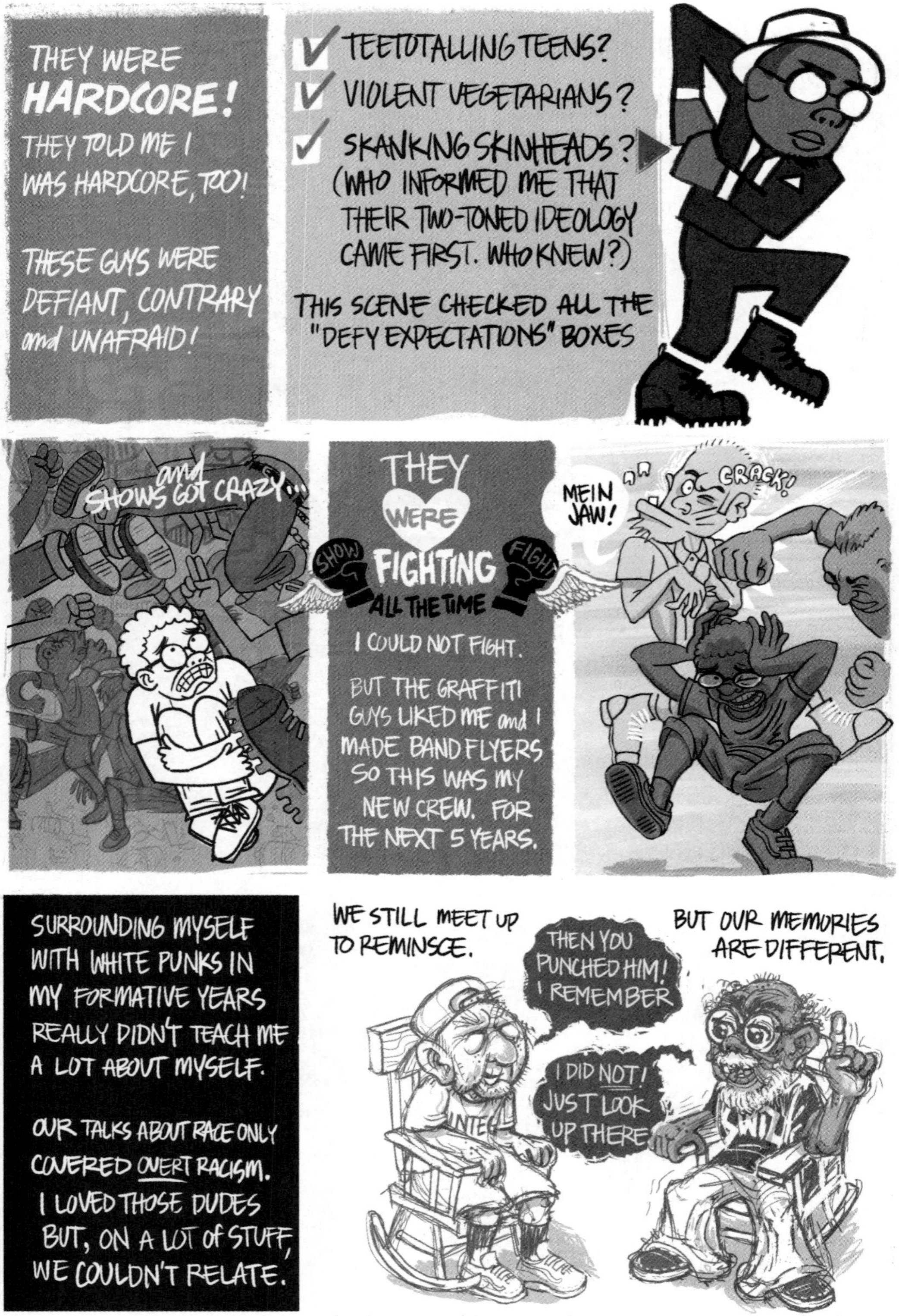
THEY WERE HARDCORE! THEY TOLD ME I WAS HARDCORE, TOO!
THESE GUYS WERE DEFIANT, CONTRARY and UNAFRAID!
TEETOTALLING TEENS?
VIOLENT VEGETARIANS?
SKANKING SKINHEADS? (WHO INFORMED ME THAT THEIR TWO-TONED IDEOLOGY CAME FIRST. WHO KNEW?)
THIS SCENE CHECKED ALL THE "DEFY EXPECTATIONS" BOXES
and SHOWS GOT CRAZY...
THEY WERE FIGHTING ALL THE TIME
SHOW
FIGHT
I COULD NOT FIGHT.
BUT THE GRAFFITI GUYS LIKED ME and I MADE BAND FLYERS SO THIS WAS MY NEW CREW. FOR THE NEXT 5 YEARS.
MEIN JAW!
CRACK!
SURROUNDING MYSELF WITH WHITE PUNKS IN MY FORMATIVE YEARS REALLY DIDN'T TEACH ME A LOT ABOUT MYSELF.
OUR TALKS ABOUT RACE ONLY COVERED OVERT RACISM. I LOVED THOSE DUDES BUT, ON A LOT OF STUFF, WE COULDN'T RELATE.
WE STILL MEET UP TO REMINSCE.
BUT OUR MEMORIES ARE DIFFERENT.
THEN YOU PUNCHED HIM! I REMEMBER
I DID NOT! JUST LOOK UP THERE

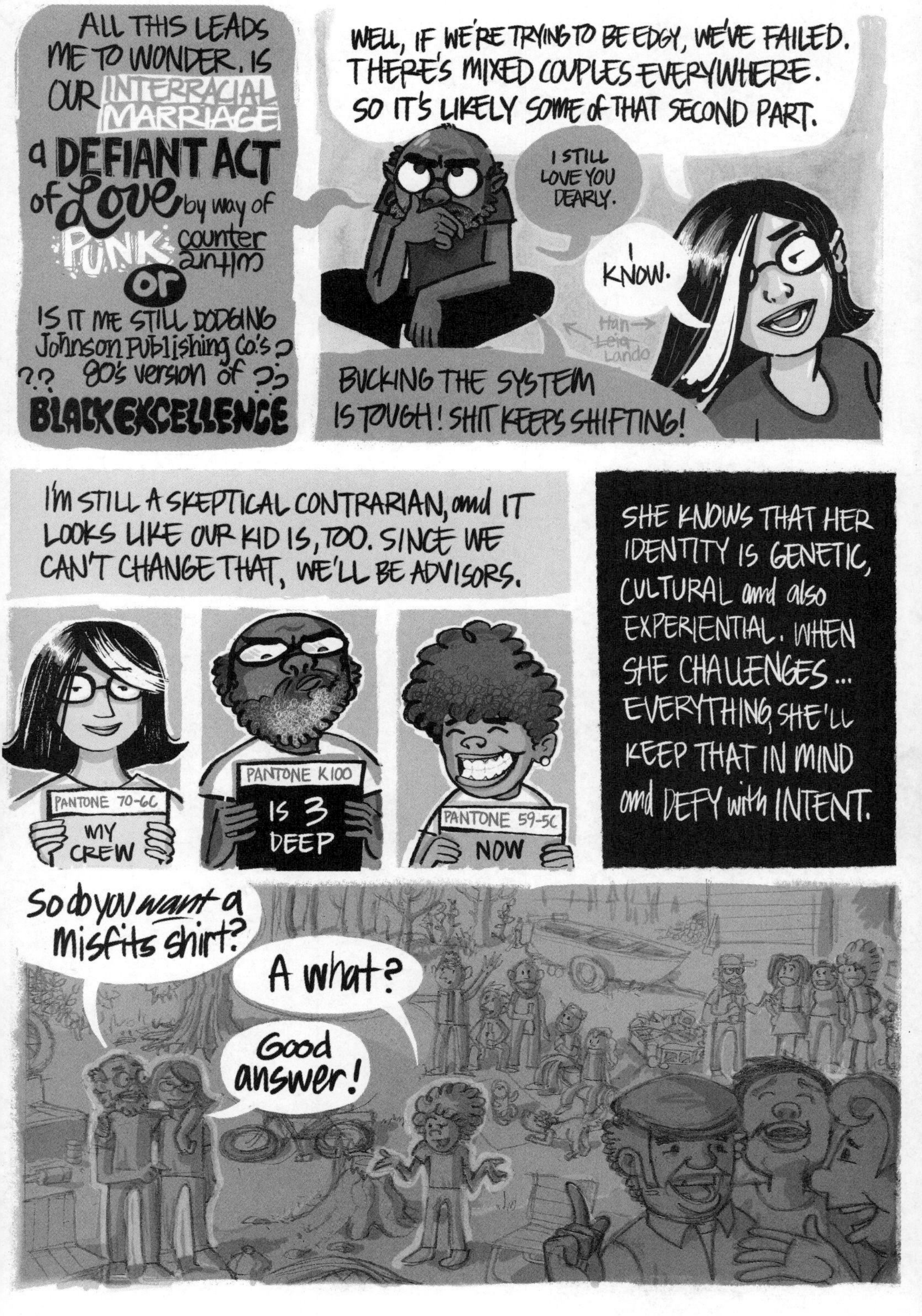
ALL THIS LEADS ME TO WONDER, IS OUR INTERRACIAL MARRIAGE a DEFIANT ACT of Love by way of PUNK counter culture or IS IT ME STILL DODGING Johnson Publishing Co.'s 80's version of BLACK EXCELLENCE ??
WELL, IF WE'RE TRYING TO BE EDGY, WE'VE FAILED. THERE'S MIXED COUPLES EVERYWHERE. SO IT'S LIKELY SOME of THAT SECOND PART.
I STILL LOVE YOU DEARLY.
I KNOW.
Han Leia Lando
BUCKING THE SYSTEM IS TOUGH! SHIT KEEPS SHIFTING!
I'M STILL A SKEPTICAL CONTRARIAN, and IT LOOKS LIKE OUR KID IS, TOO. SINCE WE CAN'T CHANGE THAT, WE'LL BE ADVISORS.
PANTONE 70-6C
MY CREW
PANTONE K100
IS 3 DEEP
PANTONE 59-5C
NOW
SHE KNOWS THAT HER IDENTITY IS GENETIC, CULTURAL and also EXPERIENTIAL. WHEN SHE CHALLENGES... EVERYTHING, SHE'LL KEEP THAT IN MIND and DEFY with INTENT.
So do you want a misfits shirt?
A what?
Good answer!

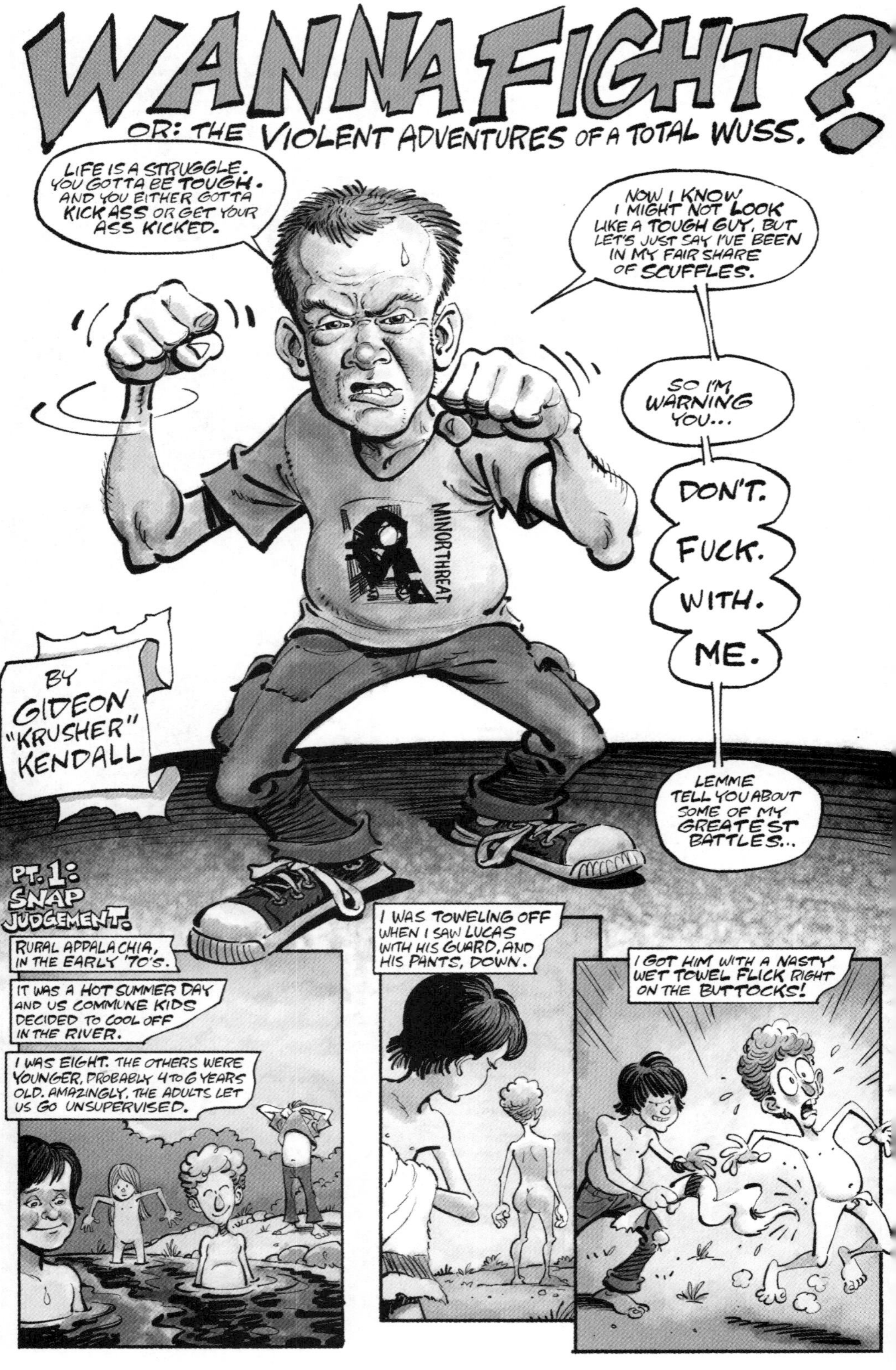
WANNA FIGHT?
OR: THE VIOLENT ADVENTURES OF A TOTAL WUSS.
LIFE IS A STRUGGLE. YOU GOTTA BE TOUGH. AND YOU EITHER GOTTA KICK ASS OR GET YOUR ASS KICKED.
NOW I KNOW I MIGHT NOT LOOK LIKE A TOUGH GUY, BUT LET'S JUST SAY I'VE BEEN IN MY FAIR SHARE OF SCUFFLES.
SO I'M WARNING YOU...
DON'T.
FUCK.
WITH.
ME.
LEMME TELL YOU ABOUT SOME OF MY GREATEST BATTLES...
MINORTHREAT
BY GIDEON "KRUSHER" KENDALL
PT. 1: SNAP JUDGEMENT!
RURAL APPALACHIA, IN THE EARLY '70'S.
IT WAS A HOT SUMMER DAY AND US COMMUNE KIDS DECIDED TO COOL OFF IN THE RIVER.
I WAS EIGHT. THE OTHERS WERE YOUNGER, PROBABLY 4 TO 6 YEARS OLD. AMAZINGLY, THE ADULTS LET US GO UNSUPERVISED.
I WAS TOWELING OFF WHEN I SAW LUCAS WITH HIS GUARD, AND HIS PANTS, DOWN.
I GOT HIM WITH A NASTY WET TOWEL FLICK RIGHT ON THE BUTTOCKS!

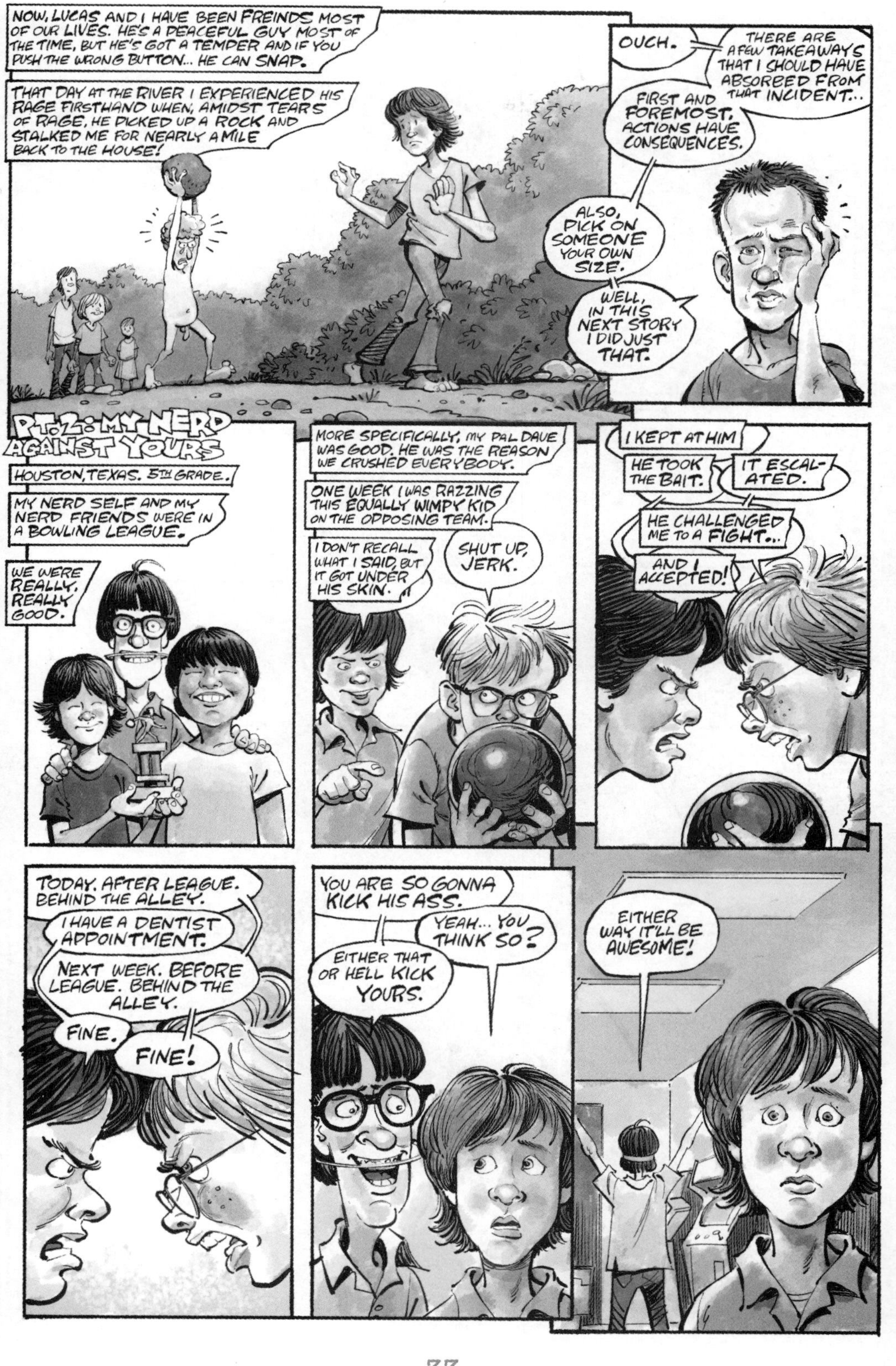
NOW, LUCAS AND I HAVE BEEN FREINDS MOST OF OUR LIVES. HE'S A PEACEFUL GUY MOST OF THE TIME, BUT HE'S GOT A TEMPER AND IF YOU PUSH THE WRONG BUTTON... HE CAN SNAP.
THAT DAY AT THE RIVER I EXPERIENCED HIS RAGE FIRSTHAND WHEN, AMIDST TEARS OF RAGE, HE PICKED UP A ROCK AND STALKED ME FOR NEARLY A MILE BACK TO THE HOUSE!
OUCH.
THERE ARE A FEW TAKEAWAYS THAT I SHOULD HAVE ABSORBED FROM THAT INCIDENT...
FIRST AND FOREMOST, ACTIONS HAVE CONSEQUENCES.
ALSO, PICK ON SOMEONE YOUR OWN SIZE.
WELL, IN THIS NEXT STORY I DID JUST THAT.
PT. 2: MY NERD AGAINST YOURS
HOUSTON, TEXAS. 5TH GRADE.
MY NERD SELF AND MY NERD FRIENDS WERE IN A BOWLING LEAGUE.
WE WERE REALLY, REALLY GOOD.
MORE SPECIFICALLY, MY PAL DAVE WAS GOOD. HE WAS THE REASON WE CRUSHED EVERYBODY.
ONE WEEK I WAS RAZZING THIS EQUALLY WIMPY KID ON THE OPPOSING TEAM.
I DON'T RECALL WHAT I SAID, BUT IT GOT UNDER HIS SKIN.
SHUT UP, JERK.
I KEPT AT HIM
HE TOOK THE BAIT.
IT ESCALATED.
HE CHALLENGED ME TO A FIGHT...
AND I ACCEPTED!
TODAY. AFTER LEAGUE. BEHIND THE ALLEY.
I HAVE A DENTIST APPOINTMENT.
NEXT WEEK. BEFORE LEAGUE. BEHIND THE ALLEY.
FINE.
FINE!
YOU ARE SO GONNA KICK HIS ASS.
YEAH... YOU THINK SO?
EITHER THAT OR HE'LL KICK YOURS.
EITHER WAY IT'LL BE AWESOME!

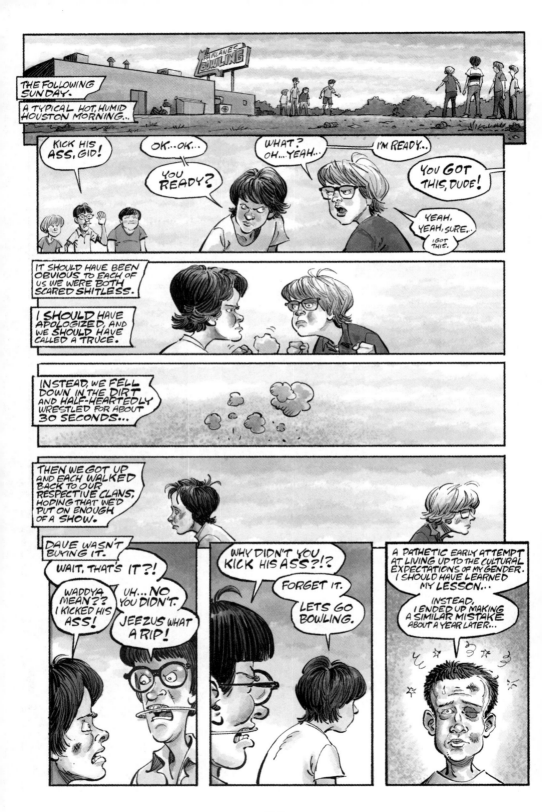

THE FOLLOWING SUNDAY.

A TYPICAL, HOT, HUMID HOUSTON MORNING...

KICK HIS ASS, GID!

OK...OK...

YOU READY?

WHAT? OH...YEAH...

I'M READY..

YOU GOT THIS, DUDE!

YEAH, YEAH, SURE.. I GOT THIS.

IT SHOULD HAVE BEEN OBVIOUS TO EACH OF US WE WERE BOTH SCARED SHITLESS.

I SHOULD HAVE APOLOGIZED, AND WE SHOULD HAVE CALLED A TRUCE.

INSTEAD, WE FELL DOWN IN THE DIRT AND HALF-HEARTEDLY WRESTLED FOR ABOUT 30 SECONDS...

THEN WE GOT UP AND EACH WALKED BACK TO OUR RESPECTIVE CLANS, HOPING THAT WE'D PUT ON ENOUGH OF A SHOW.

DAVE WASN'T BUYING IT.

WAIT, THAT'S IT?!

WADDYA MEAN?? I KICKED HIS ASS!

UH...NO YOU DIDN'T. JEEZUS WHAT A RIP!

WHY DIDN'T YOU KICK HIS ASS?!?

FORGET IT.

LETS GO BOWLING.

A PATHETIC EARLY ATTEMPT AT LIVING UP TO THE CULTURAL EXPECTATIONS OF MY GENDER. I SHOULD HAVE LEARNED MY LESSON...

INSTEAD, I ENDED UP MAKING A SIMILAR MISTAKE ABOUT A YEAR LATER...

PT. 3: LOCKER-ROOM TALK

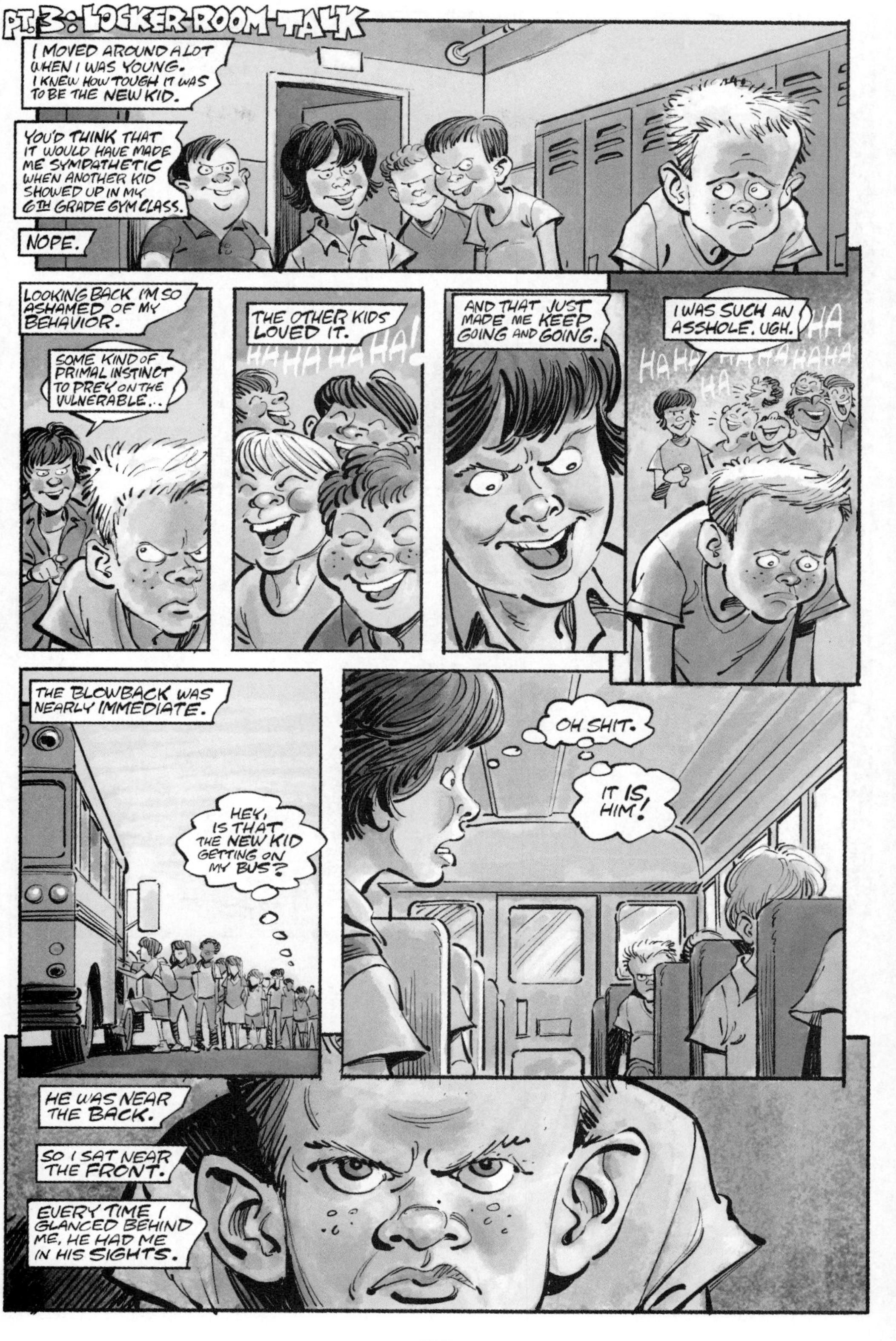
I MOVED AROUND A LOT WHEN I WAS YOUNG. I KNEW HOW TOUGH IT WAS TO BE THE NEW KID.
YOU'D THINK THAT IT WOULD HAVE MADE ME SYMPATHETIC WHEN ANOTHER KID SHOWED UP IN MY 6TH GRADE GYM CLASS.
NOPE.
LOOKING BACK I'M SO ASHAMED OF MY BEHAVIOR.
SOME KIND OF PRIMAL INSTINCT TO PREY ON THE VULNERABLE...
THE OTHER KIDS LOVED IT.
HA HA HA HA HA!
AND THAT JUST MADE ME KEEP GOING AND GOING.
I WAS SUCH AN ASSHOLE. UGH.
HA HA HA HA HA HA HA HA
THE BLOWBACK WAS NEARLY IMMEDIATE.
HEY, IS THAT THE NEW KID GETTING ON MY BUS?
OH SHIT.
IT IS HIM!
HE WAS NEAR THE BACK.
SO I SAT NEAR THE FRONT.
EVERY TIME I GLANCED BEHIND ME, HE HAD ME IN HIS SIGHTS.

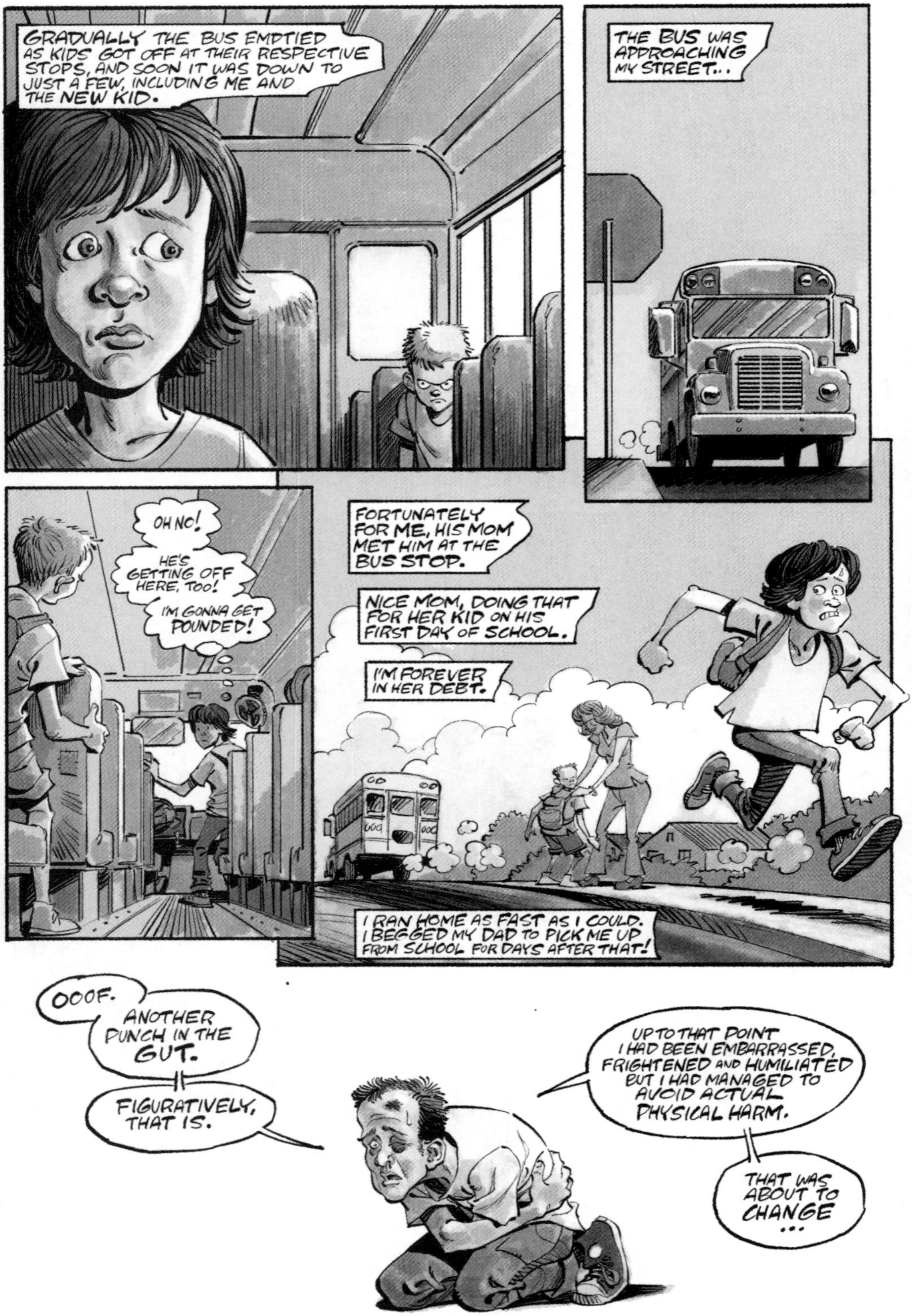
GRADUALLY THE BUS EMPTIED AS KIDS GOT OFF AT THEIR RESPECTIVE STOPS, AND SOON IT WAS DOWN TO JUST A FEW, INCLUDING ME AND THE NEW KID.
THE BUS WAS APPROACHING MY STREET...
OH NO!
HE'S GETTING OFF HERE, TOO!
I'M GONNA GET POUNDED!
FORTUNATELY FOR ME, HIS MOM MET HIM AT THE BUS STOP.
NICE MOM, DOING THAT FOR HER KID ON HIS FIRST DAY OF SCHOOL.
I'M FOREVER IN HER DEBT.
I RAN HOME AS FAST AS I COULD. I BEGGED MY DAD TO PICK ME UP FROM SCHOOL FOR DAYS AFTER THAT!
OOOF. ANOTHER PUNCH IN THE GUT.
FIGURATIVELY, THAT IS.
UP TO THAT POINT I HAD BEEN EMBARRASSED, FRIGHTENED AND HUMILIATED BUT I HAD MANAGED TO AVOID ACTUAL PHYSICAL HARM.
THAT WAS ABOUT TO CHANGE...

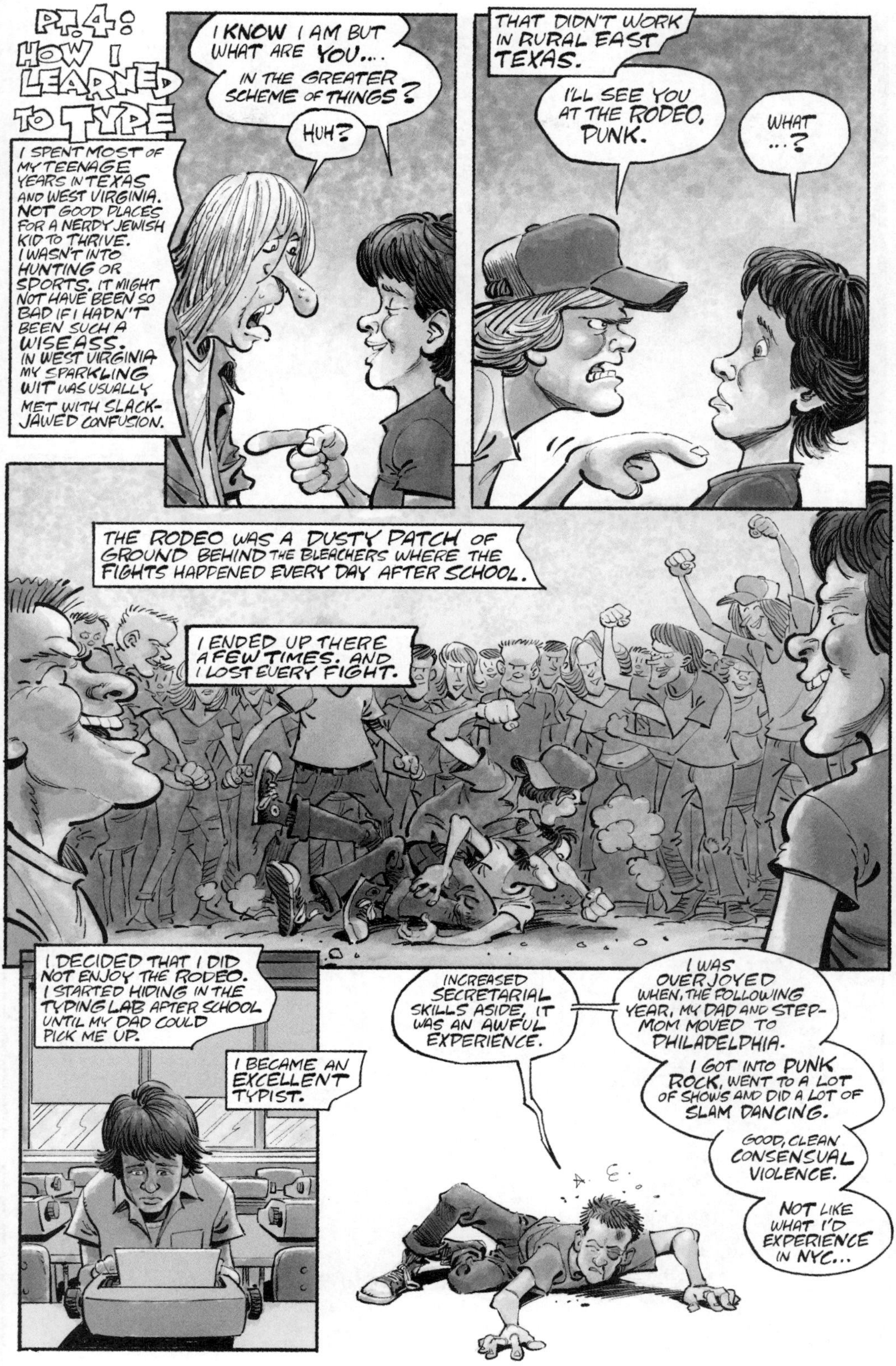
PT. 4: HOW I LEARNED TO TYPE
I SPENT MOST OF MY TEENAGE YEARS IN TEXAS AND WEST VIRGINIA. NOT GOOD PLACES FOR A NERDY JEWISH KID TO THRIVE. I WASN'T INTO HUNTING OR SPORTS. IT MIGHT NOT HAVE BEEN SO BAD IF I HADN'T BEEN SUCH A WISEASS. IN WEST VIRGINIA MY SPARKLING WIT WAS USUALLY MET WITH SLACK-JAWED CONFUSION.
I KNOW I AM BUT WHAT ARE YOU.... IN THE GREATER SCHEME OF THINGS?
HUH?
THAT DIDN'T WORK IN RURAL EAST TEXAS.
I'LL SEE YOU AT THE RODEO, PUNK.
WHAT ...?
THE RODEO WAS A DUSTY PATCH OF GROUND BEHIND THE BLEACHERS WHERE THE FIGHTS HAPPENED EVERY DAY AFTER SCHOOL.
I ENDED UP THERE A FEW TIMES. AND I LOST EVERY FIGHT.
I DECIDED THAT I DID NOT ENJOY THE RODEO. I STARTED HIDING IN THE TYPING LAB AFTER SCHOOL UNTIL MY DAD COULD PICK ME UP.
I BECAME AN EXCELLENT TYPIST.
INCREASED SECRETARIAL SKILLS ASIDE, IT WAS AN AWFUL EXPERIENCE.
I WAS OVERJOYED WHEN, THE FOLLOWING YEAR, MY DAD AND STEP-MOM MOVED TO PHILADELPHIA.
I GOT INTO PUNK ROCK, WENT TO A LOT OF SHOWS AND DID A LOT OF SLAM DANCING.
GOOD, CLEAN CONSENSUAL VIOLENCE.
NOT LIKE WHAT I'D EXPERIENCE IN NYC...

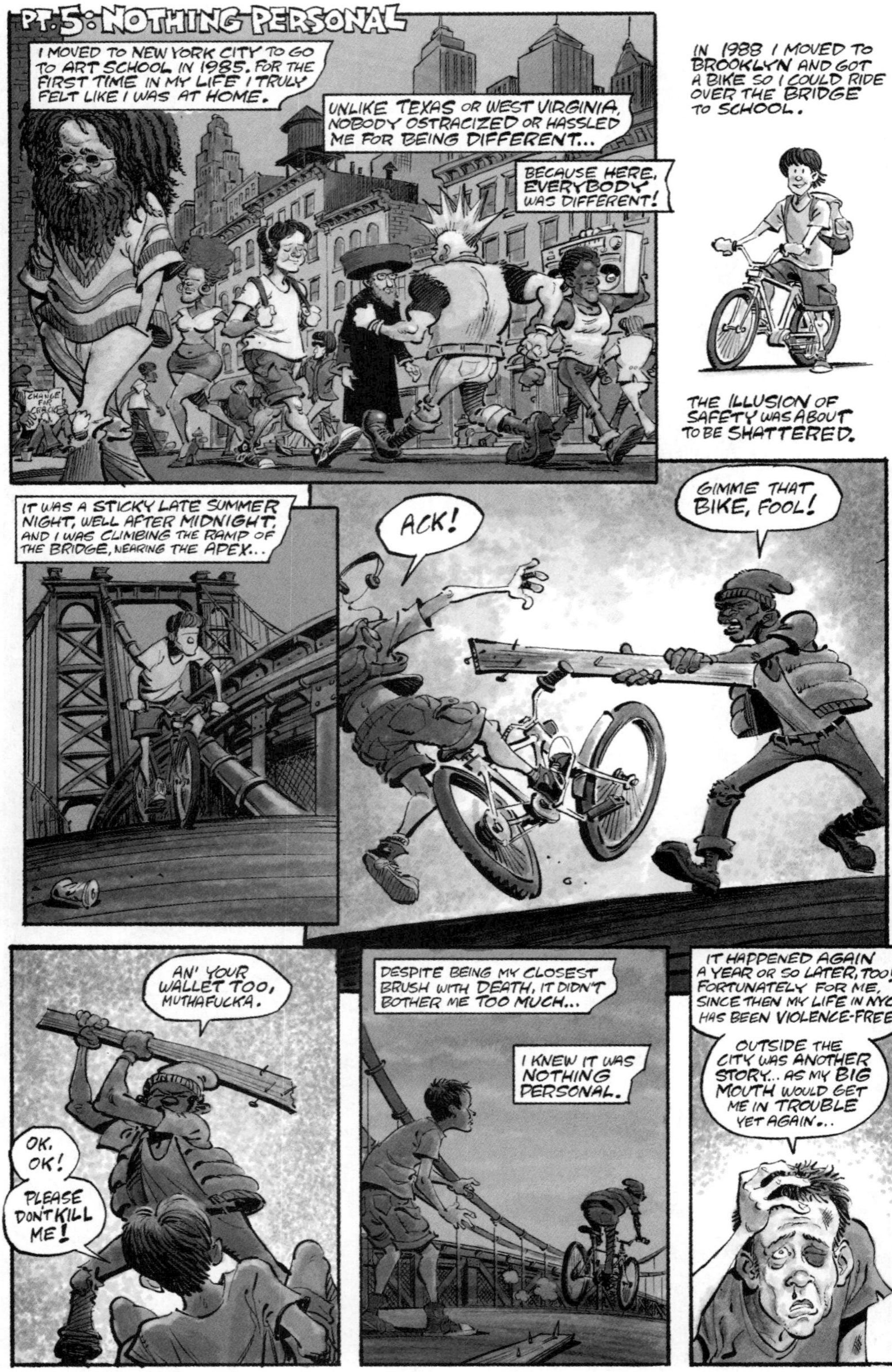

PT. 5: NOTHING PERSONAL
I MOVED TO NEW YORK CITY TO GO TO ART SCHOOL IN 1985. FOR THE FIRST TIME IN MY LIFE I TRULY FELT LIKE I WAS AT HOME.
UNLIKE TEXAS OR WEST VIRGINIA, NOBODY OSTRACIZED OR HASSLED ME FOR BEING DIFFERENT...
BECAUSE HERE, EVERYBODY WAS DIFFERENT!
IN 1988 I MOVED TO BROOKLYN AND GOT A BIKE SO I COULD RIDE OVER THE BRIDGE TO SCHOOL.
THE ILLUSION OF SAFETY WAS ABOUT TO BE SHATTERED.
IT WAS A STICKY LATE SUMMER NIGHT, WELL AFTER MIDNIGHT, AND I WAS CLIMBING THE RAMP OF THE BRIDGE, NEARING THE APEX...
ACK!
GIMME THAT BIKE, FOOL!
AN' YOUR WALLET TOO, MUTHAFUCKA.
OK, OK!
PLEASE DON'T KILL ME!
DESPITE BEING MY CLOSEST BRUSH WITH DEATH, IT DIDN'T BOTHER ME TOO MUCH...
I KNEW IT WAS NOTHING PERSONAL.
IT HAPPENED AGAIN A YEAR OR SO LATER, TOO! FORTUNATELY FOR ME, SINCE THEN MY LIFE IN NYC HAS BEEN VIOLENCE-FREE.
OUTSIDE THE CITY WAS ANOTHER STORY... AS MY BIG MOUTH WOULD GET ME IN TROUBLE YET AGAIN...

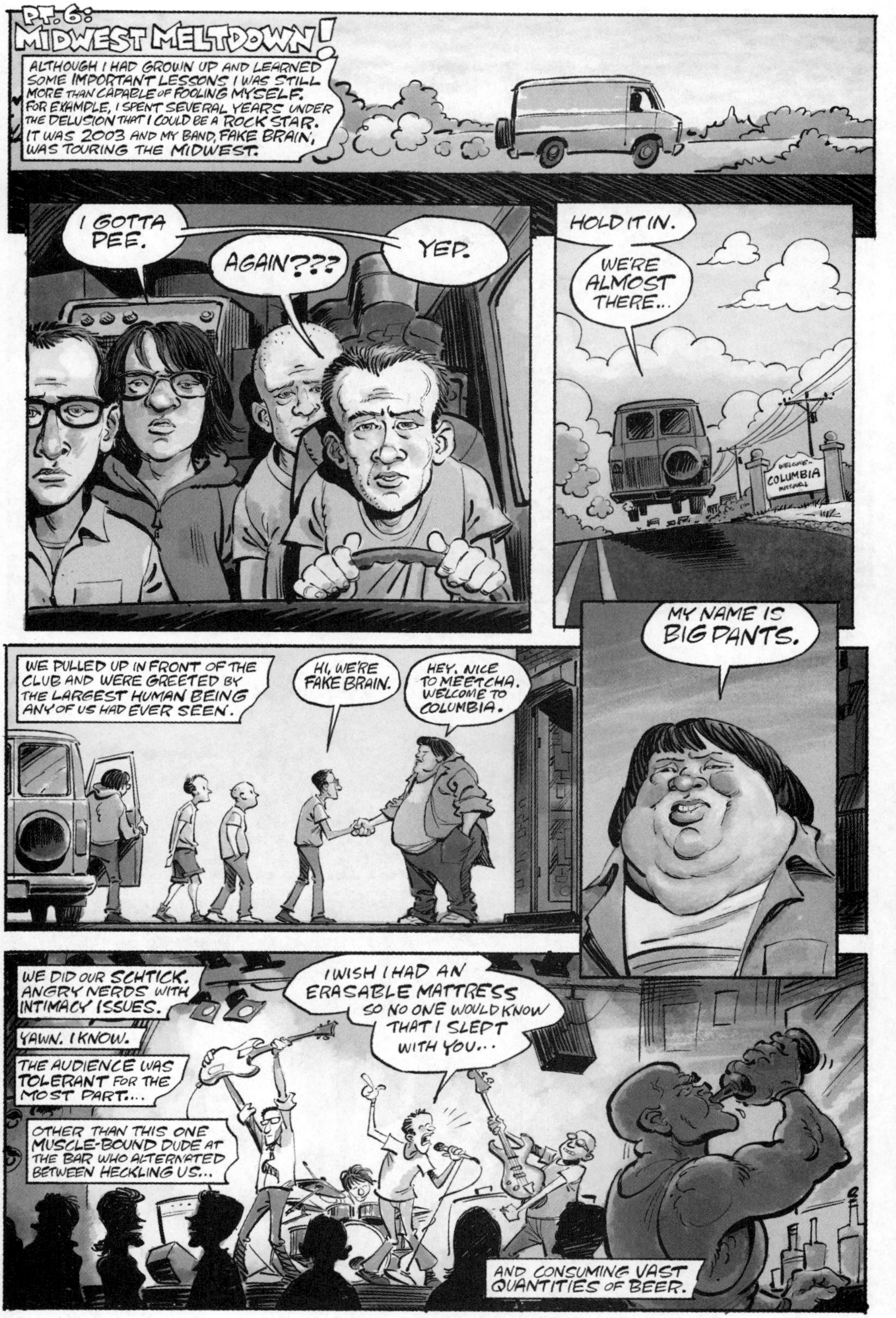
PT. 6:
MIDWEST MELTDOWN!
ALTHOUGH I HAD GROWN UP AND LEARNED SOME IMPORTANT LESSONS I WAS STILL MORE THAN CAPABLE OF FOOLING MYSELF. FOR EXAMPLE, I SPENT SEVERAL YEARS UNDER THE DELUSION THAT I COULD BE A ROCK STAR. IT WAS 2003 AND MY BAND, FAKE BRAIN, WAS TOURING THE MIDWEST.
I GOTTA PEE.
AGAIN???
YEP.
HOLD IT IN.
WE'RE ALMOST THERE...
COLUMBIA
WE PULLED UP IN FRONT OF THE CLUB AND WERE GREETED BY THE LARGEST HUMAN BEING ANY OF US HAD EVER SEEN.
HI, WE'RE FAKE BRAIN.
HEY. NICE TO MEETCHA. WELCOME TO COLUMBIA.
MY NAME IS BIG PANTS.
WE DID OUR SCHTICK. ANGRY NERDS WITH INTIMACY ISSUES.
YAWN. I KNOW.
THE AUDIENCE WAS TOLERANT FOR THE MOST PART...
I WISH I HAD AN ERASABLE MATTRESS SO NO ONE WOULD KNOW THAT I SLEPT WITH YOU...
OTHER THAN THIS ONE MUSCLE-BOUND DUDE AT THE BAR WHO ALTERNATED BETWEEN HECKLING US...
AND CONSUMING VAST QUANTITIES OF BEER.

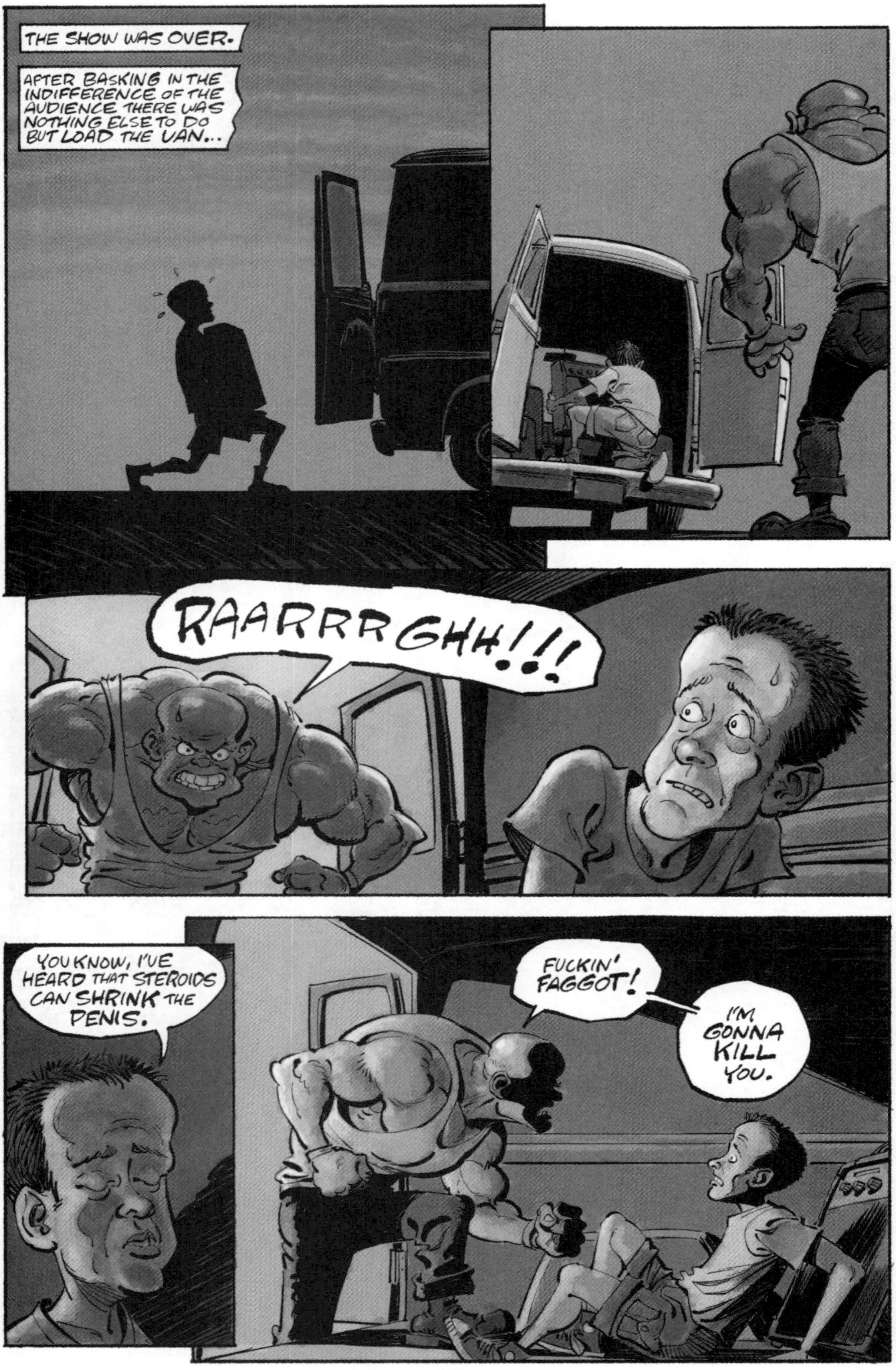
THE SHOW WAS OVER.
AFTER BASKING IN THE INDIFFERENCE OF THE AUDIENCE THERE WAS NOTHING ELSE TO DO BUT LOAD THE VAN...
RAARRRGHH!!!
YOU KNOW, I'VE HEARD THAT STEROIDS CAN SHRINK THE PENIS.
FUCKIN' FAGGOT!
I'M GONNA KILL YOU.

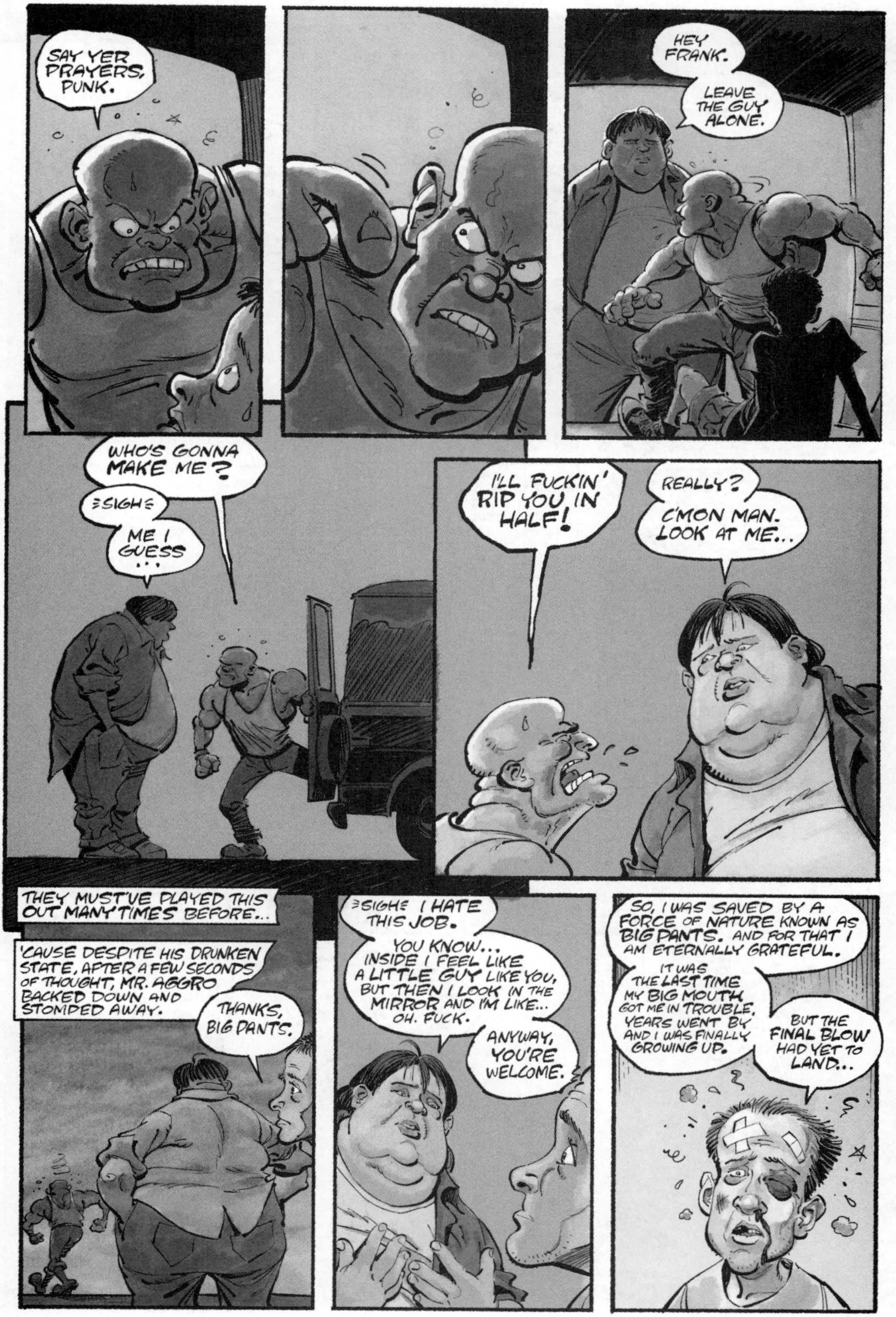
SAY YER PRAYERS, PUNK.
HEY FRANK.
LEAVE THE GUY ALONE.
WHO'S GONNA MAKE ME?
≡SIGH≡
ME I GUESS ...
I'LL FUCKIN' RIP YOU IN HALF!
REALLY?
C'MON MAN. LOOK AT ME...
THEY MUST'VE PLAYED THIS OUT MANY TIMES BEFORE...
'CAUSE DESPITE HIS DRUNKEN STATE, AFTER A FEW SECONDS OF THOUGHT, MR. AGGRO BACKED DOWN AND STOMPED AWAY.
THANKS, BIG PANTS.
≡SIGH≡ I HATE THIS JOB.
YOU KNOW... INSIDE I FEEL LIKE A LITTLE GUY LIKE YOU, BUT THEN I LOOK IN THE MIRROR AND I'M LIKE... OH. FUCK.
ANYWAY, YOU'RE WELCOME.
SO, I WAS SAVED BY A FORCE OF NATURE KNOWN AS BIG PANTS. AND FOR THAT I AM ETERNALLY GRATEFUL.
IT WAS THE LAST TIME MY BIG MOUTH GOT ME IN TROUBLE. YEARS WENT BY AND I WAS FINALLY GROWING UP.
BUT THE FINAL BLOW HAD YET TO LAND...

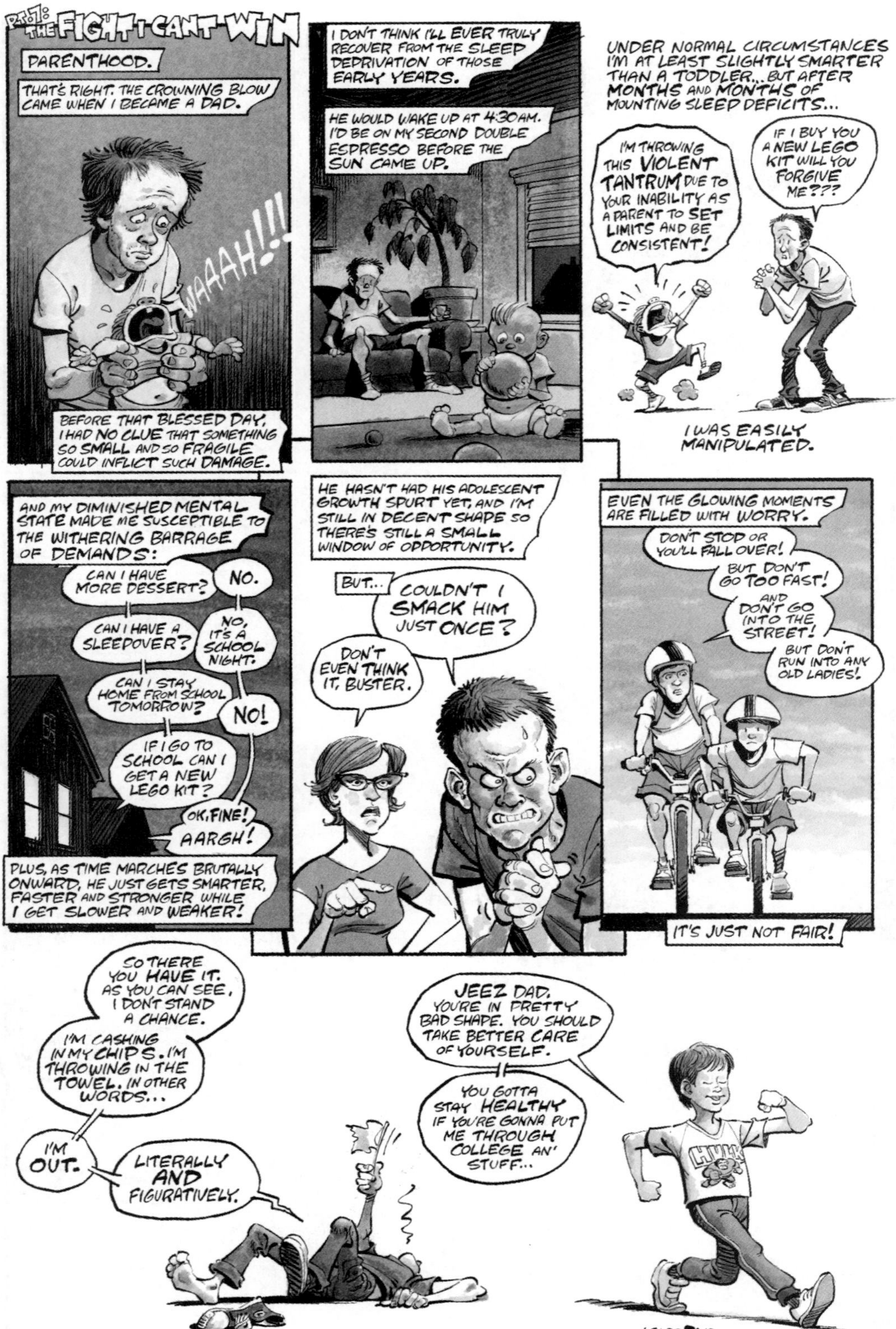
PT. 7: THE FIGHT I CAN'T WIN
PARENTHOOD.
THAT'S RIGHT. THE CROWNING BLOW CAME WHEN I BECAME A DAD.
WAAAH!!!
BEFORE THAT BLESSED DAY, I HAD NO CLUE THAT SOMETHING SO SMALL AND SO FRAGILE COULD INFLICT SUCH DAMAGE.
I DON'T THINK I'LL EVER TRULY RECOVER FROM THE SLEEP DEPRIVATION OF THOSE EARLY YEARS.
HE WOULD WAKE UP AT 4:30 AM. I'D BE ON MY SECOND DOUBLE ESPRESSO BEFORE THE SUN CAME UP.
UNDER NORMAL CIRCUMSTANCES I'M AT LEAST SLIGHTLY SMARTER THAN A TODDLER... BUT AFTER MONTHS AND MONTHS OF MOUNTING SLEEP DEFICITS...
I'M THROWING THIS VIOLENT TANTRUM DUE TO YOUR INABILITY AS A PARENT TO SET LIMITS AND BE CONSISTENT!
IF I BUY YOU A NEW LEGO KIT WILL YOU FORGIVE ME???
I WAS EASILY MANIPULATED.
AND MY DIMINISHED MENTAL STATE MADE ME SUSCEPTIBLE TO THE WITHERING BARRAGE OF DEMANDS:
CAN I HAVE MORE DESSERT?
NO.
CAN I HAVE A SLEEPOVER?
NO, IT'S A SCHOOL NIGHT.
CAN I STAY HOME FROM SCHOOL TOMORROW?
NO!
IF I GO TO SCHOOL CAN I GET A NEW LEGO KIT?
OK, FINE!
AARGH!
PLUS, AS TIME MARCHES BRUTALLY ONWARD, HE JUST GETS SMARTER, FASTER AND STRONGER WHILE I GET SLOWER AND WEAKER!
HE HASN'T HAD HIS ADOLESCENT GROWTH SPURT YET, AND I'M STILL IN DECENT SHAPE SO THERE'S STILL A SMALL WINDOW OF OPPORTUNITY.
BUT...
COULDN'T I SMACK HIM JUST ONCE?
DON'T EVEN THINK IT, BUSTER.
EVEN THE GLOWING MOMENTS ARE FILLED WITH WORRY.
DON'T STOP OR YOU'LL FALL OVER!
BUT DON'T GO TOO FAST!
AND DON'T GO INTO THE STREET!
BUT DON'T RUN INTO ANY OLD LADIES!
IT'S JUST NOT FAIR!
SO THERE YOU HAVE IT. AS YOU CAN SEE, I DON'T STAND A CHANCE.
I'M CASHING IN MY CHIPS. I'M THROWING IN THE TOWEL. IN OTHER WORDS...
I'M OUT.
LITERALLY AND FIGURATIVELY.
JEEZ DAD. YOU'RE IN PRETTY BAD SHAPE. YOU SHOULD TAKE BETTER CARE OF YOURSELF.
YOU GOTTA STAY HEALTHY IF YOU'RE GONNA PUT ME THROUGH COLLEGE AN' STUFF...
HULK
I SURRENDER!

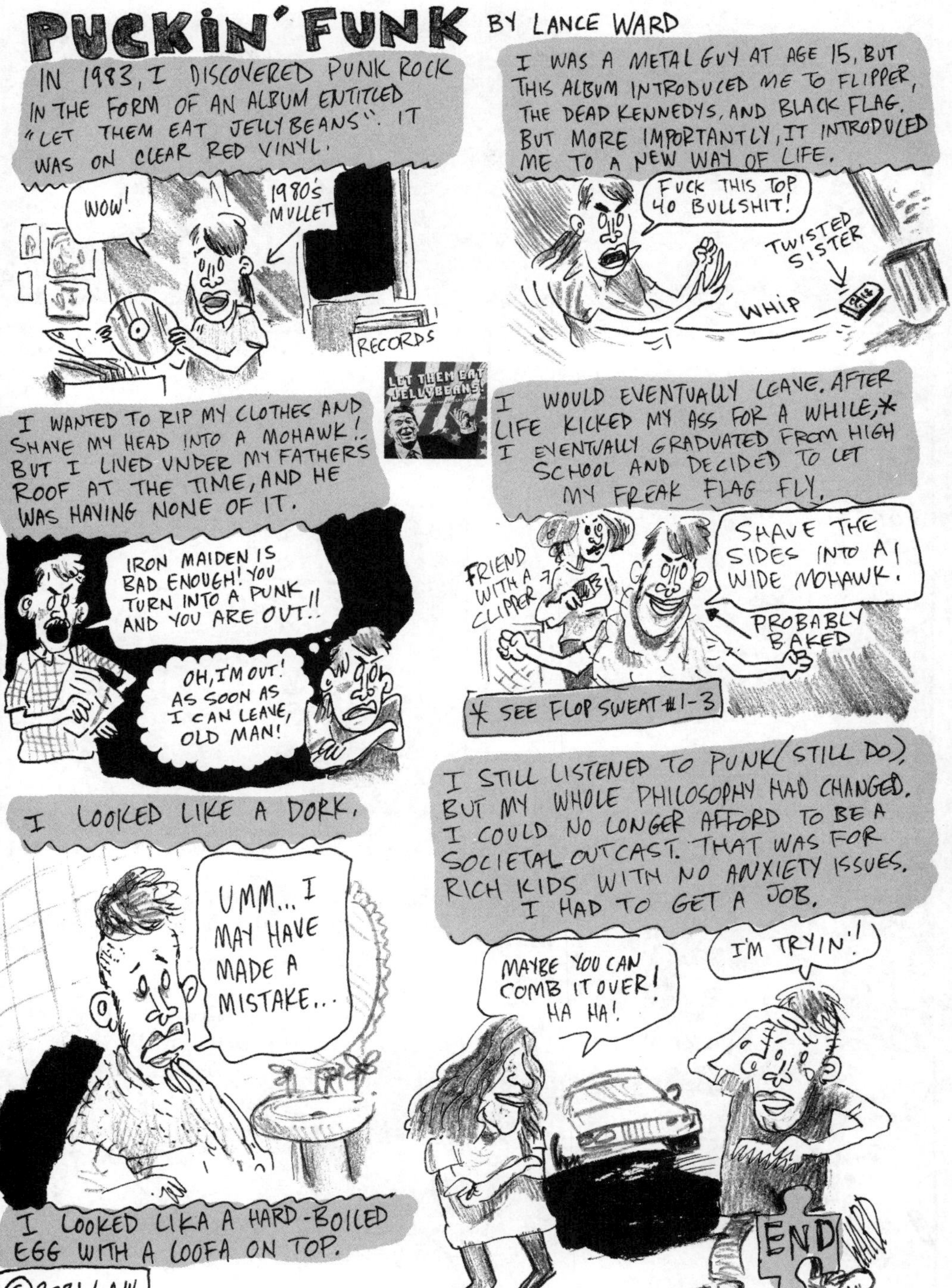
PUCKIN' FUNK BY LANCE WARD
IN 1983, I DISCOVERED PUNK ROCK IN THE FORM OF AN ALBUM ENTITLED "LET THEM EAT JELLYBEANS". IT WAS ON CLEAR RED VINYL.
WOW!
1980's MULLET
RECORDS
I WAS A METAL GUY AT AGE 15, BUT THIS ALBUM INTRODUCED ME TO FLIPPER, THE DEAD KENNEDYS, AND BLACK FLAG. BUT MORE IMPORTANTLY, IT INTRODUCED ME TO A NEW WAY OF LIFE.
FUCK THIS TOP 40 BULLSHIT!
TWISTED SISTER
WHIP
LET THEM EAT JELLYBEANS!
I WANTED TO RIP MY CLOTHES AND SHAVE MY HEAD INTO A MOHAWK! BUT I LIVED UNDER MY FATHERS ROOF AT THE TIME, AND HE WAS HAVING NONE OF IT.
IRON MAIDEN IS BAD ENOUGH! YOU TURN INTO A PUNK AND YOU ARE OUT!!
OH, I'M OUT! AS SOON AS I CAN LEAVE, OLD MAN!
I WOULD EVENTUALLY LEAVE. AFTER LIFE KICKED MY ASS FOR A WHILE,* I EVENTUALLY GRADUATED FROM HIGH SCHOOL AND DECIDED TO LET MY FREAK FLAG FLY.
FRIEND WITH A CLIPPER
SHAVE THE SIDES INTO A WIDE MOHAWK!
PROBABLY BAKED
* SEE FLOP SWEAT #1-3
I LOOKED LIKE A DORK.
UMM... I MAY HAVE MADE A MISTAKE...
I LOOKED LIKA A HARD-BOILED EGG WITH A LOOFA ON TOP.
©2021 L.A.W.
I STILL LISTENED TO PUNK (STILL DO), BUT MY WHOLE PHILOSOPHY HAD CHANGED. I COULD NO LONGER AFFORD TO BE A SOCIETAL OUTCAST. THAT WAS FOR RICH KIDS WITH NO ANXIETY ISSUES. I HAD TO GET A JOB.
MAYBE YOU CAN COMB IT OVER! HA HA!
I'M TRYIN'!
END
WARD

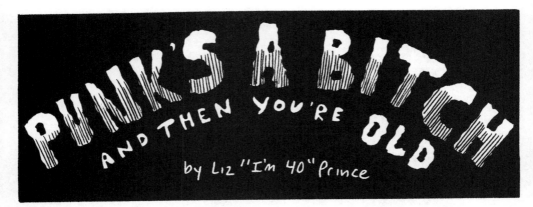

PUNK'S A BITCH AND THEN YOU'RE OLD

by Liz "I'm 40" Prince

Nostalgia is an extremely subjective thing - you can't yearn for the "good ol' days" of something you didn't live.

Unless you're a punk, then you can wax nostalgic about the heyday of CBGB's as if you weren't a toddler when it was going down.

Pfft, punk hasn't been good since '79.

"cool" "older" punk

Born in '81

GREEN DAY

Born in '78

The quickest way to prove how punk you are is to pay unyielding homage to those who came before.

SEX PISTOLS!

RAMONES!

SEX PISTOLS!

RAMONES!

Navigating that shit as a young punk in the 90's was exhausting and intimidating. And we didn't even have wikipedia as a cheat sheet!

Do you have any books on which punk bands are cool and which mean you're a poser?

LIBRARY HOURS

But I still had a lot of FUN, and it had everything to do with time and place.

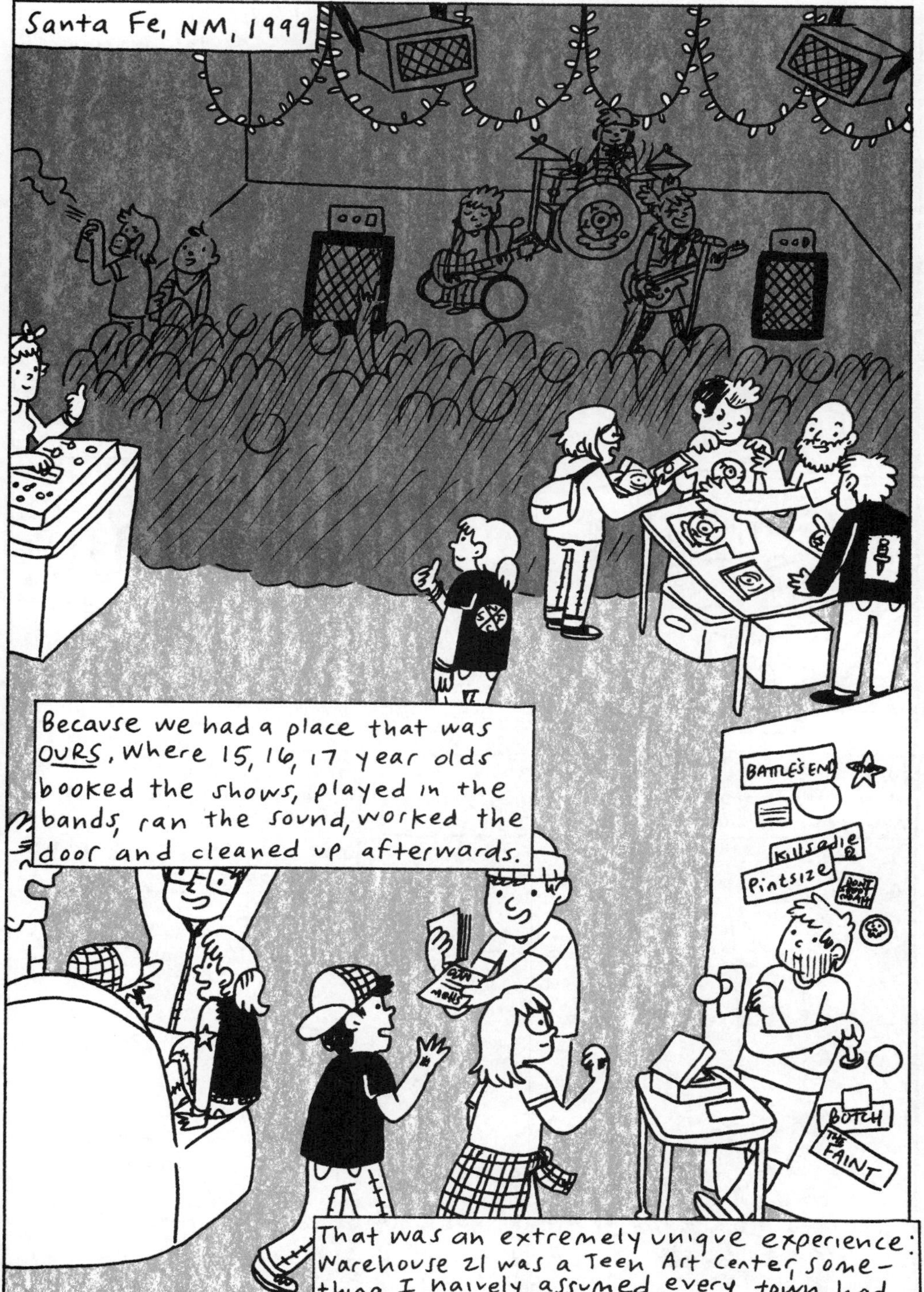

Santa Fe, NM, 1999
Because we had a place that was OURS, where 15, 16, 17 year olds booked the shows, played in the bands, ran the sound, worked the door and cleaned up afterwards.
BATTLE'S END
Killsadie
Pintsize
BOTCH
THE FAINT
That was an extremely unique experience: Warehouse 21 was a Teen Art Center, something I naively assumed every town had.

Growing up means that people and places change.

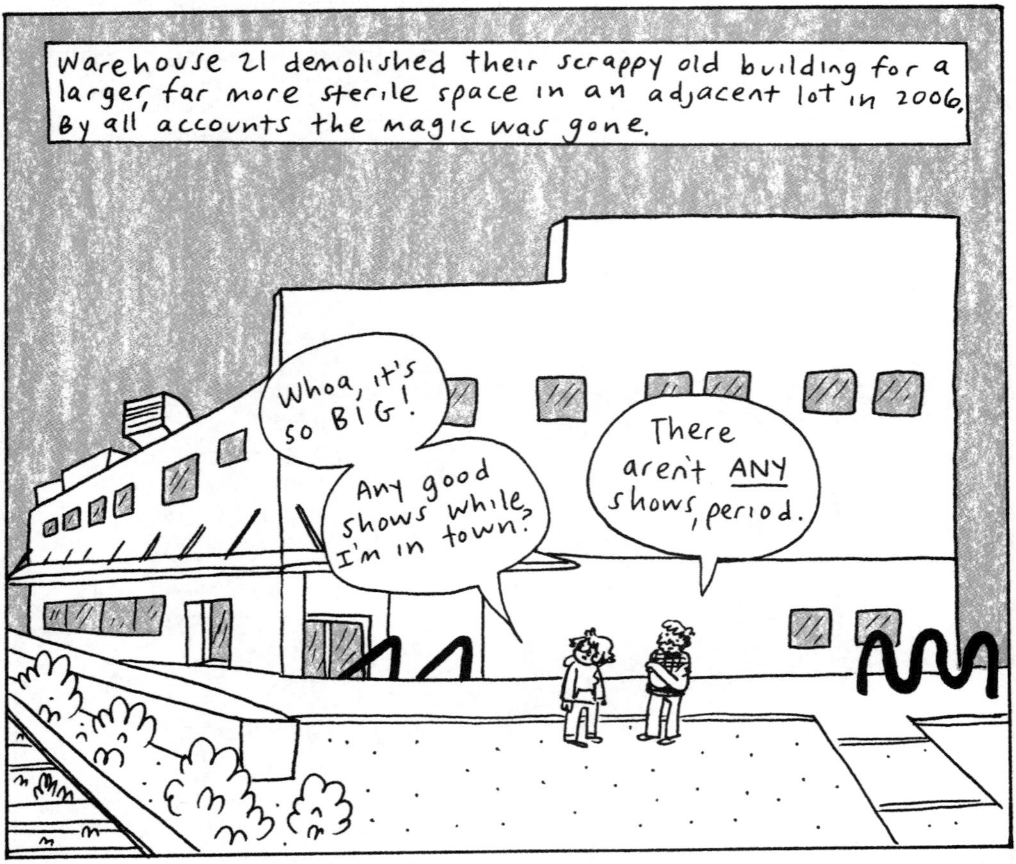

Warehouse 21 demolished their scrappy old building for a larger, far more sterile space in an adjacent lot in 2006. By all accounts the magic was gone.
Whoa, it's so BIG!
Any good shows while I'm in town?
There aren't ANY shows, period.

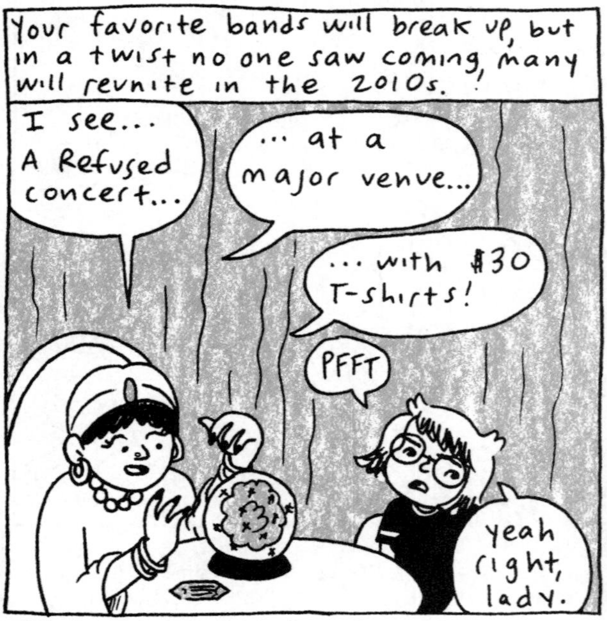

Your favorite bands will break up, but in a twist no one saw coming, many will reunite in the 2010s.
I see... A Refused concert...
... at a major venue...
... with $30 T-shirts!
PFFT
yeah right, lady.

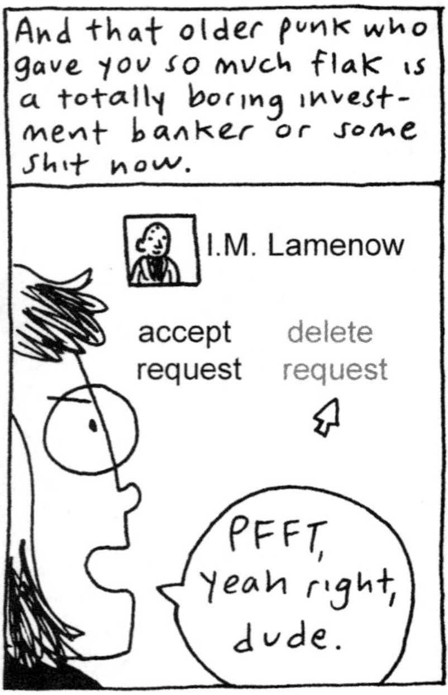

And that older punk who gave you so much flak is a totally boring investment banker or some shit now.
I.M. Lamenow
accept request
delete request
PFFT, yeah right, dude.

OK, this lady saw it coming.

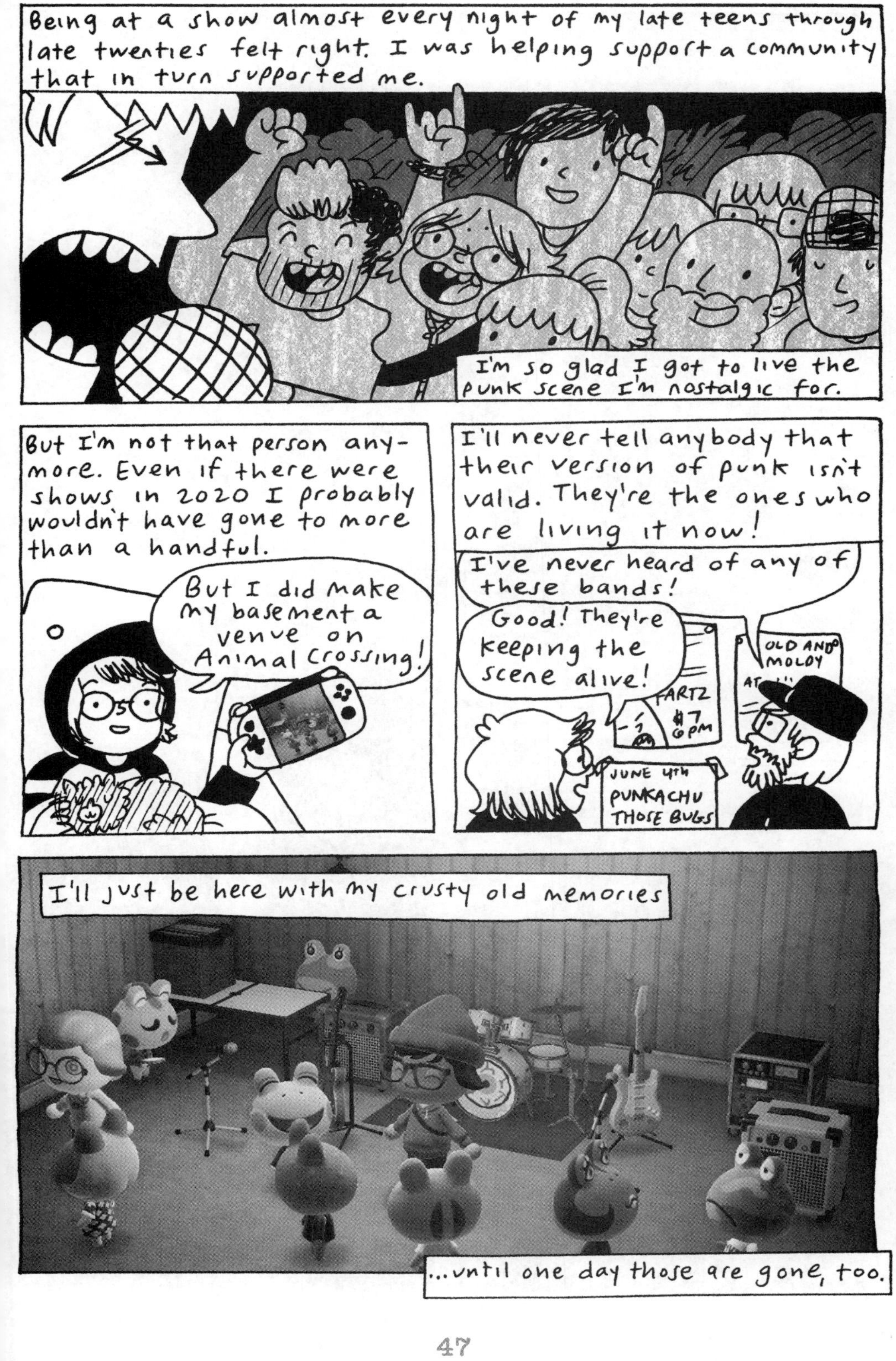
Being at a show almost every night of my late teens through late twenties felt right. I was helping support a community that in turn supported me.
I'm so glad I got to live the punk scene I'm nostalgic for.
But I'm not that person any-more. Even if there were shows in 2020 I probably wouldn't have gone to more than a handful.
But I did make my basement a venue on Animal Crossing!
I'll never tell anybody that their version of punk isn't valid. They're the ones who are living it now!
I've never heard of any of these bands!
Good! They're keeping the scene alive!
OLD AND MOLDY
FARTZ
$7
6PM
JUNE 4th
PUNKACHU
THOSE BUGS
I'll just be here with my crusty old memories
...until one day those are gone, too.

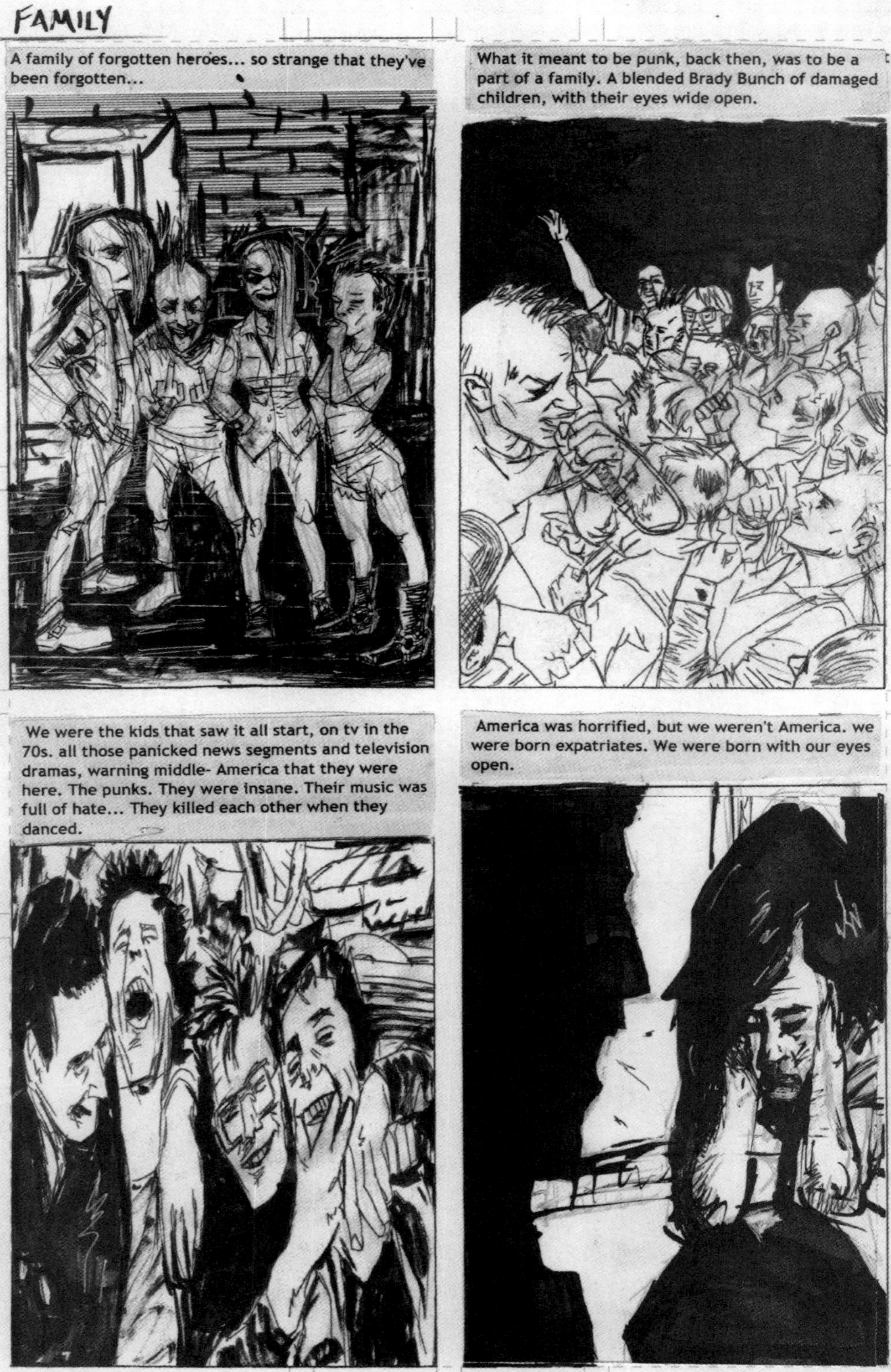
FAMILY
A family of forgotten heroes... so strange that they've been forgotten...
What it meant to be punk, back then, was to be a part of a family. A blended Brady Bunch of damaged children, with their eyes wide open.
We were the kids that saw it all start, on tv in the 70s. all those panicked news segments and television dramas, warning middle- America that they were here. The punks. They were insane. Their music was full of hate... They killed each other when they danced.
America was horrified, but we weren't America. we were born expatriates. We were born with our eyes open.

Even as we watched those shows and played with our SSP Racers, we were outsiders. Unknown to us, we even had a name, but we wouldnt hear about it for another 5 or 10 years. In the 70's the name was still being used by a band of young British musicians: They were Generation X, and so were we.

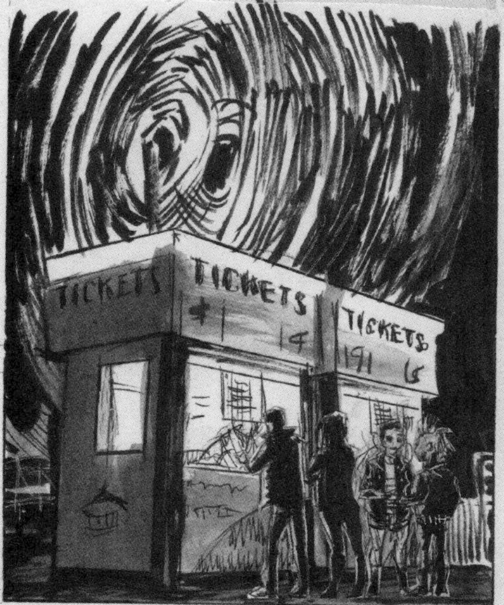

TICKETS
TICKETS
TICKETS

From the outside, (by design) punk appeared ugly, hostile, hateful. But it was fascinating, to us at least. These punks were grown-ups, but they were like us. They were what we would be, they were grown... but they were not grown up... They weren't the Hessian dirt-bags that listened to "hard-rock", and wore denim. the sullen, racist, pimply faced, long-haired guys and girls in Camaros, that the other kids (the social, normal kids that our parents liked) wanted to grow into.

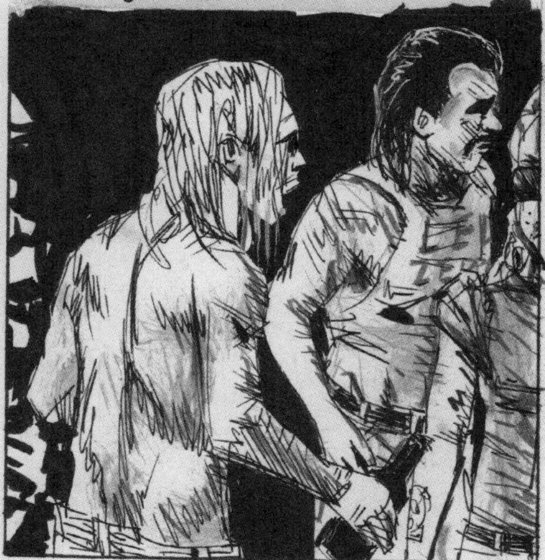

To us the mysterious punks were a living dream... superheroes. Superheroes in black leather. Living embodiments of Fonzie, that were an impossible mix of art and intention and suicidal amounts of not giving a fuck about the normal-people's world.

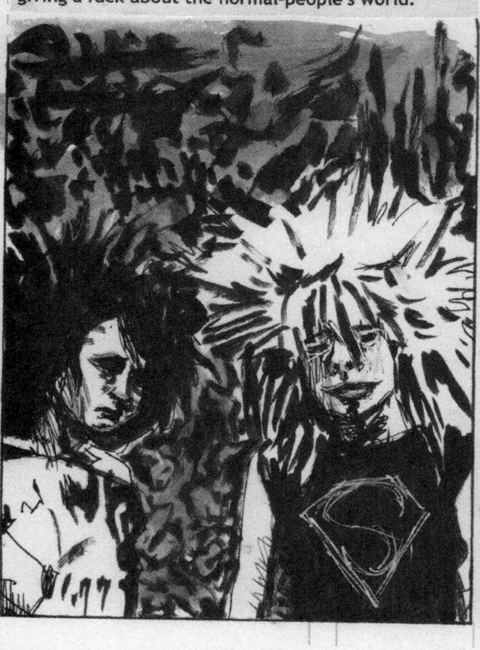

We were the whipping-boy, onto which was unloaded the fears prejudices and petty frustrations of the greater society that orbited us.

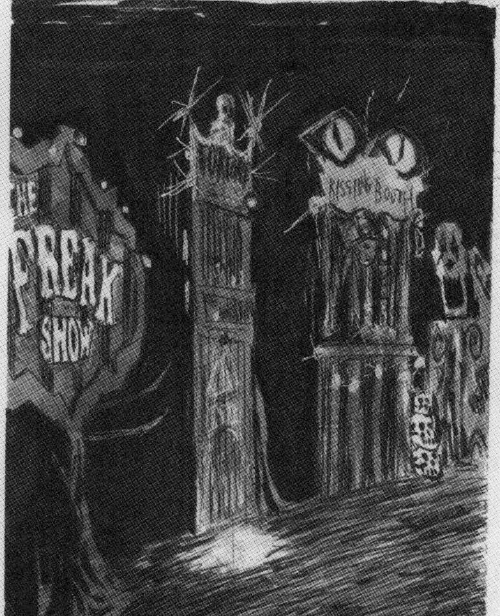

THE FREAK SHOW
KISSING

If you remove 80's punk from music and fashion, it is a framework on which to build your moral hot-rod.
When everyone else drives a BMW or Cadillac, you look at your piece of shit tin can, and know that its heart is detailed, high-compression chrome.

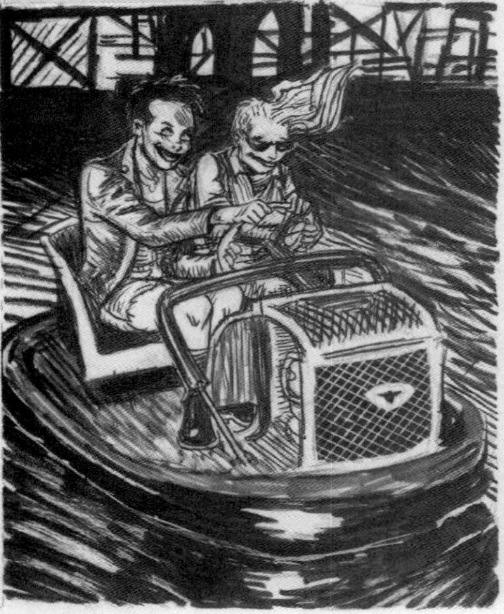

A society that mirrored, multiplied and intensified the malignant parental gaze, which was the cause of the damage that drew us together like fingers in a fist.

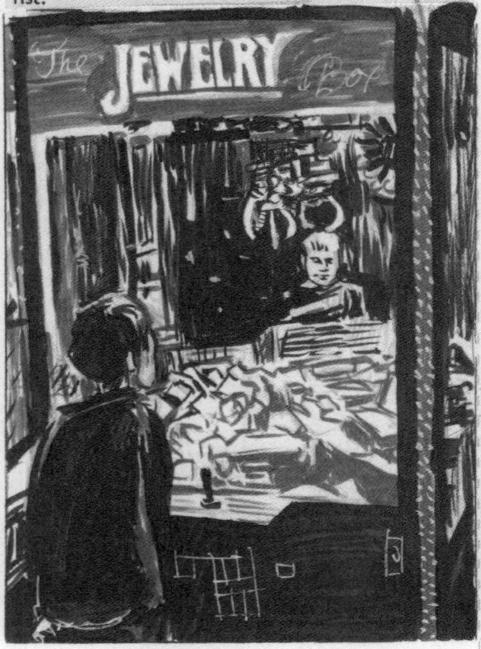
The JEWELRY Box

So we went places that we weren't supposed to go, and took our licks from society's darlings, because they realized the ugly power structure as well as we did, but they chose to embrace it instead.

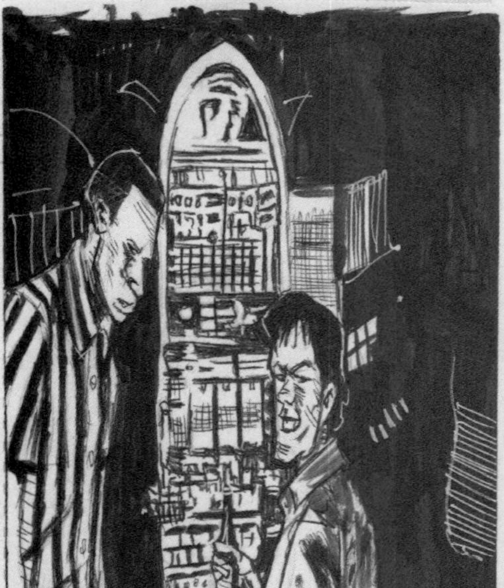

We were an entire generation of individuals that chose the martyrdom of a clean-conscience that was thrust upon you as a masochistic-morality, by an animalistic society whose only passions were fueled by selfish self-interest.

A passion for survival of the fittest based on lust and material-gain, facilitated by and nourished on, the blood and tears of the leather-bound saints.

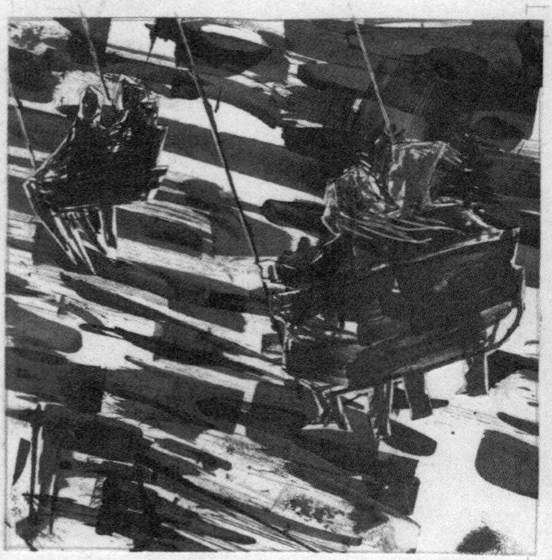

-X

How to Enjoy Breaking Your Glasses

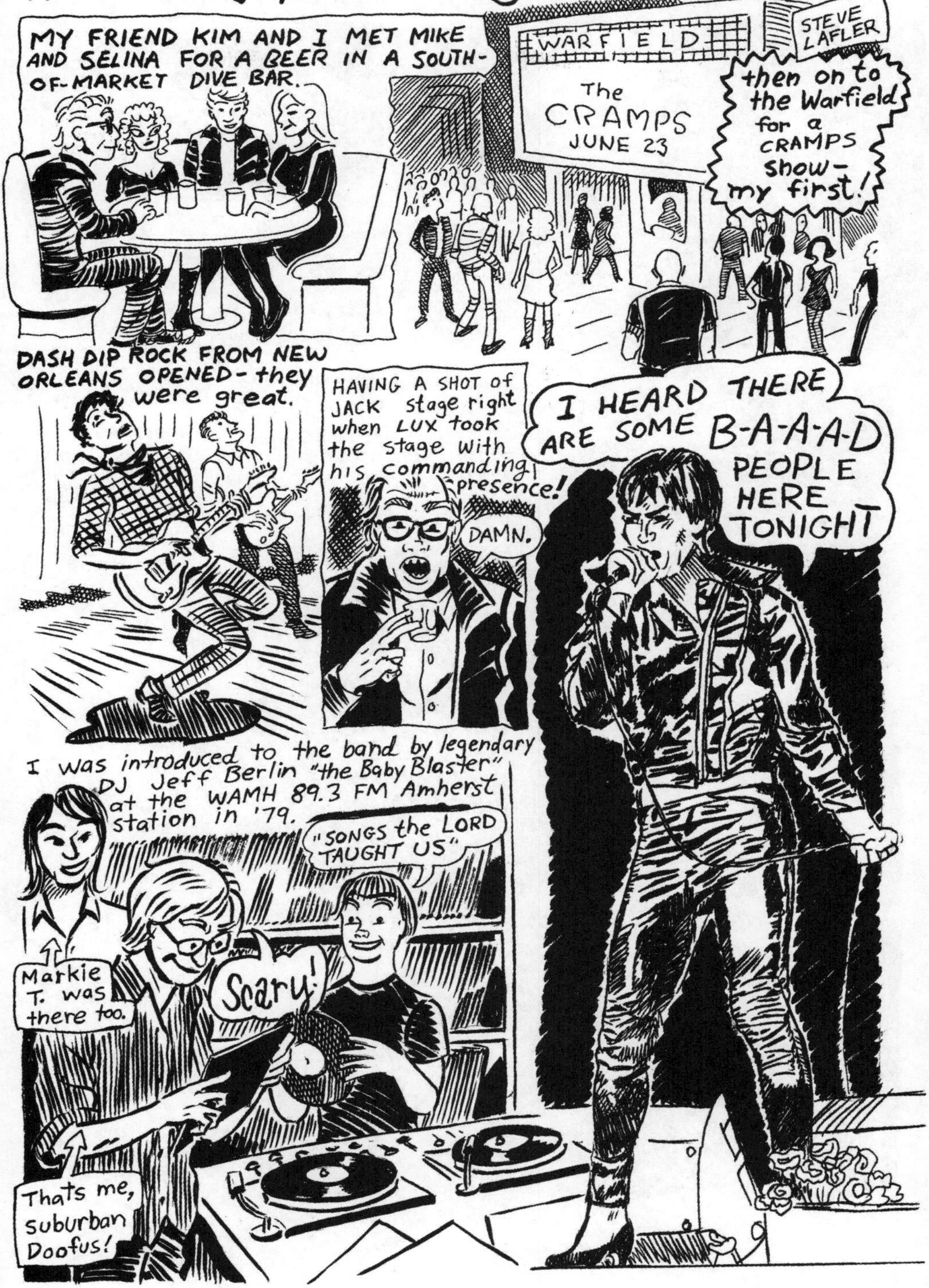

MY FRIEND KIM AND I MET MIKE AND SELINA FOR A BEER IN A SOUTH-OF-MARKET DIVE BAR.
WARFIELD
The CRAMPS JUNE 23
STEVE LAFLER
then on to the Warfield for a CRAMPS show– my first!
DASH DIP ROCK FROM NEW ORLEANS OPENED– they were great.
HAVING A SHOT of JACK stage right when LUX took the stage with his commanding presence!
DAMN.
I HEARD THERE ARE SOME B-A-A-A-D PEOPLE HERE TONIGHT
I was introduced to the band by legendary DJ Jeff Berlin "the Baby Blaster" at the WAMH 89.3 FM Amherst station in '79.
"SONGS the LORD TAUGHT US"
Markie T. was there too.
Scary!
Thats me, suburban Doofus!

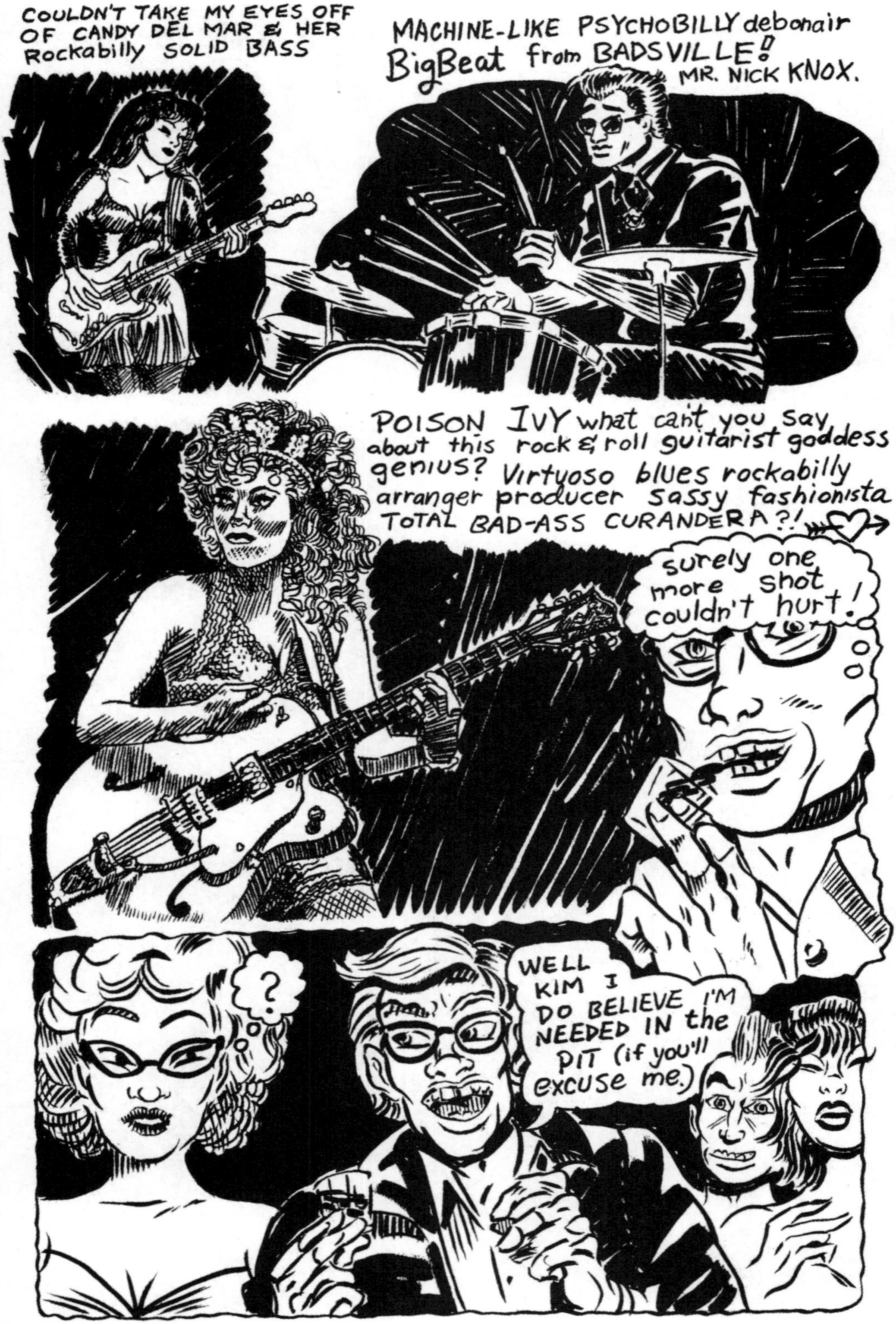
COULDN'T TAKE MY EYES OFF OF CANDY DEL MAR & HER Rockabilly SOLID BASS
MACHINE-LIKE PSYCHOBILLY debonair BigBeat from BADSVILLE! MR. NICK KNOX.
POISON IVY what can't you say about this rock & roll guitarist goddess genius? Virtuoso blues rockabilly arranger producer sassy fashionista TOTAL BAD-ASS CURANDERA?!
surely one more shot couldn't hurt!
?
WELL KIM I DO BELIEVE I'M NEEDED IN the PIT (if you'll excuse me.)

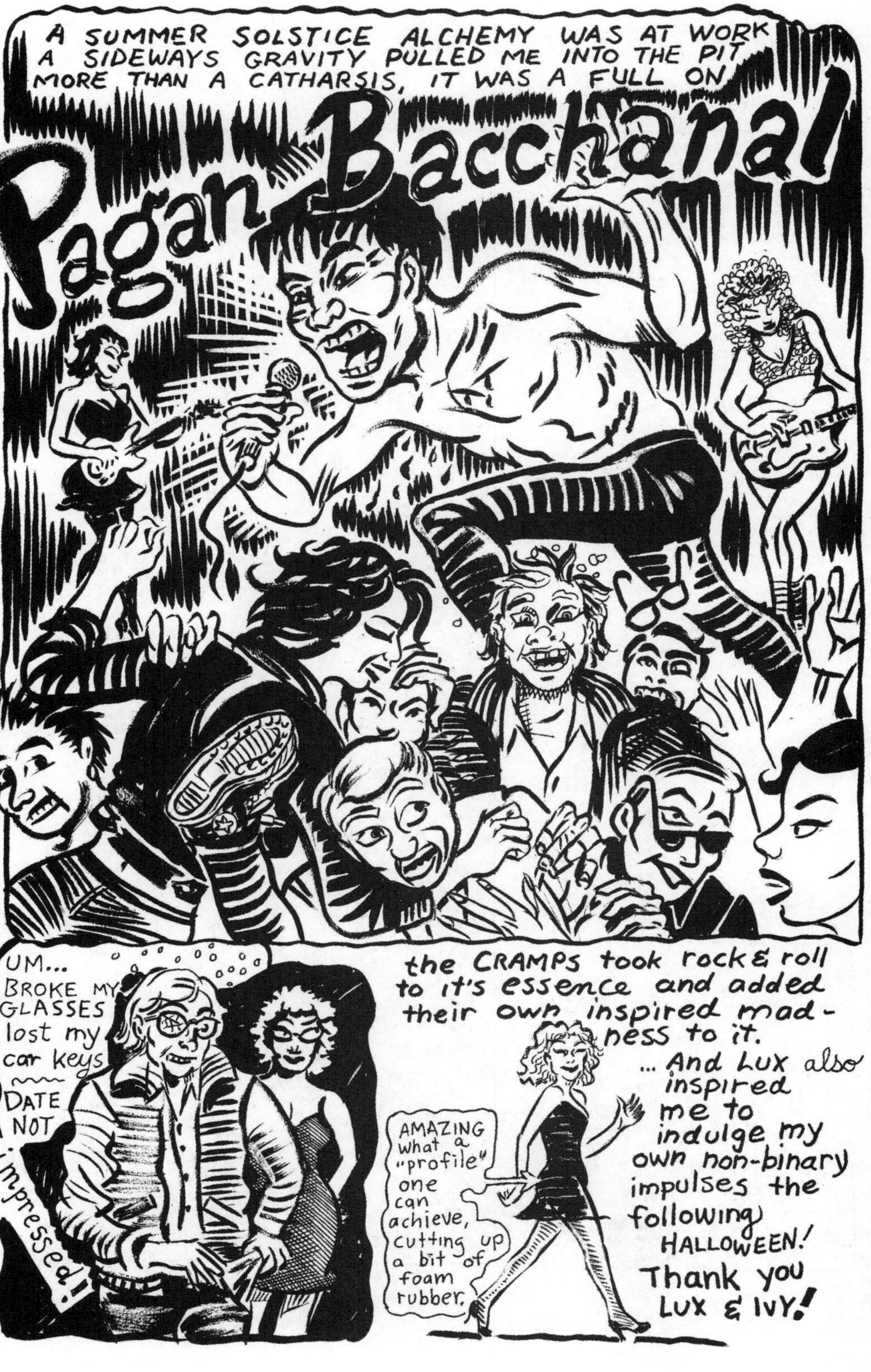
A SUMMER SOLSTICE ALCHEMY WAS AT WORK
A SIDEWAYS GRAVITY PULLED ME INTO THE PIT
MORE THAN A CATHARSIS, IT WAS A FULL ON
Pagan Bacchanal
UM... BROKE MY GLASSES lost my car keys ~ DATE NOT impressed!
the CRAMPS took rock & roll to it's essence and added their own inspired madness to it.
... And LUX also inspired me to indulge my own non-binary impulses the following HALLOWEEN!
AMAZING what a "profile" one can achieve, cutting up a bit of foam rubber.
Thank you LUX & IVY!

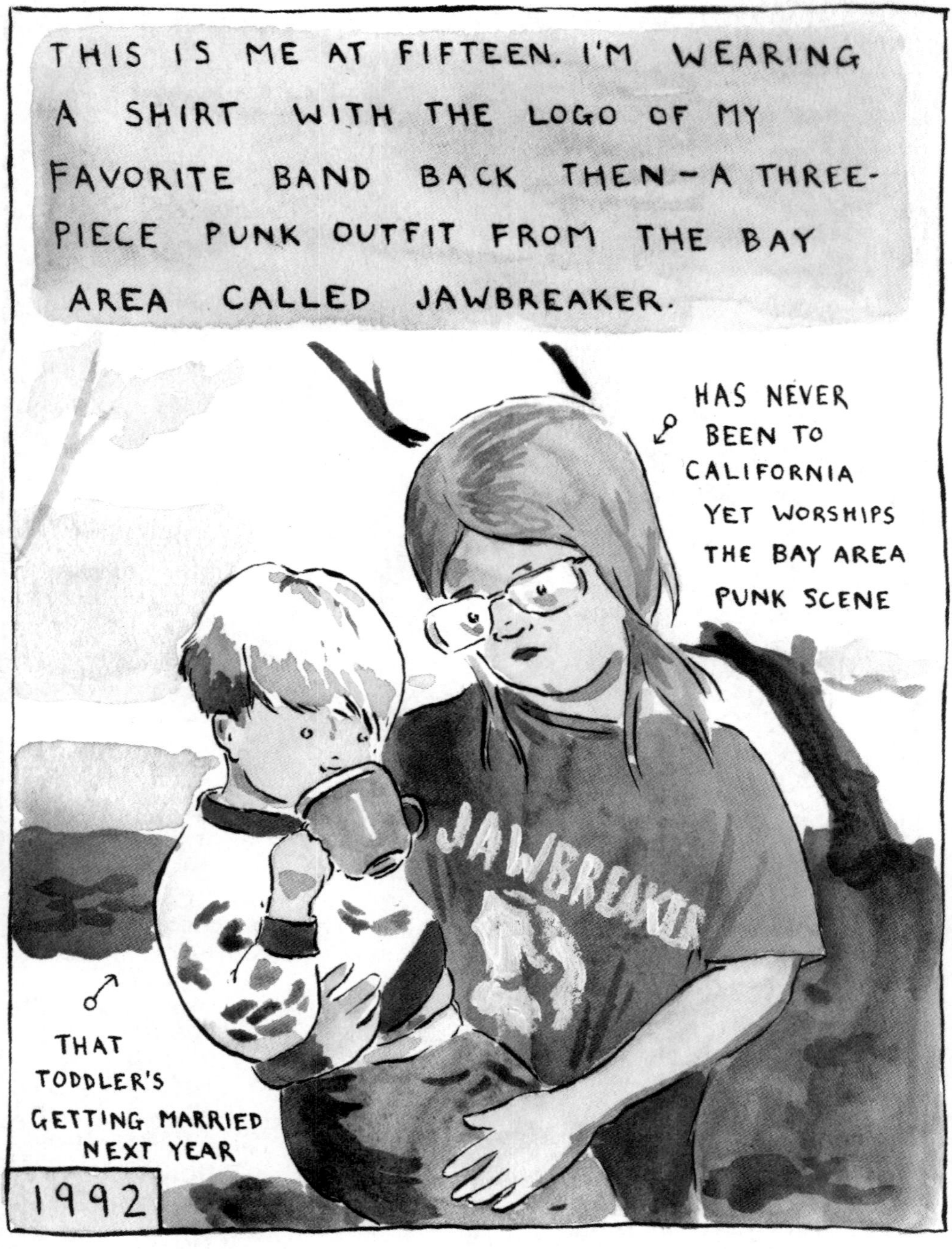
THIS IS ME AT FIFTEEN. I'M WEARING A SHIRT WITH THE LOGO OF MY FAVORITE BAND BACK THEN – A THREE-PIECE PUNK OUTFIT FROM THE BAY AREA CALLED JAWBREAKER.
HAS NEVER BEEN TO CALIFORNIA YET WORSHIPS THE BAY AREA PUNK SCENE
JAWBREAKER
THAT TODDLER'S GETTING MARRIED NEXT YEAR
1992

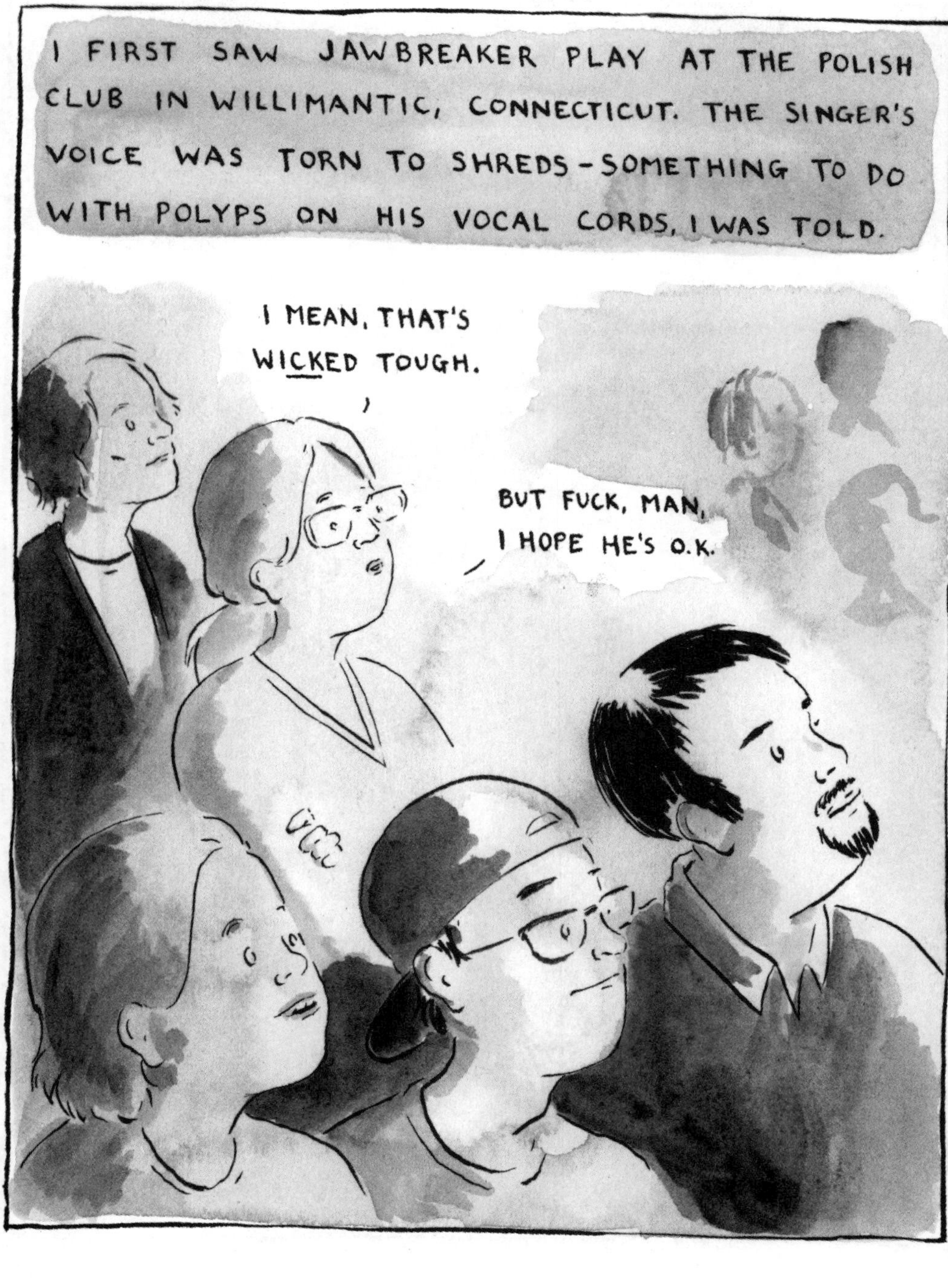
I FIRST SAW JAWBREAKER PLAY AT THE POLISH CLUB IN WILLIMANTIC, CONNECTICUT. THE SINGER'S VOICE WAS TORN TO SHREDS - SOMETHING TO DO WITH POLYPS ON HIS VOCAL CORDS, I WAS TOLD.
I MEAN, THAT'S WICKED TOUGH.
BUT FUCK, MAN, I HOPE HE'S O.K.

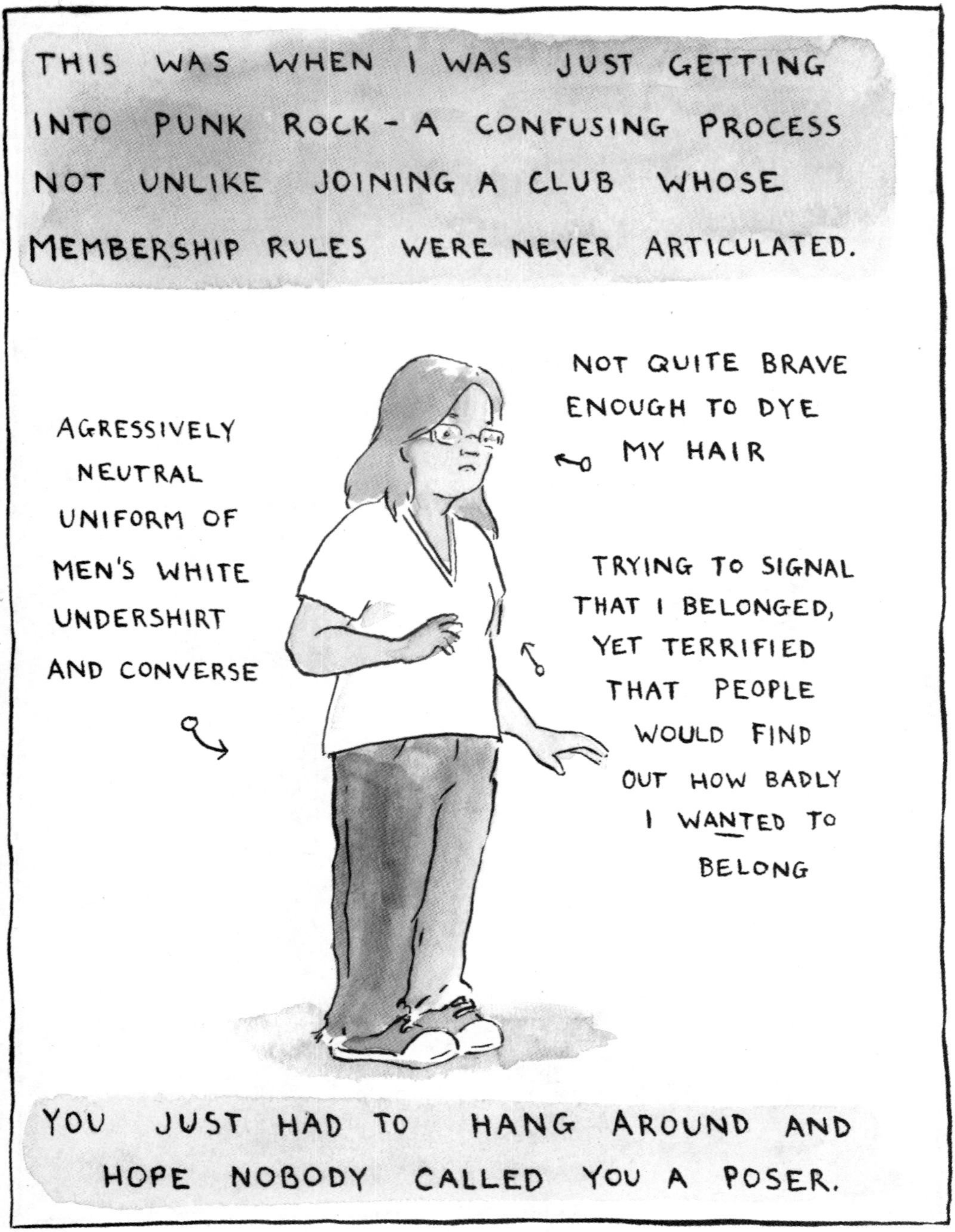
THIS WAS WHEN I WAS JUST GETTING INTO PUNK ROCK - A CONFUSING PROCESS NOT UNLIKE JOINING A CLUB WHOSE MEMBERSHIP RULES WERE NEVER ARTICULATED.
AGRESSIVELY NEUTRAL UNIFORM OF MEN'S WHITE UNDERSHIRT AND CONVERSE
NOT QUITE BRAVE ENOUGH TO DYE MY HAIR
TRYING TO SIGNAL THAT I BELONGED, YET TERRIFIED THAT PEOPLE WOULD FIND OUT HOW BADLY I WANTED TO BELONG
YOU JUST HAD TO HANG AROUND AND HOPE NOBODY CALLED YOU A POSER.

IT'S HARD TO DESCRIBE NOW
HOW THAT SCENE WORKED AND WHAT
IT MEANT TO US. BRIEFLY, WE MADE
OUR OWN FUN: WE WERE IN BANDS,
MADE FANZINES, PUT ON SHOWS IN
COMMUNITY HALLS AND BASEMENTS,
STARTED MICRO RECORD LABELS - AN
ENTIRE SUI-GENERIS MEDIA EMPIRE
RUN BY CHILDREN. BUT WE ALSO
FUNCTIONED AS A CELL OF A LARGER
NETWORK OF LIKE-MINDED PEOPLE - AND
THE LINE BETWEEN ARTIST AND FAN
WAS BLURRED, WHERE IT EXISTED AT ALL.

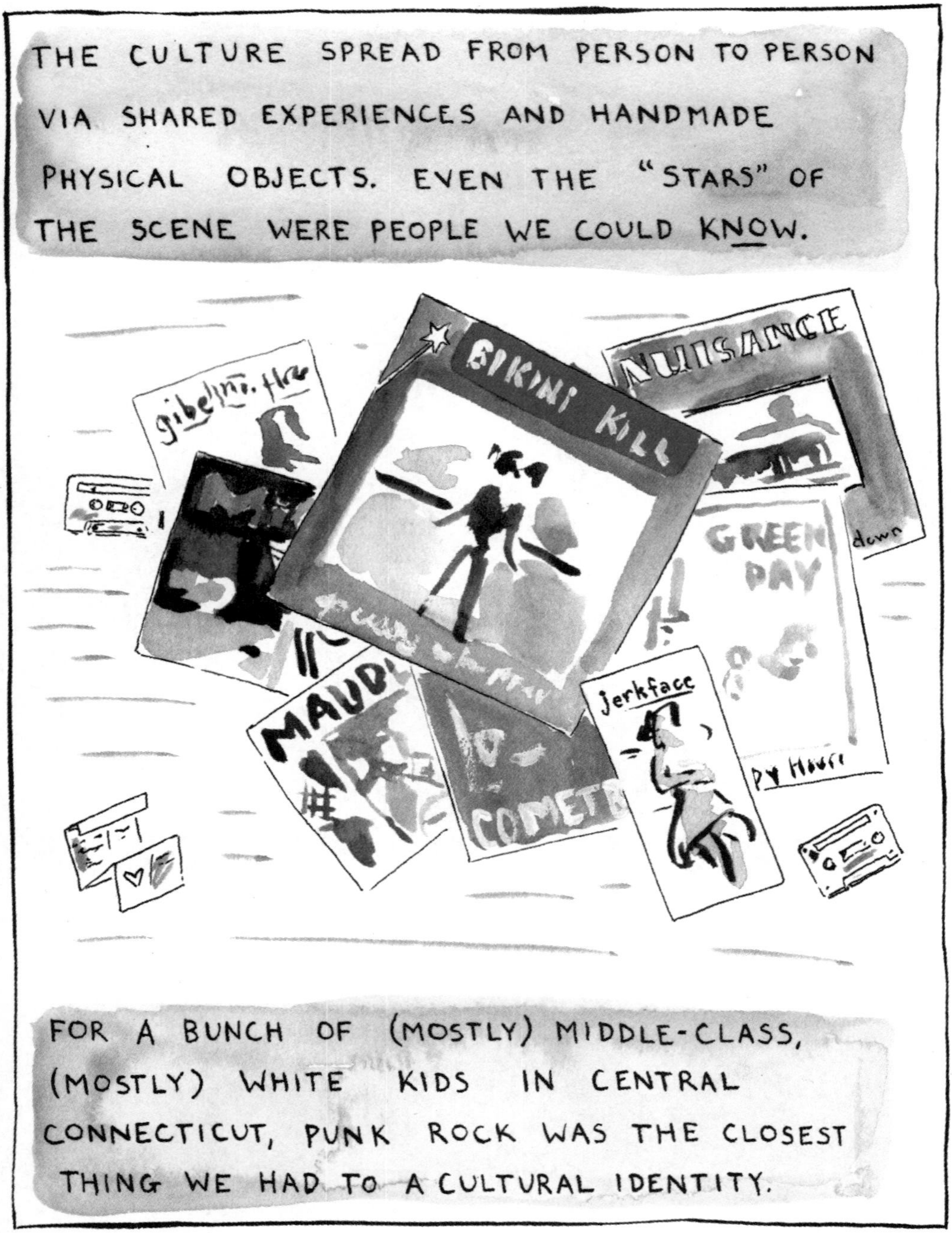
THE CULTURE SPREAD FROM PERSON TO PERSON VIA SHARED EXPERIENCES AND HANDMADE PHYSICAL OBJECTS. EVEN THE "STARS" OF THE SCENE WERE PEOPLE WE COULD KNOW.
BIKINI KILL
NUISANCE
GREEN DAY
jerkface
MAUD
COMETR
FOR A BUNCH OF (MOSTLY) MIDDLE-CLASS, (MOSTLY) WHITE KIDS IN CENTRAL CONNECTICUT, PUNK ROCK WAS THE CLOSEST THING WE HAD TO A CULTURAL IDENTITY.

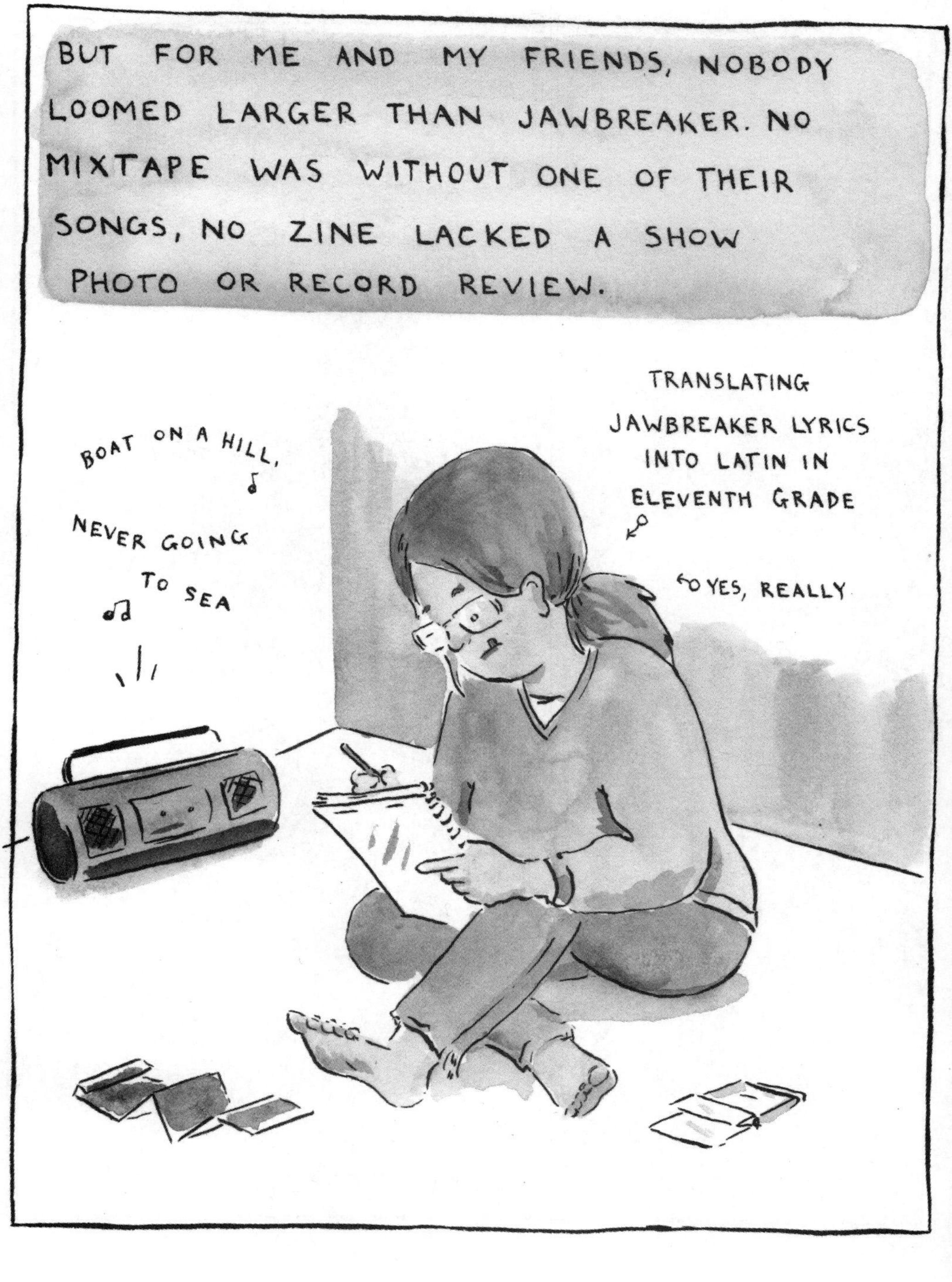

BUT FOR ME AND MY FRIENDS, NOBODY LOOMED LARGER THAN JAWBREAKER. NO MIXTAPE WAS WITHOUT ONE OF THEIR SONGS, NO ZINE LACKED A SHOW PHOTO OR RECORD REVIEW.
BOAT ON A HILL,
NEVER GOING TO SEA
TRANSLATING JAWBREAKER LYRICS INTO LATIN IN ELEVENTH GRADE
YES, REALLY

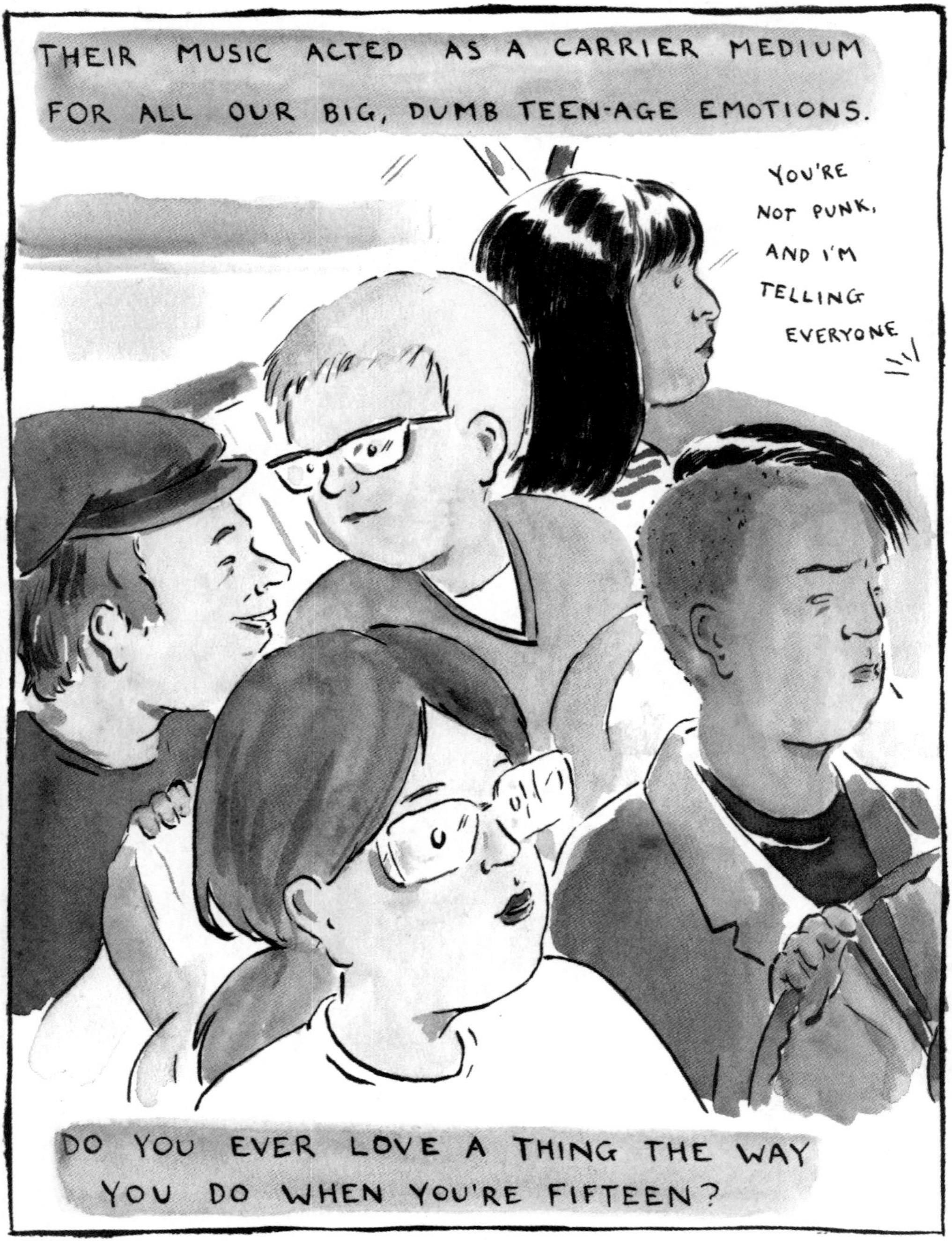
THEIR MUSIC ACTED AS A CARRIER MEDIUM FOR ALL OUR BIG, DUMB TEEN-AGE EMOTIONS.
YOU'RE NOT PUNK, AND I'M TELLING EVERYONE
DO YOU EVER LOVE A THING THE WAY YOU DO WHEN YOU'RE FIFTEEN?

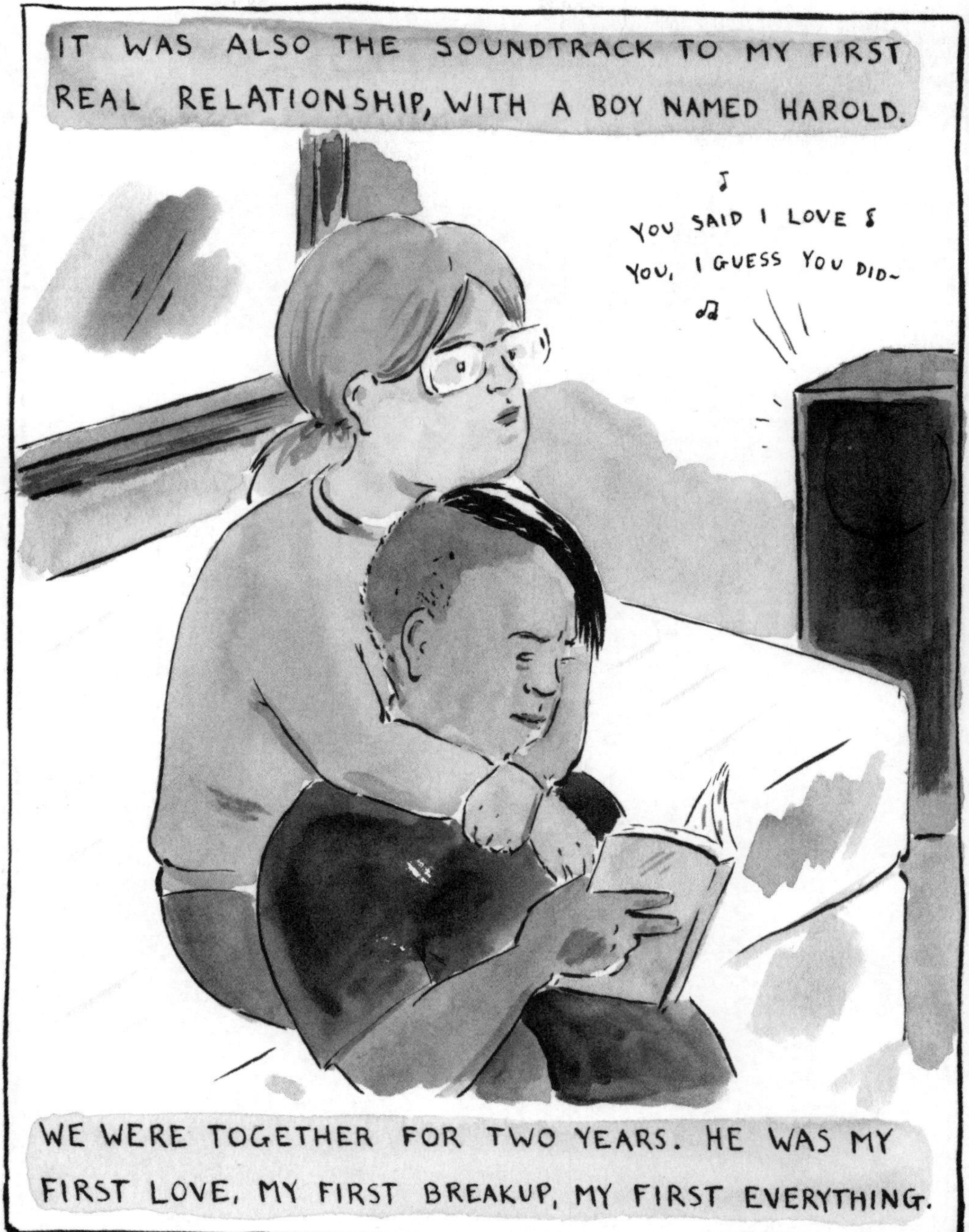
IT WAS ALSO THE SOUNDTRACK TO MY FIRST REAL RELATIONSHIP, WITH A BOY NAMED HAROLD.
YOU SAID I LOVE YOU, I GUESS YOU DID~
WE WERE TOGETHER FOR TWO YEARS. HE WAS MY FIRST LOVE, MY FIRST BREAKUP, MY FIRST EVERYTHING.

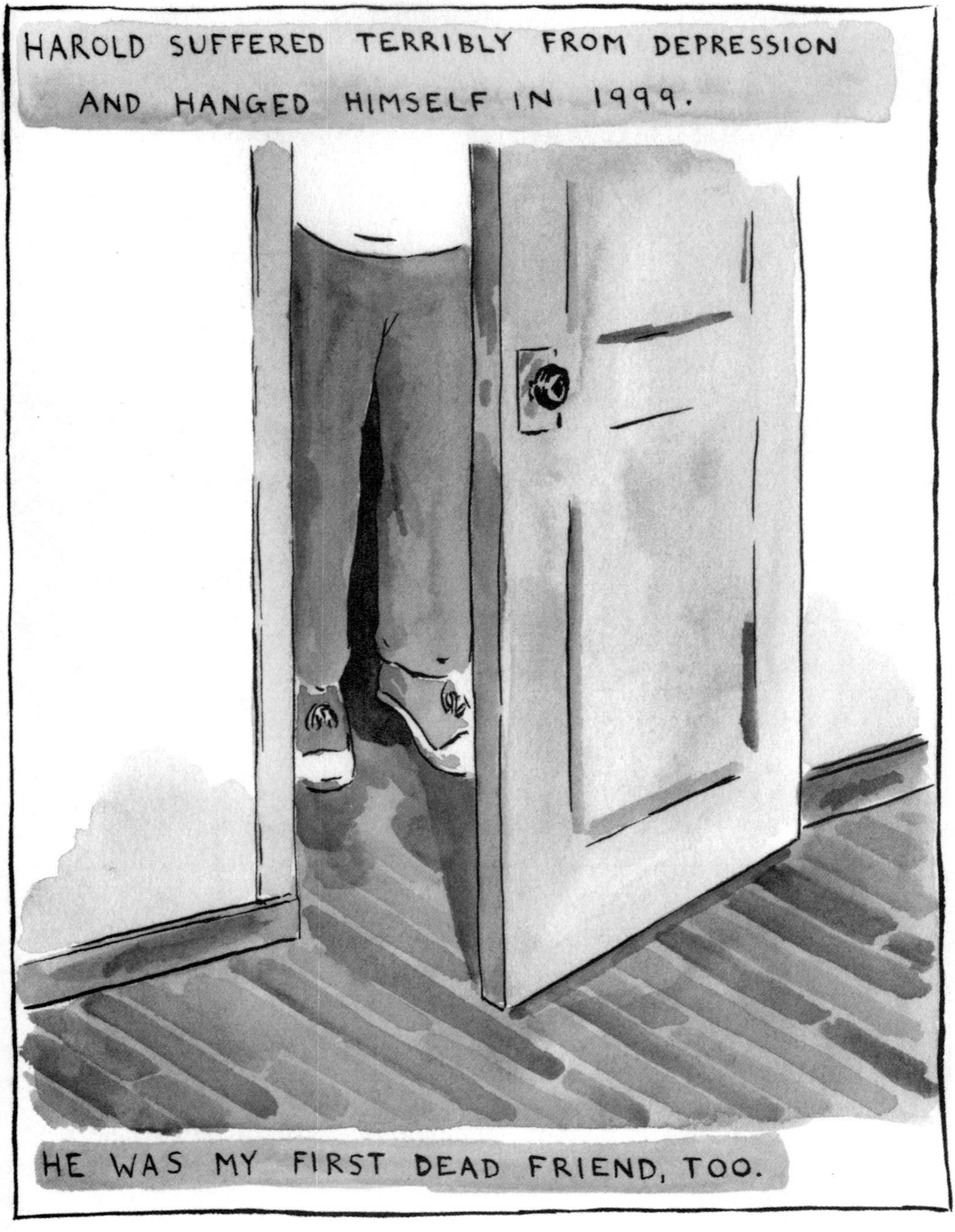
HAROLD SUFFERED TERRIBLY FROM DEPRESSION AND HANGED HIMSELF IN 1999.
HE WAS MY FIRST DEAD FRIEND, TOO.

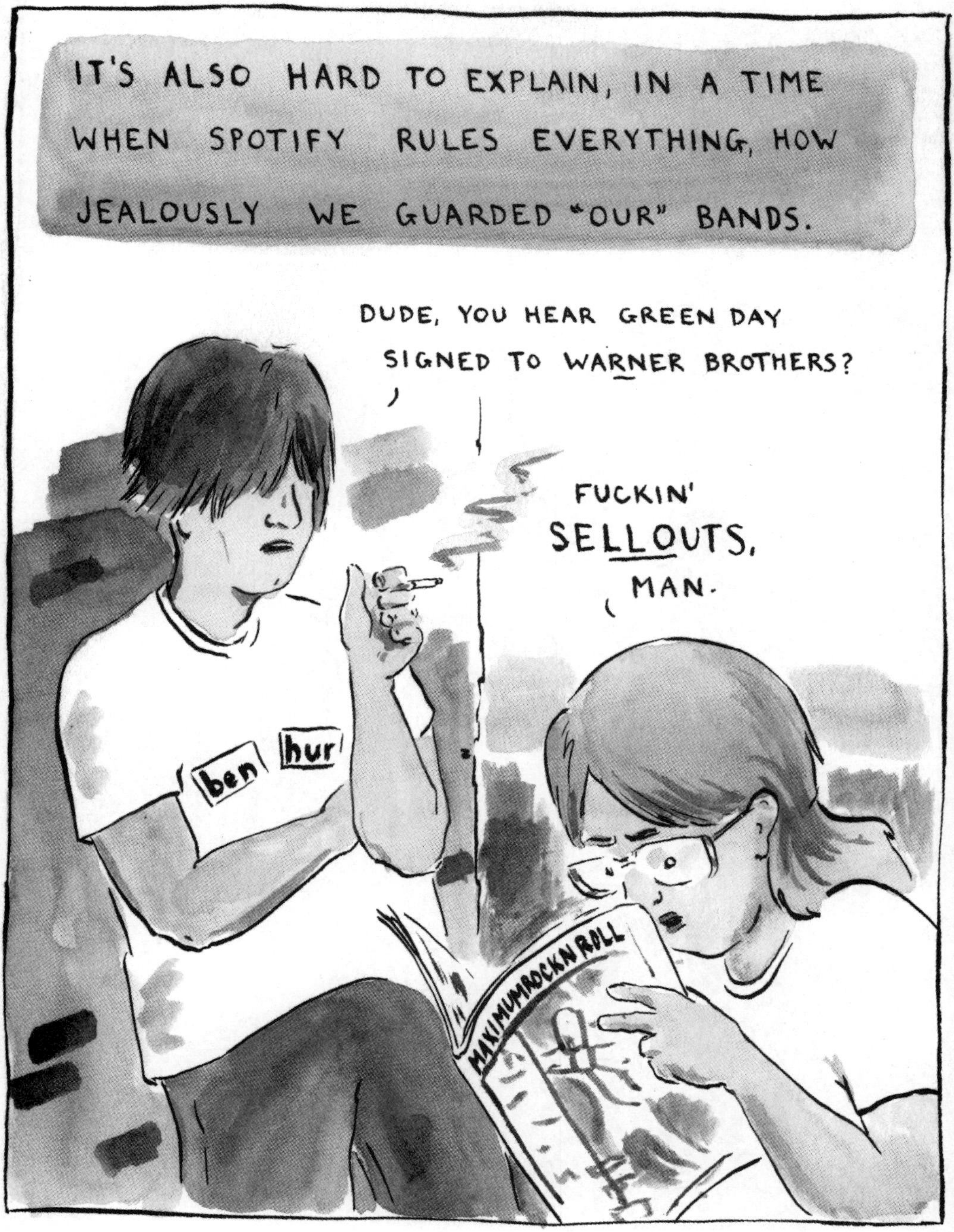
IT'S ALSO HARD TO EXPLAIN, IN A TIME WHEN SPOTIFY RULES EVERYTHING, HOW JEALOUSLY WE GUARDED "OUR" BANDS.
DUDE, YOU HEAR GREEN DAY SIGNED TO WARNER BROTHERS?
FUCKIN' SELLOUTS, MAN.
ben hur
MAXIMUMROCKNROLL

LOSING GREEN DAY TO A MAJOR WAS ONE THING, BUT WHEN JAWBREAKER SIGNED IT FELT LIKE A KNIFE IN THE BACK.
DEAD TO US!
JAWBREAKER

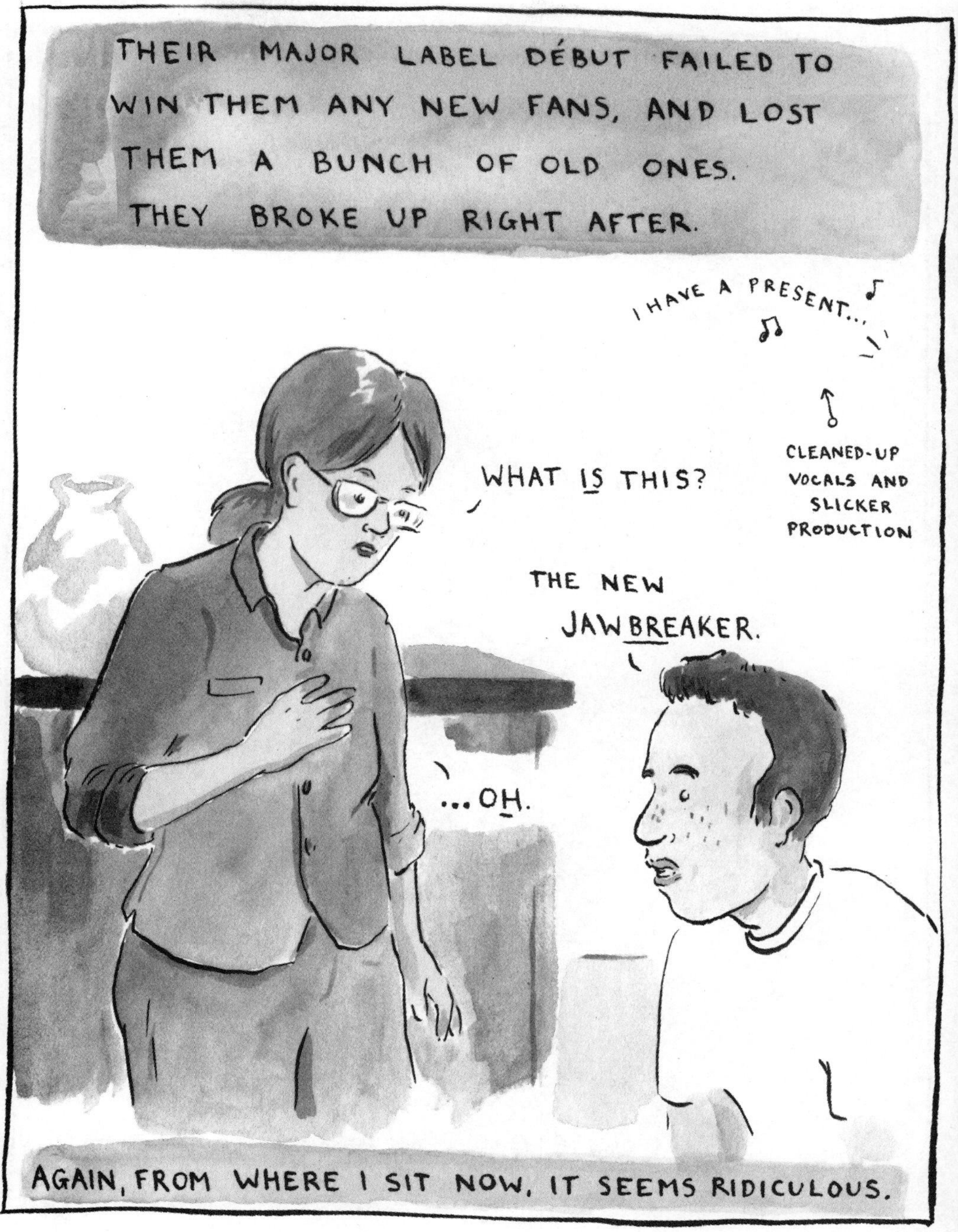
THEIR MAJOR LABEL DÉBUT FAILED TO WIN THEM ANY NEW FANS, AND LOST THEM A BUNCH OF OLD ONES. THEY BROKE UP RIGHT AFTER.
I HAVE A PRESENT...
CLEANED-UP VOCALS AND SLICKER PRODUCTION
WHAT IS THIS?
THE NEW JAWBREAKER.
...OH.
AGAIN, FROM WHERE I SIT NOW, IT SEEMS RIDICULOUS.

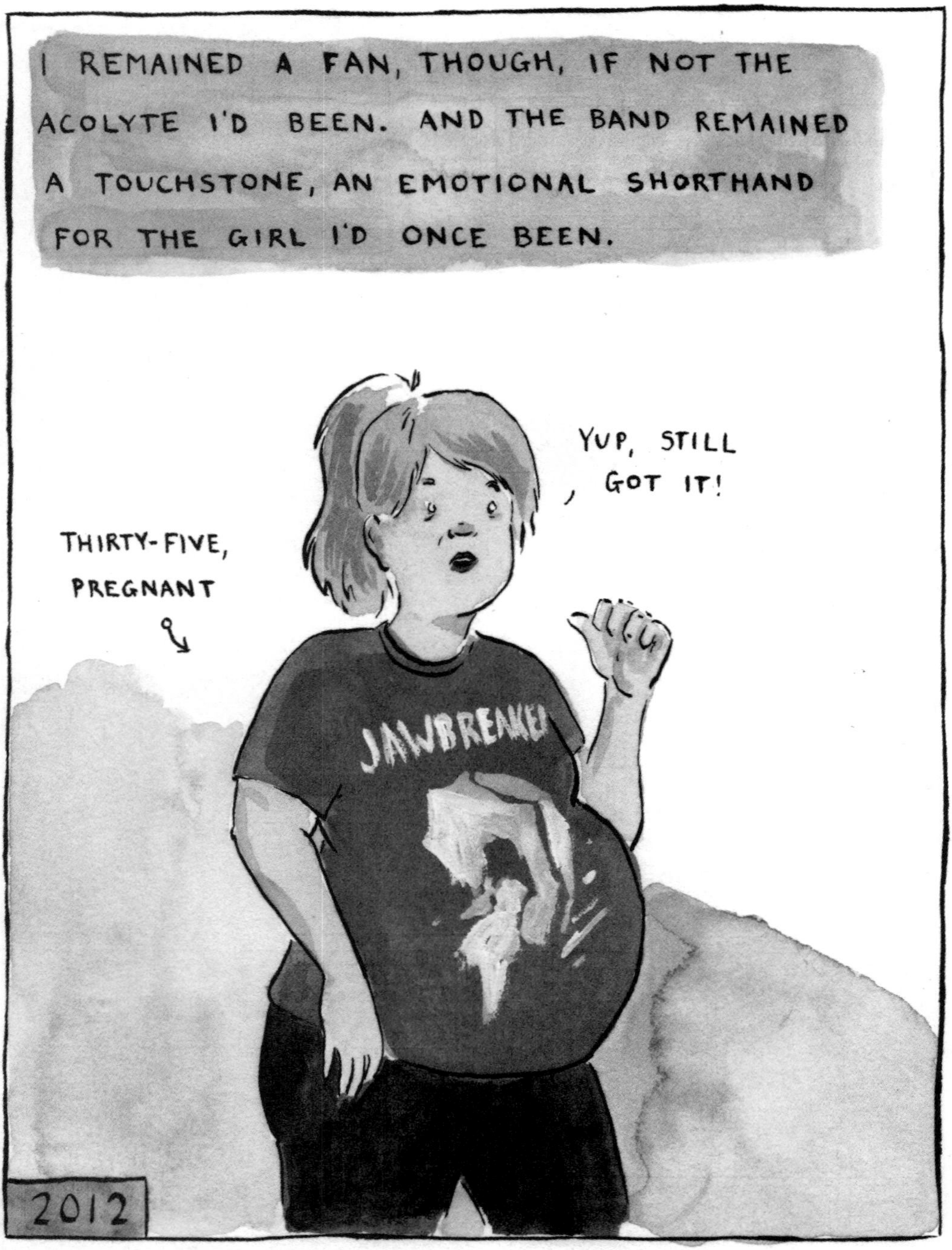
I REMAINED A FAN, THOUGH, IF NOT THE ACOLYTE I'D BEEN. AND THE BAND REMAINED A TOUCHSTONE, AN EMOTIONAL SHORTHAND FOR THE GIRL I'D ONCE BEEN.
YUP, STILL GOT IT!
THIRTY-FIVE, PREGNANT
JAWBREAKER
2012

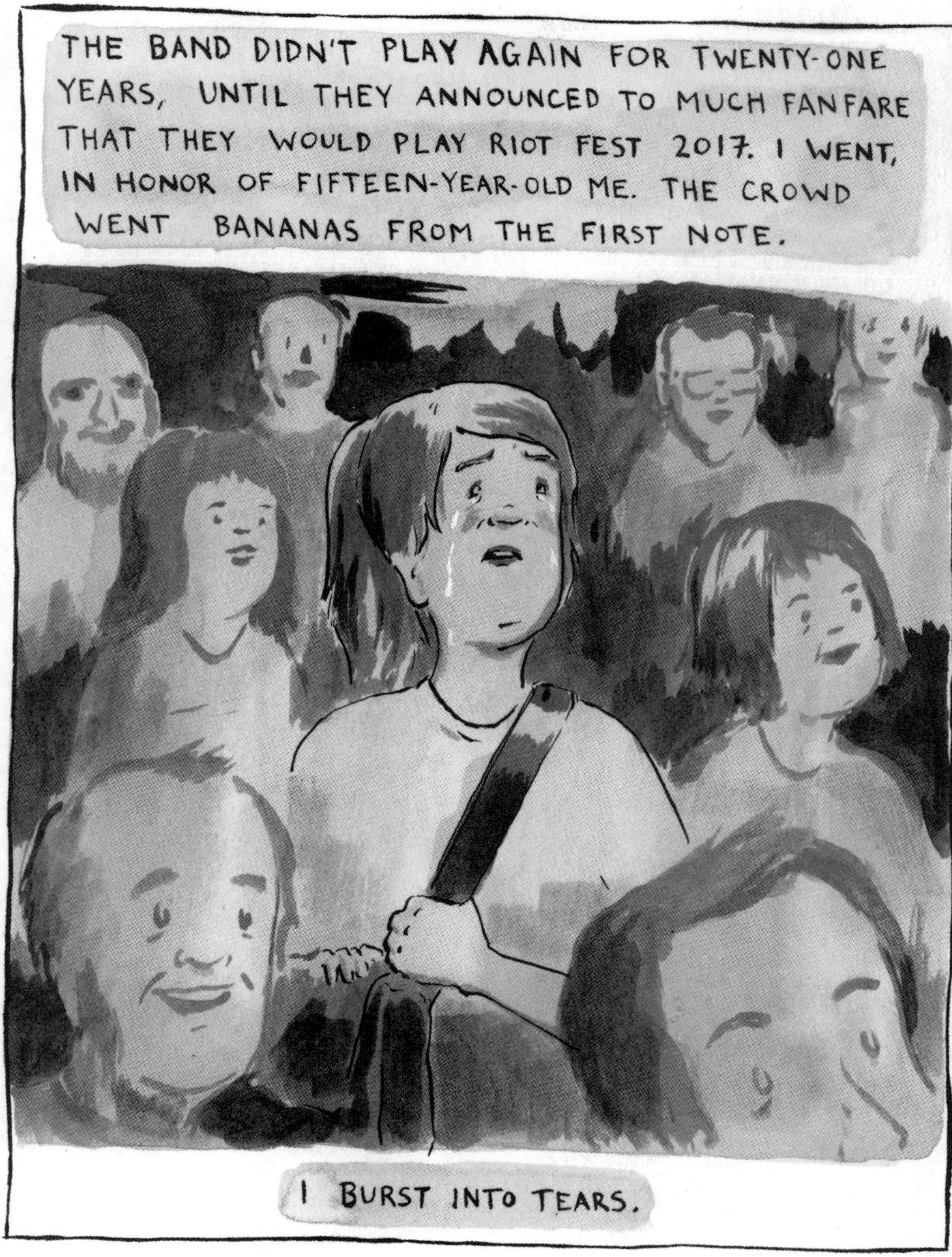
THE BAND DIDN'T PLAY AGAIN FOR TWENTY-ONE YEARS, UNTIL THEY ANNOUNCED TO MUCH FANFARE THAT THEY WOULD PLAY RIOT FEST 2017. I WENT, IN HONOR OF FIFTEEN-YEAR-OLD ME. THE CROWD WENT BANANAS FROM THE FIRST NOTE.
I BURST INTO TEARS.

I WAS STRUCK BY AN EMOTION SO
POWERFUL AND RAW THAT I HAD
A HARD TIME IDENTIFYING IT
AT FIRST: GRIEF. I STOOD THERE
IN THAT ECSTATIC CROWD AND
MOURNED. I MOURNED ALL OF US
DUMB KIDS. I MOURNED OUR GRAYING
HAIR AND SLACKENING BODIES. I
MOURNED SOME UNNAMEABLE
FORGOTTEN TRUTH I USED TO KNOW.
I MOURNED HAROLD.

I'D THOUGHT THAT I WAS THERE
FOR NOSTALGIA; TURNS OUT I WAS
THERE FOR AN OPPORTUNITY TO
GRIEVE THAT I DIDN'T KNOW
 I'D NEEDED.

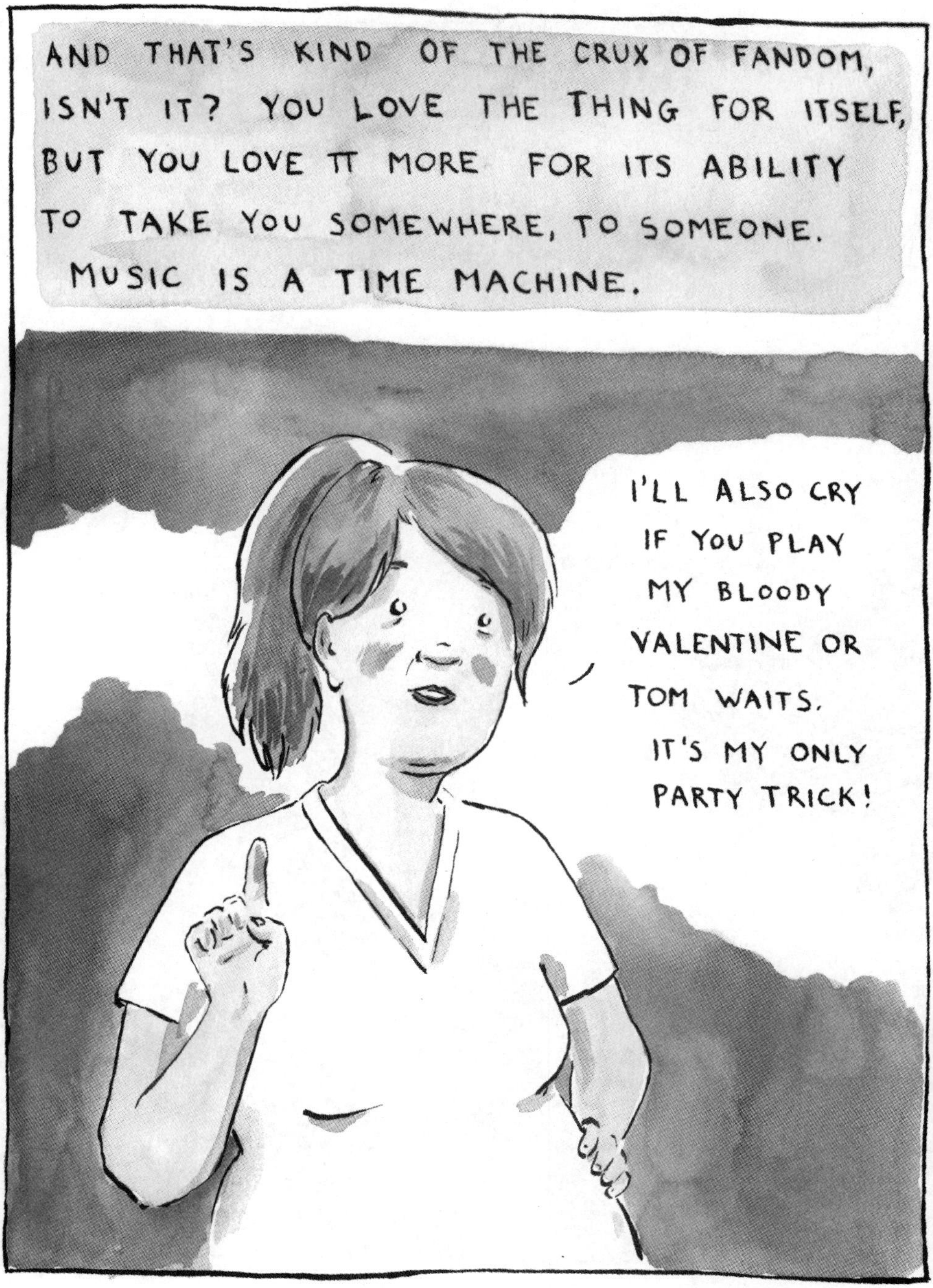
AND THAT'S KIND OF THE CRUX OF FANDOM, ISN'T IT? YOU LOVE THE THING FOR ITSELF, BUT YOU LOVE IT MORE FOR ITS ABILITY TO TAKE YOU SOMEWHERE, TO SOMEONE. MUSIC IS A TIME MACHINE.
I'LL ALSO CRY IF YOU PLAY MY BLOODY VALENTINE OR TOM WAITS. IT'S MY ONLY PARTY TRICK!

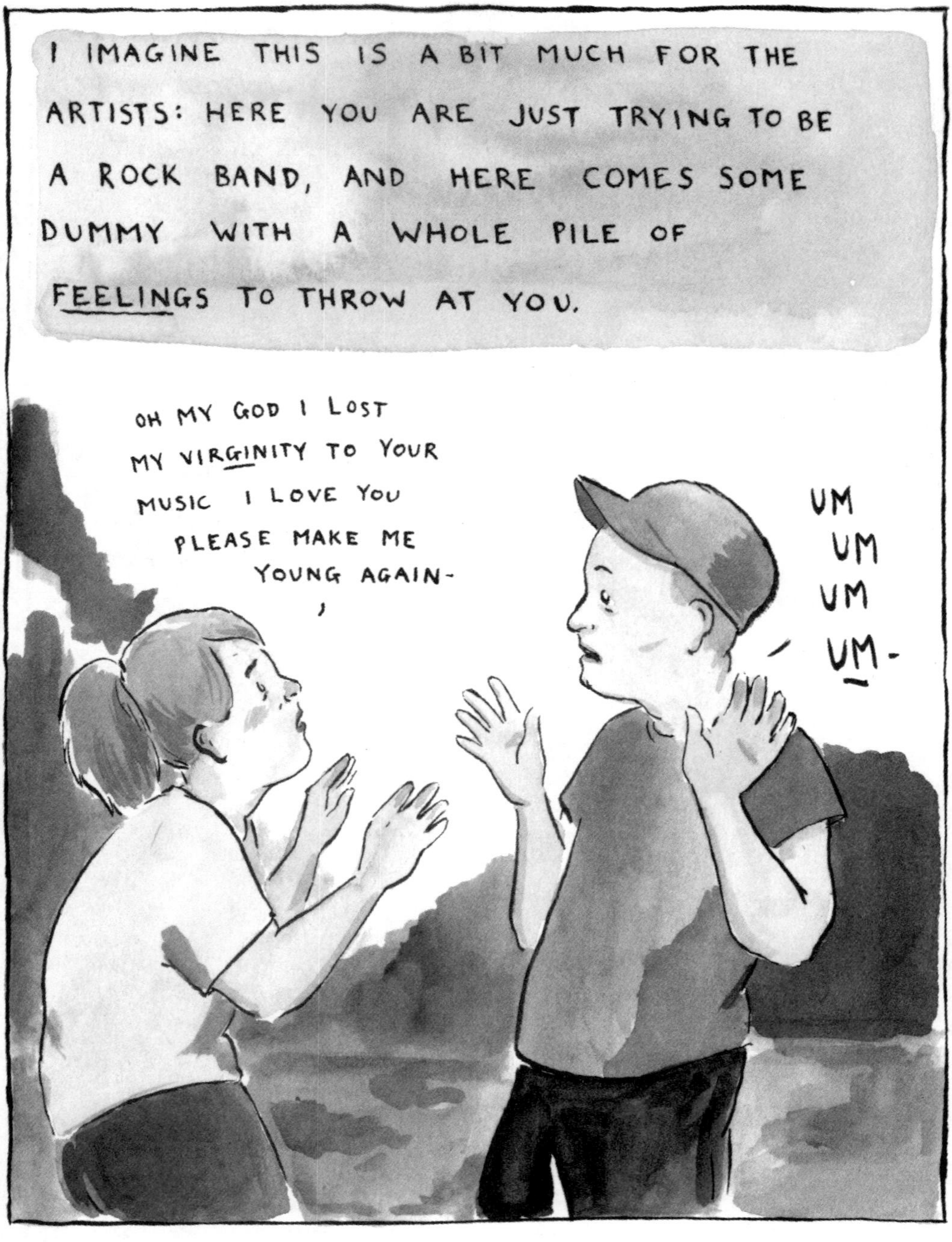
I IMAGINE THIS IS A BIT MUCH FOR THE ARTISTS: HERE YOU ARE JUST TRYING TO BE A ROCK BAND, AND HERE COMES SOME DUMMY WITH A WHOLE PILE OF FEELINGS TO THROW AT YOU.
OH MY GOD I LOST MY VIRGINITY TO YOUR MUSIC I LOVE YOU PLEASE MAKE ME YOUNG AGAIN-
UM UM UM UM-

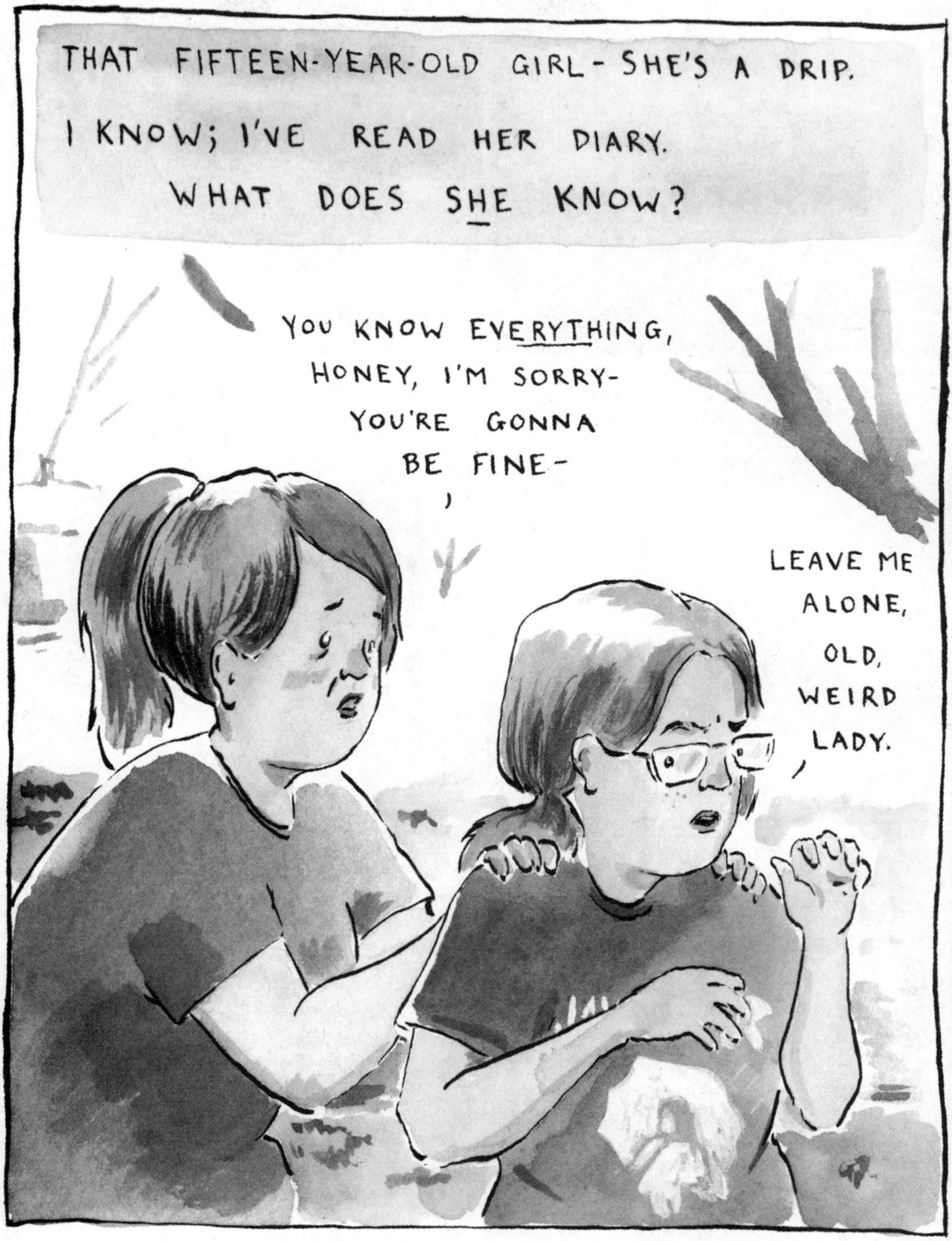
THAT FIFTEEN-YEAR-OLD GIRL - SHE'S A DRIP.
I KNOW; I'VE READ HER DIARY.
WHAT DOES SHE KNOW?
YOU KNOW EVERYTHING, HONEY, I'M SORRY- YOU'RE GONNA BE FINE-
LEAVE ME ALONE, OLD, WEIRD LADY.

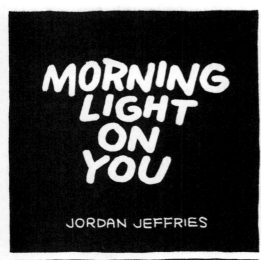

MORNING LIGHT ON YOU

JORDAN JEFFRIES

I RECENTLY WATCHED EPHRAIM ASILI'S FILM *THE INHERITANCE*

CLICK CLICK

TAP TAP

WHICH DEPICTS THE DYNAMICS OF A NASCENT BLACK SOCIALIST COLLECTIVE.

IN AN EARLY SCENE, CHARACTERS READ FROM MAO AND QUOTE AMIRI BARAKA

AS THEY GRAPPLE WITH THE ROLE OF ART IN AIDING REVOLUTION.

WE ARE TAUGHT TO DENY THE FORCE OF ART.

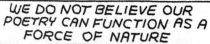

WE DO NOT BELIEVE OUR POETRY CAN FUNCTION AS A FORCE OF NATURE

TO TRANSFORM, AND CLEANSE, AND DESTROY, AND RESURRECT.

WE SETTLE FOR BEING CRAFTPERSONS

FASHIONING CUNNING LITTLE ARTIFACTS DEVILS USE TO DRINK BLOOD.

WE ARE THE GOOD MANNERS OF VAMPIRES.

WE ARE THE GOOD MANNERS OF *VAMPIRES.*

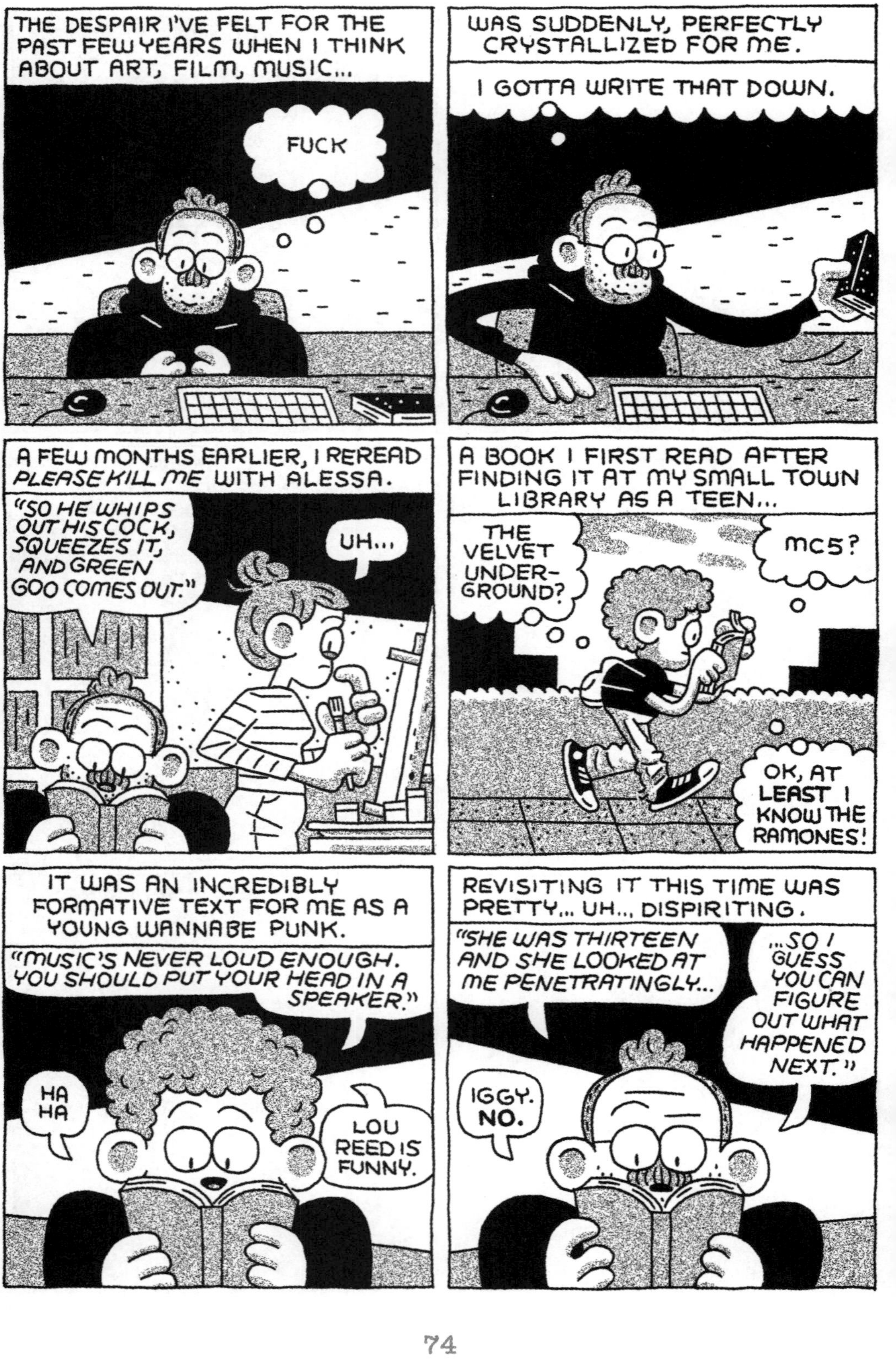
THE DESPAIR I'VE FELT FOR THE PAST FEW YEARS WHEN I THINK ABOUT ART, FILM, MUSIC...
FUCK
WAS SUDDENLY, PERFECTLY CRYSTALLIZED FOR ME.
I GOTTA WRITE THAT DOWN.
A FEW MONTHS EARLIER, I REREAD *PLEASE KILL ME* WITH ALESSA.
"SO HE WHIPS OUT HIS COCK, SQUEEZES IT, AND GREEN GOO COMES OUT."
UH...
A BOOK I FIRST READ AFTER FINDING IT AT MY SMALL TOWN LIBRARY AS A TEEN...
THE VELVET UNDER-GROUND?
MC5?
OK, AT **LEAST** I KNOW THE RAMONES!
IT WAS AN INCREDIBLY FORMATIVE TEXT FOR ME AS A YOUNG WANNABE PUNK.
"MUSIC'S NEVER LOUD ENOUGH. YOU SHOULD PUT YOUR HEAD IN A SPEAKER."
HA HA
LOU REED IS FUNNY.
REVISITING IT THIS TIME WAS PRETTY... UH... DISPIRITING.
"SHE WAS THIRTEEN AND SHE LOOKED AT ME PENETRATINGLY...
...SO I GUESS YOU CAN FIGURE OUT WHAT HAPPENED NEXT."
IGGY. **NO.**

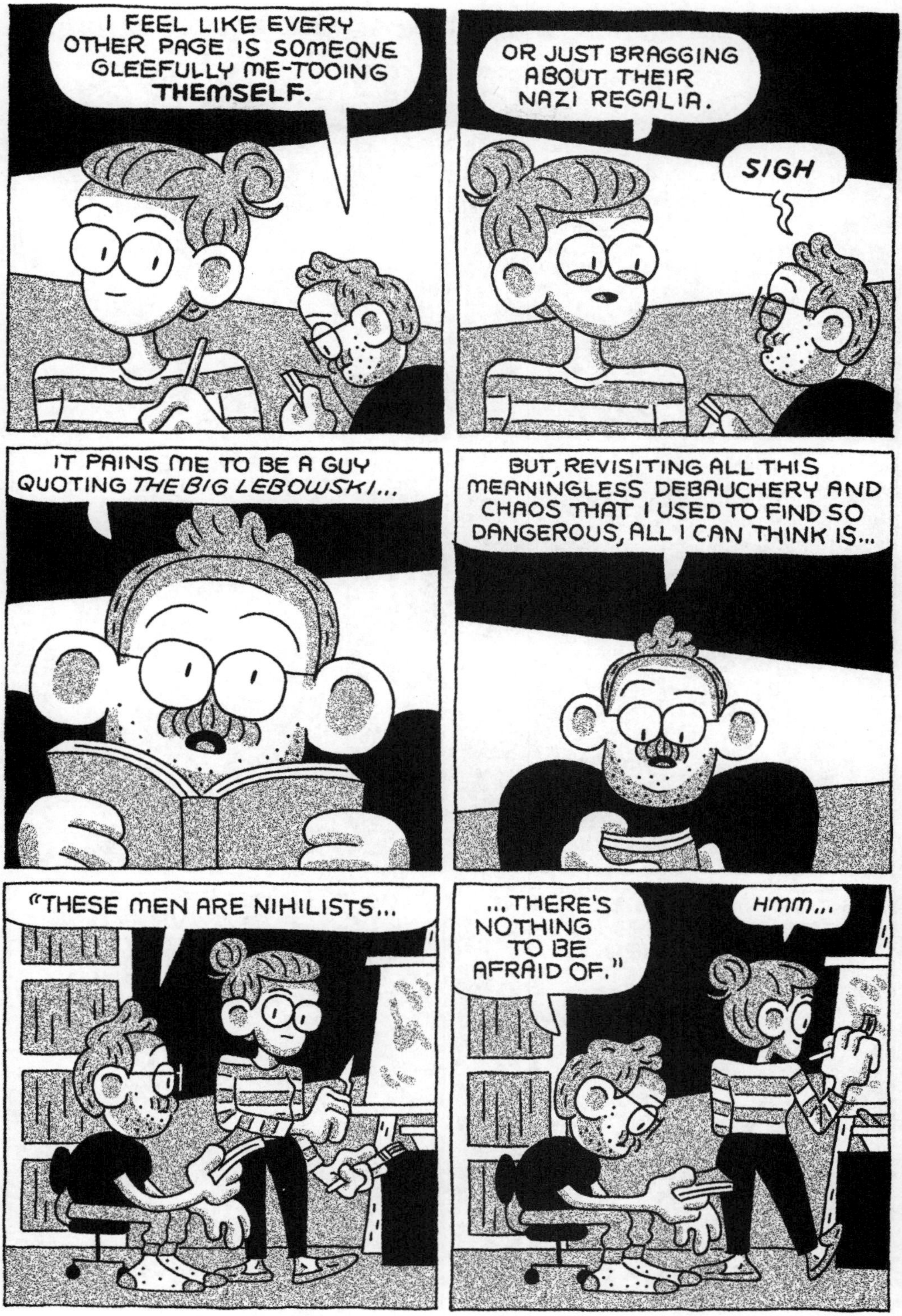
I FEEL LIKE EVERY OTHER PAGE IS SOMEONE GLEEFULLY ME-TOOING **THEMSELF.**
OR JUST BRAGGING ABOUT THEIR NAZI REGALIA.
SIGH
IT PAINS ME TO BE A GUY QUOTING *THE BIG LEBOWSKI*...
BUT, REVISITING ALL THIS MEANINGLESS DEBAUCHERY AND CHAOS THAT I USED TO FIND SO DANGEROUS, ALL I CAN THINK IS...
"THESE MEN ARE NIHILISTS...
...THERE'S NOTHING TO BE AFRAID OF."
HMM...

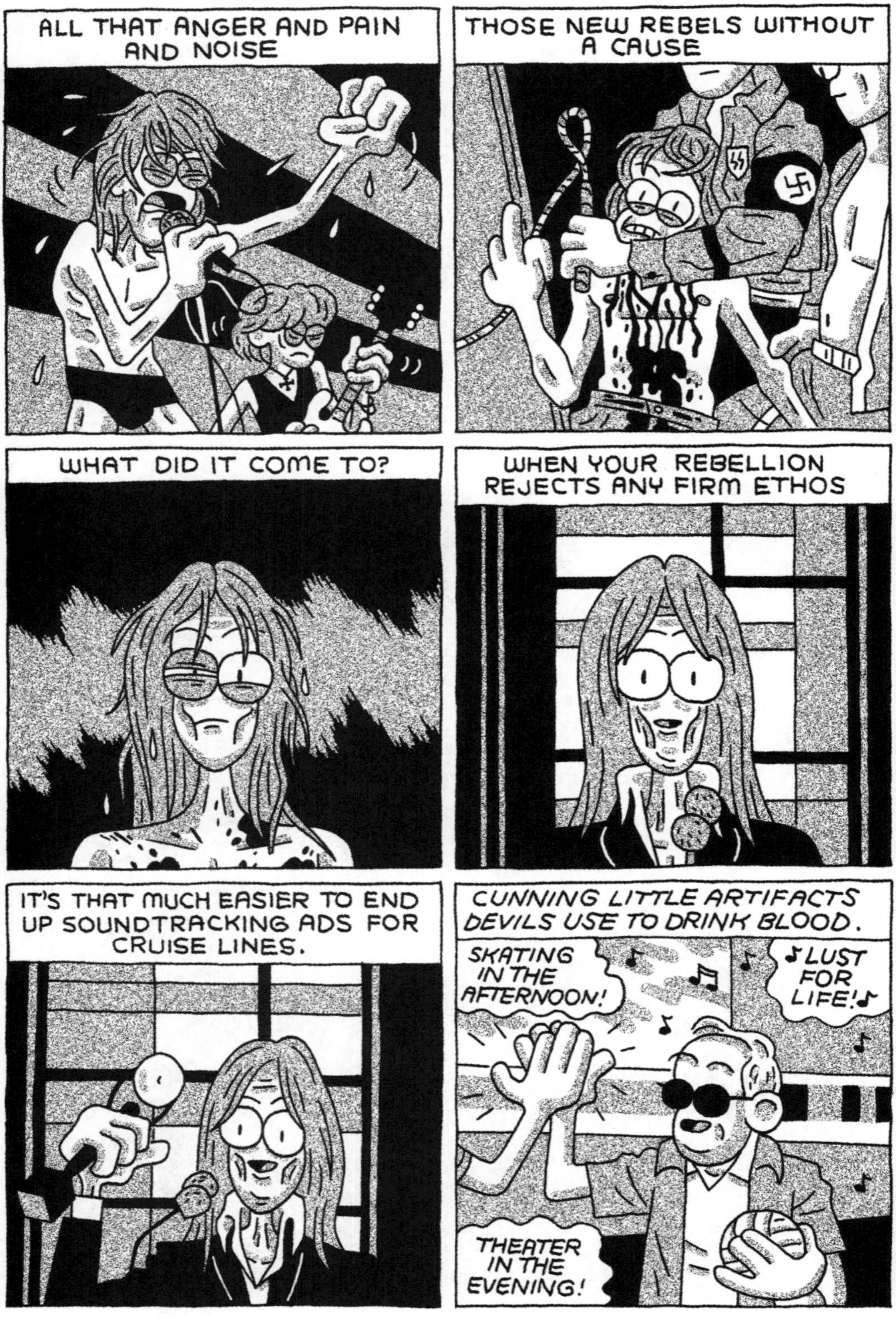
ALL THAT ANGER AND PAIN AND NOISE
THOSE NEW REBELS WITHOUT A CAUSE
WHAT DID IT COME TO?
WHEN YOUR REBELLION REJECTS ANY FIRM ETHOS
IT'S THAT MUCH EASIER TO END UP SOUNDTRACKING ADS FOR CRUISE LINES.
CUNNING LITTLE ARTIFACTS DEVILS USE TO DRINK BLOOD.
SKATING IN THE AFTERNOON!
LUST FOR LIFE!
THEATER IN THE EVENING!

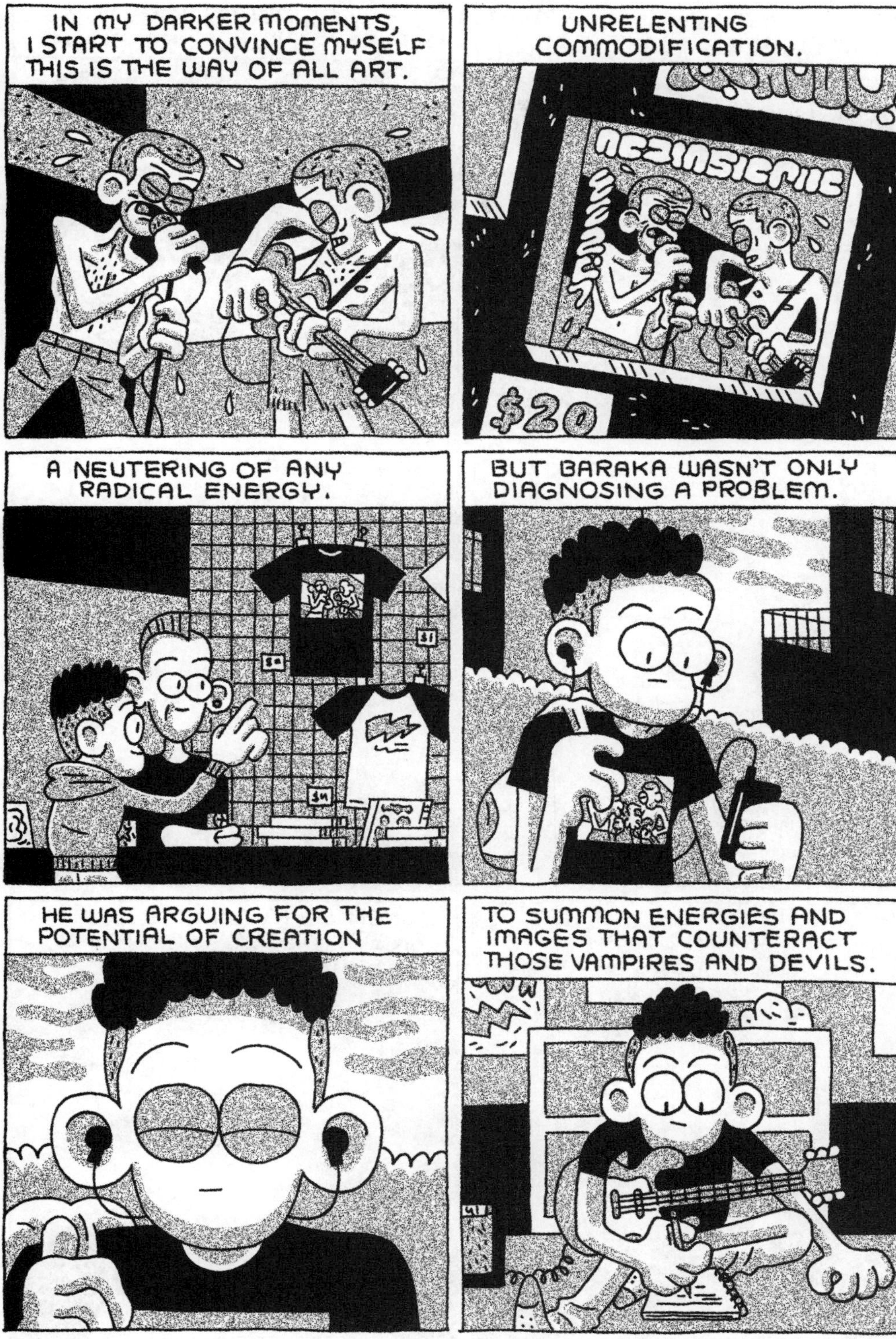
IN MY DARKER MOMENTS, I START TO CONVINCE MYSELF THIS IS THE WAY OF ALL ART.
UNRELENTING COMMODIFICATION.
$20
A NEUTERING OF ANY RADICAL ENERGY.
BUT BARAKA WASN'T ONLY DIAGNOSING A PROBLEM.
HE WAS ARGUING FOR THE POTENTIAL OF CREATION
TO SUMMON ENERGIES AND IMAGES THAT COUNTERACT THOSE VAMPIRES AND DEVILS.

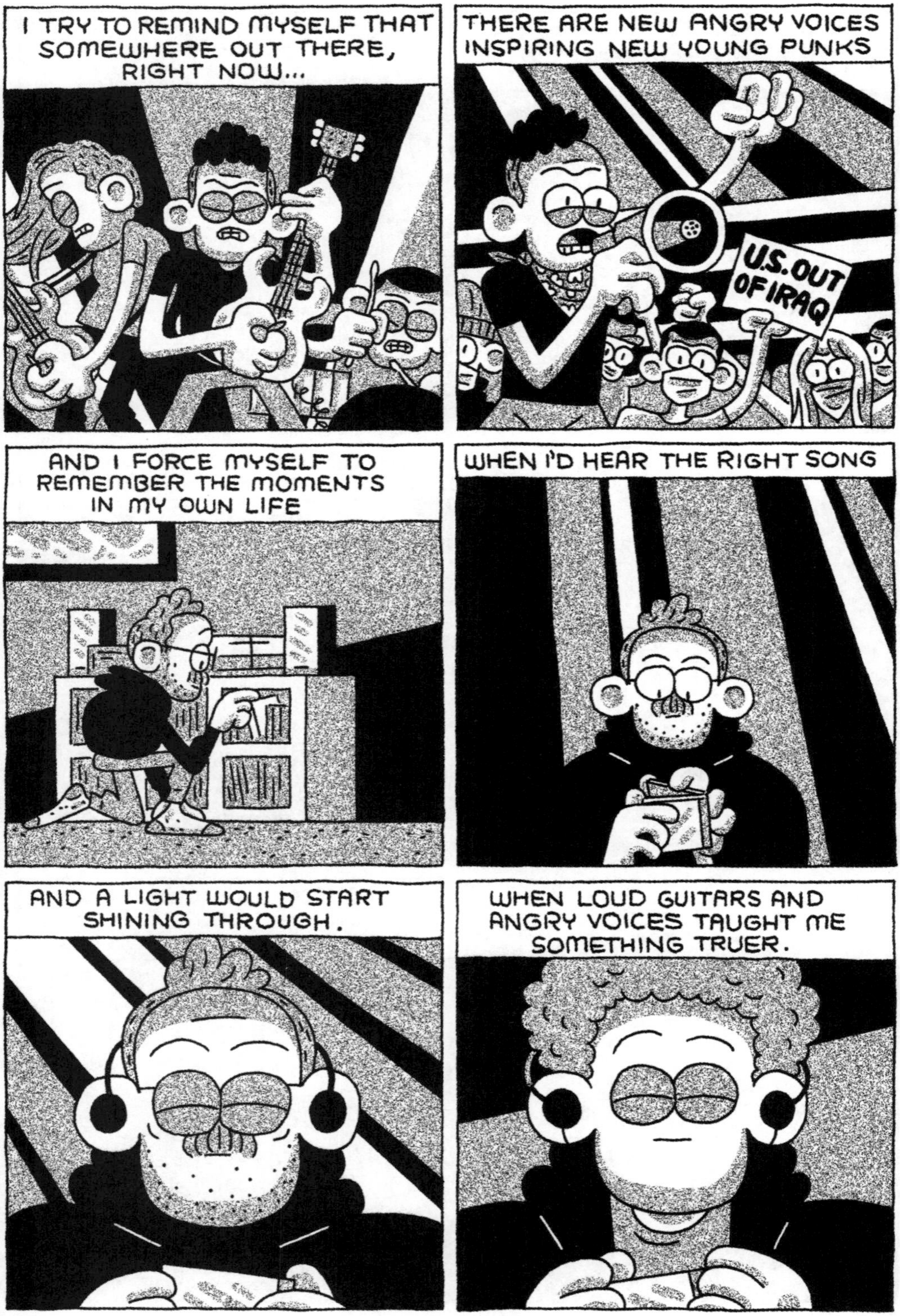
I TRY TO REMIND MYSELF THAT SOMEWHERE OUT THERE, RIGHT NOW...
THERE ARE NEW ANGRY VOICES INSPIRING NEW YOUNG PUNKS
U.S. OUT OF IRAQ
AND I FORCE MYSELF TO REMEMBER THE MOMENTS IN MY OWN LIFE
WHEN I'D HEAR THE RIGHT SONG
AND A LIGHT WOULD START SHINING THROUGH.
WHEN LOUD GUITARS AND ANGRY VOICES TAUGHT ME SOMETHING TRUER.

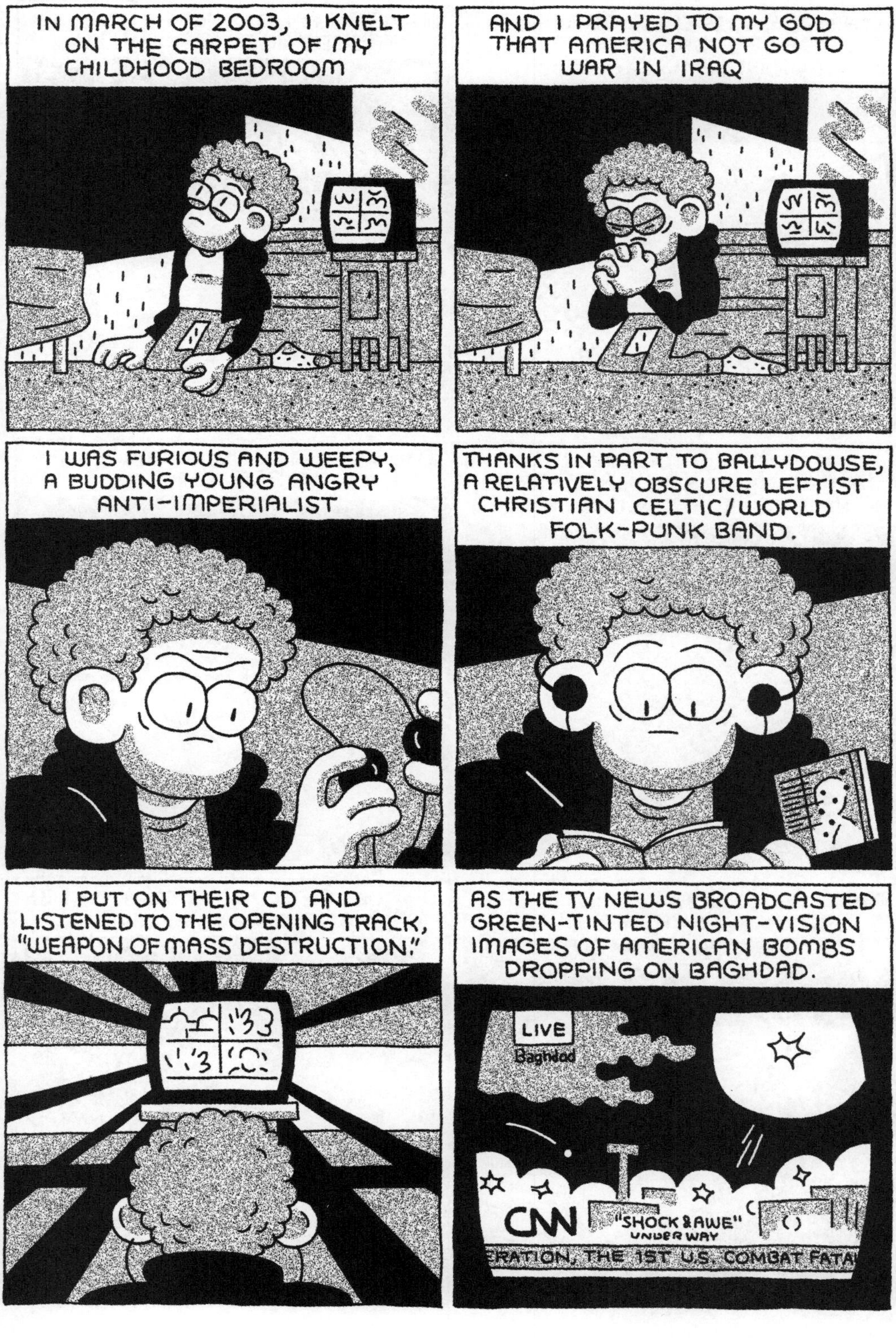
IN MARCH OF 2003, I KNELT ON THE CARPET OF MY CHILDHOOD BEDROOM
AND I PRAYED TO MY GOD THAT AMERICA NOT GO TO WAR IN IRAQ
I WAS FURIOUS AND WEEPY, A BUDDING YOUNG ANGRY ANTI-IMPERIALIST
THANKS IN PART TO BALLYDOWSE, A RELATIVELY OBSCURE LEFTIST CHRISTIAN CELTIC/WORLD FOLK-PUNK BAND.
I PUT ON THEIR CD AND LISTENED TO THE OPENING TRACK, "WEAPON OF MASS DESTRUCTION."
AS THE TV NEWS BROADCASTED GREEN-TINTED NIGHT-VISION IMAGES OF AMERICAN BOMBS DROPPING ON BAGHDAD.
LIVE
Baghdad
CNN
"SHOCK & AWE" UNDER WAY
ERATION, THE 1ST U.S. COMBAT FATA

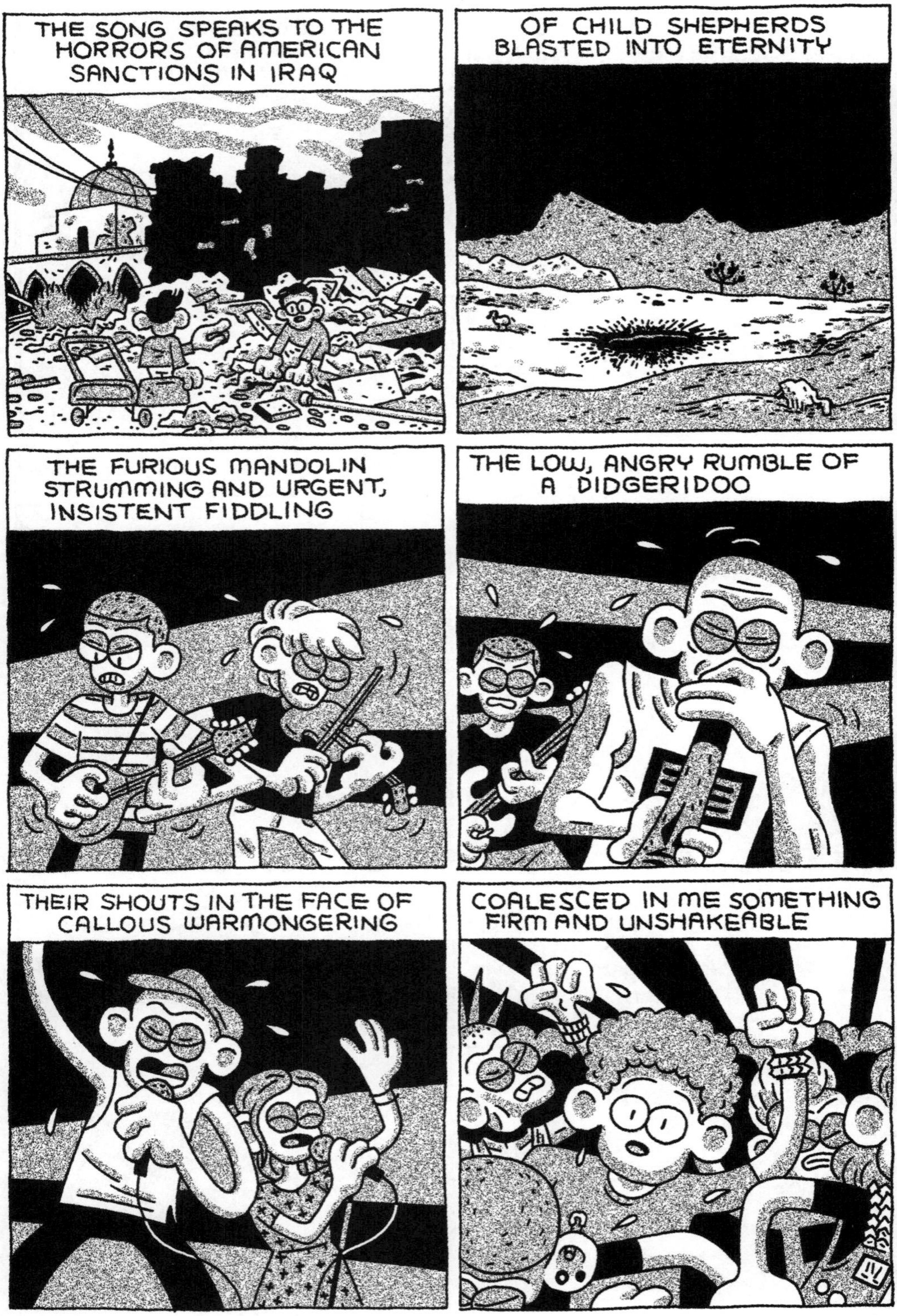
THE SONG SPEAKS TO THE HORRORS OF AMERICAN SANCTIONS IN IRAQ
OF CHILD SHEPHERDS BLASTED INTO ETERNITY
THE FURIOUS MANDOLIN STRUMMING AND URGENT, INSISTENT FIDDLING
THE LOW, ANGRY RUMBLE OF A DIDGERIDOO
THEIR SHOUTS IN THE FACE OF CALLOUS WARMONGERING
COALESCED IN ME SOMETHING FIRM AND UNSHAKEABLE

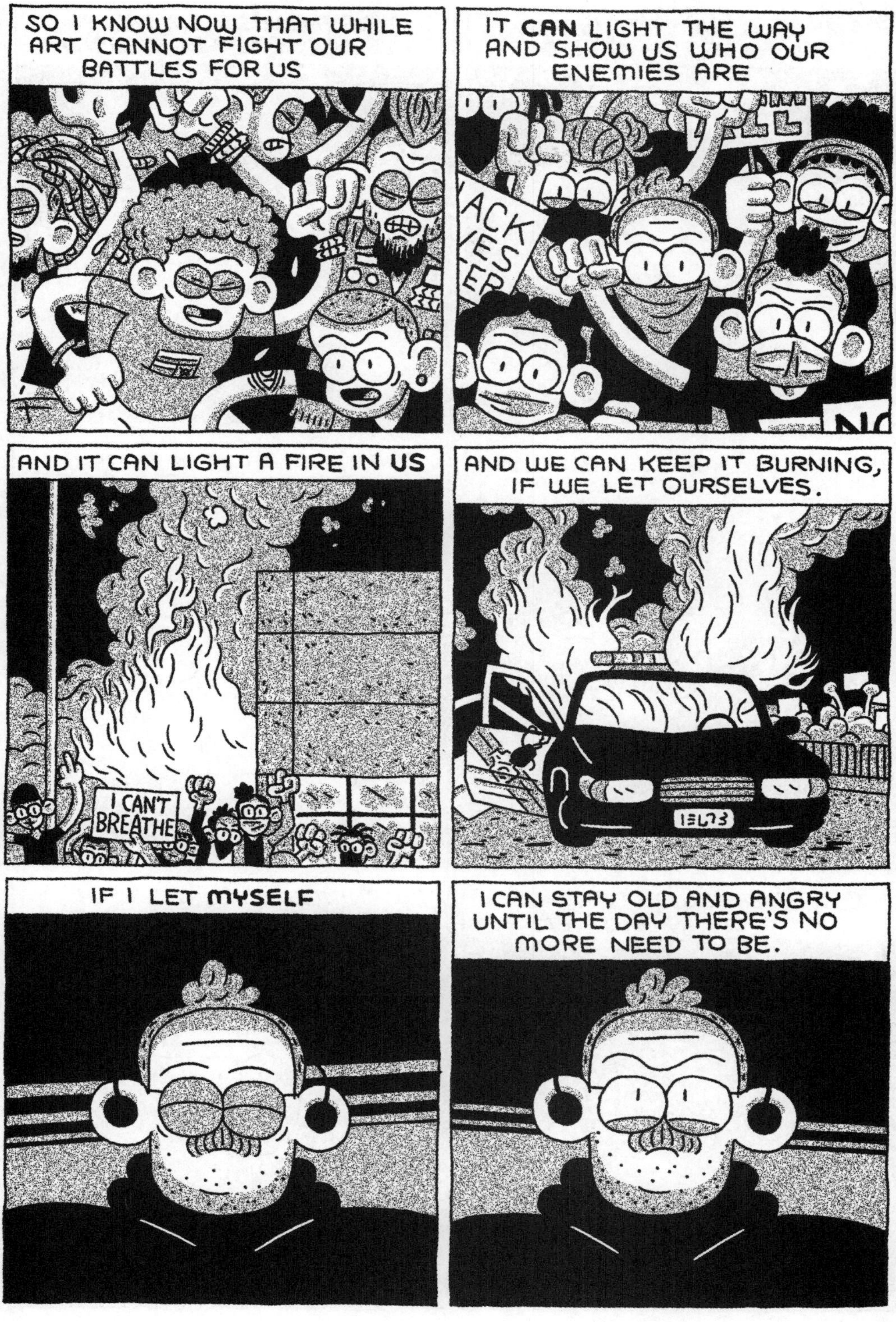
SO I KNOW NOW THAT WHILE ART CANNOT FIGHT OUR BATTLES FOR US
IT **CAN** LIGHT THE WAY AND SHOW US WHO OUR ENEMIES ARE
AND IT CAN LIGHT A FIRE IN **US**
I CAN'T BREATHE
AND WE CAN KEEP IT BURNING, IF WE LET OURSELVES.
IF I LET **MYSELF**
I CAN STAY OLD AND ANGRY UNTIL THE DAY THERE'S NO MORE NEED TO BE.

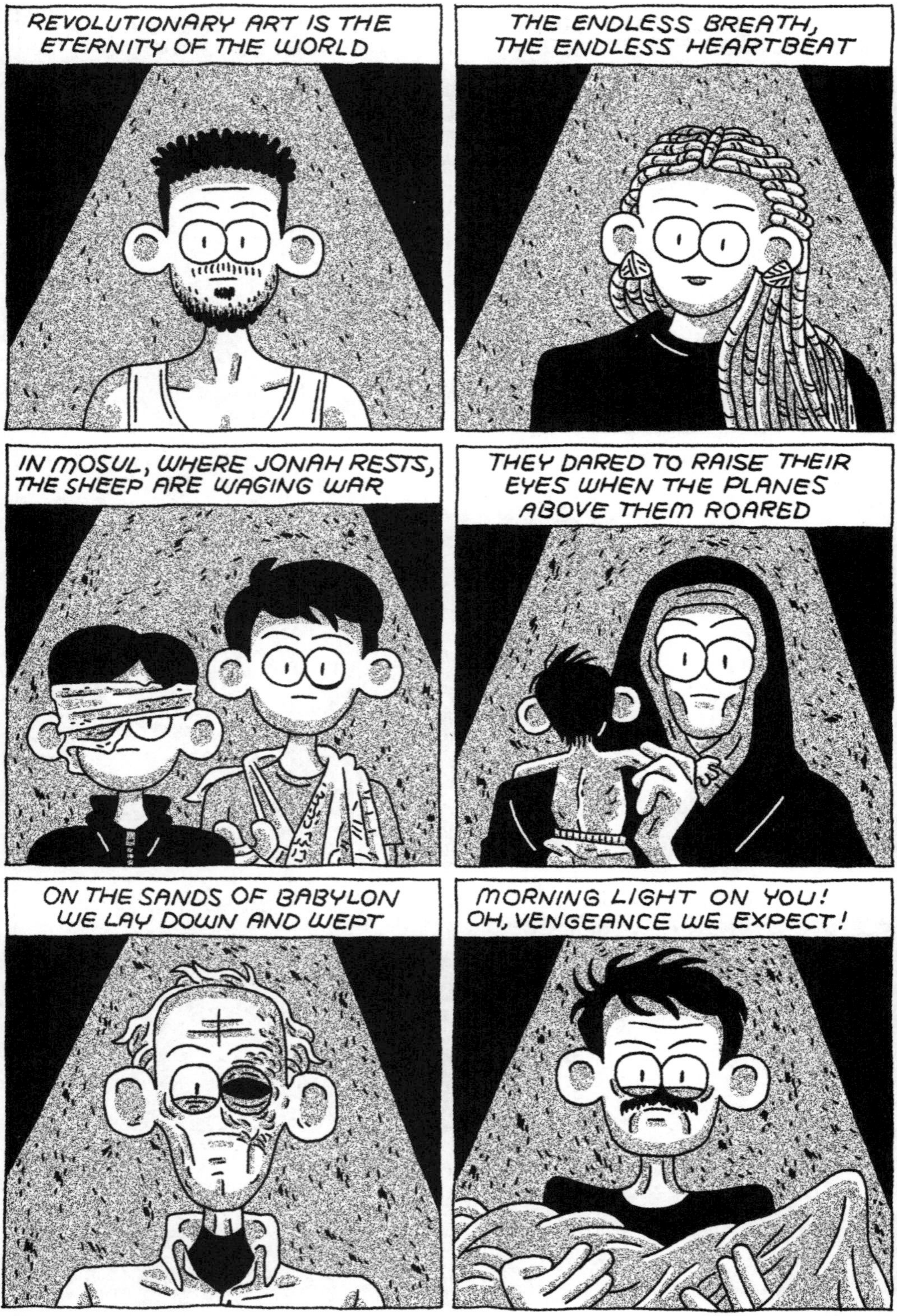
REVOLUTIONARY ART IS THE ETERNITY OF THE WORLD
THE ENDLESS BREATH, THE ENDLESS HEARTBEAT
IN MOSUL, WHERE JONAH RESTS, THE SHEEP ARE WAGING WAR
THEY DARED TO RAISE THEIR EYES WHEN THE PLANES ABOVE THEM ROARED
ON THE SANDS OF BABYLON WE LAY DOWN AND WEPT
MORNING LIGHT ON YOU! OH, VENGEANCE WE EXPECT!

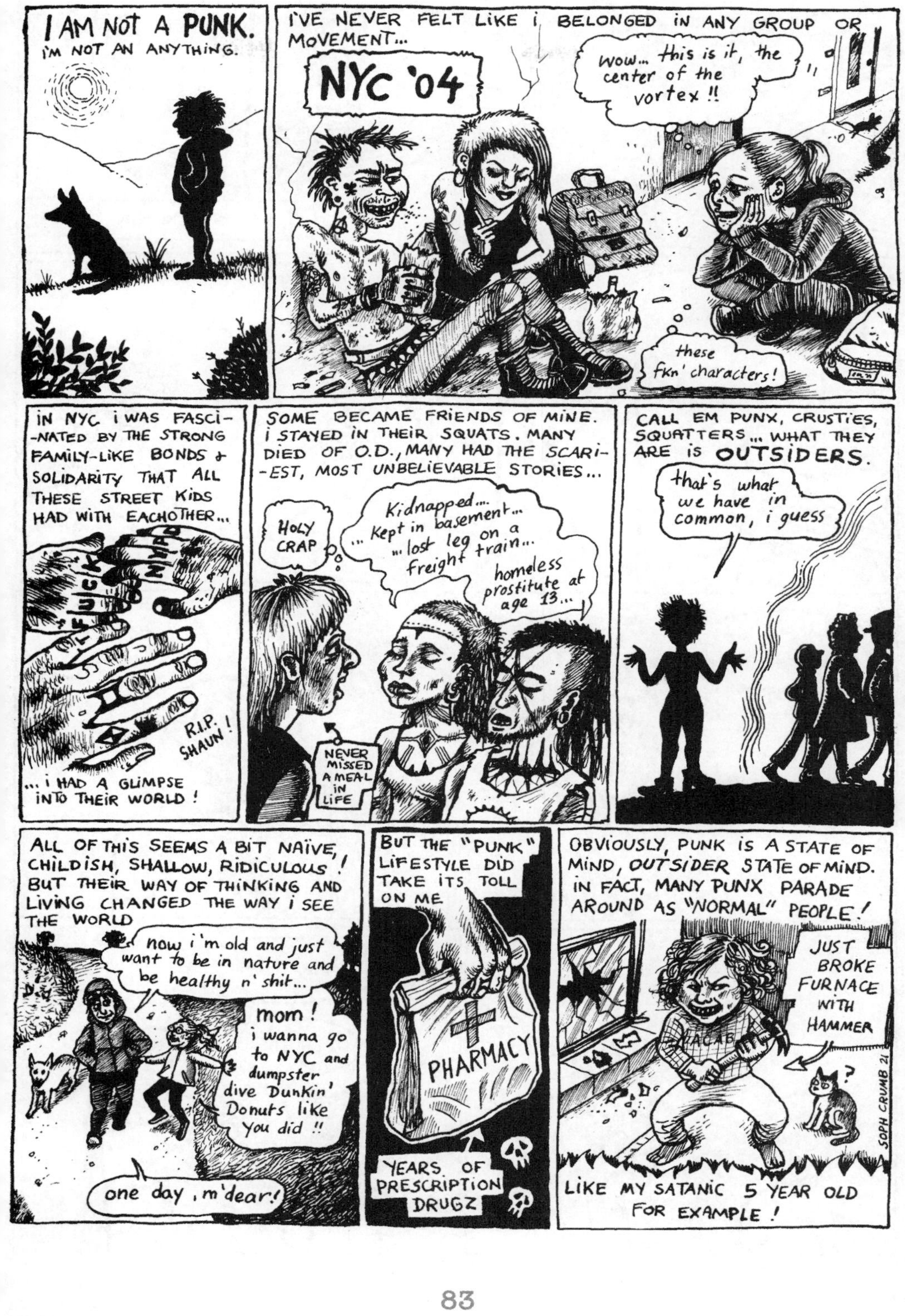
I AM NOT A PUNK.
I'M NOT AN ANYTHING.
I'VE NEVER FELT LIKE i BELONGED IN ANY GROUP OR MOVEMENT...
NYC '04
wow... this is it, the center of the vortex !!
these fkn' characters!
IN NYC i WAS FASCI-NATED BY THE STRONG FAMILY-LIKE BONDS & SOLIDARITY THAT ALL THESE STREET KIDS HAD WITH EACHOTHER...
R.I.P. SHAUN!
... i HAD A GLIMPSE INTO THEIR WORLD!
SOME BECAME FRIENDS OF MINE. i STAYED IN THEIR SQUATS. MANY DIED OF O.D., MANY HAD THE SCARI-EST, MOST UNBELIEVABLE STORIES...
HOLY CRAP
Kidnapped... ... Kept in basement... ... lost leg on a freight train...
homeless prostitute at age 13...
NEVER MISSED A MEAL IN LIFE
CALL EM PUNX, CRUSTIES, SQUATTERS... WHAT THEY ARE IS OUTSIDERS.
that's what we have in common, i guess
ALL OF THIS SEEMS A BIT NAÏVE, CHILDISH, SHALLOW, RIDICULOUS! BUT THEIR WAY OF THINKING AND LIVING CHANGED THE WAY i SEE THE WORLD
now i'm old and just want to be in nature and be healthy n' shit...
mom! i wanna go to NYC and dumpster dive Dunkin' Donuts like you did !!
one day, m'dear!
BUT THE "PUNK" LIFESTYLE DID TAKE ITS TOLL ON ME
PHARMACY
YEARS OF PRESCRIPTION DRUGZ
OBVIOUSLY, PUNK IS A STATE OF MIND, OUTSIDER STATE OF MIND. IN FACT, MANY PUNX PARADE AROUND AS "NORMAL" PEOPLE!
JUST BROKE FURNACE WITH HAMMER
?
SOPH CRUMB 21
LIKE MY SATANIC 5 YEAR OLD FOR EXAMPLE!

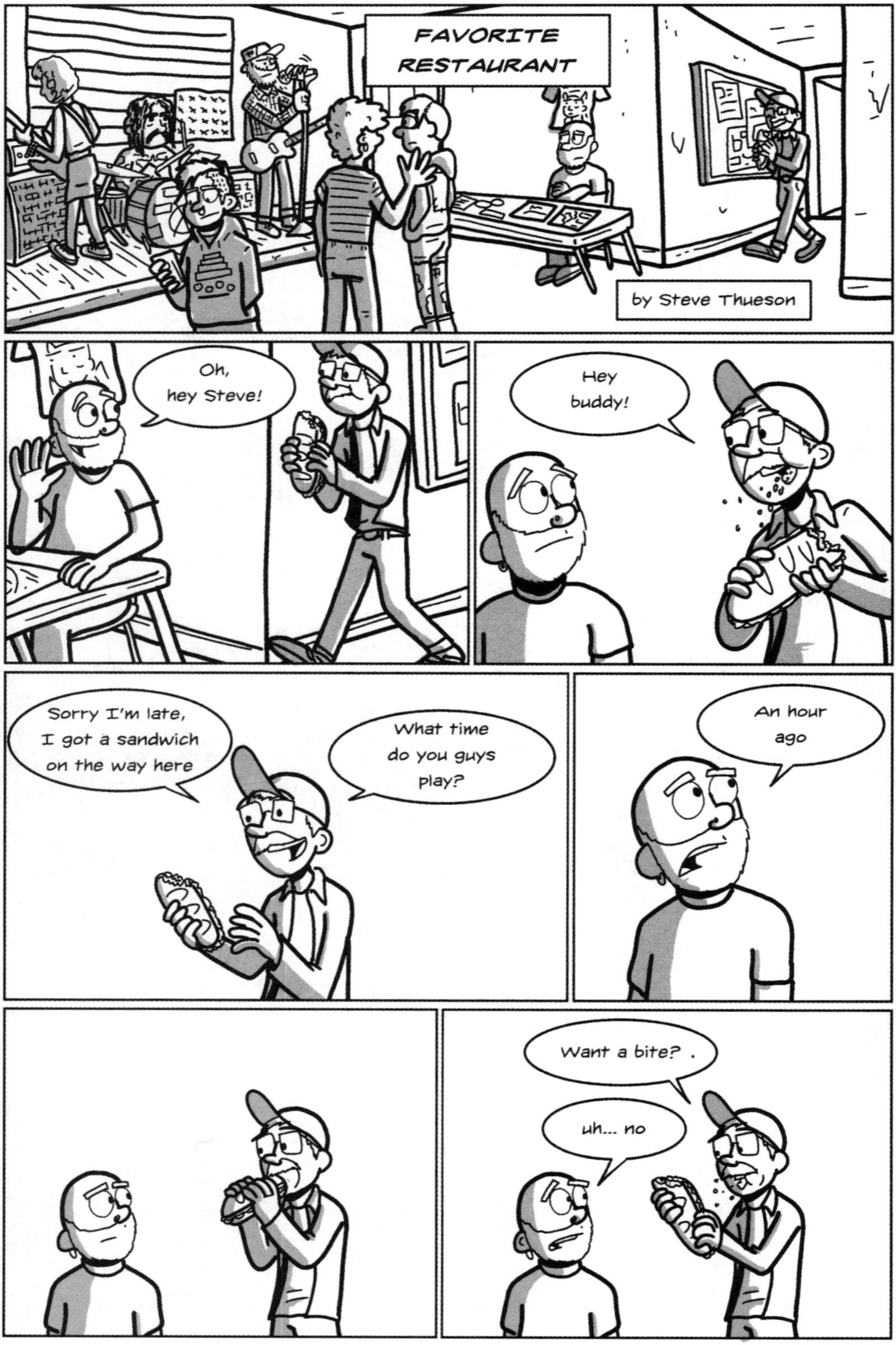
FAVORITE RESTAURANT
by Steve Thueson
Oh, hey Steve!
Hey buddy!
Sorry I'm late, I got a sandwich on the way here
What time do you guys play?
An hour ago
Want a bite? .
uh... no

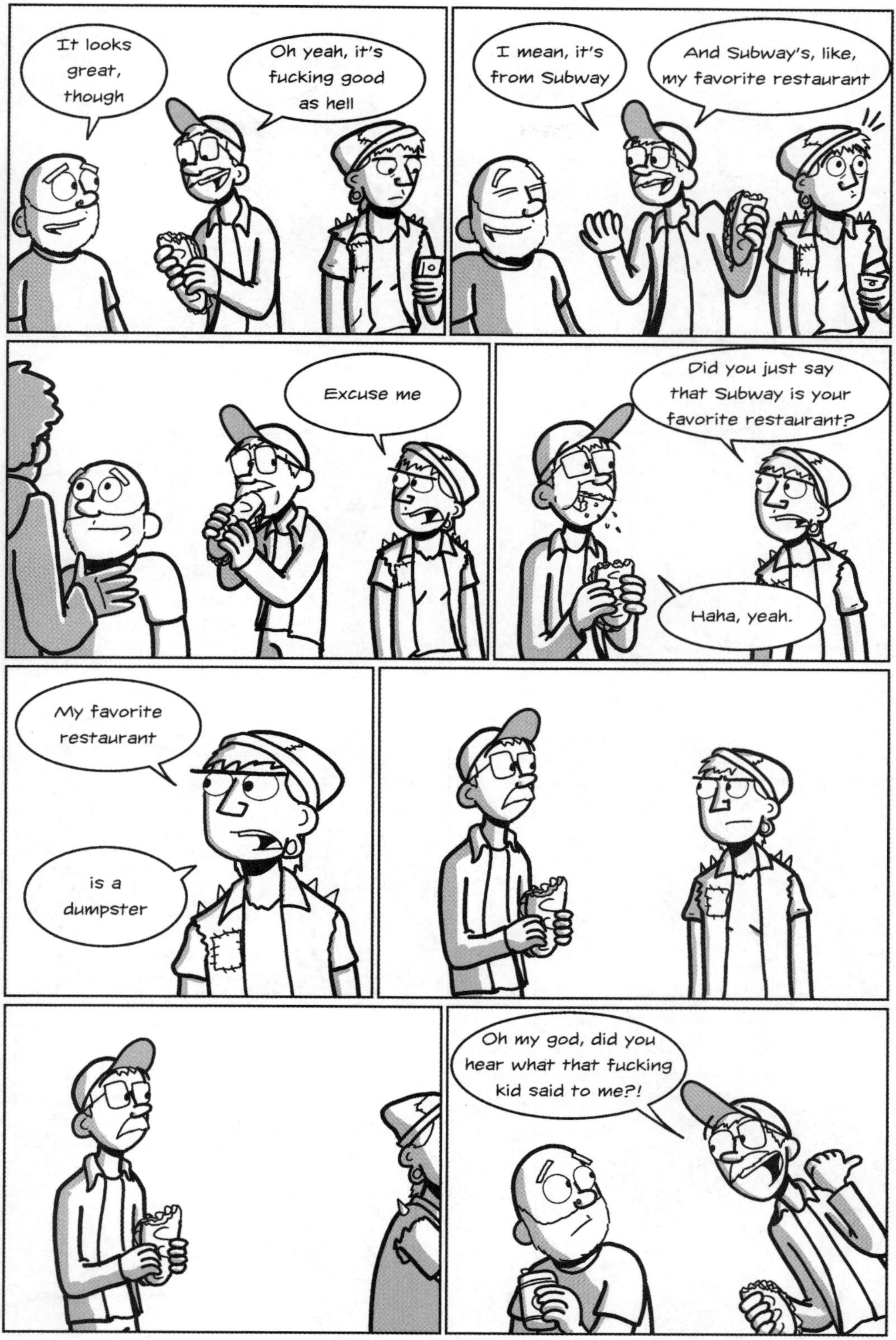
It looks great, though
Oh yeah, it's fucking good as hell
I mean, it's from Subway
And Subway's, like, my favorite restaurant
Excuse me
Did you just say that Subway is your favorite restaurant?
Haha, yeah.
My favorite restaurant
is a dumpster
Oh my god, did you hear what that fucking kid said to me?!

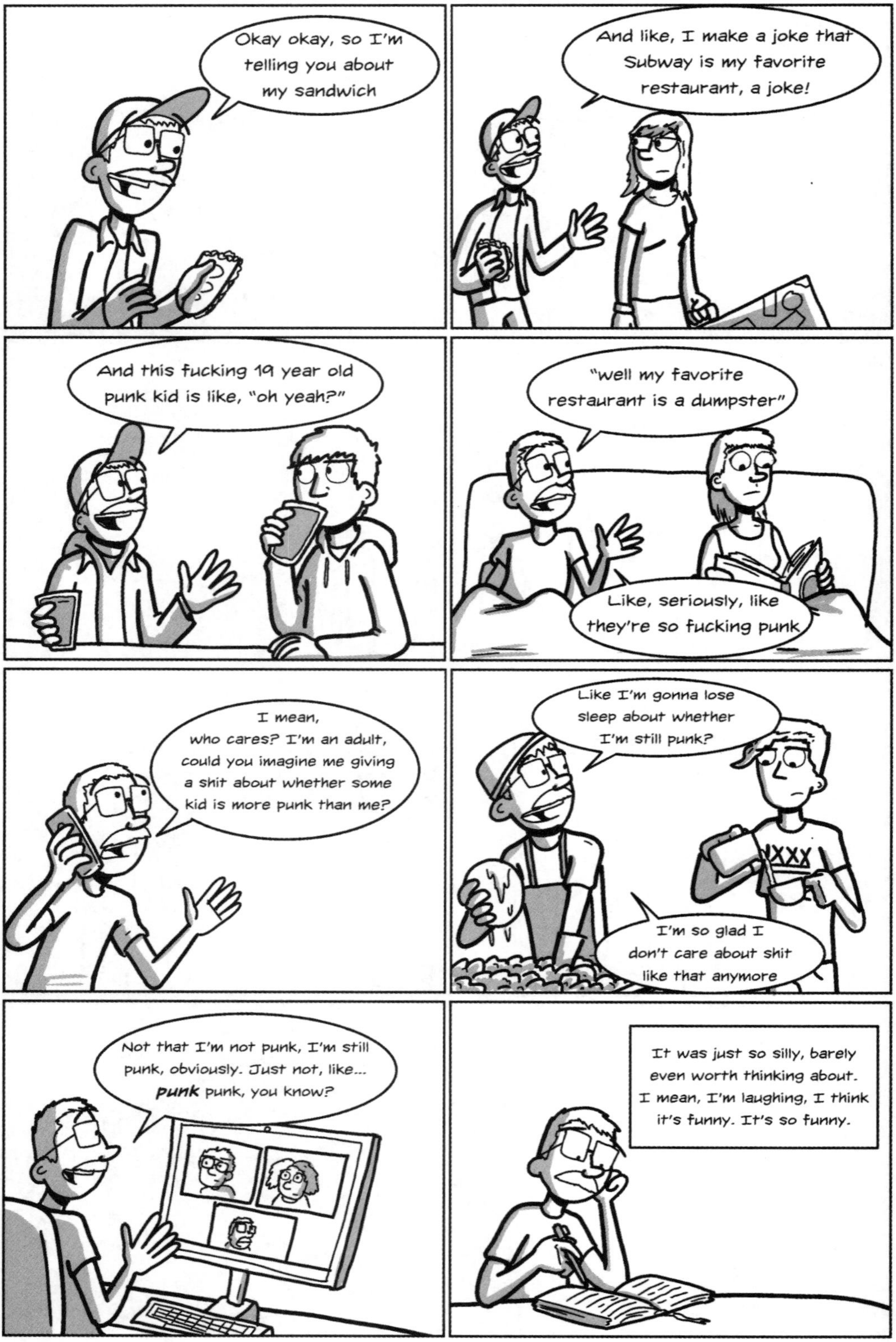

Okay okay, so I'm telling you about my sandwich
And like, I make a joke that Subway is my favorite restaurant, a joke!
And this fucking 19 year old punk kid is like, "oh yeah?"
"well my favorite restaurant is a dumpster"
Like, seriously, like they're so fucking punk
I mean, who cares? I'm an adult, could you imagine me giving a shit about whether some kid is more punk than me?
Like I'm gonna lose sleep about whether I'm still punk?
XXX
I'm so glad I don't care about shit like that anymore
Not that I'm not punk, I'm still punk, obviously. Just not, like... **punk** punk, you know?
It was just so silly, barely even worth thinking about. I mean, I'm laughing, I think it's funny. It's so funny.

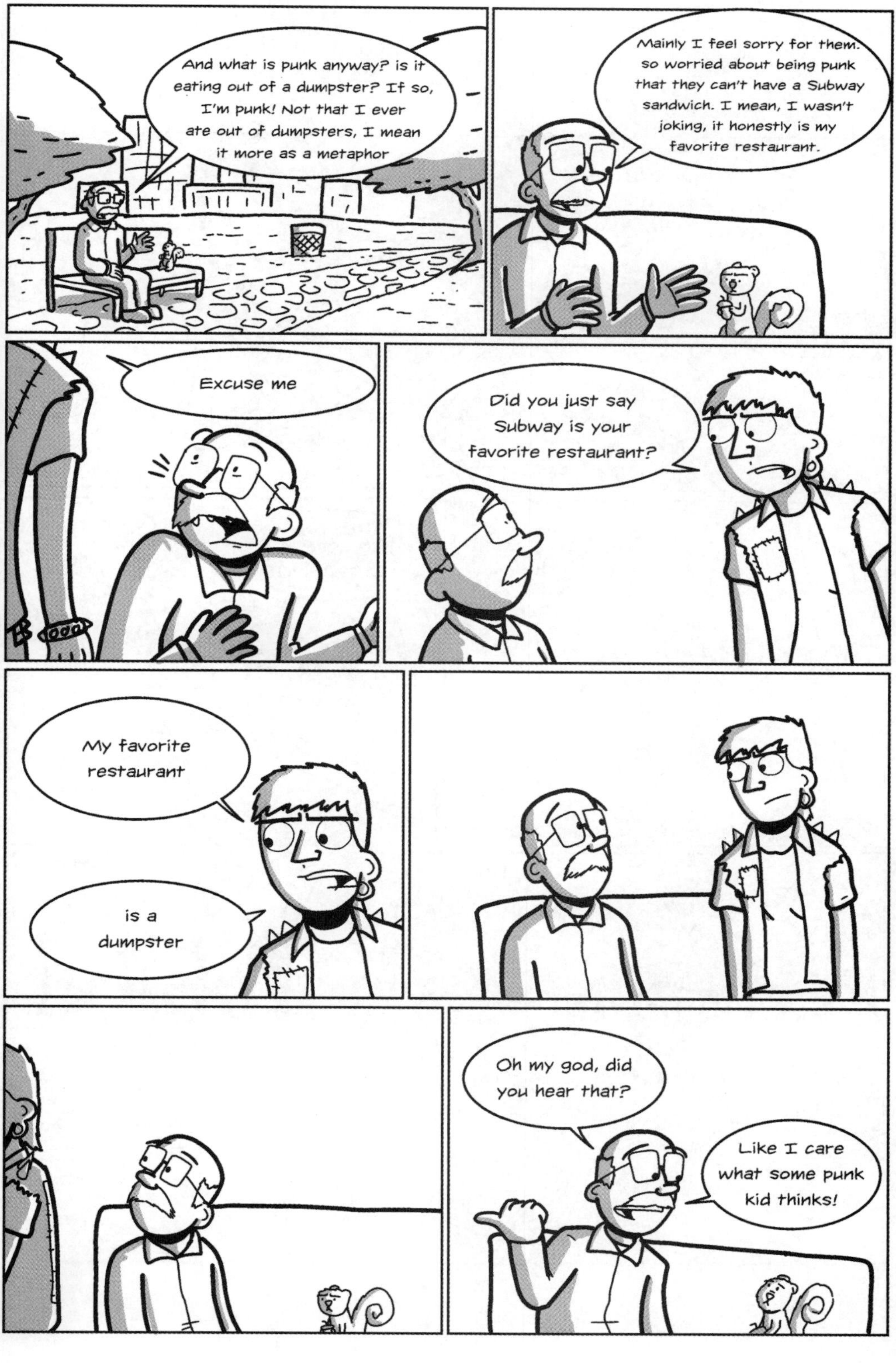
And what is punk anyway? is it eating out of a dumpster? If so, I'm punk! Not that I ever ate out of dumpsters, I mean it more as a metaphor
Mainly I feel sorry for them. so worried about being punk that they can't have a Subway sandwich. I mean, I wasn't joking, it honestly is my favorite restaurant.
Excuse me
Did you just say Subway is your favorite restaurant?
My favorite restaurant
is a dumpster
Oh my god, did you hear that?
Like I care what some punk kid thinks!

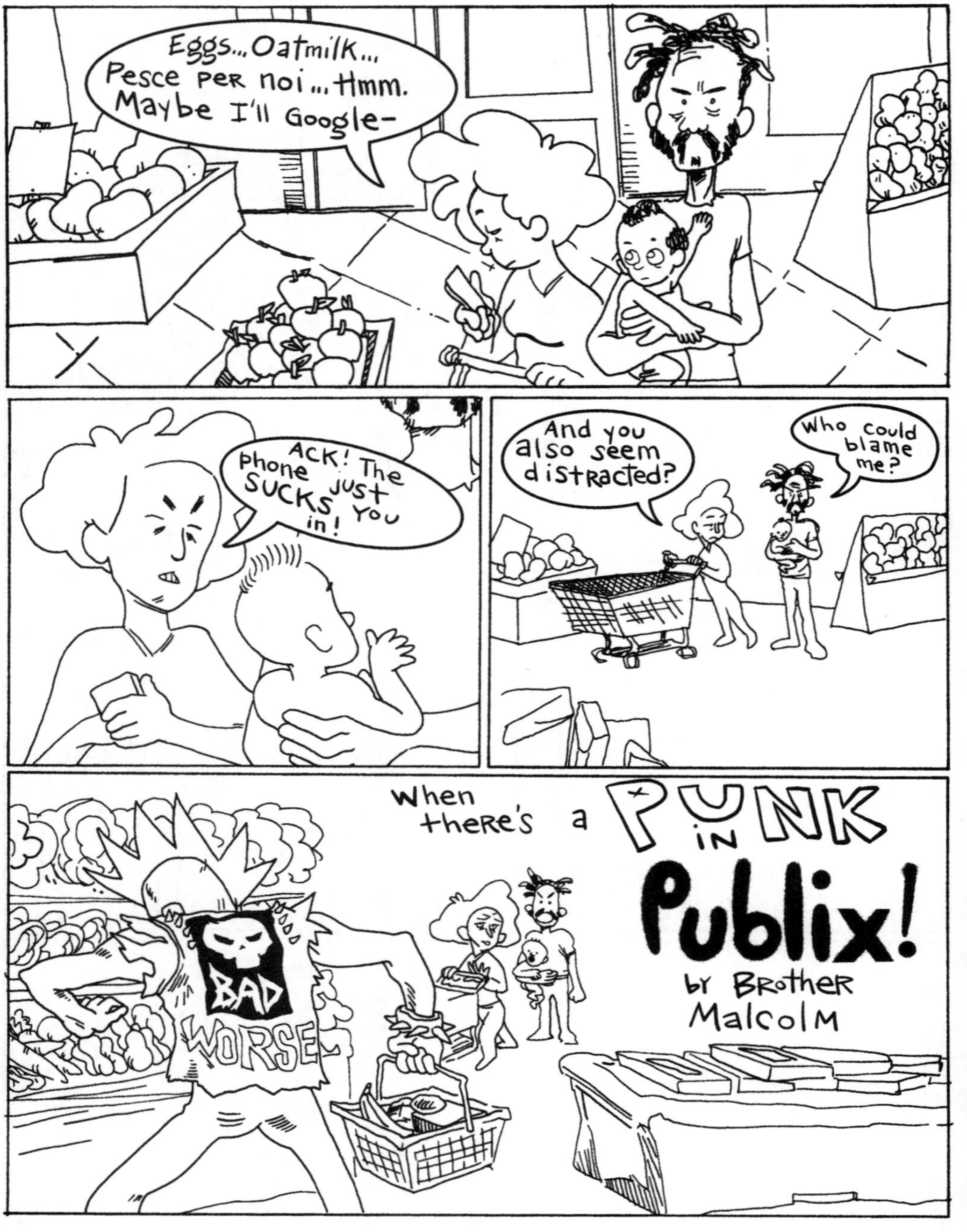
Eggs... Oatmilk... Pesce per noi... Hmm. Maybe I'll Google-
ACK! The phone just SUCKS you in!
And you also seem distracted?
Who could blame me?
When there's a PUNK in Publix!
by Brother Malcolm
BAD WORSE

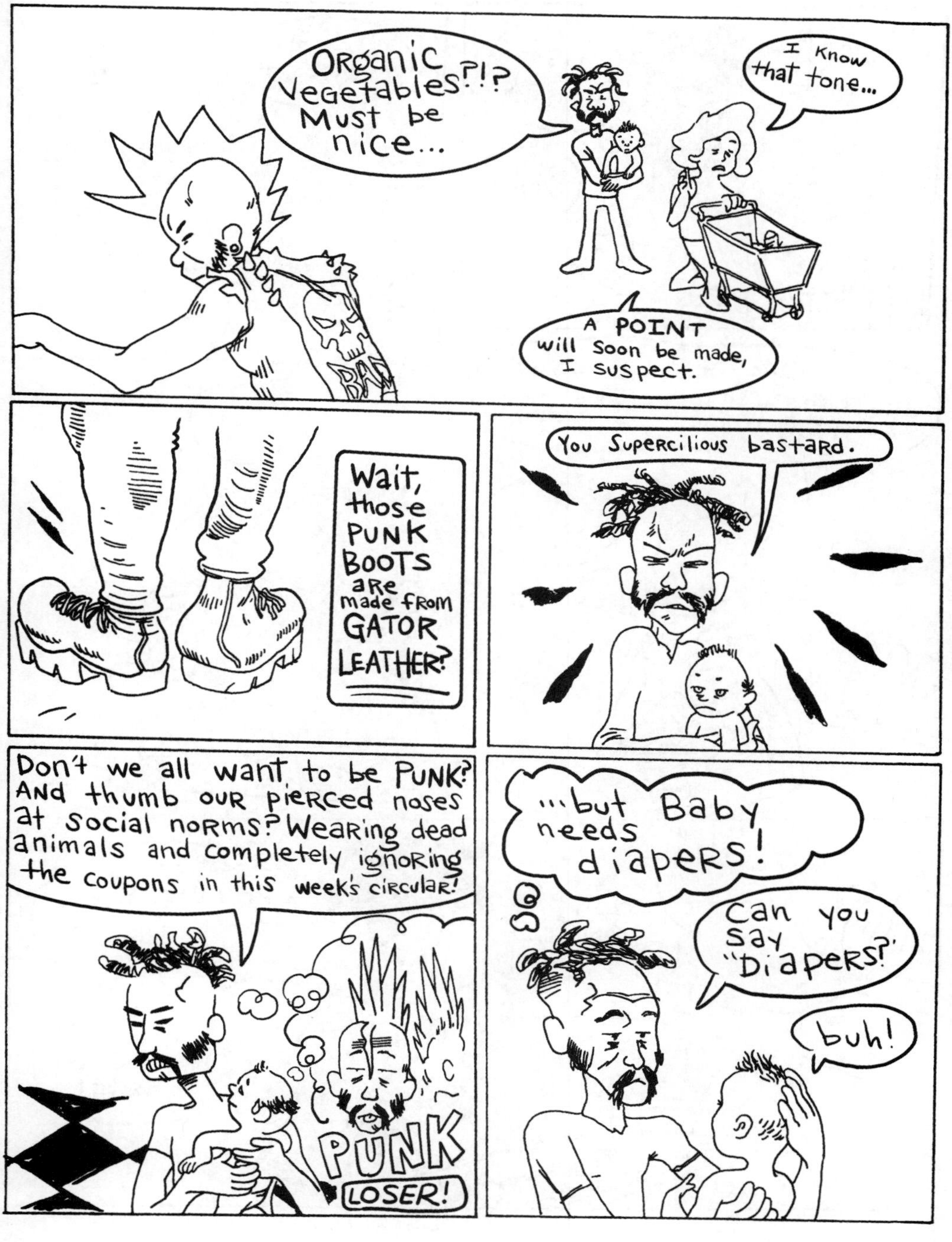

Organic Vegetables?!? Must be nice...
I know that tone...
A POINT will soon be made, I suspect.
BAD
Wait, those PUNK BOOTS are made from GATOR LEATHER?
You supercilious bastard.
Don't we all want to be PUNK? And thumb our pierced noses at social norms? Wearing dead animals and completely ignoring the coupons in this week's circular!
PUNK
LOSER!
...but Baby needs diapers!
Can you say "Diapers?"
buh!

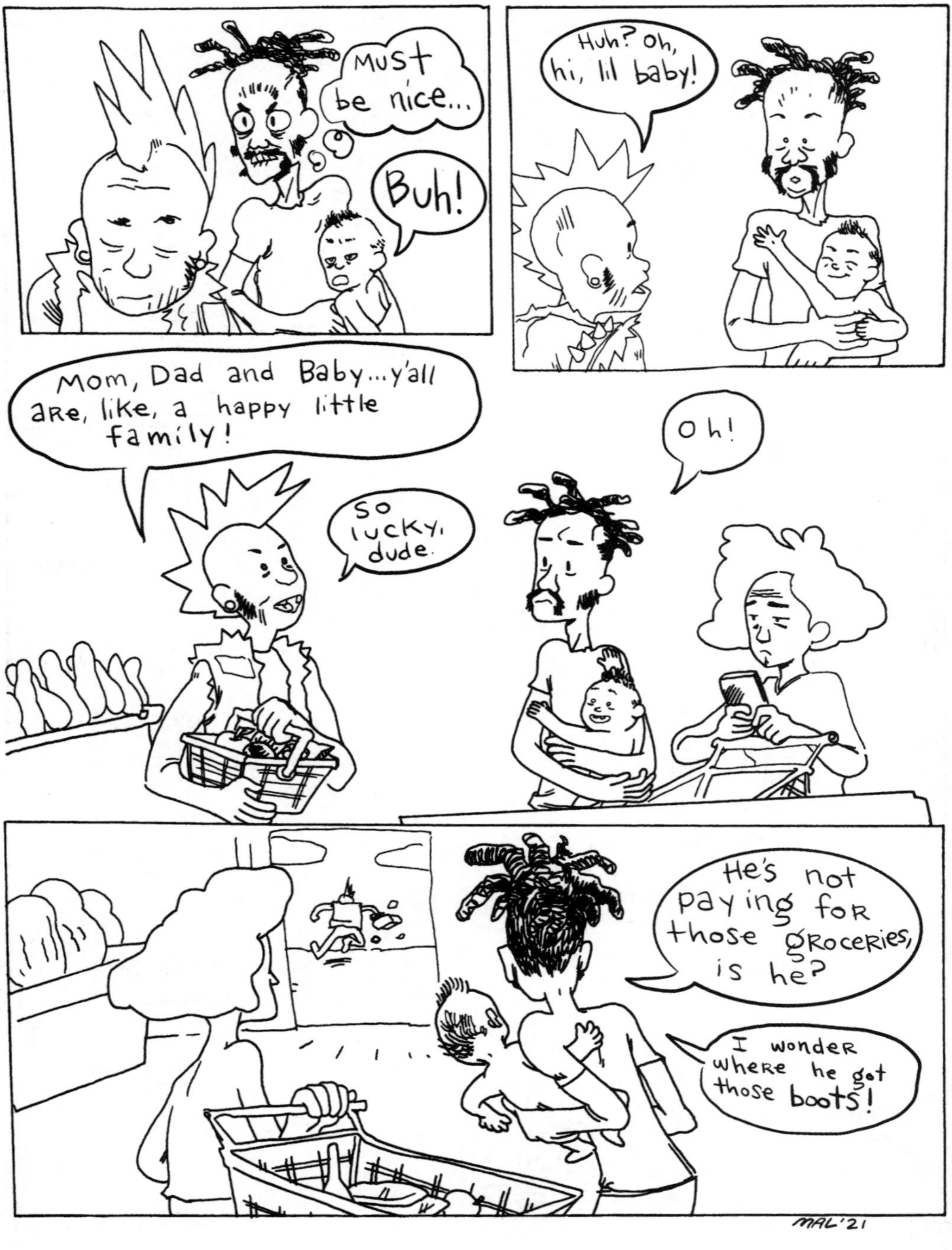
Must be nice...
Buh!
Huh? Oh, hi, lil baby!
Mom, Dad and Baby...y'all are, like, a happy little family!
So lucky, dude.
Oh!
He's not paying for those groceries, is he?
I wonder where he got those boots!
MAL '21

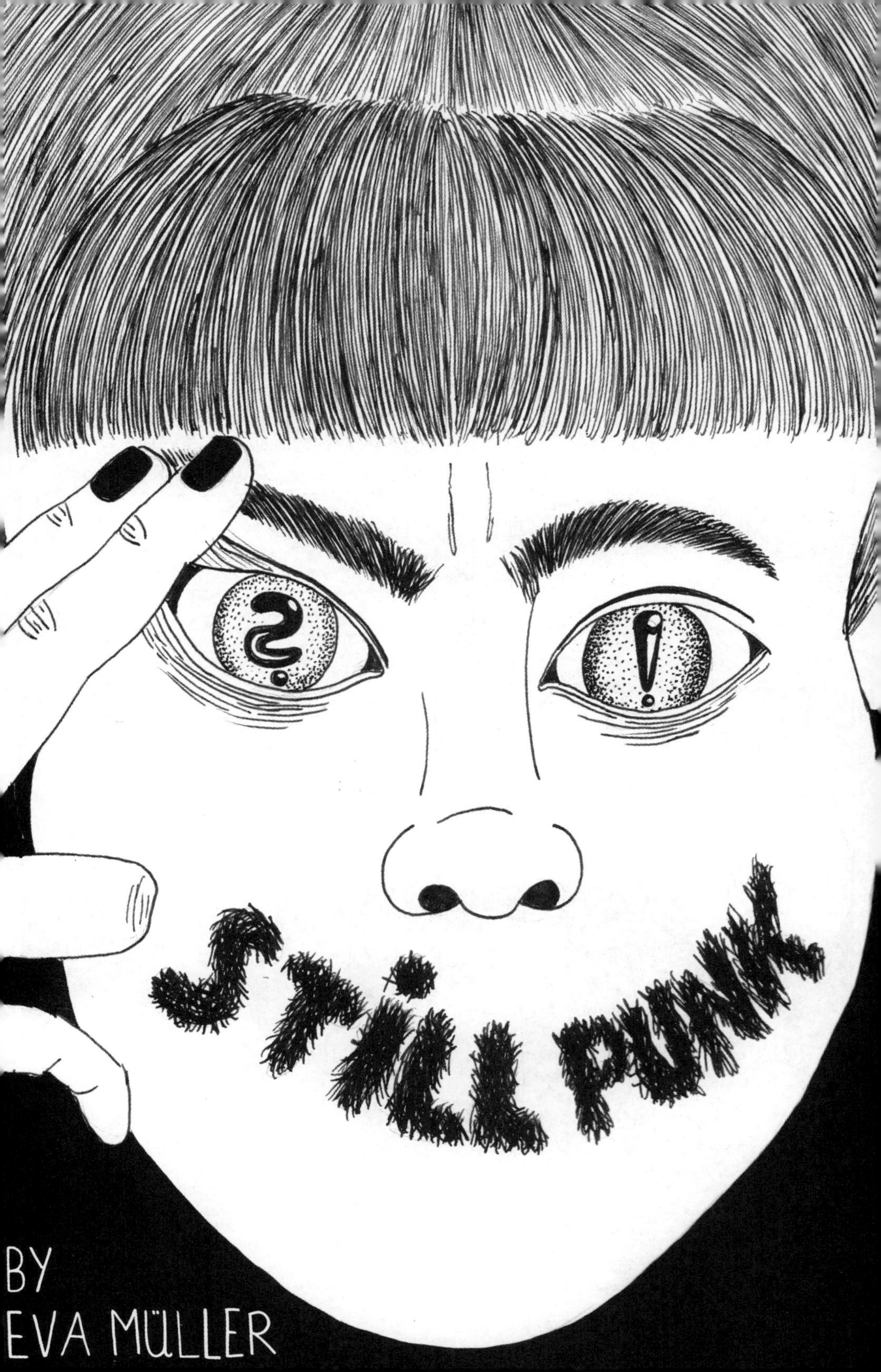
STILL PUNK
BY
EVA MÜLLER

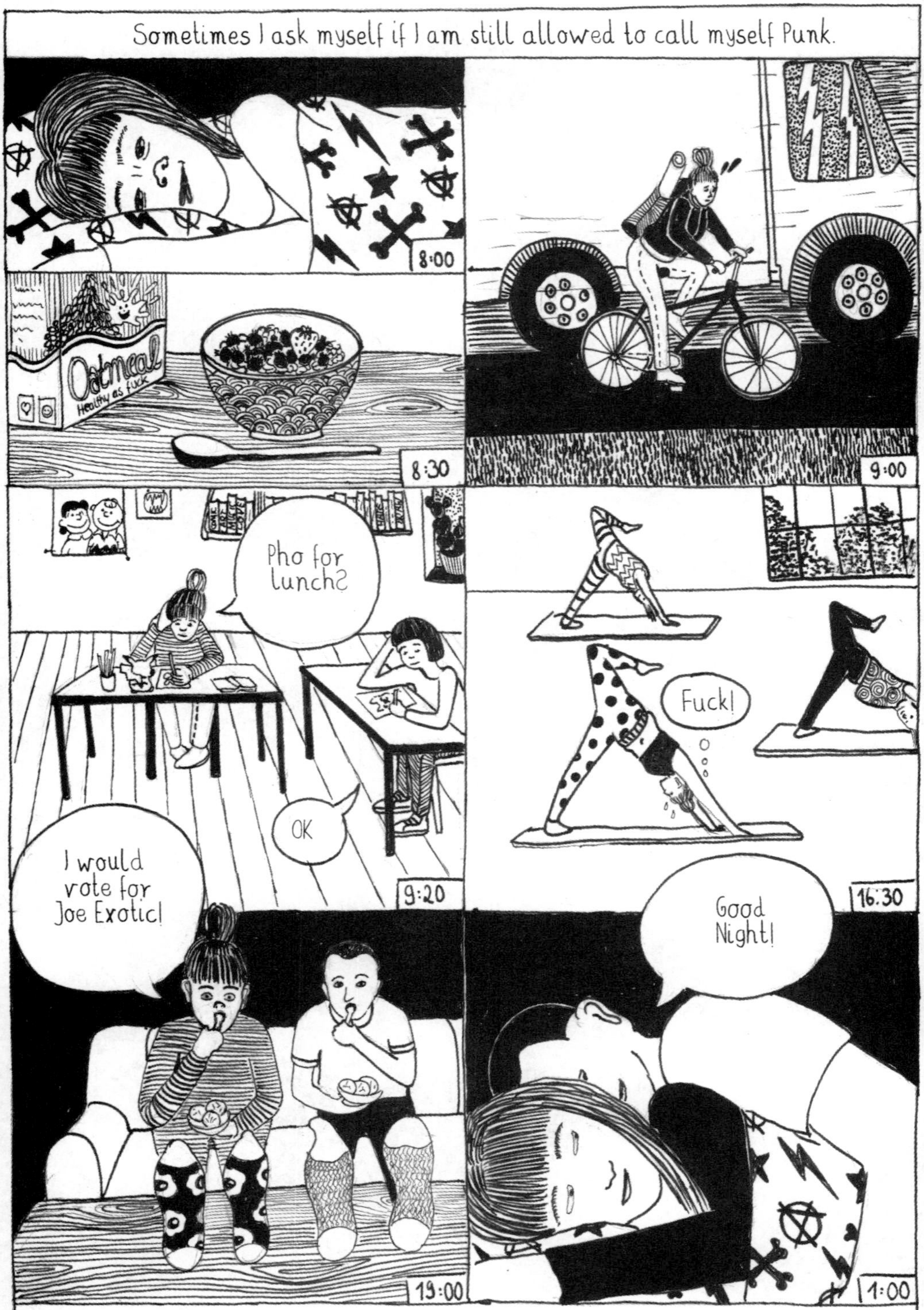
Sometimes I ask myself if I am still allowed to call myself Punk.
8:00
Oatmeal
Healthy as fuck
8:30
9:00
Pho for lunch?
OK
9:20
Fuck!
16:30
I would vote for Joe Exotic!
19:00
Good Night!
1:00
I have a very regular life now.

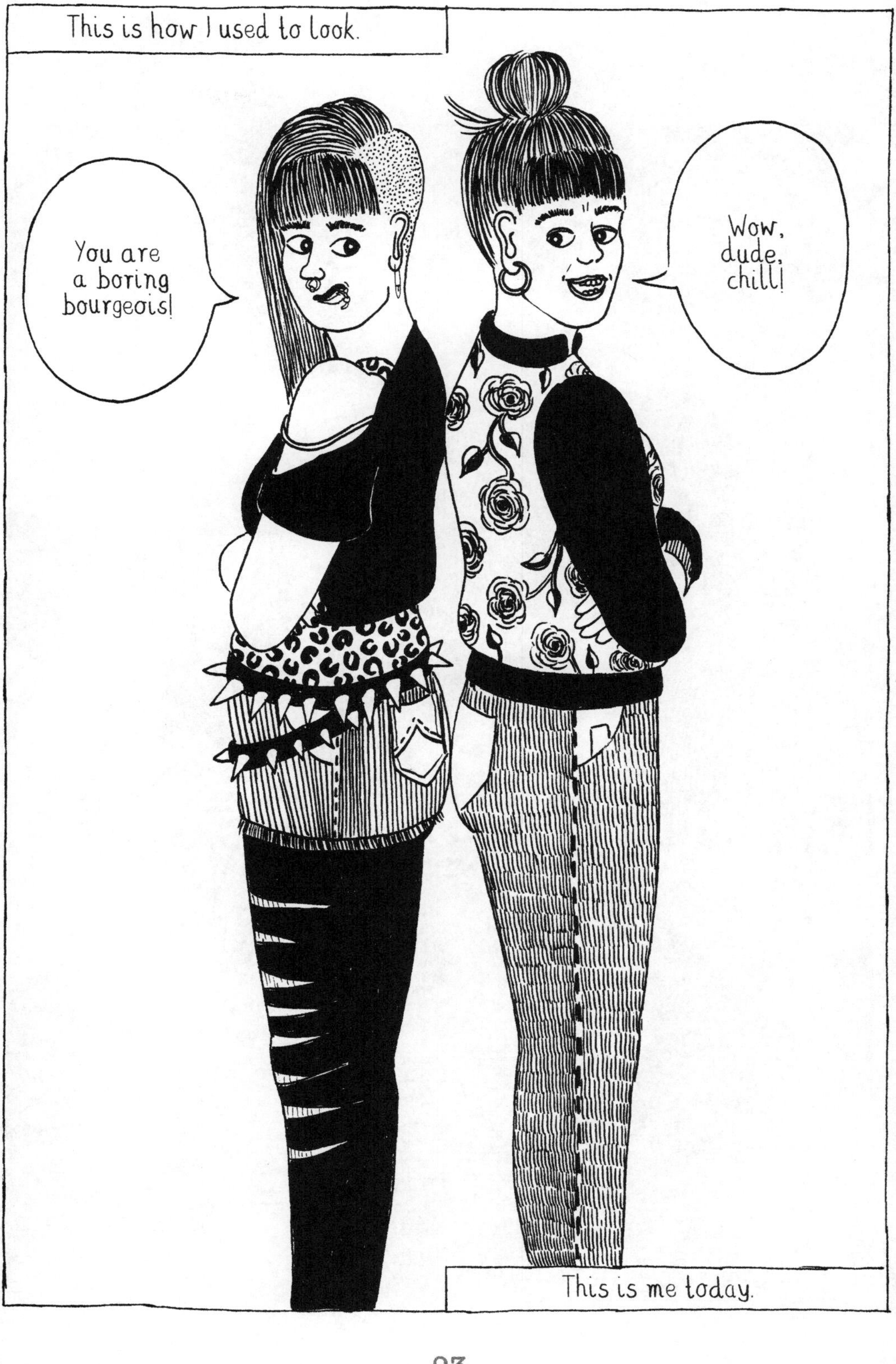

This is how I used to look.
You are a boring bourgeois!
Wow, dude, chill!
This is me today.

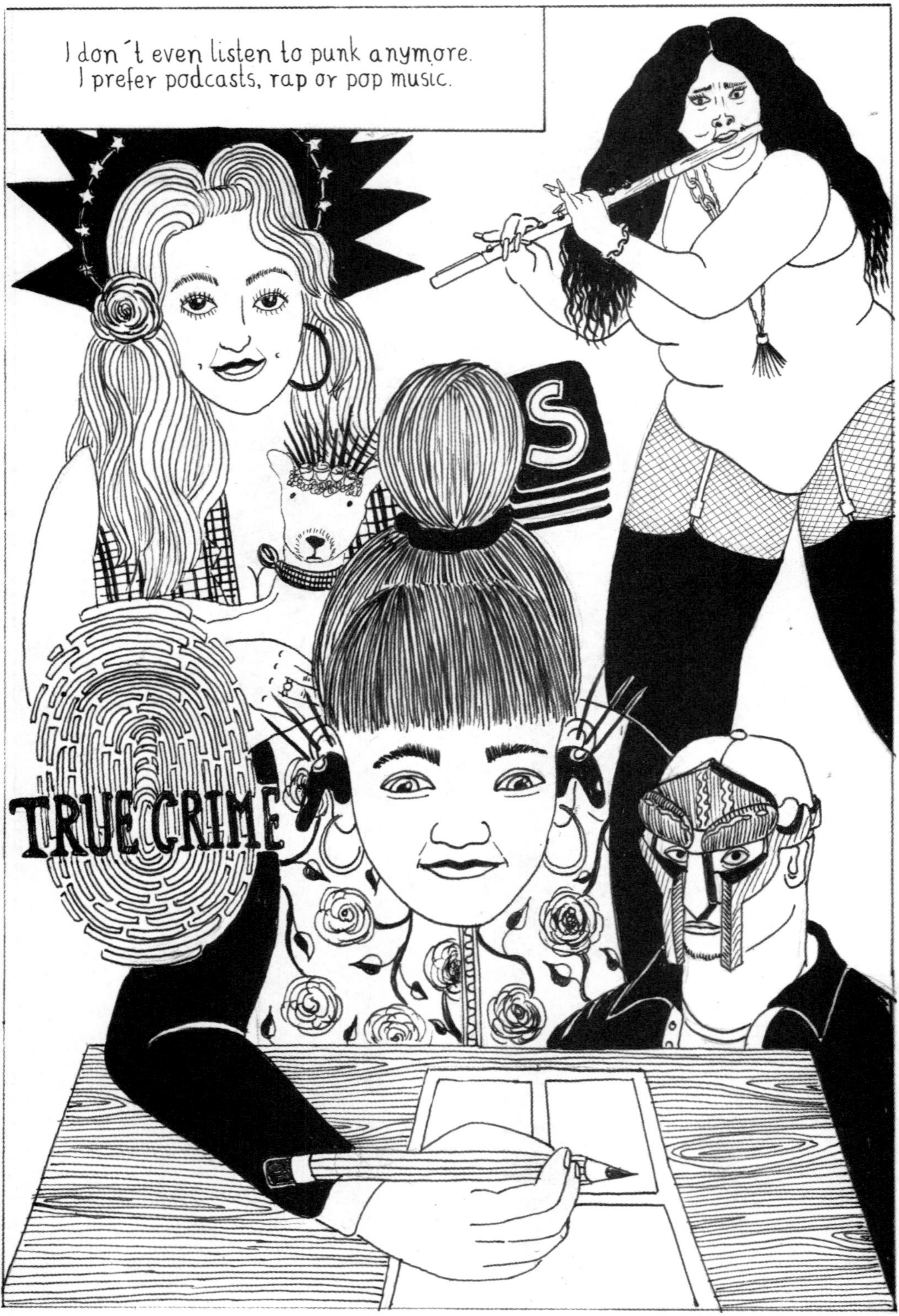
I don´t even listen to punk anymore.
I prefer podcasts, rap or pop music.
TRUE CRIME
S

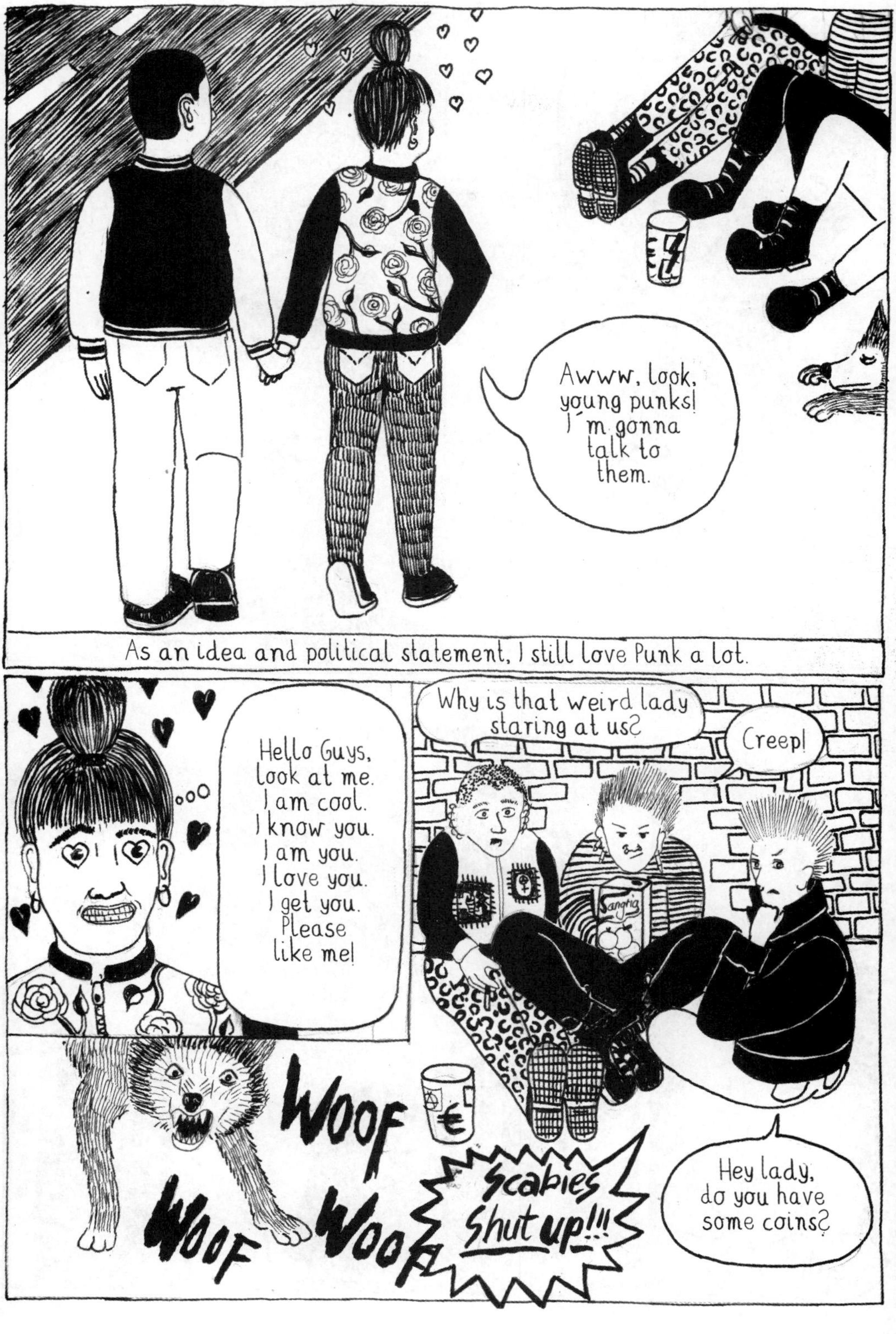

Awww, look, young punks! I'm gonna talk to them.
As an idea and political statement, I still love Punk a lot.
Hello Guys, look at me. I am cool. I know you. I am you. I love you. I get you. Please like me!
Why is that weird lady staring at us?
Creep!
WOOF
WOOF
WOOF
Scabies Shut up!!!
Hey lady, do you have some coins?

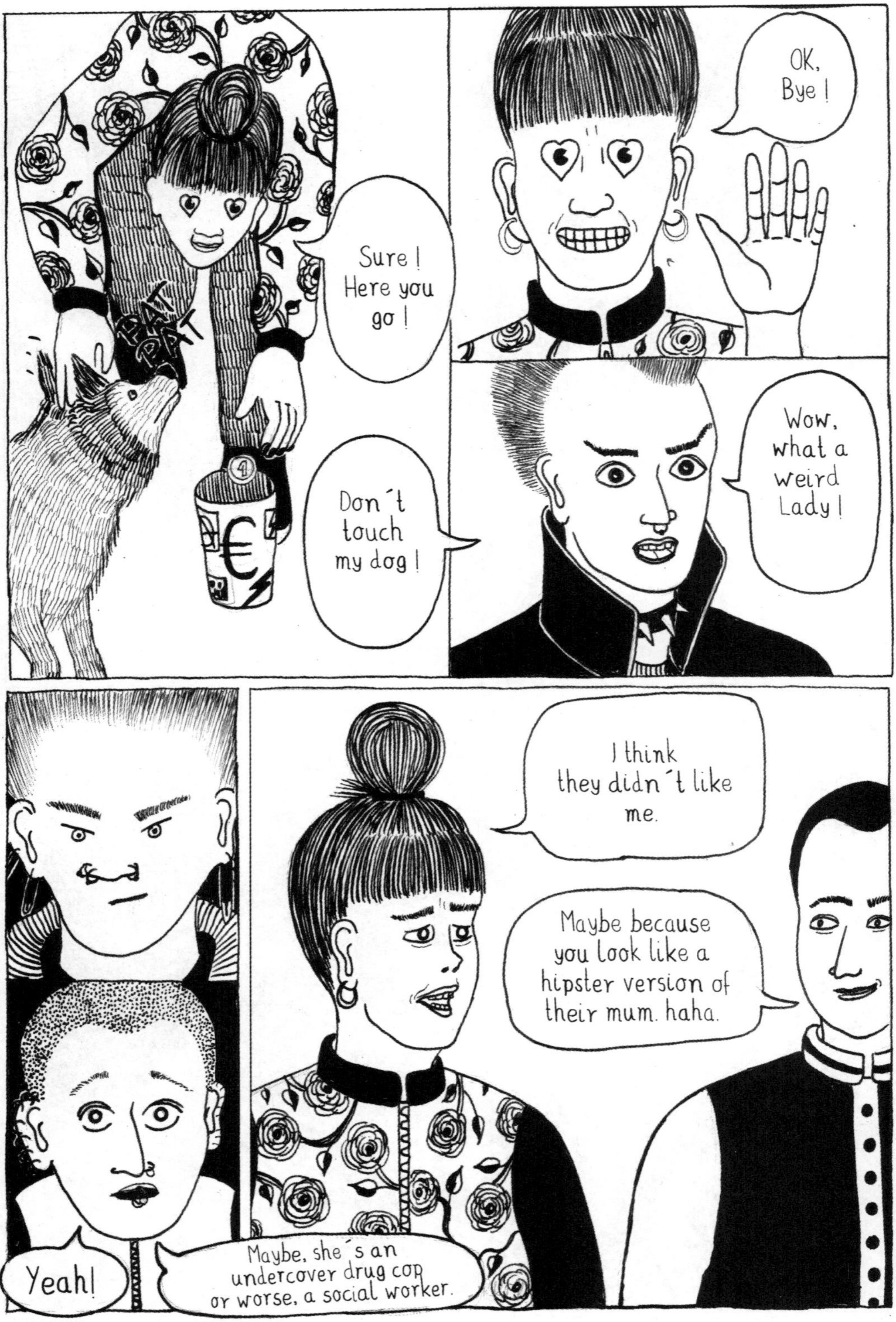
Sure! Here you go!
PAT PAT PAT
Don´t touch my dog!
OK, Bye!
Wow, what a weird Lady!
Yeah!
Maybe, she´s an undercover drug cop or worse, a social worker.
I think they didn´t like me.
Maybe because you look like a hipster version of their mum. haha.

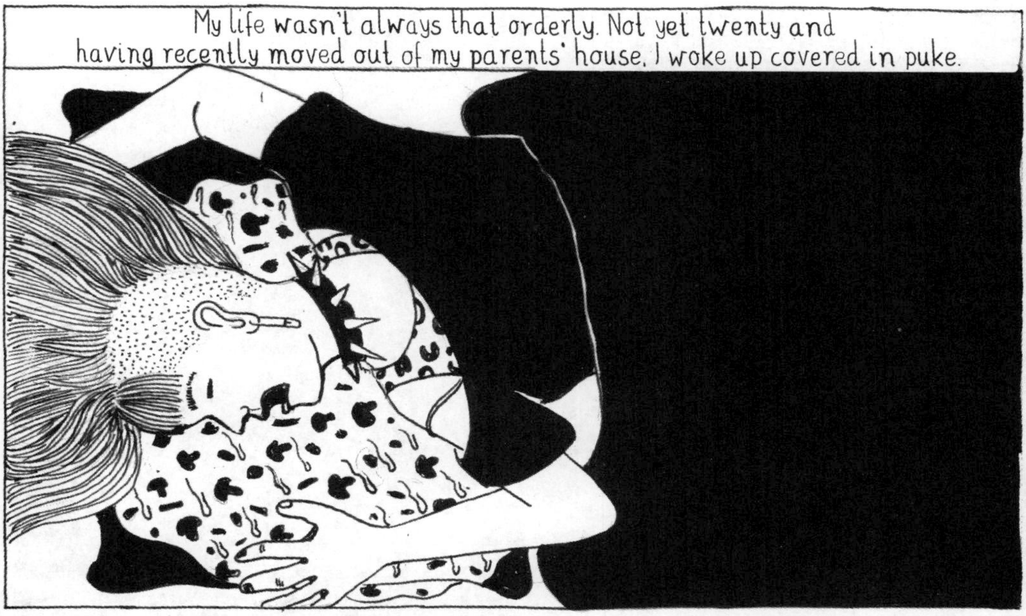
My life wasn't always that orderly. Not yet twenty and having recently moved out of my parents' house, I woke up covered in puke.

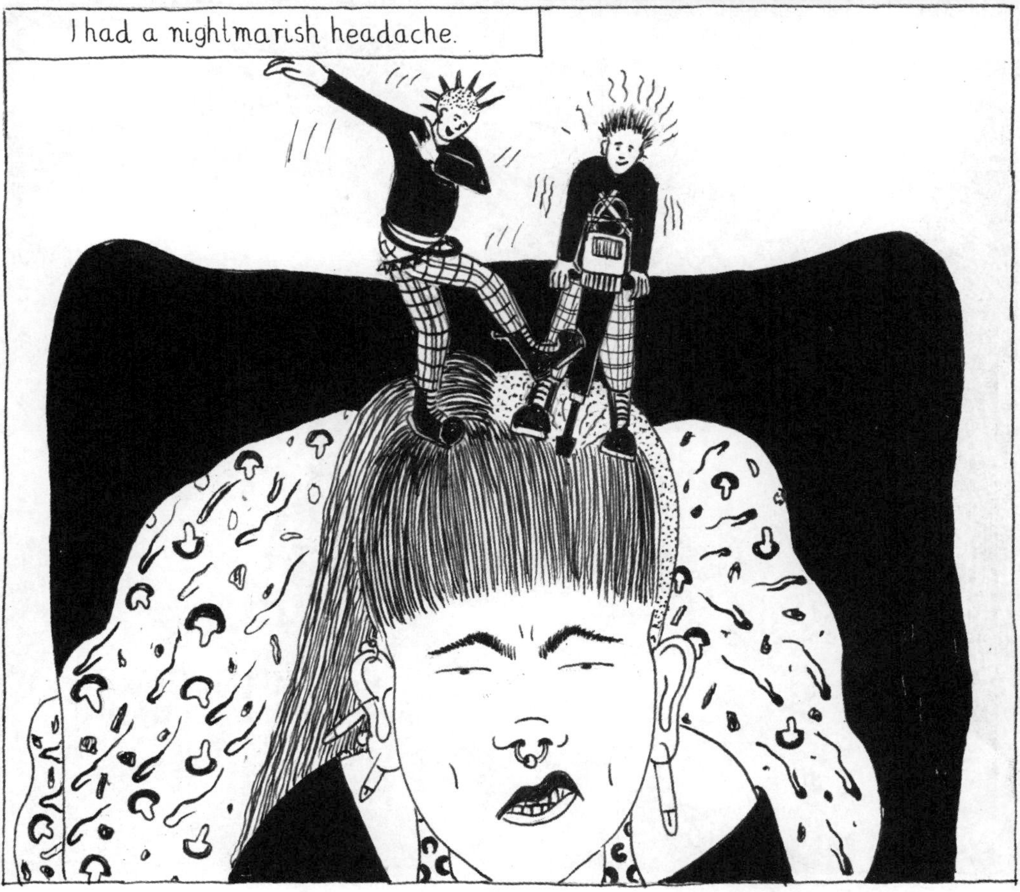
I had a nightmarish headache.

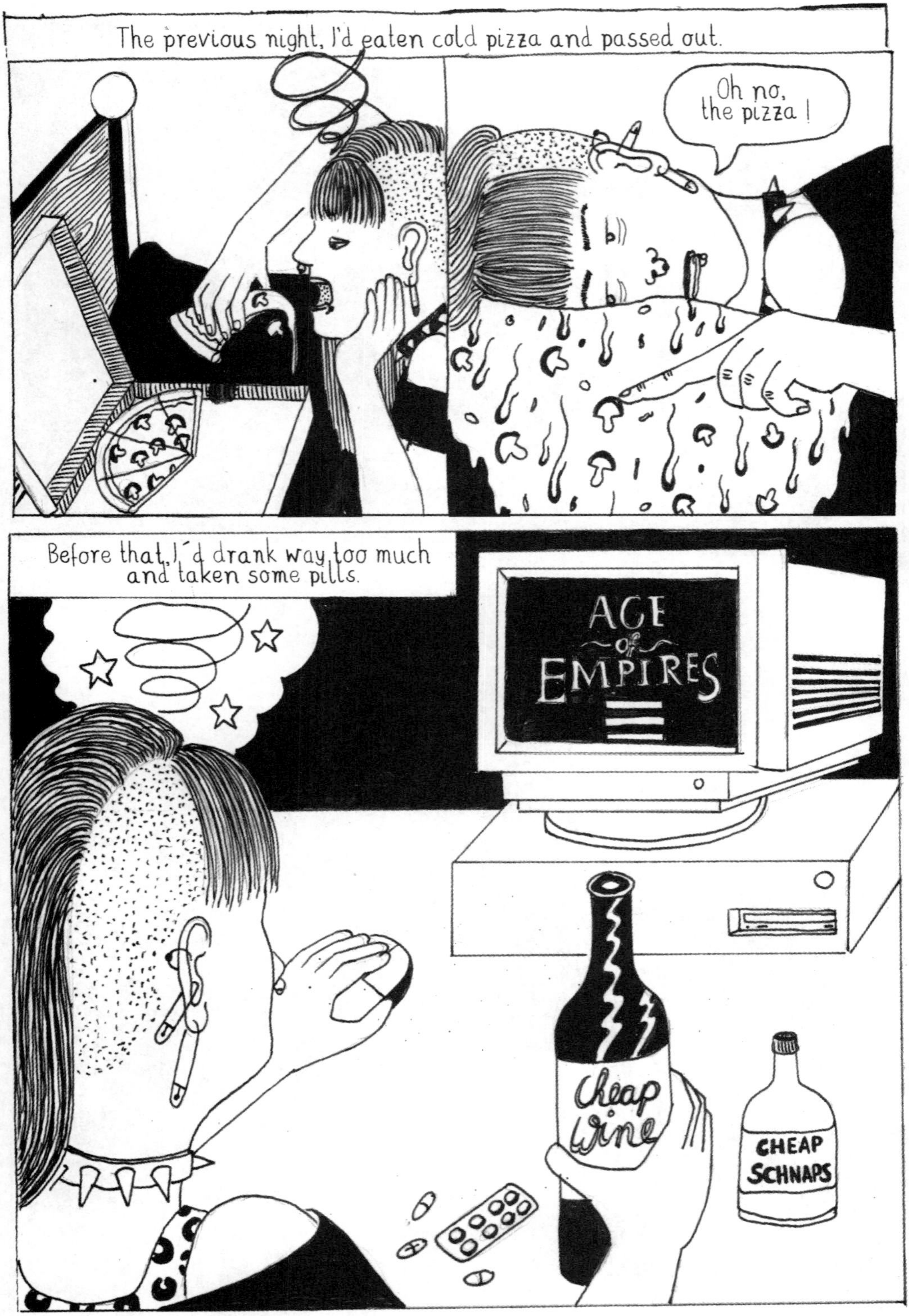
The previous night, I'd eaten cold pizza and passed out.
Oh no, the pizza !
Before that, I´d drank way too much and taken some pills.
AGE of EMPIRES
Cheap Wine
CHEAP SCHNAPS

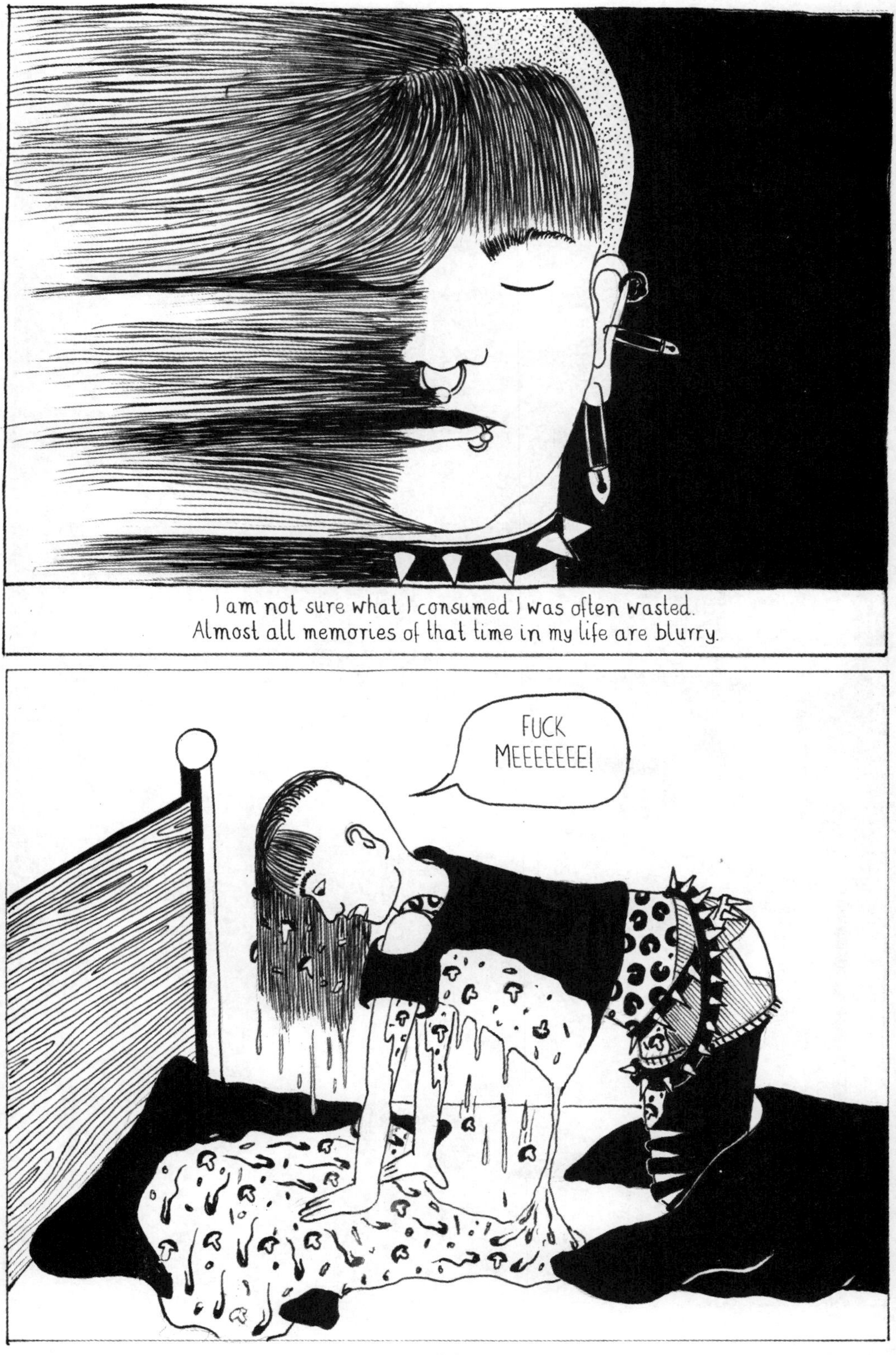
I am not sure what I consumed I was often wasted.
Almost all memories of that time in my life are blurry.
FUCK MEEEEEEE!

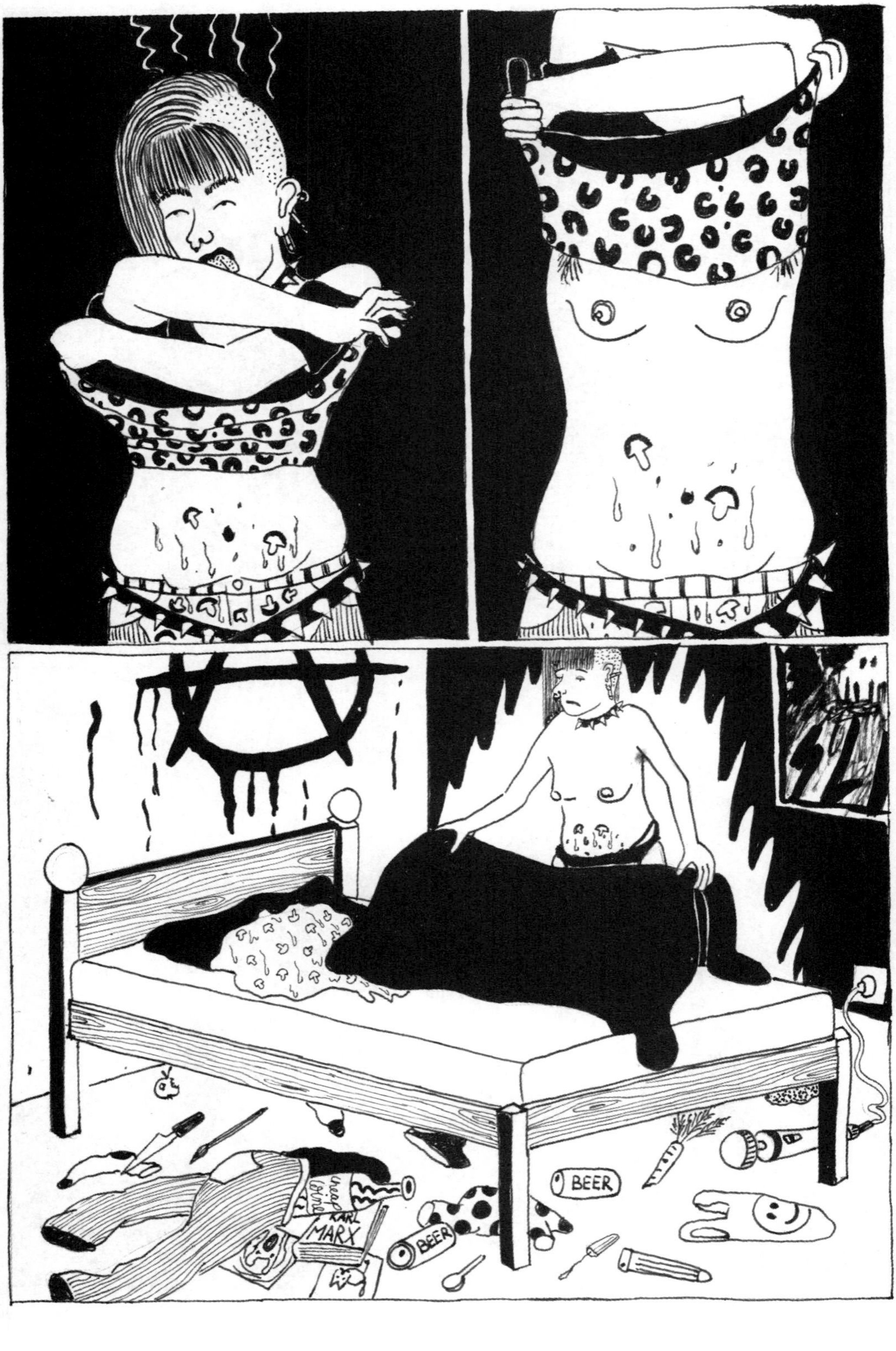
cheap wine
KARL MARX
BEER
BEER

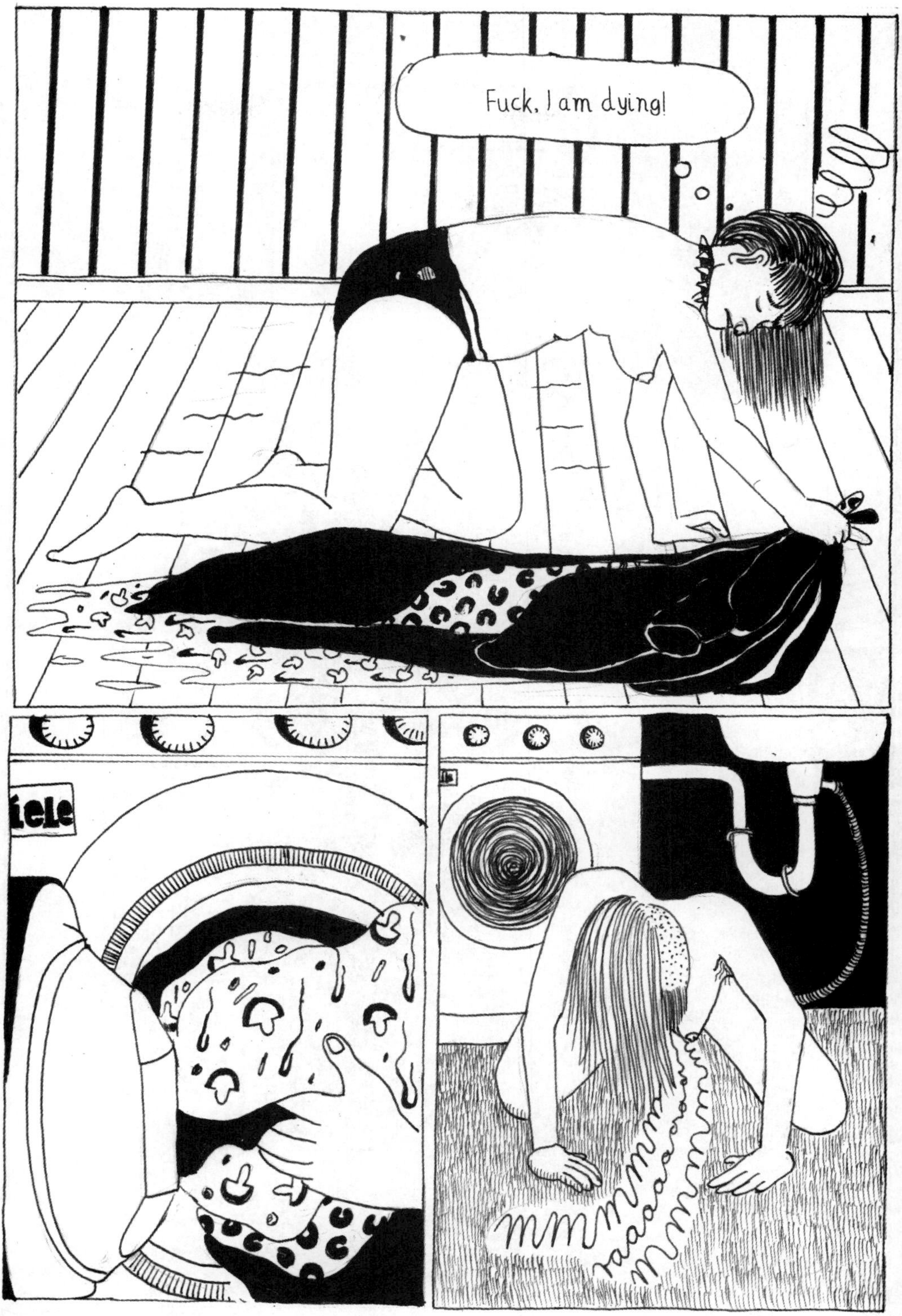
Fuck, I am dying!

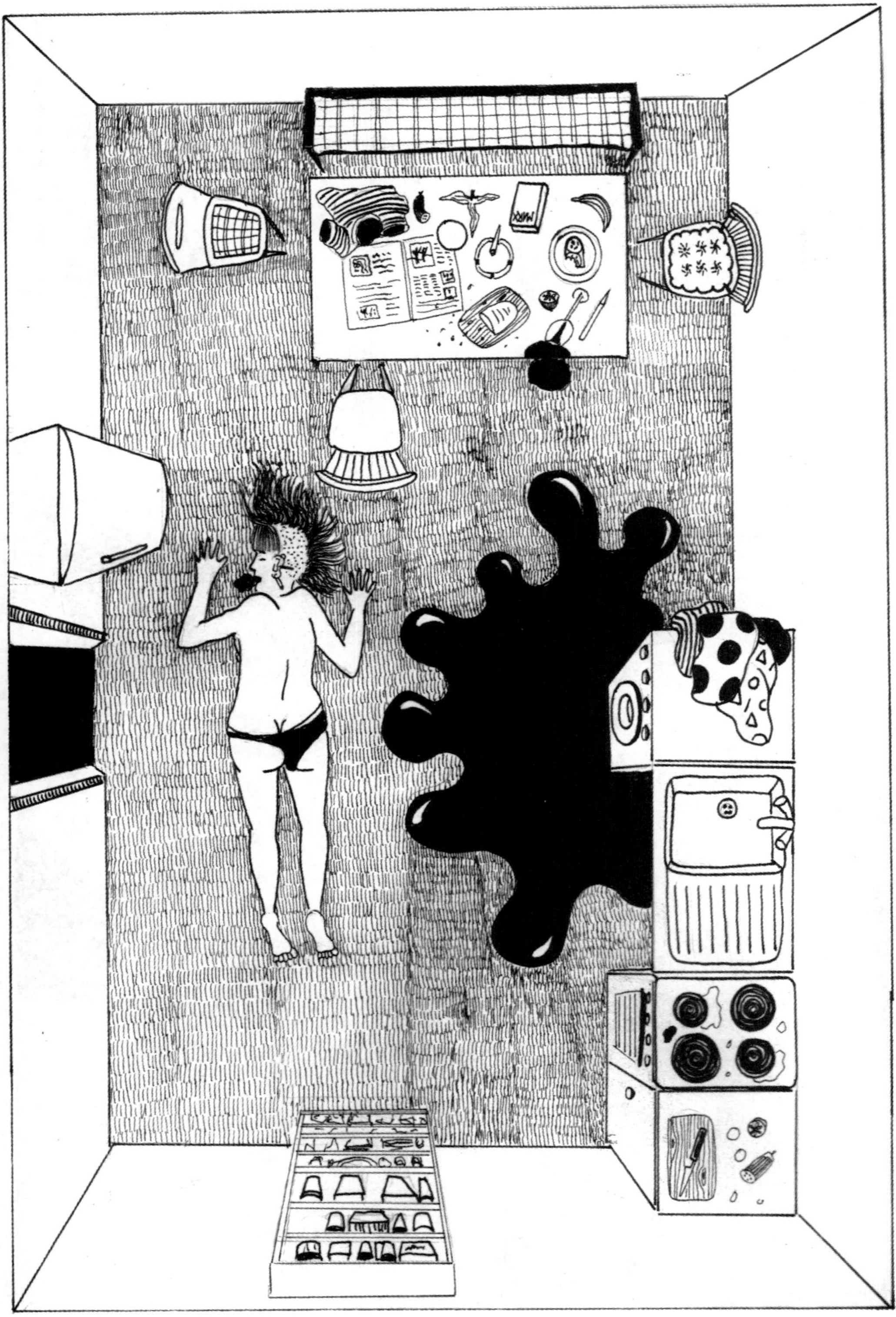

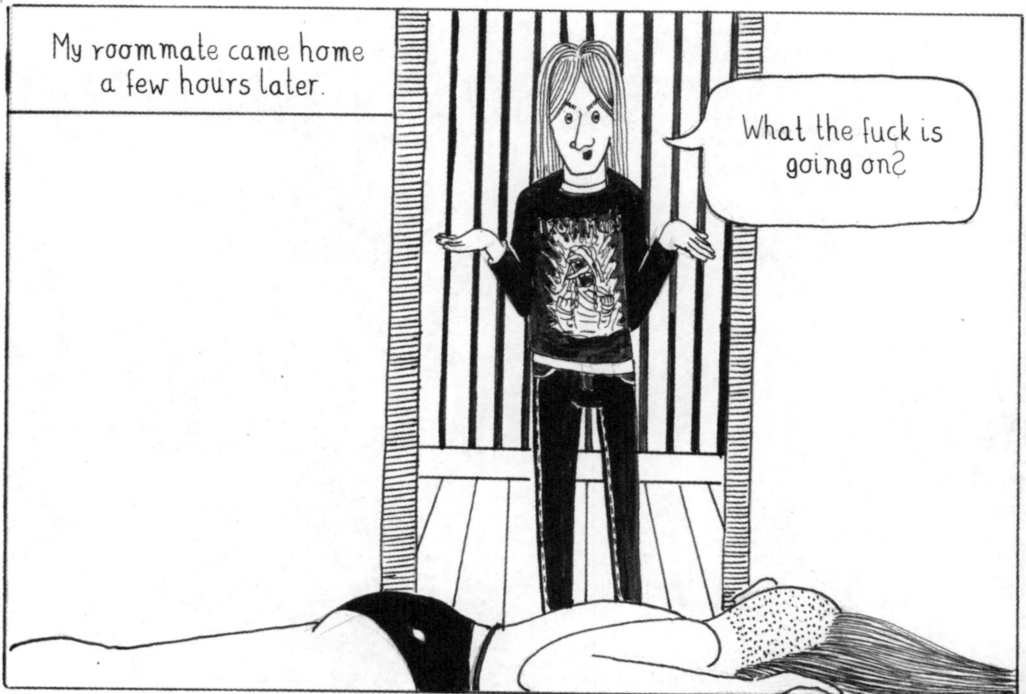
My roommate came home a few hours later.
What the fuck is going on?

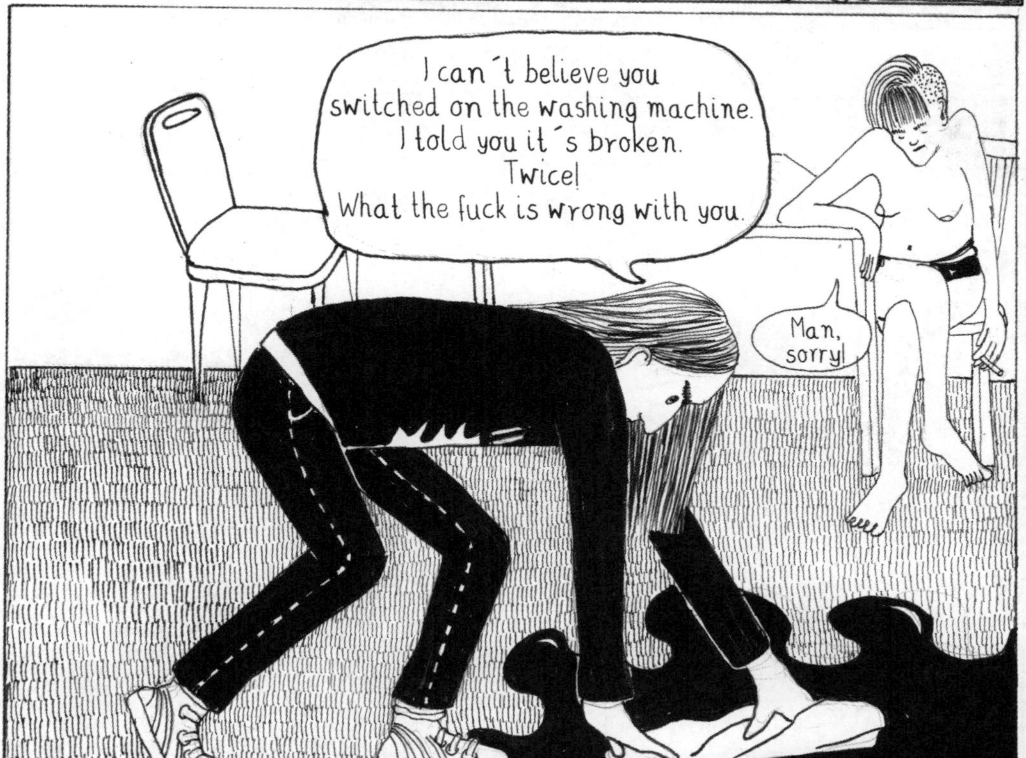
I can´t believe you switched on the washing machine. I told you it´s broken. Twice! What the fuck is wrong with you.
Man, sorry!

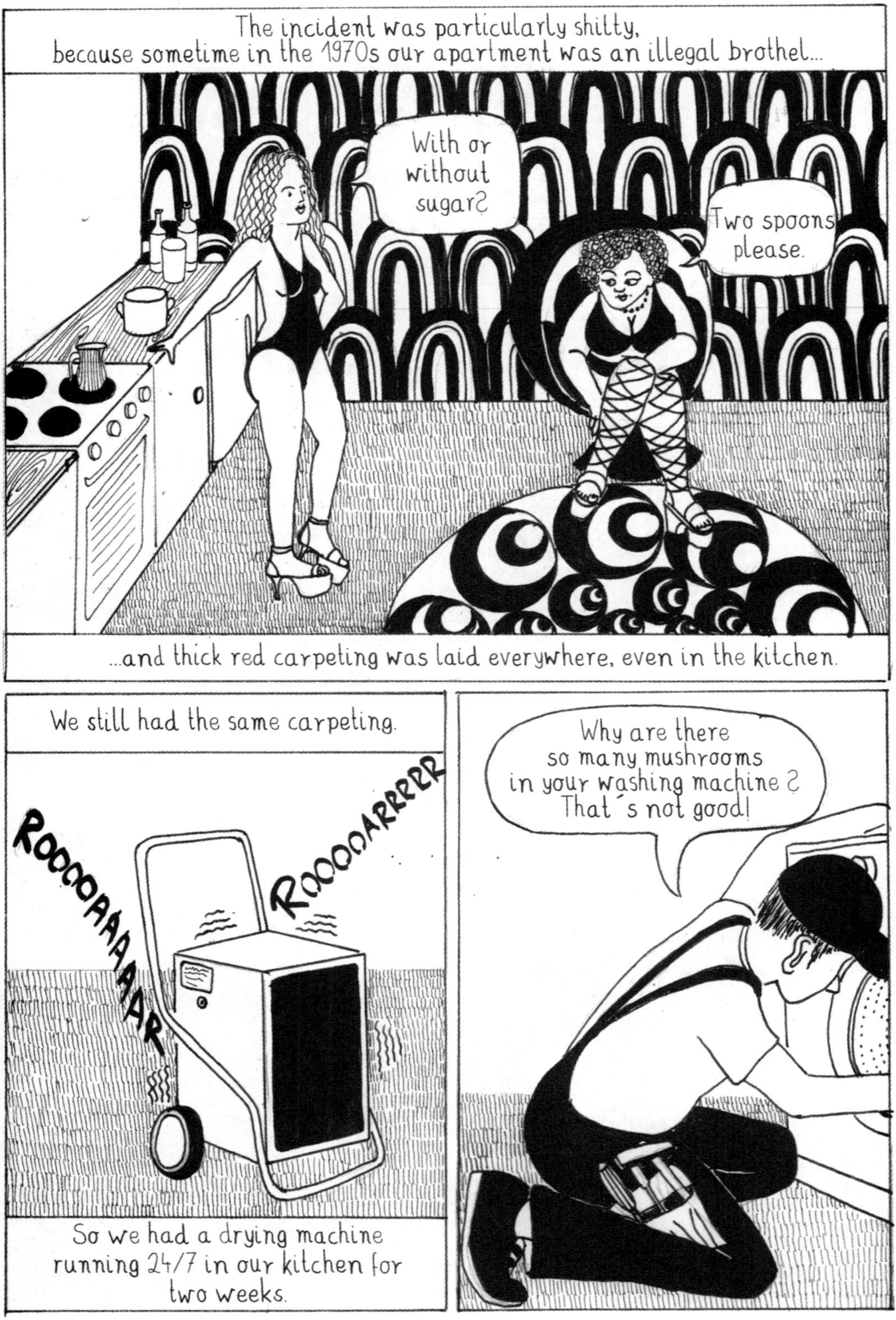
The incident was particularly shitty,
because sometime in the 1970s our apartment was an illegal brothel...
With or without sugar?
Two spoons please.
...and thick red carpeting was laid everywhere, even in the kitchen.
We still had the same carpeting.
ROOOOAAAAAAR
ROOOOARRRRR
So we had a drying machine running 24/7 in our kitchen for two weeks.
Why are there so many mushrooms in your washing machine? That´s not good!

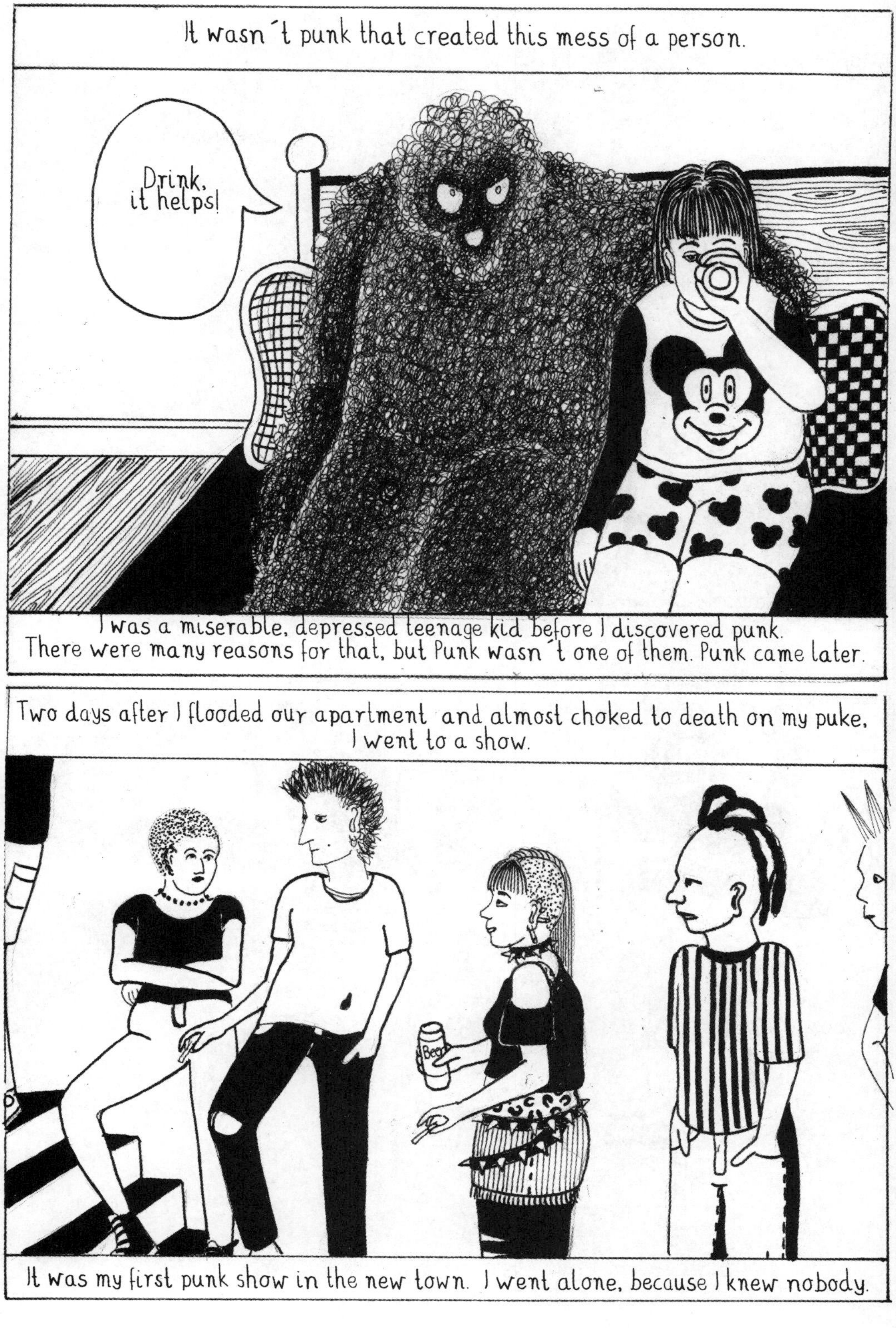

It wasn´t punk that created this mess of a person.
Drink, it helps!
I was a miserable, depressed teenage kid before I discovered punk. There were many reasons for that, but Punk wasn´t one of them. Punk came later.
Two days after I flooded our apartment and almost choked to death on my puke, I went to a show.
Beer
It was my first punk show in the new town. I went alone, because I knew nobody.

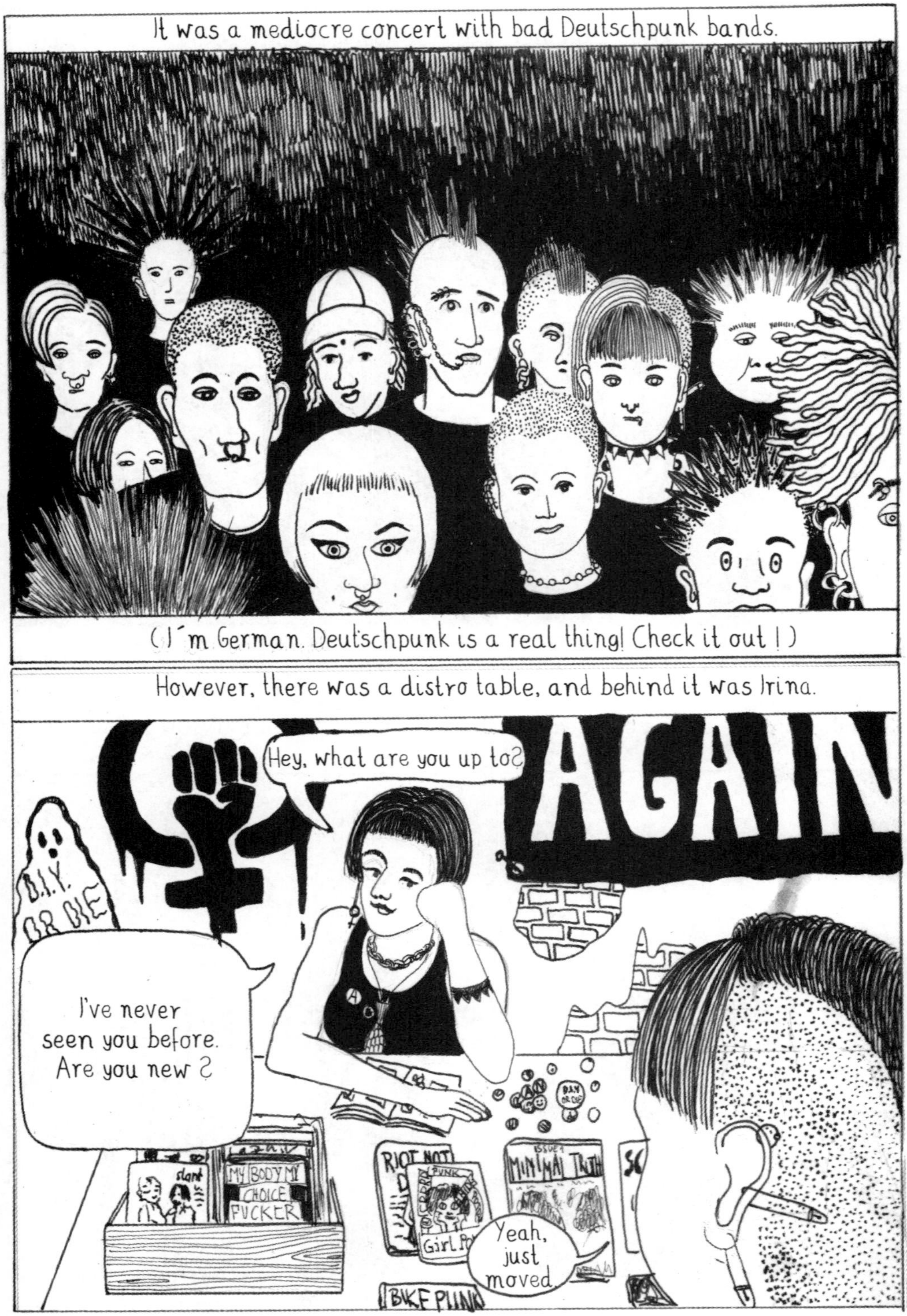
It was a mediocre concert with bad Deutschpunk bands.
(I´m German. Deutschpunk is a real thing! Check it out!)
However, there was a distro table, and behind it was Irina.
AGAIN
Hey, what are you up to?
D.I.Y. OR DIE
I've never seen you before. Are you new?
MY BODY MY CHOICE FUCKER
slant
RIOT NOT
PUNK
Girl Po
MINIMAL TRUTH
Yeah, just moved.
BIKE PUNK

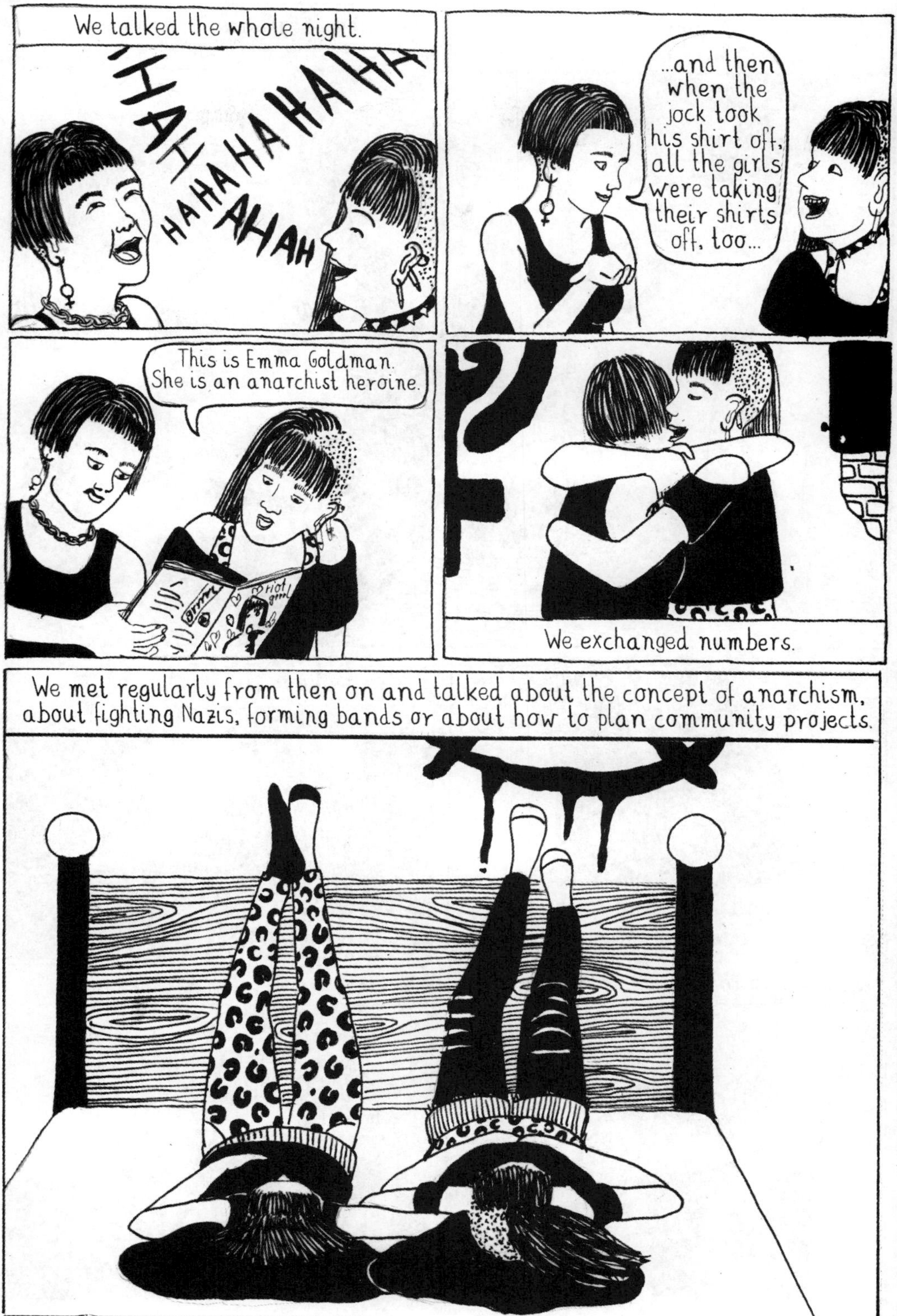

We talked the whole night.
...and then when the jock took his shirt off, all the girls were taking their shirts off, too...
This is Emma Goldman. She is an anarchist heroine.
We exchanged numbers.
We met regularly from then on and talked about the concept of anarchism, about fighting Nazis, forming bands or about how to plan community projects.

We went to political group meetings and, I met Irina's friends. My drinking and drug use faded in the backround and wasn't such a problem anymore.

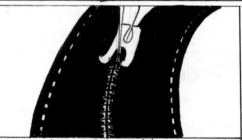

Instead, I learned how to sew a cool bag from old bike tubes...

...or make a skirt out of an old pair of Jeans.

I learned how to save food from dumpsters...

...and cook for many people.

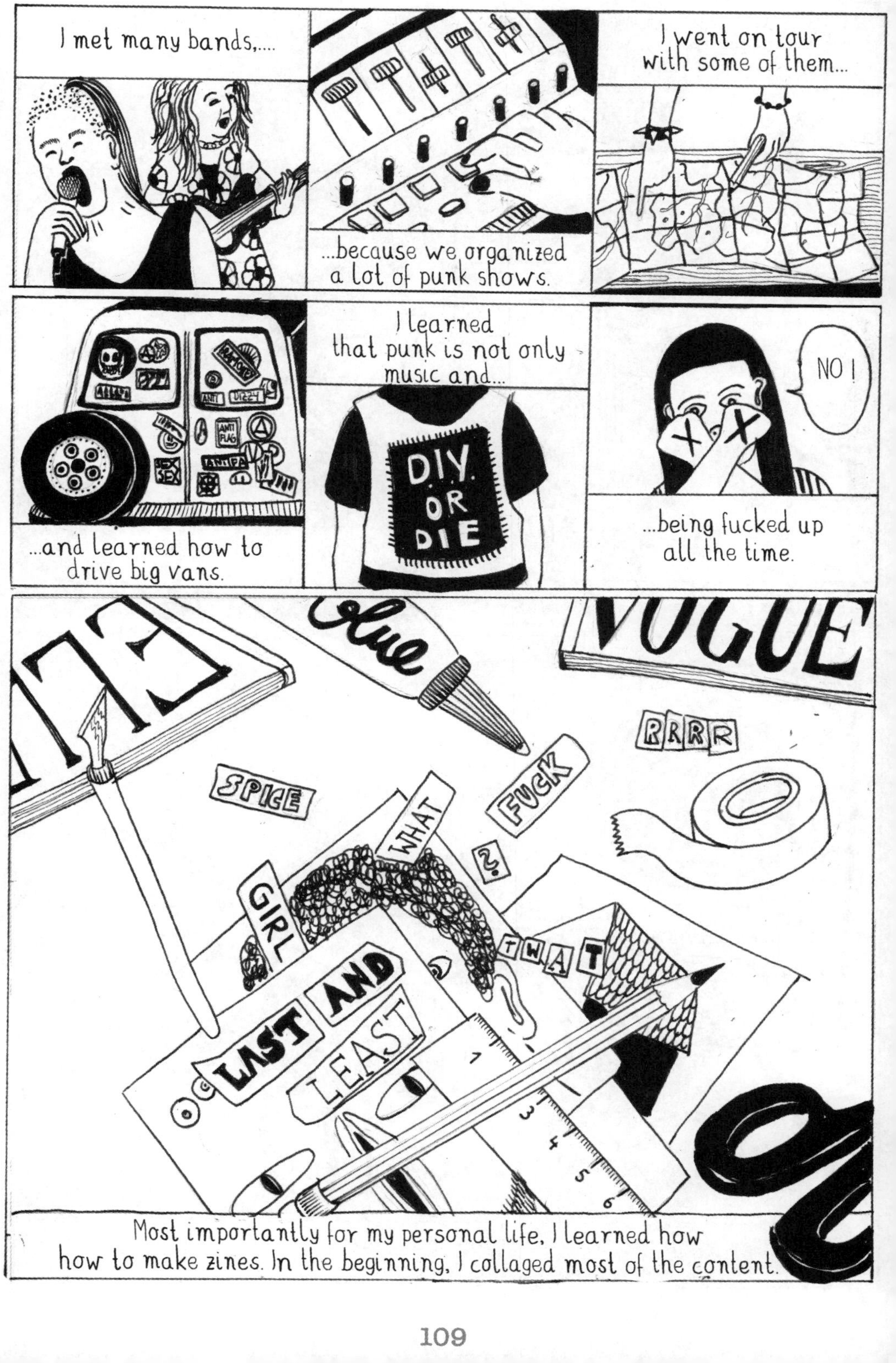
I met many bands,....
...because we organized a lot of punk shows.
I went on tour with some of them...
...and learned how to drive big vans.
I learned that punk is not only music and...
D.I.Y. OR DIE
NO!
...being fucked up all the time.
glue
VOGUE
RRRR
SPICE
WHAT
FUCK
?
GIRL
TWAT
LAST AND LEAST
Most importantly for my personal life, I learned how how to make zines. In the beginning, I collaged most of the content.

Then I started to draw it by myself. Sometimes the drawings were just scrawly lines,...
... but it didn't matter because it was punk.
My friends have been very encouraging.
The drawings are amazing!
Really cool!
MACHO PUNX FVCK OFF
DROWNED
#5
And also the writing is so smart and intense. I love it.
STORTEBEKER
KAIA WILSON
LIVE
bring your ping pong rack
26. JULY
PINK TANK ENTERTAINMENT
DROWNED
#7
CITY BOMBING
3. AUGUST
PINK TANK FESTIVAL
Rote Flora
LITTLE RASCALS
The Cunts
From then on, I made hundreds of band posters, T-shirts, record covers, flyers and zines.

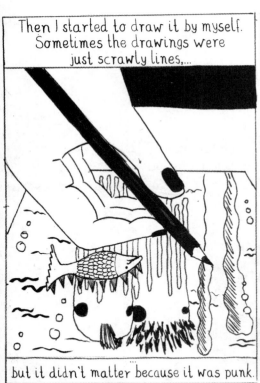

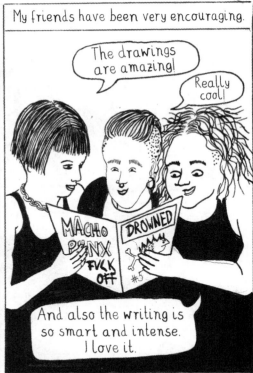

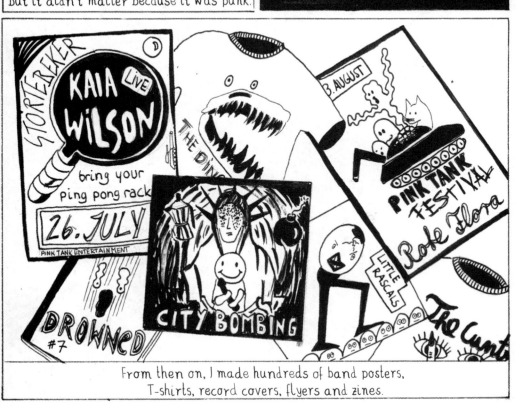

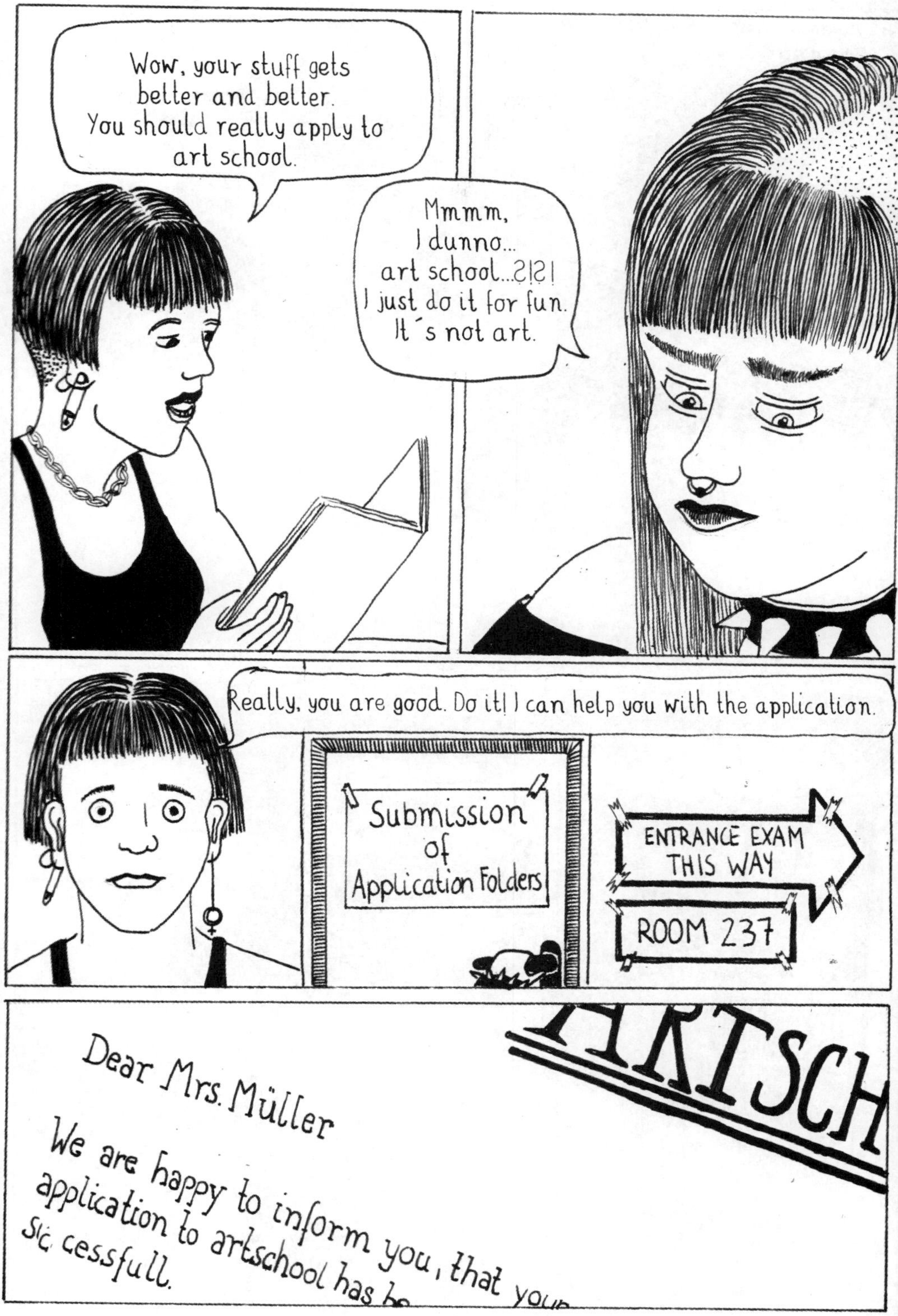

Wow, your stuff gets better and better. You should really apply to art school.
Mmmm, I dunno... art school...?!?! I just do it for fun. It´s not art.
Really, you are good. Do it! I can help you with the application.
Submission of Application Folders
ENTRANCE EXAM THIS WAY
ROOM 237
ARTSCH
Dear Mrs. Müller
We are happy to inform you, that your application to artschool has be
successfull.

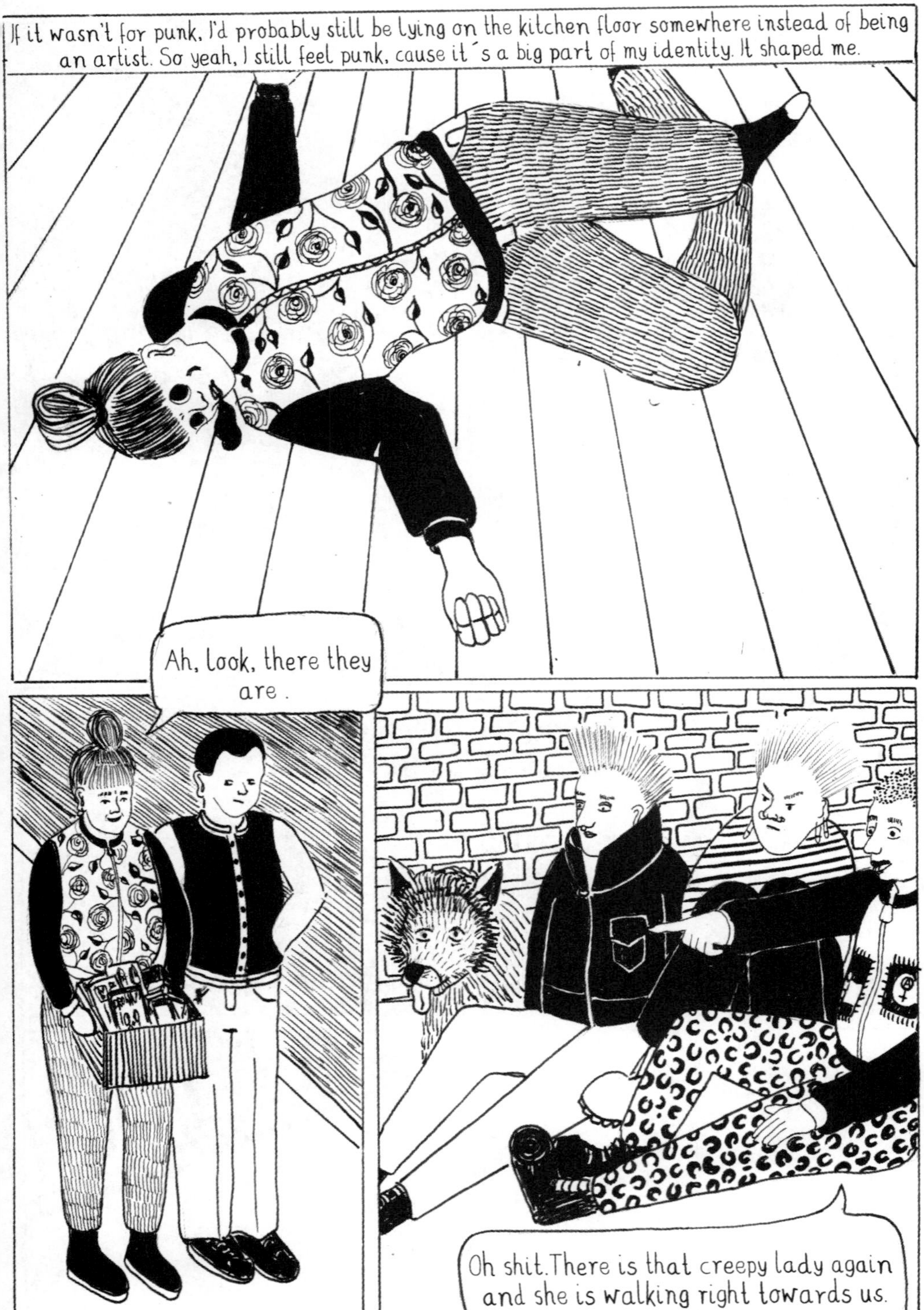
If it wasn't for punk, I'd probably still be lying on the kitchen floor somewhere instead of being an artist. So yeah, I still feel punk, cause it´s a big part of my identity. It shaped me.
Ah, look, there they are.
Oh shit. There is that creepy lady again and she is walking right towards us.

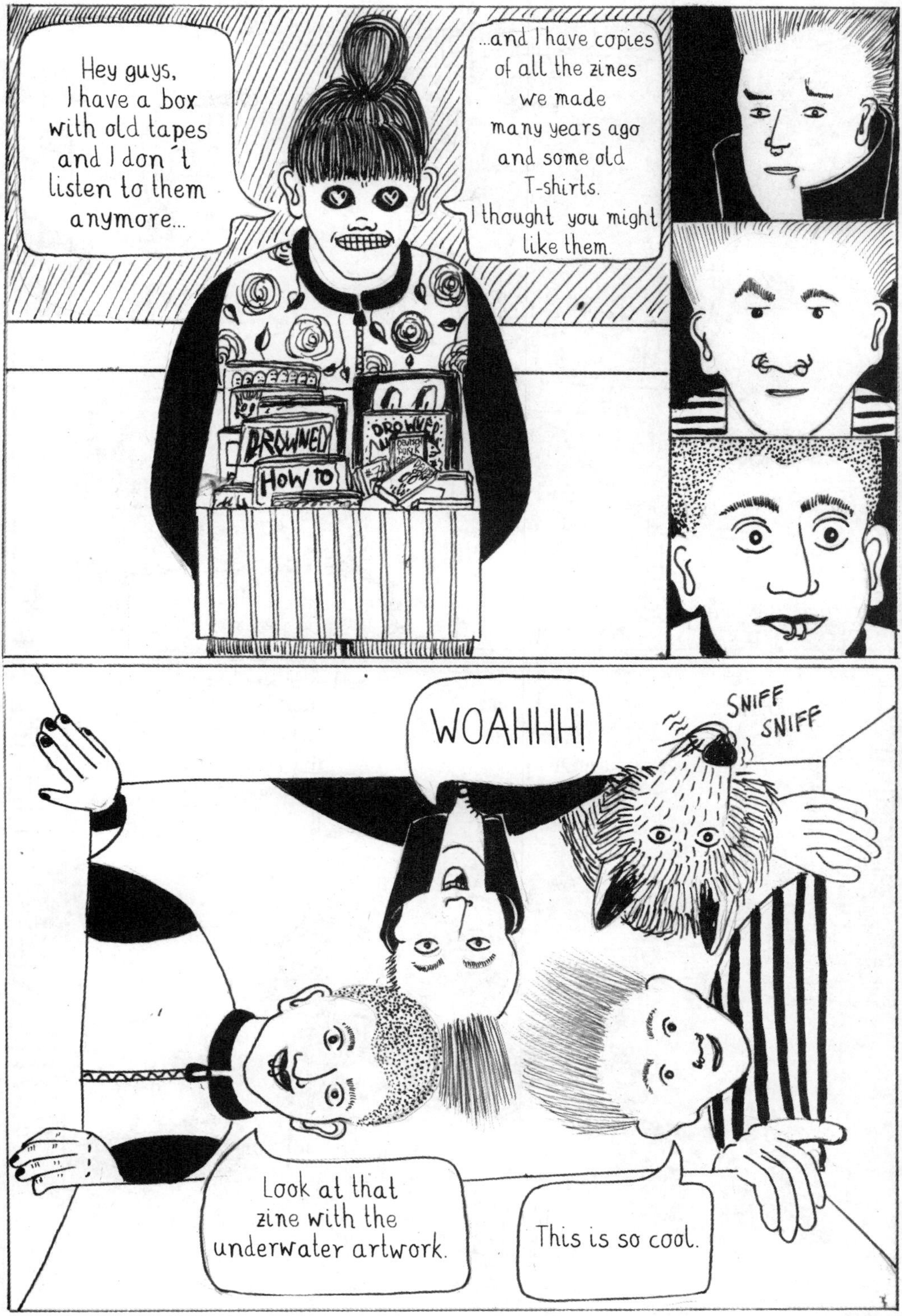
Hey guys, I have a box with old tapes and I don´t listen to them anymore...
...and I have copies of all the zines we made many years ago and some old T-shirts. I thought you might like them.
DROWNED
HOW TO
WOAHHH!
SNIFF SNIFF
Look at that zine with the underwater artwork.
This is so cool.

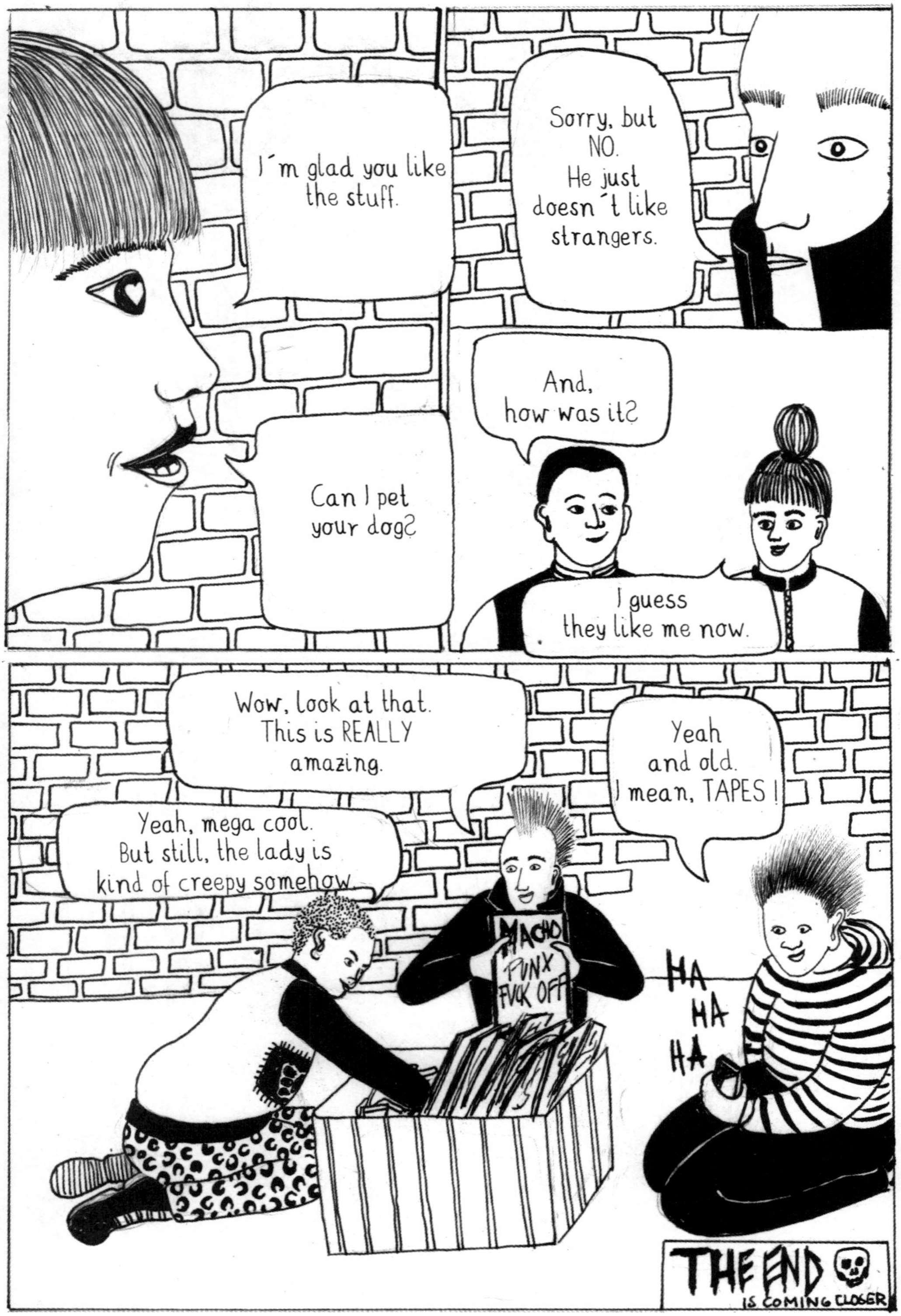
I´m glad you like the stuff.
Can I pet your dogS
Sorry, but NO. He just doesn´t like strangers.
And, how was itS
I guess they like me now.
Wow, look at that. This is REALLY amazing.
Yeah and old. I mean, TAPES !
Yeah, mega cool. But still, the lady is kind of creepy somehow.
MACHO PUNX FUCK OFF
HA HA HA
THE END IS COMING CLOSER

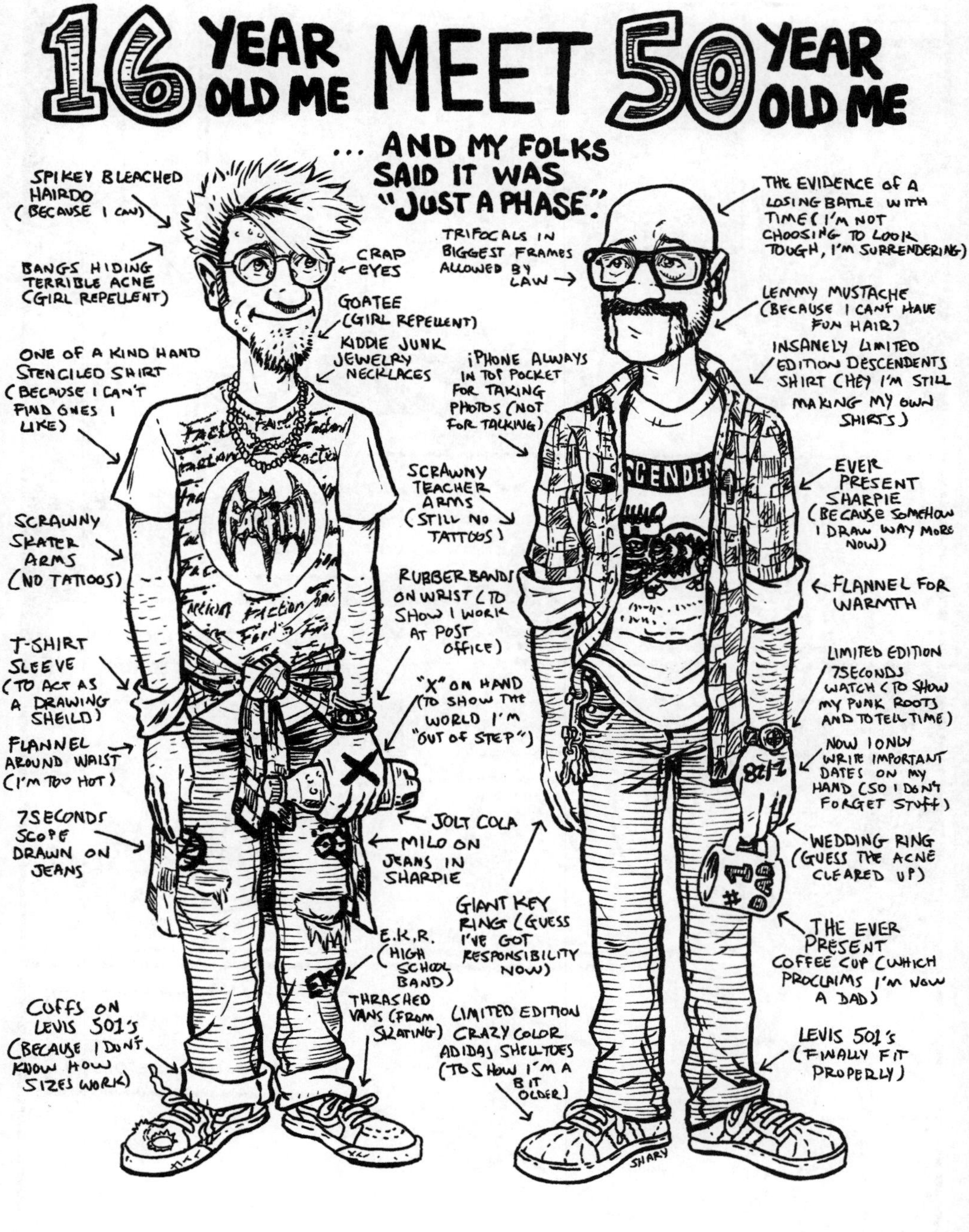
16 YEAR OLD ME MEET 50 YEAR OLD ME
... AND MY FOLKS SAID IT WAS "JUST A PHASE".
SPIKEY BLEACHED HAIRDO (BECAUSE I CAN)
BANGS HIDING TERRIBLE ACNE (GIRL REPELLENT)
CRAP EYES
GOATEE (GIRL REPELLENT)
KIDDIE JUNK JEWELRY NECKLACES
ONE OF A KIND HAND STENCILED SHIRT (BECAUSE I CAN'T FIND ONES I LIKE)
SCRAWNY SKATER ARMS (NO TATTOOS)
T-SHIRT SLEEVE (TO ACT AS A DRAWING SHEILD)
FLANNEL AROUND WAIST (I'M TOO HOT)
7SECONDS SCOPE DRAWN ON JEANS
RUBBER BANDS ON WRIST (TO SHOW I WORK AT POST OFFICE)
"X" ON HAND (TO SHOW THE WORLD I'M "OUT OF STEP")
JOLT COLA
MILO ON JEANS IN SHARPIE
E.K.R. (HIGH SCHOOL BAND)
THRASHED VANS (FROM SKATING)
CUFFS ON LEVIS 501'S (BECAUSE I DON'T KNOW HOW SIZES WORK)
THE EVIDENCE OF A LOSING BATTLE WITH TIME (I'M NOT CHOOSING TO LOOK TOUGH, I'M SURRENDERING)
TRIFOCALS IN BIGGEST FRAMES ALLOWED BY LAW
LEMMY MUSTACHE (BECAUSE I CAN'T HAVE FUN HAIR)
INSANELY LIMITED EDITION DESCENDENTS SHIRT (HEY I'M STILL MAKING MY OWN SHIRTS)
iPHONE ALWAYS IN TOP POCKET FOR TAKING PHOTOS (NOT FOR TALKING)
SCRAWNY TEACHER ARMS (STILL NO TATTOOS)
EVER PRESENT SHARPIE (BECAUSE SOMEHOW I DRAW WAY MORE NOW)
FLANNEL FOR WARMTH
LIMITED EDITION 7SECONDS WATCH (TO SHOW MY PUNK ROOTS AND TO TELL TIME)
NOW I ONLY WRITE IMPORTANT DATES ON MY HAND (SO I DON'T FORGET STUFF)
WEDDING RING (GUESS THE ACNE CLEARED UP)
GIANT KEY RING (GUESS I'VE GOT RESPONSIBILITY NOW)
THE EVER PRESENT COFFEE CUP (WHICH PROCLAIMS I'M NOW A DAD)
LIMITED EDITION CRAZY COLOR ADIDAS SHELLTOES (TO SHOW I'M A BIT OLDER)
LEVIS 501'S (FINALLY FIT PROPERLY)
SHARY

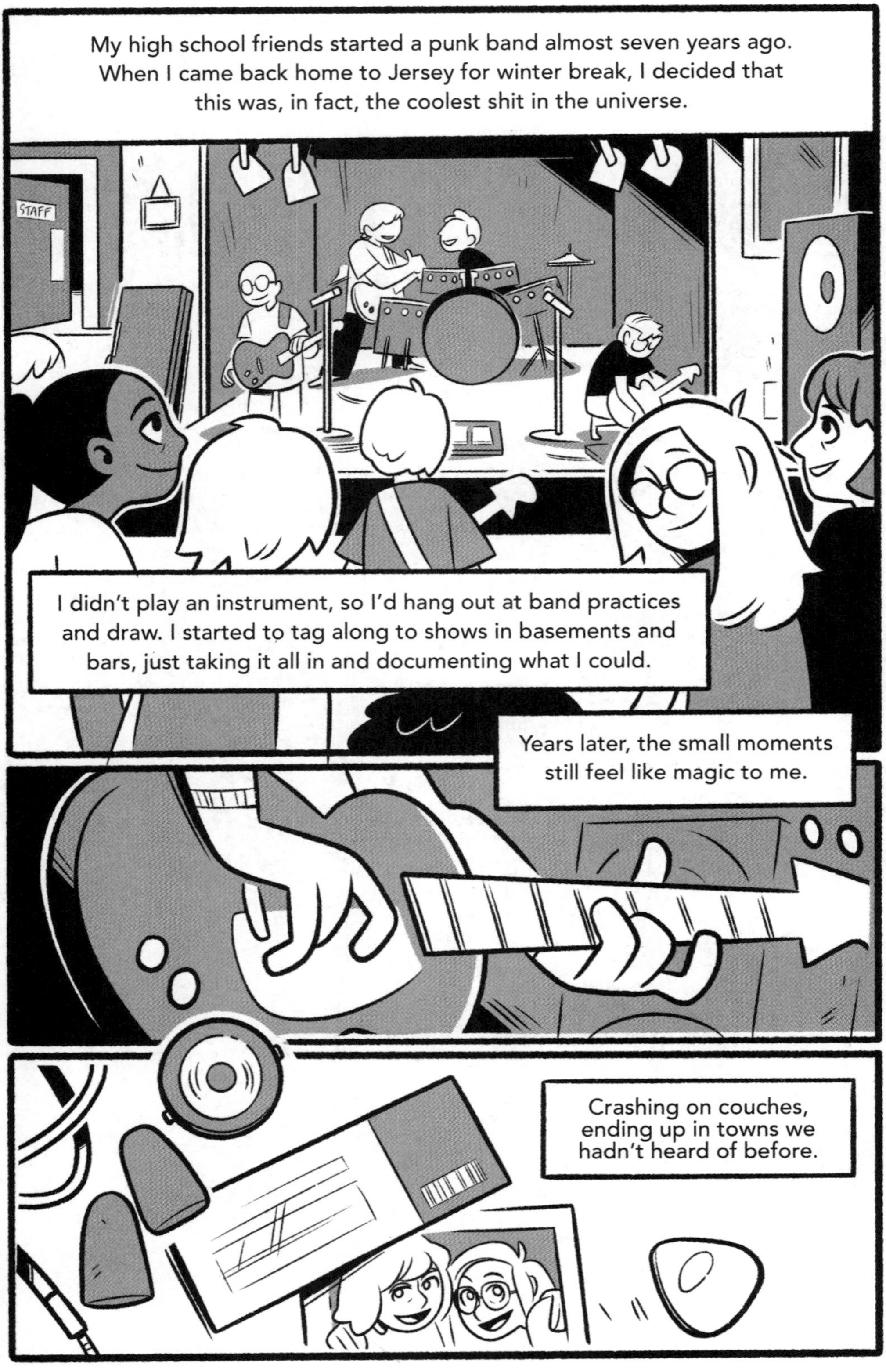
My high school friends started a punk band almost seven years ago. When I came back home to Jersey for winter break, I decided that this was, in fact, the coolest shit in the universe.
STAFF
I didn't play an instrument, so I'd hang out at band practices and draw. I started to tag along to shows in basements and bars, just taking it all in and documenting what I could.
Years later, the small moments still feel like magic to me.
Crashing on couches, ending up in towns we hadn't heard of before.

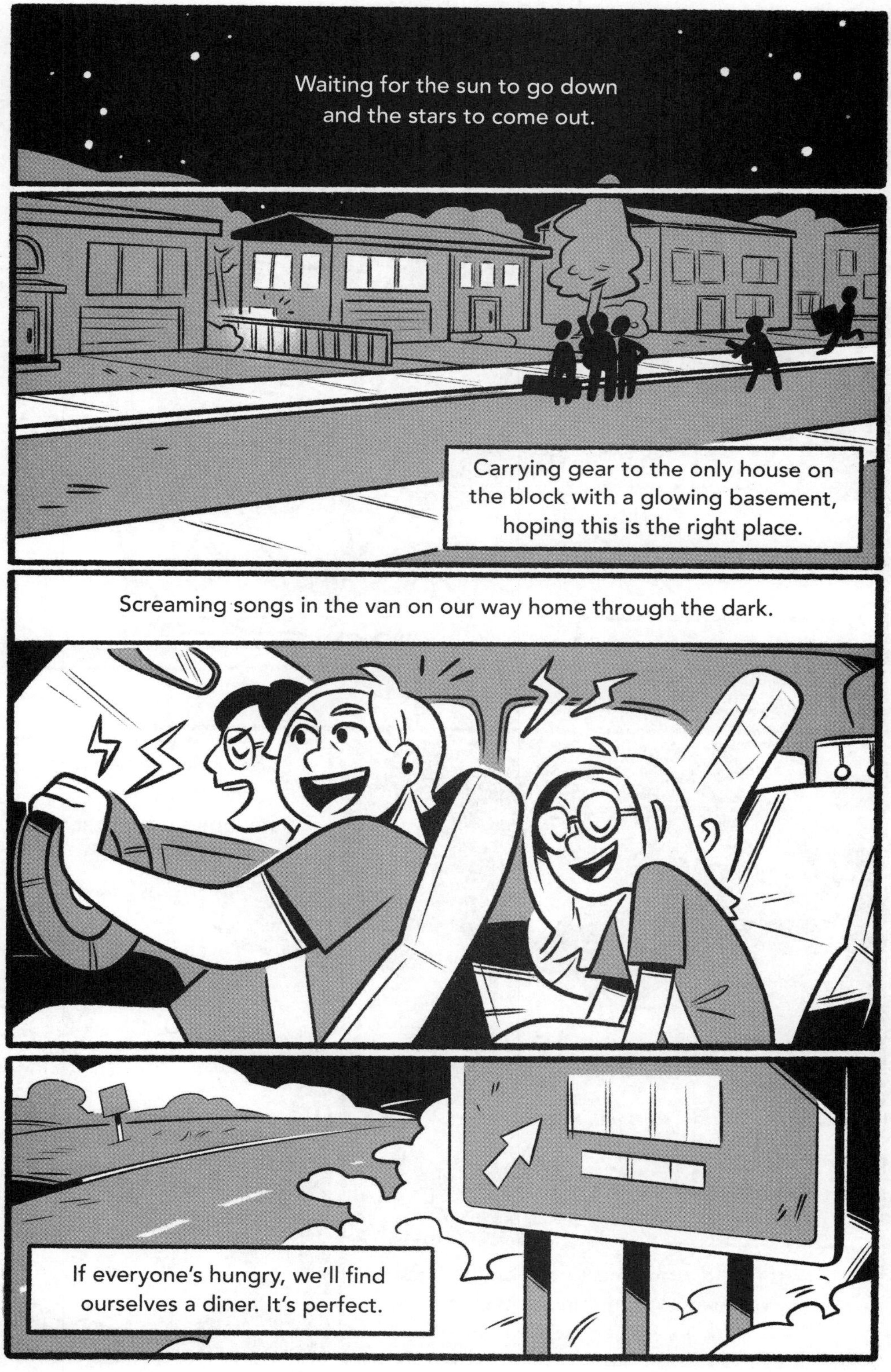

Waiting for the sun to go down and the stars to come out.
Carrying gear to the only house on the block with a glowing basement, hoping this is the right place.
Screaming songs in the van on our way home through the dark.
If everyone's hungry, we'll find ourselves a diner. It's perfect.

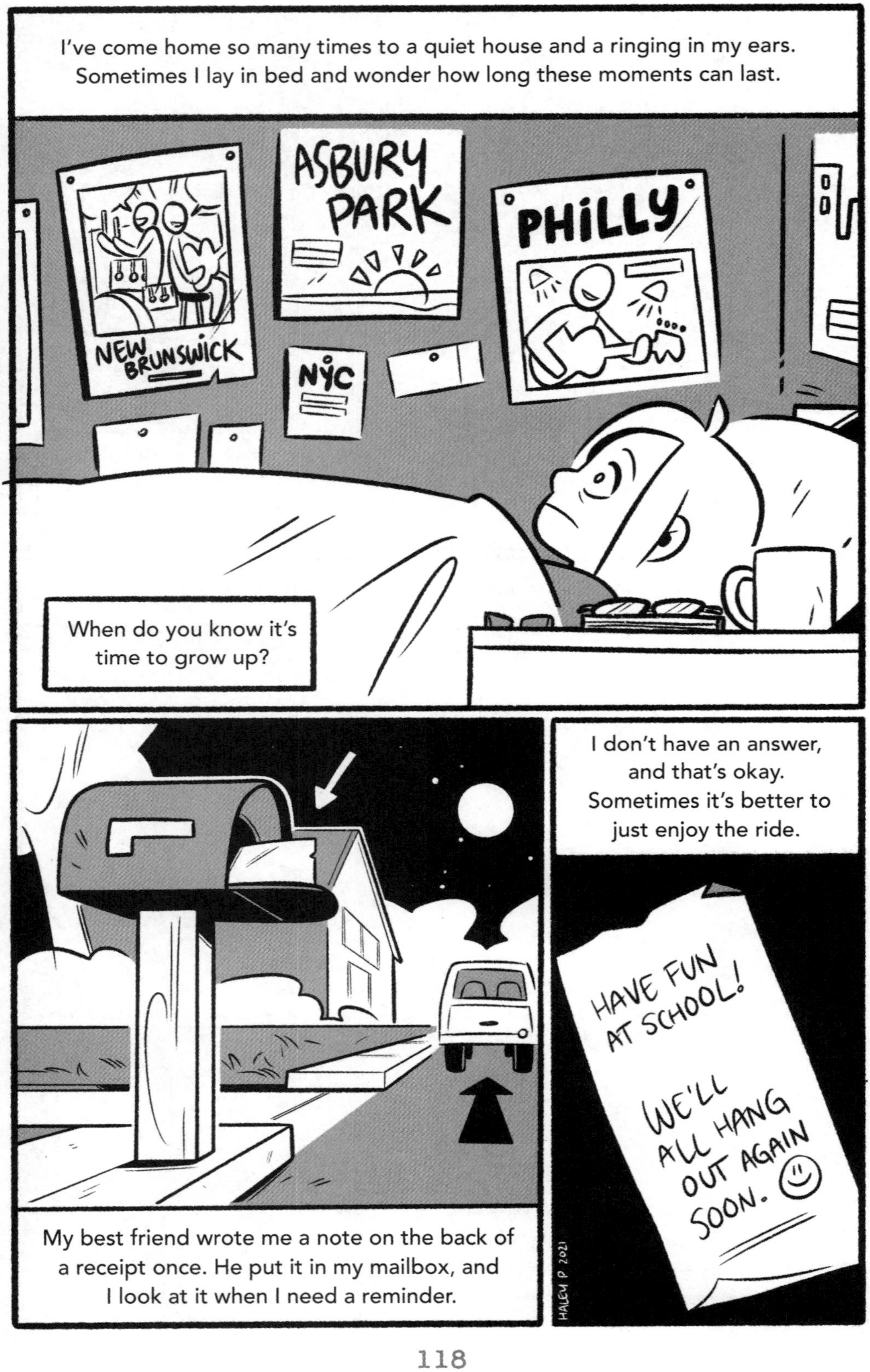
I've come home so many times to a quiet house and a ringing in my ears. Sometimes I lay in bed and wonder how long these moments can last.
NEW BRUNSWICK
ASBURY PARK
NYC
PHILLY
When do you know it's time to grow up?
My best friend wrote me a note on the back of a receipt once. He put it in my mailbox, and I look at it when I need a reminder.
I don't have an answer, and that's okay. Sometimes it's better to just enjoy the ride.
HAVE FUN AT SCHOOL!
WE'LL ALL HANG OUT AGAIN SOON.
HALEY P 2021

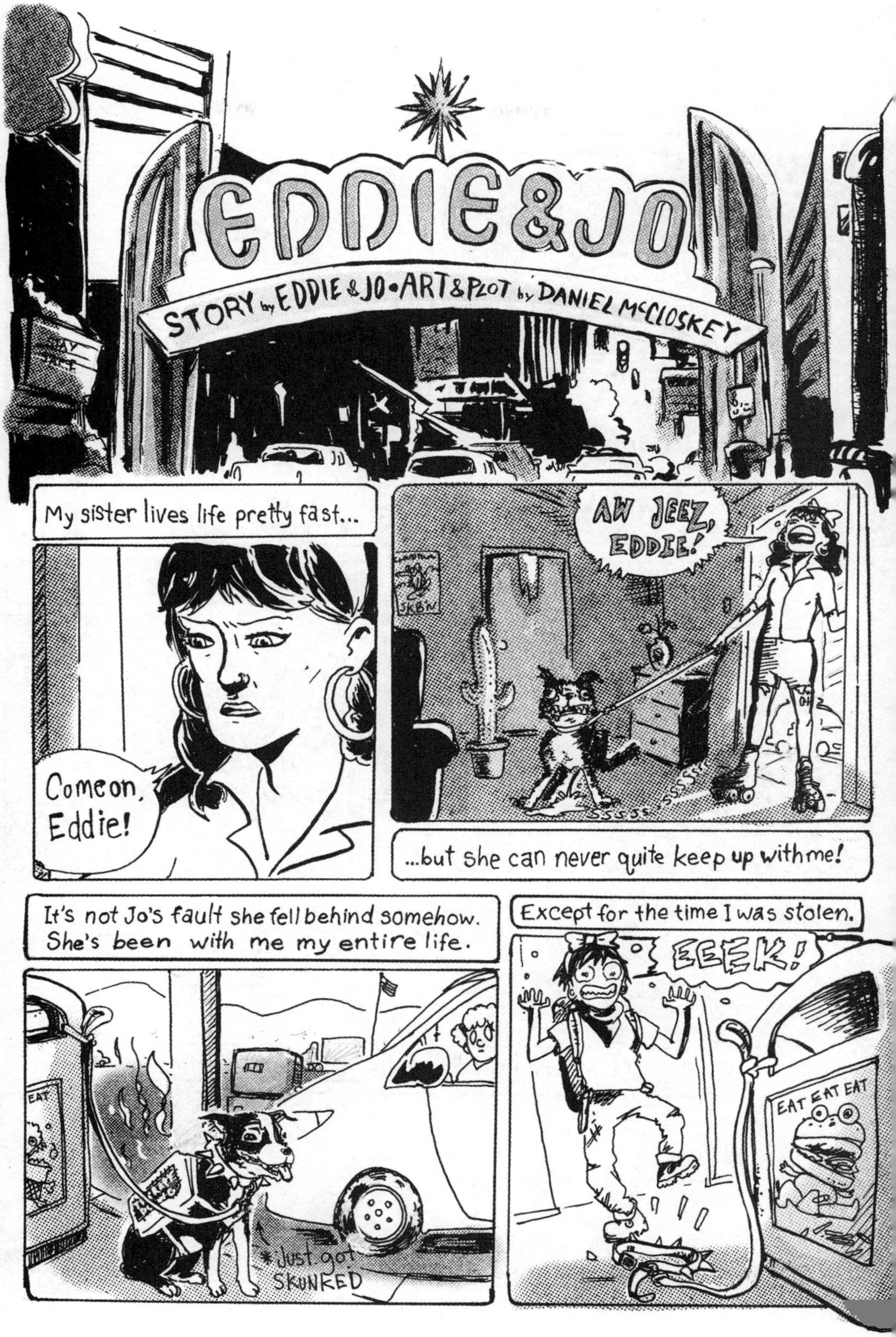
EDDIE & JO
STORY by EDDIE & JO • ART & PLOT by DANIEL McCLOSKEY
My sister lives life pretty fast...
Comeon, Eddie!
AW JEEZ, EDDIE!
...but she can never quite keep up with me!
It's not Jo's fault she fell behind somehow. She's been with me my entire life.
* Just got SKUNKED
Except for the time I was stolen.
EEEK!
EAT EAT EAT

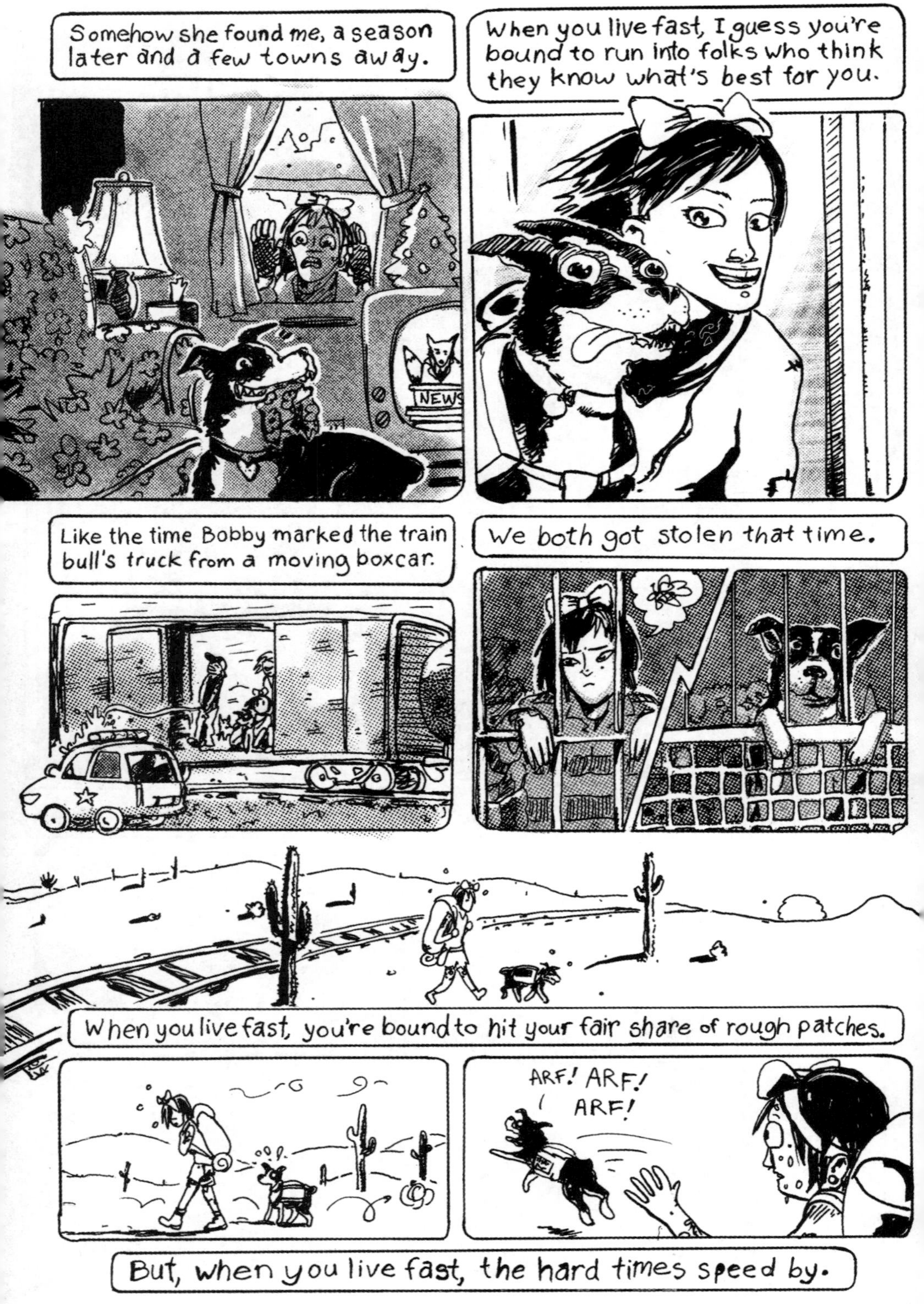
Somehow she found me, a season later and a few towns away.
When you live fast, I guess you're bound to run into folks who think they know what's best for you.
NEWS
Like the time Bobby marked the train bull's truck from a moving boxcar.
We both got stolen that time.
When you live fast, you're bound to hit your fair share of rough patches.
ARF! ARF! ARF!
But, when you live fast, the hard times speed by.

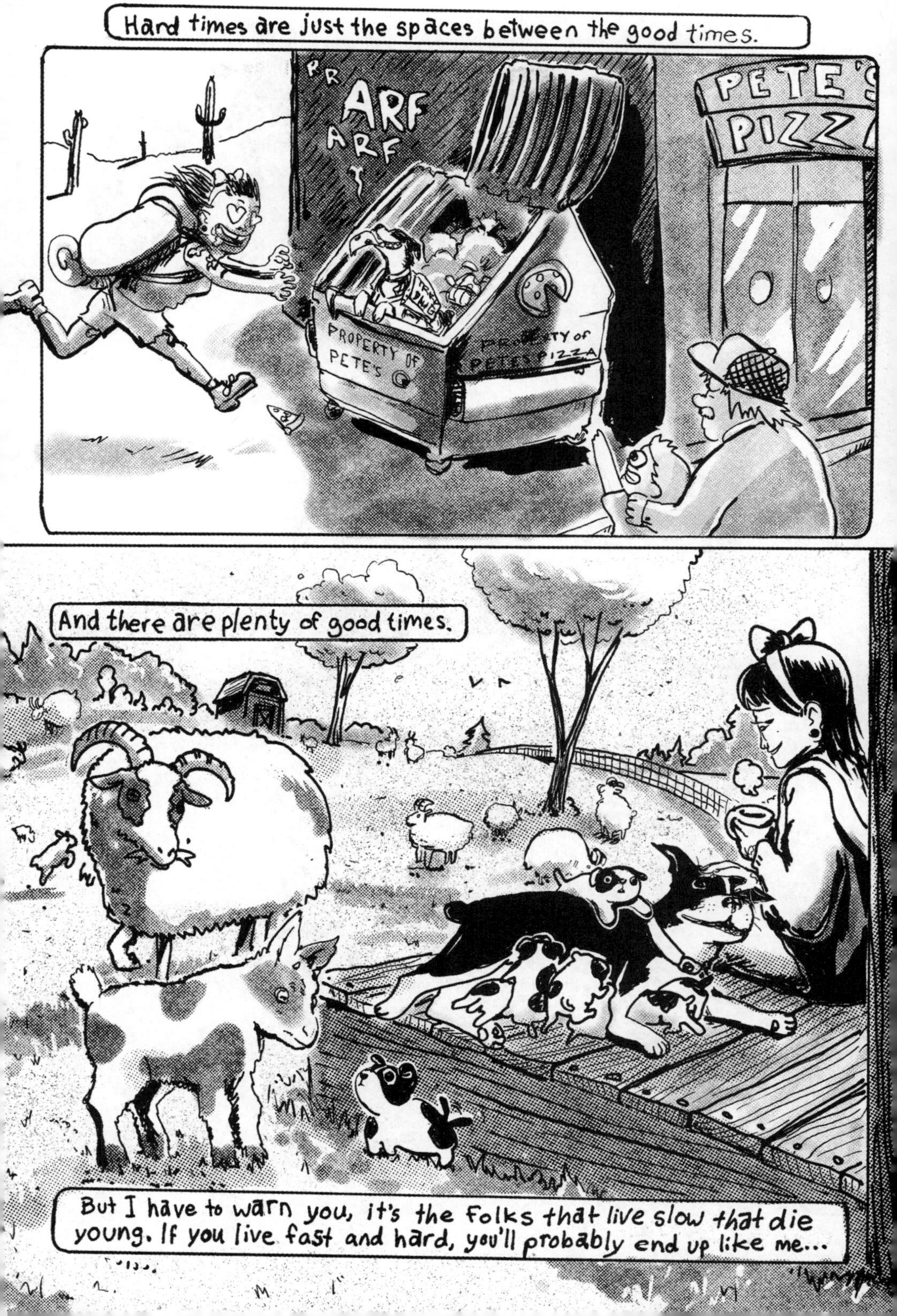

Hard times are just the spaces between the good times.
RR
ARF
ARF
PETE'S
PIZZ
PROPERTY OF PETE'S
PROPERTY OF PETE'S PIZZA
And there are plenty of good times.
But I have to warn you, it's the folks that live slow that die young. If you live fast and hard, you'll probably end up like me...

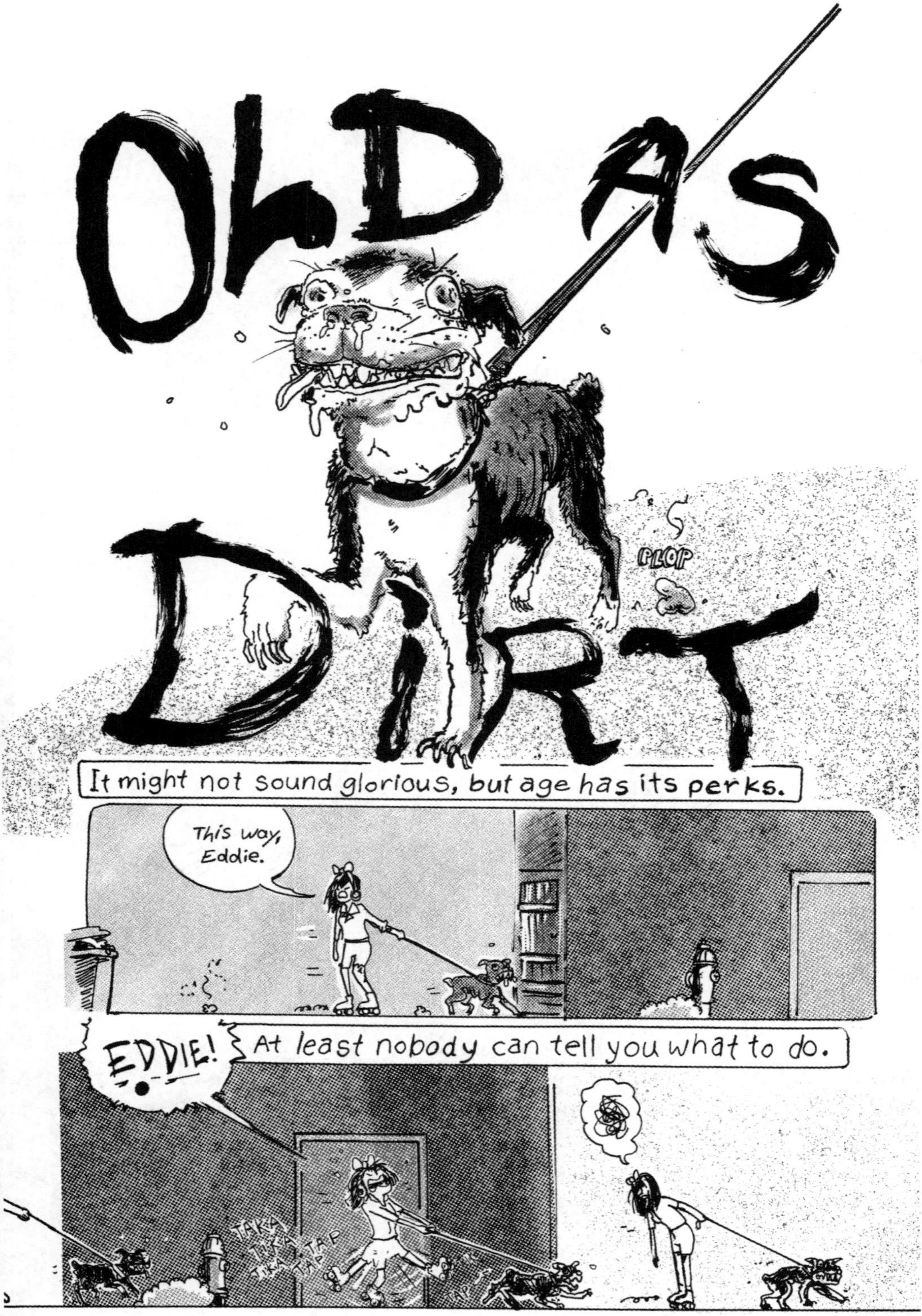

OLD AS DIRT
PLOP
It might not sound glorious, but age has its perks.
This way, Eddie.
EDDIE!
At least nobody can tell you what to do.
TAKA TAKA TAKA TAP TAP

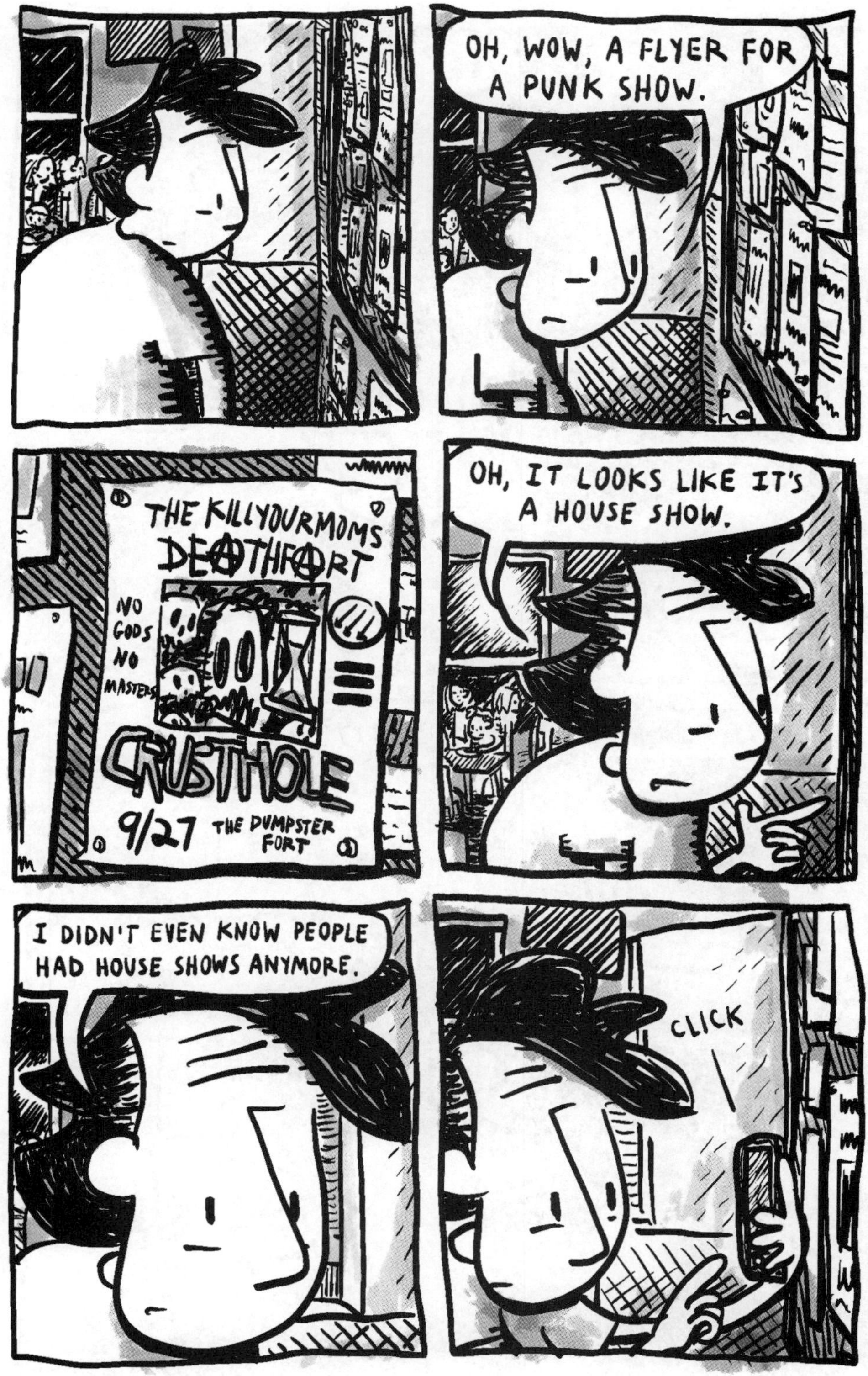
OH, WOW, A FLYER FOR A PUNK SHOW.
THE KILLYOURMOMS
DEATHFART
NO GODS NO MASTERS
CRUSTHOLE
9/27 THE DUMPSTER FORT
OH, IT LOOKS LIKE IT'S A HOUSE SHOW.
I DIDN'T EVEN KNOW PEOPLE HAD HOUSE SHOWS ANYMORE.
CLICK

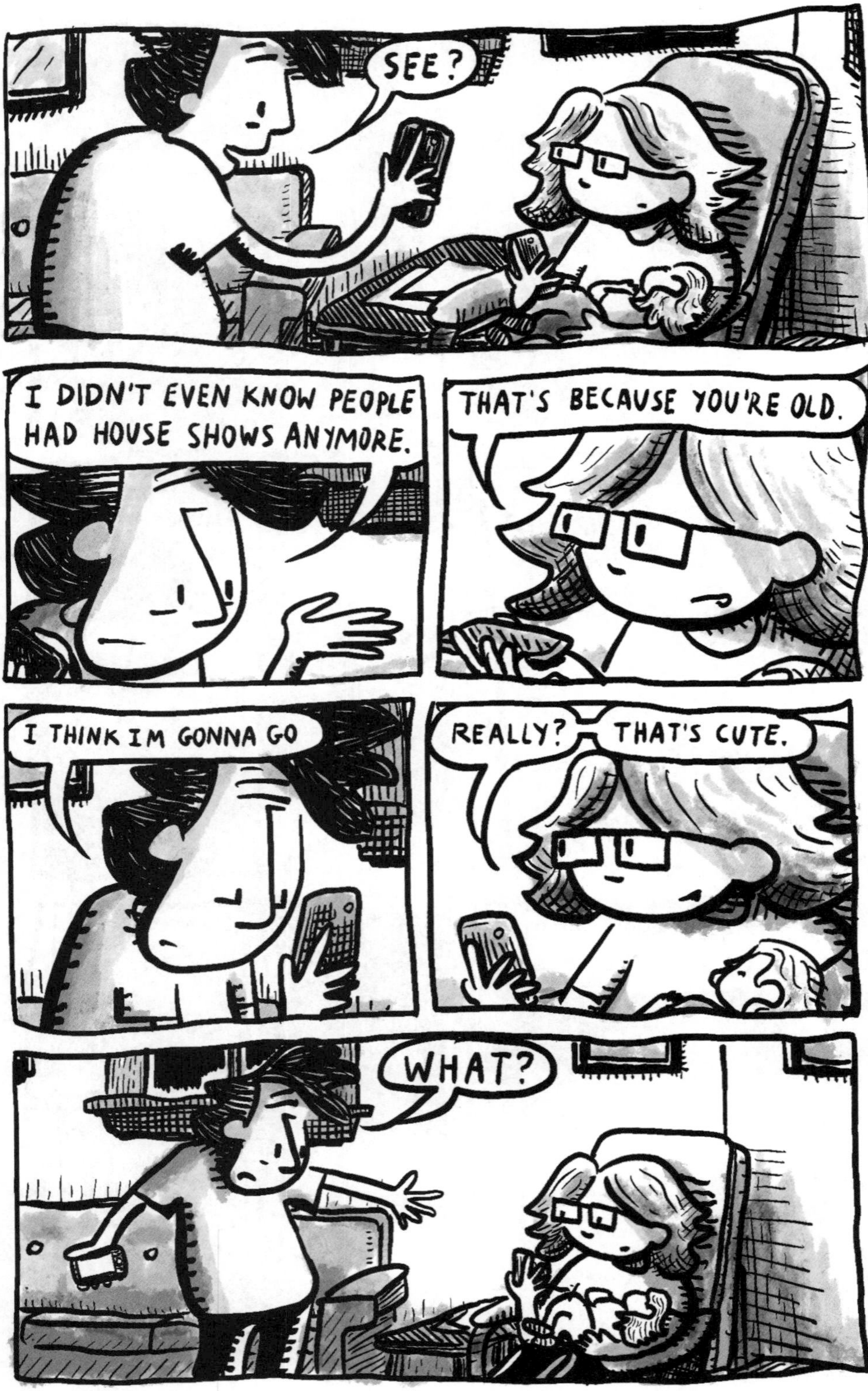
SEE?
I DIDN'T EVEN KNOW PEOPLE HAD HOUSE SHOWS ANYMORE.
THAT'S BECAUSE YOU'RE OLD.
I THINK IM GONNA GO
REALLY?
THAT'S CUTE.
WHAT?

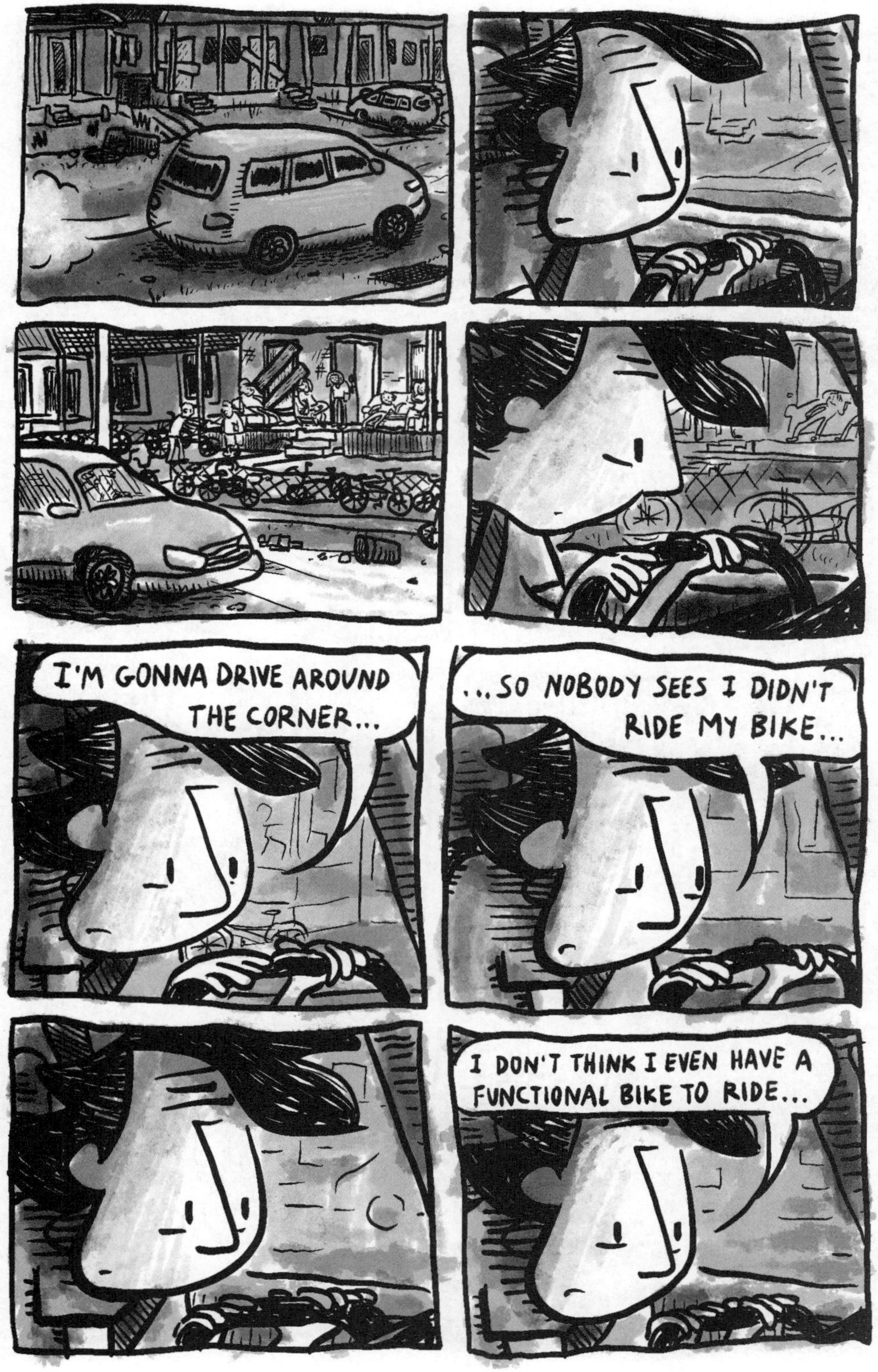
I'M GONNA DRIVE AROUND THE CORNER...
...SO NOBODY SEES I DIDN'T RIDE MY BIKE...
I DON'T THINK I EVEN HAVE A FUNCTIONAL BIKE TO RIDE...

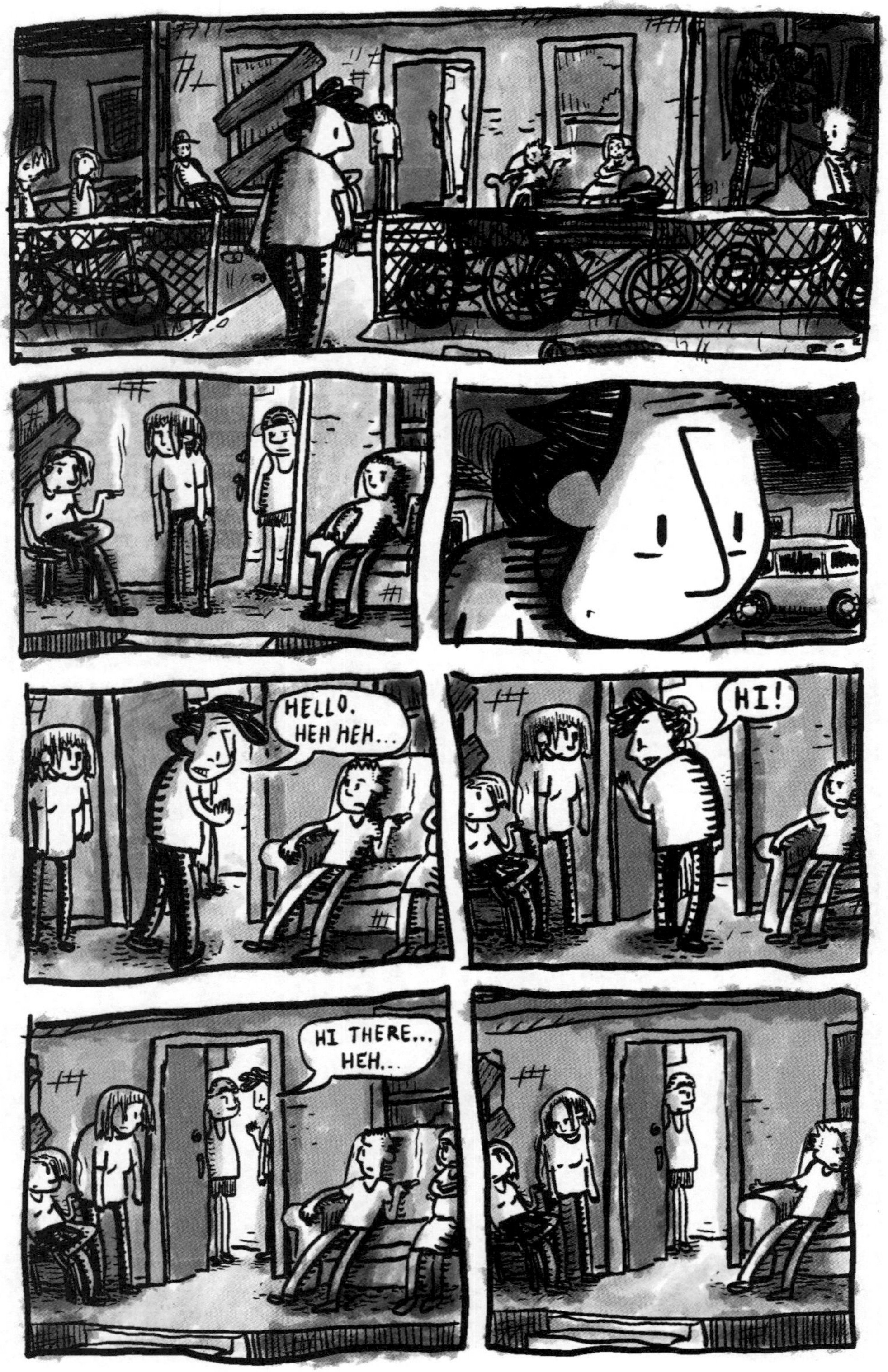
HELLO. HEH HEH...
HI!
HI THERE... HEH...

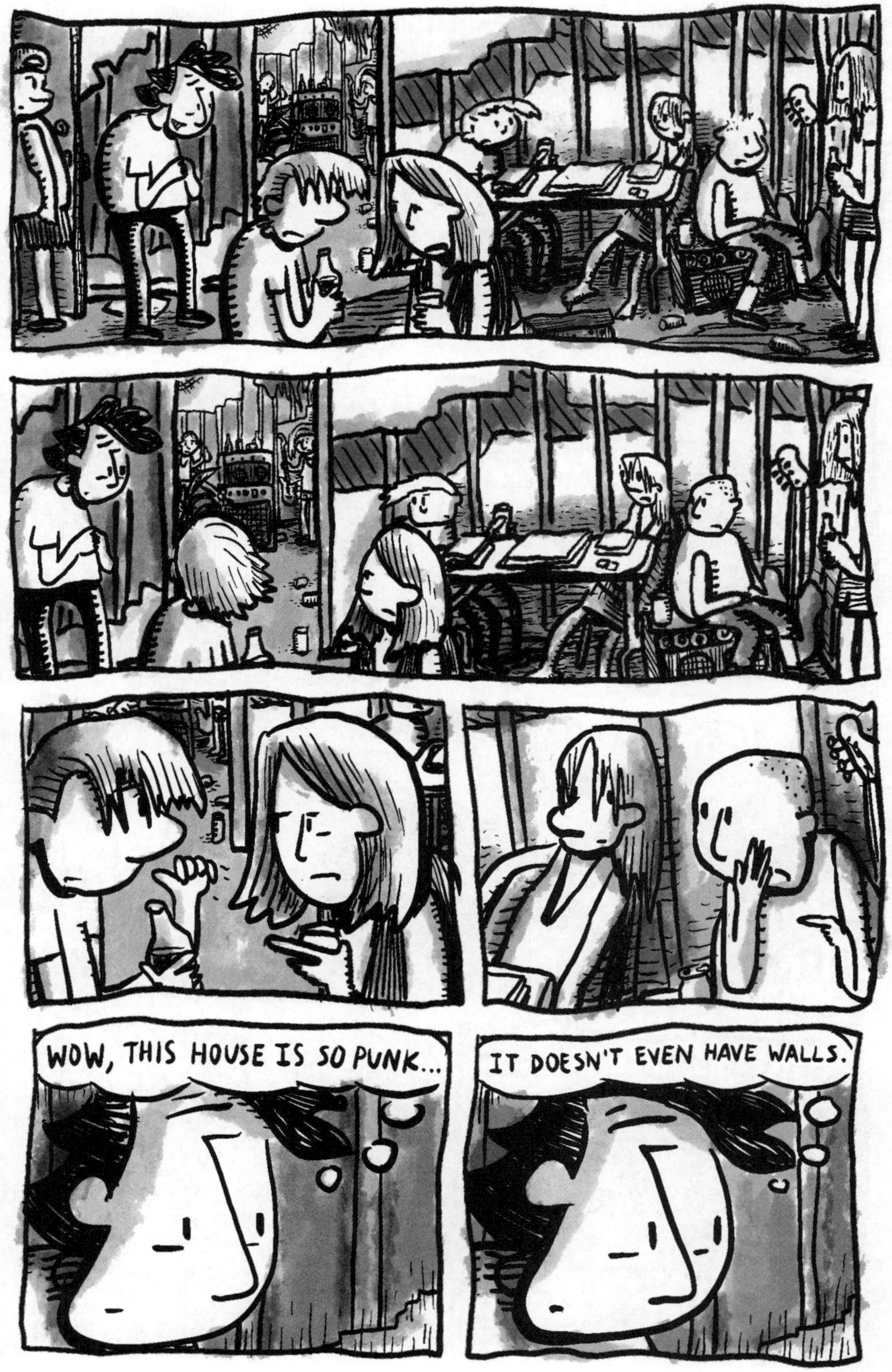
WOW, THIS HOUSE IS SO PUNK...
IT DOESN'T EVEN HAVE WALLS.

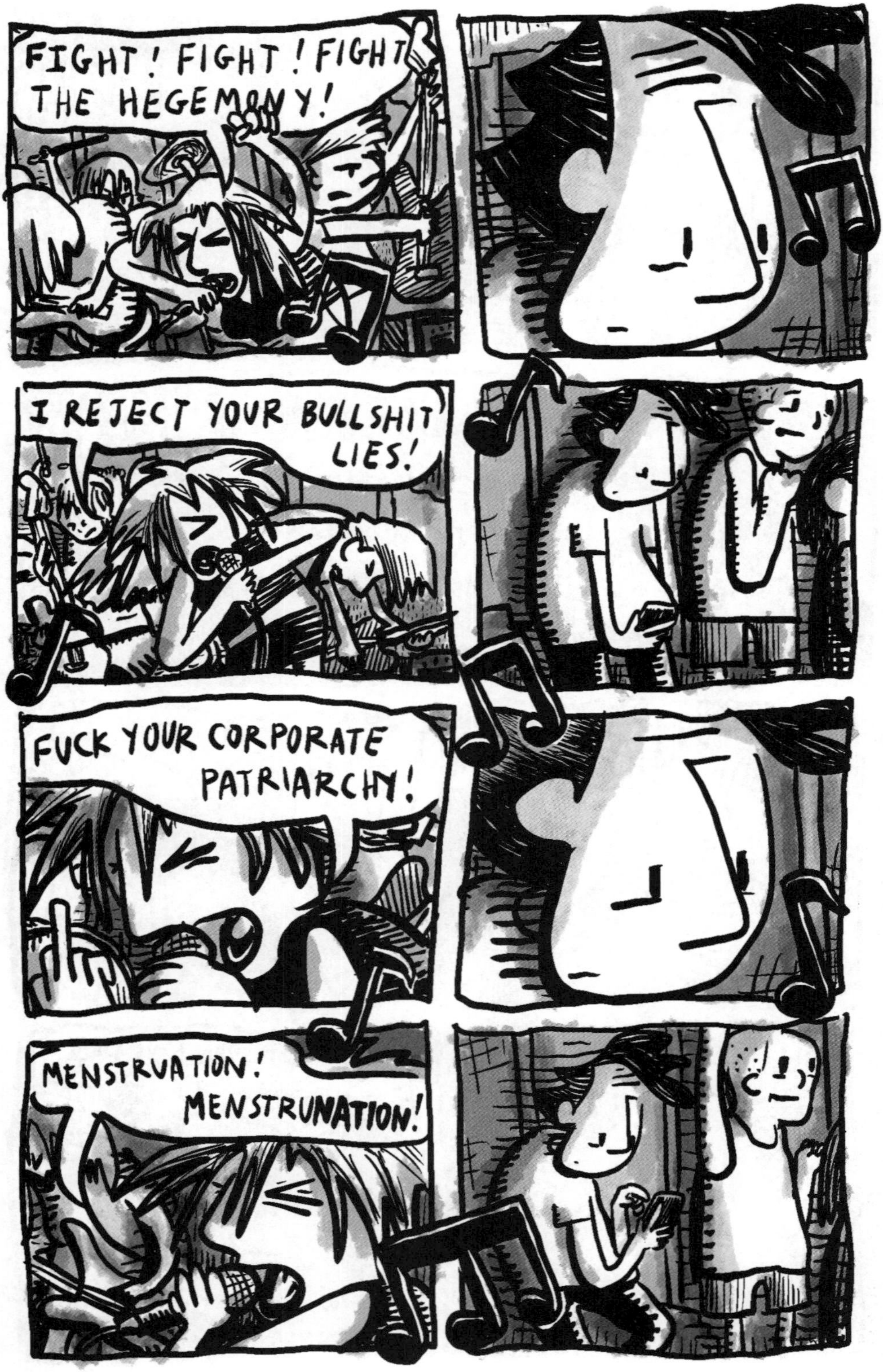
FIGHT! FIGHT! FIGHT THE HEGEMONY!
I REJECT YOUR BULLSHIT LIES!
FUCK YOUR CORPORATE PATRIARCHY!
MENSTRUATION! MENSTRUNATION!

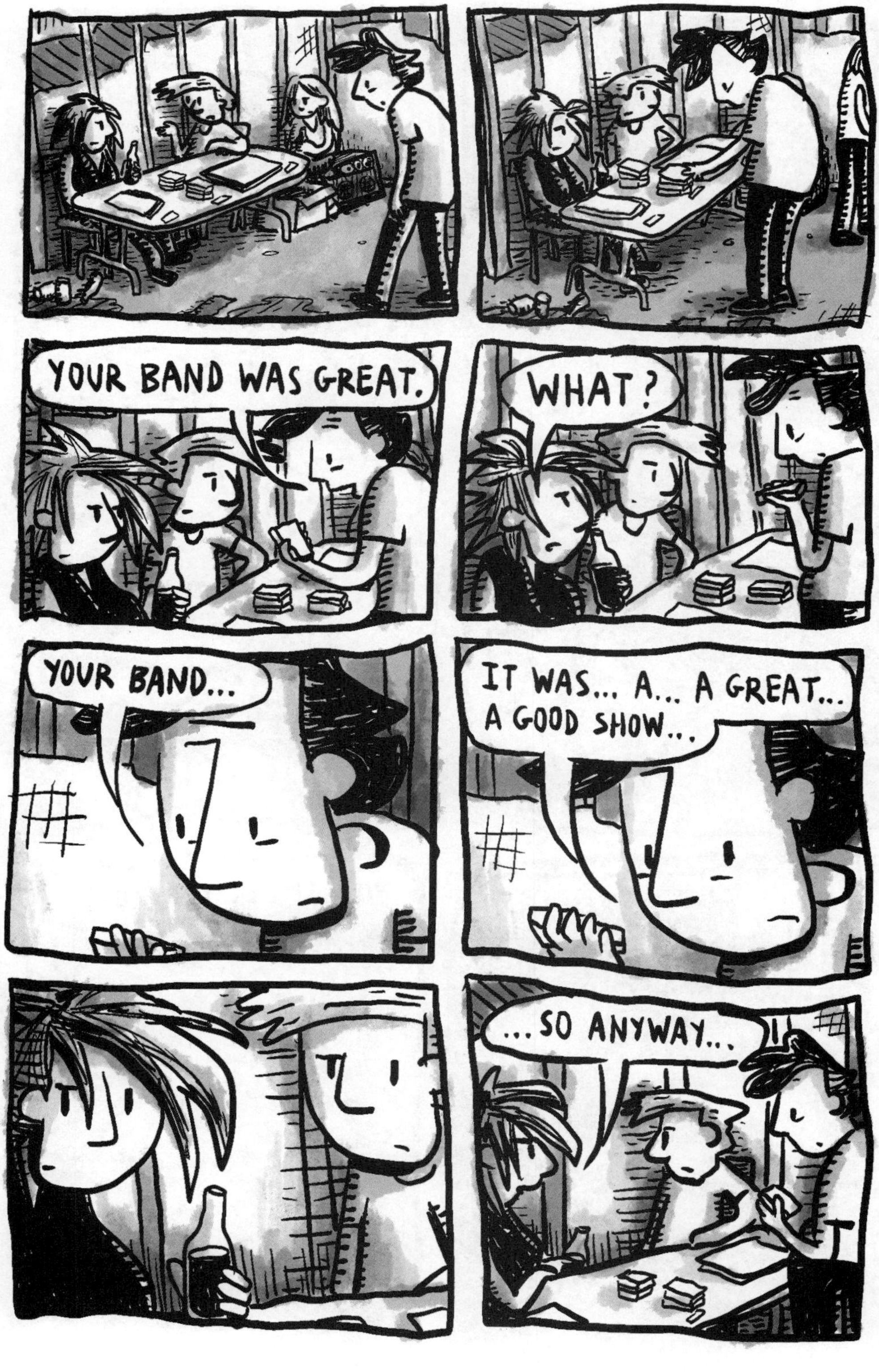

YOUR BAND WAS GREAT.
WHAT?
YOUR BAND...
IT WAS... A... A GREAT... A GOOD SHOW...
...SO ANYWAY...

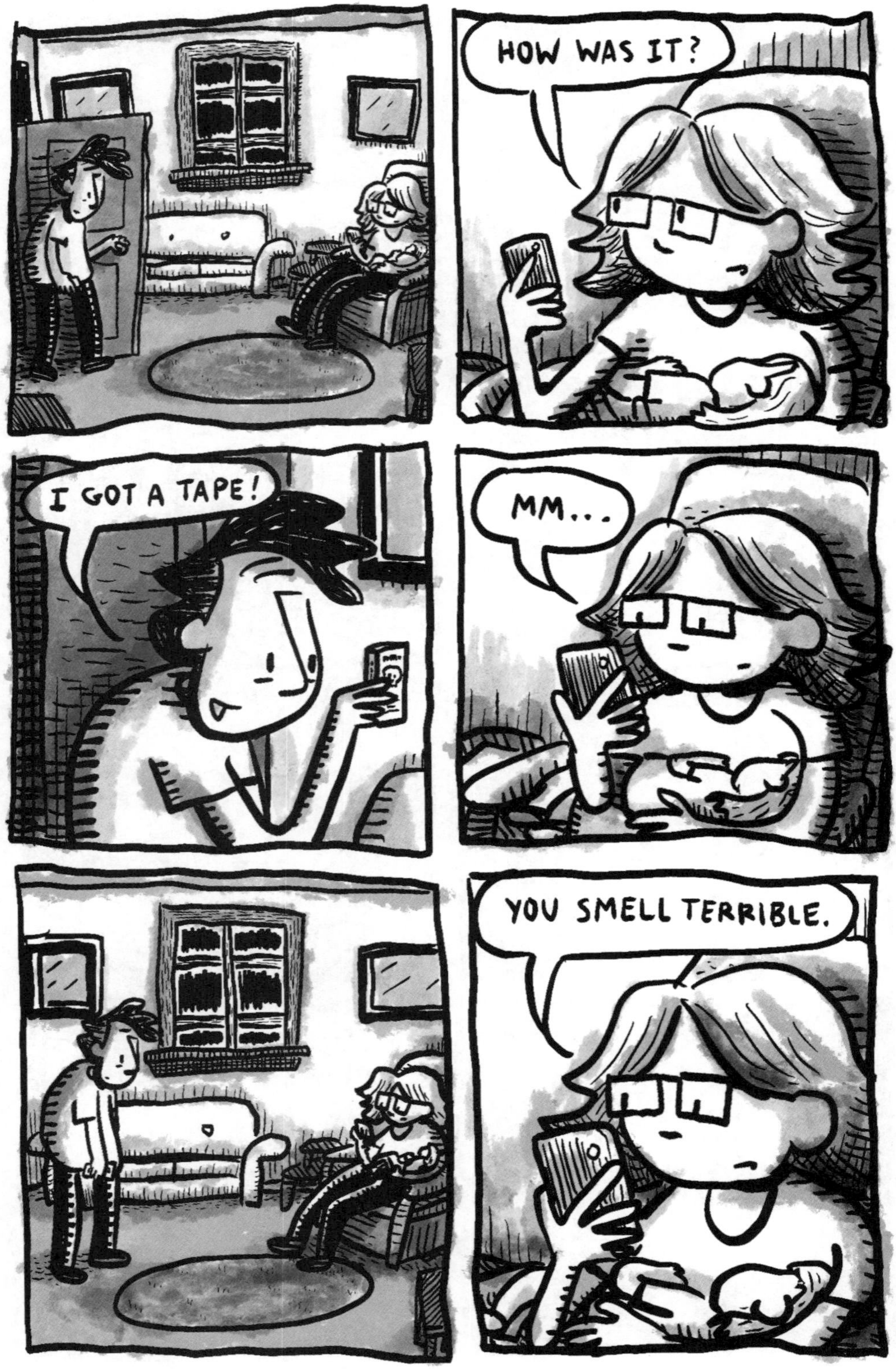
HOW WAS IT?
I GOT A TAPE!
MM...
YOU SMELL TERRIBLE.

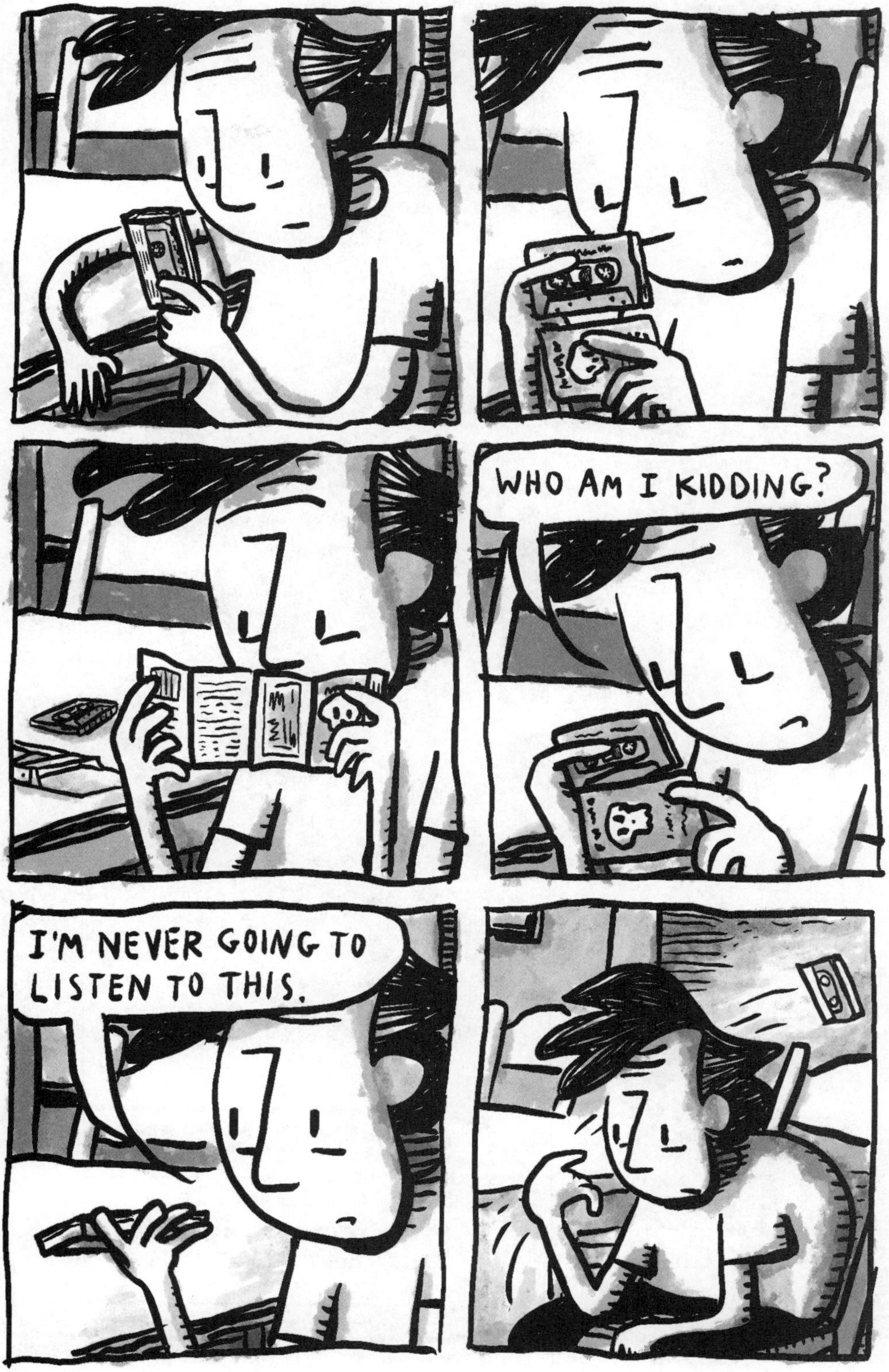
WHO AM I KIDDING?
I'M NEVER GOING TO LISTEN TO THIS.

Oi! x OR OY?

Are you a TRUE PUNK?

Or an OLD KVETCH?

Take our quiz to find out!*

By Sam Grinberg

Read each scenario to determine your outcome.

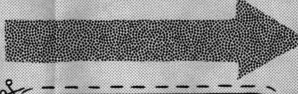

"This quiz changed my life."
-Ronnie Regicide

*If unsatisfied with results of quiz please send reason for dispute and $100 check to Birdcage Bottom Books, LLC.

Panel 1

A drink would be nice...but I have to get up early for work tomorrow and I don't want that *21+ wristband* to get stuck to my arm hair.

OY? ☐ OR Oi? ☐ | **THE CORRECT ANSWER IS: OY!** You're old! You'd rather be sober than agitate your "delicate" arm hair.

Panel 2

Wow, their new CD is really *$20??* Wait! Here we go- I can get it on Amazon *much* cheaper. *Prime, baby!*

CD - $20

OY? ☐ OR Oi? ☐ | **THE CORRECT ANSWER IS: OY!** You're old! And cheap! Support the band *firsthand, jerk!*

Panel 3

I forgot to eat dinner-but all they have is shitty pizza. I guess I have no choice. Wha- $10 for *ONE* slice? *Forget that!* I'll wait till after the show.

PIZZA

OY? ☐ OR Oi? ☐ | **THE CORRECT ANSWER IS: OY!** You're old! Bite the bullet and deal with the shitty pizza!

Panel 4

Oh my god - has the music *always* been *this* loud? Jesus Christ! They have to be kidding with this volume! I need earplugs, *stat!*

STARBAND BALLROOM EXIT MERCH

OY? ☐ OR Oi? ☐ | **THE CORRECT ANSWER IS: OY!** You're old! Earplugs. 'Nuff said.

Panel 5

The sound guy *must* remember what this place was like before they renovated. This new design makes absolutely no sense...it's so hard to see the stage. Architecture should be built with a purpose in mind- not purely for a cool *'aesthetic".* Form *follows* function, *god damnit!*

OY? ☐ OR Oi? ☐ | **THE CORRECT ANSWER IS: OY!** You're old! And rambling! The sound guy is not interested in what it was like "back in the day." He's older than you! And busy!

Panel 6

Who are these opening bands? I haven't heard of any of them - *and I can see why.* Kids will listen to anything these days. I guess it's less about the music now and more about the *fashion.*

FOLLOW US ON INSTAGRAM

OY? ☐ OR Oi? ☐ | **THE CORRECT ANSWER IS: OY!** You're old! And spouting "old man" clichés! You also just referred to the crowd as "Kids". *Need we say more?*

Panel 7

I'm *soo* thirsty - but the bar is too crowded. *Share?* You couldn't *pay me* to share a bottle of water with someone here. I'd rather *die.*

AGAINST BRIE!

OY? ☐ OR Oi? ☐ | **THE CORRECT ANSWER IS: OY!** You're old! Just share the damn bottle and get over it! Communal water is a mainstay of surviving a good show!

Panel 8

I'm going to stand *allll* the way in the back. That's how you *really* enjoy the music and *actually* take in the experience. Not like those *primitives* running in circles and shoving each other.

OY? ☐ OR Oi? ☐ | **THE CORRECT ANSWER IS: OY!** You're old! You're not fooling anyone. *We know* why you're standing in the back.

Panel 9

This night is lasting *forever.* I can barely keep my eyes open. My feet hurt. Since when did the headliner go on at *11pm?* Ok, I'll leave after the first song. That's enough for me to say I saw them live. Plus I'll beat the traffic getting out of here. *Siri,* where is the closest White Castle?

OY? ☐ OR Oi? ☐ | **THE CORRECT ANSWER IS: Oi!** Congratulations! You're a *true punk!* What's more \m/ than a crave case?

©SAM GRINBERG 2021

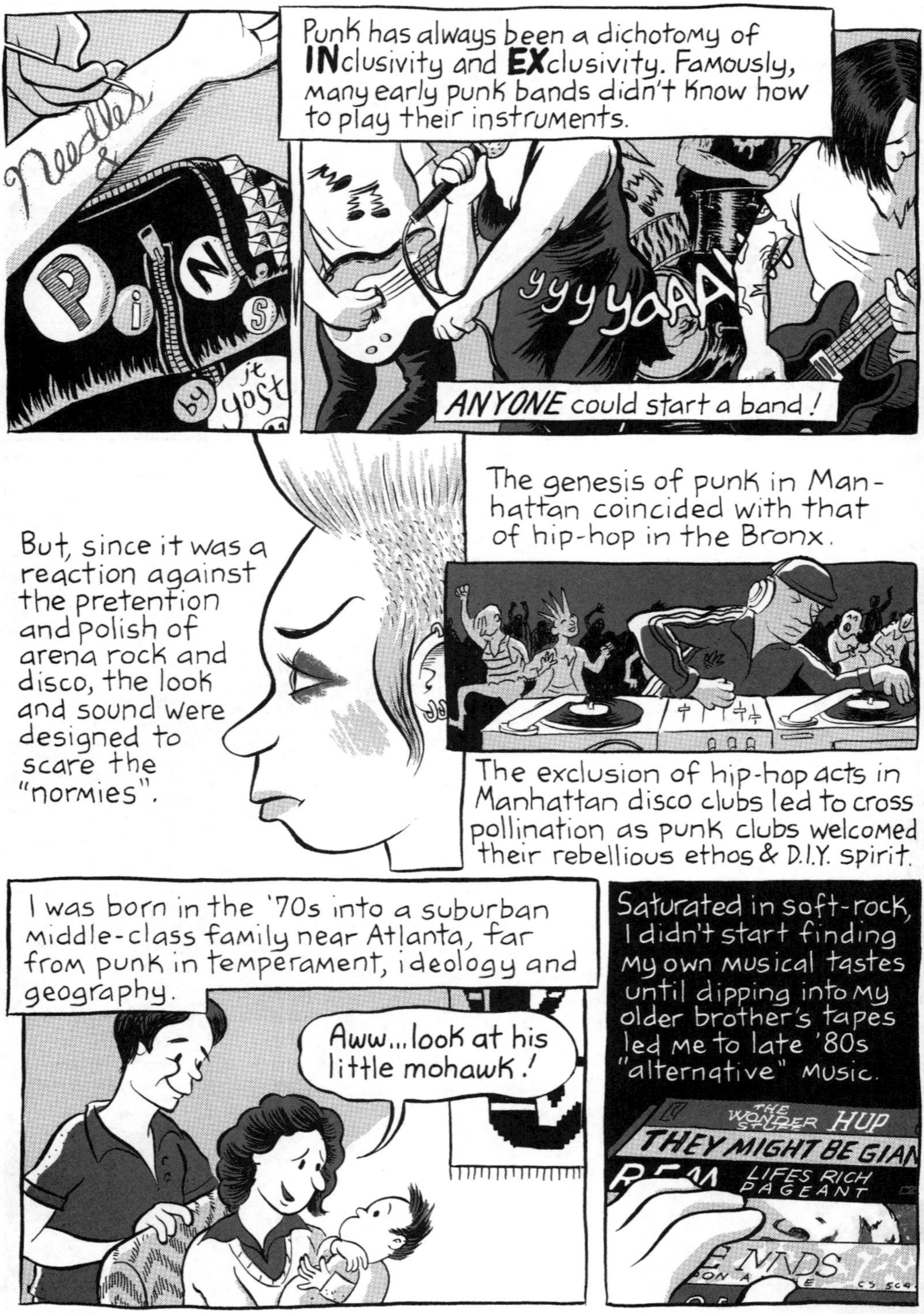
Needles & Pins
by jt yost
Punk has always been a dichotomy of INclusivity and EXclusivity. Famously, many early punk bands didn't know how to play their instruments.
yyyyaAA
ANYONE could start a band!
But, since it was a reaction against the pretention and polish of arena rock and disco, the look and sound were designed to scare the "normies".
The genesis of punk in Manhattan coincided with that of hip-hop in the Bronx.
The exclusion of hip-hop acts in Manhattan disco clubs led to cross pollination as punk clubs welcomed their rebellious ethos & D.I.Y. spirit.
I was born in the '70s into a suburban middle-class family near Atlanta, far from punk in temperament, ideology and geography.
Aww... look at his little mohawk!
Saturated in soft-rock, I didn't start finding my own musical tastes until dipping into my older brother's tapes led me to late '80s "alternative" music.
THE WONDER STUFF HUP
THEY MIGHT BE GIAN
LIFES RICH PAGEANT

I started watching MTV's "120 Minutes" religiously and getting recommendations from my local record shop.

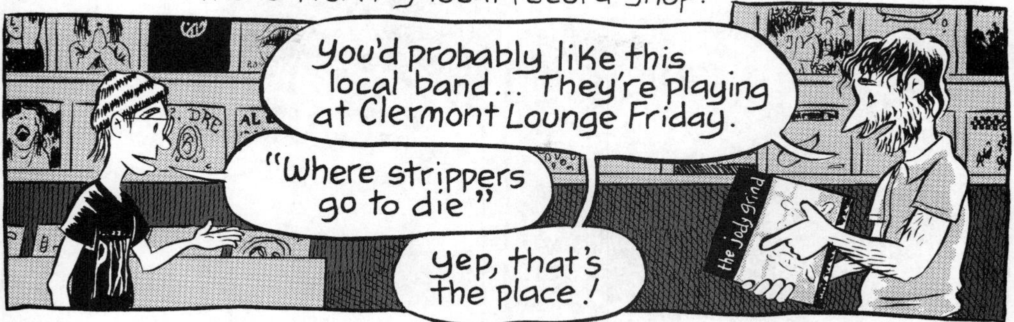
You'd probably like this local band... They're playing at Clermont Lounge Friday.
"Where strippers go to die"
yep, that's the place!
the jody grind

I'd also occaisionally buy albums based solely on the album cover art...

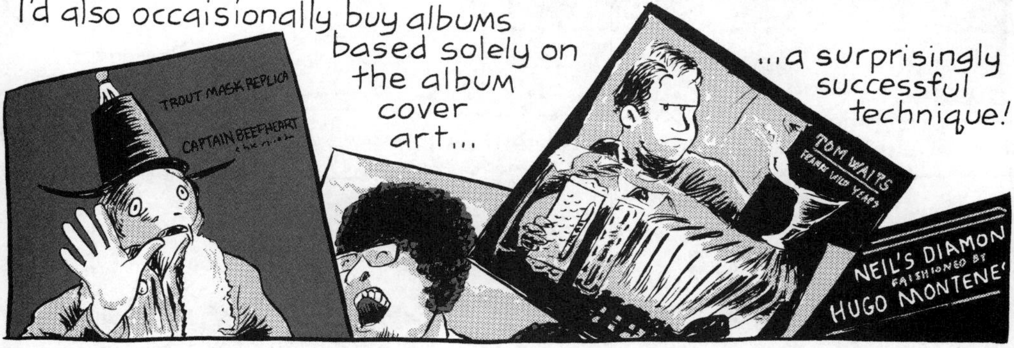
TROUT MASK REPLICA
CAPTAIN BEEFHEART
TOM WAITS
FRANKS WILD YEARS
NEIL'S DIAMON
FASHIONED BY
HUGO MONTENE

...a surprisingly successful technique!

Around this time, I started dressing like a mentally ill octogenarian golfing clown and experimenting with uninviting hairstyles.

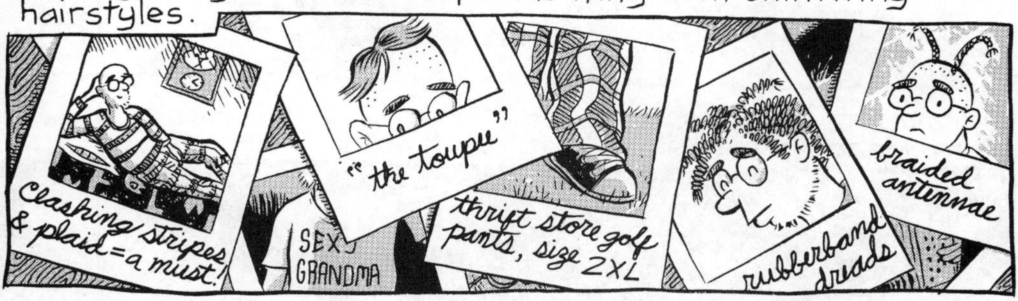
Clashing stripes & plaid = a must!
"the toupee"
SEXY GRANDMA
thrift store golf pants, size 2XL
rubberband dreads
braided antennae

I defended these choices with some righteous nonsense.

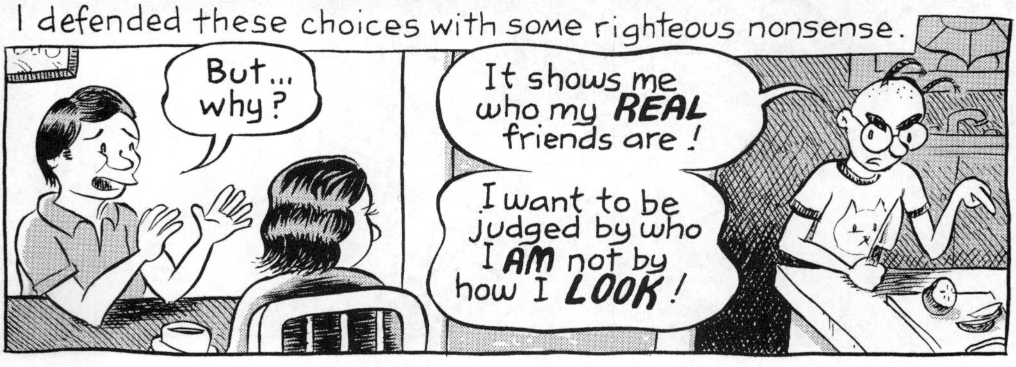
But... why?
It shows me who my **REAL** friends are!
I want to be judged by who I **AM** not by how I **LOOK**!

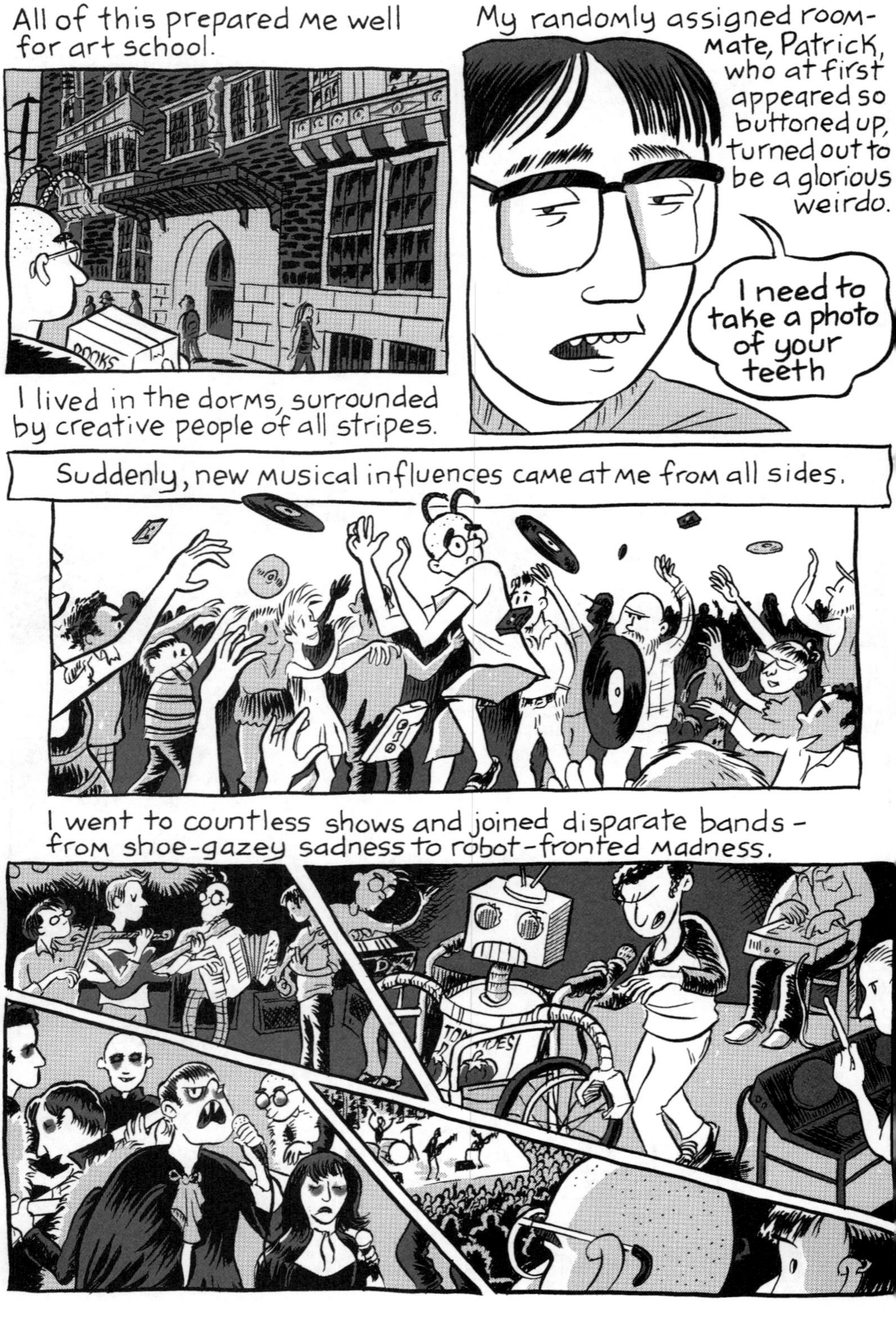
All of this prepared me well for art school.
I lived in the dorms, surrounded by creative people of all stripes.
My randomly assigned room-mate, Patrick, who at first appeared so buttoned up, turned out to be a glorious weirdo.
I need to take a photo of your teeth
Suddenly, new musical influences came at me from all sides.
I went to countless shows and joined disparate bands - from shoe-gazey sadness to robot-fronted madness.

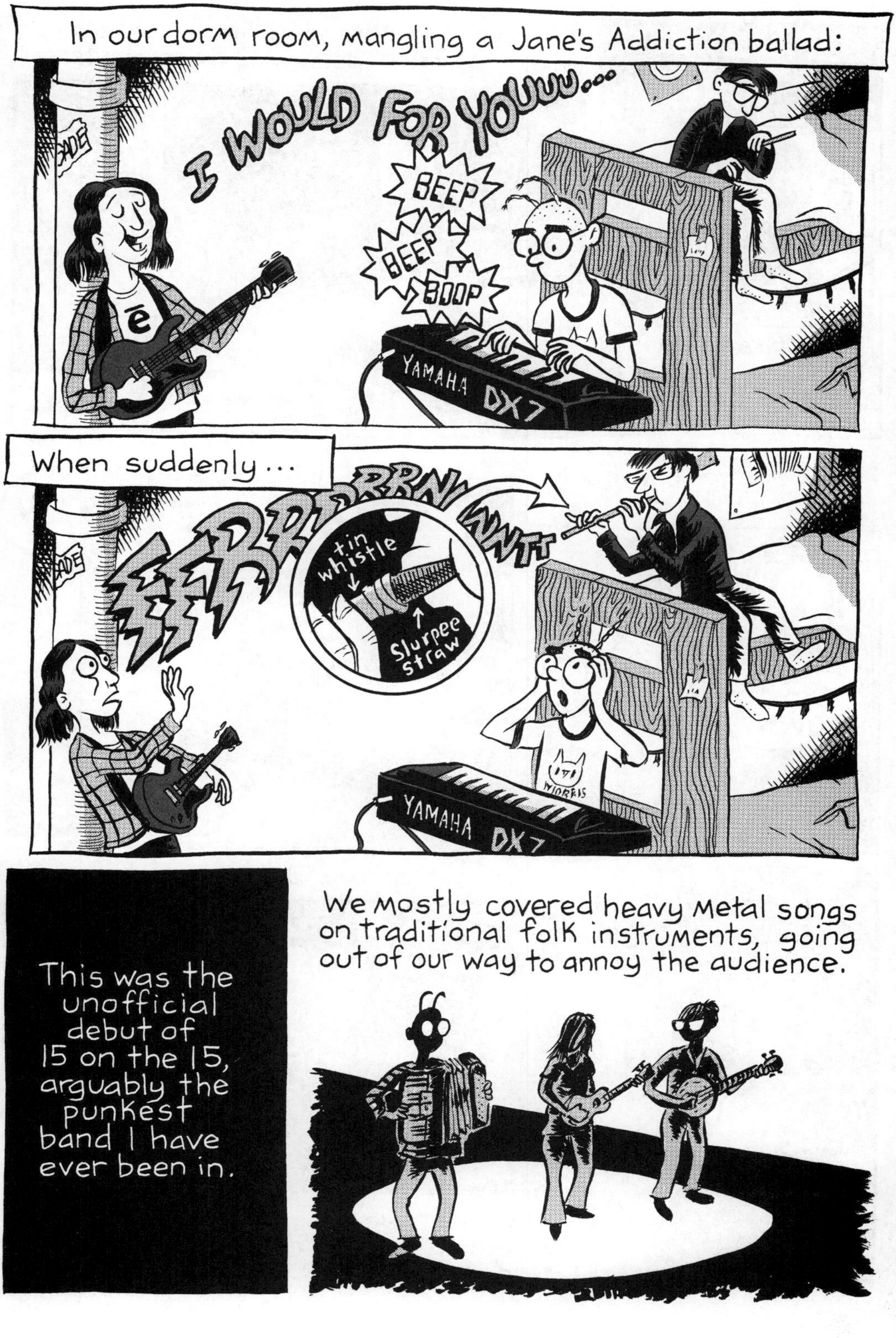
In our dorm room, mangling a Jane's Addiction ballad:
I WOULD FOR YOUUU...
BEEP
BEEP
BOOP
YAMAHA DX7
When suddenly...
tin whistle
Slurpee straw
YAMAHA DX7
This was the unofficial debut of 15 on the 15, arguably the punkest band I have ever been in.
We mostly covered heavy metal songs on traditional folk instruments, going out of our way to annoy the audience.

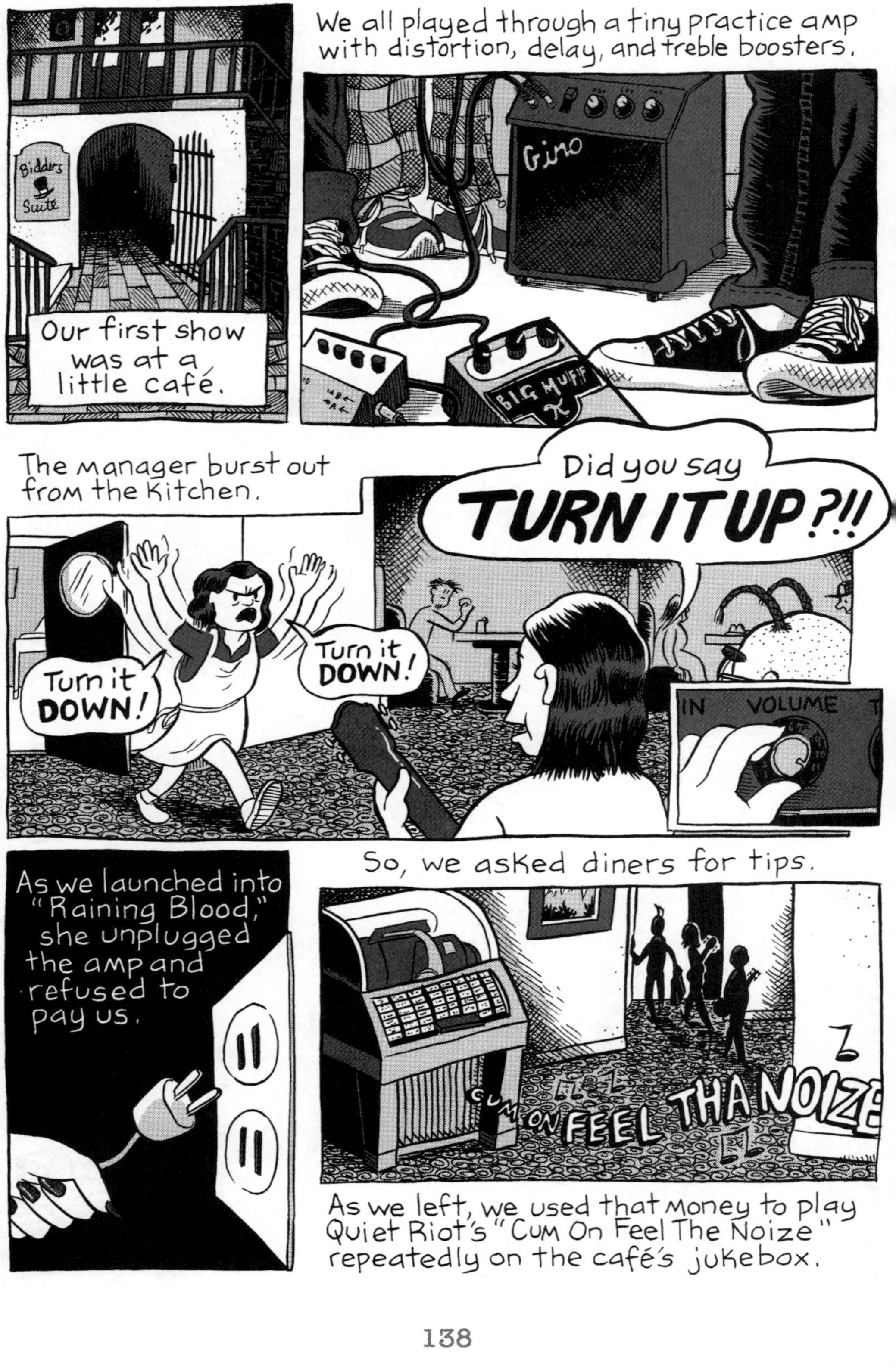
Our first show was at a little café.
We all played through a tiny practice amp with distortion, delay, and treble boosters.
Gino
BIG MUFF
The manager burst out from the Kitchen.
Turn it DOWN!
Turn it DOWN!
Did you say TURN IT UP?!!
IN VOLUME
As we launched into "Raining Blood," she unplugged the amp and refused to pay us.
So, we asked diners for tips.
CUM ON FEEL THA NOIZE
As we left, we used that money to play Quiet Riot's "Cum On Feel The Noize" repeatedly on the café's jukebox.

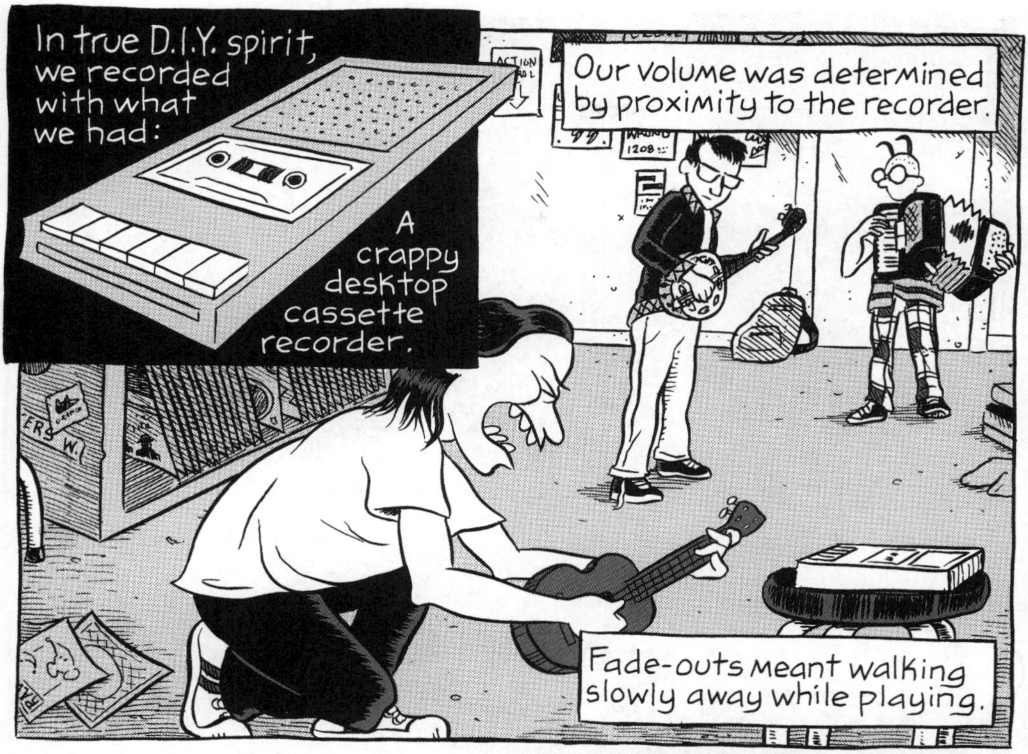
In true D.I.Y. spirit, we recorded with what we had:
A crappy desktop cassette recorder.
Our volume was determined by proximity to the recorder.
Fade-outs meant walking slowly away while playing.

Before one show that stands out in my mind, Patrick used spray paint to fix his hair into a towering tri-hawk.

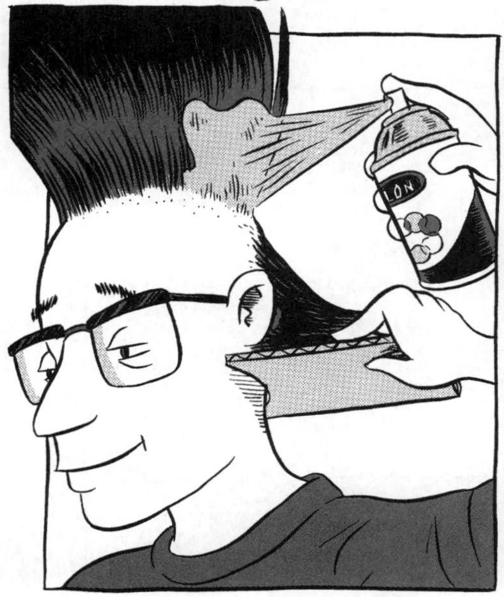

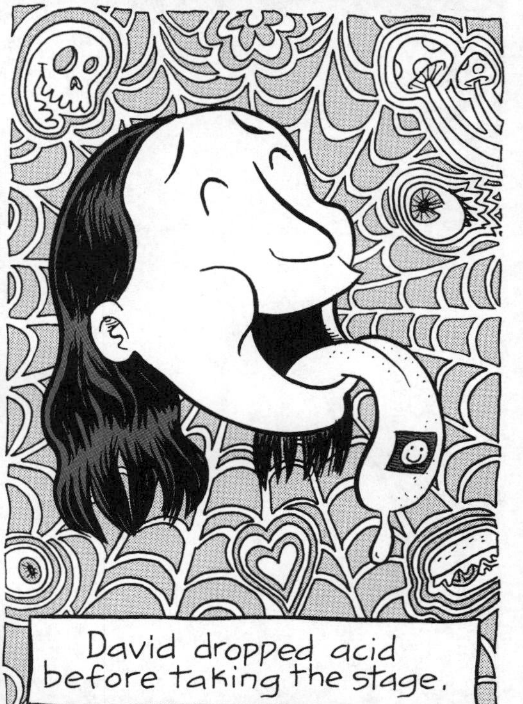
David dropped acid before taking the stage.

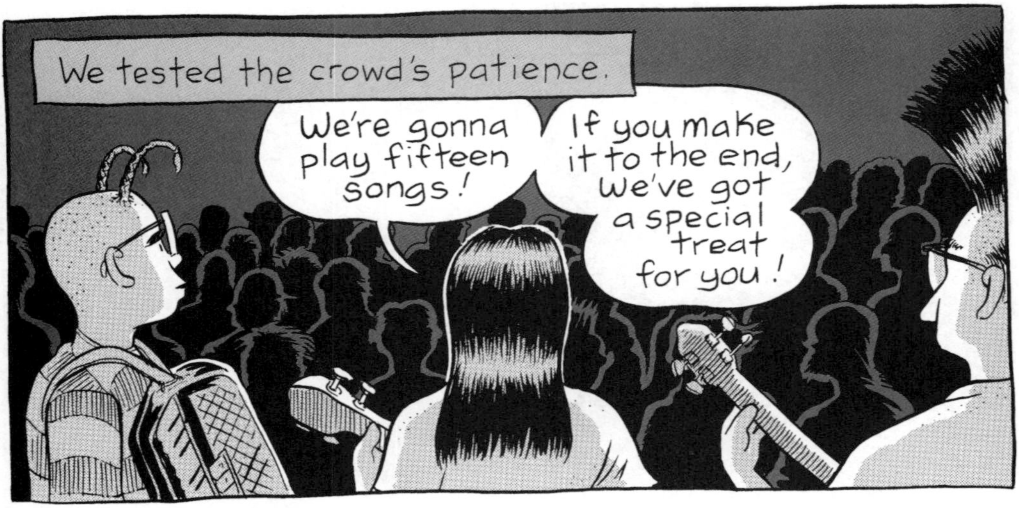
We tested the crowd's patience.
We're gonna play fifteen songs!
If you make it to the end, we've got a special treat for you!

The "treat" was a cover of The Smiths' "How Soon Is Now?", a song that sounds horrific with staccato banjo playing the heavily sustained lead guitar riff.

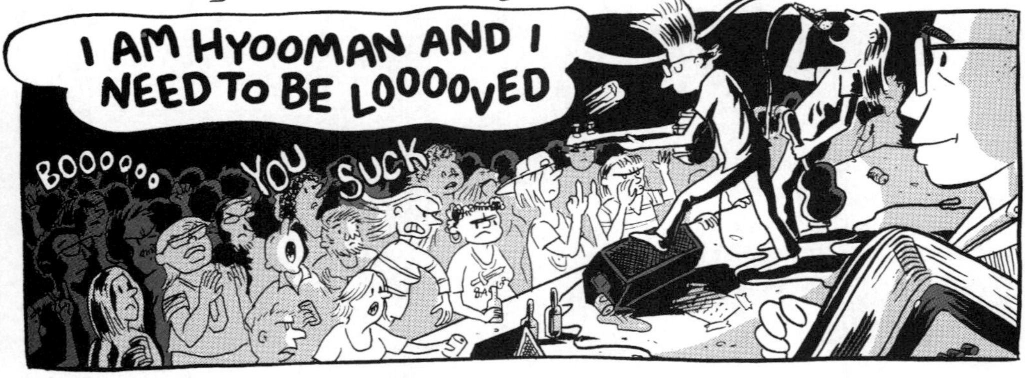
I AM HYOOMAN AND I NEED TO BE LOOOOVED
BOOOOOO
YOU SUCK

A feud was started with Vapor Rhinos, a local band we'd never met. We'd talk shit at our shows and called a local paper until they sent a reporter to our apartment.

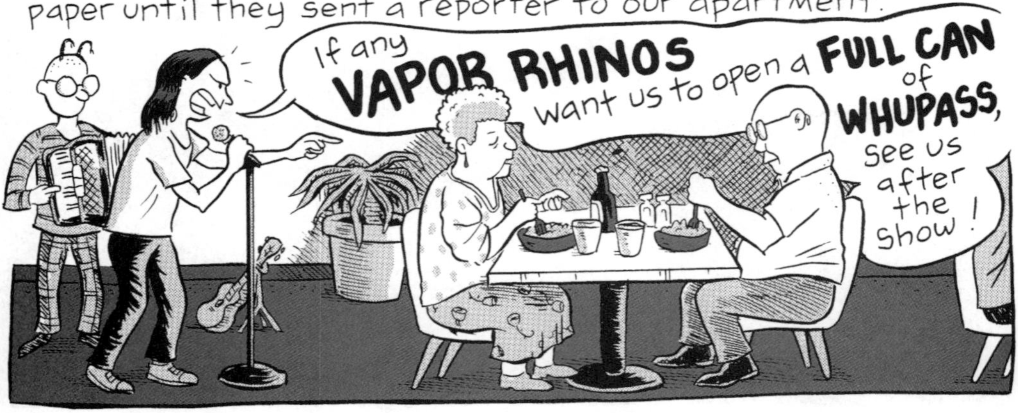
If any VAPOR RHINOS want us to open a FULL CAN of WHUPASS, see us after the show!

We lived in the lower half of a mansion built by tobacco heiresses in the 1920s.

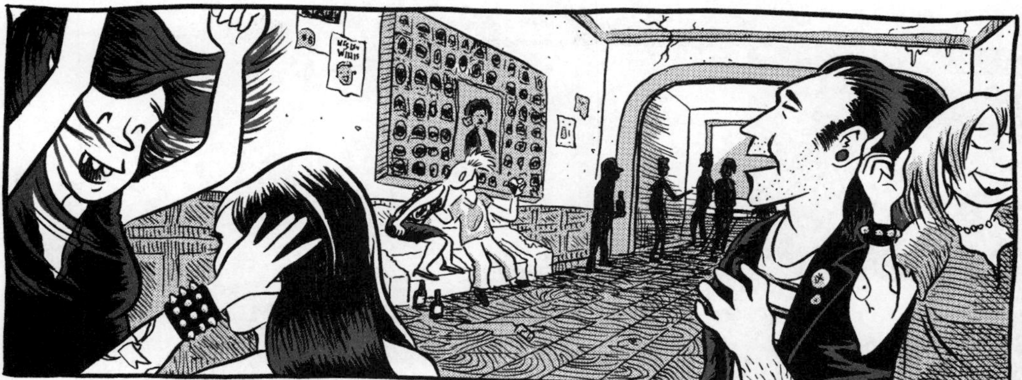

It became a punk house destroyed by house shows and careless art school kids with no parental guidance.

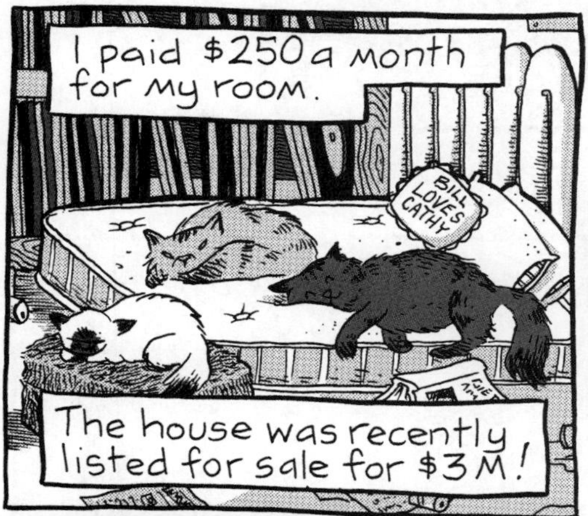
I paid $250 a month for my room.
BILL LOVES CATHY
The house was recently listed for sale for $3M!

Anyway, the article referred to our house as a commune.

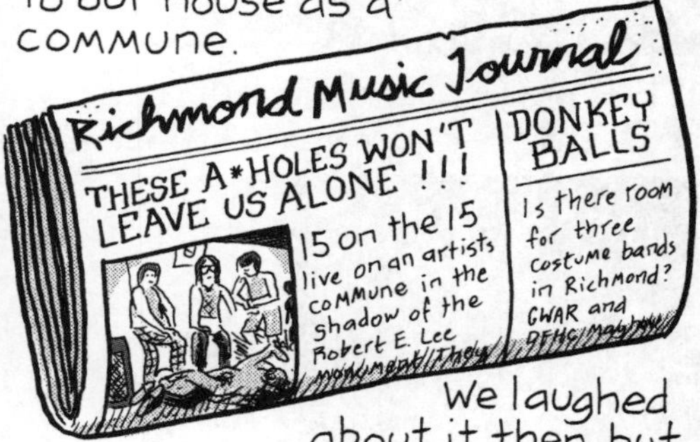
Richmond Music Journal
THESE A*HOLES WON'T LEAVE US ALONE!!!
15 on the 15 live on an artists commune in the shadow of the Robert E. Lee
DONKEY BALLS
Is there room for three costume bands in Richmond? GWAR and

We laughed about it then, but there's a kernel of truth in it.

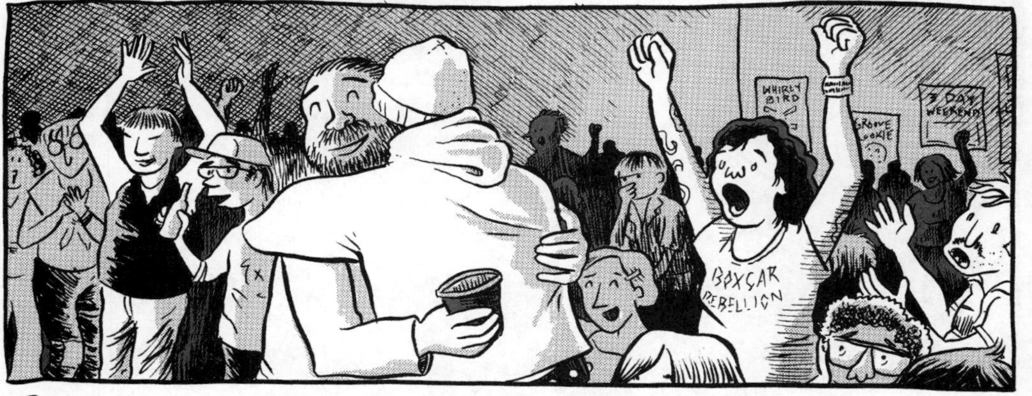
WHIRLY BIRD
3 DAY WEEKEND
BOXCAR REBELLION

Richmond, VA was a hotbed of punk and hardcore bands in the '90s, and there was a spirit of comraderie and collaboration rather than competition.

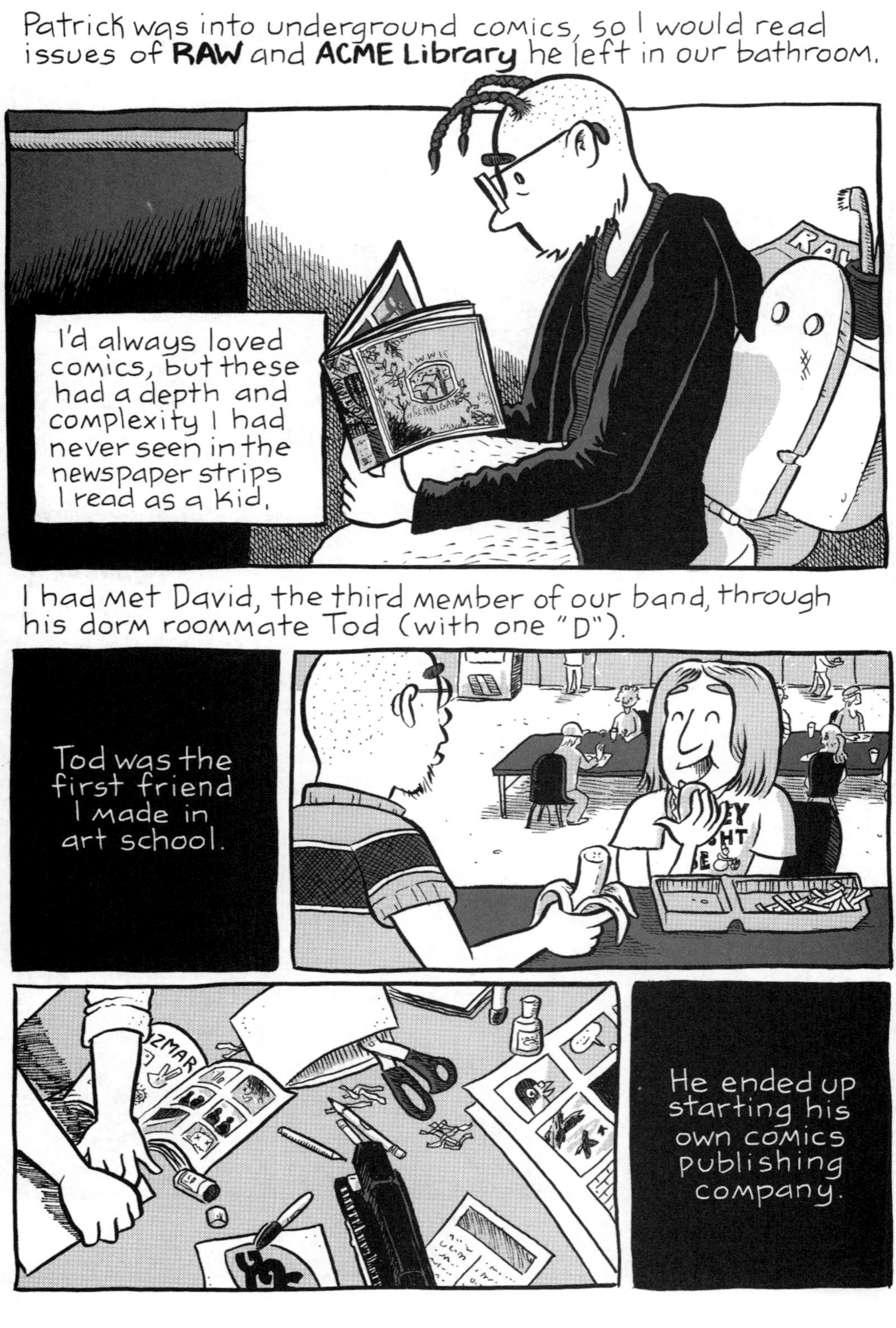
Patrick was into underground comics, so I would read issues of RAW and ACME Library he left in our bathroom.
I'd always loved comics, but these had a depth and complexity I had never seen in the newspaper strips I read as a kid.
I had met David, the third member of our band, through his dorm roommate Tod (with one "D").
Tod was the first friend I made in art school.
He ended up starting his own comics publishing company.

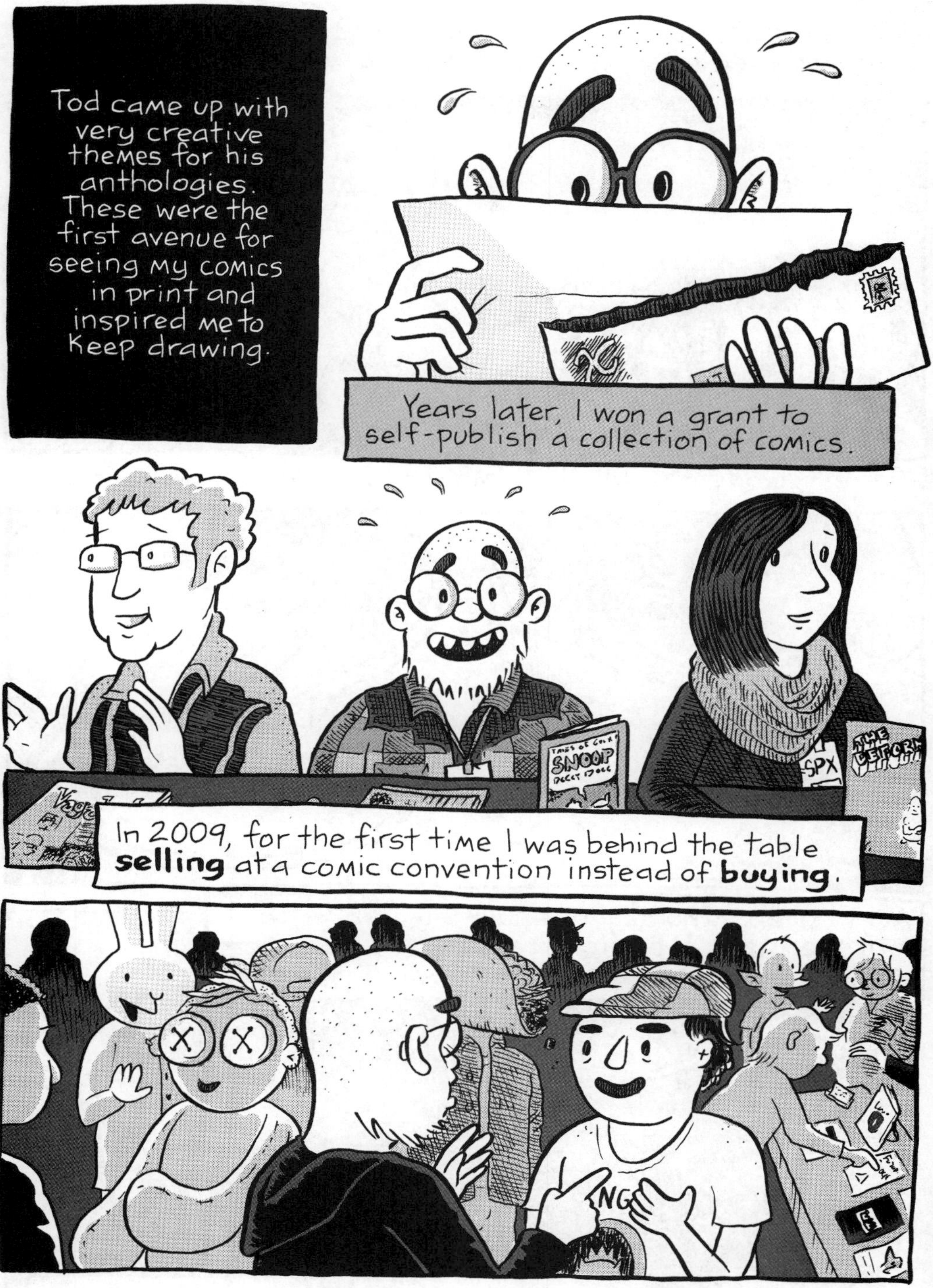
Tod came up with very creative themes for his anthologies. These were the first avenue for seeing my comics in print and inspired me to keep drawing.
Years later, I won a grant to self-publish a collection of comics.
SNOOP
SPX
In 2009, for the first time I was behind the table **selling** at a comic convention instead of **buying**.

I met other Xeric grant recipients and began forming friendships within the community.

Maybe it's a low bar for entry, but I immediately felt accepted and supported much as with the music community years earlier.

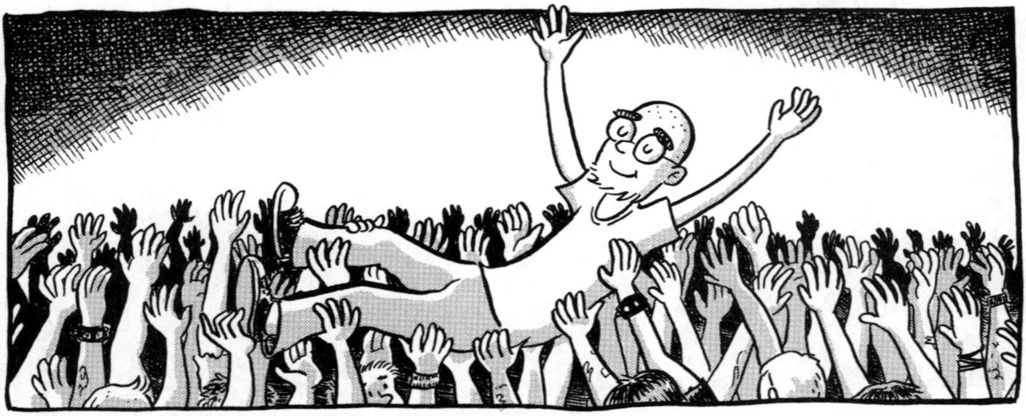

Some friends straddle both my music and arts communities.

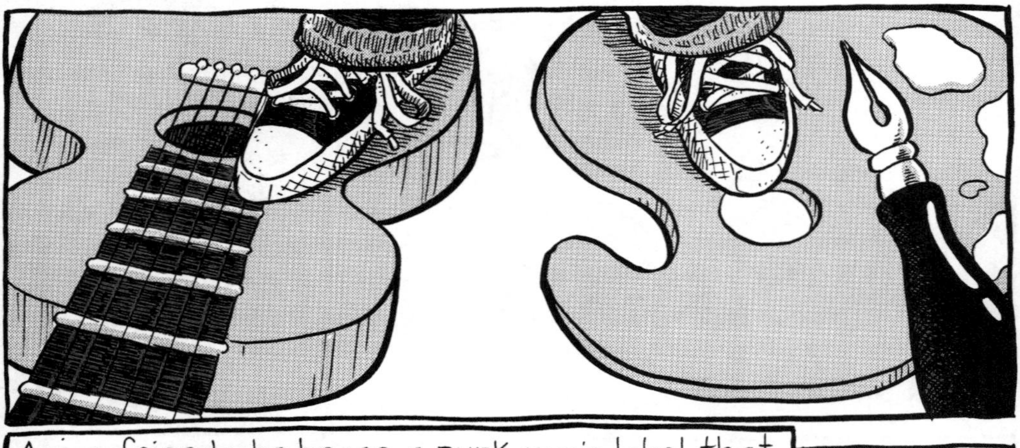

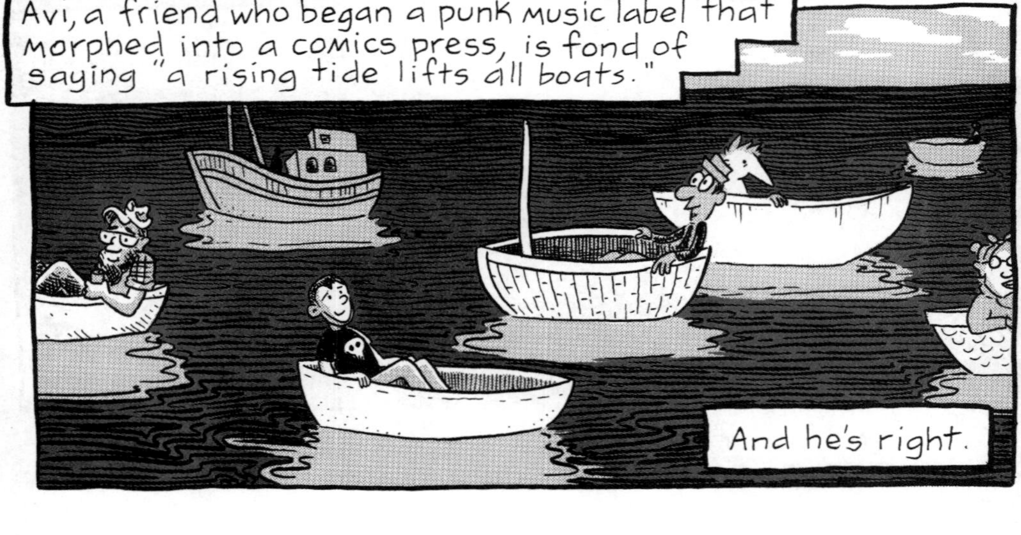
Avi, a friend who began a punk music label that morphed into a comics press, is fond of saying "a rising tide lifts all boats."
And he's right.

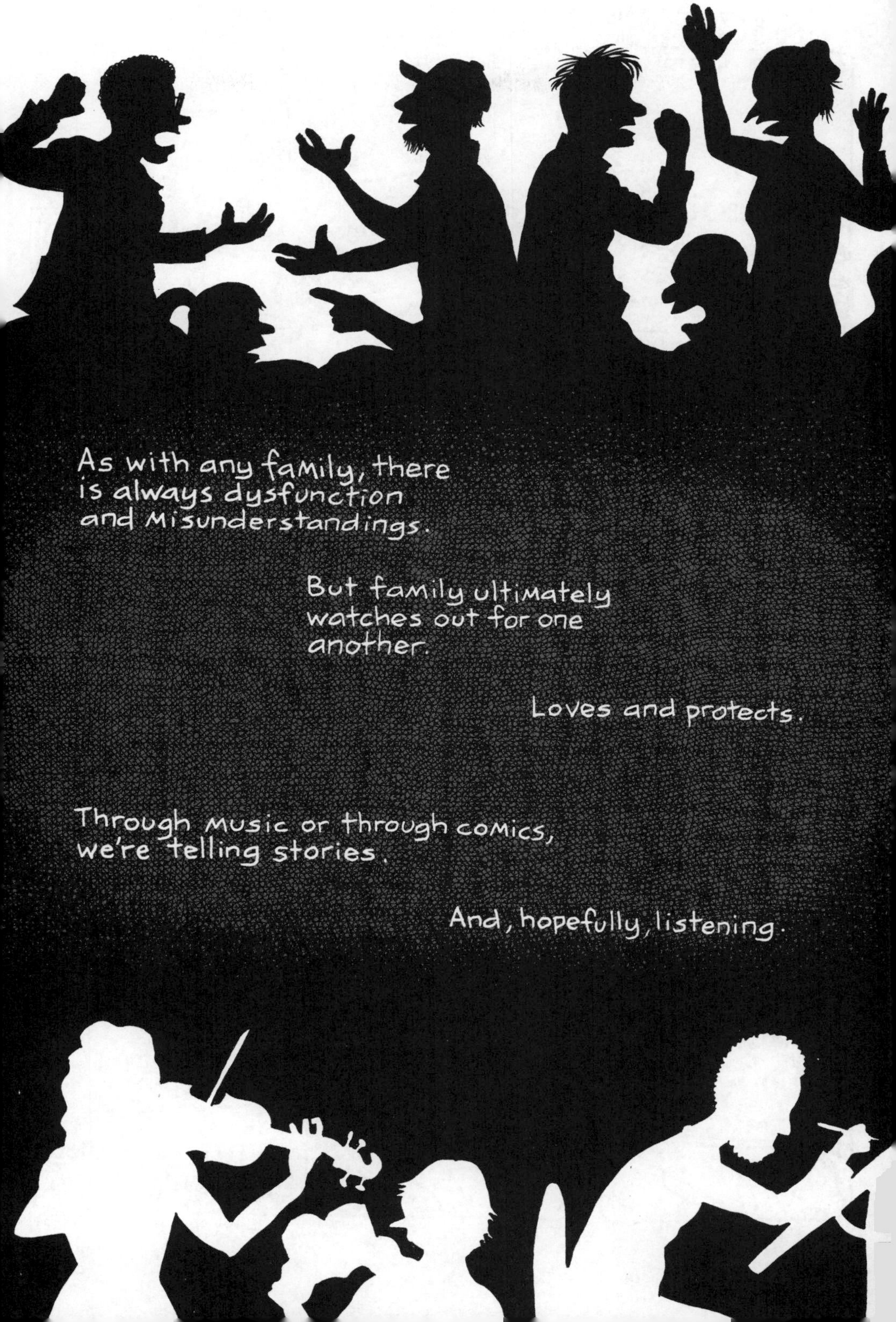
As with any family, there is always dysfunction and misunderstandings.
But family ultimately watches out for one another.
Loves and protects.
Through music or through comics, we're telling stories.
And, hopefully, listening.

NICE PEOPLE CLEAN PEOPLE

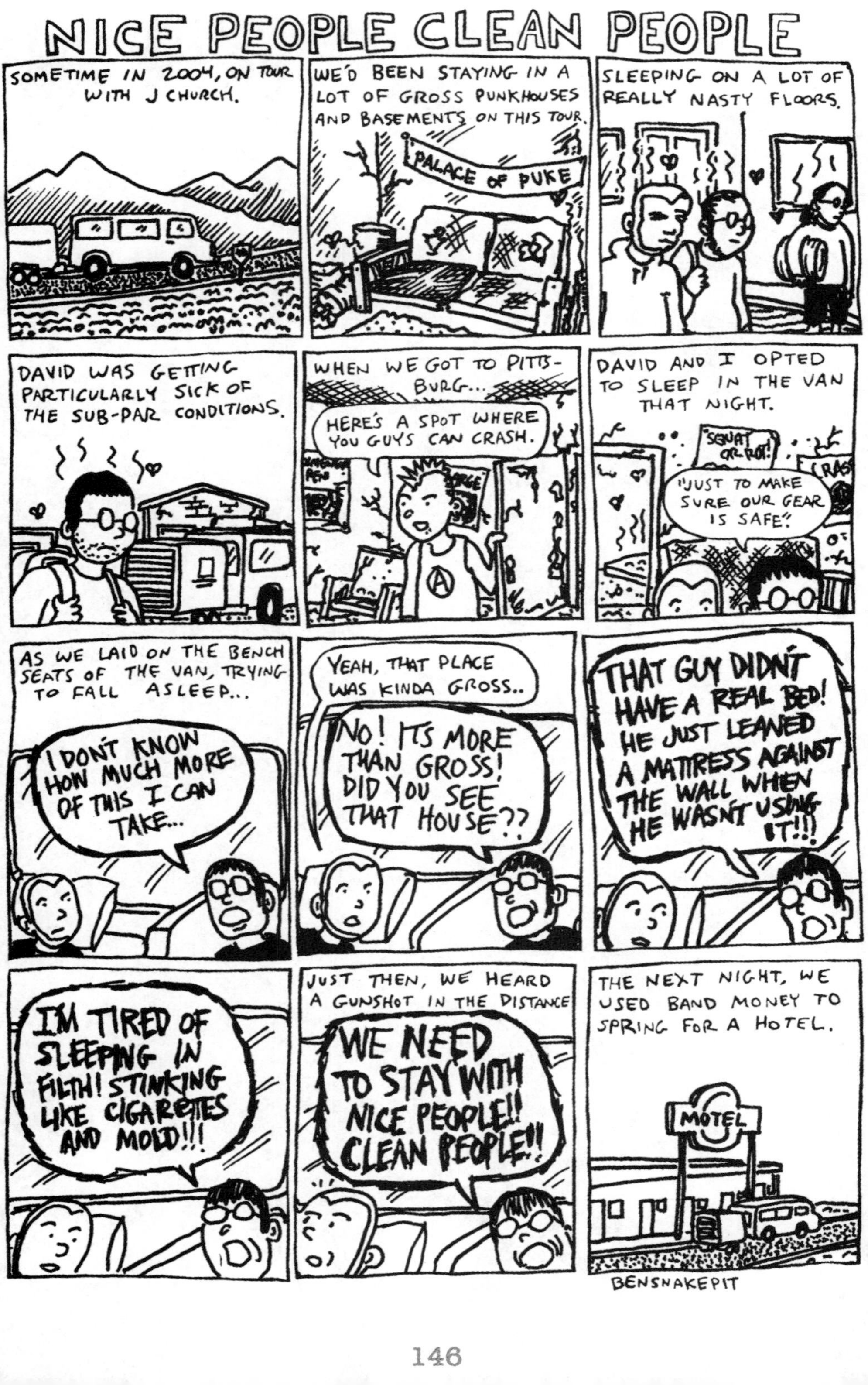
SOMETIME IN 2004, ON TOUR WITH J CHURCH.
WE'D BEEN STAYING IN A LOT OF GROSS PUNKHOUSES AND BASEMENTS ON THIS TOUR.
PALACE OF PUKE
SLEEPING ON A LOT OF REALLY NASTY FLOORS.
DAVID WAS GETTING PARTICULARLY SICK OF THE SUB-PAR CONDITIONS.
WHEN WE GOT TO PITTSBURG...
HERE'S A SPOT WHERE YOU GUYS CAN CRASH.
DAVID AND I OPTED TO SLEEP IN THE VAN THAT NIGHT.
SQUAT OR ROT!
"JUST TO MAKE SURE OUR GEAR IS SAFE."
AS WE LAID ON THE BENCH SEATS OF THE VAN, TRYING TO FALL ASLEEP...
I DON'T KNOW HOW MUCH MORE OF THIS I CAN TAKE...
YEAH, THAT PLACE WAS KINDA GROSS..
NO! ITS MORE THAN GROSS! DID YOU SEE THAT HOUSE??
THAT GUY DIDN'T HAVE A REAL BED! HE JUST LEANED A MATTRESS AGAINST THE WALL WHEN HE WASN'T USING IT!!!
I'M TIRED OF SLEEPING IN FILTH! STINKING LIKE CIGARETTES AND MOLD!!!
JUST THEN, WE HEARD A GUNSHOT IN THE DISTANCE
WE NEED TO STAY WITH NICE PEOPLE!! CLEAN PEOPLE!!
THE NEXT NIGHT, WE USED BAND MONEY TO SPRING FOR A HOTEL.
MOTEL

BENSNAKEPIT

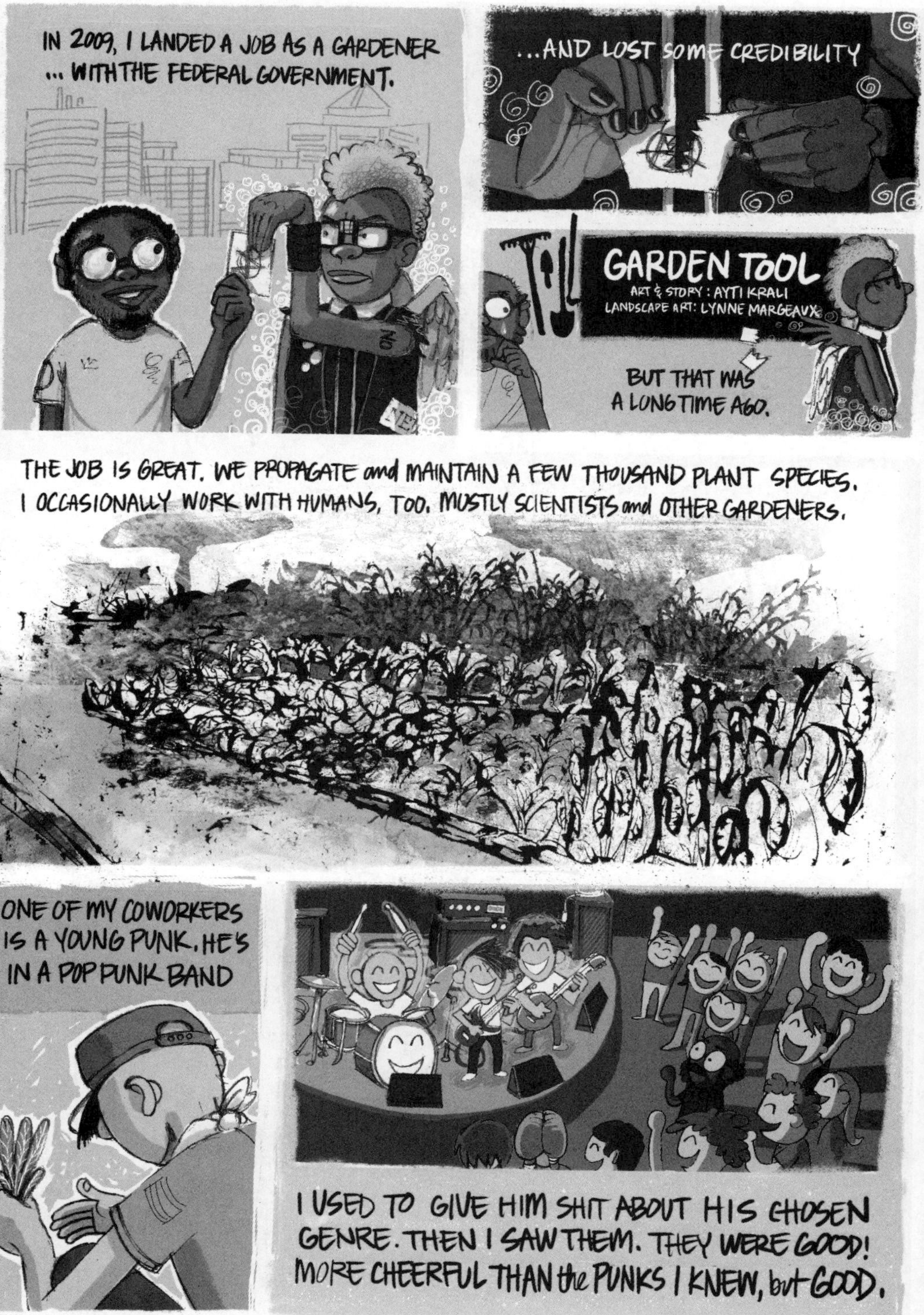
IN 2009, I LANDED A JOB AS A GARDENER ... WITH THE FEDERAL GOVERNMENT.
...AND LOST SOME CREDIBILITY
GARDEN TOOL
ART & STORY: AYTI KRALI
LANDSCAPE ART: LYNNE MARGEAUX
BUT THAT WAS A LONG TIME AGO.
THE JOB IS GREAT. WE PROPAGATE and MAINTAIN A FEW THOUSAND PLANT SPECIES. I OCCASIONALLY WORK WITH HUMANS, TOO. MOSTLY SCIENTISTS and OTHER GARDENERS.
ONE OF MY COWORKERS IS A YOUNG PUNK. HE'S IN A POP PUNK BAND
I USED TO GIVE HIM SHIT ABOUT HIS CHOSEN GENRE. THEN I SAW THEM. THEY WERE GOOD! MORE CHEERFUL THAN the PUNKS I KNEW, but GOOD.

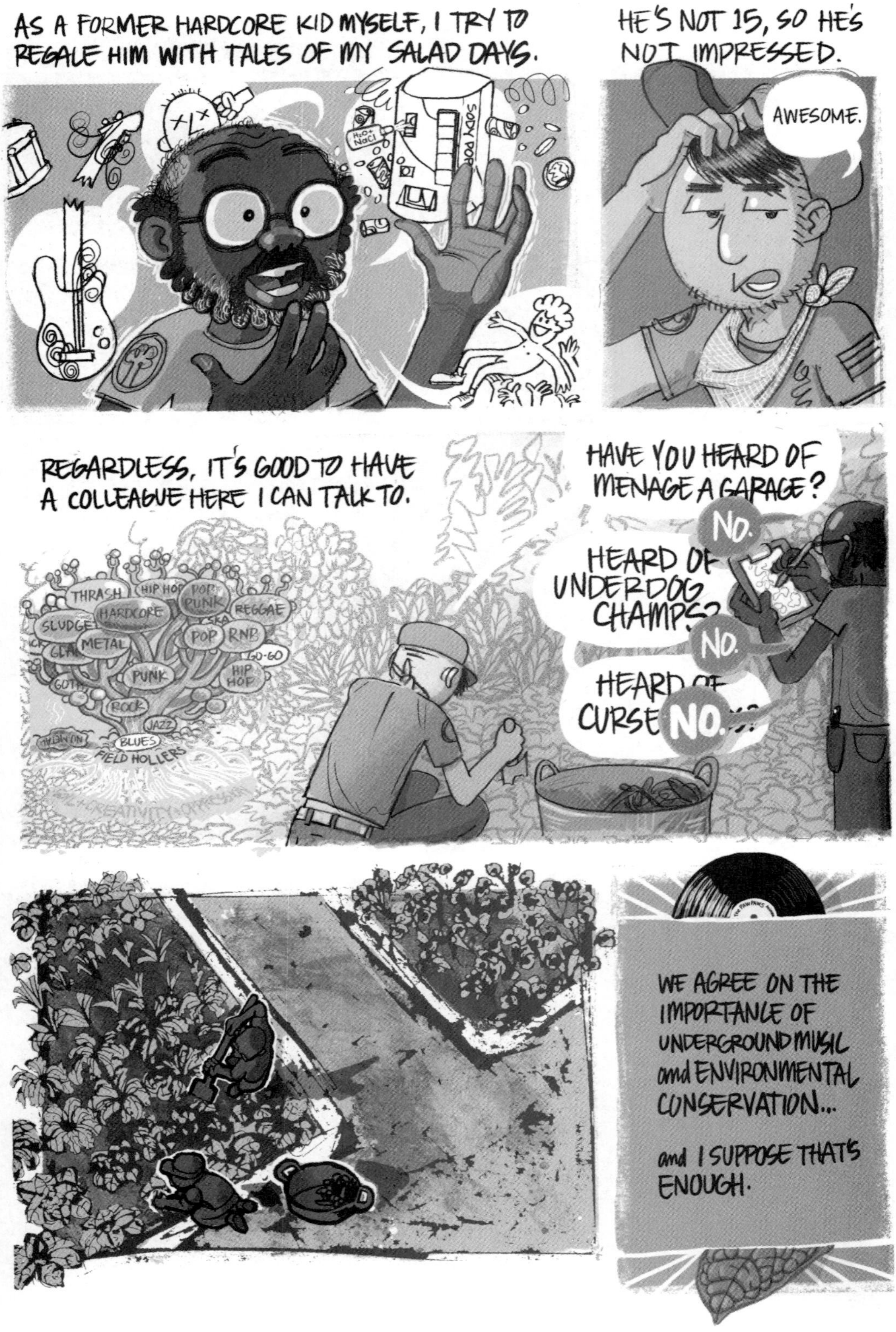
AS A FORMER HARDCORE KID MYSELF, I TRY TO REGALE HIM WITH TALES OF MY SALAD DAYS.
HE'S NOT 15, SO HE'S NOT IMPRESSED.
AWESOME.
REGARDLESS, IT'S GOOD TO HAVE A COLLEAGUE HERE I CAN TALK TO.
THRASH
HIP HOP
POP PUNK
HARDCORE
REGGAE
SLUDGE
SKA
METAL
POP
RNB
GO-GO
PUNK
HIP HOP
ROCK
JAZZ
BLUES
FIELD HOLLERS
HAVE YOU HEARD OF MENAGE A GARAGE?
NO.
HEARD OF UNDERDOG CHAMPS?
NO.
HEARD OF CURSE
NO.
WE AGREE ON THE IMPORTANCE OF UNDERGROUND MUSIC and ENVIRONMENTAL CONSERVATION...
and I SUPPOSE THAT'S ENOUGH.

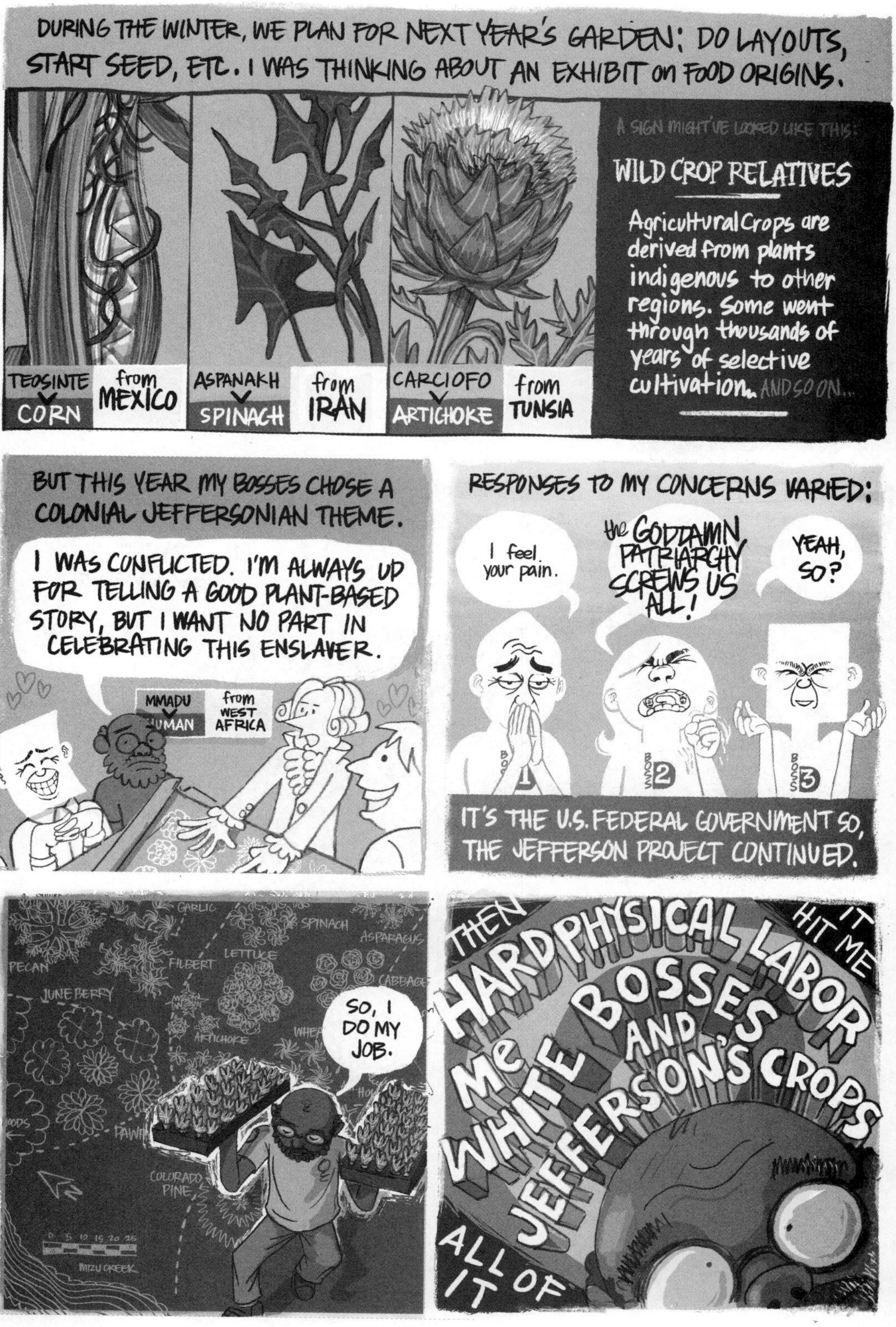
DURING THE WINTER, WE PLAN FOR NEXT YEAR'S GARDEN: DO LAYOUTS, START SEED, ETC. I WAS THINKING ABOUT AN EXHIBIT on FOOD ORIGINS.
TEOSINTE
CORN
from MEXICO
ASPANAKH
SPINACH
from IRAN
CARCIOFO
ARTICHOKE
from TUNSIA
A SIGN MIGHT'VE LOOKED LIKE THIS:
WILD CROP RELATIVES
Agricultural Crops are derived from plants indigenous to other regions. Some went through thousands of years of selective cultivation... AND SO ON...
BUT THIS YEAR MY BOSSES CHOSE A COLONIAL JEFFERSONIAN THEME.
I WAS CONFLICTED. I'M ALWAYS UP FOR TELLING A GOOD PLANT-BASED STORY, BUT I WANT NO PART IN CELEBRATING THIS ENSLAVER.
MMADU
UMAN
from WEST AFRICA
RESPONSES TO MY CONCERNS VARIED:
I feel your pain.
the GODDAMN PATRIARCHY SCREWS US ALL!
YEAH, SO?
BOSS 1
BOSS 2
BOSS 3
IT'S THE U.S. FEDERAL GOVERNMENT SO, THE JEFFERSON PROJECT CONTINUED.
GARLIC
SPINACH
ASPARAGUS
LETTUCE
FILBERT
PECAN
CABBAGE
JUNE BERRY
ARTICHOKE
COLORADO PINE
0 5 10 15 20 25
MIZU CREEK
SO, I DO MY JOB.
THEN IT HIT ME
HARD PHYSICAL LABOR
Me
WHITE BOSSES
AND
JEFFERSON'S CROPS
ALL OF IT

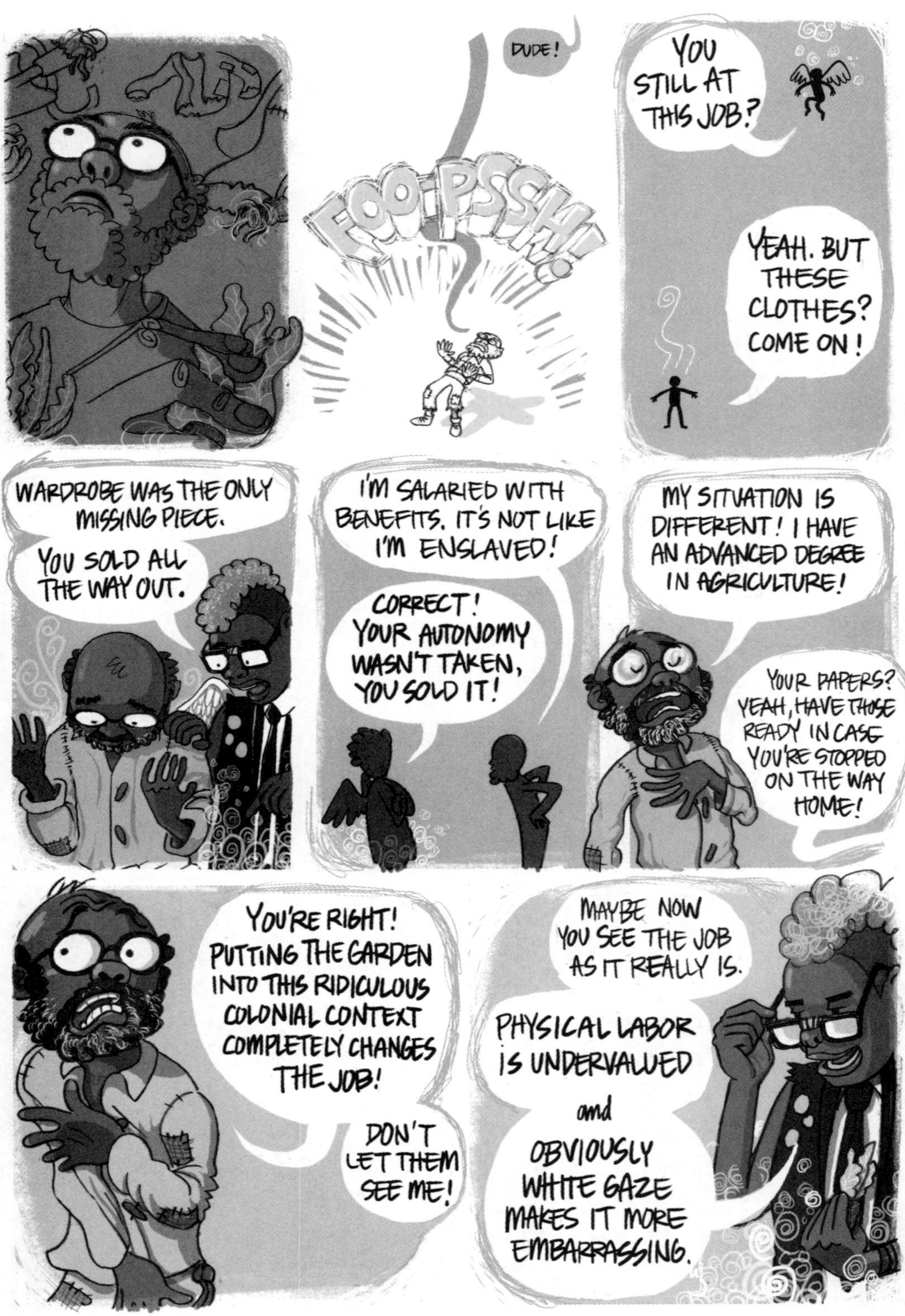
DUDE!
FOO-PSSH!
YOU STILL AT THIS JOB?
YEAH. BUT THESE CLOTHES? COME ON!
WARDROBE WAS THE ONLY MISSING PIECE.
YOU SOLD ALL THE WAY OUT.
I'M SALARIED WITH BENEFITS. IT'S NOT LIKE I'M ENSLAVED!
CORRECT! YOUR AUTONOMY WASN'T TAKEN, YOU SOLD IT!
MY SITUATION IS DIFFERENT! I HAVE AN ADVANCED DEGREE IN AGRICULTURE!
YOUR PAPERS? YEAH, HAVE THOSE READY IN CASE YOU'RE STOPPED ON THE WAY HOME!
YOU'RE RIGHT! PUTTING THE GARDEN INTO THIS RIDICULOUS COLONIAL CONTEXT COMPLETELY CHANGES THE JOB!
DON'T LET THEM SEE ME!
MAYBE NOW YOU SEE THE JOB AS IT REALLY IS.
PHYSICAL LABOR IS UNDERVALUED
and
OBVIOUSLY WHITE GAZE MAKES IT MORE EMBARRASSING.

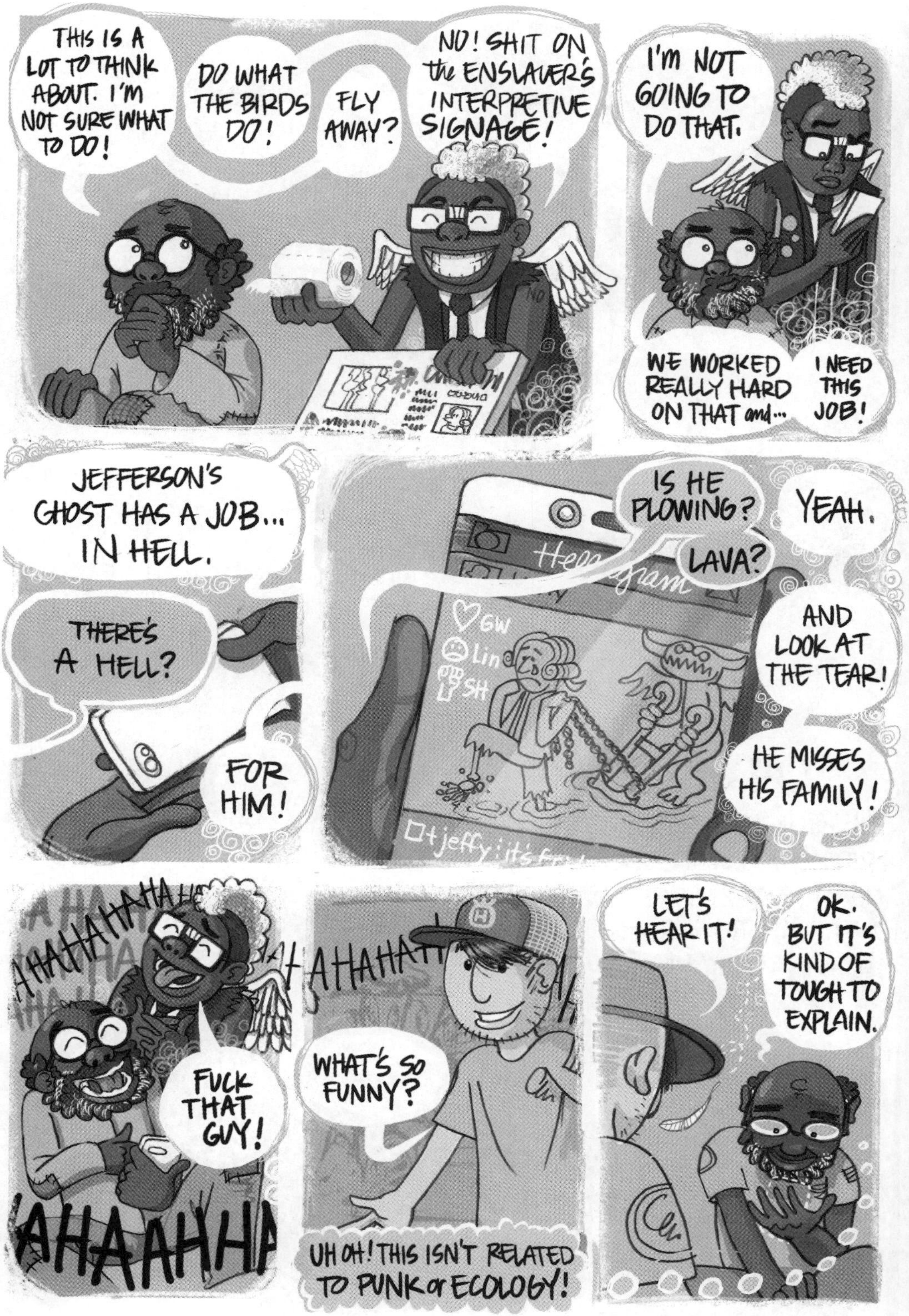
THIS IS A LOT TO THINK ABOUT. I'M NOT SURE WHAT TO DO!
DO WHAT THE BIRDS DO!
FLY AWAY?
NO! SHIT ON the ENSLAVER'S INTERPRETIVE SIGNAGE!
I'M NOT GOING TO DO THAT.
WE WORKED REALLY HARD ON THAT and...
I NEED THIS JOB!
JEFFERSON'S GHOST HAS A JOB... IN HELL.
THERE'S A HELL?
FOR HIM!
IS HE PLOWING?
LAVA?
YEAH.
AND LOOK AT THE TEAR!
HE MISSES HIS FAMILY!
HAHAHAHAHA
FUCK THAT GUY!
AHAAHHA
HAHAHA
WHAT'S SO FUNNY?
UH OH! THIS ISN'T RELATED TO PUNK or ECOLOGY!
LET'S HEAR IT!
OK. BUT IT'S KIND OF TOUGH TO EXPLAIN.

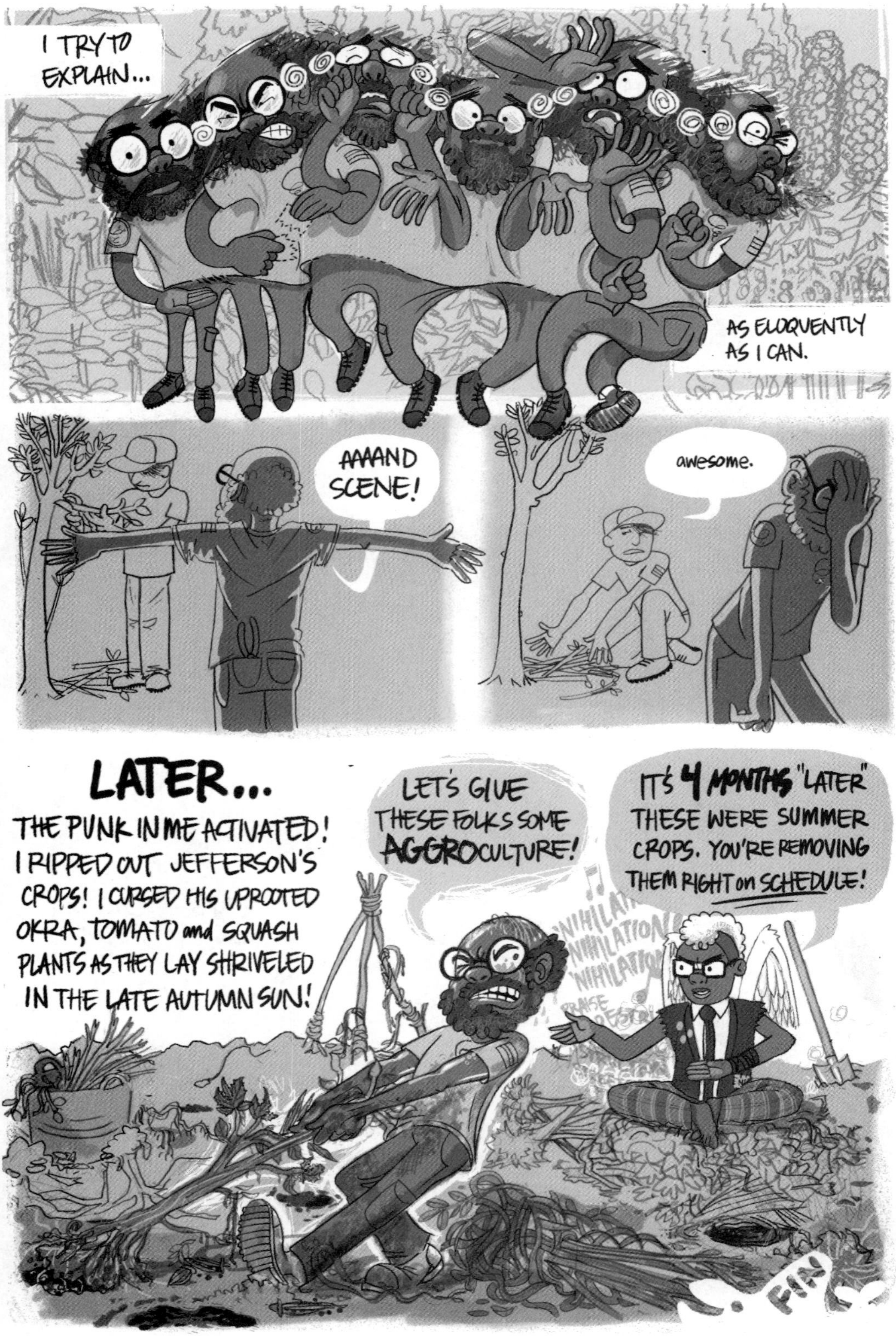
I TRY TO EXPLAIN...
AS ELOQUENTLY AS I CAN.
AAAAND SCENE!
awesome.
LATER...
THE PUNK IN ME ACTIVATED! I RIPPED OUT JEFFERSON'S CROPS! I CURSED HIS UPROOTED OKRA, TOMATO and SQUASH PLANTS AS THEY LAY SHRIVELED IN THE LATE AUTUMN SUN!
LET'S GIVE THESE FOLKS SOME AGGROCULTURE!
IT'S 4 MONTHS "LATER" THESE WERE SUMMER CROPS. YOU'RE REMOVING THEM RIGHT on SCHEDULE!
FIN

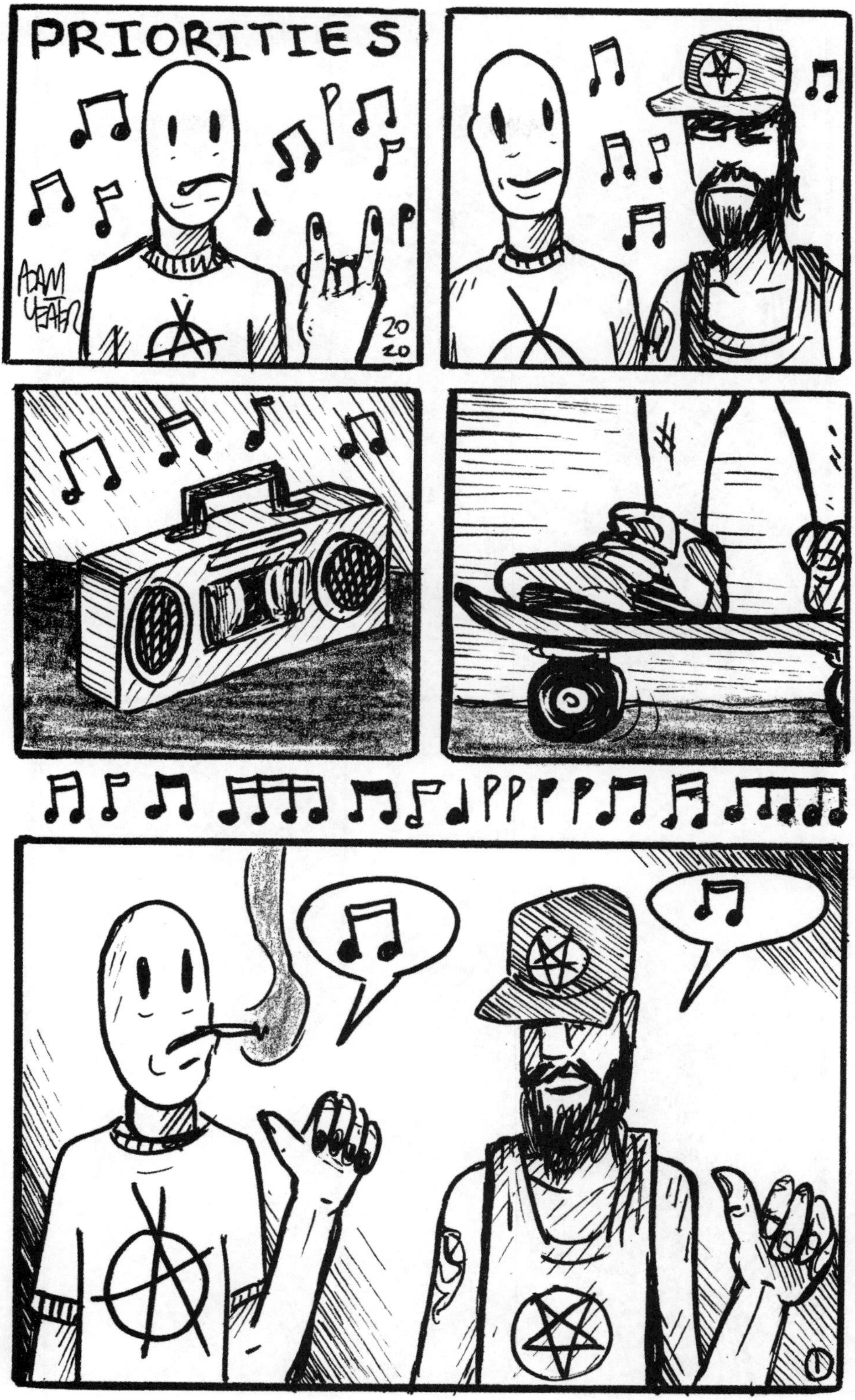
PRIORITIES
ADAM YEAH
20 20
1

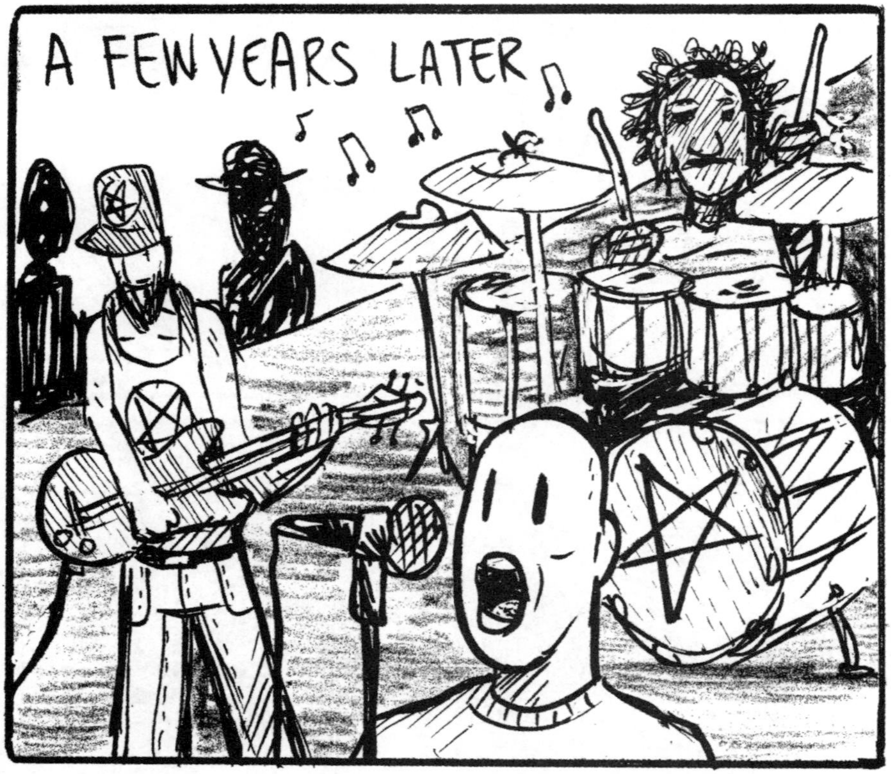
A FEW YEARS LATER

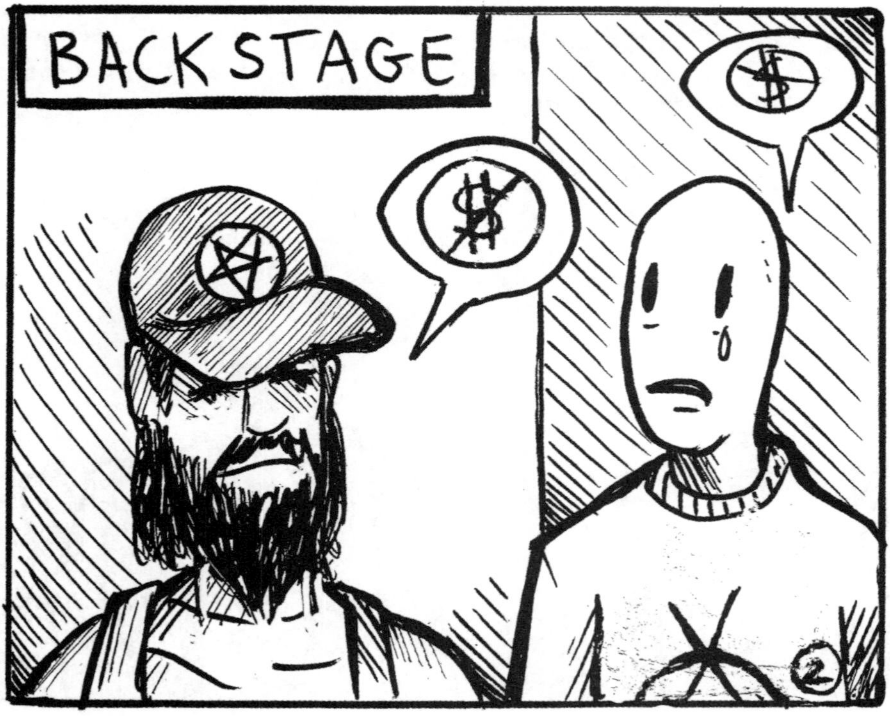
BACKSTAGE

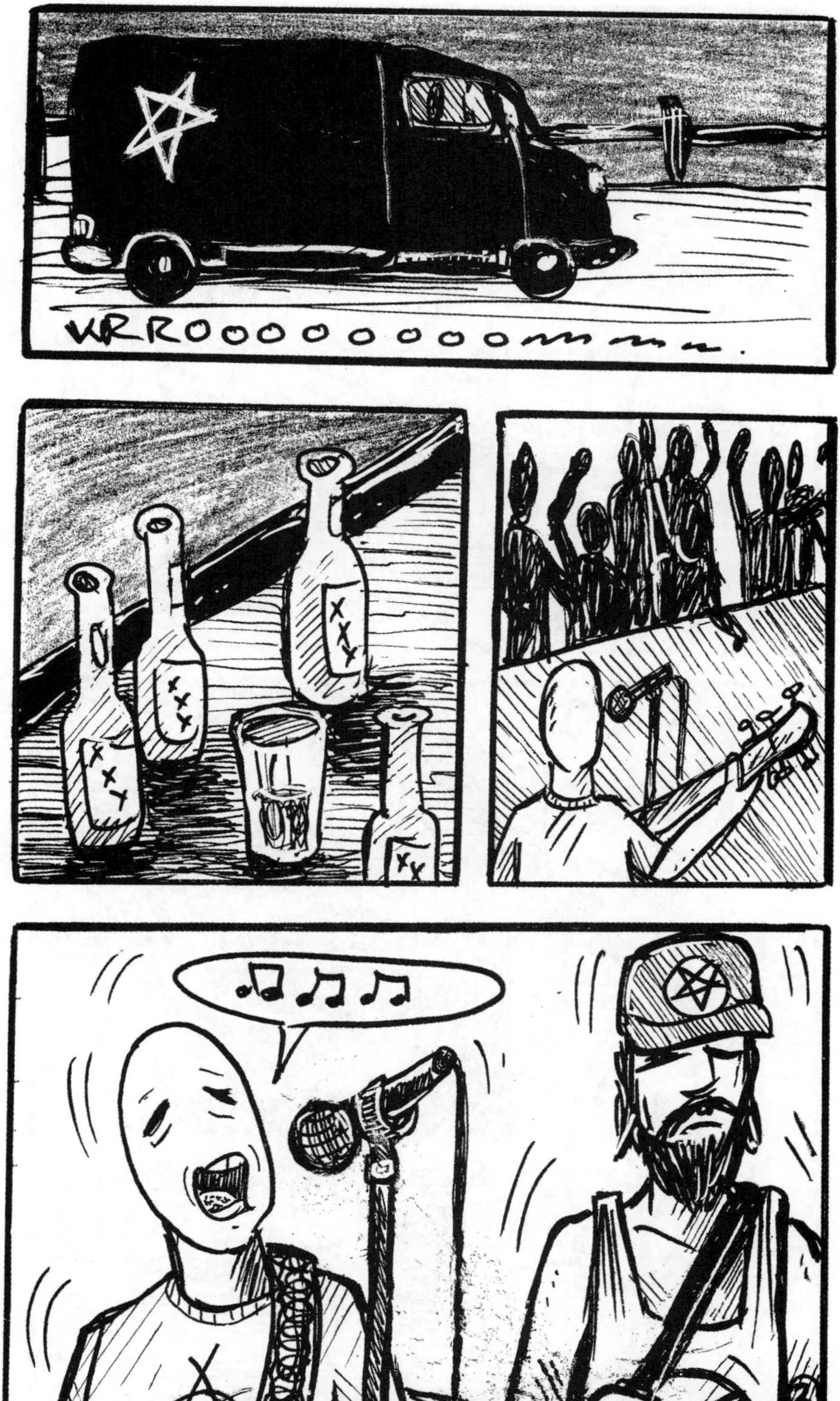
VRROOOOOOOOmmm...
XXX
XXX
XXX
XXX
XX

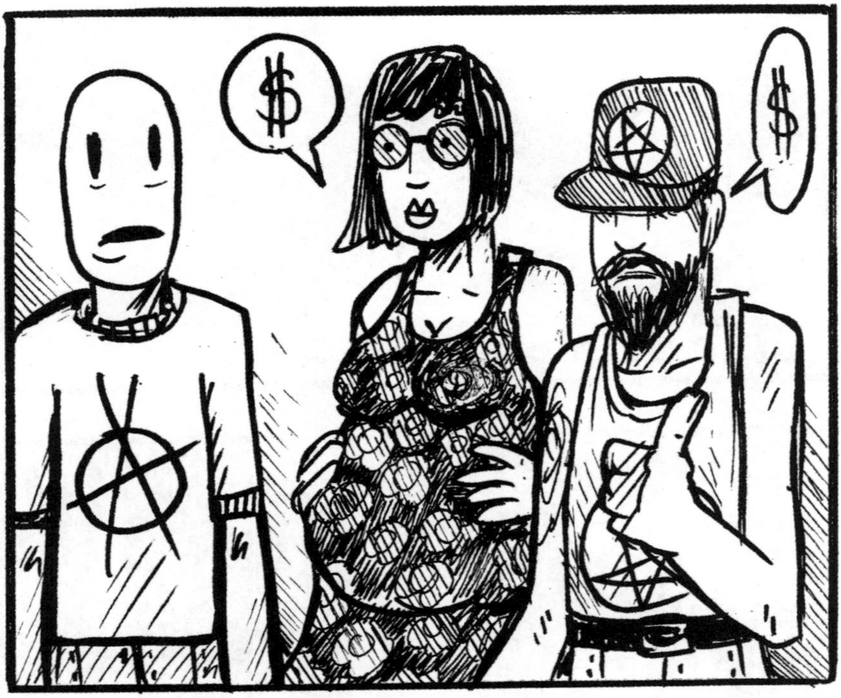
$
$

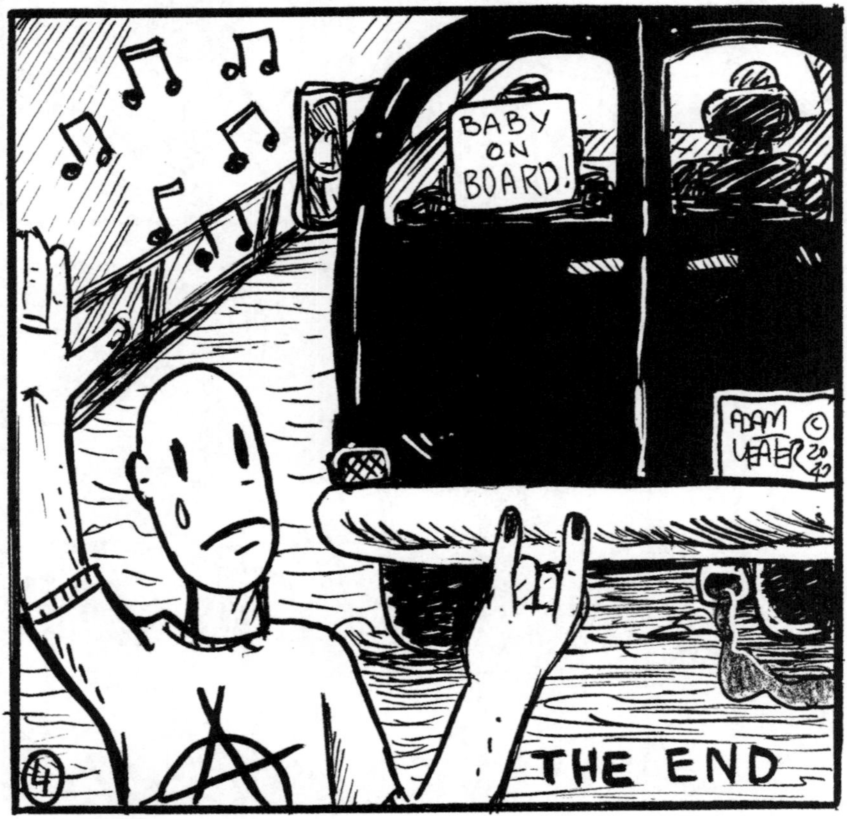
BABY ON BOARD!
ADAM YEATER © 2017
4
THE END

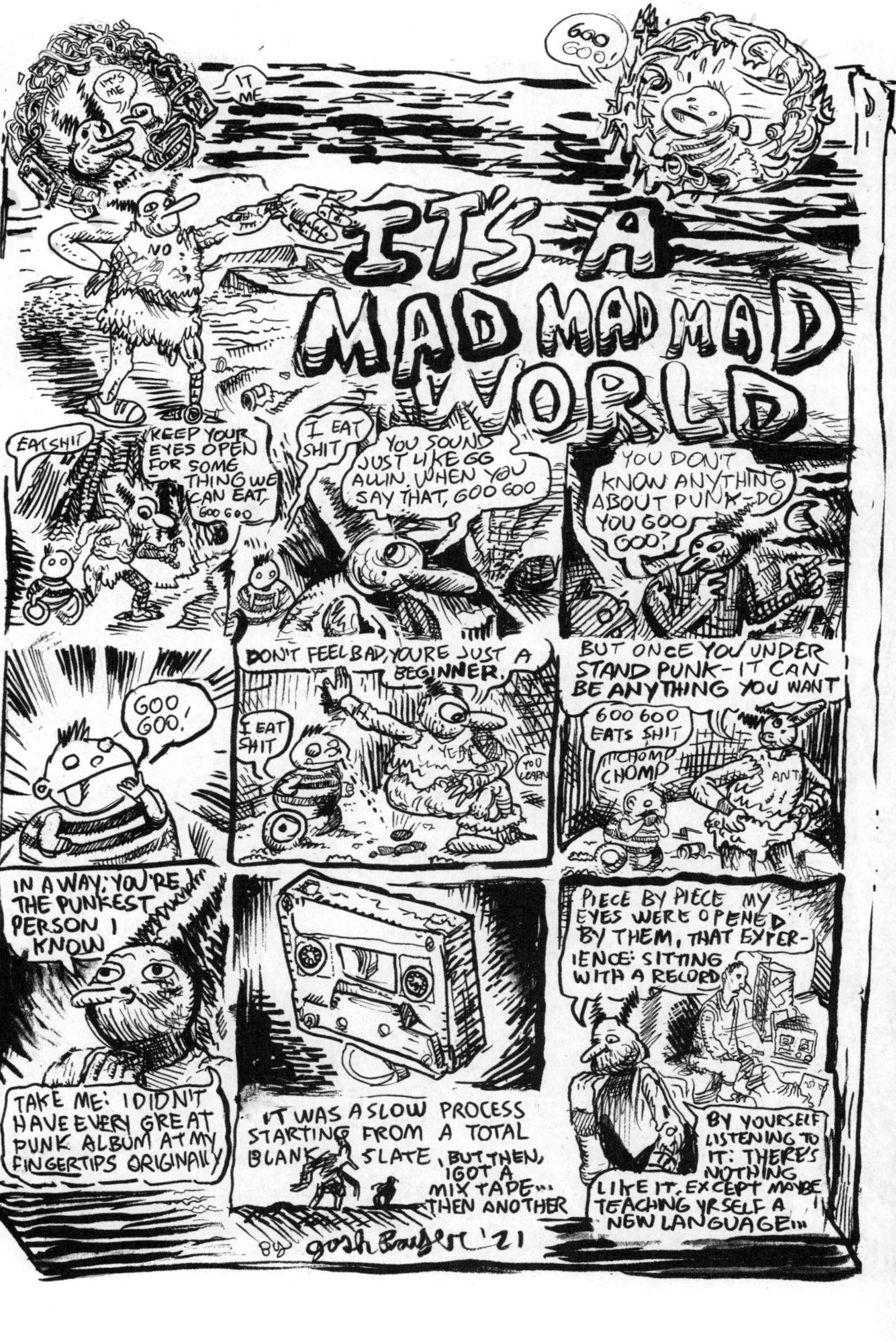
IT'S ME
IT ME
GOO GOO!
ANTI
NO
IT'S A MAD MAD MAD WORLD
EAT SHIT
KEEP YOUR EYES OPEN FOR SOME THING WE CAN EAT, GOO GOO
I EAT SHIT
YOU SOUND JUST LIKE GG ALLIN WHEN YOU SAY THAT, GOO GOO
YOU DON'T KNOW ANYTHING ABOUT PUNK-DO YOU GOO GOO?
GOO GOO!
DON'T FEEL BAD, YOU'RE JUST A BEGINNER.
I EAT SHIT
YEAH
YOU LEARN
BUT ONCE YOU UNDERSTAND PUNK- IT CAN BE ANYTHING YOU WANT
GOO GOO EATS SHIT
CHOMP CHOMP
ANTI
IN A WAY, YOU'RE THE PUNKEST PERSON I KNOW
TAKE ME: I DIDN'T HAVE EVERY GREAT PUNK ALBUM AT MY FINGERTIPS ORIGINALLY
IT WAS A SLOW PROCESS STARTING FROM A TOTAL BLANK SLATE, BUT THEN, I GOT A MIX TAPE... THEN ANOTHER
PIECE BY PIECE MY EYES WERE OPENED BY THEM, THAT EXPERIENCE: SITTING WITH A RECORD
BY YOURSELF LISTENING TO IT: THERE'S NOTHING LIKE IT, EXCEPT MAYBE TEACHING YRSELF A NEW LANGUAGE...
By Josh Bayer '21

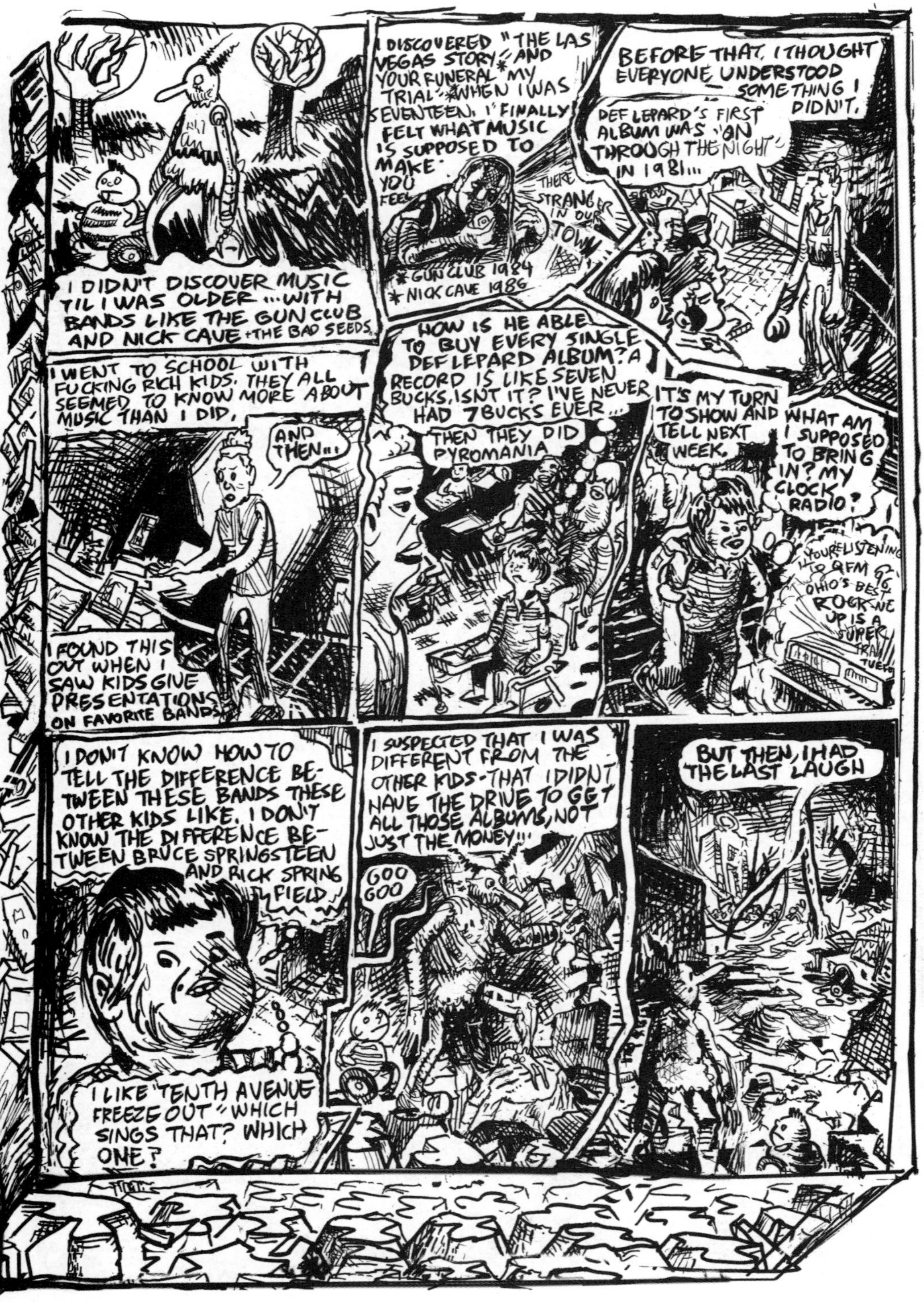
I DIDN'T DISCOVER MUSIC TIL I WAS OLDER ...WITH BANDS LIKE THE GUN CLUB AND NICK CAVE + THE BAD SEEDS
I DISCOVERED "THE LAS VEGAS STORY"* AND YOUR FUNERAL* MY TRIAL"* WHEN I WAS SEVENTEEN, I FINALLY FELT WHAT MUSIC IS SUPPOSED TO MAKE YOU FEEL
THERE STRANGER IN OUR TOWN
*GUN CLUB 1984
*NICK CAVE 1986
BEFORE THAT, I THOUGHT EVERYONE UNDERSTOOD SOMETHING I DIDN'T.
DEF LEPARD'S FIRST ALBUM WAS "ON THROUGH THE NIGHT" IN 1981...
I WENT TO SCHOOL WITH FUCKING RICH KIDS. THEY ALL SEEMED TO KNOW MORE ABOUT MUSIC THAN I DID.
AND THEN...
I FOUND THIS OUT WHEN I SAW KIDS GIVE PRESENTATIONS ON FAVORITE BANDS.
HOW IS HE ABLE TO BUY EVERY SINGLE DEF LEPARD ALBUM? A RECORD IS LIKE SEVEN BUCKS, ISNT IT? I'VE NEVER HAD 7 BUCKS EVER...
THEN THEY DID PYROMANIA
IT'S MY TURN TO SHOW AND TELL NEXT WEEK.
WHAT AM I SUPPOSED TO BRING IN? MY CLOCK RADIO?
YOU'RE LISTENING TO QFM 96 OHIO'S BEST ROCK
I DON'T KNOW HOW TO TELL THE DIFFERENCE BETWEEN THESE BANDS THESE OTHER KIDS LIKE. I DON'T KNOW THE DIFFERENCE BETWEEN BRUCE SPRINGSTEEN AND RICK SPRINGFIELD.
I LIKE "TENTH AVENUE FREEZE OUT" WHICH SINGS THAT? WHICH ONE?
I SUSPECTED THAT I WAS DIFFERENT FROM THE OTHER KIDS - THAT I DIDN'T HAVE THE DRIVE TO GET ALL THOSE ALBUMS, NOT JUST THE MONEY!!
GOO GOO
BUT THEN, I HAD THE LAST LAUGH

SALE COUPON BEST

ABANDON SUPERMAR

I UNDERSTOOD HOW ALEX FELT IN "A CLOCKWORK ORANGE" WHEN HE HEARD BEETHOVEN

GOO GOO

PENNIES

I WAS TRANSPORTED THE SAME WAY HE WAS

MUSIC THE ONLY COUNTER WEIGHT TO THE VIOLENCE AND HORROR INSIDE.

A SERIES OF

SNFU IF YOU SWEAR

CATCH NOISE

MY ALARM RINGING MILK TO MY DISM GO DISM BACK R THERE R KILL

CASSETTES SERVED AS MY ENTRYWAY YOU COULD CRAM A LOT OF MUSIC IN THEM...

REALLY DON WANNA GO BUT I NEED MONEY SO

A FRIEND FROM MY HIGH SCHOOL GAVE ME A TAPE THAT CONTAINED SNFU'S 2ND ALBUM.

THAT RECORD WAS A HUGE EYE-OPENER FOR ME. I DIDN'T KNOW SONGS COULD SPEAK SO PLAINLY -- OR THAT YOU COULD TACKLE SUCH CONTENT.

ANTI

KEEPS ME PINNED

I'M LOOKING AT MY CEILING IT'S LOOKING BACK AT ME

SONGS ABOUT GOING TO A JOB YOU DREAD ("MONEY MATTERS", "THE CEILING") ABOUT GROWING OLD, ("I FORGET" "HE'S NOT GETTING OLDER, HE'S GETTING BITTER") SONGS ABOUT FEAR ("I'M REAL SCARED" "SCARECROW") I COULD FEEL THOSE SONGS CHANGING ME...

I COULD FEEL THAT RECORD CHANGING ME, GOO-GOO,

GOO GOO

I THOUGHT YOU HAD TO LISTEN TO ROMANTIC ALTERNATIVE MUSIC TO BE AN ARTIST... LIKE THE SMITHS OR...

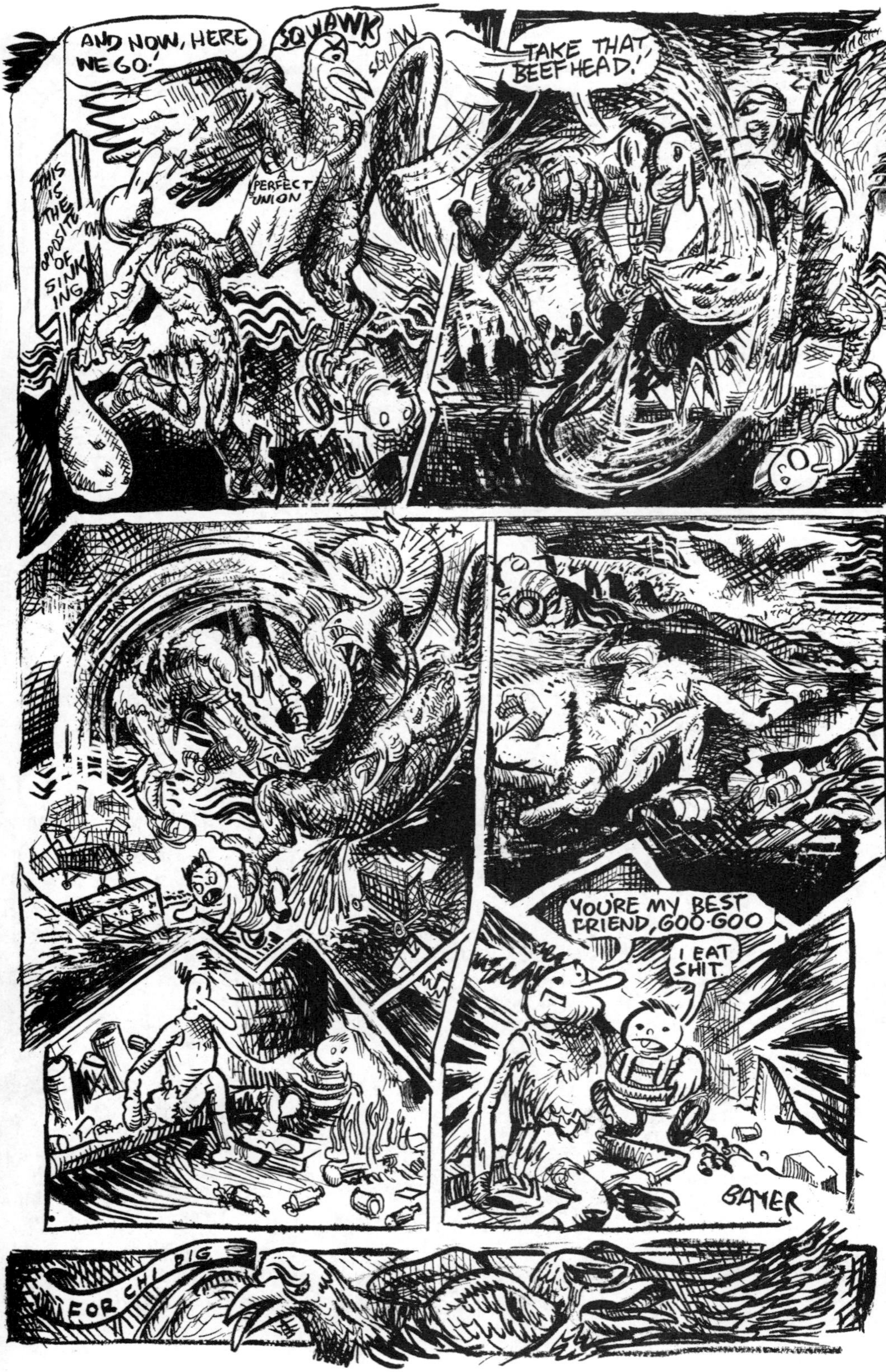
AND NOW, HERE WE GO!
SQUAWK
SQUAW
THIS IS THE OPPOSITE OF SINKING
A PERFECT UNION
TAKE THAT BEEFHEAD!
YOU'RE MY BEST FRIEND, GOO-GOO
I EAT SHIT.
BAYER
FOR CHI PIG

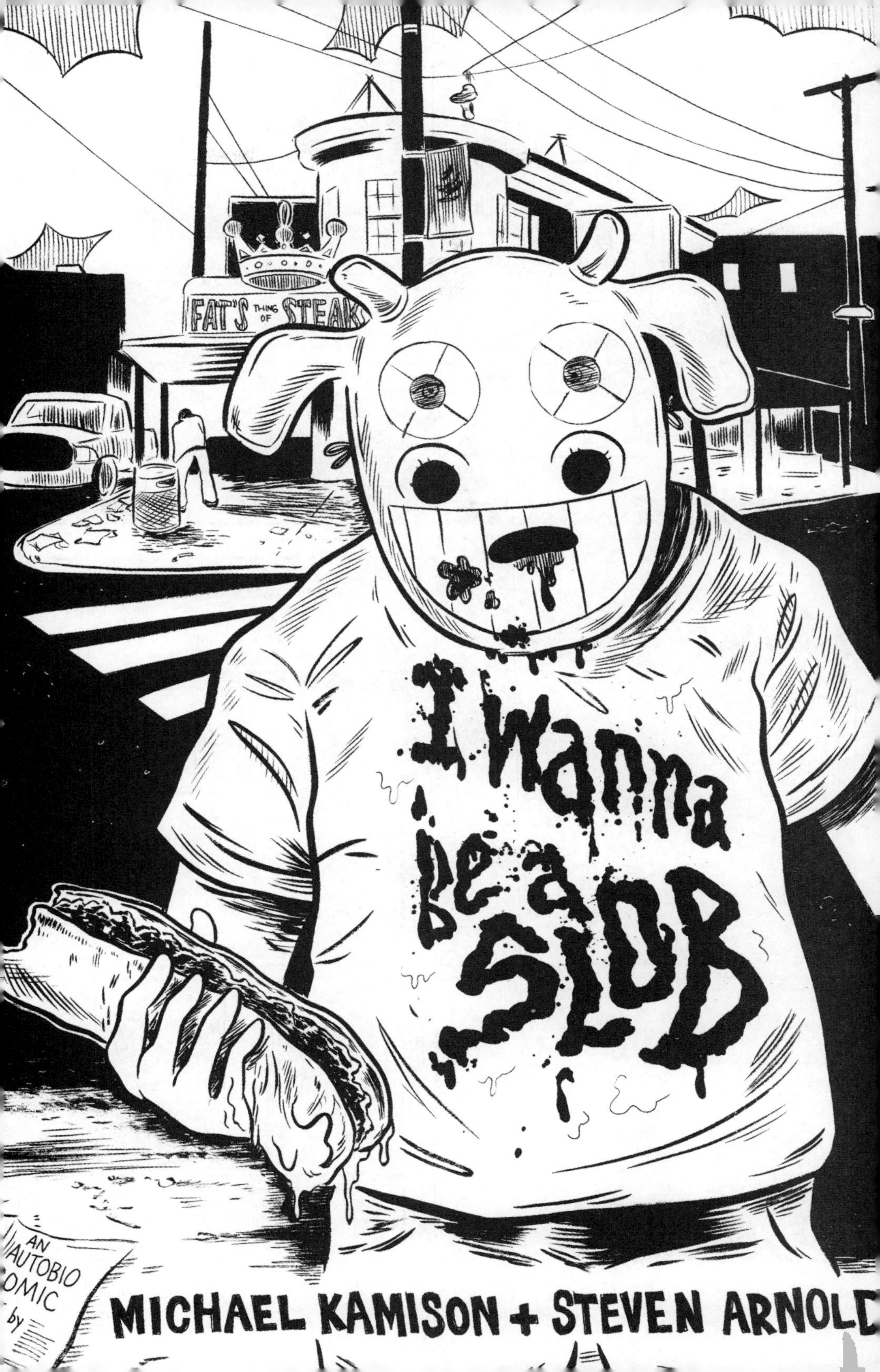
FAT'S THING OF STEAKS
I wanna be a SLOB
AN AUTOBIO COMIC by
MICHAEL KAMISON + STEVEN ARNOLD

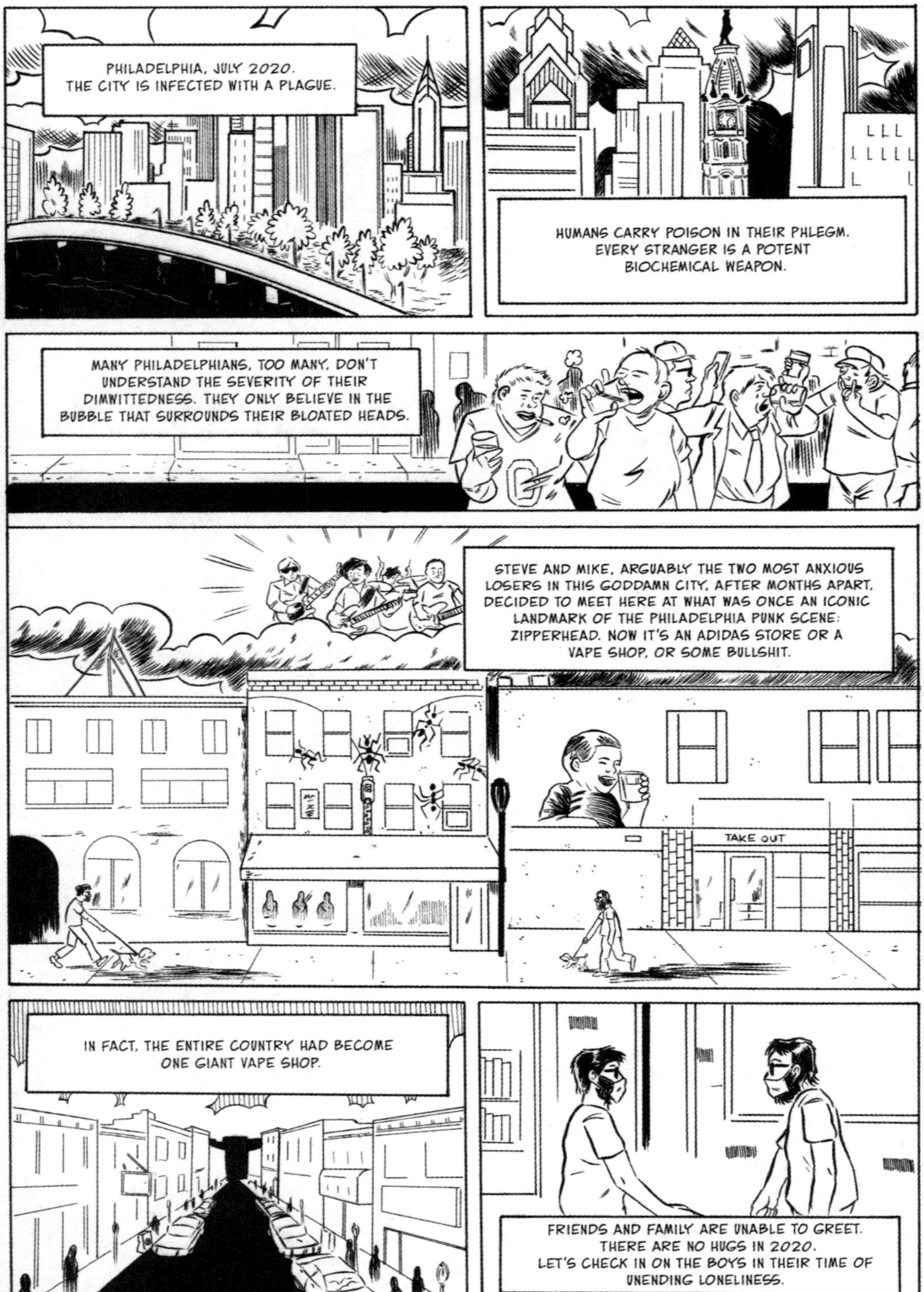
PHILADELPHIA, JULY 2020.
THE CITY IS INFECTED WITH A PLAGUE.
HUMANS CARRY POISON IN THEIR PHLEGM. EVERY STRANGER IS A POTENT BIOCHEMICAL WEAPON.
MANY PHILADELPHIANS, TOO MANY, DON'T UNDERSTAND THE SEVERITY OF THEIR DIMWITTEDNESS. THEY ONLY BELIEVE IN THE BUBBLE THAT SURROUNDS THEIR BLOATED HEADS.
STEVE AND MIKE, ARGUABLY THE TWO MOST ANXIOUS LOSERS IN THIS GODDAMN CITY, AFTER MONTHS APART, DECIDED TO MEET HERE AT WHAT WAS ONCE AN ICONIC LANDMARK OF THE PHILADELPHIA PUNK SCENE: ZIPPERHEAD. NOW IT'S AN ADIDAS STORE OR A VAPE SHOP, OR SOME BULLSHIT.
TAKE OUT
IN FACT, THE ENTIRE COUNTRY HAD BECOME ONE GIANT VAPE SHOP.
FRIENDS AND FAMILY ARE UNABLE TO GREET. THERE ARE NO HUGS IN 2020. LET'S CHECK IN ON THE BOYS IN THEIR TIME OF UNENDING LONELINESS.

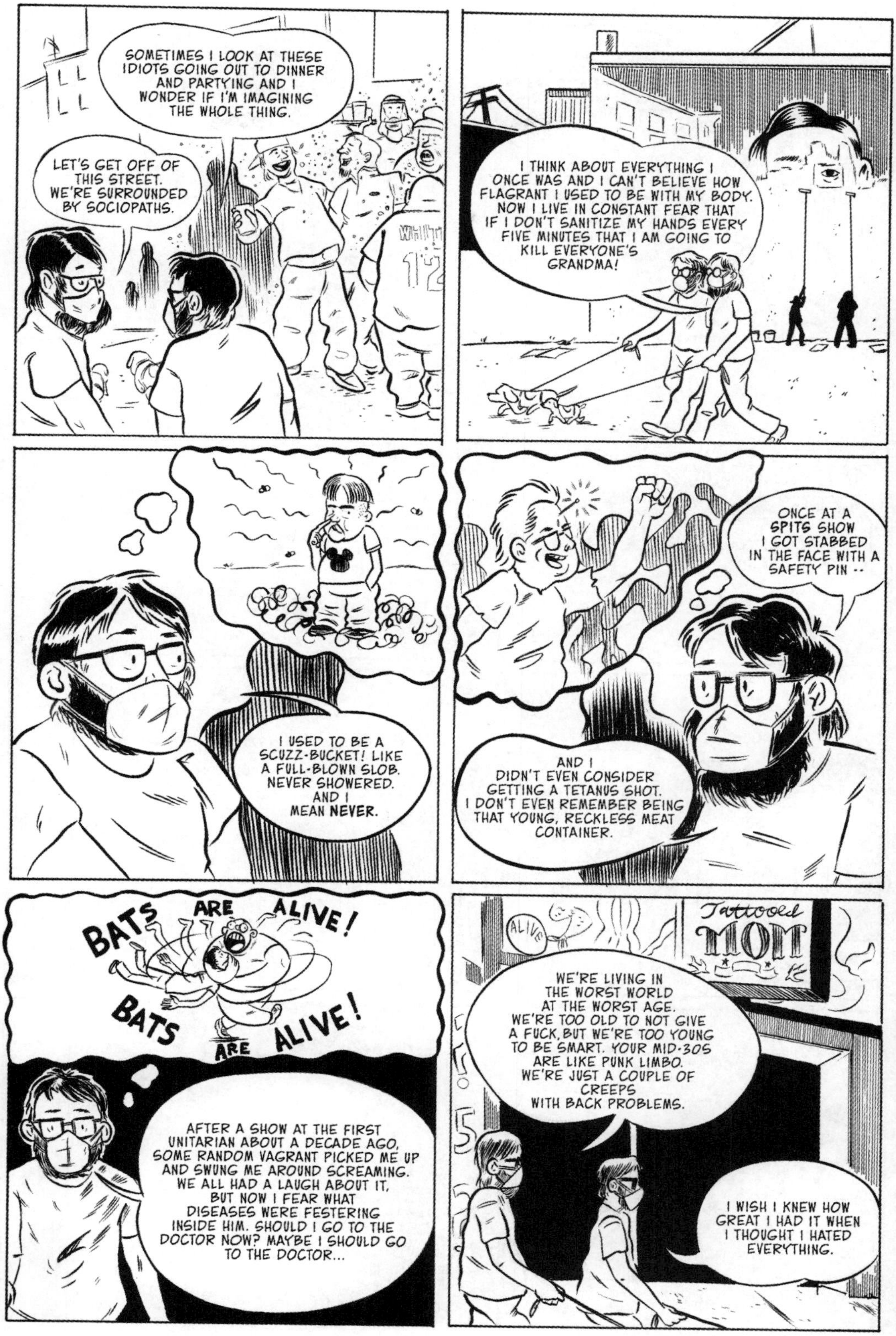
SOMETIMES I LOOK AT THESE IDIOTS GOING OUT TO DINNER AND PARTYING AND I WONDER IF I'M IMAGINING THE WHOLE THING.
LET'S GET OFF OF THIS STREET. WE'RE SURROUNDED BY SOCIOPATHS.
I THINK ABOUT EVERYTHING I ONCE WAS AND I CAN'T BELIEVE HOW FLAGRANT I USED TO BE WITH MY BODY. NOW I LIVE IN CONSTANT FEAR THAT IF I DON'T SANITIZE MY HANDS EVERY FIVE MINUTES THAT I AM GOING TO KILL EVERYONE'S GRANDMA!
I USED TO BE A SCUZZ-BUCKET! LIKE A FULL-BLOWN SLOB. NEVER SHOWERED. AND I MEAN NEVER.
ONCE AT A SPITS SHOW I GOT STABBED IN THE FACE WITH A SAFETY PIN --
AND I DIDN'T EVEN CONSIDER GETTING A TETANUS SHOT. I DON'T EVEN REMEMBER BEING THAT YOUNG, RECKLESS MEAT CONTAINER.
BATS ARE ALIVE! BATS ARE ALIVE!
AFTER A SHOW AT THE FIRST UNITARIAN ABOUT A DECADE AGO, SOME RANDOM VAGRANT PICKED ME UP AND SWUNG ME AROUND SCREAMING. WE ALL HAD A LAUGH ABOUT IT, BUT NOW I FEAR WHAT DISEASES WERE FESTERING INSIDE HIM. SHOULD I GO TO THE DOCTOR NOW? MAYBE I SHOULD GO TO THE DOCTOR...
ALIVE
Tattooed MOM
WE'RE LIVING IN THE WORST WORLD AT THE WORST AGE. WE'RE TOO OLD TO NOT GIVE A FUCK, BUT WE'RE TOO YOUNG TO BE SMART. YOUR MID-30S ARE LIKE PUNK LIMBO. WE'RE JUST A COUPLE OF CREEPS WITH BACK PROBLEMS.
I WISH I KNEW HOW GREAT I HAD IT WHEN I THOUGHT I HATED EVERYTHING.

THE BULLSHIT OF THIS PANDEMIC HAS HAD ME REFLECTING A LOT ABOUT THE RISE AND FALL OF MY PUNK YEARS, YA KNOW?

IT WAS THE FIRST DAY OF 7TH GRADE WHEN I BEFRIENDED DAN AND JOE. THEY WERE UNLIKE ANYONE I EVER KNEW BEFORE. FOR WHATEVER REASON, THEY LIKED ME. PROBABLY BECAUSE I WAS SO AWKWARD AND SELF-DEPRECATING THAT I MADE THEM LAUGH. WE HAD SOME MUSIC IN COMMON, BUT MOST I HADN'T HEARD OF.

FX Punk in drublic NOFX Punk in drublic N
RANCID ... and out come the wolves
Dude Ranch Blink 182 I
FUGAZI · 13 SONGS   DISCHORD 36

THANKS, BUT I DON'T HAVE A CD PLAYER.

OK, FRED FLINTSTONE.

MY PARENTS WOULDN'T BUY ME ONE, SO I USED THE RECENTLY INSTALLED COMPUTER'S CD-ROM DRIVE TO LISTEN.

SOMETHING CHANGED THAT DAY. I KNEW WHAT I WANTED TO BE: A PUNK.

THE ENERGY, THE LOOK. THEY LOOKED HOW I FELT. LIKE AN OUTSIDER, BUT THEY HAD THE COURAGE TO SHOUT ABOUT IT.

EVENTUALLY I GOT A DISCMAN FOR MY BIRTHDAY. THEN I SPENT ALL MY ALLOWANCE AND LAWN CUTTING MONEY ON MUSIC.

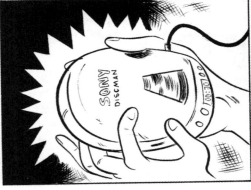

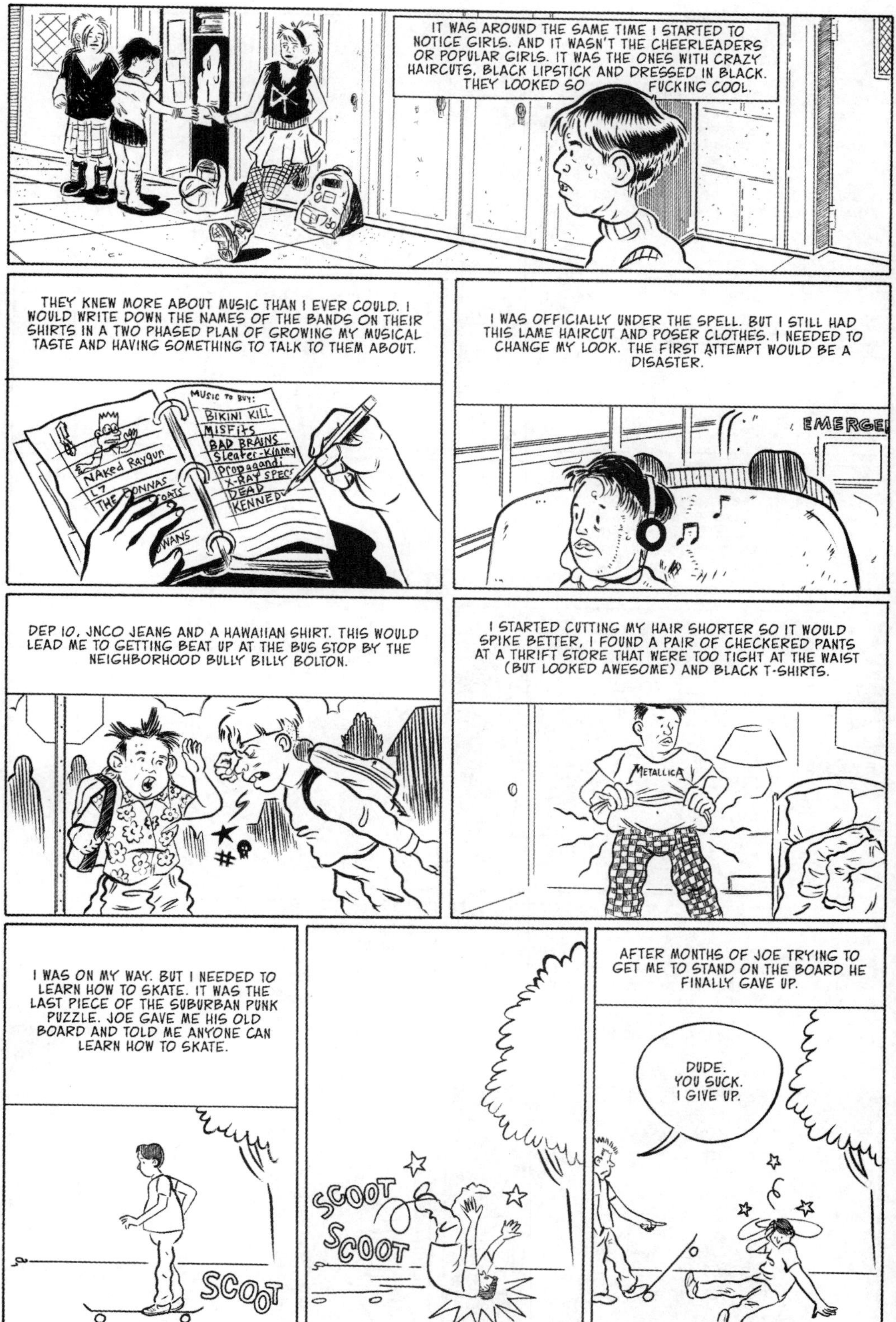

IT WAS AROUND THE SAME TIME I STARTED TO NOTICE GIRLS. AND IT WASN'T THE CHEERLEADERS OR POPULAR GIRLS. IT WAS THE ONES WITH CRAZY HAIRCUTS, BLACK LIPSTICK AND DRESSED IN BLACK. THEY LOOKED SO FUCKING COOL.
THEY KNEW MORE ABOUT MUSIC THAN I EVER COULD. I WOULD WRITE DOWN THE NAMES OF THE BANDS ON THEIR SHIRTS IN A TWO PHASED PLAN OF GROWING MY MUSICAL TASTE AND HAVING SOMETHING TO TALK TO THEM ABOUT.
MUSIC TO BUY:
BIKINI KILL
MISFits
BAD BRAINS
Sleater-Kinney
Propagandi
X-RAY SPECS
DEAD
KENNED
NAKed Raygun
L7
THE DONNAS
I WAS OFFICIALLY UNDER THE SPELL. BUT I STILL HAD THIS LAME HAIRCUT AND POSER CLOTHES. I NEEDED TO CHANGE MY LOOK. THE FIRST ATTEMPT WOULD BE A DISASTER.
EMERGE
DEP 10, JNCO JEANS AND A HAWAIIAN SHIRT. THIS WOULD LEAD ME TO GETTING BEAT UP AT THE BUS STOP BY THE NEIGHBORHOOD BULLY BILLY BOLTON.
I STARTED CUTTING MY HAIR SHORTER SO IT WOULD SPIKE BETTER, I FOUND A PAIR OF CHECKERED PANTS AT A THRIFT STORE THAT WERE TOO TIGHT AT THE WAIST (BUT LOOKED AWESOME) AND BLACK T-SHIRTS.
METALLICA
I WAS ON MY WAY. BUT I NEEDED TO LEARN HOW TO SKATE. IT WAS THE LAST PIECE OF THE SUBURBAN PUNK PUZZLE. JOE GAVE ME HIS OLD BOARD AND TOLD ME ANYONE CAN LEARN HOW TO SKATE.
SCOOT
SCOOT
SCOOT
AFTER MONTHS OF JOE TRYING TO GET ME TO STAND ON THE BOARD HE FINALLY GAVE UP.
DUDE. YOU SUCK. I GIVE UP.

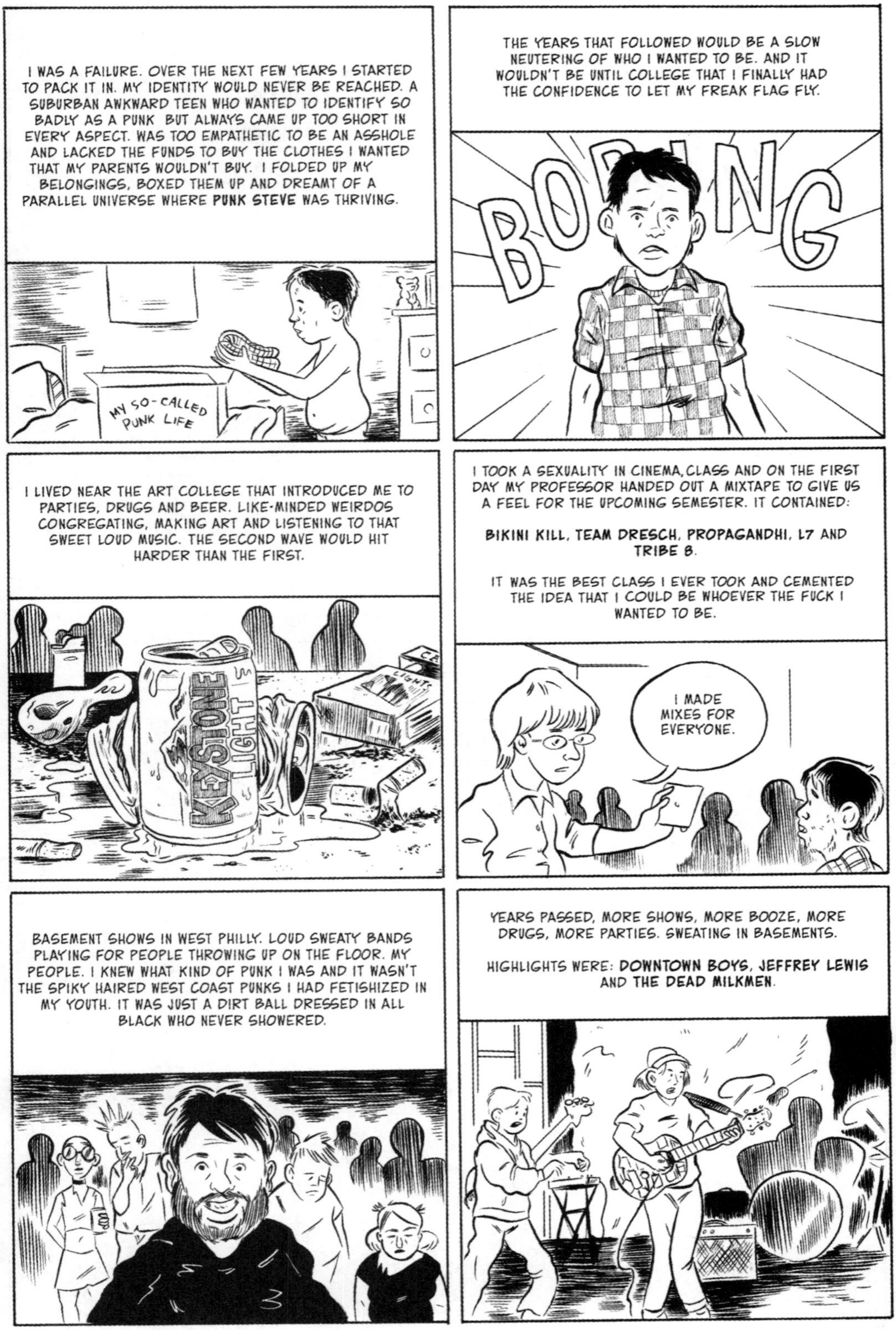
I WAS A FAILURE. OVER THE NEXT FEW YEARS I STARTED TO PACK IT IN. MY IDENTITY WOULD NEVER BE REACHED. A SUBURBAN AWKWARD TEEN WHO WANTED TO IDENTIFY SO BADLY AS A PUNK BUT ALWAYS CAME UP TOO SHORT IN EVERY ASPECT. WAS TOO EMPATHETIC TO BE AN ASSHOLE AND LACKED THE FUNDS TO BUY THE CLOTHES I WANTED THAT MY PARENTS WOULDN'T BUY. I FOLDED UP MY BELONGINGS, BOXED THEM UP AND DREAMT OF A PARALLEL UNIVERSE WHERE **PUNK STEVE** WAS THRIVING.
MY SO-CALLED PUNK LIFE
THE YEARS THAT FOLLOWED WOULD BE A SLOW NEUTERING OF WHO I WANTED TO BE. AND IT WOULDN'T BE UNTIL COLLEGE THAT I FINALLY HAD THE CONFIDENCE TO LET MY FREAK FLAG FLY.
I LIVED NEAR THE ART COLLEGE THAT INTRODUCED ME TO PARTIES, DRUGS AND BEER. LIKE-MINDED WEIRDOS CONGREGATING, MAKING ART AND LISTENING TO THAT SWEET LOUD MUSIC. THE SECOND WAVE WOULD HIT HARDER THAN THE FIRST.
KEYSTONE LIGHT
I TOOK A SEXUALITY IN CINEMA, CLASS AND ON THE FIRST DAY MY PROFESSOR HANDED OUT A MIXTAPE TO GIVE US A FEEL FOR THE UPCOMING SEMESTER. IT CONTAINED:
BIKINI KILL, **TEAM DRESCH**, **PROPAGANDHI**, **L7** AND **TRIBE 8**.
IT WAS THE BEST CLASS I EVER TOOK AND CEMENTED THE IDEA THAT I COULD BE WHOEVER THE FUCK I WANTED TO BE.
I MADE MIXES FOR EVERYONE.
BASEMENT SHOWS IN WEST PHILLY. LOUD SWEATY BANDS PLAYING FOR PEOPLE THROWING UP ON THE FLOOR. MY PEOPLE. I KNEW WHAT KIND OF PUNK I WAS AND IT WASN'T THE SPIKY HAIRED WEST COAST PUNKS I HAD FETISHIZED IN MY YOUTH. IT WAS JUST A DIRT BALL DRESSED IN ALL BLACK WHO NEVER SHOWERED.
YEARS PASSED, MORE SHOWS, MORE BOOZE, MORE DRUGS, MORE PARTIES. SWEATING IN BASEMENTS.
HIGHLIGHTS WERE: **DOWNTOWN BOYS**, **JEFFREY LEWIS** AND **THE DEAD MILKMEN**.

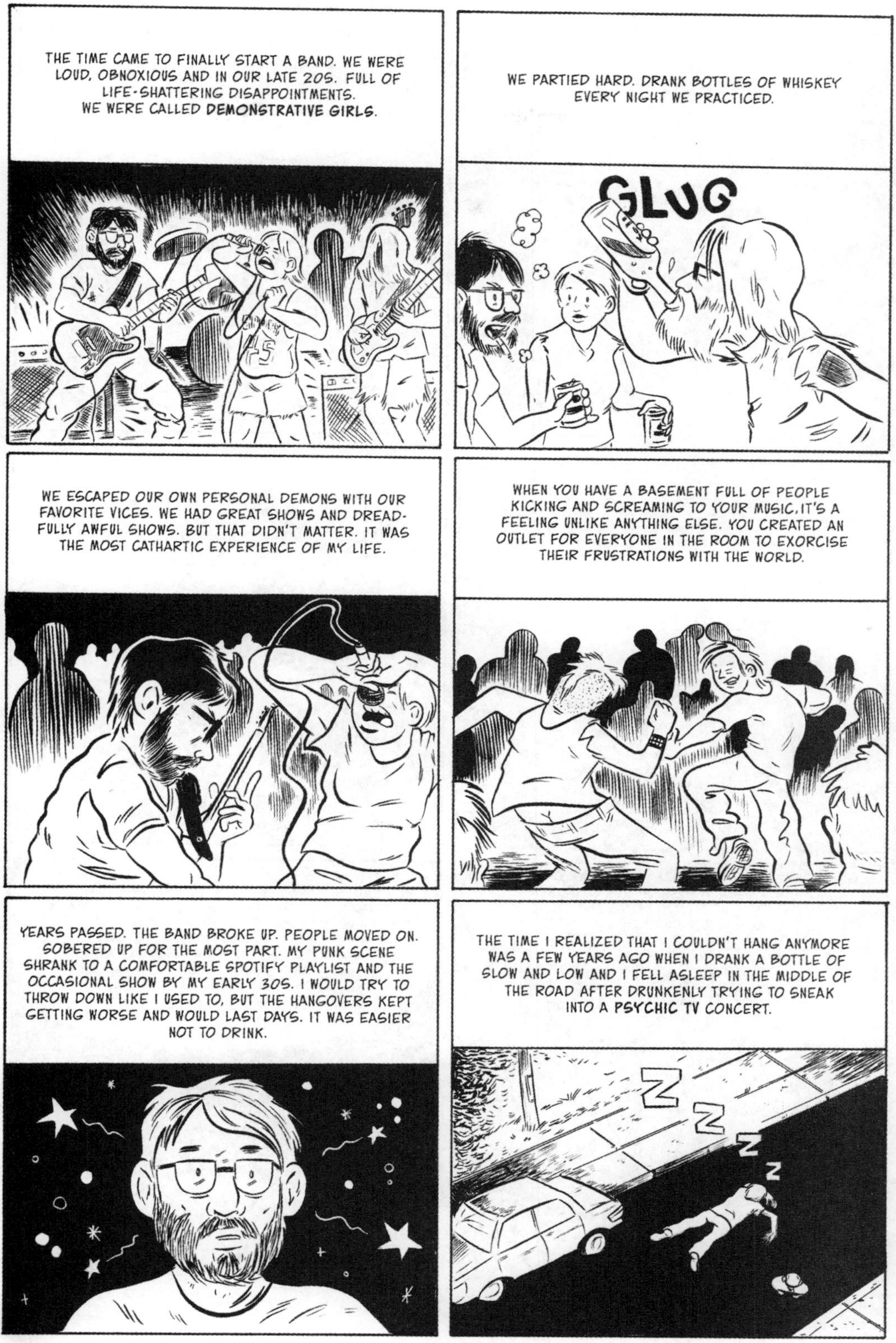
THE TIME CAME TO FINALLY START A BAND. WE WERE LOUD, OBNOXIOUS AND IN OUR LATE 20S. FULL OF LIFE-SHATTERING DISAPPOINTMENTS. WE WERE CALLED **DEMONSTRATIVE GIRLS**.
WE PARTIED HARD. DRANK BOTTLES OF WHISKEY EVERY NIGHT WE PRACTICED.
GLUG
WE ESCAPED OUR OWN PERSONAL DEMONS WITH OUR FAVORITE VICES. WE HAD GREAT SHOWS AND DREAD-FULLY AWFUL SHOWS. BUT THAT DIDN'T MATTER. IT WAS THE MOST CATHARTIC EXPERIENCE OF MY LIFE.
WHEN YOU HAVE A BASEMENT FULL OF PEOPLE KICKING AND SCREAMING TO YOUR MUSIC, IT'S A FEELING UNLIKE ANYTHING ELSE. YOU CREATED AN OUTLET FOR EVERYONE IN THE ROOM TO EXORCISE THEIR FRUSTRATIONS WITH THE WORLD.
YEARS PASSED. THE BAND BROKE UP. PEOPLE MOVED ON. SOBERED UP FOR THE MOST PART. MY PUNK SCENE SHRANK TO A COMFORTABLE SPOTIFY PLAYLIST AND THE OCCASIONAL SHOW BY MY EARLY 30S. I WOULD TRY TO THROW DOWN LIKE I USED TO, BUT THE HANGOVERS KEPT GETTING WORSE AND WOULD LAST DAYS. IT WAS EASIER NOT TO DRINK.
THE TIME I REALIZED THAT I COULDN'T HANG ANYMORE WAS A FEW YEARS AGO WHEN I DRANK A BOTTLE OF SLOW AND LOW AND I FELL ASLEEP IN THE MIDDLE OF THE ROAD AFTER DRUNKENLY TRYING TO SNEAK INTO A **PSYCHIC TV** CONCERT.
Z Z Z Z

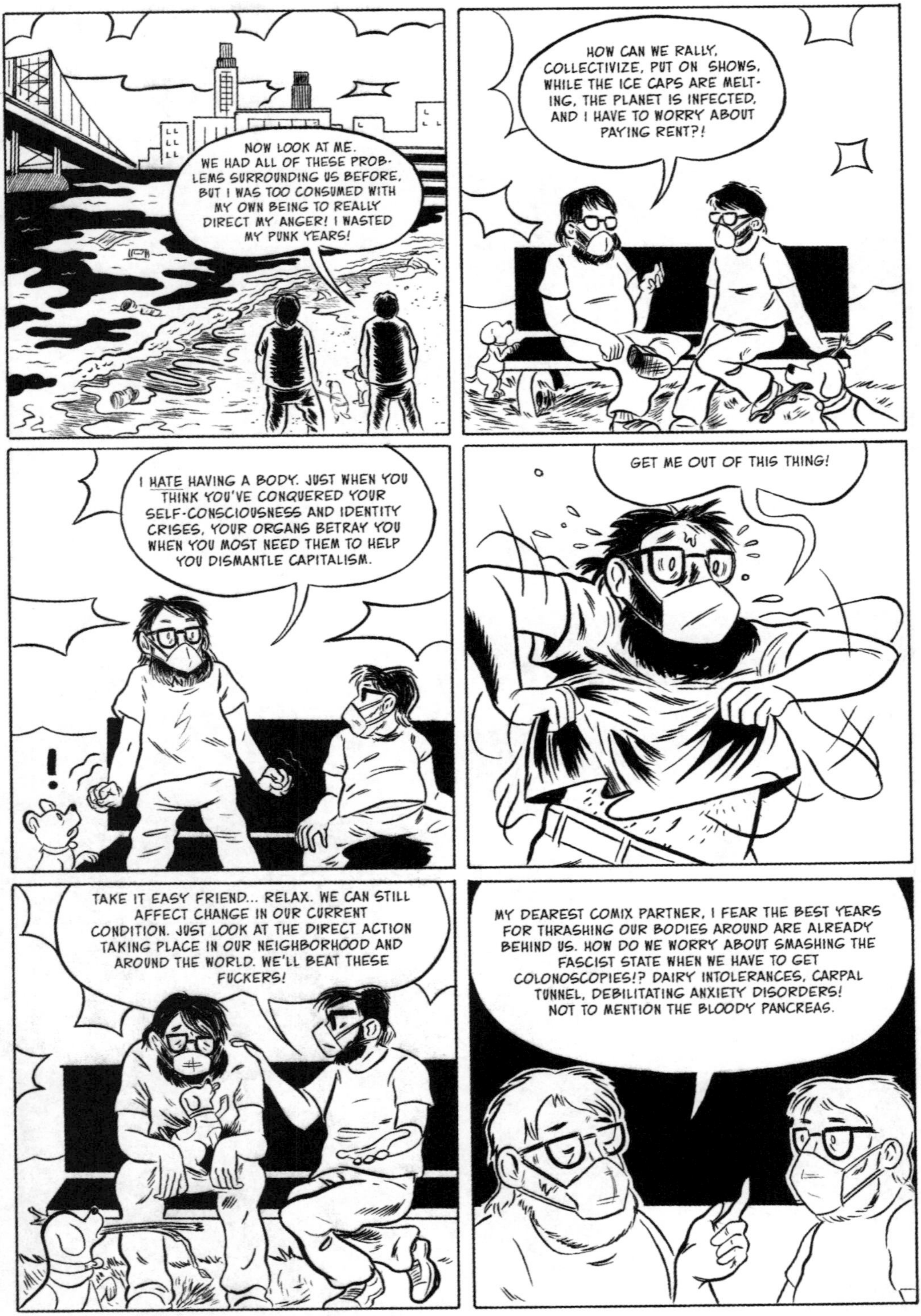
NOW LOOK AT ME. WE HAD ALL OF THESE PROBLEMS SURROUNDING US BEFORE, BUT I WAS TOO CONSUMED WITH MY OWN BEING TO REALLY DIRECT MY ANGER! I WASTED MY PUNK YEARS!
HOW CAN WE RALLY, COLLECTIVIZE, PUT ON SHOWS, WHILE THE ICE CAPS ARE MELTING, THE PLANET IS INFECTED, AND I HAVE TO WORRY ABOUT PAYING RENT?!
I HATE HAVING A BODY. JUST WHEN YOU THINK YOU'VE CONQUERED YOUR SELF-CONSCIOUSNESS AND IDENTITY CRISES, YOUR ORGANS BETRAY YOU WHEN YOU MOST NEED THEM TO HELP YOU DISMANTLE CAPITALISM.
!
GET ME OUT OF THIS THING!
TAKE IT EASY FRIEND... RELAX. WE CAN STILL AFFECT CHANGE IN OUR CURRENT CONDITION. JUST LOOK AT THE DIRECT ACTION TAKING PLACE IN OUR NEIGHBORHOOD AND AROUND THE WORLD. WE'LL BEAT THESE FUCKERS!
MY DEAREST COMIX PARTNER, I FEAR THE BEST YEARS FOR THRASHING OUR BODIES AROUND ARE ALREADY BEHIND US. HOW DO WE WORRY ABOUT SMASHING THE FASCIST STATE WHEN WE HAVE TO GET COLONOSCOPIES!? DAIRY INTOLERANCES, CARPAL TUNNEL, DEBILITATING ANXIETY DISORDERS! NOT TO MENTION THE BLOODY PANCREAS.

I'LL BE ANGRY WITH THAT GODDAMN ENZYME FACTORY FOR THE REST OF MY DAYS!

IT WAS THE NIGHT THE QUARANTINE WAS ANNOUNCED THAT I FELT THE PAIN.

IT WAS ALL CONSUMING, LIKE A KNIFE TWISTING FROM MY THROAT TO MY GUTS. I WAS CONVINCED THAT I WAS DYING.

I WAS A SACK OF GALLSTONES. APPARENTLY ONE OF THEM HAD LODGED ITSELF IN MY PANCREATIC DUCT AND CAUSED A VIOLENT INFLAMMATION. I WAS PUMPED FULL OF PAIN MEDS AND FLUIDS, BUT NOTHING SEEMED TO QUELL THE MENACE THAT WAS FESTERING INSIDE.

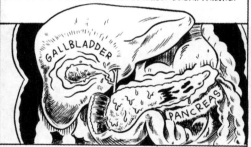

MY PANCREAS WAS NECROTIZING, WHICH IS JUST A SPED-UP WAY OF PUMMELING ME TOWARDS THE INEVITABILITY THAT ALL OF OUR BODIES MUST EXPERIENCE: ORGAN FAILURE.

GALLBLADDER

PANCREAS

I WAS KEPT ON A STEADY SUPPLY OF DILAUDID, WHICH IS LIKE MORPHINE ON SPEED. I WAS BLOATED WITH 60LBS OF WATER WEIGHT. WITH EVERY INCREASING DOSE I BECAME MORE DELUSIONAL AND PARANOID, BUT ENTIRELY INCAPACITATED.

I WAS CONVINCED THAT THE HOSPITAL STAFF WERE CONSPIRING AGAINST ME.

PLEASE, HELP ME. GET ME OUT OF HERE. ARE YOU IN ON IT TOO??

THEN I WENT SEPTIC.

BY APRIL, I HAD FIVE SURGERIES TO SCRAPE THE DEAD TISSUE FROM INSIDE MY PANCREAS.

IN MAY, I WAS UP TO 10.

WHAT'S WORSE, BECAUSE OF COVID I WAS UNABLE TO HAVE ANY VISITORS, SO I WAS TRAPPED IN THIS CRONENBERGIAN HELLSCAPE WITH LEAKING WOUNDS, COVERED IN MY OWN FILTH, AND I NEVER FELT THE COMFORT OF ANOTHER HUMAN.

OCCASIONALLY TESS WOULD SNEAK INTO MY ROOM DURING HER LUNCH BREAKS, BUT WAS QUICKLY ESCORTED OUT BY OTHER NURSES. WE WERE ALL HELD CAPTIVE BY OUR FEAR OF EACH OTHER'S BODIES. THE INVISIBLE TERROR HAUNTED THAT BLEACH-SCENTED PRISON.

PLEASE! TAKE ME WITH YOU! I WANT TO BE HOME WITH YOU!

MY ENTIRE WORLD WAS CONSUMED WITH CONSTANT EXISTENTIAL PANIC, BUT I WAS COMPLETELY HELPLESS IN MY DEGENERATING LIVING CORPSE. YOU KNOW THAT HOSPITAL SCENE IN *JACOB'S LADDER*? IT WAS LIKE THAT, BUT I NEVER WOKE UP.

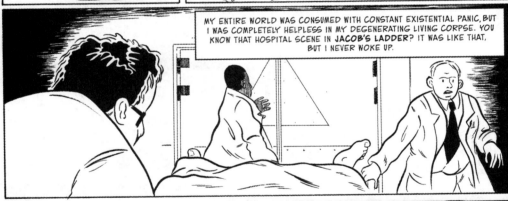

THE ONLY TIME I EVER FELT A SOOTHING HAND WAS DURING THE TIME I SPENT IN THE ICU WHEN MY NURSE COMFORTED ME WHILE THEY DRAINED THE TOXIC FLUID THAT WAS SURROUNDING MY LUNGS. IT WAS A BLISSFUL REPRIEVE AMONG AN APOCALYPTIC NIGHTMARE.

I'VE SINCE FORGOTTEN HER NAME AND FACE, BUT WHEREVER SHE IS OUT THERE I HOPE SHE UNDERSTANDS THE MAGNITUDE OF THAT FLEETING MOMENT OF HUMAN CONNECTION THAT I WILL REMEMBER TILL I'M COVERED IN DIRT.

ON MAY 25TH, AS I WAS FINALLY GAINING ENOUGH STRENGTH TO STAND, YET ANOTHER BLACK MAN WAS MURDERED BY THE VENOMOUS POLICE IN THIS WORLD POLLUTED BY HATRED AND SYSTEMIC GENOCIDE.

YOU WOULD THINK IN A TIME WHERE ALL HUMANS ARE UNANIMOUSLY SUFFERING FROM A PARALYZING ILLNESS THAT WAS RAPIDLY DESTROYING OUR COMMUNITIES THAT WE COULD UNITE TO PUT AN END TO THESE COUNTLESS TRAGEDIES AT THE HANDS OF BLOODTHIRSTY COPS. BUT THAT WAS NOT THE CASE. BIGOTRY HAD PREVAILED. THE CANCER OF RACISM WAS STILL THE MOST DANGEROUS PANDEMIC PLAGUING HUMANITY.

THAT NIGHT, I COULD FEEL THE STREETS OF THE CITY BUZZING WITH BOILED-OVER FRUSTRATION AND HOPELESSNESS.

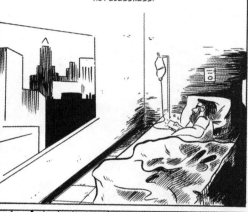

DESPITE MY IMPROVING HEALTH, THOSE NIGHTS WERE THE MOST DEVASTATING.

FOR DAYS, I WATCHED THE COLLECTIVE FIGHT AGAINST STATE-FUNDED SLAUGHTER PLAY OUT IN FRONT OF MY WINDOW.

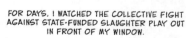

I WANT TO GO OUTSIDE. I NEED TO BE WITH PEOPLE.

WHAT YOU NEED IS REST! YOU DON'T WANT TO GO OUT THERE WITH ALL THAT CRAZINESS.

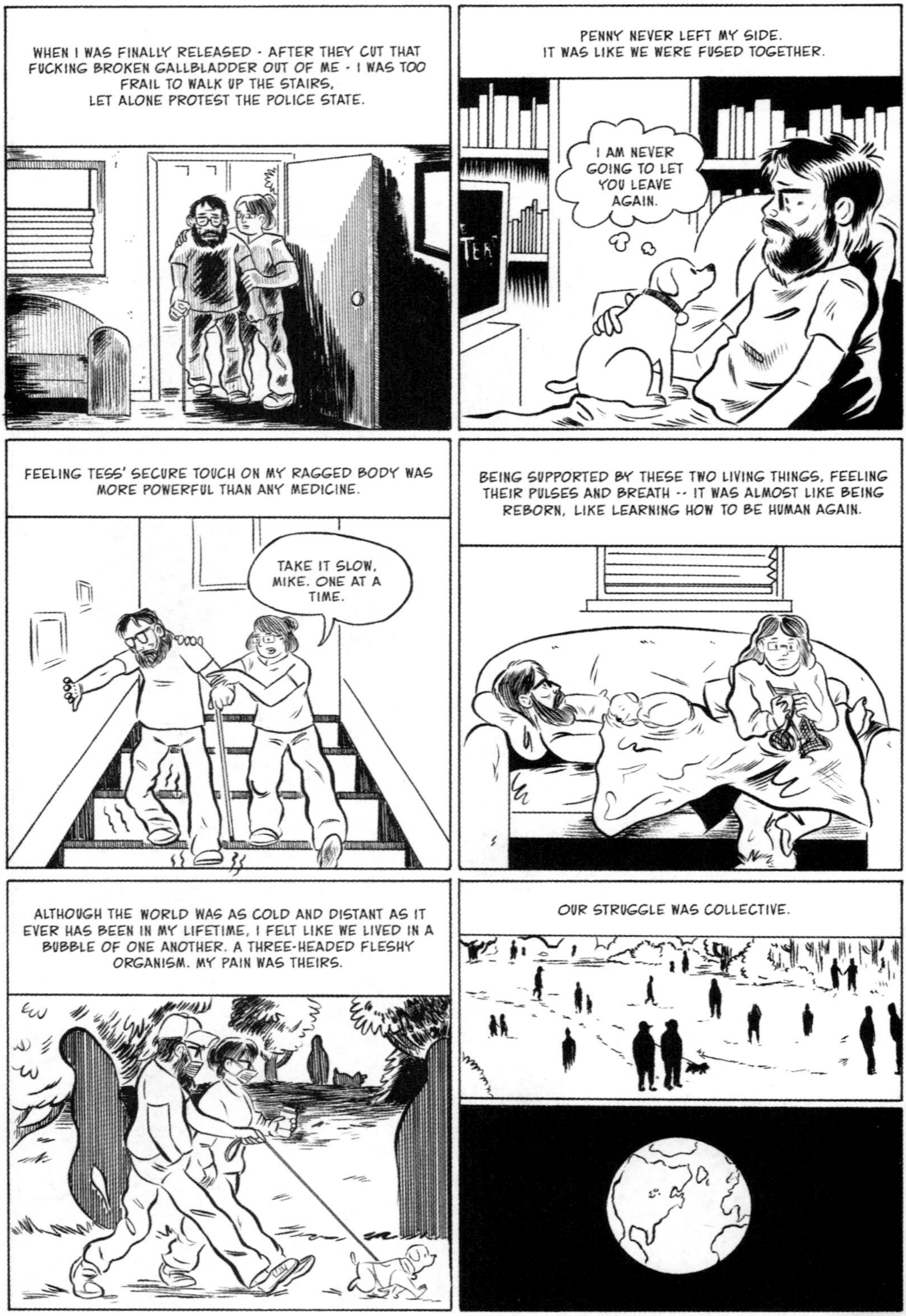
WHEN I WAS FINALLY RELEASED - AFTER THEY CUT THAT FUCKING BROKEN GALLBLADDER OUT OF ME - I WAS TOO FRAIL TO WALK UP THE STAIRS, LET ALONE PROTEST THE POLICE STATE.
PENNY NEVER LEFT MY SIDE. IT WAS LIKE WE WERE FUSED TOGETHER.
I AM NEVER GOING TO LET YOU LEAVE AGAIN.
FEELING TESS' SECURE TOUCH ON MY RAGGED BODY WAS MORE POWERFUL THAN ANY MEDICINE.
TAKE IT SLOW, MIKE. ONE AT A TIME.
BEING SUPPORTED BY THESE TWO LIVING THINGS, FEELING THEIR PULSES AND BREATH -- IT WAS ALMOST LIKE BEING REBORN, LIKE LEARNING HOW TO BE HUMAN AGAIN.
ALTHOUGH THE WORLD WAS AS COLD AND DISTANT AS IT EVER HAS BEEN IN MY LIFETIME, I FELT LIKE WE LIVED IN A BUBBLE OF ONE ANOTHER. A THREE-HEADED FLESHY ORGANISM. MY PAIN WAS THEIRS.
OUR STRUGGLE WAS COLLECTIVE.

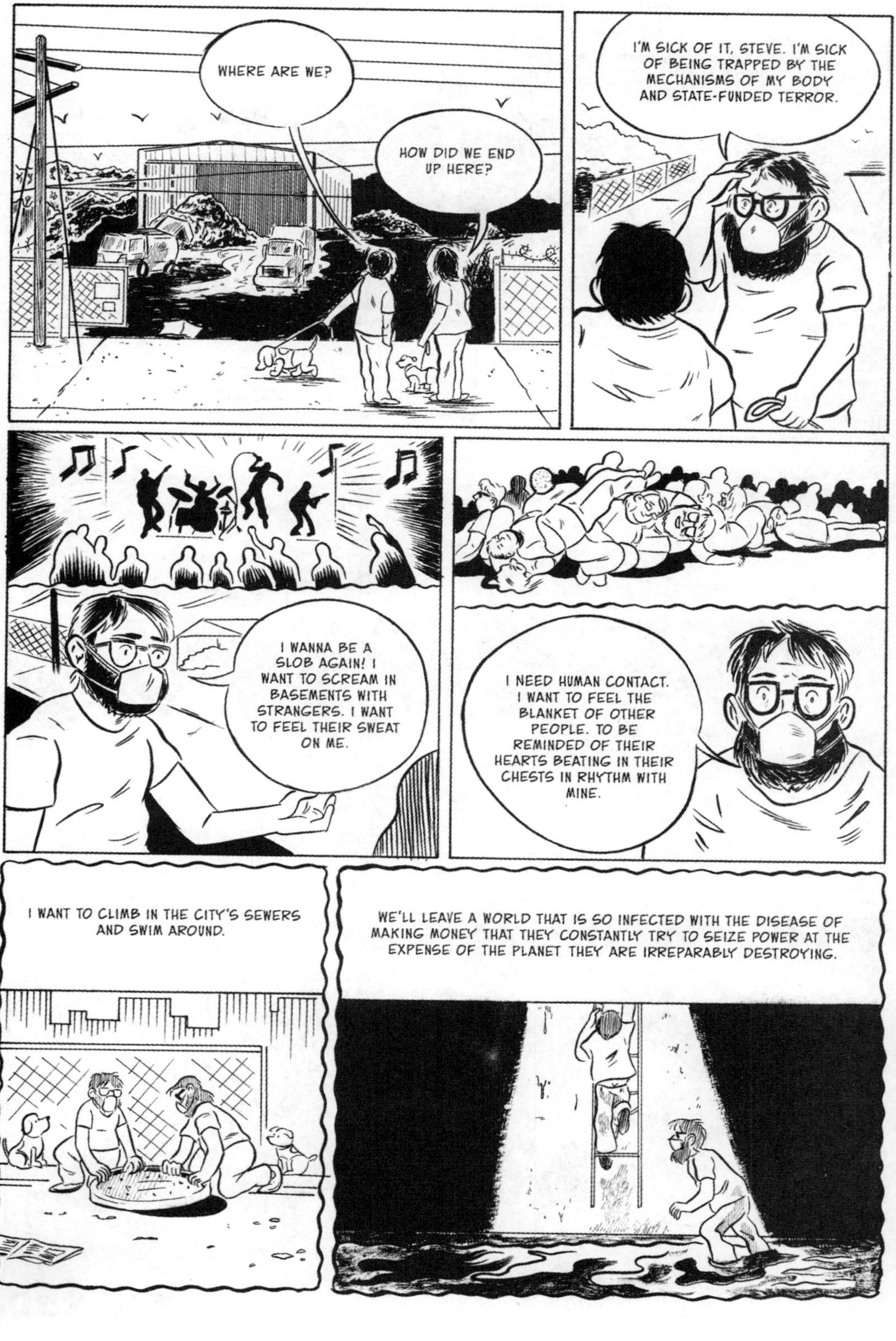
WHERE ARE WE?
HOW DID WE END UP HERE?
I'M SICK OF IT, STEVE. I'M SICK OF BEING TRAPPED BY THE MECHANISMS OF MY BODY AND STATE-FUNDED TERROR.
I WANNA BE A SLOB AGAIN! I WANT TO SCREAM IN BASEMENTS WITH STRANGERS. I WANT TO FEEL THEIR SWEAT ON ME.
I NEED HUMAN CONTACT. I WANT TO FEEL THE BLANKET OF OTHER PEOPLE. TO BE REMINDED OF THEIR HEARTS BEATING IN THEIR CHESTS IN RHYTHM WITH MINE.
I WANT TO CLIMB IN THE CITY'S SEWERS AND SWIM AROUND.
WE'LL LEAVE A WORLD THAT IS SO INFECTED WITH THE DISEASE OF MAKING MONEY THAT THEY CONSTANTLY TRY TO SEIZE POWER AT THE EXPENSE OF THE PLANET THEY ARE IRREPARABLY DESTROYING.

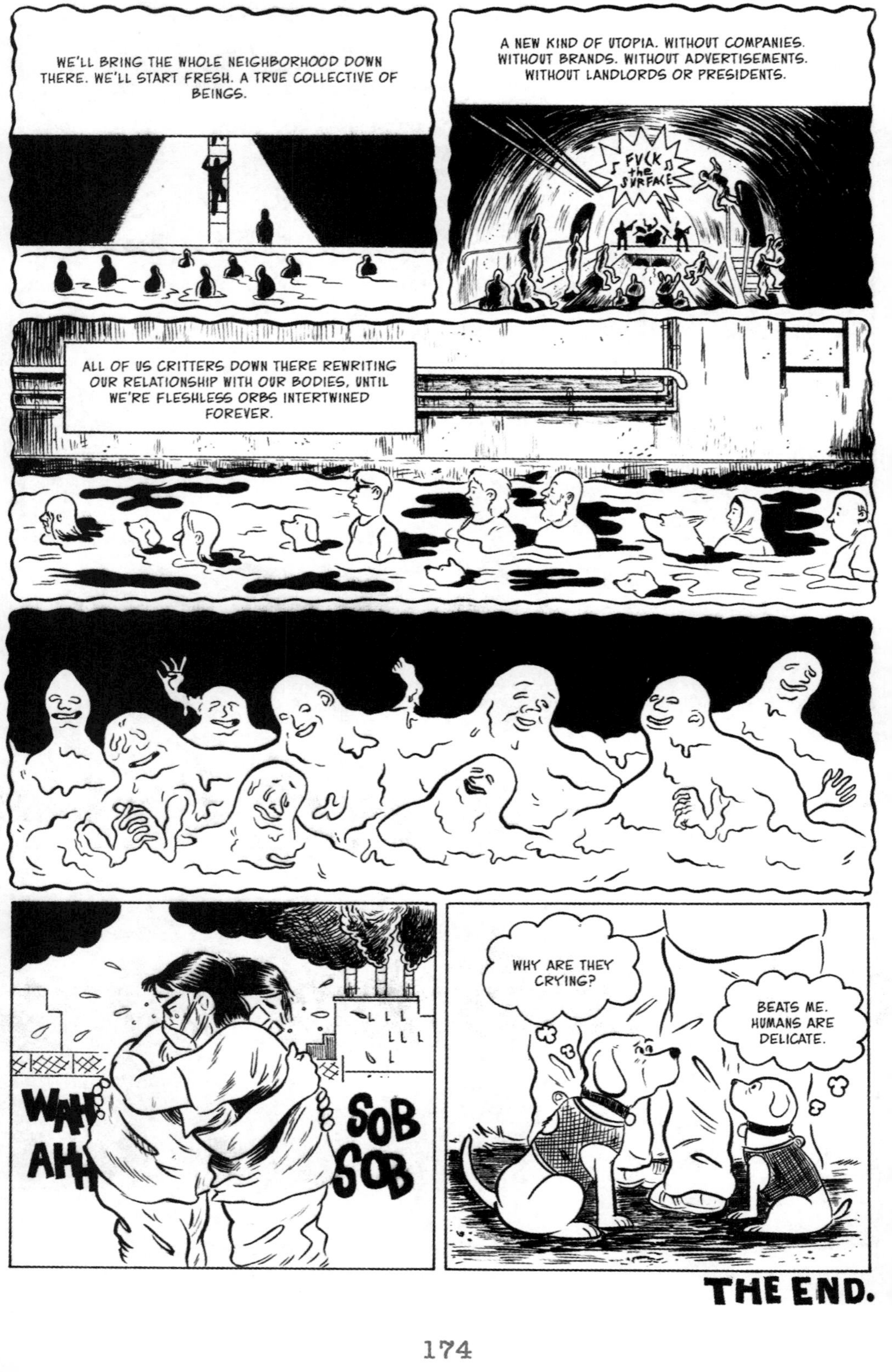
WE'LL BRING THE WHOLE NEIGHBORHOOD DOWN THERE. WE'LL START FRESH. A TRUE COLLECTIVE OF BEINGS.
A NEW KIND OF UTOPIA. WITHOUT COMPANIES. WITHOUT BRANDS. WITHOUT ADVERTISEMENTS. WITHOUT LANDLORDS OR PRESIDENTS.
FUCK the SURFACE
ALL OF US CRITTERS DOWN THERE REWRITING OUR RELATIONSHIP WITH OUR BODIES, UNTIL WE'RE FLESHLESS ORBS INTERTWINED FOREVER.
WAHH AHH
SOB SOB
WHY ARE THEY CRYING?
BEATS ME. HUMANS ARE DELICATE.

THE END.

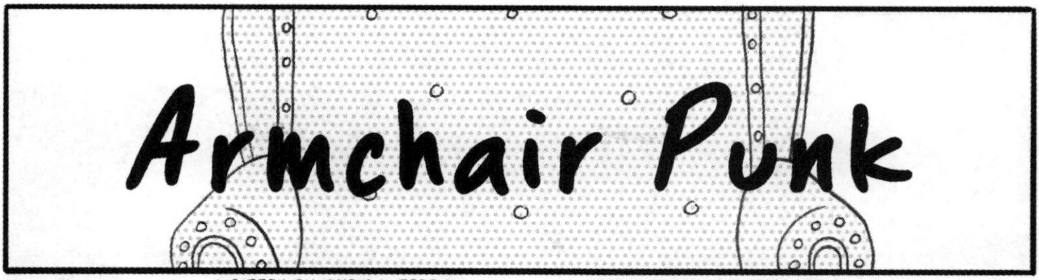
Armchair Punk

WRITTEN BY: CHRIS L. TERRY DRAWN BY: ANDREA PEARSON

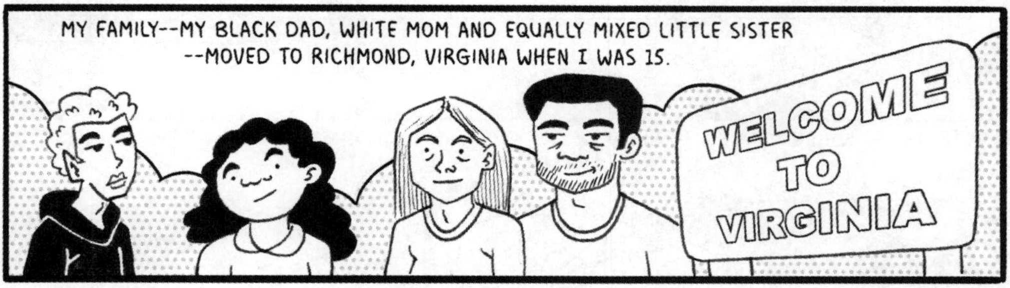
MY FAMILY--MY BLACK DAD, WHITE MOM AND EQUALLY MIXED LITTLE SISTER --MOVED TO RICHMOND, VIRGINIA WHEN I WAS 15.
WELCOME TO VIRGINIA

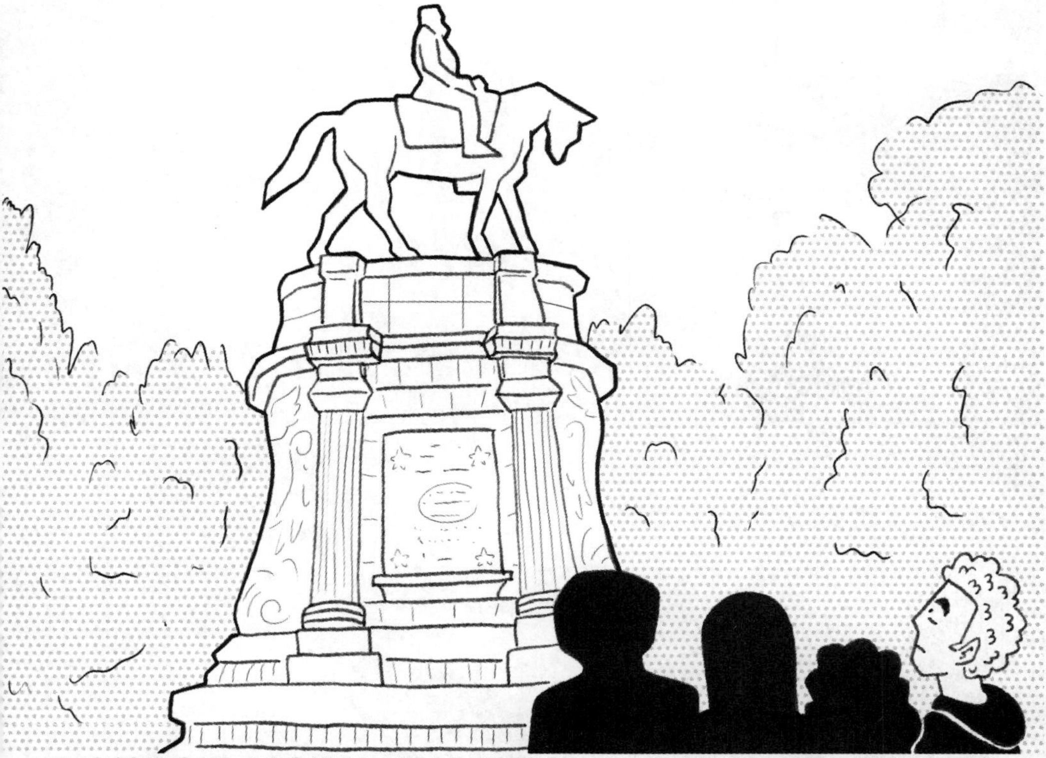

OUR APARTMENT SAT IN THE SHADOW OF A HUGE STATUE OF CONFEDERATE GENERAL ROBERT E. LEE. I COULDN'T BELIEVE THAT MY NEW CITY WAS HONORING THE WHITE MEN WHO FOUGHT TO OWN PEOPLE WHO LOOKED LIKE ME.

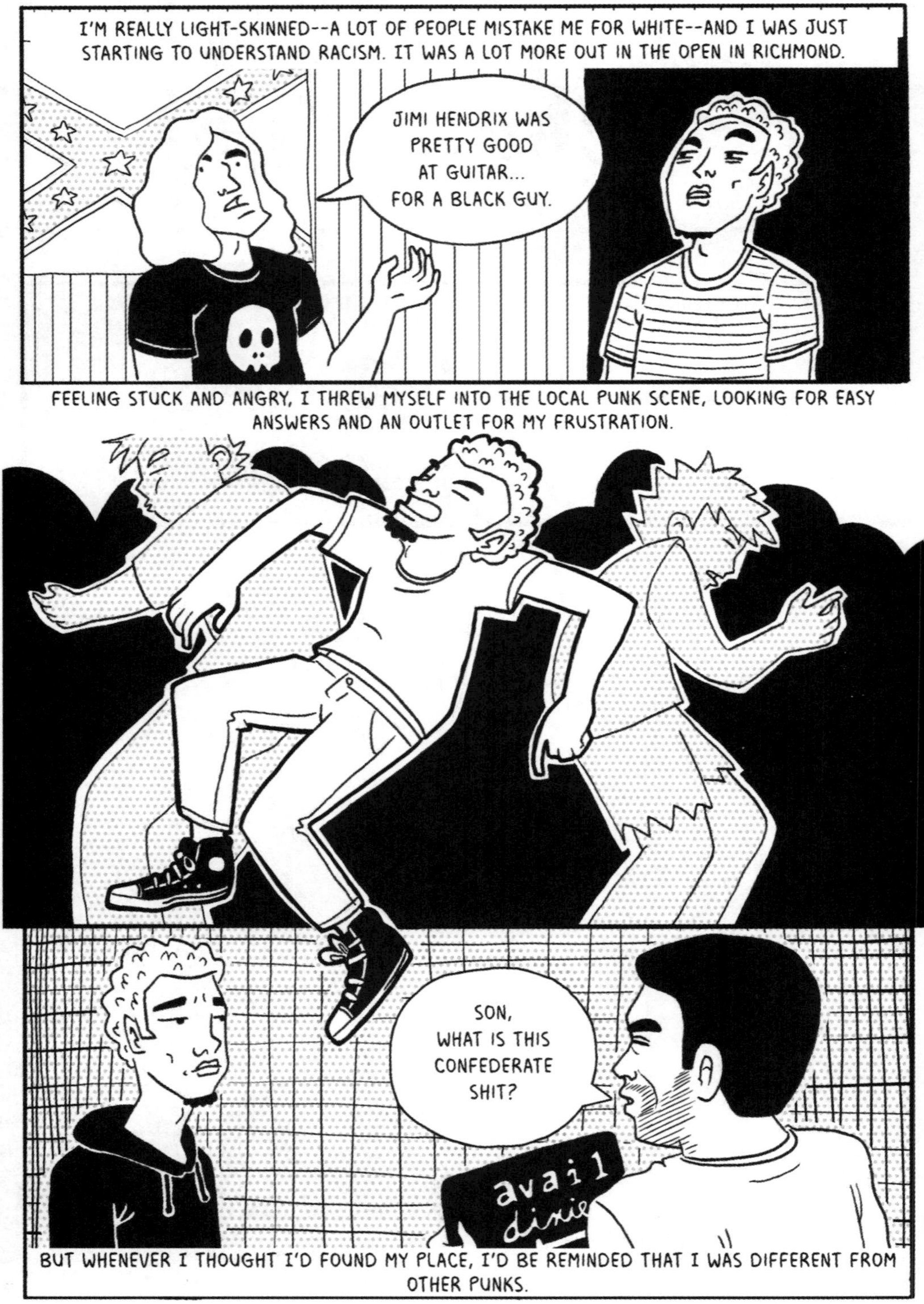
I'M REALLY LIGHT-SKINNED--A LOT OF PEOPLE MISTAKE ME FOR WHITE--AND I WAS JUST STARTING TO UNDERSTAND RACISM. IT WAS A LOT MORE OUT IN THE OPEN IN RICHMOND.
JIMI HENDRIX WAS PRETTY GOOD AT GUITAR... FOR A BLACK GUY.
FEELING STUCK AND ANGRY, I THREW MYSELF INTO THE LOCAL PUNK SCENE, LOOKING FOR EASY ANSWERS AND AN OUTLET FOR MY FRUSTRATION.
SON, WHAT IS THIS CONFEDERATE SHIT?
avail
dixie
BUT WHENEVER I THOUGHT I'D FOUND MY PLACE, I'D BE REMINDED THAT I WAS DIFFERENT FROM OTHER PUNKS.

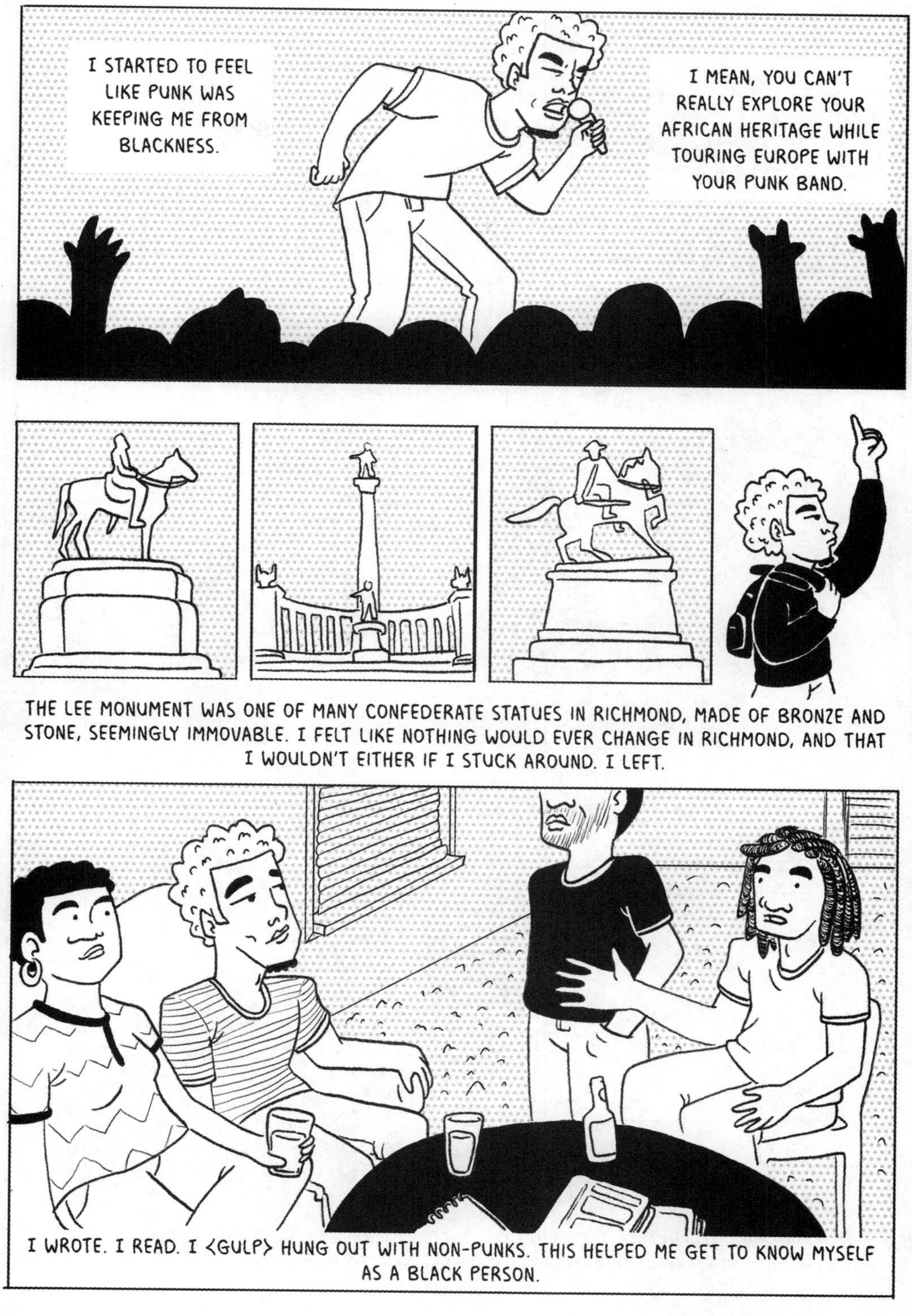
I STARTED TO FEEL LIKE PUNK WAS KEEPING ME FROM BLACKNESS.
I MEAN, YOU CAN'T REALLY EXPLORE YOUR AFRICAN HERITAGE WHILE TOURING EUROPE WITH YOUR PUNK BAND.
THE LEE MONUMENT WAS ONE OF MANY CONFEDERATE STATUES IN RICHMOND, MADE OF BRONZE AND STONE, SEEMINGLY IMMOVABLE. I FELT LIKE NOTHING WOULD EVER CHANGE IN RICHMOND, AND THAT I WOULDN'T EITHER IF I STUCK AROUND. I LEFT.
I WROTE. I READ. I <GULP> HUNG OUT WITH NON-PUNKS. THIS HELPED ME GET TO KNOW MYSELF AS A BLACK PERSON.

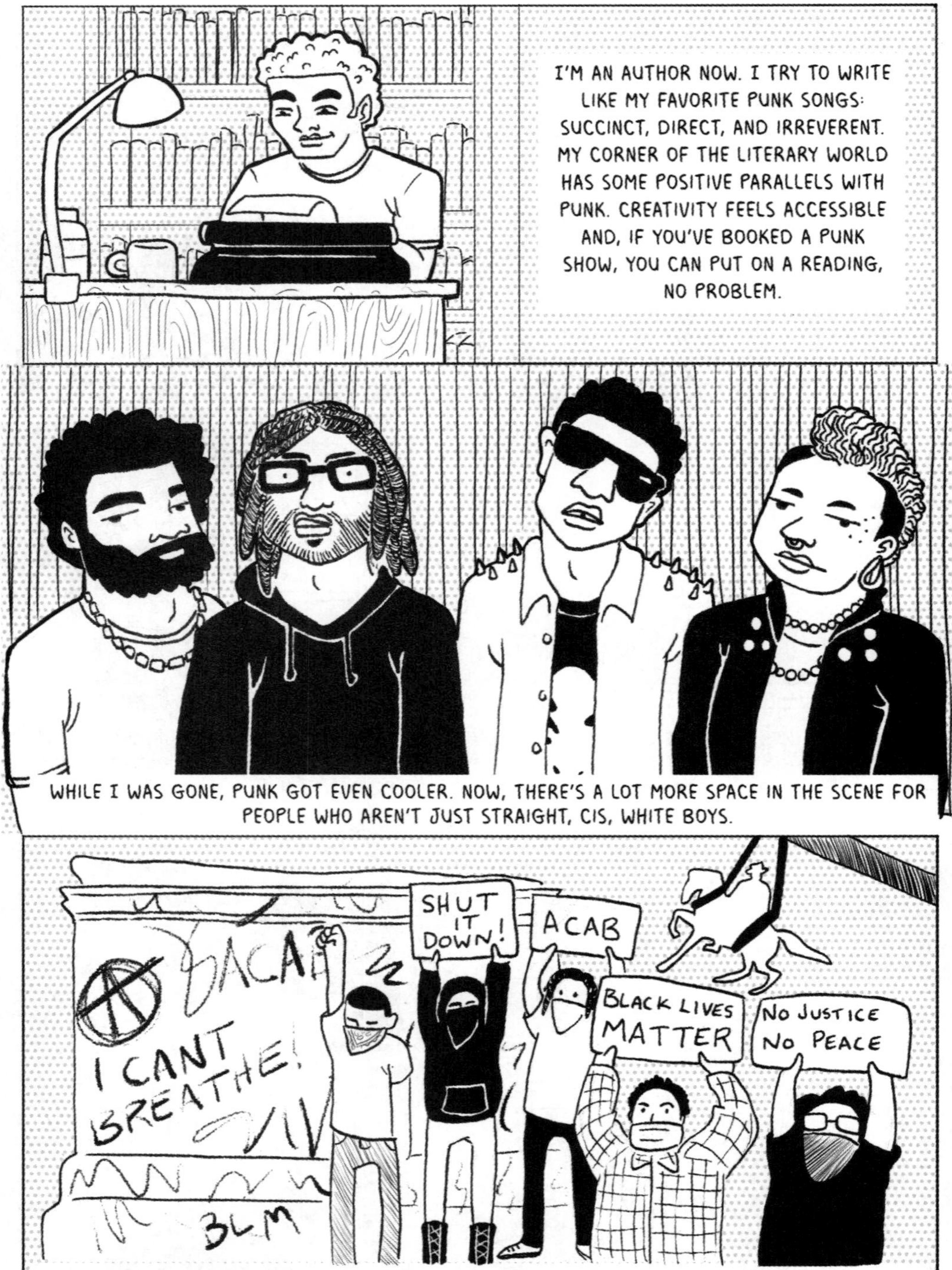
I'M AN AUTHOR NOW. I TRY TO WRITE LIKE MY FAVORITE PUNK SONGS: SUCCINCT, DIRECT, AND IRREVERENT. MY CORNER OF THE LITERARY WORLD HAS SOME POSITIVE PARALLELS WITH PUNK. CREATIVITY FEELS ACCESSIBLE AND, IF YOU'VE BOOKED A PUNK SHOW, YOU CAN PUT ON A READING, NO PROBLEM.
WHILE I WAS GONE, PUNK GOT EVEN COOLER. NOW, THERE'S A LOT MORE SPACE IN THE SCENE FOR PEOPLE WHO AREN'T JUST STRAIGHT, CIS, WHITE BOYS.
ACAB
I CANT BREATHE!
BLM
SHUT IT DOWN!
ACAB
BLACK LIVES MATTER
NO JUSTICE NO PEACE
THIS NEW GENERATION IS TEARING DOWN CONFEDERATE MONUMENTS AND THE WHITE SUPREMACIST INFRASTRUCTURE. THINGS THAT ONCE SEEMED IMMOVABLE ARE STARTING TO MOVE.

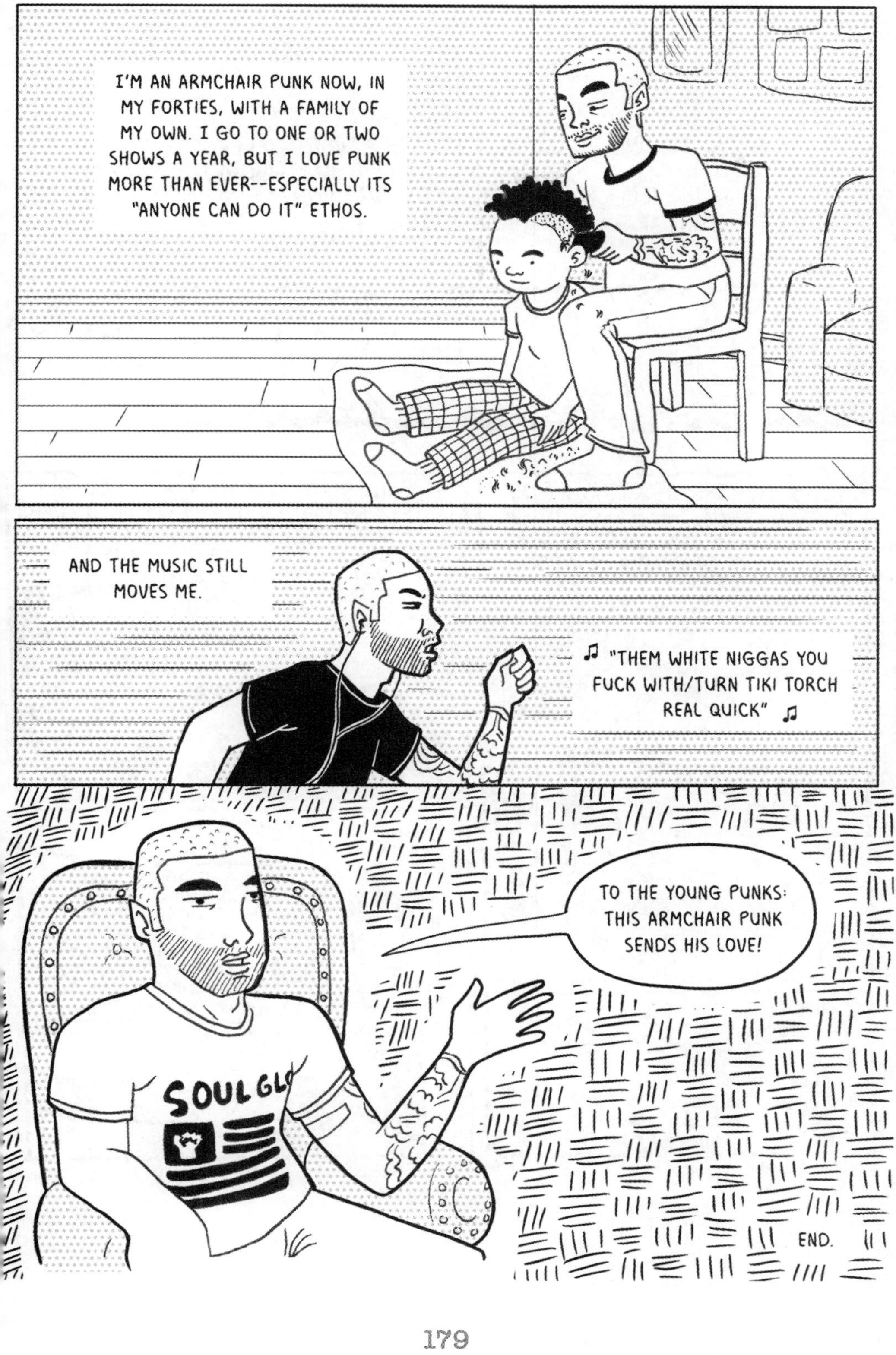
I'M AN ARMCHAIR PUNK NOW, IN MY FORTIES, WITH A FAMILY OF MY OWN. I GO TO ONE OR TWO SHOWS A YEAR, BUT I LOVE PUNK MORE THAN EVER--ESPECIALLY ITS "ANYONE CAN DO IT" ETHOS.
AND THE MUSIC STILL MOVES ME.
♫ "THEM WHITE NIGGAS YOU FUCK WITH/TURN TIKI TORCH REAL QUICK" ♫
TO THE YOUNG PUNKS: THIS ARMCHAIR PUNK SENDS HIS LOVE!
END.

BEING A TOWNIE PUNK CAN LEAVE YOU WITH A WARPED PERSPECTIVE OF TIME. ONE DAY, YOU'LL LOOK AROUND & TAKE A MENTAL INVENTORY OF HOW THINGS HAVE CHANGED & REALIZE THAT THE CIRCLE IS NOW COMPLETE. THIS IS THE TRUE STORY OF HOW I UNWITTINGLY CROSSED OVER & JOINED THE RANKS OF THE "IN MY DAY"ERS. THIS IS HOW I BECAME

OLD MAN BERKELEY*

WELCOME SISTER.
FREE LEONARD

TEENAGERS BE TEXTIN'. WE USED TO LEAVE NOTES FOR EACH OTHER IN AN OLD SHOE WE KEPT ON TOP OF THE BART STATION ELEVATOR IN DOWNTOWN BERKELEY.
MEET ME AT NEUTRON AT 5.
GUNK
MY BRIEF STINT AS A HACKER OCCURRED IN 1980 WHEN ME & MY BROTHER DISCOVERED WE COULD UNSCRAMBLE THE PLAYBOY CHANNEL BY PUSHING A 5-NUMBER SEQUENCE ON THE CABLE BOX.
DID IT WORK?
YES, HELLO. MY CHILD SWALLOWED A FUNNY PILL. IT'S ROUND & YELLOW...
MY FRIENDS WOULD COP PILLS IN THE TENDERLOIN & THEN CALL THE POISON CONTROL HOTLINE TO MAKE SURE THEY DIDN'T BUY SOMETHING THAT WOULD KILL THEM.
PHONE
I SEE... WILL HE HAVE TO GET HIS STOMACH PUMPED OR WILL HE JUST FEEL KINDA FLOATY?
WE AREN'T ON THE SAME PAGE AT KARAOKE.
YOU'RE MY WONDERWALL
YES!
HAW! HAW!
YAS KWEEN!
???

*"OLD MAN BERKELEY" COINED BY FELLOW OMB EMMA DEBONCOEUR

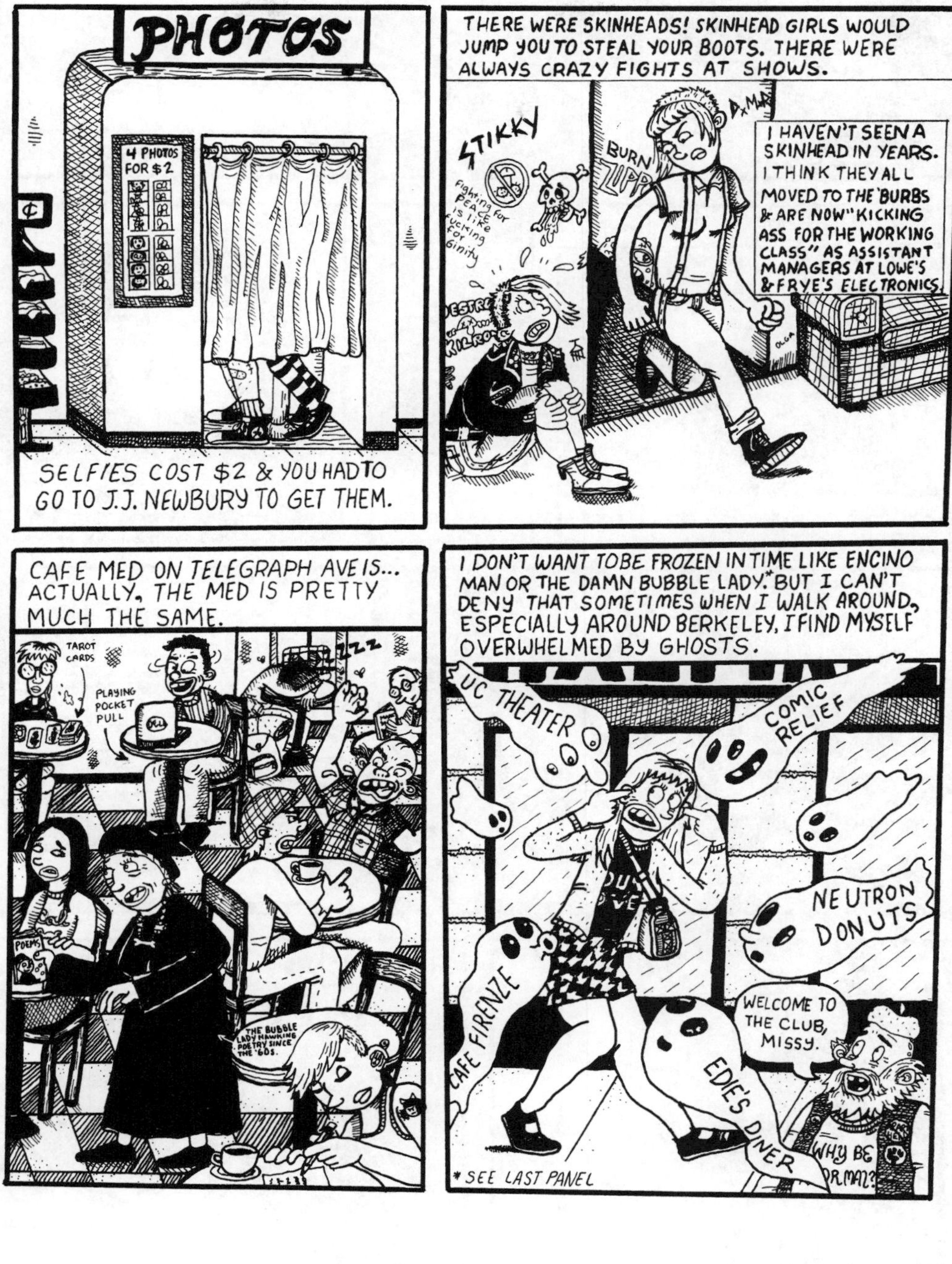
PHOTOS
4 PHOTOS FOR $2
SELFIES COST $2 & YOU HAD TO GO TO J.J. NEWBURY TO GET THEM.
THERE WERE SKINHEADS! SKINHEAD GIRLS WOULD JUMP YOU TO STEAL YOUR BOOTS. THERE WERE ALWAYS CRAZY FIGHTS AT SHOWS.
STIKKY
BURN
I HAVEN'T SEEN A SKINHEAD IN YEARS. I THINK THEY ALL MOVED TO THE 'BURBS & ARE NOW "KICKING ASS FOR THE WORKING CLASS" AS ASSISTANT MANAGERS AT LOWE'S & FRYE'S ELECTRONICS.
CAFE MED ON TELEGRAPH AVE IS... ACTUALLY, THE MED IS PRETTY MUCH THE SAME.
TAROT CARDS
PLAYING POCKET PULL
ZZZ
POEMS
THE BUBBLE LADY HAWKING POETRY SINCE THE '60S.
I DON'T WANT TO BE FROZEN IN TIME LIKE ENCINO MAN OR THE DAMN BUBBLE LADY.* BUT I CAN'T DENY THAT SOMETIMES WHEN I WALK AROUND, ESPECIALLY AROUND BERKELEY, I FIND MYSELF OVERWHELMED BY GHOSTS.
UC THEATER
COMIC RELIEF
NEUTRON DONUTS
CAFE FIRENZE
EDIE'S DINER
WELCOME TO THE CLUB, MISSY.
WHY BE NORMAL?
* SEE LAST PANEL

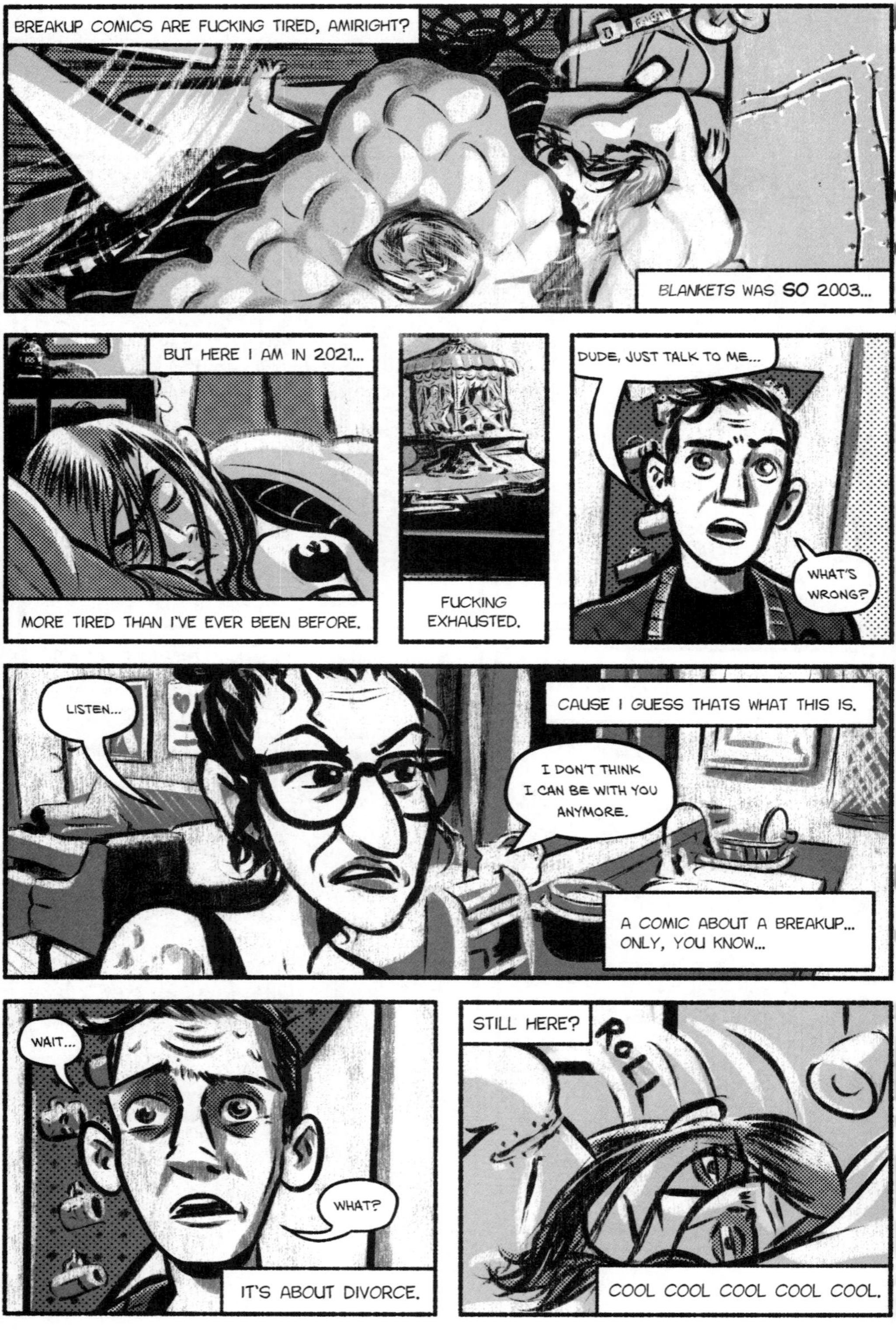
BREAKUP COMICS ARE FUCKING TIRED, AMIRIGHT?
BLANKETS WAS SO 2003...
BUT HERE I AM IN 2021...
MORE TIRED THAN I'VE EVER BEEN BEFORE.
FUCKING EXHAUSTED.
DUDE, JUST TALK TO ME...
WHAT'S WRONG?
LISTEN...
CAUSE I GUESS THATS WHAT THIS IS.
I DON'T THINK I CAN BE WITH YOU ANYMORE.
A COMIC ABOUT A BREAKUP... ONLY, YOU KNOW...
WAIT...
WHAT?
IT'S ABOUT DIVORCE.
STILL HERE?
ROLL
COOL COOL COOL COOL COOL.

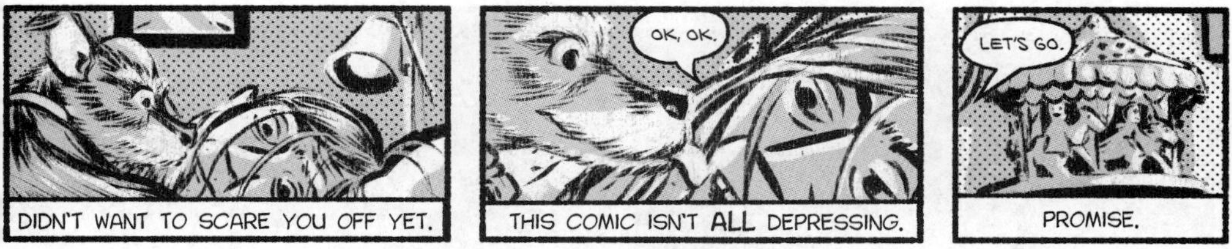
DIDN'T WANT TO SCARE YOU OFF YET.
OK, OK.
THIS COMIC ISN'T ALL DEPRESSING.
LET'S GO.
PROMISE.

UNSTUCK

KETTNER 2021'

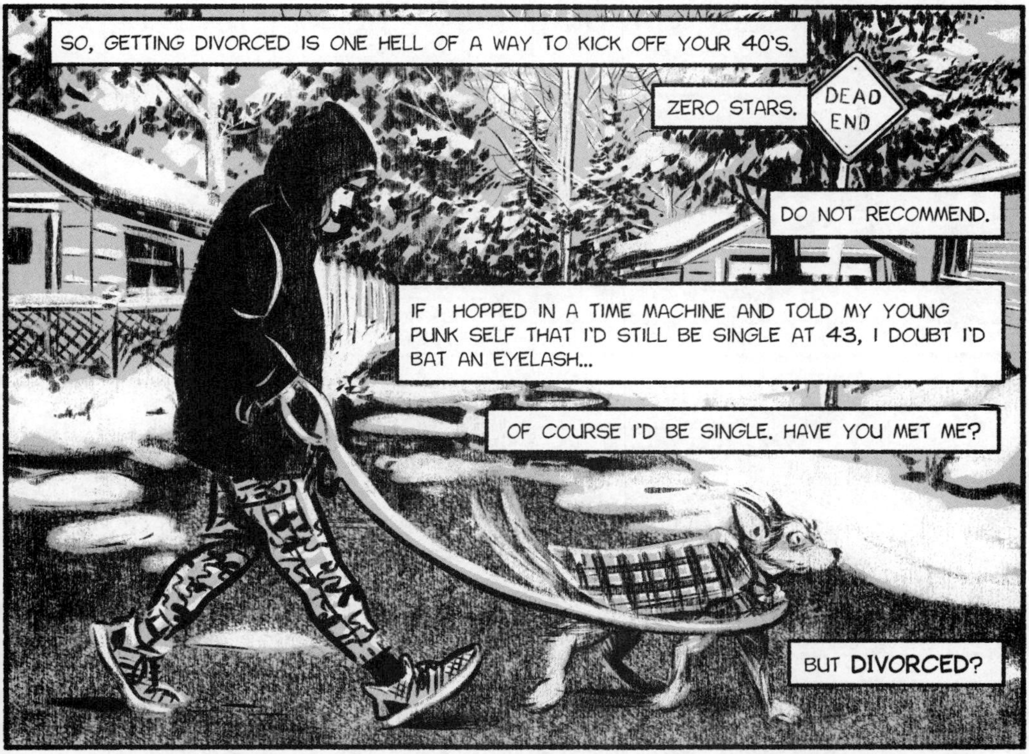
SO, GETTING DIVORCED IS ONE HELL OF A WAY TO KICK OFF YOUR 40'S.
ZERO STARS.
DEAD END
DO NOT RECOMMEND.
IF I HOPPED IN A TIME MACHINE AND TOLD MY YOUNG PUNK SELF THAT I'D STILL BE SINGLE AT 43, I DOUBT I'D BAT AN EYELASH...
OF COURSE I'D BE SINGLE. HAVE YOU MET ME?
BUT DIVORCED?

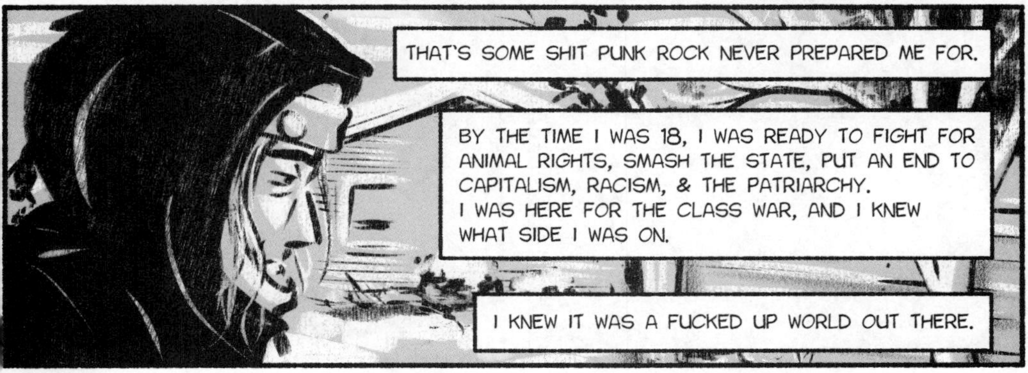
THAT'S SOME SHIT PUNK ROCK NEVER PREPARED ME FOR.
BY THE TIME I WAS 18, I WAS READY TO FIGHT FOR ANIMAL RIGHTS, SMASH THE STATE, PUT AN END TO CAPITALISM, RACISM, & THE PATRIARCHY.
I WAS HERE FOR THE CLASS WAR, AND I KNEW WHAT SIDE I WAS ON.
I KNEW IT WAS A FUCKED UP WORLD OUT THERE.

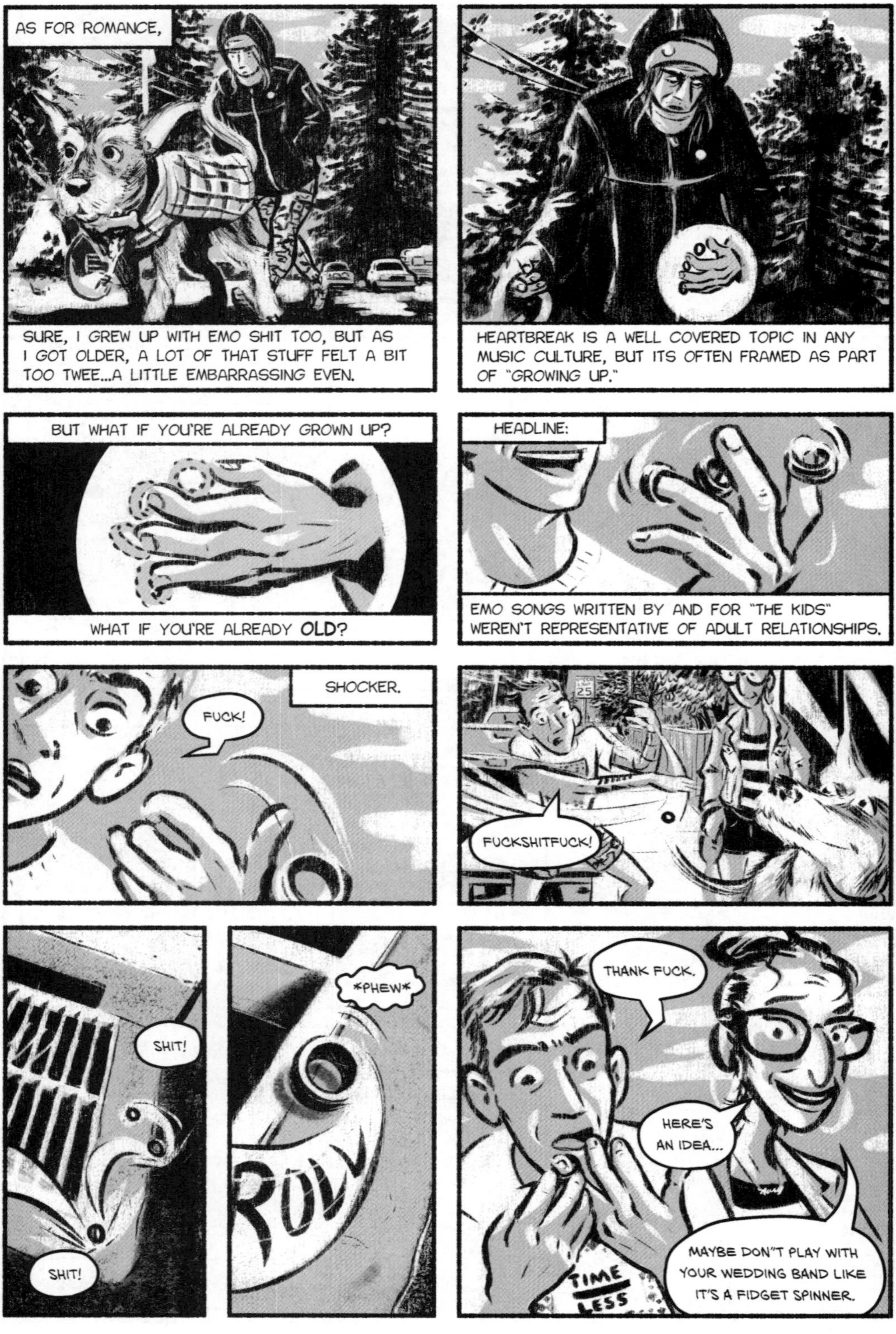
AS FOR ROMANCE,
SURE, I GREW UP WITH EMO SHIT TOO, BUT AS I GOT OLDER, A LOT OF THAT STUFF FELT A BIT TOO TWEE...A LITTLE EMBARRASSING EVEN.
HEARTBREAK IS A WELL COVERED TOPIC IN ANY MUSIC CULTURE, BUT ITS OFTEN FRAMED AS PART OF "GROWING UP."
BUT WHAT IF YOU'RE ALREADY GROWN UP?
WHAT IF YOU'RE ALREADY **OLD**?
HEADLINE:
EMO SONGS WRITTEN BY AND FOR "THE KIDS" WEREN'T REPRESENTATIVE OF ADULT RELATIONSHIPS.
SHOCKER.
FUCK!
25
FUCKSHITFUCK!
SHIT!
SHIT!
PHEW
ROLL
THANK FUCK.
HERE'S AN IDEA...
MAYBE DON'T PLAY WITH YOUR WEDDING BAND LIKE IT'S A FIDGET SPINNER.
TIME LESS

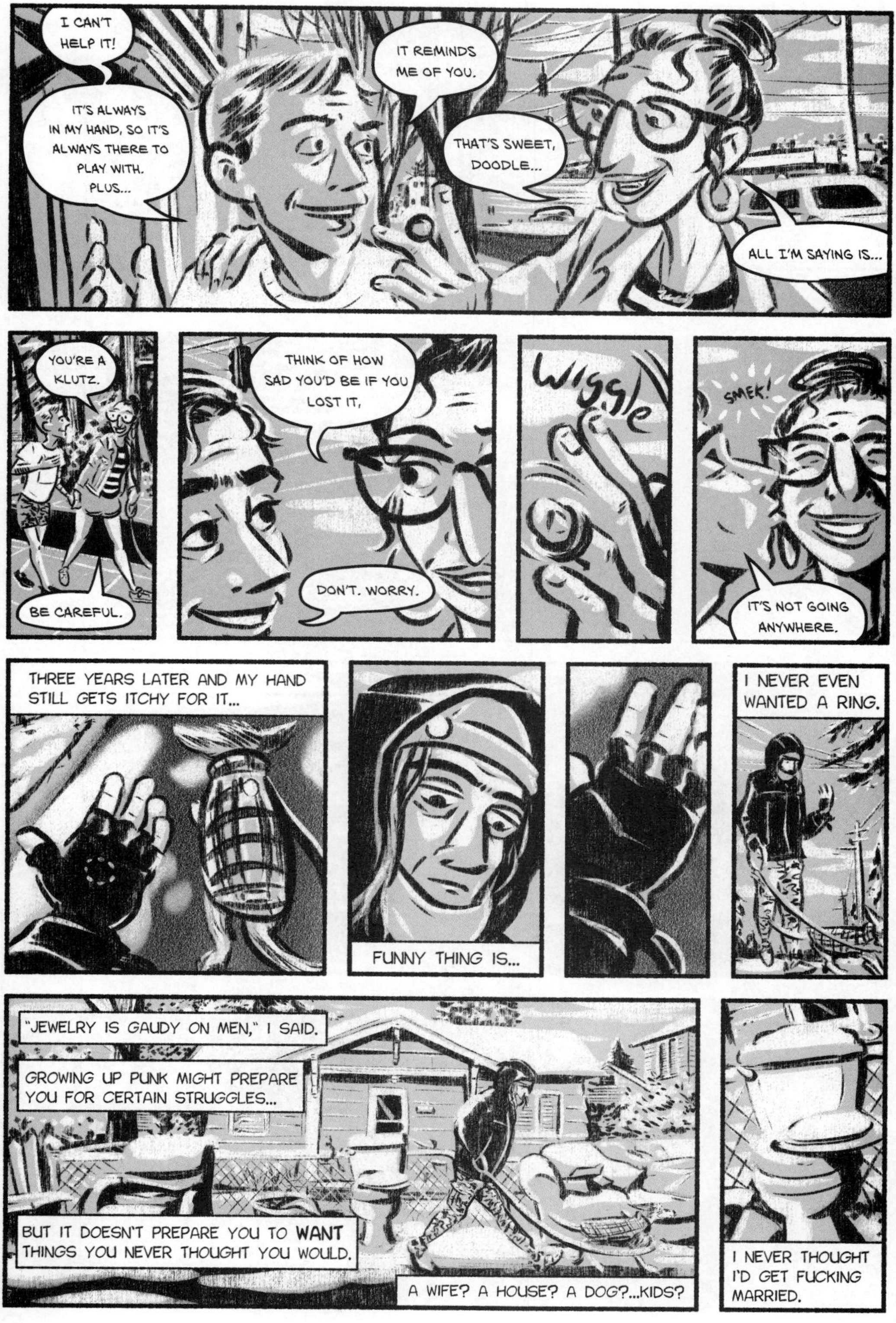
I CAN'T HELP IT!
IT'S ALWAYS IN MY HAND, SO IT'S ALWAYS THERE TO PLAY WITH. PLUS...
IT REMINDS ME OF YOU.
THAT'S SWEET, DOODLE...
ALL I'M SAYING IS...
YOU'RE A KLUTZ.
BE CAREFUL.
THINK OF HOW SAD YOU'D BE IF YOU LOST IT,
DON'T. WORRY.
Wiggle
SMEK!
IT'S NOT GOING ANYWHERE.
THREE YEARS LATER AND MY HAND STILL GETS ITCHY FOR IT...
FUNNY THING IS...
I NEVER EVEN WANTED A RING.
"JEWELRY IS GAUDY ON MEN," I SAID.
GROWING UP PUNK MIGHT PREPARE YOU FOR CERTAIN STRUGGLES...
BUT IT DOESN'T PREPARE YOU TO **WANT** THINGS YOU NEVER THOUGHT YOU WOULD.
A WIFE? A HOUSE? A DOG?...KIDS?
I NEVER THOUGHT I'D GET FUCKING MARRIED.

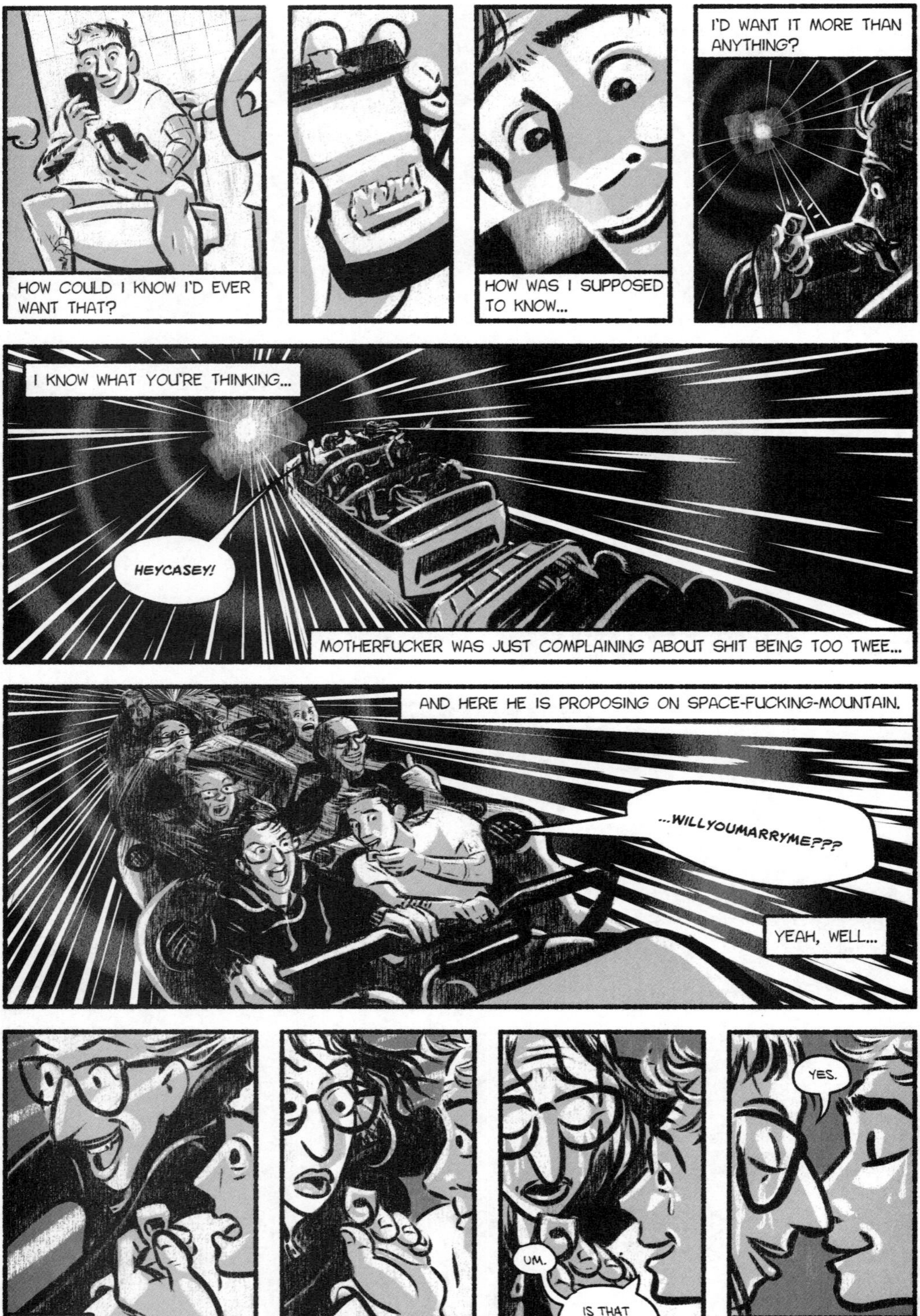
HOW COULD I KNOW I'D EVER WANT THAT?
HOW WAS I SUPPOSED TO KNOW...
I'D WANT IT MORE THAN ANYTHING?
I KNOW WHAT YOU'RE THINKING...
HEYCASEY!
MOTHERFUCKER WAS JUST COMPLAINING ABOUT SHIT BEING TOO TWEE...
AND HERE HE IS PROPOSING ON SPACE-FUCKING-MOUNTAIN.
...WILLYOUMARRYME???
YEAH, WELL...
SUE ME,
UM.
IS THAT A YES?
YES.
IT WAS NICE.

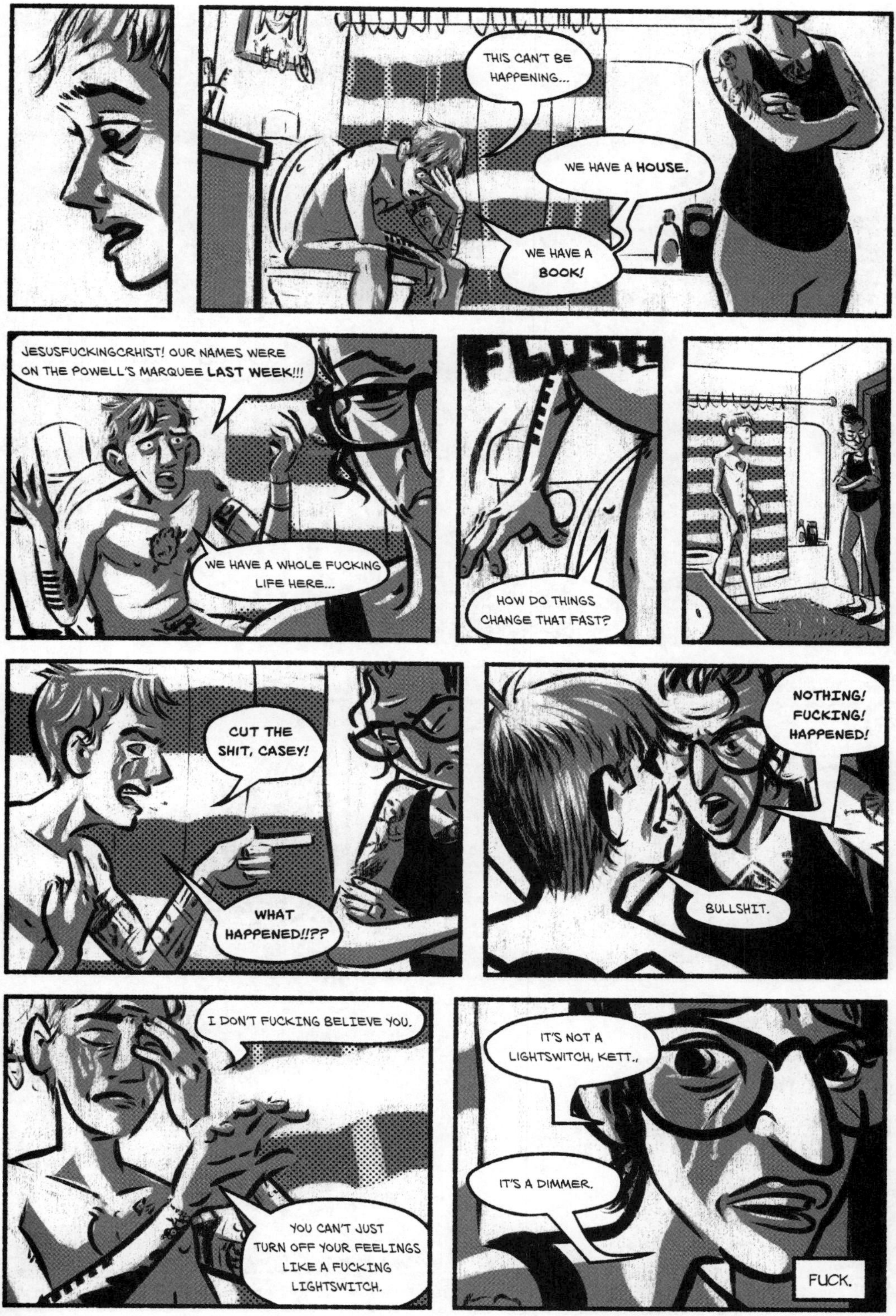
THIS CAN'T BE HAPPENING...
WE HAVE A HOUSE.
WE HAVE A BOOK!
JESUSFUCKINGCRHIST! OUR NAMES WERE ON THE POWELL'S MARQUEE LAST WEEK!!!
WE HAVE A WHOLE FUCKING LIFE HERE...
HOW DO THINGS CHANGE THAT FAST?
CUT THE SHIT, CASEY!
WHAT HAPPENED!!??
NOTHING! FUCKING! HAPPENED!
BULLSHIT.
I DON'T FUCKING BELIEVE YOU.
YOU CAN'T JUST TURN OFF YOUR FEELINGS LIKE A FUCKING LIGHTSWITCH.
IT'S NOT A LIGHTSWITCH, KETT.,
IT'S A DIMMER.
FUCK.

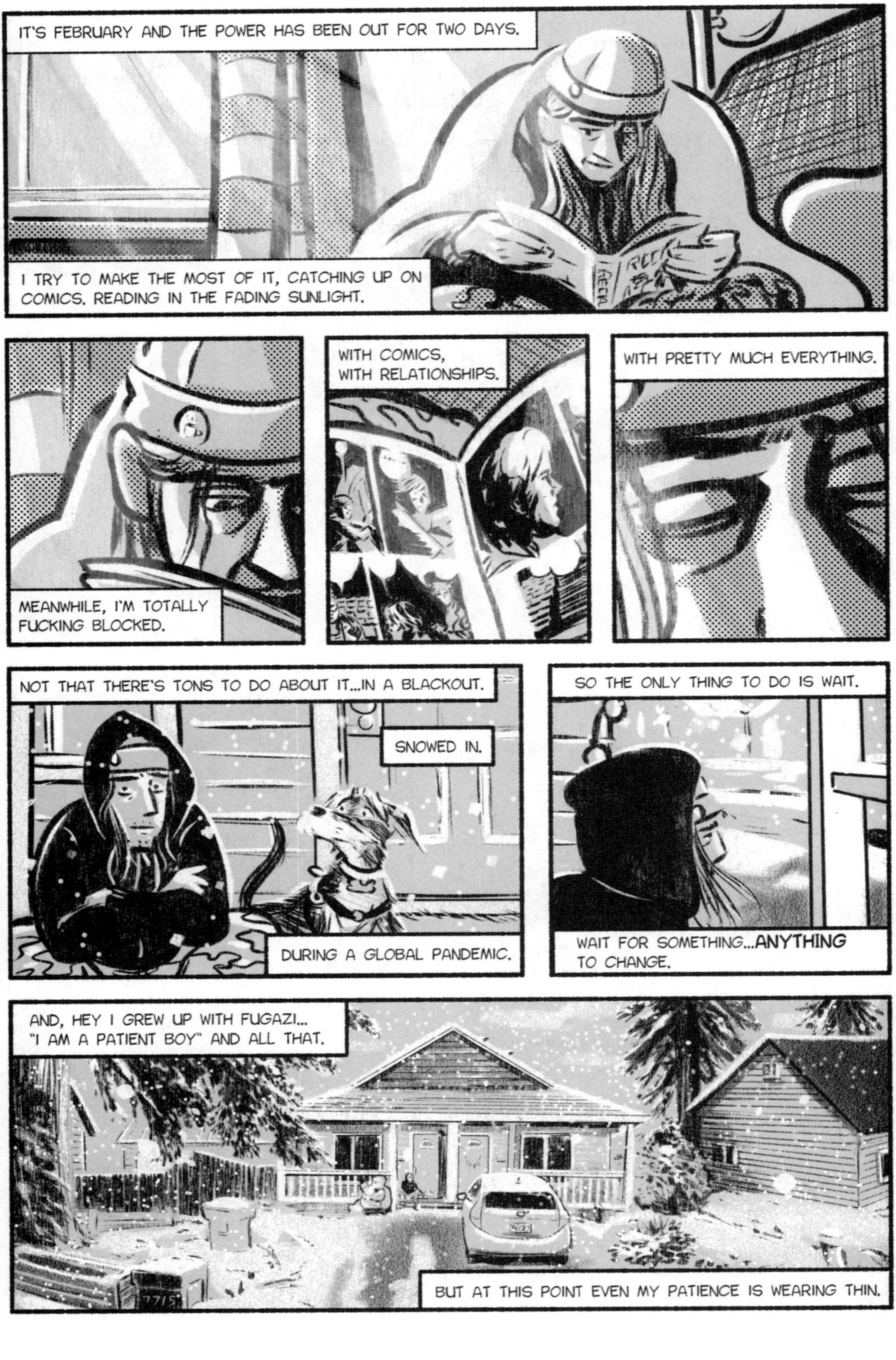
IT'S FEBRUARY AND THE POWER HAS BEEN OUT FOR TWO DAYS.
I TRY TO MAKE THE MOST OF IT, CATCHING UP ON COMICS. READING IN THE FADING SUNLIGHT.
MEANWHILE, I'M TOTALLY FUCKING BLOCKED.
WITH COMICS, WITH RELATIONSHIPS.
WITH PRETTY MUCH EVERYTHING.
NOT THAT THERE'S TONS TO DO ABOUT IT...IN A BLACKOUT.
SNOWED IN.
DURING A GLOBAL PANDEMIC.
SO THE ONLY THING TO DO IS WAIT.
WAIT FOR SOMETHING...**ANYTHING** TO CHANGE.
AND, HEY I GREW UP WITH FUGAZI... "I AM A PATIENT BOY" AND ALL THAT.
BUT AT THIS POINT EVEN MY PATIENCE IS WEARING THIN.

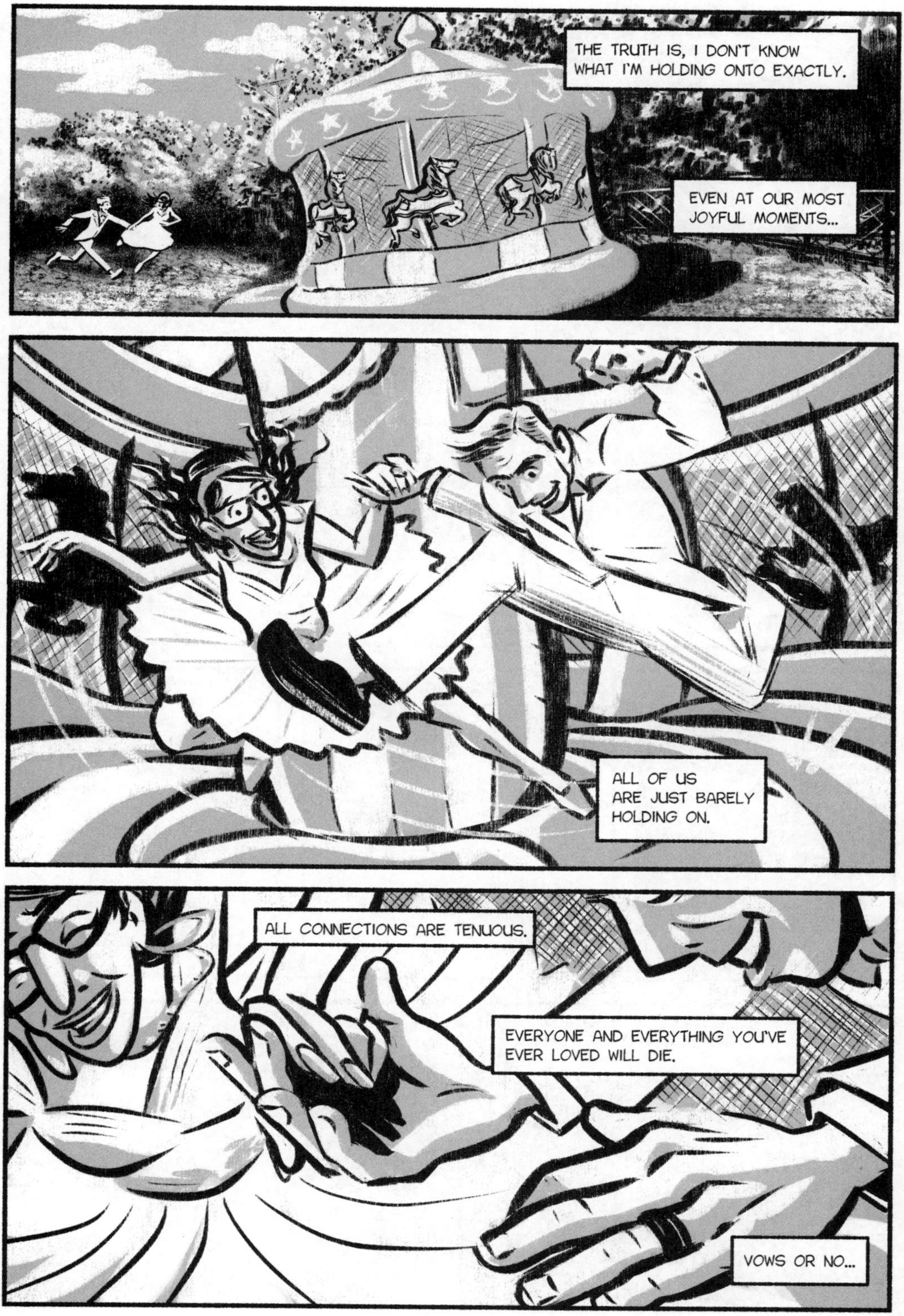
THE TRUTH IS, I DON'T KNOW WHAT I'M HOLDING ONTO EXACTLY.
EVEN AT OUR MOST JOYFUL MOMENTS...
ALL OF US ARE JUST BARELY HOLDING ON.
ALL CONNECTIONS ARE TENUOUS.
EVERYONE AND EVERYTHING YOU'VE EVER LOVED WILL DIE.
VOWS OR NO...

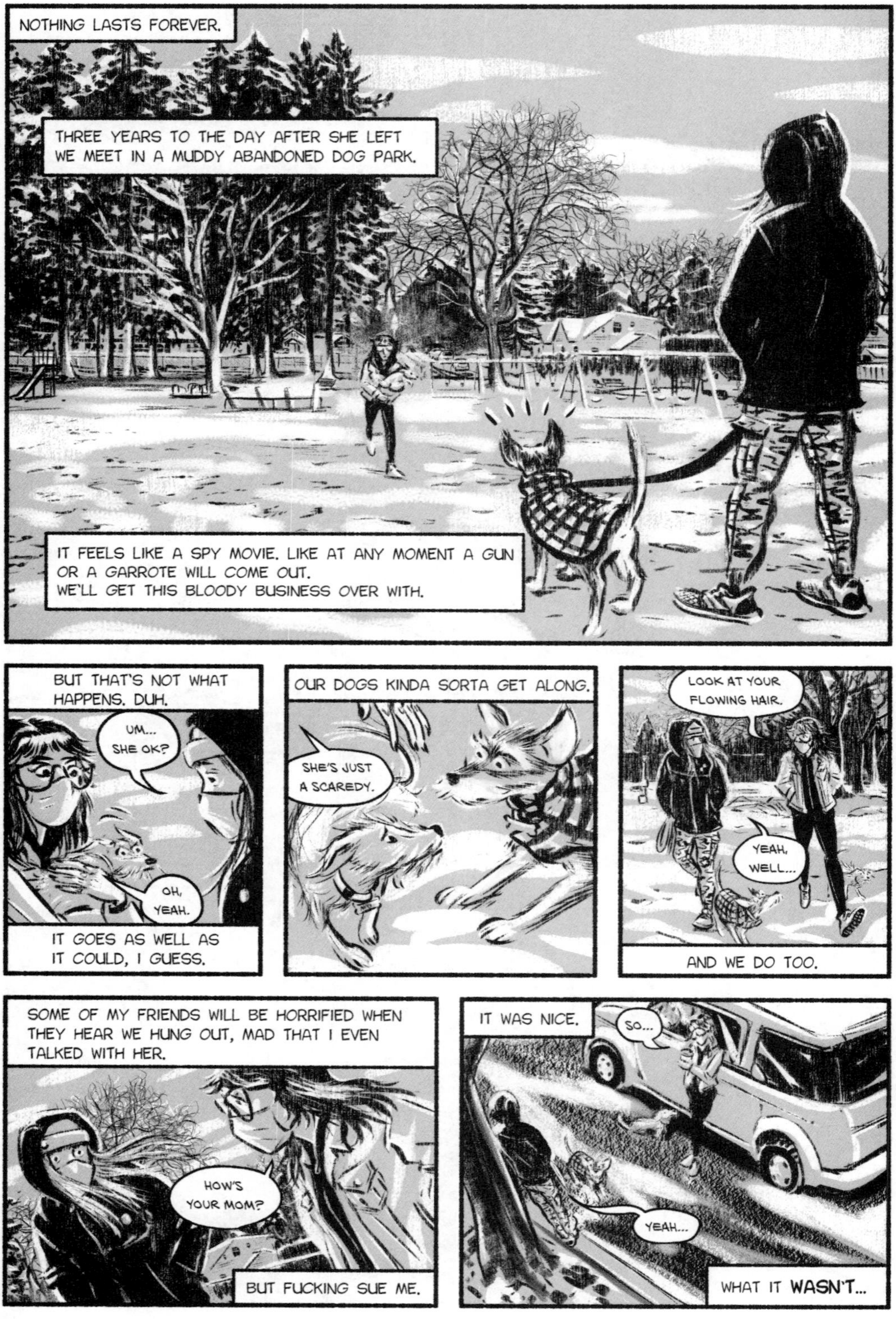
NOTHING LASTS FOREVER.
THREE YEARS TO THE DAY AFTER SHE LEFT WE MEET IN A MUDDY ABANDONED DOG PARK.
IT FEELS LIKE A SPY MOVIE. LIKE AT ANY MOMENT A GUN OR A GARROTE WILL COME OUT.
WE'LL GET THIS BLOODY BUSINESS OVER WITH.
BUT THAT'S NOT WHAT HAPPENS. DUH.
UM... SHE OK?
OH, YEAH.
IT GOES AS WELL AS IT COULD, I GUESS.
OUR DOGS KINDA SORTA GET ALONG.
SHE'S JUST A SCAREDY.
LOOK AT YOUR FLOWING HAIR.
YEAH, WELL...
AND WE DO TOO.
SOME OF MY FRIENDS WILL BE HORRIFIED WHEN THEY HEAR WE HUNG OUT, MAD THAT I EVEN TALKED WITH HER.
HOW'S YOUR MOM?
BUT FUCKING SUE ME.
IT WAS NICE.
SO...
YEAH...
WHAT IT **WASN'T**...

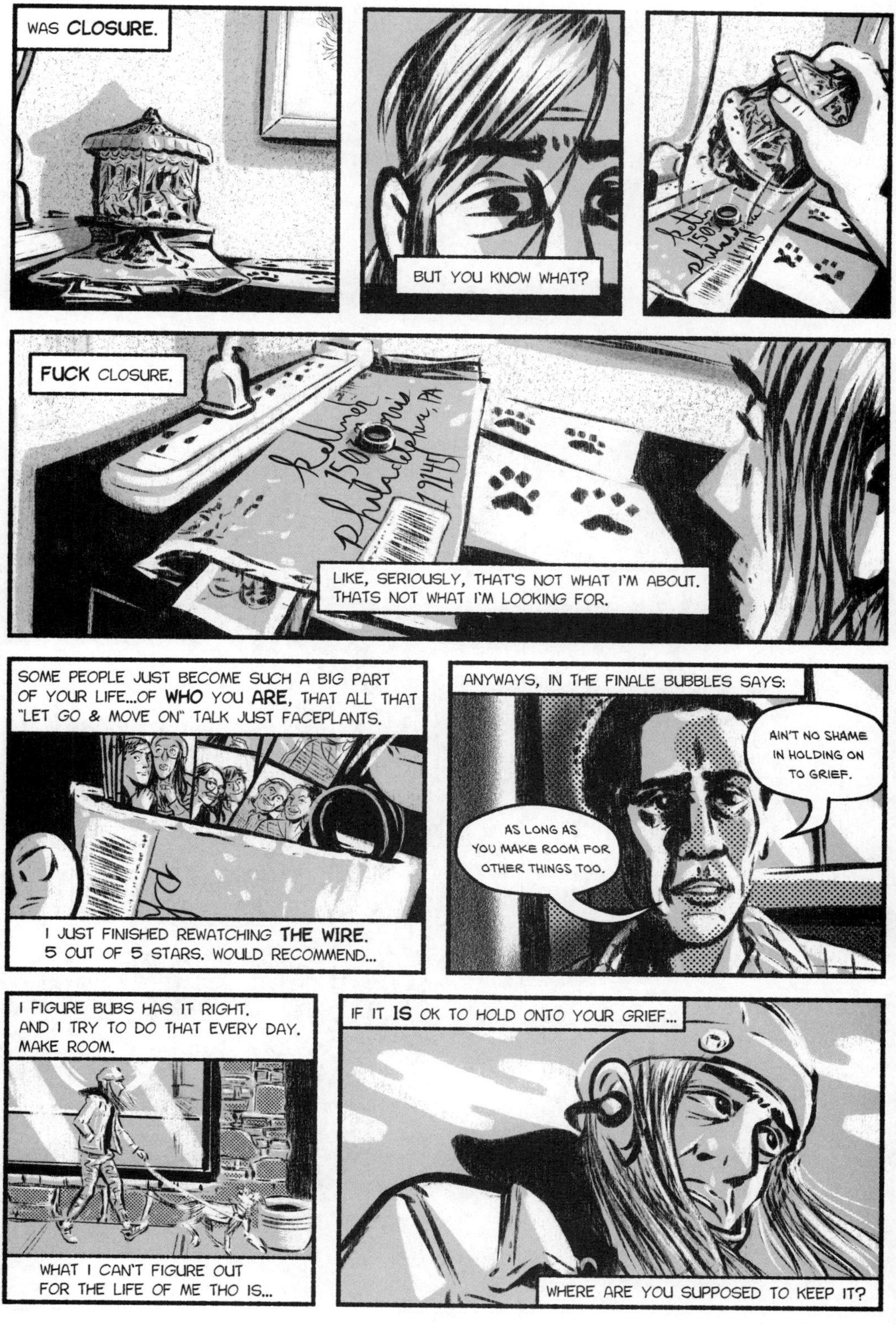
WAS CLOSURE.
BUT YOU KNOW WHAT?
FUCK CLOSURE.
LIKE, SERIOUSLY, THAT'S NOT WHAT I'M ABOUT. THATS NOT WHAT I'M LOOKING FOR.
SOME PEOPLE JUST BECOME SUCH A BIG PART OF YOUR LIFE...OF WHO YOU ARE, THAT ALL THAT "LET GO & MOVE ON" TALK JUST FACEPLANTS.
I JUST FINISHED REWATCHING THE WIRE. 5 OUT OF 5 STARS. WOULD RECOMMEND...
ANYWAYS, IN THE FINALE BUBBLES SAYS:
AIN'T NO SHAME IN HOLDING ON TO GRIEF.
AS LONG AS YOU MAKE ROOM FOR OTHER THINGS TOO.
I FIGURE BUBS HAS IT RIGHT. AND I TRY TO DO THAT EVERY DAY. MAKE ROOM.
WHAT I CAN'T FIGURE OUT FOR THE LIFE OF ME THO IS...
IF IT IS OK TO HOLD ONTO YOUR GRIEF...
WHERE ARE YOU SUPPOSED TO KEEP IT?

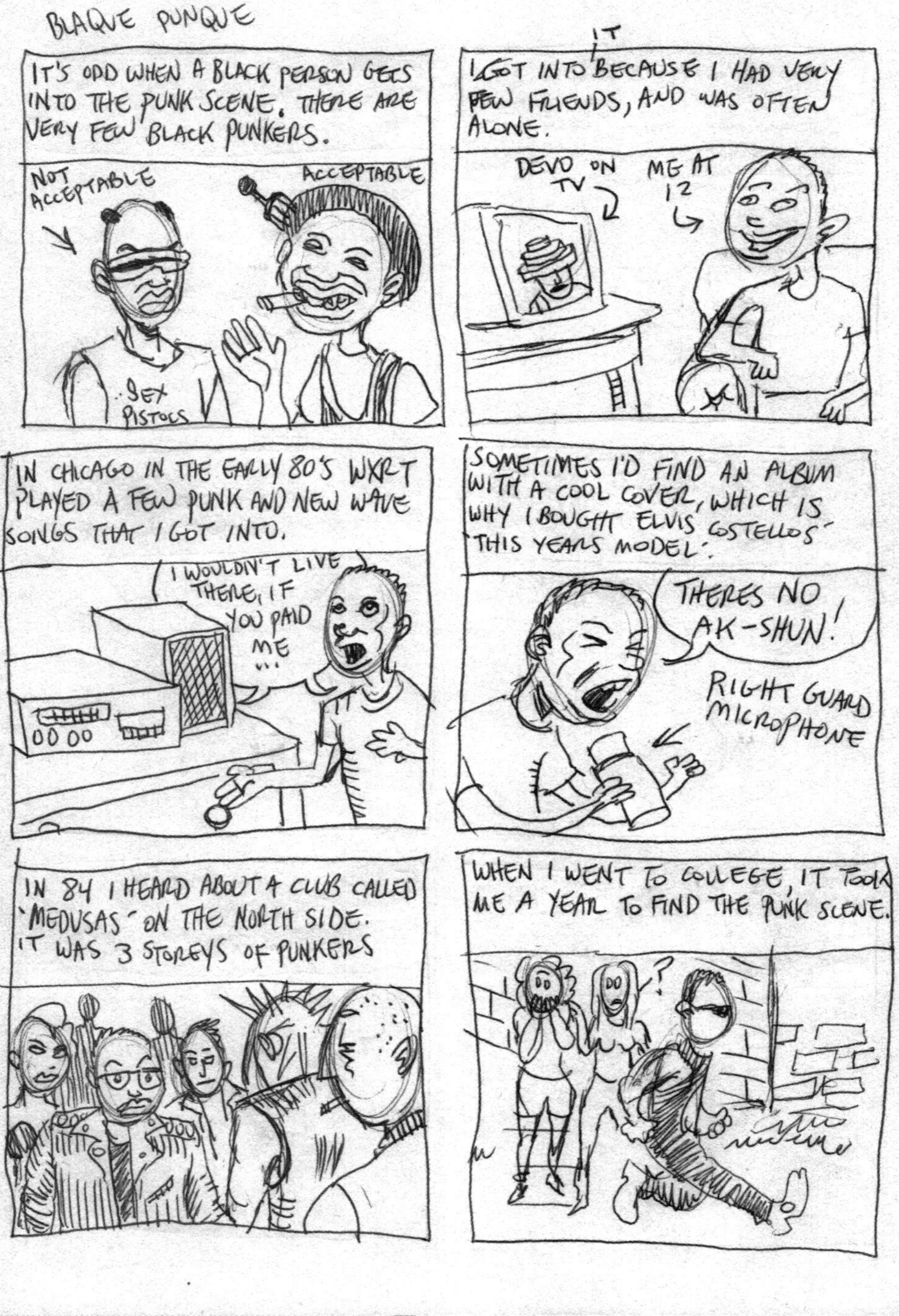
BLAQUE PUNQUE
IT'S ODD WHEN A BLACK PERSON GETS INTO THE PUNK SCENE. THERE ARE VERY FEW BLACK PUNKERS.
NOT ACCEPTABLE
ACCEPTABLE
SEX PISTOLS
I GOT INTO IT BECAUSE I HAD VERY FEW FRIENDS, AND WAS OFTEN ALONE.
DEVO ON TV
ME AT 12
IN CHICAGO IN THE EARLY 80'S WXRT PLAYED A FEW PUNK AND NEW WAVE SONGS THAT I GOT INTO.
I WOULDN'T LIVE THERE, IF YOU PAID ME...
SOMETIMES I'D FIND AN ALBUM WITH A COOL COVER, WHICH IS WHY I BOUGHT ELVIS COSTELLOS' 'THIS YEARS MODEL'.
THERES NO AK-SHUN!
RIGHT GUARD MICROPHONE
IN 84 I HEARD ABOUT A CLUB CALLED 'MEDUSAS' ON THE NORTH SIDE. IT WAS 3 STOREYS OF PUNKERS
WHEN I WENT TO COLLEGE, IT TOOK ME A YEAR TO FIND THE PUNK SCENE.
?

I WORE A FROHAWK OFF AND ON FOR FOUR YEARS. THIS WAS OFTEN MISTAKEN FOR MR.T WORSHIP.
I PITY THE FOOL! HA HA HA!
I THINK I DATED 3 OR FOUR GIRLS IN MY 6 YEARS OF COLLEGE, NONE OF THEM STUCK WITH ME VERY LONG.
HE WAS NICE, BUT I CANT DATE A BLACK MAN... MY PARENTS THREATENED TO CUT ME OFF!
WHEN I MOVED TO AUSTIN, I COULD SEE SHOWS EVERY NIGHT, BUT I CHOSE TO CHASE WOMEN.
EXCUSE ME, WILL YOU BY ME A DRINK?
HEY THERE, TALK TO ME!
I GOT A BUNCH OF TATTOOS AND LET MY HAIR DREAD.
Mr X
IN THE LATE NINETIES AUSTIN COLLAPSED UNDER CONSERVATIVE AND HIPSTER PRESSURES, SO I STOPPED GOING OUT.
FAMILY VALUES
WHITE TRASH CHIC
BAH!
NOWADAYS I LOOK ON MY PUNK BACKGROUND AS STRANGE, BUT CAN'T PICTURE WHAT I'D HAVE BEEN DOING WITHOUT IT.
I'DA BEEN A WHOLE NUTHER PERSON.
-X

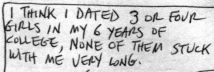

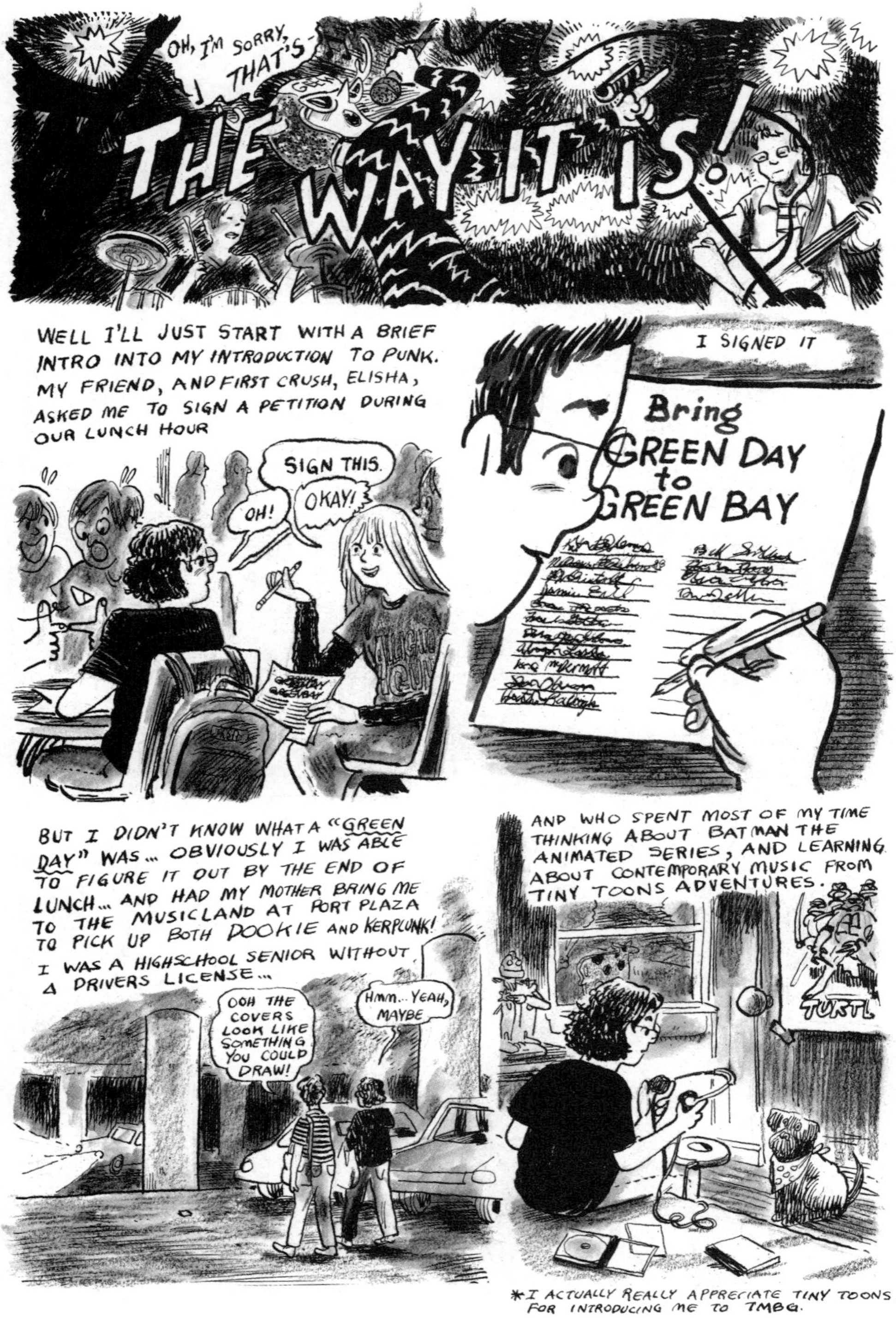

OH, I'M SORRY, THAT'S-
THE WAY IT IS!
WELL I'LL JUST START WITH A BRIEF INTRO INTO MY INTRODUCTION TO PUNK. MY FRIEND, AND FIRST CRUSH, ELISHA, ASKED ME TO SIGN A PETITION DURING OUR LUNCH HOUR
SIGN THIS.
OH!
OKAY!
I SIGNED IT
Bring GREEN DAY to GREEN BAY
BUT I DIDN'T KNOW WHAT A "GREEN DAY" WAS... OBVIOUSLY I WAS ABLE TO FIGURE IT OUT BY THE END OF LUNCH... AND HAD MY MOTHER BRING ME TO THE MUSICLAND AT PORT PLAZA TO PICK UP BOTH DOOKIE AND KERPLUNK!
I WAS A HIGHSCHOOL SENIOR WITHOUT A DRIVERS LICENSE...
OOH THE COVERS LOOK LIKE SOMETHING YOU COULD DRAW!
Hmm... YEAH, MAYBE
AND WHO SPENT MOST OF MY TIME THINKING ABOUT BATMAN THE ANIMATED SERIES, AND LEARNING ABOUT CONTEMPORARY MUSIC FROM TINY TOONS ADVENTURES.*
TURTL
*I ACTUALLY REALLY APPRECIATE TINY TOONS FOR INTRODUCING ME TO TMBG.

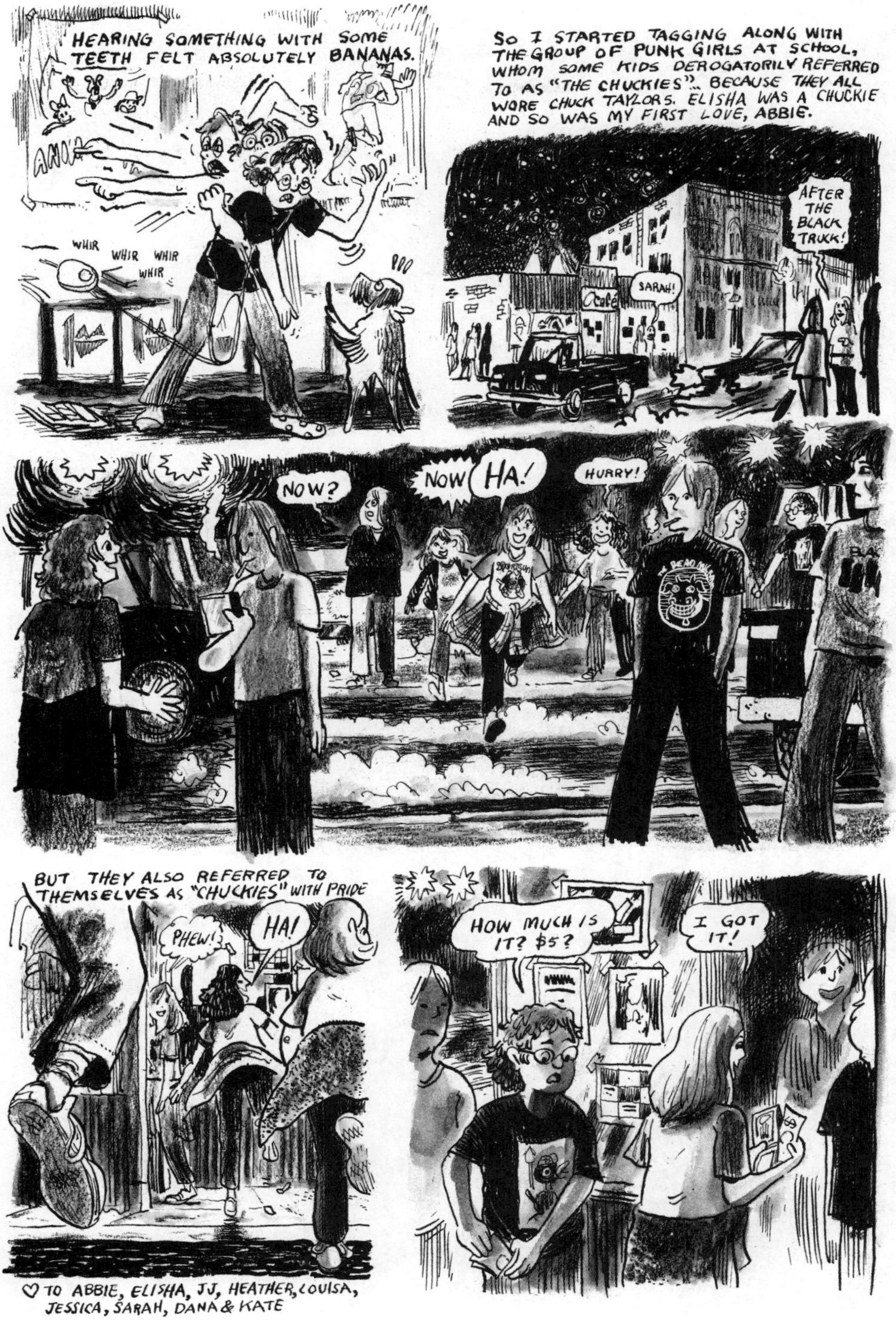
HEARING SOMETHING WITH SOME TEETH FELT ABSOLUTELY BANANAS.
WHIR WHIR WHIR WHIR
SO I STARTED TAGGING ALONG WITH THE GROUP OF PUNK GIRLS AT SCHOOL, WHOM SOME KIDS DEROGATORILY REFERRED TO AS "THE CHUCKIES"... BECAUSE THEY ALL WORE CHUCK TAYLORS. ELISHA WAS A CHUCKIE AND SO WAS MY FIRST LOVE, ABBIE.
AFTER THE BLACK TRUCK!
SARAH!
Cafe
NOW?
NOW
HA!
HURRY!
BUT THEY ALSO REFERRED TO THEMSELVES AS "CHUCKIES" WITH PRIDE
PHEW!
HA!
HOW MUCH IS IT? $5?
I GOT IT!
♡ TO ABBIE, ELISHA, JJ, HEATHER, LOUISA, JESSICA, SARAH, DANA & KATE

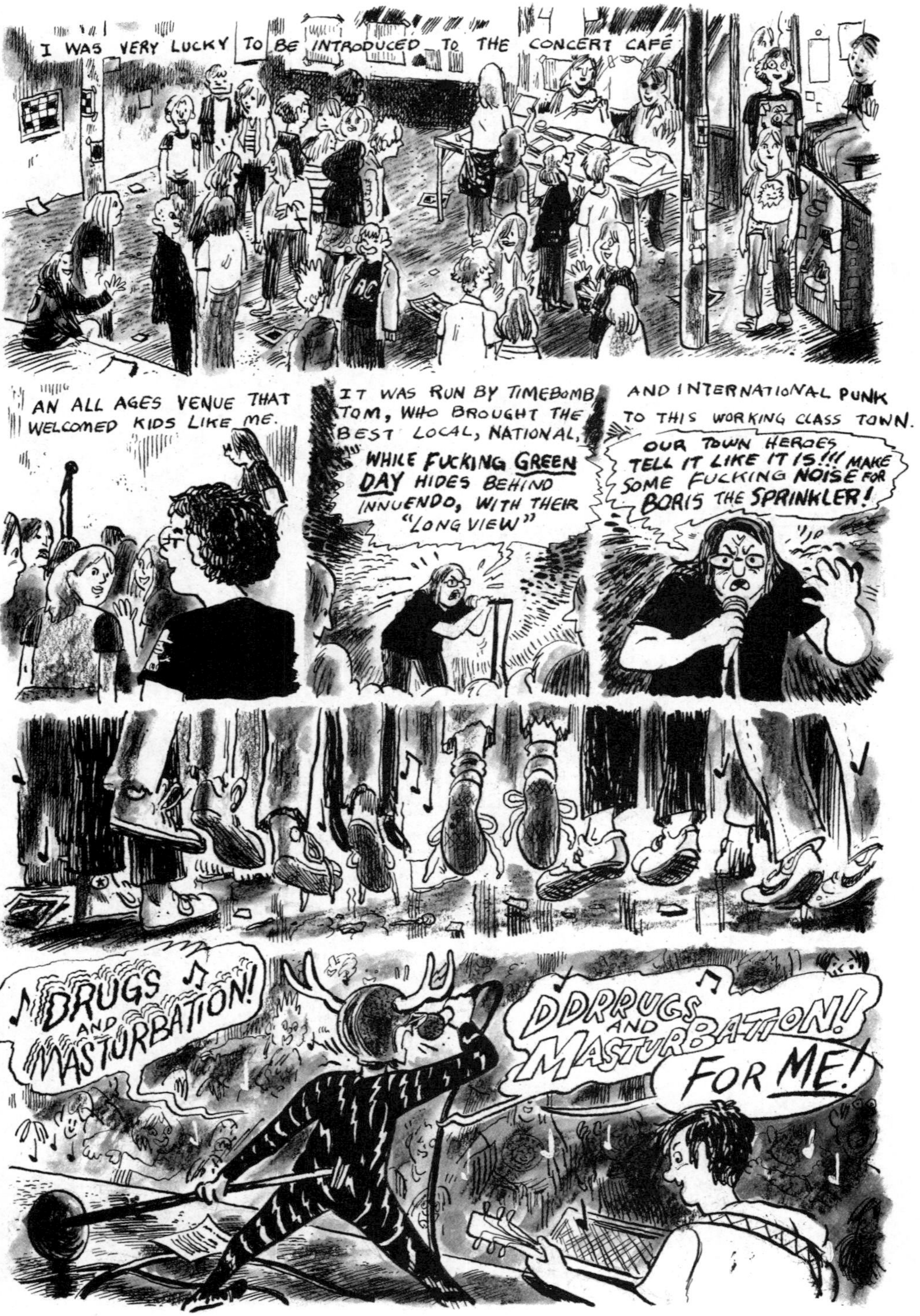
I WAS VERY LUCKY TO BE INTRODUCED TO THE CONCERT CAFÉ
AN ALL AGES VENUE THAT WELCOMED KIDS LIKE ME.
IT WAS RUN BY TIMEBOMB TOM, WHO BROUGHT THE BEST LOCAL, NATIONAL,
WHILE FUCKING GREEN DAY HIDES BEHIND INNUENDO, WITH THEIR "LONG VIEW"
AND INTERNATIONAL PUNK TO THIS WORKING CLASS TOWN.
OUR TOWN HEROES TELL IT LIKE IT IS!!! MAKE SOME FUCKING NOISE FOR BORIS THE SPRINKLER!
DRUGS AND MASTURBATION!
DDRRUGS AND MASTURBATION! FOR ME!

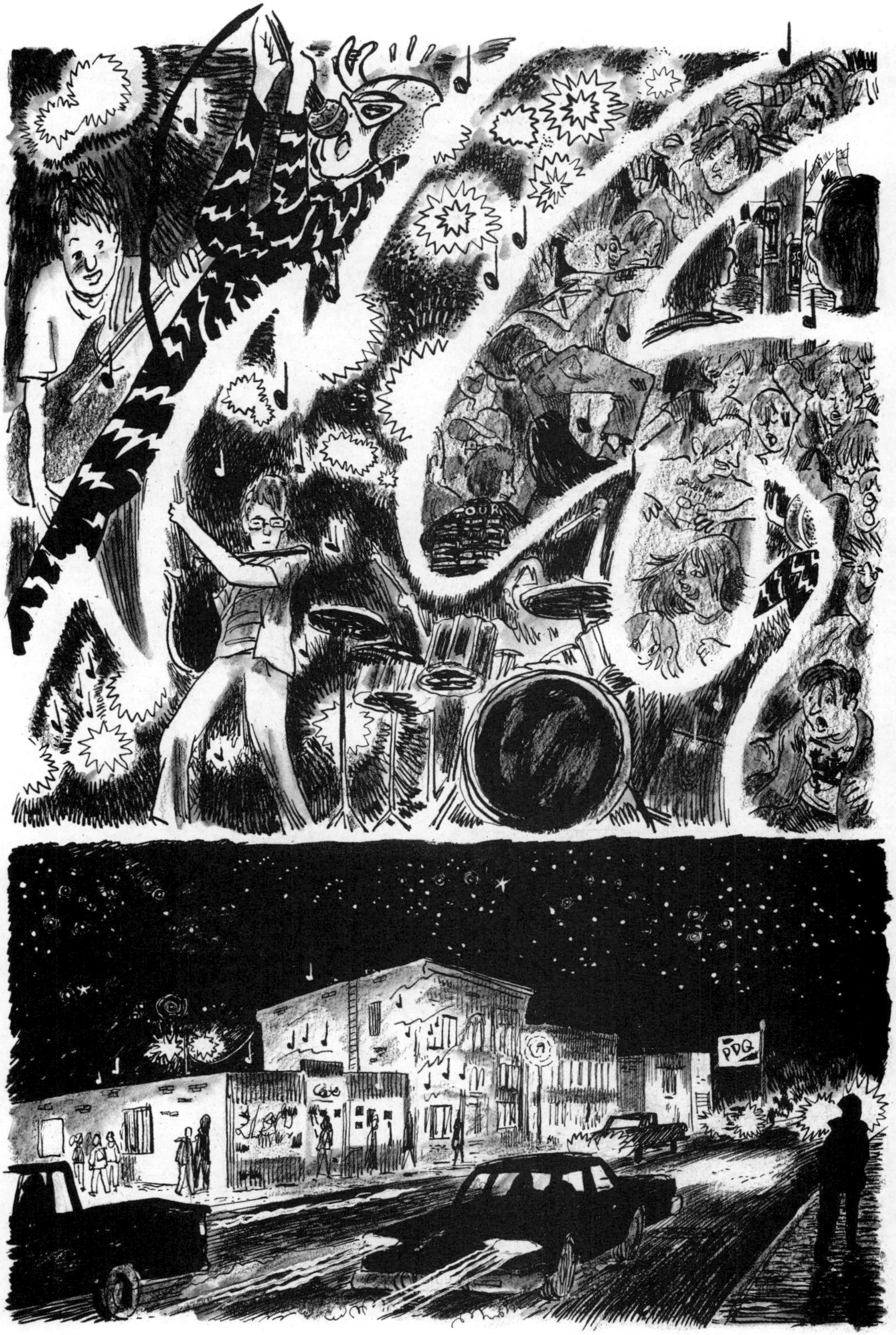
FOUR
PDQ

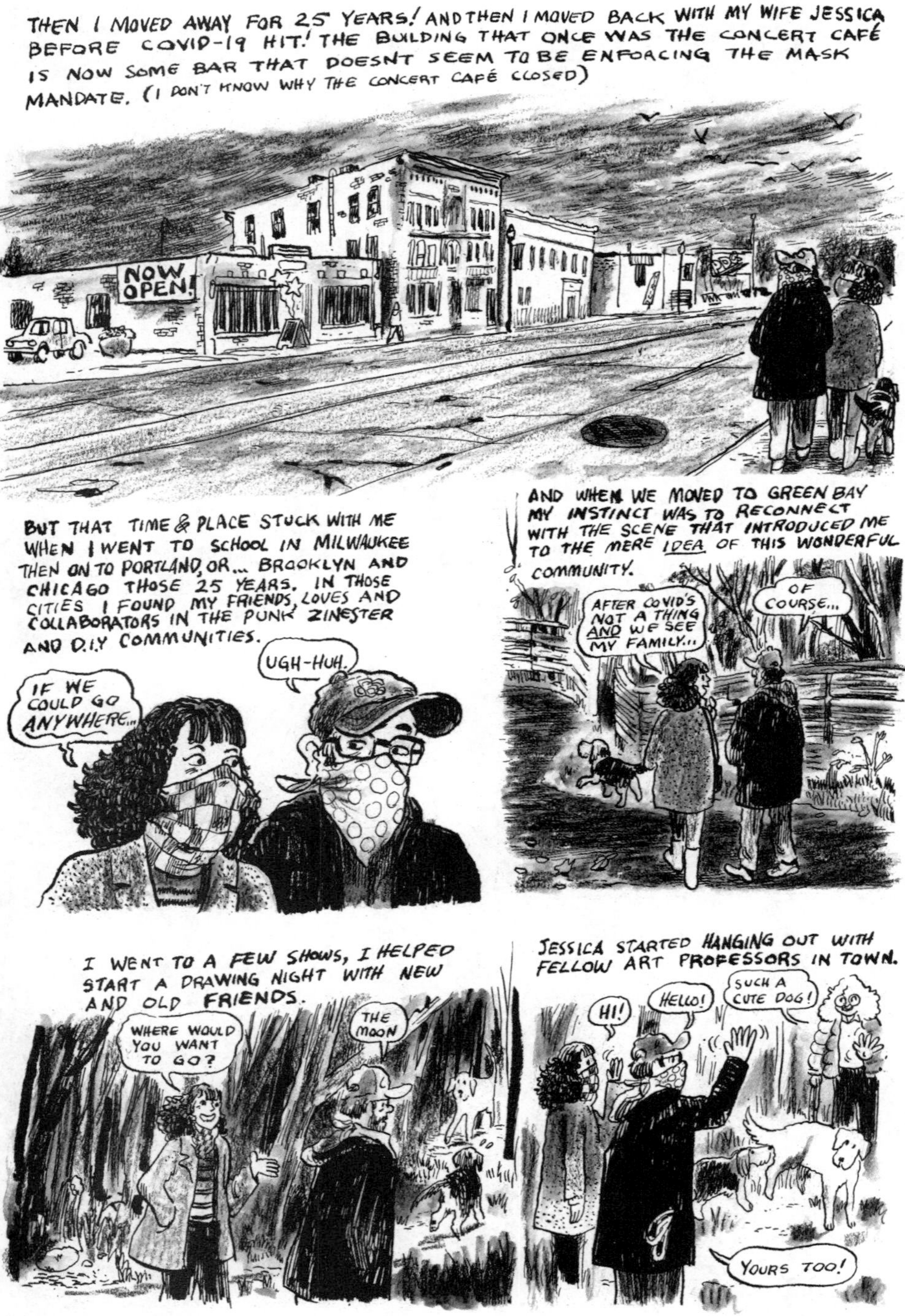
THEN I MOVED AWAY FOR 25 YEARS! AND THEN I MOVED BACK WITH MY WIFE JESSICA BEFORE COVID-19 HIT! THE BUILDING THAT ONCE WAS THE CONCERT CAFÉ IS NOW SOME BAR THAT DOESN'T SEEM TO BE ENFORCING THE MASK MANDATE. (I DON'T KNOW WHY THE CONCERT CAFÉ CLOSED)
NOW OPEN!
BUT THAT TIME & PLACE STUCK WITH ME WHEN I WENT TO SCHOOL IN MILWAUKEE THEN ON TO PORTLAND, OR... BROOKLYN AND CHICAGO THOSE 25 YEARS. IN THOSE CITIES I FOUND MY FRIENDS, LOVES AND COLLABORATORS IN THE PUNK ZINESTER AND D.I.Y COMMUNITIES.
IF WE COULD GO ANYWHERE...
UGH-HUH.
AND WHEN WE MOVED TO GREEN BAY MY INSTINCT WAS TO RECONNECT WITH THE SCENE THAT INTRODUCED ME TO THE MERE IDEA OF THIS WONDERFUL COMMUNITY.
AFTER COVID'S NOT A THING AND WE SEE MY FAMILY...
OF COURSE...
I WENT TO A FEW SHOWS, I HELPED START A DRAWING NIGHT WITH NEW AND OLD FRIENDS.
WHERE WOULD YOU WANT TO GO?
THE MOON
JESSICA STARTED HANGING OUT WITH FELLOW ART PROFESSORS IN TOWN.
HI!
HELLO!
SUCH A CUTE DOG!
YOURS TOO!

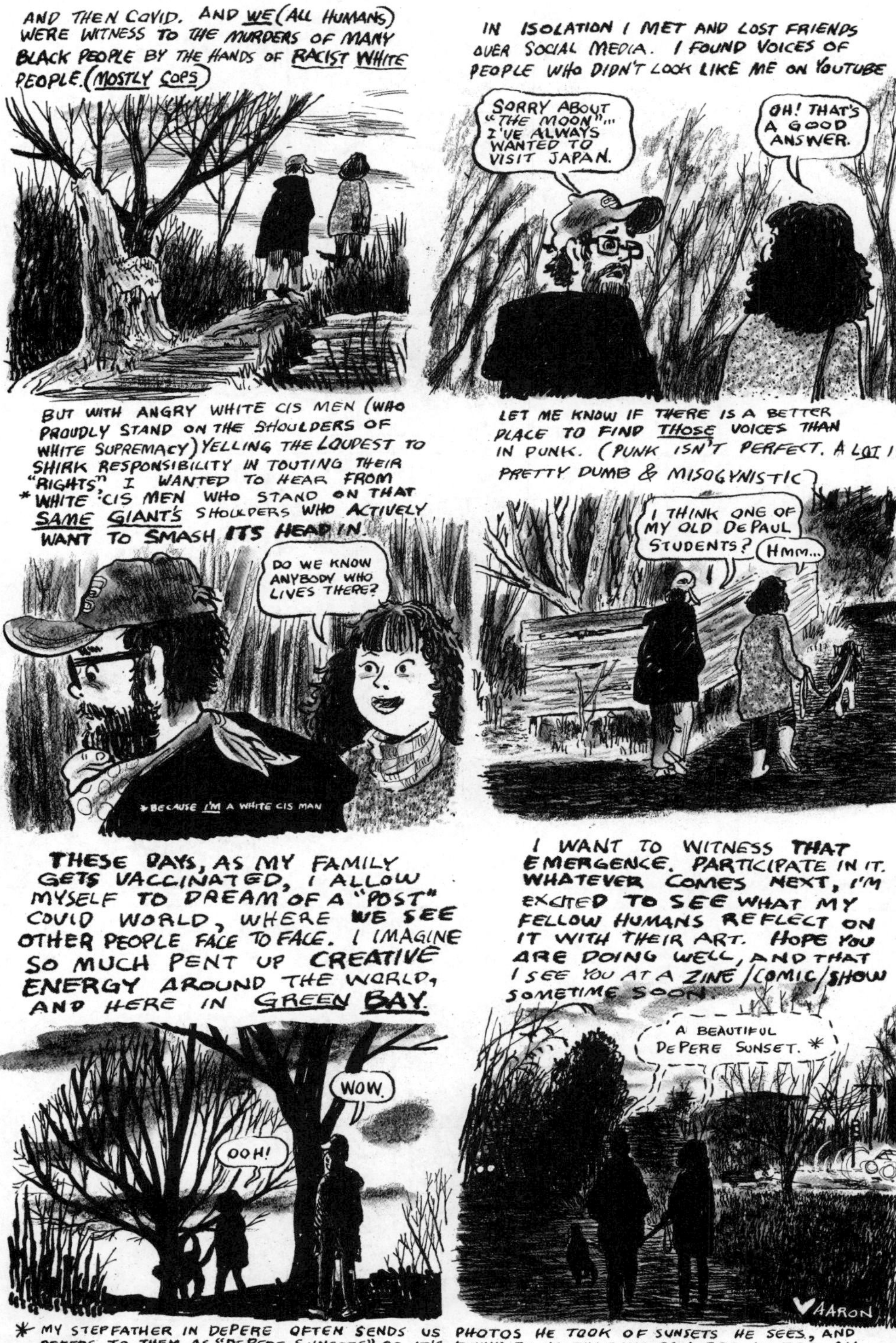
AND THEN COVID. AND WE (ALL HUMANS) WERE WITNESS TO THE MURDERS OF MANY BLACK PEOPLE BY THE HANDS OF RACIST WHITE PEOPLE. (MOSTLY COPS)
IN ISOLATION I MET AND LOST FRIENDS OVER SOCIAL MEDIA. I FOUND VOICES OF PEOPLE WHO DIDN'T LOOK LIKE ME ON YOUTUBE
SORRY ABOUT "THE MOON"... I'VE ALWAYS WANTED TO VISIT JAPAN.
OH! THAT'S A GOOD ANSWER.
BUT WITH ANGRY WHITE CIS MEN (WHO PROUDLY STAND ON THE SHOULDERS OF WHITE SUPREMACY) YELLING THE LOUDEST TO SHIRK RESPONSIBILITY IN TOUTING THEIR "RIGHTS" I WANTED TO HEAR FROM *WHITE CIS MEN WHO STAND ON THAT SAME GIANT'S SHOULDERS WHO ACTIVELY WANT TO SMASH ITS HEAD IN.
DO WE KNOW ANYBODY WHO LIVES THERE?
*BECAUSE I'M A WHITE CIS MAN
LET ME KNOW IF THERE IS A BETTER PLACE TO FIND THOSE VOICES THAN IN PUNK. (PUNK ISN'T PERFECT. A LOT IS PRETTY DUMB & MISOGYNISTIC)
I THINK ONE OF MY OLD DEPAUL STUDENTS?
HMM...
THESE DAYS, AS MY FAMILY GETS VACCINATED, I ALLOW MYSELF TO DREAM OF A "POST" COVID WORLD, WHERE WE SEE OTHER PEOPLE FACE TO FACE. I IMAGINE SO MUCH PENT UP CREATIVE ENERGY AROUND THE WORLD, AND HERE IN GREEN BAY.
WOW.
OOH!
I WANT TO WITNESS THAT EMERGENCE. PARTICIPATE IN IT. WHATEVER COMES NEXT, I'M EXCITED TO SEE WHAT MY FELLOW HUMANS REFLECT ON IT WITH THEIR ART. HOPE YOU ARE DOING WELL, AND THAT I SEE YOU AT A ZINE/COMIC/SHOW SOMETIME SOON.
A BEAUTIFUL DEPERE SUNSET. *
AARON
* MY STEPFATHER IN DEPERE OFTEN SENDS US PHOTOS HE TOOK OF SUNSETS HE SEES, AND REFERS TO THEM AS "DEPERE SUNSETS" SO IT'S FUNNY TO US THAT WE CAN SEE IT TOO, ALL THE WAY IN GREEN BAY (A 20 MINUTE BIKE RIDE)

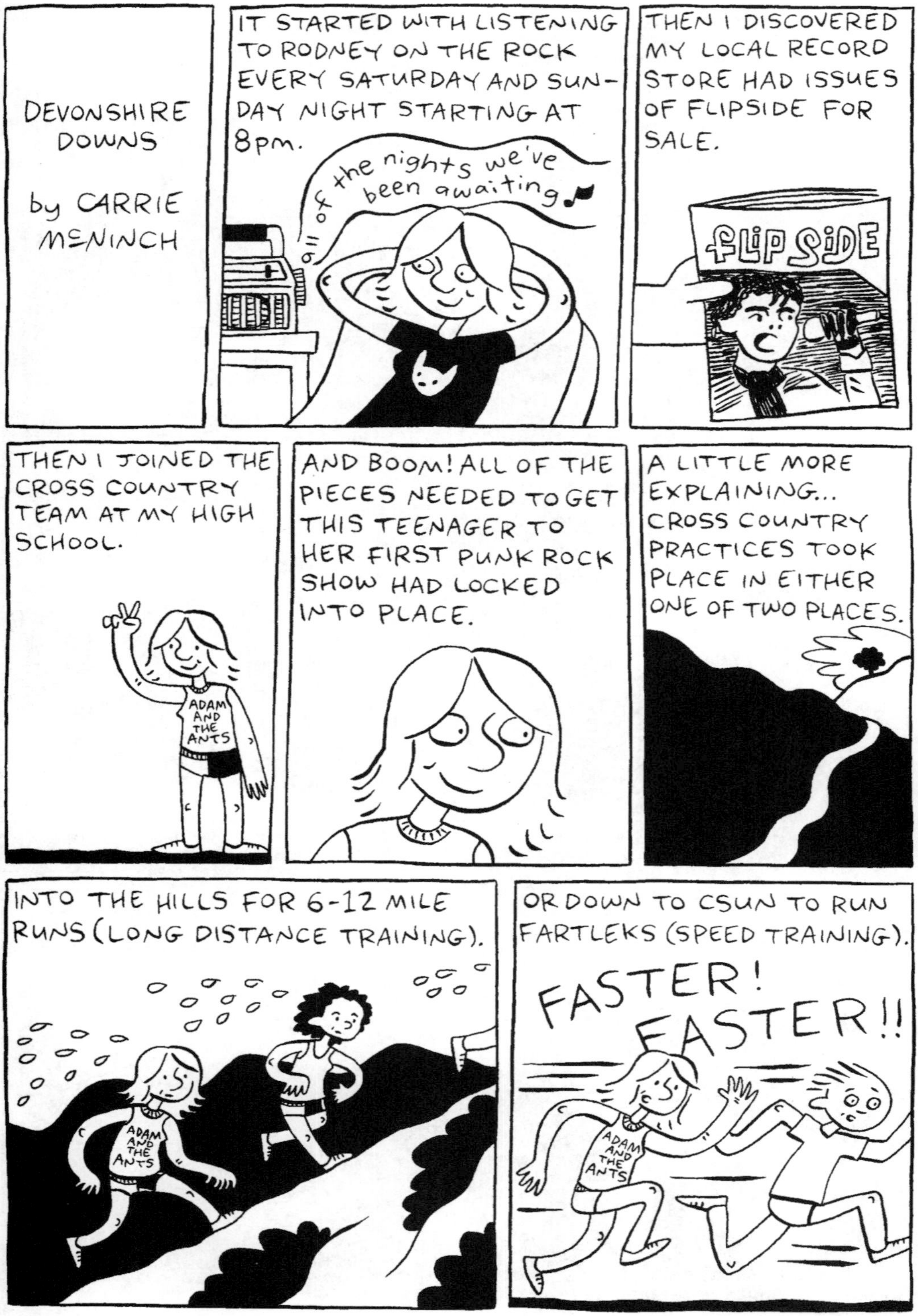
DEVONSHIRE DOWNS
by CARRIE McNINCH
IT STARTED WITH LISTENING TO RODNEY ON THE ROCK EVERY SATURDAY AND SUNDAY NIGHT STARTING AT 8pm.
...of the nights we've been awaiting
THEN I DISCOVERED MY LOCAL RECORD STORE HAD ISSUES OF FLIPSIDE FOR SALE.
FLIPSIDE
THEN I JOINED THE CROSS COUNTRY TEAM AT MY HIGH SCHOOL.
ADAM AND THE ANTS
AND BOOM! ALL OF THE PIECES NEEDED TO GET THIS TEENAGER TO HER FIRST PUNK ROCK SHOW HAD LOCKED INTO PLACE.
A LITTLE MORE EXPLAINING... CROSS COUNTRY PRACTICES TOOK PLACE IN EITHER ONE OF TWO PLACES.
INTO THE HILLS FOR 6-12 MILE RUNS (LONG DISTANCE TRAINING).
ADAM AND THE ANTS
OR DOWN TO CSUN TO RUN FARTLEKS (SPEED TRAINING).
FASTER! FASTER!!
ADAM AND THE ANTS

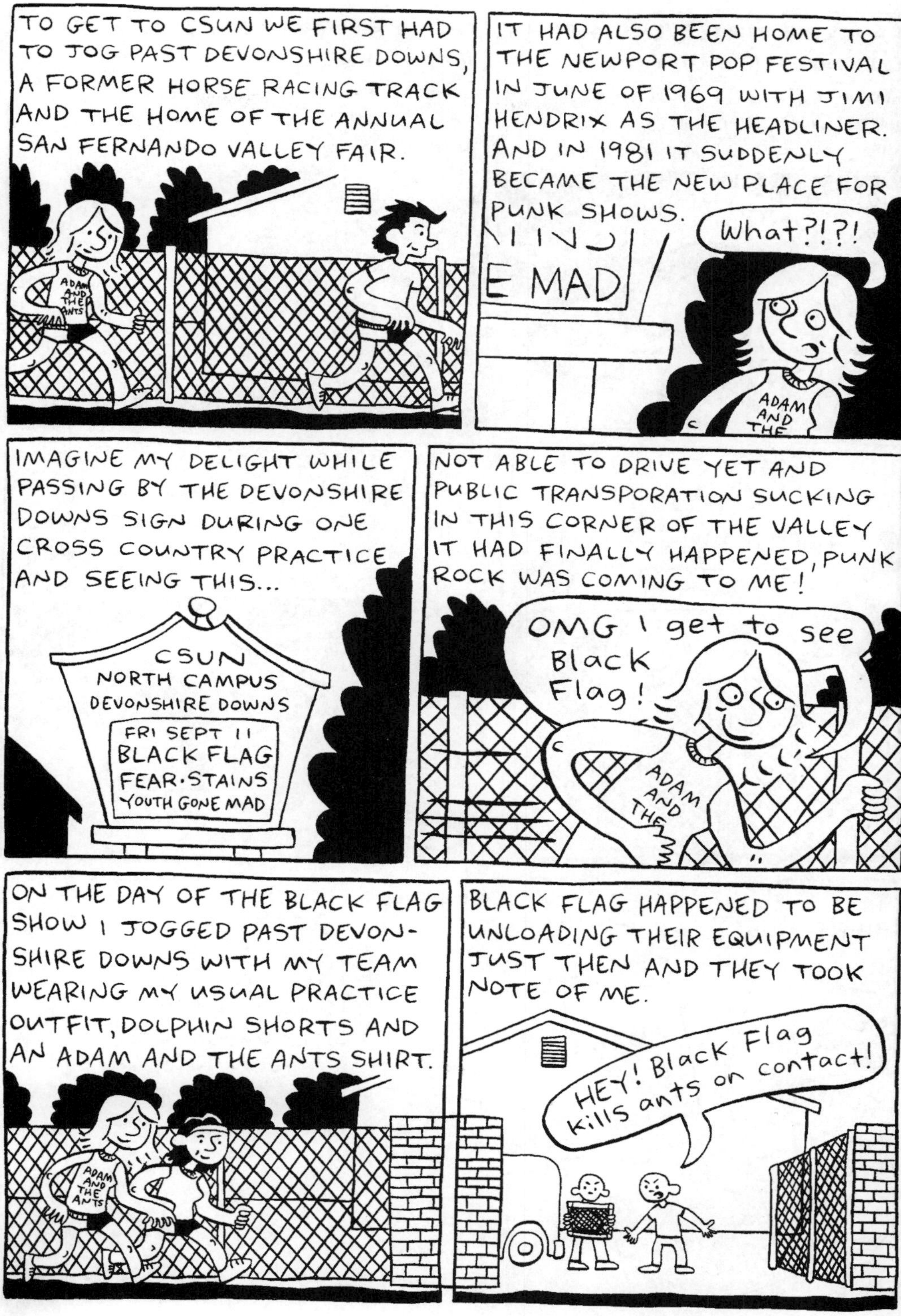
TO GET TO CSUN WE FIRST HAD TO JOG PAST DEVONSHIRE DOWNS, A FORMER HORSE RACING TRACK AND THE HOME OF THE ANNUAL SAN FERNANDO VALLEY FAIR.
ADAM AND THE ANTS
IT HAD ALSO BEEN HOME TO THE NEWPORT POP FESTIVAL IN JUNE OF 1969 WITH JIMI HENDRIX AS THE HEADLINER. AND IN 1981 IT SUDDENLY BECAME THE NEW PLACE FOR PUNK SHOWS.
E MAD
What?!?!
ADAM AND THE
IMAGINE MY DELIGHT WHILE PASSING BY THE DEVONSHIRE DOWNS SIGN DURING ONE CROSS COUNTRY PRACTICE AND SEEING THIS...
CSUN
NORTH CAMPUS
DEVONSHIRE DOWNS
FRI SEPT 11
BLACK FLAG
FEAR·STAINS
YOUTH GONE MAD
NOT ABLE TO DRIVE YET AND PUBLIC TRANSPORATION SUCKING IN THIS CORNER OF THE VALLEY IT HAD FINALLY HAPPENED, PUNK ROCK WAS COMING TO ME!
OMG I get to see Black Flag!
ADAM AND THE
ON THE DAY OF THE BLACK FLAG SHOW I JOGGED PAST DEVONSHIRE DOWNS WITH MY TEAM WEARING MY USUAL PRACTICE OUTFIT, DOLPHIN SHORTS AND AN ADAM AND THE ANTS SHIRT.
ADAM AND THE ANTS
BLACK FLAG HAPPENED TO BE UNLOADING THEIR EQUIPMENT JUST THEN AND THEY TOOK NOTE OF ME.
HEY! Black Flag kills ants on contact!

LATER ON THAT EVENING I PUT ON ANOTHER SHIRT AND WENT TO MY FIRST HARDCORE SHOW WITH A COUPLE KIDS FROM MY CROSS COUNTRY TEAM.

We are tired of your abuse try to stop us ♪♪

THE NEXT SHOW COMING UP AT DEVONSHIRE DOWNS WAS THE CRAMPS. MY LIKE-MINDED COMRADES AND I (LONG DISTANCE RUNNERS HAVE A TENDENCY TO BE INTO GOOD MUSIC) DECIDED TO FIGURE OUT A WAY TO GET IN THE SHOW FOR FREE.

It's in our backyard.

There's gotta be a way.

DURING FARTLEK PRACTICE WE NOTICED A WAY.

Is this... unlocked?

Yes, it is!

ON HALLOWEEN NIGHT WE SNUCK IN THROUGH AN UNLOCKED BACK GATE THAT NO ONE WOULD KNOW WAS THERE UNLESS THEY JOGGED BY IT 2 OR 3 TIMES A WEEK.

I got a garbage brain that's drivin' me insane ♪♪

THE SNEAKING INTO SHOWS AT DEVONSHIRE DOWNS CONTINUED.

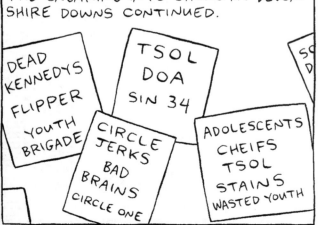

DEAD KENNEDYS
FLIPPER
YOUTH BRIGADE

TSOL
DOA
SIN 34

CIRCLE JERKS
BAD BRAINS
CIRCLE ONE

ADOLESCENTS
CHEIFS
TSOL
STAINS
WASTED YOUTH

DIDN'T LET UP UNTIL AFTER I GRADUATED HIGH SCHOOL AND MOVED TO HOLLYWOOD.

Goodbye San Fernando Valley!

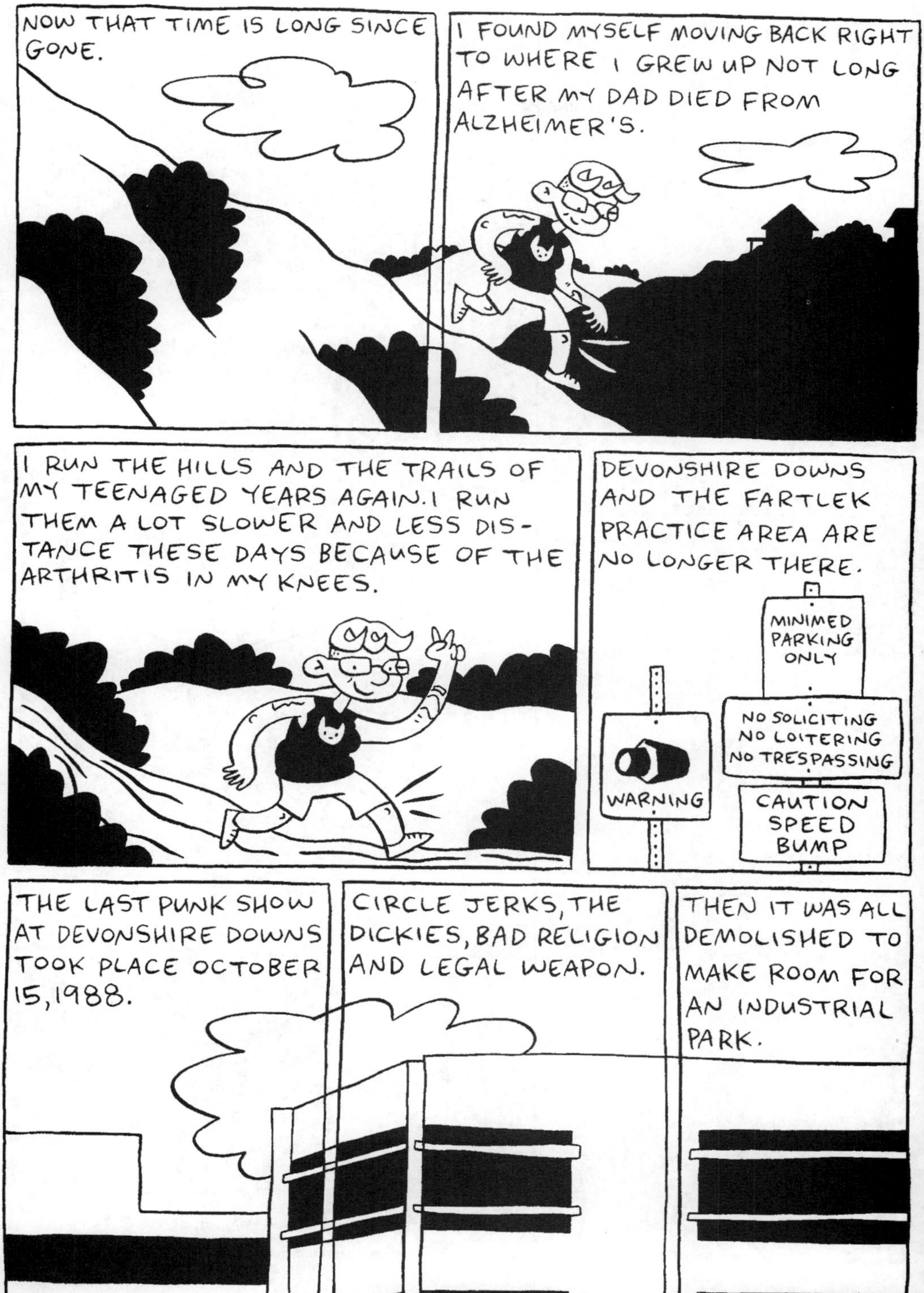
NOW THAT TIME IS LONG SINCE GONE.
I FOUND MYSELF MOVING BACK RIGHT TO WHERE I GREW UP NOT LONG AFTER MY DAD DIED FROM ALZHEIMER'S.
I RUN THE HILLS AND THE TRAILS OF MY TEENAGED YEARS AGAIN. I RUN THEM A LOT SLOWER AND LESS DISTANCE THESE DAYS BECAUSE OF THE ARTHRITIS IN MY KNEES.
DEVONSHIRE DOWNS AND THE FARTLEK PRACTICE AREA ARE NO LONGER THERE.
MINIMED PARKING ONLY
NO SOLICITING NO LOITERING NO TRESPASSING
WARNING
CAUTION SPEED BUMP
THE LAST PUNK SHOW AT DEVONSHIRE DOWNS TOOK PLACE OCTOBER 15, 1988.
CIRCLE JERKS, THE DICKIES, BAD RELIGION AND LEGAL WEAPON.
THEN IT WAS ALL DEMOLISHED TO MAKE ROOM FOR AN INDUSTRIAL PARK.

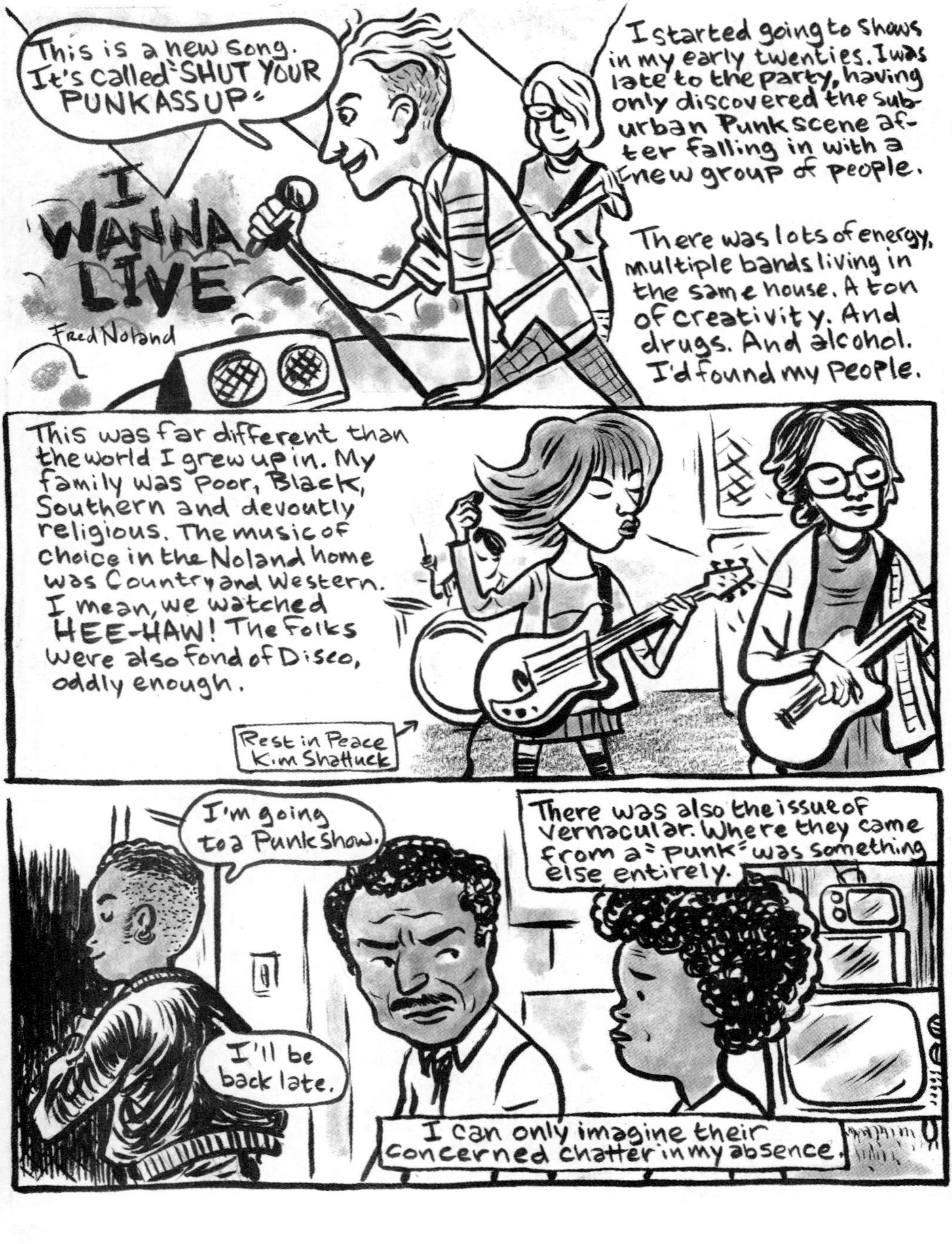
This is a new song. It's called "SHUT YOUR PUNKASS UP."
I started going to shows in my early twenties. I was late to the party, having only discovered the suburban Punk scene after falling in with a new group of people.
I WANNA LIVE
Fred Noland
There was lots of energy, multiple bands living in the same house. A ton of creativity. And drugs. And alcohol. I'd found my people.
This was far different than the world I grew up in. My family was poor, Black, Southern and devoutly religious. The music of choice in the Noland home was Country and Western. I mean, we watched HEE-HAW! The folks were also fond of Disco, oddly enough.
Rest in Peace Kim Shattuck
I'm going to a Punk show.
There was also the issue of vernacular. Where they came from a "punk" was something else entirely.
I'll be back late.
I can only imagine their concerned chatter in my absence.

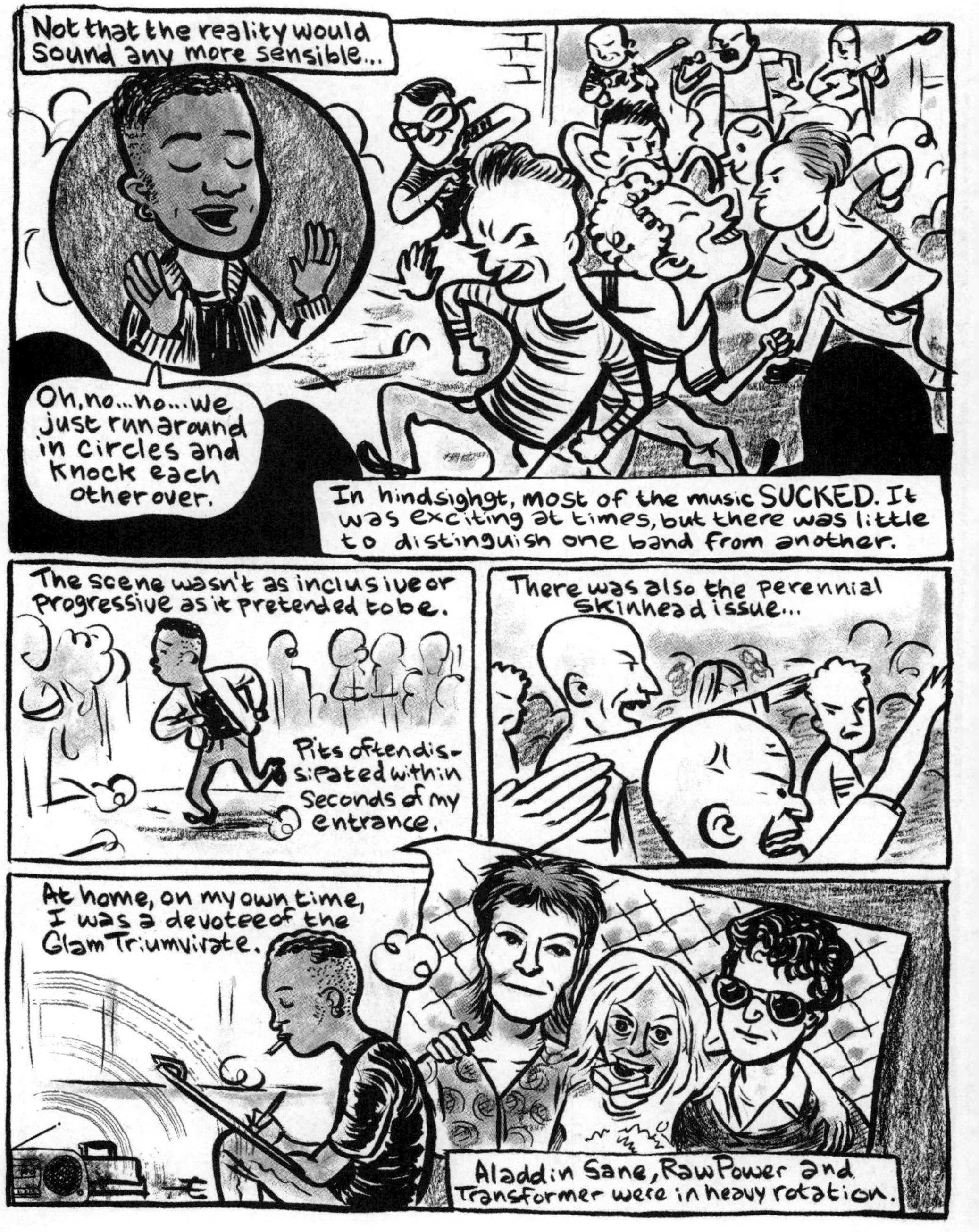

Not that the reality would sound any more sensible...
Oh, no... no... we just run around in circles and knock each other over.
In hindsighgt, most of the music SUCKED. It was exciting at times, but there was little to distinguish one band from another.
The scene wasn't as inclusive or progressive as it pretended to be.
Pits often dissipated within seconds of my entrance.
There was also the perennial skinhead issue...
At home, on my own time, I was a devotee of the Glam Triumvirate.
Aladdin Sane, Raw Power and Transformer were in heavy rotation.

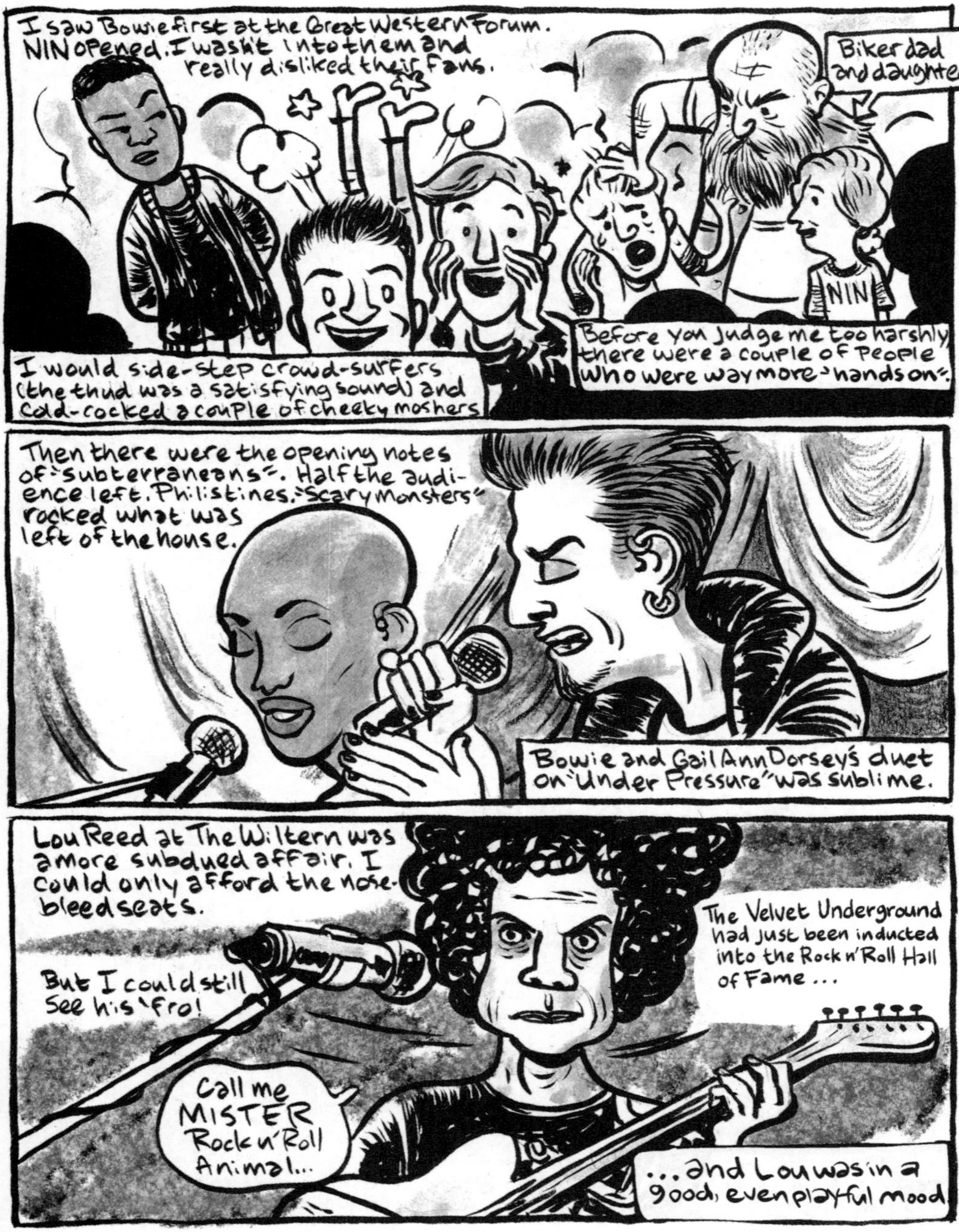
I saw Bowie first at the Great Western Forum. NIN opened. I wasn't into them and really disliked their fans.
Biker dad and daughter
NIN
I would side-step crowd-surfers (the thud was a satisfying sound) and cold-cocked a couple of cheeky moshers
Before you judge me too harshly there were a couple of people who were way more "hands on".
Then there were the opening notes of "Subterraneans". Half the audience left. Philistines. "Scary Monsters" rocked what was left of the house.
Bowie and Gail Ann Dorsey's duet on "Under Pressure" was sublime.
Lou Reed at The Wiltern was a more subdued affair. I could only afford the nose-bleed seats.
But I could still see his 'fro!
The Velvet Underground had just been inducted into the Rock n' Roll Hall of Fame ...
Call me MISTER Rock n' Roll Animal...
... and Lou was in a good, even playful mood

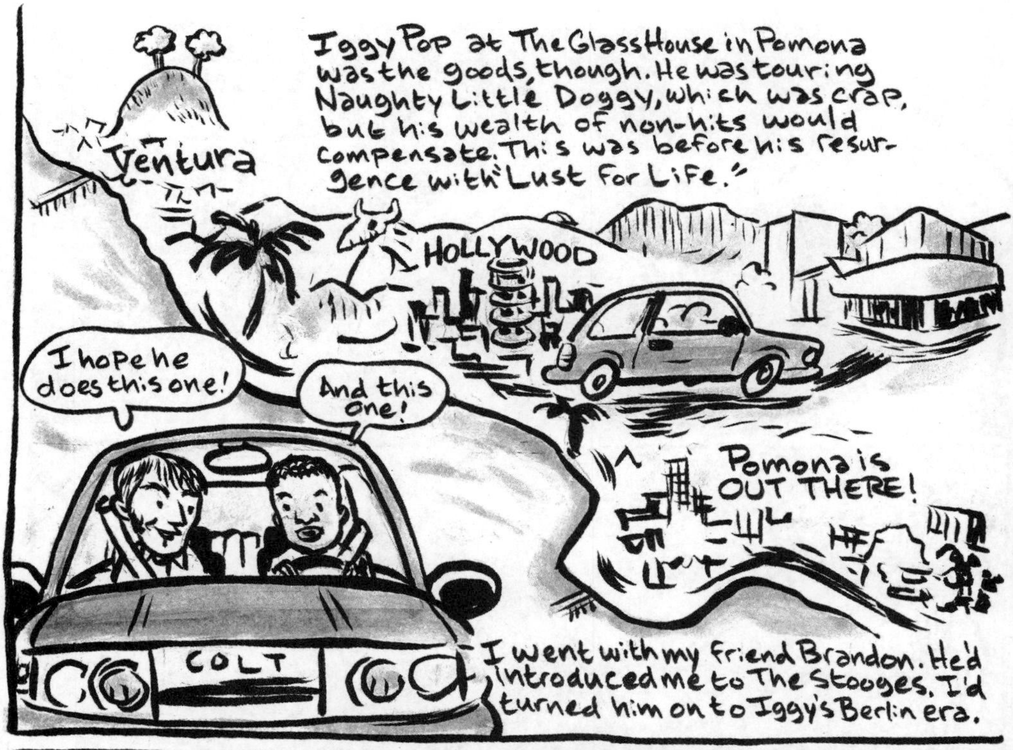
Iggy Pop at The GlassHouse in Pomona was the goods, though. He was touring Naughty Little Doggy, which was crap, but his wealth of non-hits would compensate. This was before his resurgence with "Lust for Life."
Ventura
HOLLYWOOD
I hope he does this one!
And this one!
Pomona is OUT THERE!
COLT
I went with my friend Brandon. He'd introduced me to The Stooges. I'd turned him on to Iggy's Berlin era.
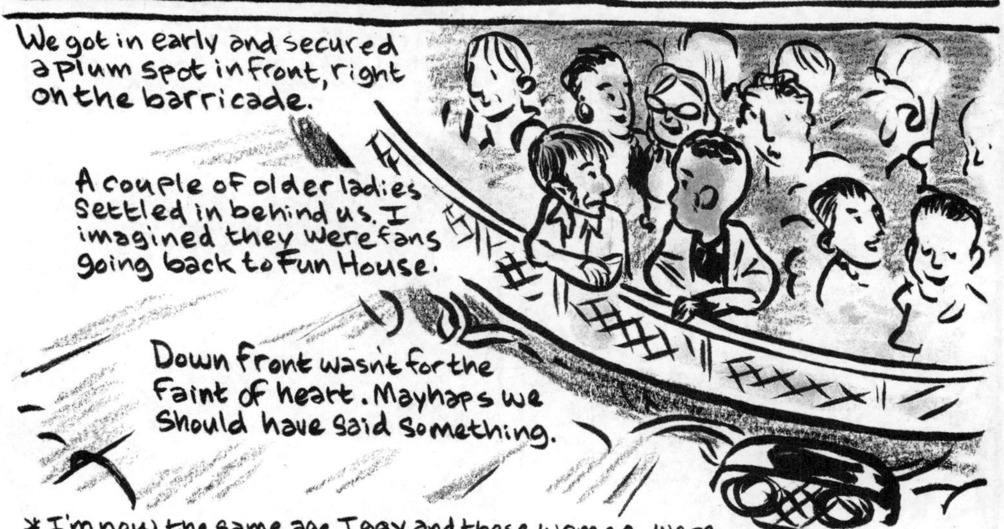
We got in early and secured a plum spot in front, right on the barricade.
A couple of older ladies settled in behind us. I imagined they were fans going back to Fun House.
Down front wasn't for the faint of heart. Mayhaps we should have said something.
* I'm now the same age Iggy and these women were.

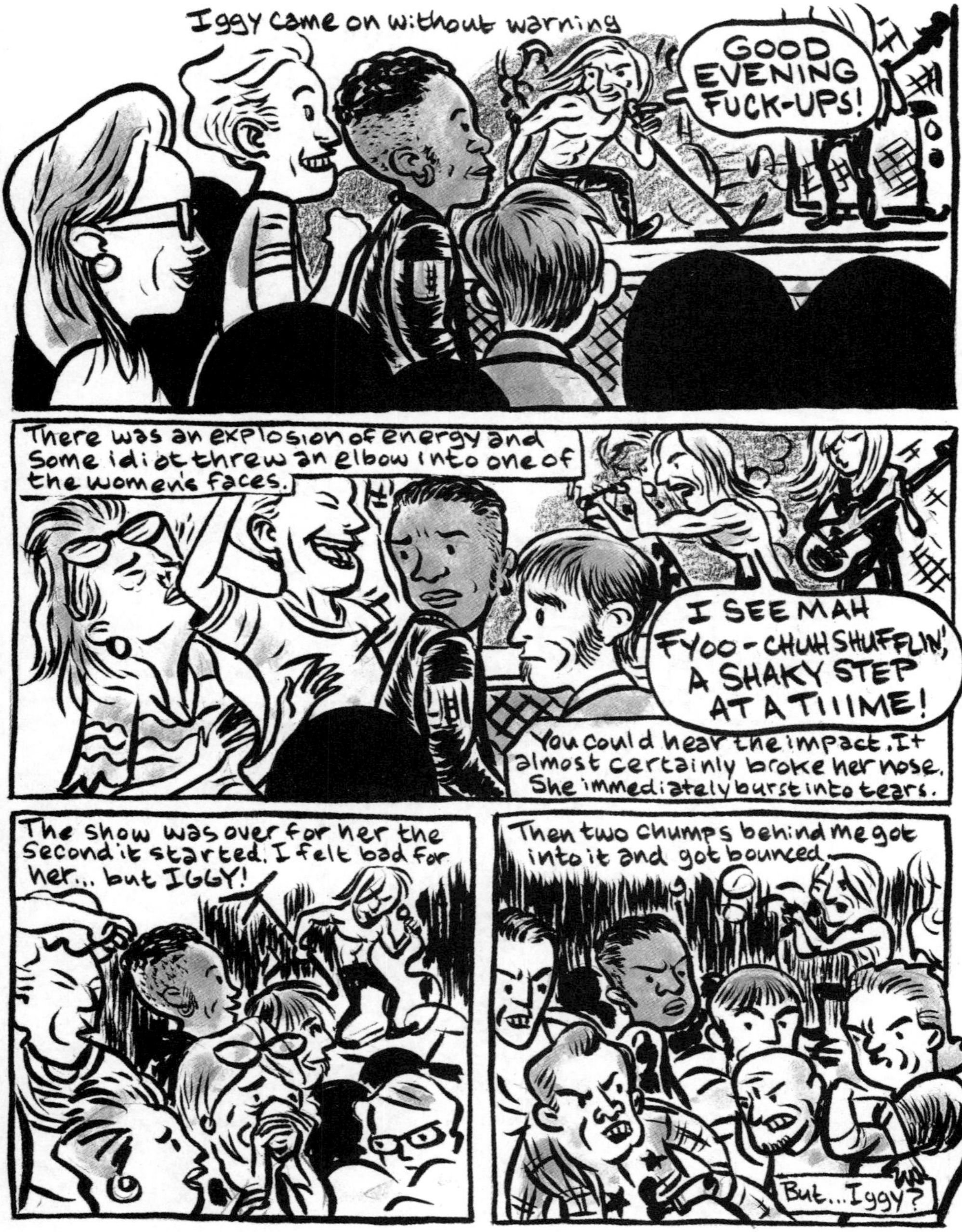
Iggy came on without warning
GOOD EVENING FUCK-UPS!
There was an explosion of energy and some idiot threw an elbow into one of the women's faces.
I SEE MAH FYOO-CHUH SHUFFLIN', A SHAKY STEP AT A TIIIME!
You could hear the impact. It almost certainly broke her nose. She immediately burst into tears.
The show was over for her the second it started. I felt bad for her... but IGGY!
Then two chumps behind me got into it and got bounced.
But... Iggy?

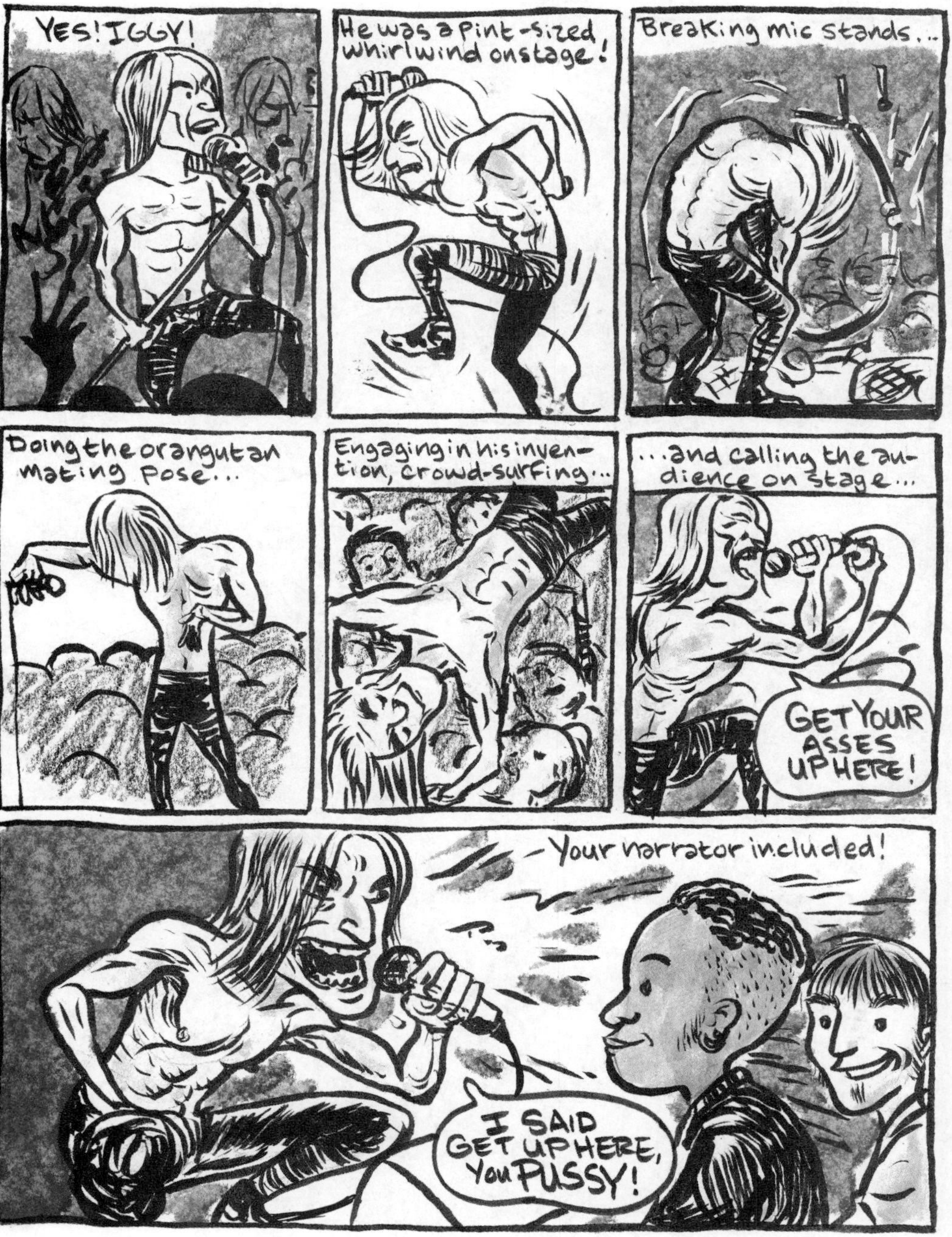
YES! IGGY!
He was a pint-sized whirlwind onstage!
Breaking mic stands...
Doing the orangutan mating pose...
Engaging in his invention, crowd-surfing...
...and calling the audience on stage...
GET YOUR ASSES UP HERE!
-Your narrator included!
I SAID GET UP HERE, You PUSSY!

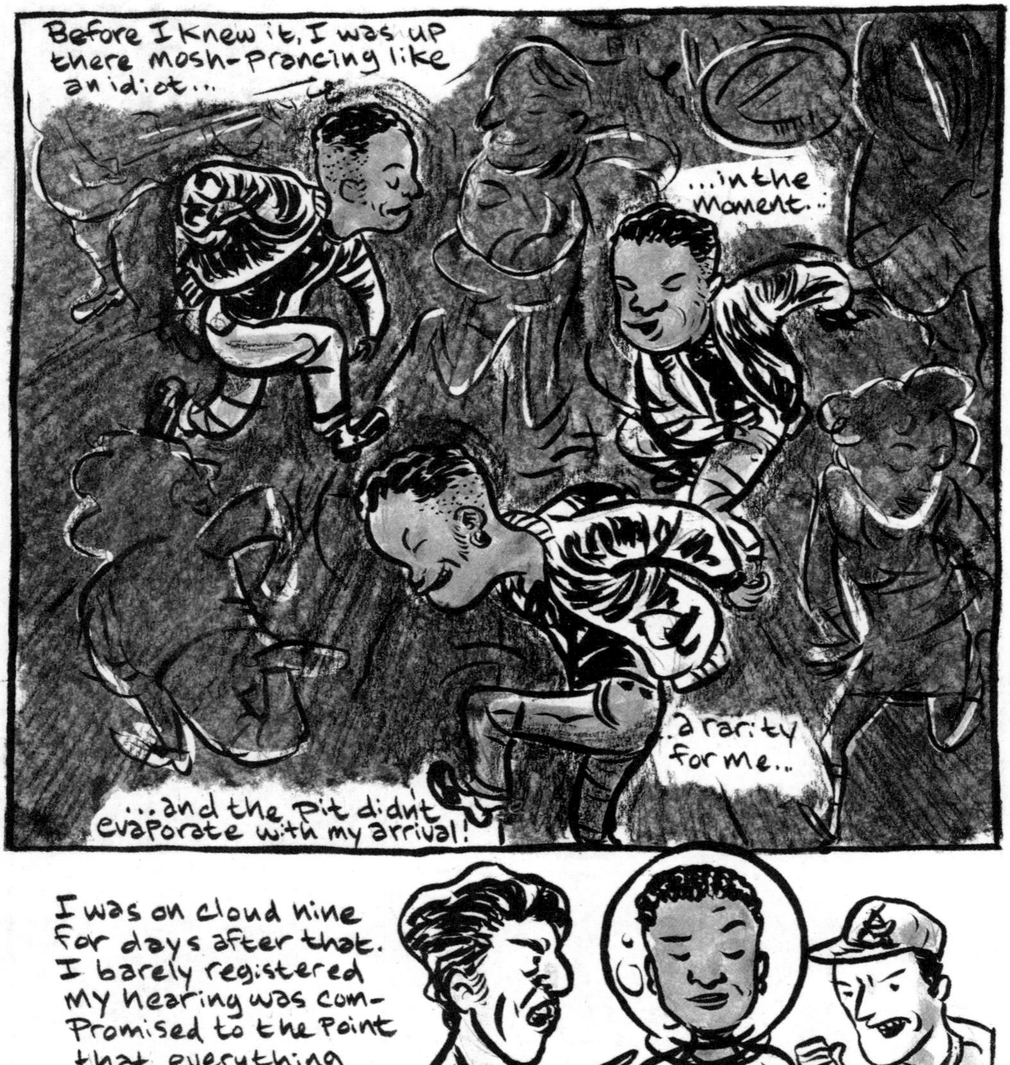
Before I knew it, I was up there mosh-prancing like an idiot...
...in the moment...
...a rarity for me...
...and the pit didnt evaporate with my arrival!

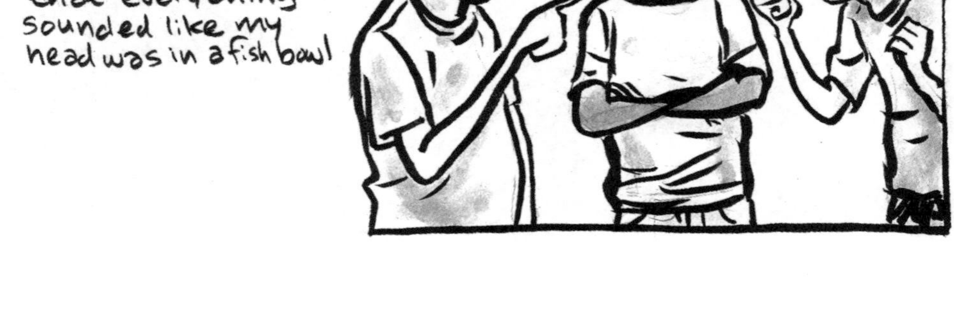
I was on cloud nine for days after that. I barely registered my hearing was compromised to the point that everything sounded like my head was in a fish bowl

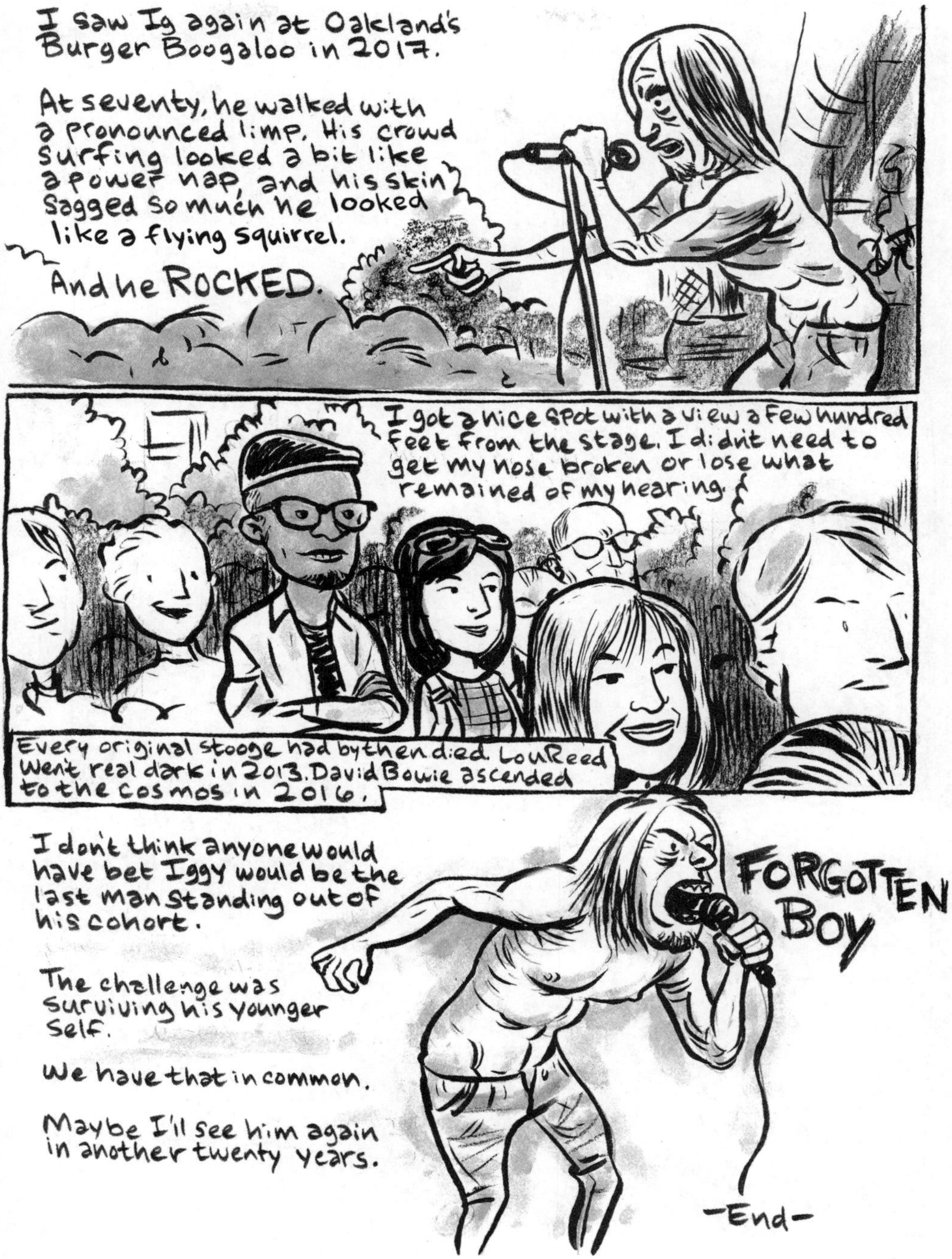
I saw Ig again at Oakland's Burger Boogaloo in 2017.
At seventy, he walked with a pronounced limp. His crowd surfing looked a bit like a power nap, and his skin sagged so much he looked like a flying squirrel.
And he ROCKED.
I got a nice spot with a view a few hundred feet from the stage. I didn't need to get my nose broken or lose what remained of my hearing.
Every original stooge had by then died. Lou Reed went real dark in 2013. David Bowie ascended to the cosmos in 2016.
I don't think anyone would have bet Iggy would be the last man standing out of his cohort.
The challenge was surviving his younger self.
We have that in common.
Maybe I'll see him again in another twenty years.
FORGOTTEN BOY
-End-

(NOT) TOO TOUGH TO DIE BY FRANK GROSZ

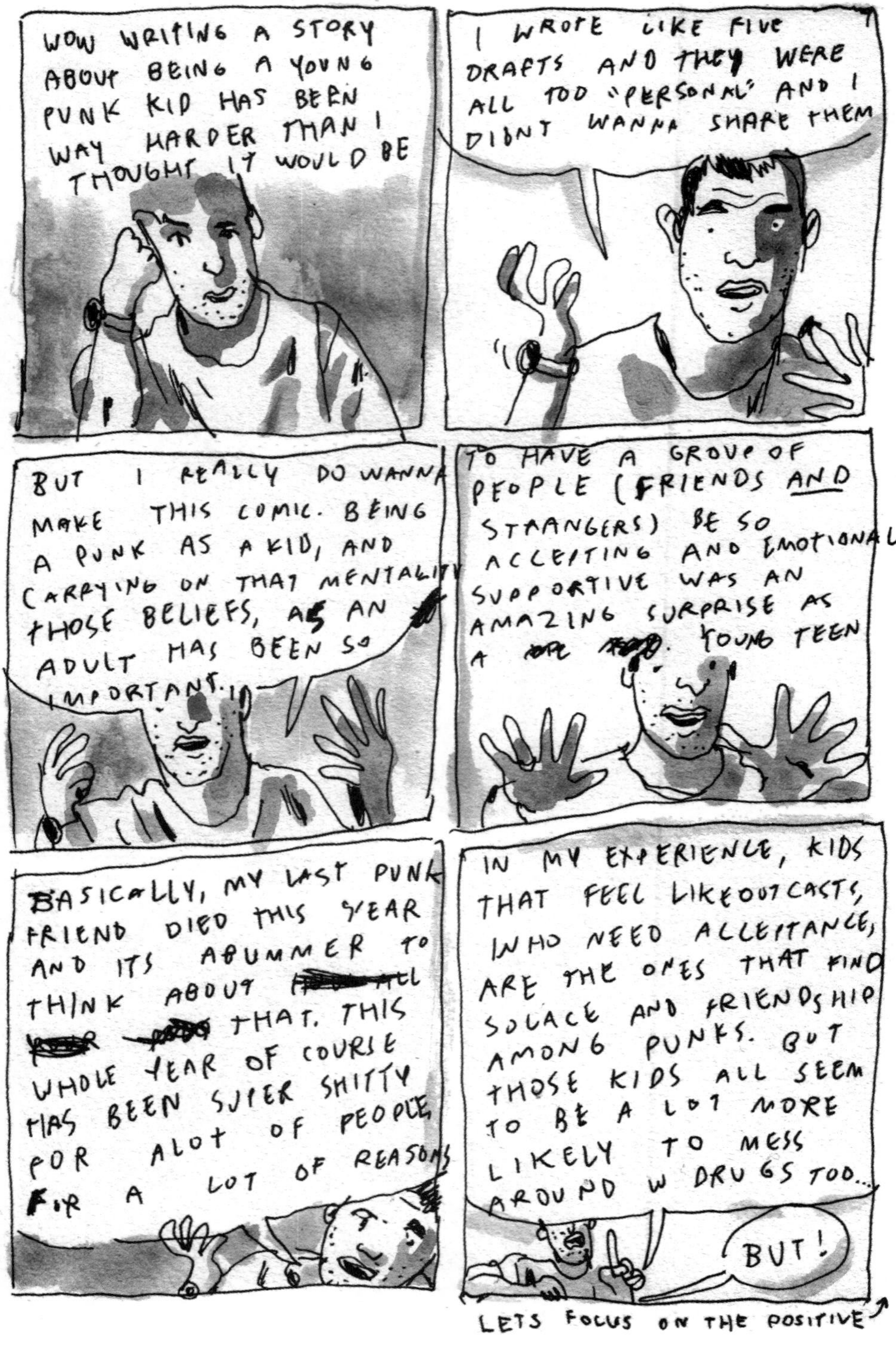
WOW WRITING A STORY ABOUT BEING A YOUNG PUNK KID HAS BEEN WAY HARDER THAN I THOUGHT IT WOULD BE
I WROTE LIKE FIVE DRAFTS AND THEY WERE ALL TOO "PERSONAL" AND I DIDNT WANNA SHARE THEM
BUT I REALLY DO WANNA MAKE THIS COMIC. BEING A PUNK AS A KID, AND CARRYING ON THAT MENTALITY THOSE BELIEFS, AS AN ADULT HAS BEEN SO IMPORTANT.
TO HAVE A GROUP OF PEOPLE (FRIENDS AND STRANGERS) BE SO ACCEPTING AND EMOTIONALLY SUPPORTIVE WAS AN AMAZING SURPRISE AS A YOUNG TEEN
BASICALLY, MY LAST PUNK FRIEND DIED THIS YEAR AND ITS A BUMMER TO THINK ABOUT THAT. THIS WHOLE YEAR OF COURSE HAS BEEN SUPER SHITTY FOR ALOT OF PEOPLE FOR A LOT OF REASONS
IN MY EXPERIENCE, KIDS THAT FEEL LIKE OUTCASTS, WHO NEED ACCEPTANCE, ARE THE ONES THAT FIND SOLACE AND FRIENDSHIP AMONG PUNKS. BUT THOSE KIDS ALL SEEM TO BE A LOT MORE LIKELY TO MESS AROUND W DRUGS TOO...
BUT!
LETS FOCUS ON THE POSITIVE

TALKING WITH OTHER KIDS WHO KNEW THE GOVERNMUNT DOESN'T CARE ABOUT ITS CITIZENS, THAT CORPORATIONS DONT CARE ABOUT THEIR CUSTOMERS, AND THAT COPS DONT CARE ABOUT THE PEOPLE THEYRE SUPPOSED TO PROTECT? ~~DROP REALLY~~ ~~XXXXXXXXX~~ THAT EVERY ONE WHO LIVES ON EARTH DOESN'T CARE ABOUT IT?

I HAD GREAT CONVERSATIONS W MY PUNK PALS AND THEY FORMED MY ATTITUDE IN LIFE, ~~XXX~~ THE ONE I STILL HOLD TODAY.

FOR ME, BEING PUNK WASN'T SO MUCH ABOUT THE MUSIC (WHICH I LOVED) OR THE FASHION (WHICH I IRONICALLY COULDNT AFFORD TO MAKE) OR ~~XXX~~ EVEN THE ART (WHICH SEEMED CONTRIVED TO A LITTLE 14 YEAR OLD PESSIMIST)

~~XXX~~ THE BASIC MESSAGE OF CARE AND ACCEPTANCE IS WHAT PUNK REALLY MEANT TO ME. AND WRITING THAT OUT MAKES MY MIND GO ON SO MANY CHURCH/RELIGION INSTITUTIONS -BEING- REPLACED- WITH- PUNK- OUTREACH- CENTER TANGENT THAT I SHOULD JUST STOP NOW.

BEING A PUNK KID CHANGED MY LIFE FOR THE BETTER AND IT WOULD BE A DISSERVICE TO THE MOVEMENT TO NOT SPEND A COUPLE HOURS MAKING THIS COMIC.

EVEN THOUGH ITS ~~XXX~~ NOT SPECIFICALLY ABOUT MY PUNK EXPERIENCE, IF THERES ONE THING I LEARNED ABOUT BEING PUNK ITS THAT ANY THING IS PUNK WITH THE RIGHT ATTITUDE.

STAY COOL GUYS!

FRANK GROSZ 2020

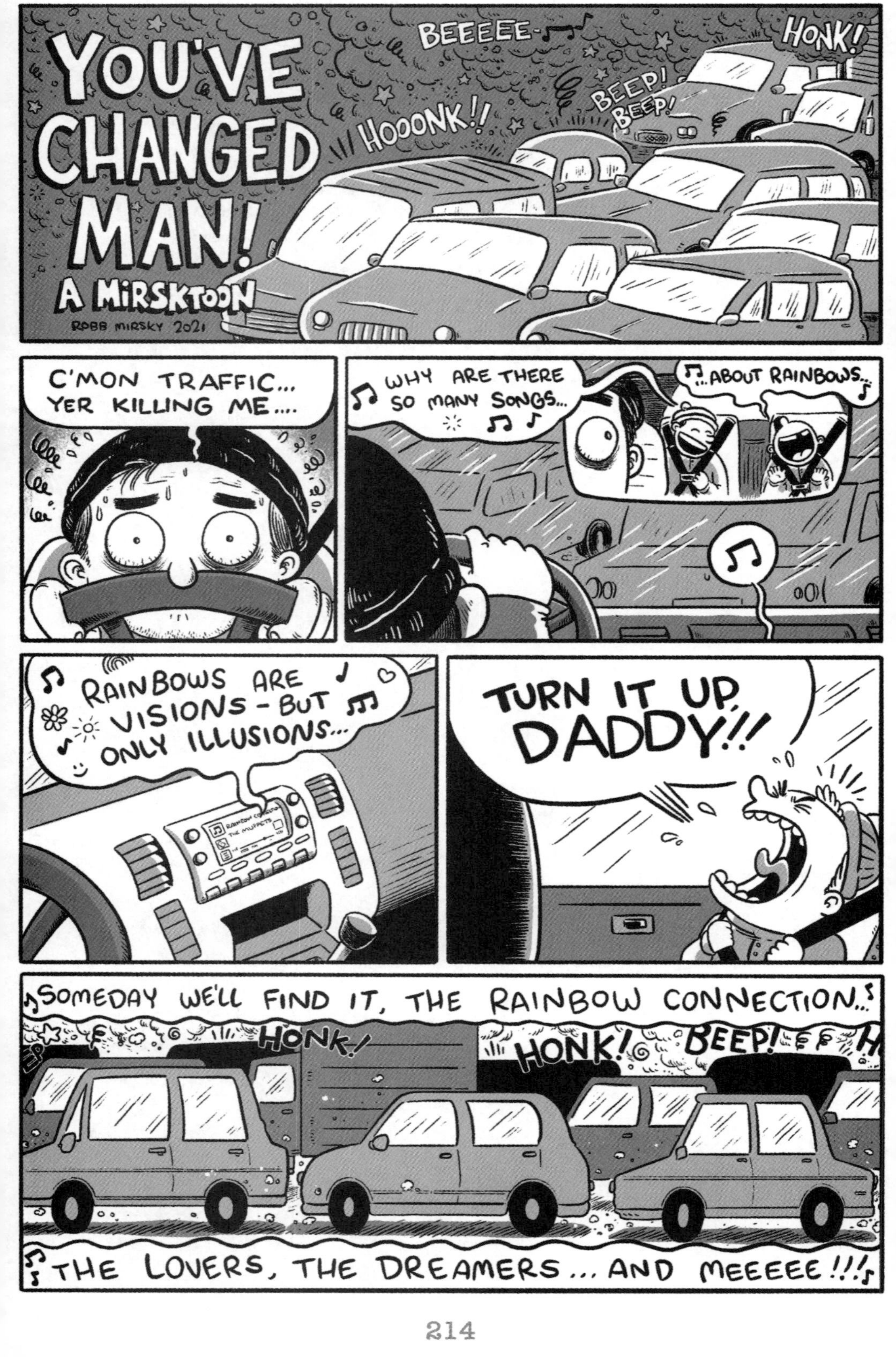
YOU'VE CHANGED MAN!
A MIRSKTOON
ROBB MIRSKY 2021
BEEEEE-
HONK!
BEEP! BEEP!
HOOONK!!
C'MON TRAFFIC... YER KILLING ME....
WHY ARE THERE SO MANY SONGS...
...ABOUT RAINBOWS...
RAINBOWS ARE VISIONS - BUT ONLY ILLUSIONS...
TURN IT UP, DADDY!!!
SOMEDAY WE'LL FIND IT, THE RAINBOW CONNECTION...
HONK!
HONK!
BEEP!
THE LOVERS, THE DREAMERS ... AND MEEEEE!!!

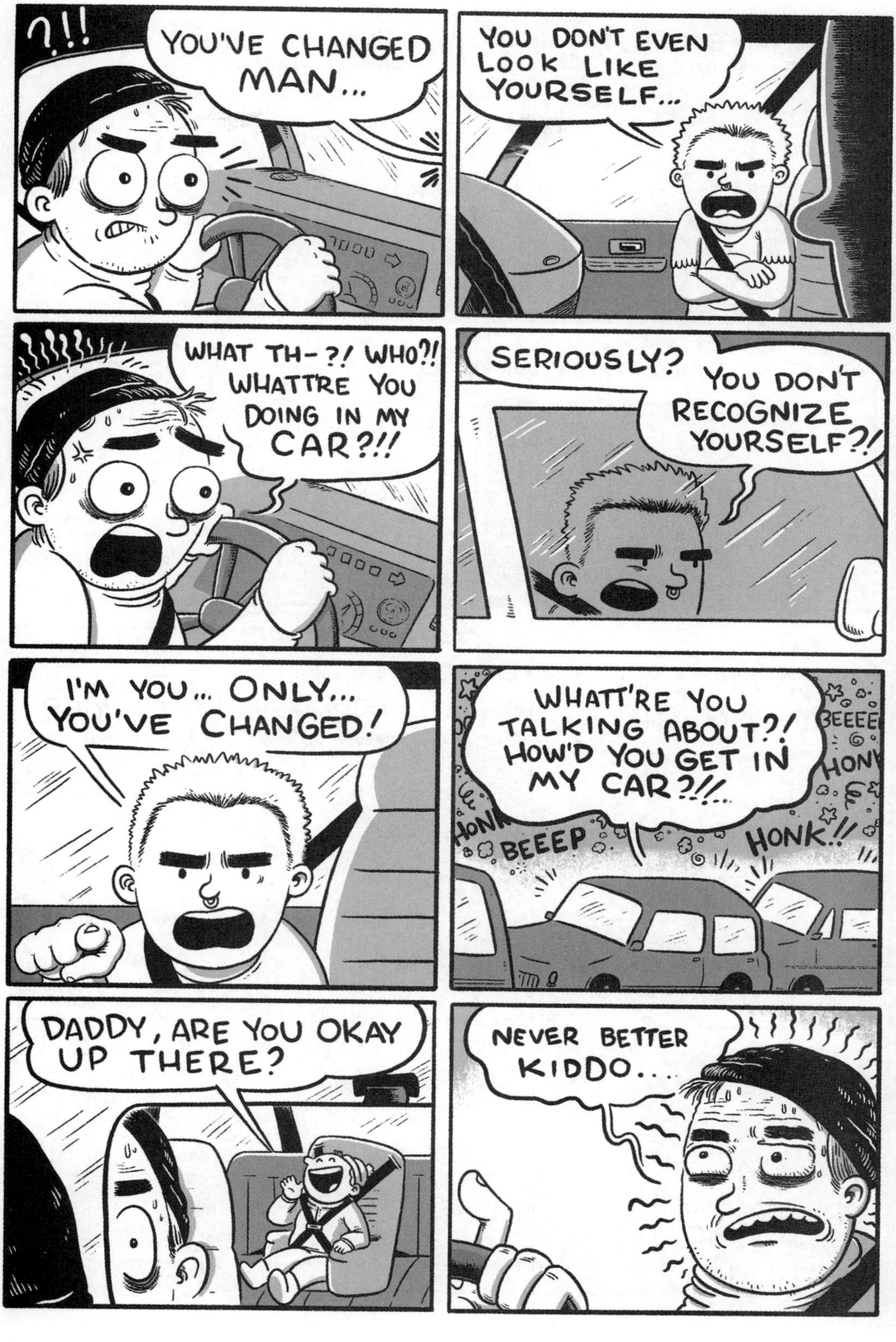
?!!
YOU'VE CHANGED MAN...
YOU DON'T EVEN LOOK LIKE YOURSELF...
WHAT TH-?! WHO?! WHATT'RE YOU DOING IN MY CAR?!!
SERIOUSLY?
YOU DON'T RECOGNIZE YOURSELF?!
I'M YOU... ONLY... YOU'VE CHANGED!
WHATT'RE YOU TALKING ABOUT?! HOW'D YOU GET IN MY CAR?!!...
BEEEE
HONK
HONK
BEEEP
HONK!!
DADDY, ARE YOU OKAY UP THERE?
NEVER BETTER KIDDO...

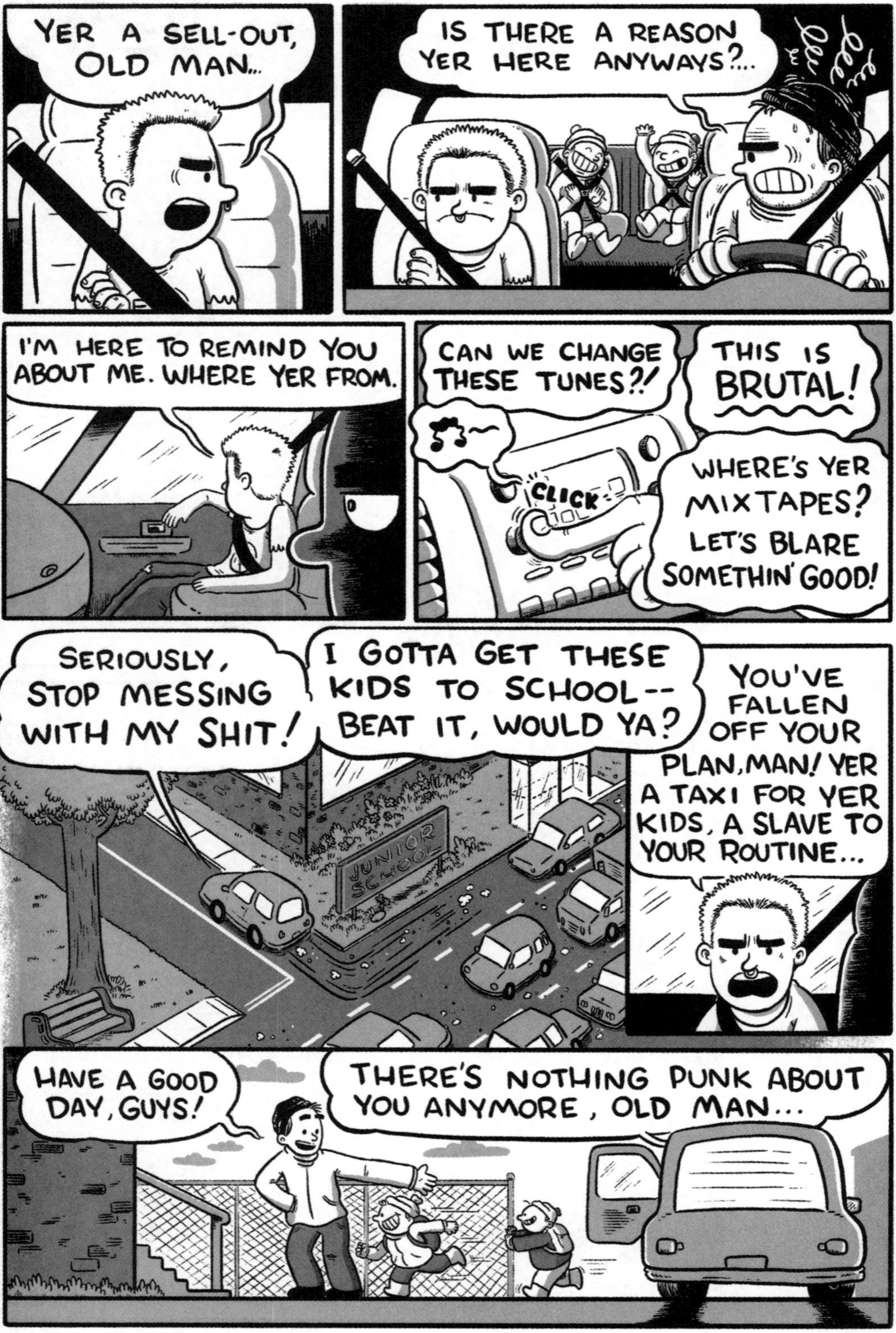
YER A SELL-OUT, OLD MAN...
IS THERE A REASON YER HERE ANYWAYS?...
I'M HERE TO REMIND YOU ABOUT ME. WHERE YER FROM.
CAN WE CHANGE THESE TUNES?!
THIS IS BRUTAL!
CLICK
WHERE'S YER MIXTAPES? LET'S BLARE SOMETHIN' GOOD!
SERIOUSLY, STOP MESSING WITH MY SHIT!
I GOTTA GET THESE KIDS TO SCHOOL-- BEAT IT, WOULD YA?
YOU'VE FALLEN OFF YOUR PLAN, MAN! YER A TAXI FOR YER KIDS, A SLAVE TO YOUR ROUTINE...
JUNIOR SCHOOL
HAVE A GOOD DAY, GUYS!
THERE'S NOTHING PUNK ABOUT YOU ANYMORE, OLD MAN...

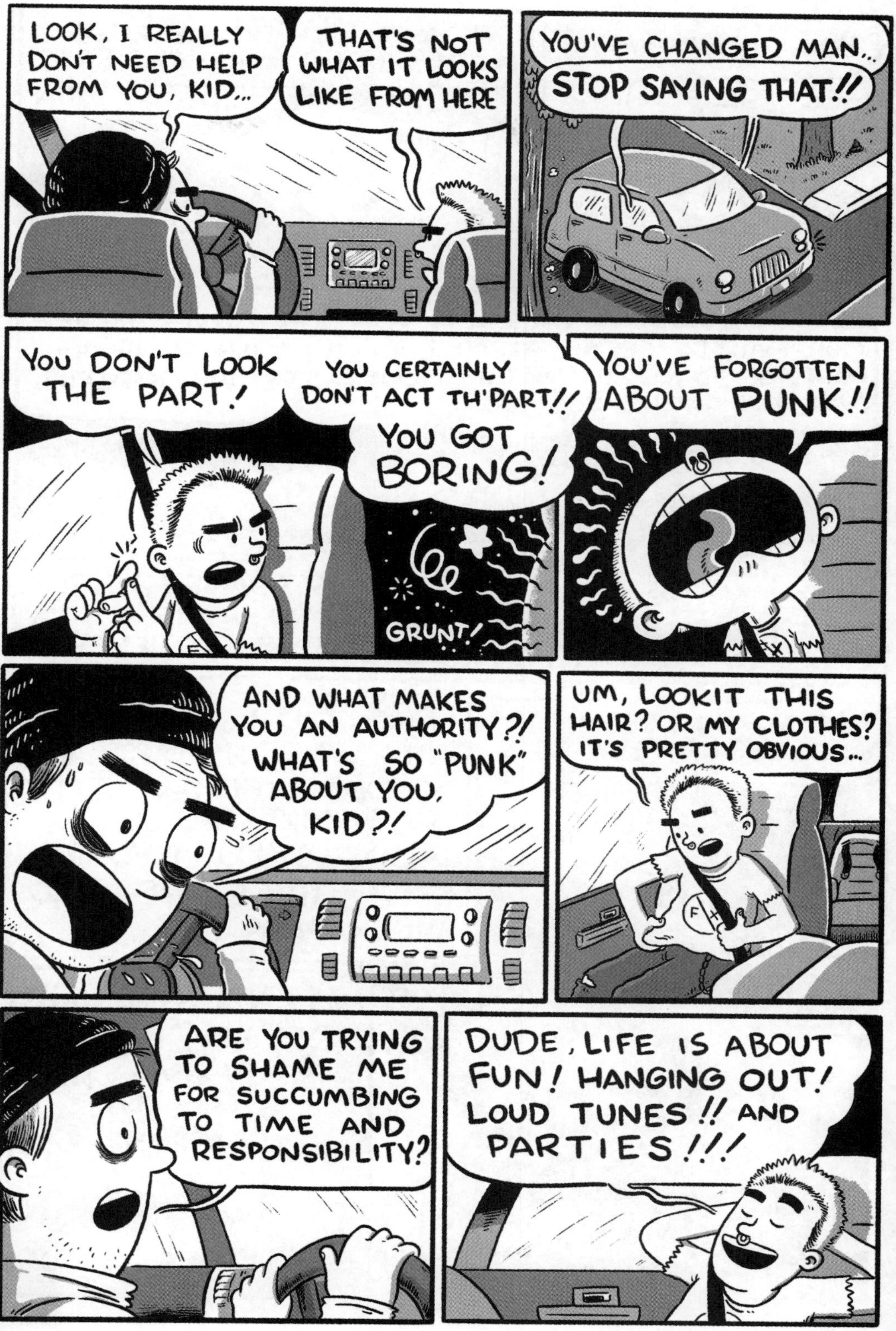
LOOK, I REALLY DON'T NEED HELP FROM YOU, KID...
THAT'S NOT WHAT IT LOOKS LIKE FROM HERE
YOU'VE CHANGED MAN...
STOP SAYING THAT!!
YOU DON'T LOOK THE PART!
YOU CERTAINLY DON'T ACT TH'PART!!
YOU GOT BORING!
GRUNT!
YOU'VE FORGOTTEN ABOUT PUNK!!
AND WHAT MAKES YOU AN AUTHORITY?! WHAT'S SO "PUNK" ABOUT YOU, KID?!
UM, LOOKIT THIS HAIR? OR MY CLOTHES? IT'S PRETTY OBVIOUS...
ARE YOU TRYING TO SHAME ME FOR SUCCUMBING TO TIME AND RESPONSIBILITY?
DUDE, LIFE IS ABOUT FUN! HANGING OUT! LOUD TUNES!! AND PARTIES!!!

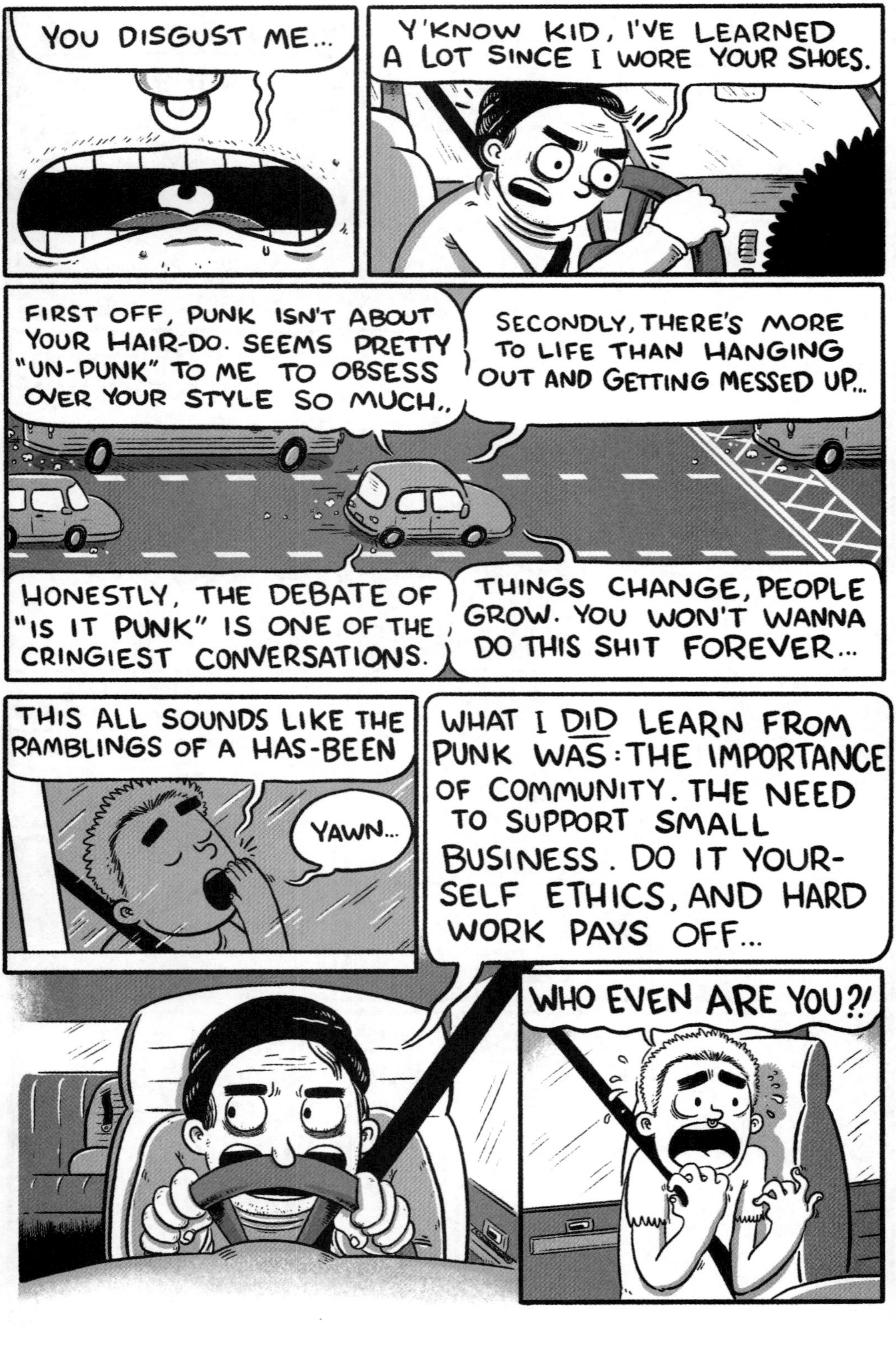
YOU DISGUST ME...
Y'KNOW KID, I'VE LEARNED A LOT SINCE I WORE YOUR SHOES.
FIRST OFF, PUNK ISN'T ABOUT YOUR HAIR-DO. SEEMS PRETTY "UN-PUNK" TO ME TO OBSESS OVER YOUR STYLE SO MUCH..
SECONDLY, THERE'S MORE TO LIFE THAN HANGING OUT AND GETTING MESSED UP...
HONESTLY, THE DEBATE OF "IS IT PUNK" IS ONE OF THE CRINGIEST CONVERSATIONS.
THINGS CHANGE, PEOPLE GROW. YOU WON'T WANNA DO THIS SHIT FOREVER...
THIS ALL SOUNDS LIKE THE RAMBLINGS OF A HAS-BEEN
YAWN...
WHAT I DID LEARN FROM PUNK WAS: THE IMPORTANCE OF COMMUNITY. THE NEED TO SUPPORT SMALL BUSINESS. DO IT YOURSELF ETHICS, AND HARD WORK PAYS OFF...
WHO EVEN ARE YOU?!

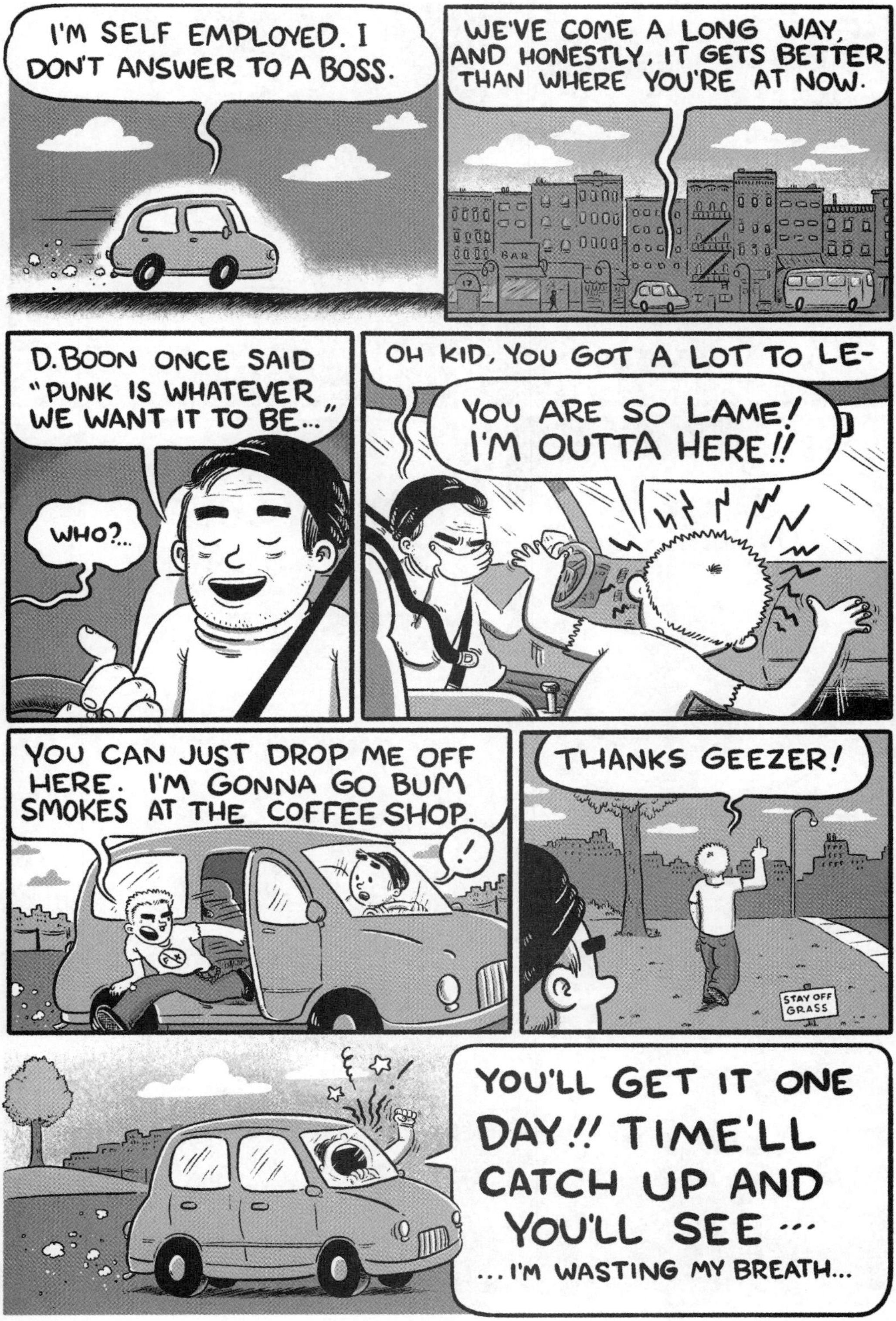
I'M SELF EMPLOYED. I DON'T ANSWER TO A BOSS.
WE'VE COME A LONG WAY, AND HONESTLY, IT GETS BETTER THAN WHERE YOU'RE AT NOW.
BAR
D. BOON ONCE SAID "PUNK IS WHATEVER WE WANT IT TO BE..."
WHO?...
OH KID, YOU GOT A LOT TO LE-
YOU ARE SO LAME! I'M OUTTA HERE!!
YOU CAN JUST DROP ME OFF HERE. I'M GONNA GO BUM SMOKES AT THE COFFEE SHOP.
!
THANKS GEEZER!
STAY OFF GRASS
YOU'LL GET IT ONE DAY!! TIME'LL CATCH UP AND YOU'LL SEE ...
... I'M WASTING MY BREATH...

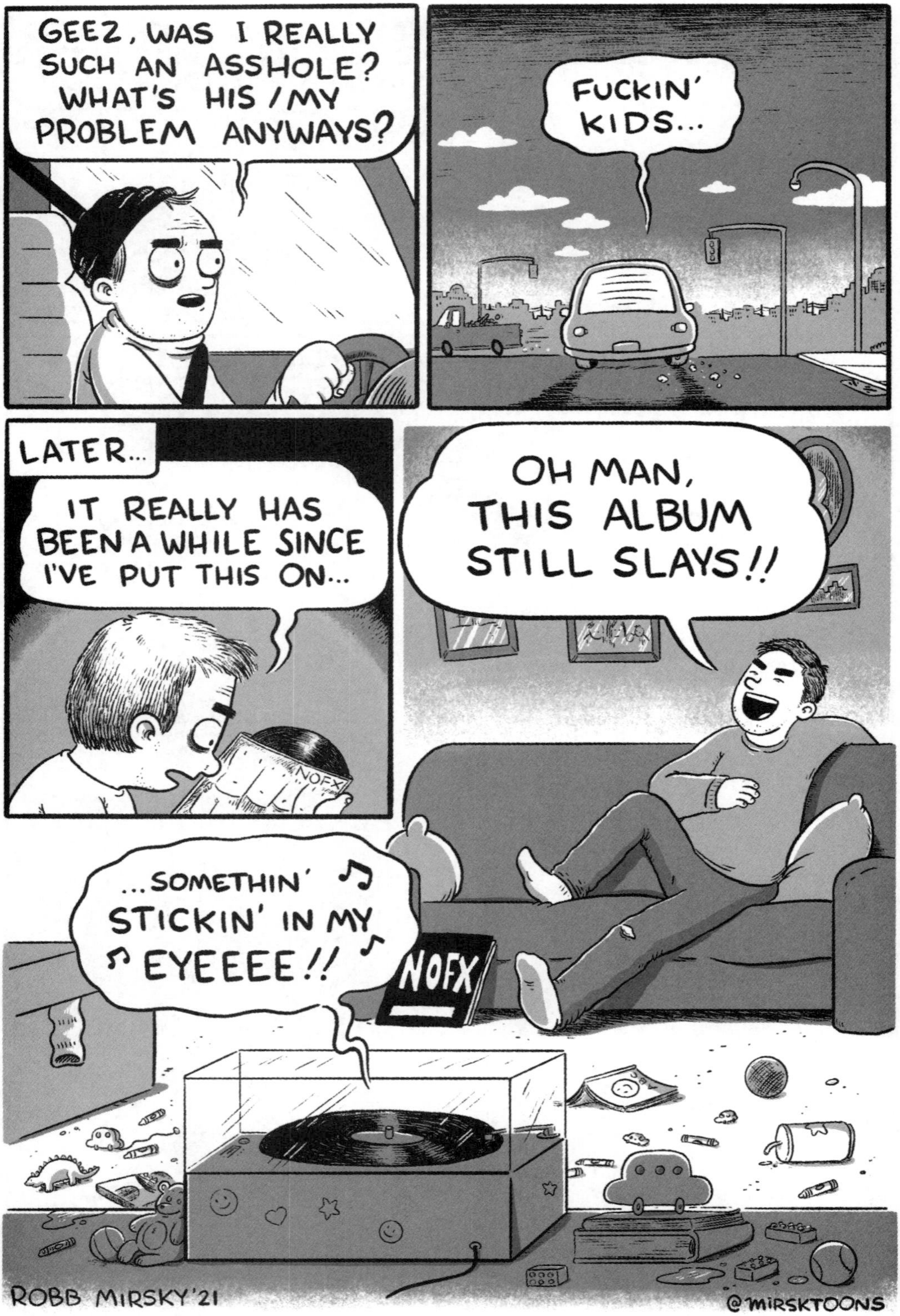
GEEZ, WAS I REALLY SUCH AN ASSHOLE? WHAT'S HIS / MY PROBLEM ANYWAYS?
FUCKIN' KIDS...
LATER...
IT REALLY HAS BEEN A WHILE SINCE I'VE PUT THIS ON...
NOFX
OH MAN, THIS ALBUM STILL SLAYS!!
...SOMETHIN' STICKIN' IN MY EYEEEE!!
NOFX
ROBB MIRSKY '21
@MIRSKTOONS

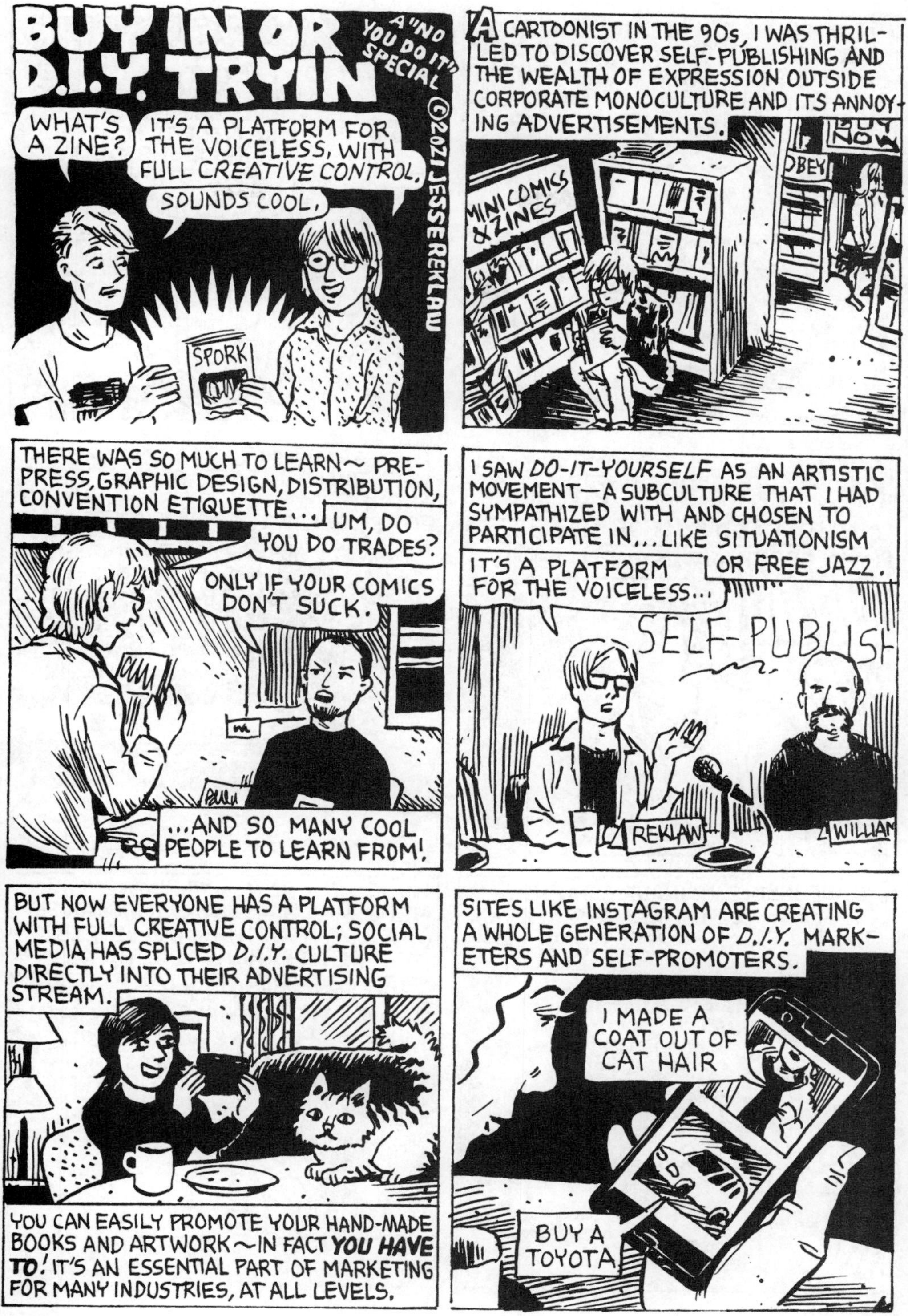
BUY IN OR D.I.Y. TRYIN
A "NO YOU DO IT" SPECIAL
©2021 JESSE REKLAW
WHAT'S A ZINE?
IT'S A PLATFORM FOR THE VOICELESS, WITH FULL CREATIVE CONTROL.
SOUNDS COOL.
SPORK
AS A CARTOONIST IN THE 90s, I WAS THRILLED TO DISCOVER SELF-PUBLISHING AND THE WEALTH OF EXPRESSION OUTSIDE CORPORATE MONOCULTURE AND ITS ANNOYING ADVERTISEMENTS.
MINICOMICS & ZINES
OBEY
BUY NOW
THERE WAS SO MUCH TO LEARN ~ PRE-PRESS, GRAPHIC DESIGN, DISTRIBUTION, CONVENTION ETIQUETTE...
UM, DO YOU DO TRADES?
ONLY IF YOUR COMICS DON'T SUCK.
...AND SO MANY COOL PEOPLE TO LEARN FROM!
I SAW DO-IT-YOURSELF AS AN ARTISTIC MOVEMENT—A SUBCULTURE THAT I HAD SYMPATHIZED WITH AND CHOSEN TO PARTICIPATE IN... LIKE SITUATIONISM OR FREE JAZZ.
IT'S A PLATFORM FOR THE VOICELESS...
SELF-PUBLISH
REKLAW
WILLIAM
BUT NOW EVERYONE HAS A PLATFORM WITH FULL CREATIVE CONTROL; SOCIAL MEDIA HAS SPLICED D.I.Y. CULTURE DIRECTLY INTO THEIR ADVERTISING STREAM.
YOU CAN EASILY PROMOTE YOUR HAND-MADE BOOKS AND ARTWORK ~ IN FACT YOU HAVE TO! IT'S AN ESSENTIAL PART OF MARKETING FOR MANY INDUSTRIES, AT ALL LEVELS.
SITES LIKE INSTAGRAM ARE CREATING A WHOLE GENERATION OF D.I.Y. MARKETERS AND SELF-PROMOTERS.
I MADE A COAT OUT OF CAT HAIR
BUY A TOYOTA

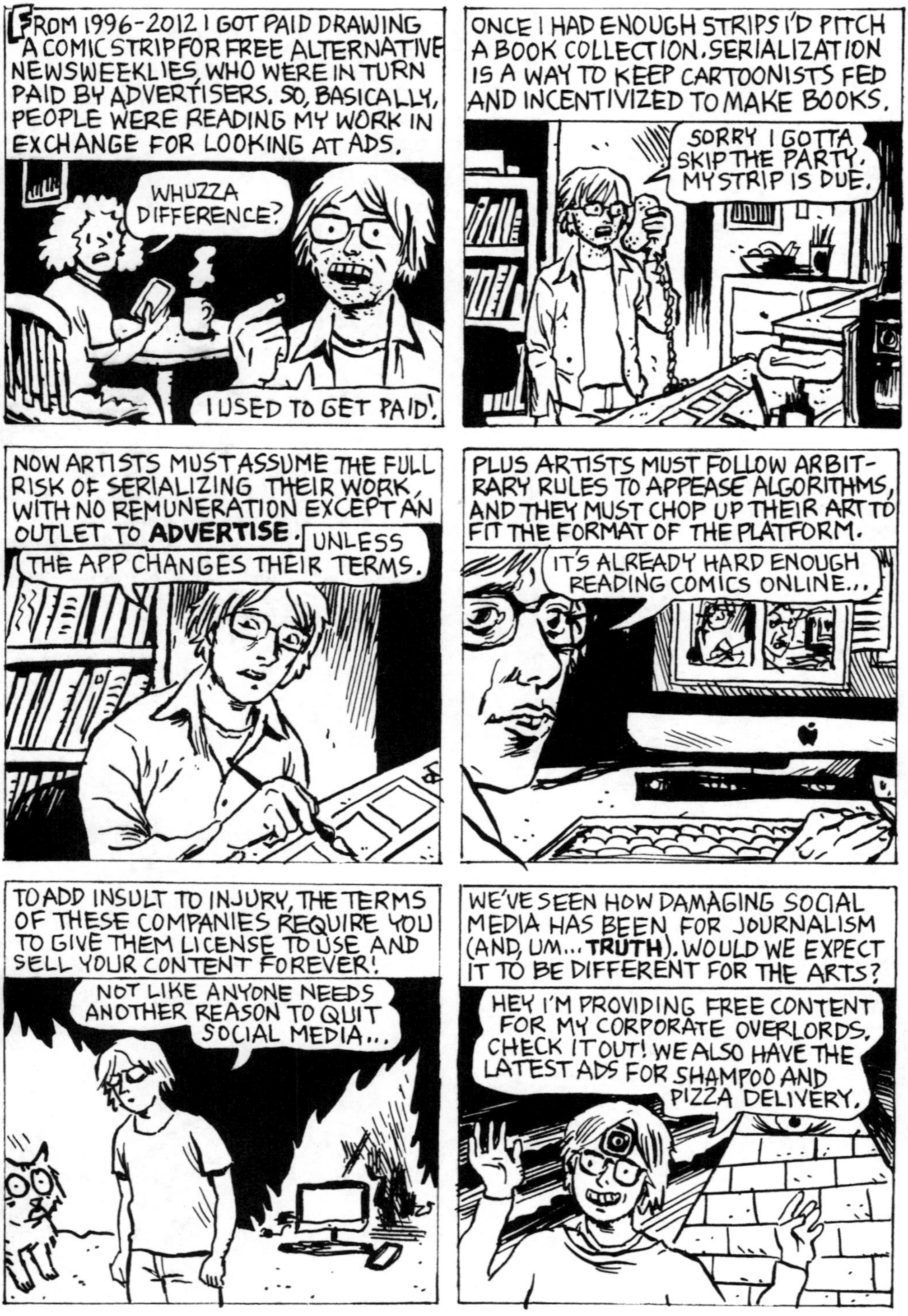
FROM 1996-2012 I GOT PAID DRAWING A COMIC STRIP FOR FREE ALTERNATIVE NEWSWEEKLIES, WHO WERE IN TURN PAID BY ADVERTISERS. SO, BASICALLY, PEOPLE WERE READING MY WORK IN EXCHANGE FOR LOOKING AT ADS.
WHUZZA DIFFERENCE?
I USED TO GET PAID!
ONCE I HAD ENOUGH STRIPS I'D PITCH A BOOK COLLECTION. SERIALIZATION IS A WAY TO KEEP CARTOONISTS FED AND INCENTIVIZED TO MAKE BOOKS.
SORRY I GOTTA SKIP THE PARTY. MY STRIP IS DUE.
NOW ARTISTS MUST ASSUME THE FULL RISK OF SERIALIZING THEIR WORK, WITH NO REMUNERATION EXCEPT AN OUTLET TO **ADVERTISE**.
UNLESS THE APP CHANGES THEIR TERMS.
PLUS ARTISTS MUST FOLLOW ARBITRARY RULES TO APPEASE ALGORITHMS, AND THEY MUST CHOP UP THEIR ART TO FIT THE FORMAT OF THE PLATFORM.
IT'S ALREADY HARD ENOUGH READING COMICS ONLINE...
TO ADD INSULT TO INJURY, THE TERMS OF THESE COMPANIES REQUIRE YOU TO GIVE THEM LICENSE TO USE AND SELL YOUR CONTENT FOREVER!
NOT LIKE ANYONE NEEDS ANOTHER REASON TO QUIT SOCIAL MEDIA...
WE'VE SEEN HOW DAMAGING SOCIAL MEDIA HAS BEEN FOR JOURNALISM (AND, UM... **TRUTH**). WOULD WE EXPECT IT TO BE DIFFERENT FOR THE ARTS?
HEY I'M PROVIDING FREE CONTENT FOR MY CORPORATE OVERLORDS. CHECK IT OUT! WE ALSO HAVE THE LATEST ADS FOR SHAMPOO AND PIZZA DELIVERY.

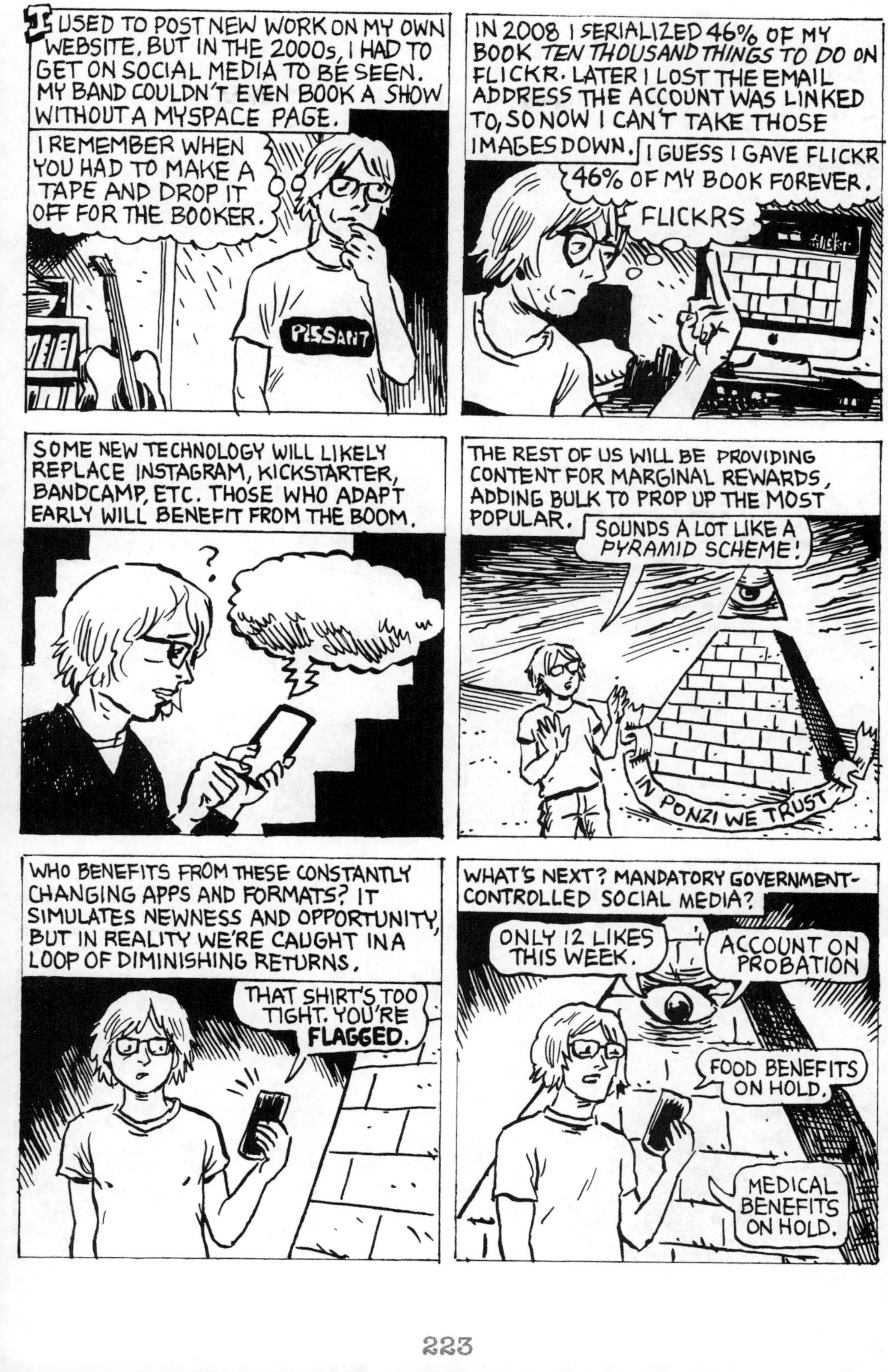
I USED TO POST NEW WORK ON MY OWN WEBSITE, BUT IN THE 2000s, I HAD TO GET ON SOCIAL MEDIA TO BE SEEN. MY BAND COULDN'T EVEN BOOK A SHOW WITHOUT A MYSPACE PAGE.
I REMEMBER WHEN YOU HAD TO MAKE A TAPE AND DROP IT OFF FOR THE BOOKER.
PISSANT
IN 2008 I SERIALIZED 46% OF MY BOOK TEN THOUSAND THINGS TO DO ON FLICKR. LATER I LOST THE EMAIL ADDRESS THE ACCOUNT WAS LINKED TO, SO NOW I CAN'T TAKE THOSE IMAGES DOWN.
I GUESS I GAVE FLICKR 46% OF MY BOOK FOREVER.
FLICKRS
SOME NEW TECHNOLOGY WILL LIKELY REPLACE INSTAGRAM, KICKSTARTER, BANDCAMP, ETC. THOSE WHO ADAPT EARLY WILL BENEFIT FROM THE BOOM.
?
THE REST OF US WILL BE PROVIDING CONTENT FOR MARGINAL REWARDS, ADDING BULK TO PROP UP THE MOST POPULAR.
SOUNDS A LOT LIKE A PYRAMID SCHEME!
IN PONZI WE TRUST
WHO BENEFITS FROM THESE CONSTANTLY CHANGING APPS AND FORMATS? IT SIMULATES NEWNESS AND OPPORTUNITY, BUT IN REALITY WE'RE CAUGHT IN A LOOP OF DIMINISHING RETURNS.
THAT SHIRT'S TOO TIGHT. YOU'RE FLAGGED.
WHAT'S NEXT? MANDATORY GOVERNMENT-CONTROLLED SOCIAL MEDIA?
ONLY 12 LIKES THIS WEEK.
ACCOUNT ON PROBATION
FOOD BENEFITS ON HOLD.
MEDICAL BENEFITS ON HOLD.

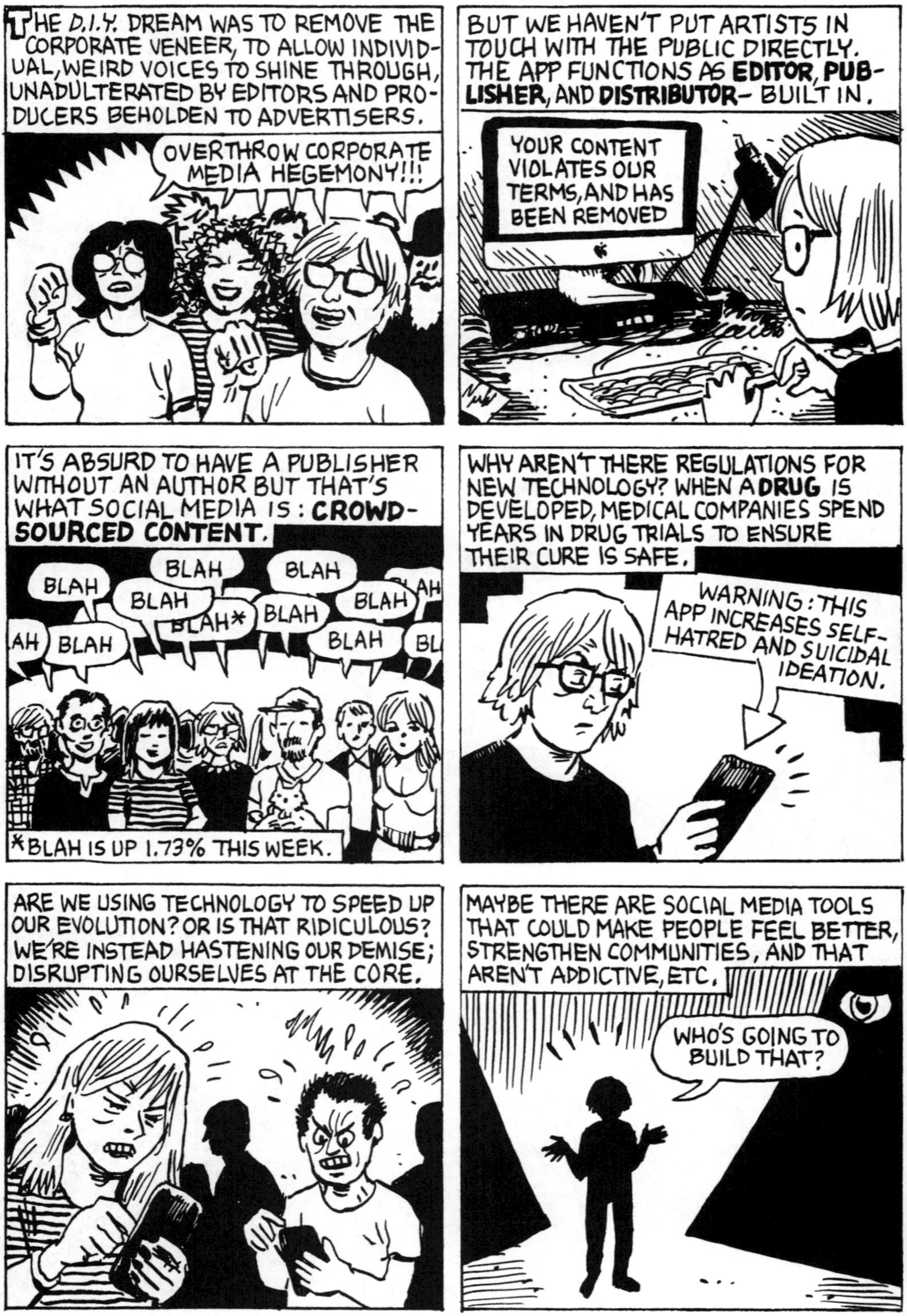
THE D.I.Y. DREAM WAS TO REMOVE THE CORPORATE VENEER, TO ALLOW INDIVIDUAL, WEIRD VOICES TO SHINE THROUGH, UNADULTERATED BY EDITORS AND PRODUCERS BEHOLDEN TO ADVERTISERS.
OVERTHROW CORPORATE MEDIA HEGEMONY!!!
BUT WE HAVEN'T PUT ARTISTS IN TOUCH WITH THE PUBLIC DIRECTLY. THE APP FUNCTIONS AS **EDITOR**, **PUBLISHER**, AND **DISTRIBUTOR**– BUILT IN.
YOUR CONTENT VIOLATES OUR TERMS, AND HAS BEEN REMOVED
IT'S ABSURD TO HAVE A PUBLISHER WITHOUT AN AUTHOR BUT THAT'S WHAT SOCIAL MEDIA IS: **CROWD-SOURCED CONTENT**.
BLAH
BLAH
BLAH
BLAH
BLAH*
BLAH
BLAH
BLAH
BLAH
*BLAH IS UP 1.73% THIS WEEK.
WHY AREN'T THERE REGULATIONS FOR NEW TECHNOLOGY? WHEN A **DRUG** IS DEVELOPED, MEDICAL COMPANIES SPEND YEARS IN DRUG TRIALS TO ENSURE THEIR CURE IS SAFE.
WARNING: THIS APP INCREASES SELF-HATRED AND SUICIDAL IDEATION.
ARE WE USING TECHNOLOGY TO SPEED UP OUR EVOLUTION? OR IS THAT RIDICULOUS? WE'RE INSTEAD HASTENING OUR DEMISE; DISRUPTING OURSELVES AT THE CORE.
MAYBE THERE ARE SOCIAL MEDIA TOOLS THAT COULD MAKE PEOPLE FEEL BETTER, STRENGTHEN COMMUNITIES, AND THAT AREN'T ADDICTIVE, ETC.
WHO'S GOING TO BUILD THAT?

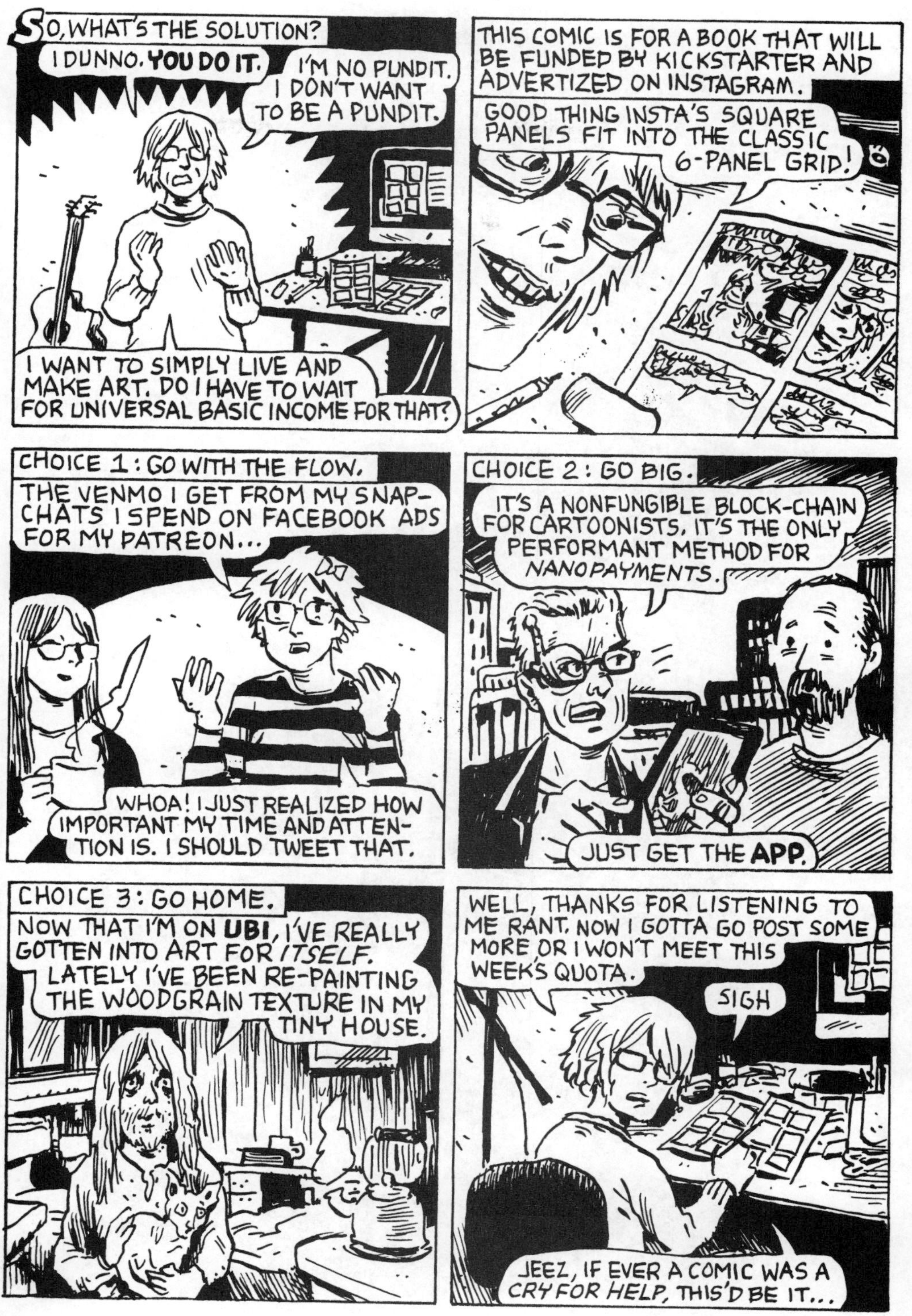
SO, WHAT'S THE SOLUTION?
I DUNNO. **YOU DO IT.**
I'M NO PUNDIT. I DON'T WANT TO BE A PUNDIT.
I WANT TO SIMPLY LIVE AND MAKE ART. DO I HAVE TO WAIT FOR UNIVERSAL BASIC INCOME FOR THAT?
THIS COMIC IS FOR A BOOK THAT WILL BE FUNDED BY KICKSTARTER AND ADVERTIZED ON INSTAGRAM.
GOOD THING INSTA'S SQUARE PANELS FIT INTO THE CLASSIC 6-PANEL GRID!
CHOICE 1: GO WITH THE FLOW.
THE VENMO I GET FROM MY SNAPCHATS I SPEND ON FACEBOOK ADS FOR MY PATREON...
WHOA! I JUST REALIZED HOW IMPORTANT MY TIME AND ATTENTION IS. I SHOULD TWEET THAT.
CHOICE 2: GO BIG.
IT'S A NONFUNGIBLE BLOCK-CHAIN FOR CARTOONISTS. IT'S THE ONLY PERFORMANT METHOD FOR *NANOPAYMENTS*.
JUST GET THE **APP**.
CHOICE 3: GO HOME.
NOW THAT I'M ON **UBI**, I'VE REALLY GOTTEN INTO ART FOR *ITSELF*.
LATELY I'VE BEEN RE-PAINTING THE WOODGRAIN TEXTURE IN MY TINY HOUSE.
WELL, THANKS FOR LISTENING TO ME RANT. NOW I GOTTA GO POST SOME MORE OR I WON'T MEET THIS WEEK'S QUOTA.
SIGH
JEEZ, IF EVER A COMIC WAS A *CRY FOR HELP*, THIS'D BE IT...

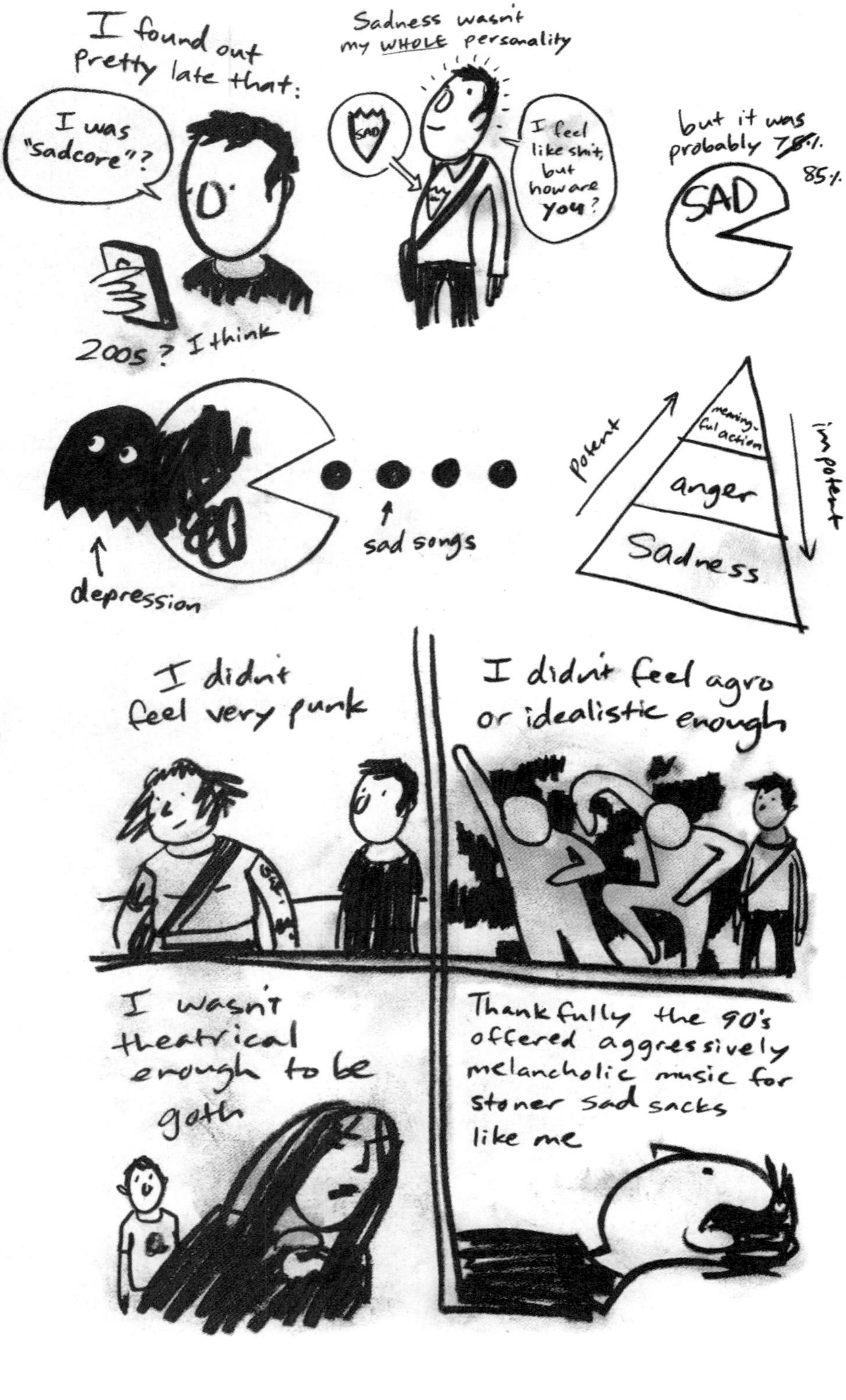
I found out pretty late that:
I was "sadcore"?
2005? I think
Sadness wasn't my WHOLE personality
SAD
I feel like shit, but how are you?
but it was probably 75% 85%
SAD
depression
sad songs
potent
meaning-ful action
anger
Sadness
impotent
I didn't feel very punk
I didn't feel agro or idealistic enough
I wasn't theatrical enough to be goth
Thankfully the 90's offered aggressively melancholic music for stoner sad sacks like me

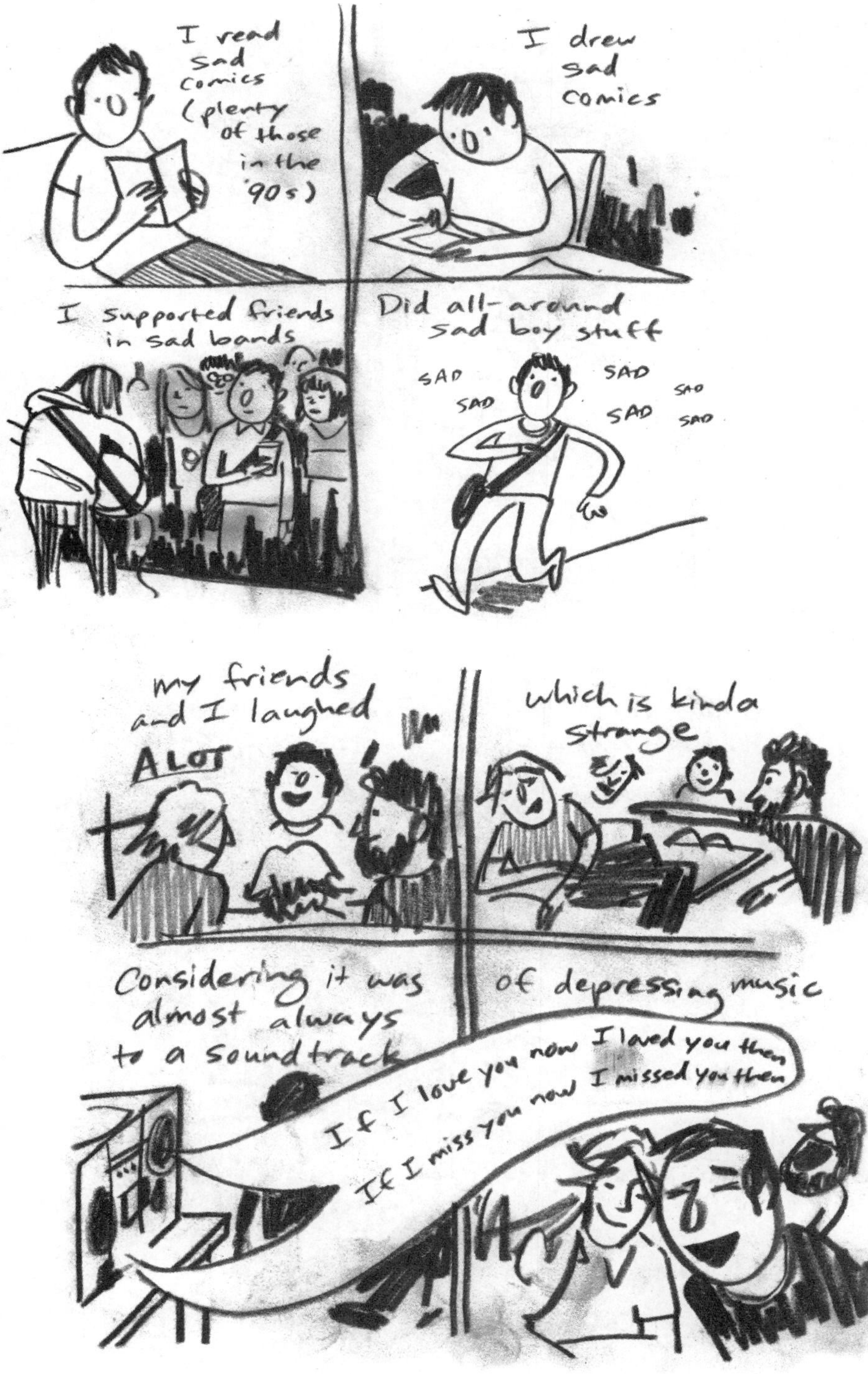
I read sad comics (plenty of those in the '90s)
I drew sad comics
I supported friends in sad bands
Did all-around sad boy stuff
SAD
SAD
SAD
SAD
SAD
SAD
my friends and I laughed
ALOT
which is kinda strange
Considering it was almost always to a soundtrack
of depressing music
If I love you now I loved you then
If I miss you now I missed you then

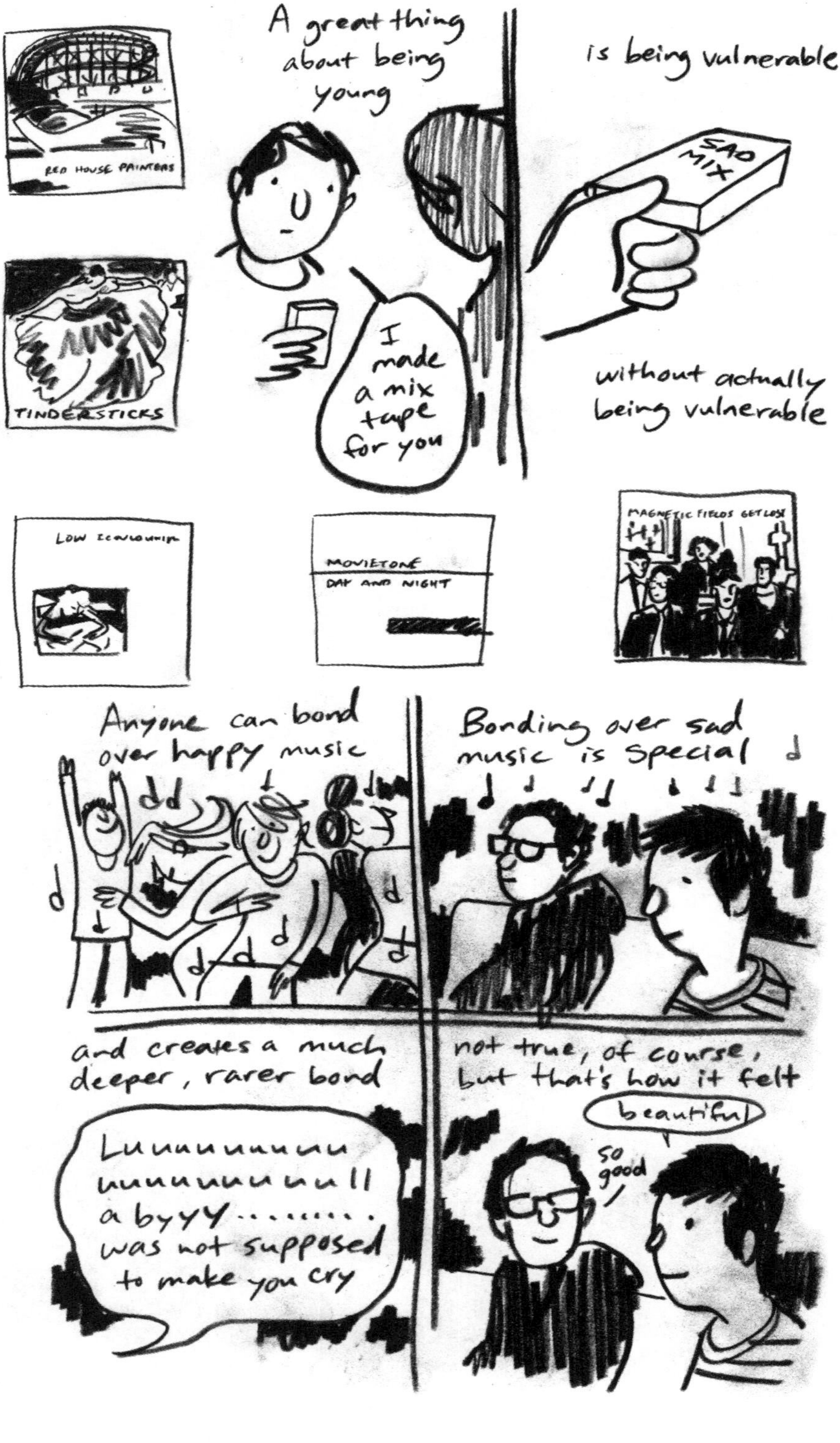
RED HOUSE PAINTERS
TINDERSTICKS
A great thing about being young
I made a mix tape for you
is being vulnerable
SAD MIX
without actually being vulnerable
MOVIETONE
DAY AND NIGHT
MAGNETIC FIELDS GET LOST
Anyone can bond over happy music
Bonding over sad music is Special
and creates a much deeper, rarer bond
Luuuuuuuuu uuuuuuuuull abyyY........ was not supposed to make you cry
not true, of course, but that's how it felt
beautiful
so good

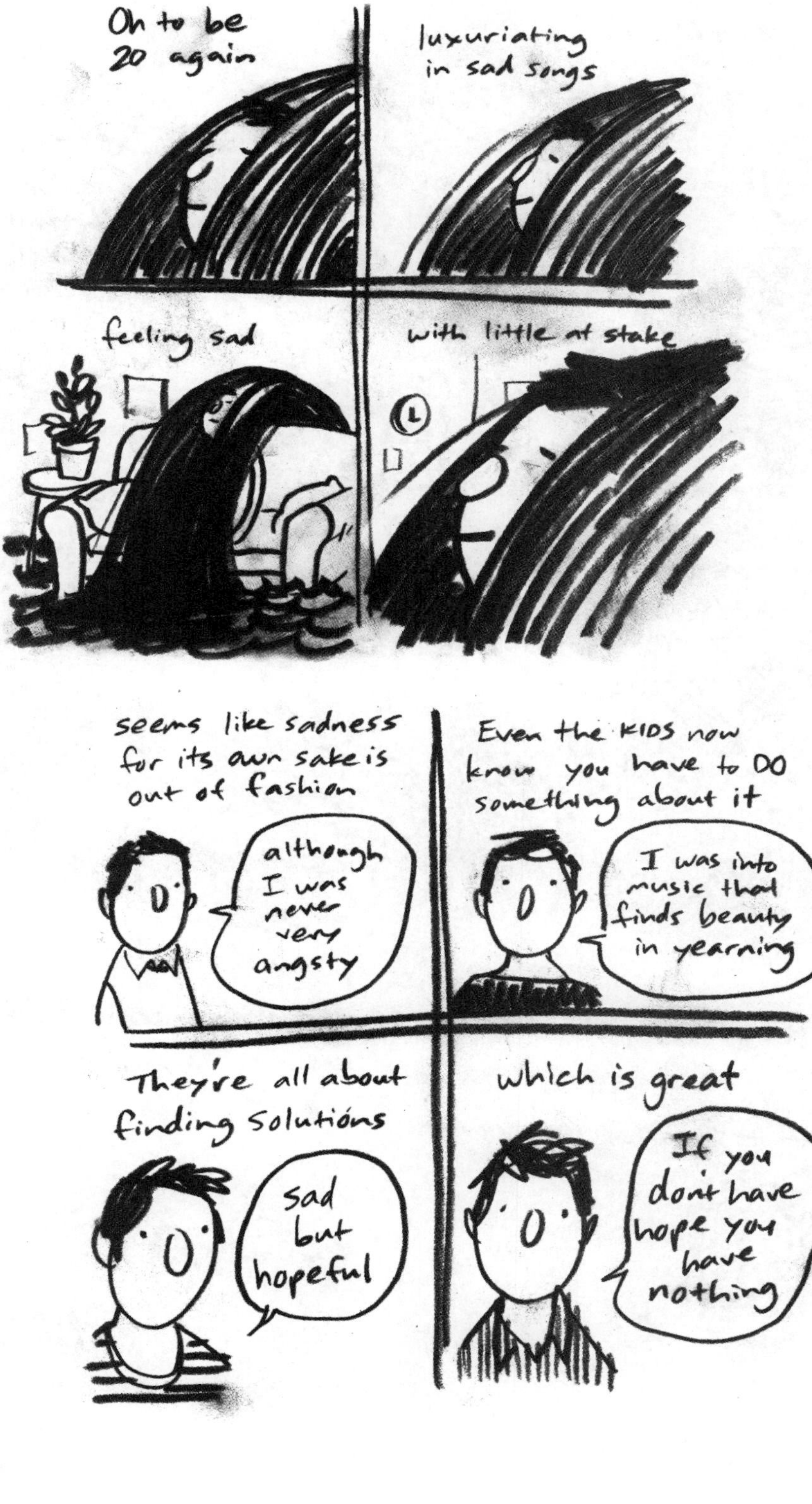
Oh to be 20 again
luxuriating in sad songs
feeling sad
with little at stake
seems like sadness for its own sake is out of fashion
although I was never very angsty
Even the KIDS now know you have to DO something about it
I was into music that finds beauty in yearning
They're all about finding solutions
sad but hopeful
which is great
If you don't have hope you have nothing

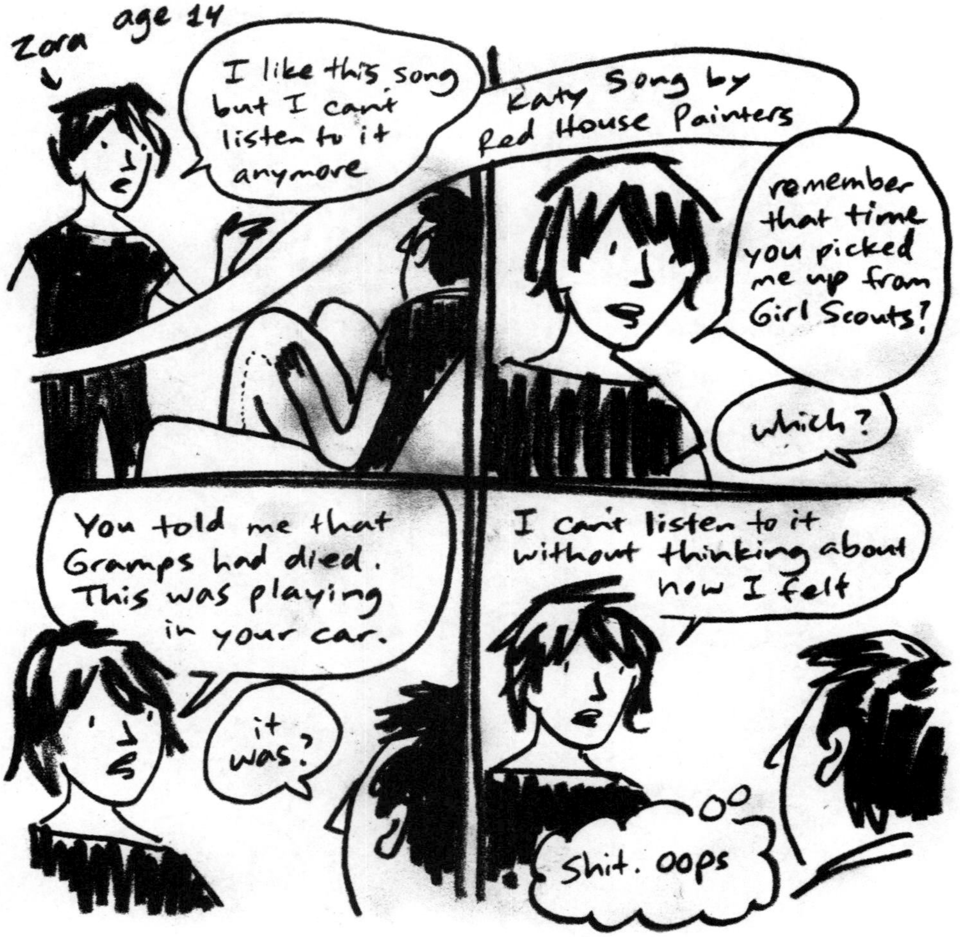
Zora age 14
I like this song but I can't listen to it anymore
Katy Song by Red House Painters
remember that time you picked me up from Girl Scouts?
which?
You told me that Gramps had died. This was playing in your car.
it was?
I can't listen to it without thinking about how I felt
Shit. oops

" Now that I'm older and sub-space is colder
Just wanna say something true "
— David Berman

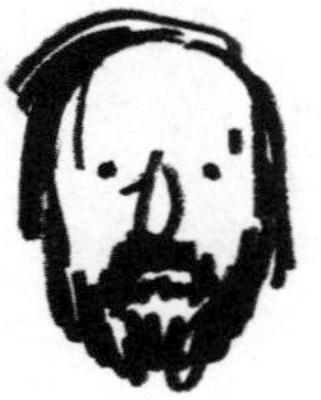

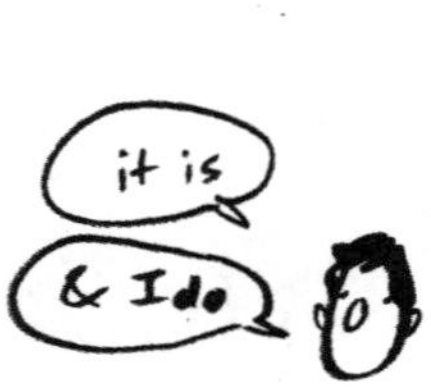
it is
& Ido

Adam Meuse

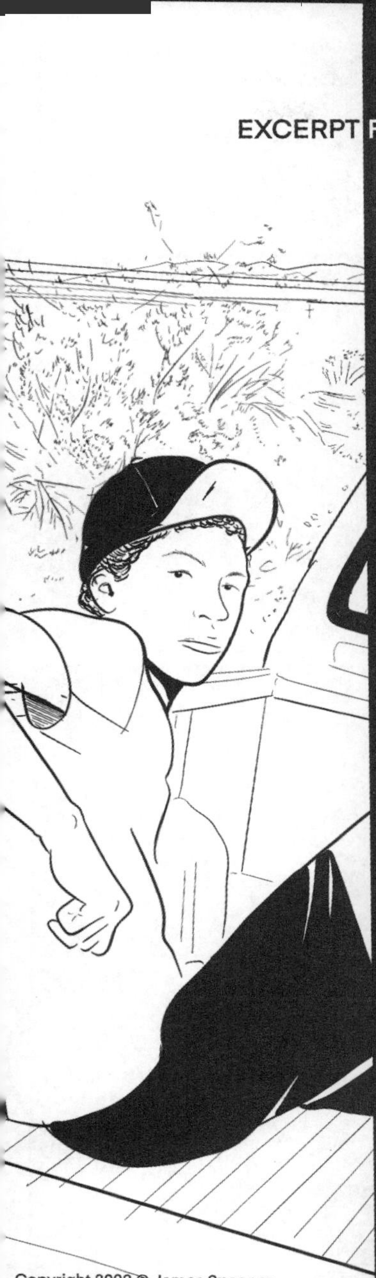

EXCERPT FROM **THE HIGH DESERT**

A GRAPHIC MEMOIR

BY JAMES SPOONER

SPOONER'S

NO FUN

REPRINTED FROM RAZORCAKE

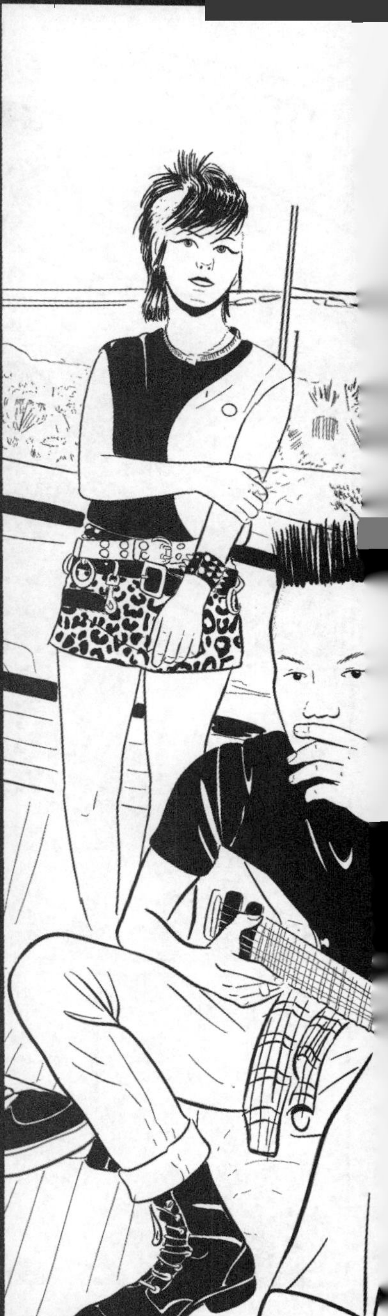

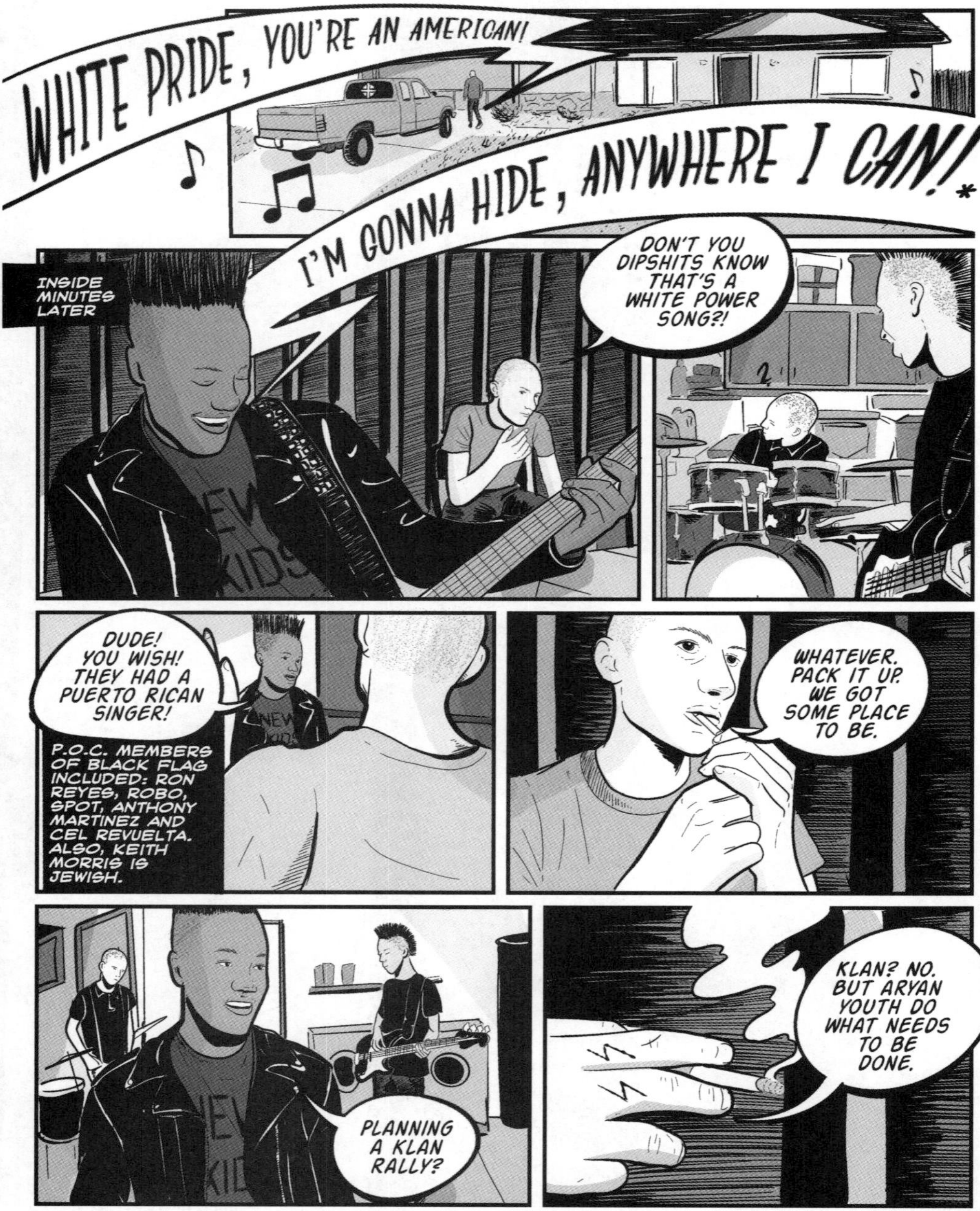
WHITE PRIDE, YOU'RE AN AMERICAN!
I'M GONNA HIDE, ANYWHERE I CAN!*
INSIDE MINUTES LATER
DON'T YOU DIPSHITS KNOW THAT'S A WHITE POWER SONG?!
DUDE! YOU WISH! THEY HAD A PUERTO RICAN SINGER!
P.O.C. MEMBERS OF BLACK FLAG INCLUDED: RON REYES, ROBO, SPOT, ANTHONY MARTINEZ AND CEL REVUELTA. ALSO, KEITH MORRIS IS JEWISH.
WHATEVER. PACK IT UP. WE GOT SOME PLACE TO BE.
PLANNING A KLAN RALLY?
KLAN? NO. BUT ARYAN YOUTH DO WHAT NEEDS TO BE DONE.

*BLACK FLAG- WHITE MINORITY

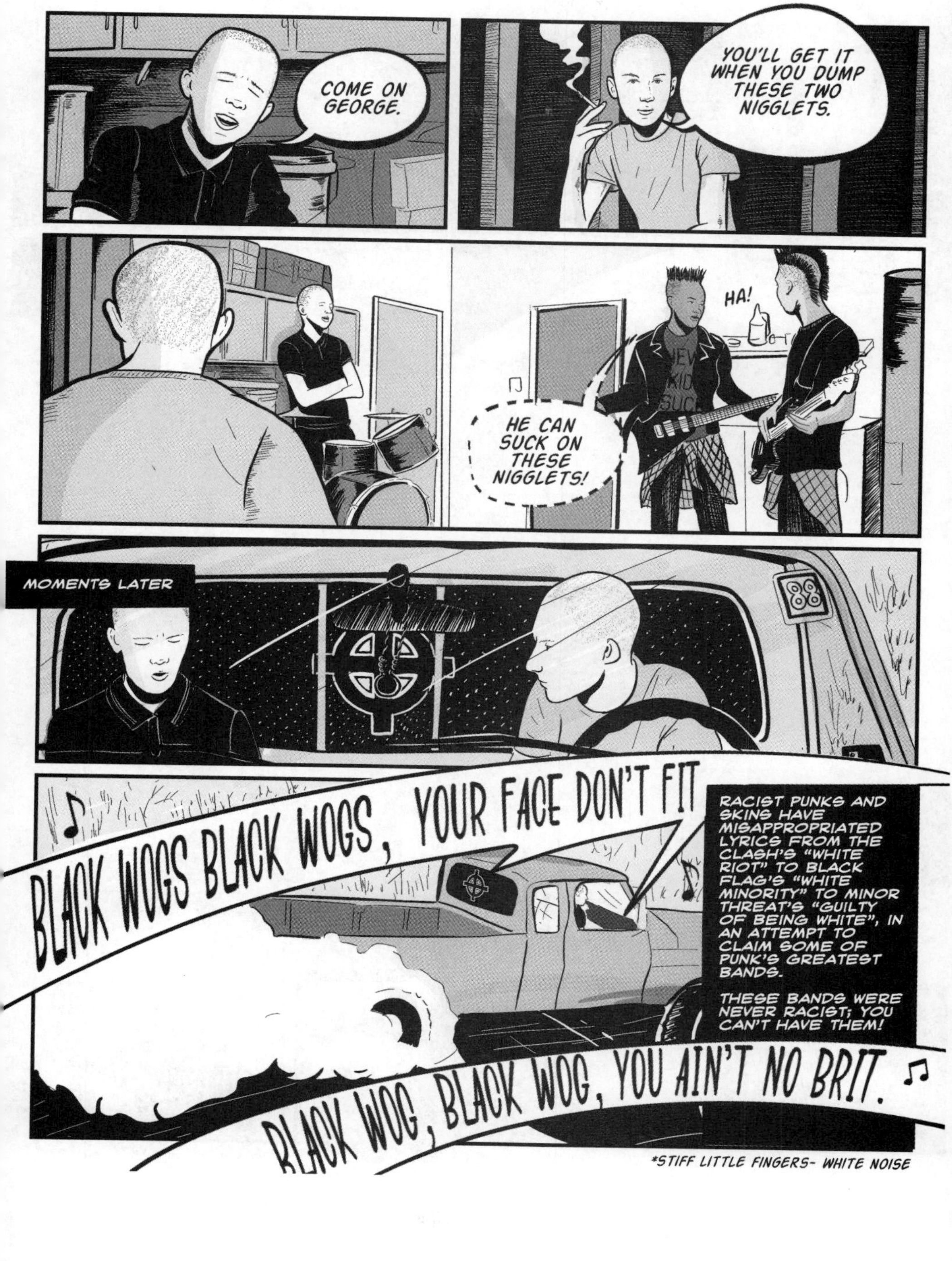
COME ON GEORGE.
YOU'LL GET IT WHEN YOU DUMP THESE TWO NIGGLETS.
HA!
HE CAN SUCK ON THESE NIGGLETS!
MOMENTS LATER
88
♪ BLACK WOGS BLACK WOGS, YOUR FACE DON'T FIT
RACIST PUNKS AND SKINS HAVE MISAPPROPRIATED LYRICS FROM THE CLASH'S "WHITE RIOT" TO BLACK FLAG'S "WHITE MINORITY" TO MINOR THREAT'S "GUILTY OF BEING WHITE", IN AN ATTEMPT TO CLAIM SOME OF PUNK'S GREATEST BANDS.
THESE BANDS WERE NEVER RACIST; YOU CAN'T HAVE THEM!
BLACK WOG, BLACK WOG, YOU AIN'T NO BRIT. ♪

*STIFF LITTLE FINGERS- WHITE NOISE

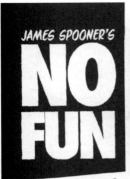

JAMES SPOONER'S

NO FUN

BEAUTY STANDARDS

HAIR IS A HUGE PART OF IDENTIFYING OUR SUBCULTURAL "TRIBES" IE: PUNKS, METAL HEADS, GOTHS, ETC...

IN THE 80'S THIS FELT AS TRUE AS EVER.

IN 7TH GRADE, MORE THAN ANYTHING, I WANTED TONY HAWK HAIR...

ME

AND THUS BEGAN A LONG BOUT WITH SELF HATE.

BY 9TH GRADE I TAMED MY NATURAL AFRO WITH A 40 MINUTE DAILY RITUAL OF HAIRSPRAY AND BLOW DRYING TO FORM TWO CAREFULLY PRESSED MOHAWKS.

EVERYONE KNOWS I'M PUNK NOW!

UPON MY MOVE TO NEW YORK AND SEEING OTHER BLACK PUNKS I FOUND MYSELF GAINING A SENSE OF PRIDE AROUND MY HAIR (AND BLACKNESS IN GENERAL).

HE IS COOL.

HE'S COOL TOO!

BUT AFTER A FEW YEARS IN THE EARLY 90S EMO SCENE I DESPERATELY WANTED TO LOOK THE PART.

WHAT KIND OF STUFF ARE YOU INTO?

MOSS ICON, MOHINDER, JULIA...

MY HAIR WAS BETRAYING ME...

THE HIGH WATERS AND STRIPED SWEATER DON'T GIVE IT AWAY?

I HAD READ MALCOLM X. I WAS AWARE OF THE IMPLICATIONS BEHIND CHEMICAL STRAIGHTENERS, BUT I TOLD MYSELF I WAS DIFFERENT.

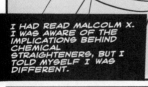

I'M NOT "TRYING TO BE WHITE", I JUST WANT TO FIT IN WITH MY SCENE.*

EVENTUALLY, IN AN ACT OF REBELLION AGAINST ALL THINGS WHITE, I CUT THE PERM.

*WHO WERE MOSTLY WHITE KIDS.

BY THE TIME I STOPPED REACTING TO WHITE BEAUTY STANDARDS I WAS IN MY MID 20S.

IT TOOK OVER 10 YEARS TO DISCOVER MY HAIR'S TRUE TEXTURE...

WHOA! LOOK AT THESE CURLS!

JUST IN TIME TO START LOSING MY HAIR ALL TOGETHER!

HOLD UP! IS THAT A BALD SPOT?!

BZZZZZZZ

OH WELL.

@SPOONERSNOFUN

J. SPOONER '14

234

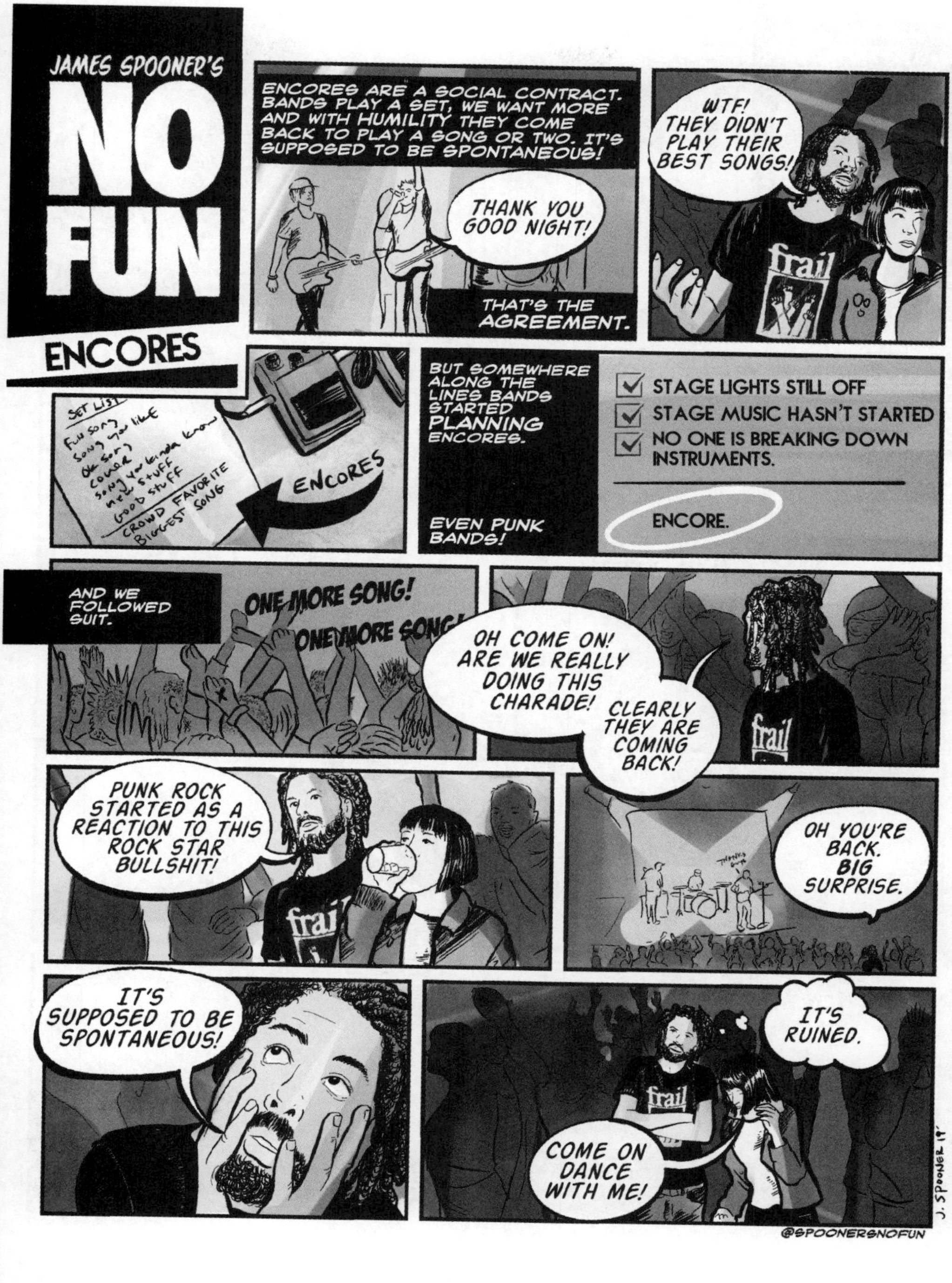

JAMES SPOONER'S
NO FUN
ENCORES
ENCORES ARE A SOCIAL CONTRACT. BANDS PLAY A SET, WE WANT MORE AND WITH HUMILITY THEY COME BACK TO PLAY A SONG OR TWO. IT'S SUPPOSED TO BE SPONTANEOUS!
THANK YOU GOOD NIGHT!
THAT'S THE AGREEMENT.
WTF! THEY DIDN'T PLAY THEIR BEST SONGS!
frail
SET LIST
CROWD FAVORITE
BIGGEST SONG
ENCORES
BUT SOMEWHERE ALONG THE LINES BANDS STARTED PLANNING ENCORES.
EVEN PUNK BANDS!
STAGE LIGHTS STILL OFF
STAGE MUSIC HASN'T STARTED
NO ONE IS BREAKING DOWN INSTRUMENTS.
ENCORE.
AND WE FOLLOWED SUIT.
ONE MORE SONG!
ONE MORE SONG!
OH COME ON! ARE WE REALLY DOING THIS CHARADE!
CLEARLY THEY ARE COMING BACK!
PUNK ROCK STARTED AS A REACTION TO THIS ROCK STAR BULLSHIT!
OH YOU'RE BACK. BIG SURPRISE.
IT'S SUPPOSED TO BE SPONTANEOUS!
IT'S RUINED.
COME ON DANCE WITH ME!
J. SPOONER 19'
@SPOONERSNOFUN

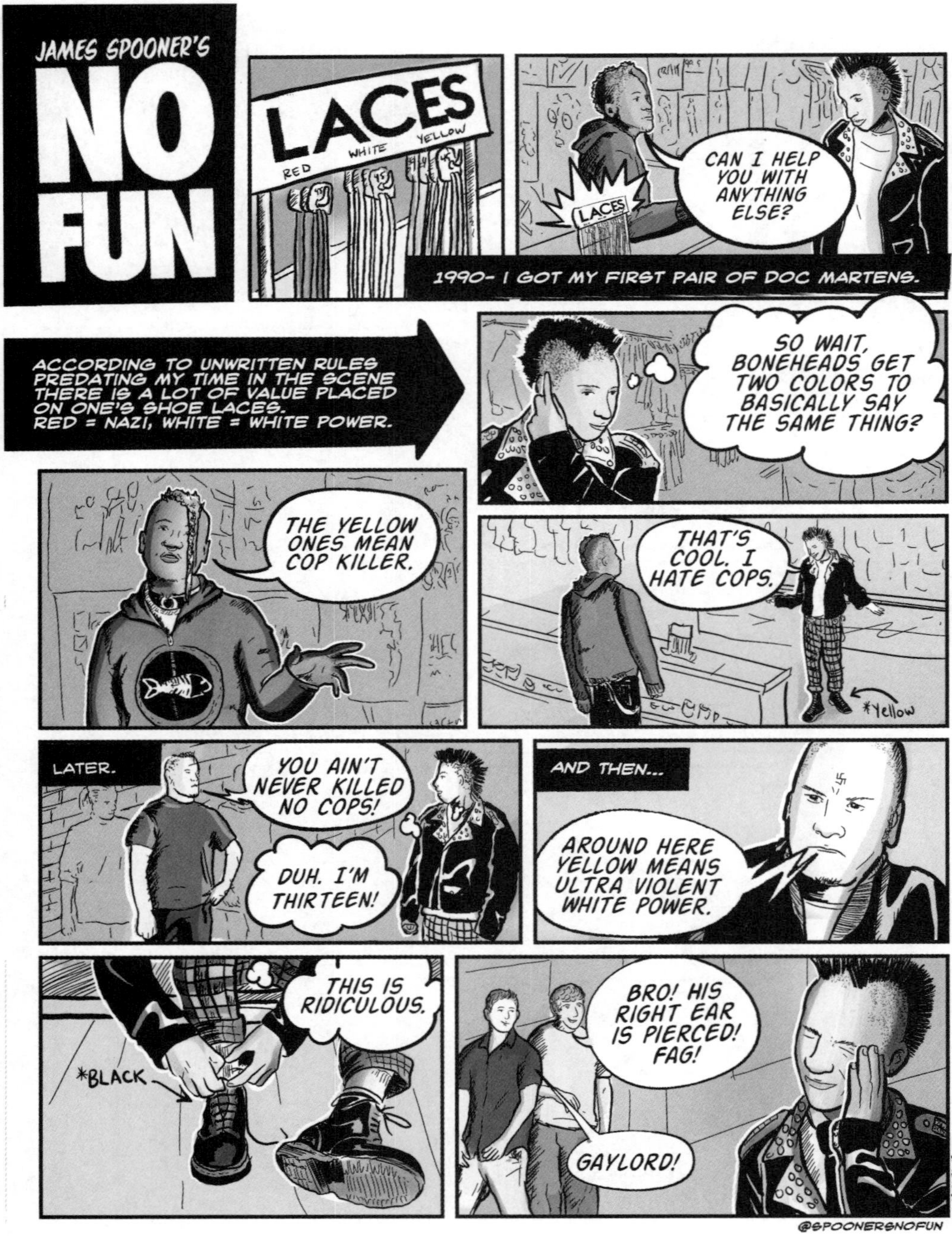
JAMES SPOONER'S
NO FUN
LACES
RED WHITE YELLOW
LACES
CAN I HELP YOU WITH ANYTHING ELSE?
1990- I GOT MY FIRST PAIR OF DOC MARTENS.
ACCORDING TO UNWRITTEN RULES PREDATING MY TIME IN THE SCENE THERE IS A LOT OF VALUE PLACED ON ONE'S SHOE LACES. RED = NAZI, WHITE = WHITE POWER.
SO WAIT, BONEHEADS GET TWO COLORS TO BASICALLY SAY THE SAME THING?
THE YELLOW ONES MEAN COP KILLER.
THAT'S COOL. I HATE COPS.
*Yellow
LATER.
YOU AIN'T NEVER KILLED NO COPS!
DUH. I'M THIRTEEN!
AND THEN...
AROUND HERE YELLOW MEANS ULTRA VIOLENT WHITE POWER.
THIS IS RIDICULOUS.
*BLACK
BRO! HIS RIGHT EAR IS PIERCED! FAG!
GAYLORD!
J. SPOONER 19

@SPOONERSNOFUN

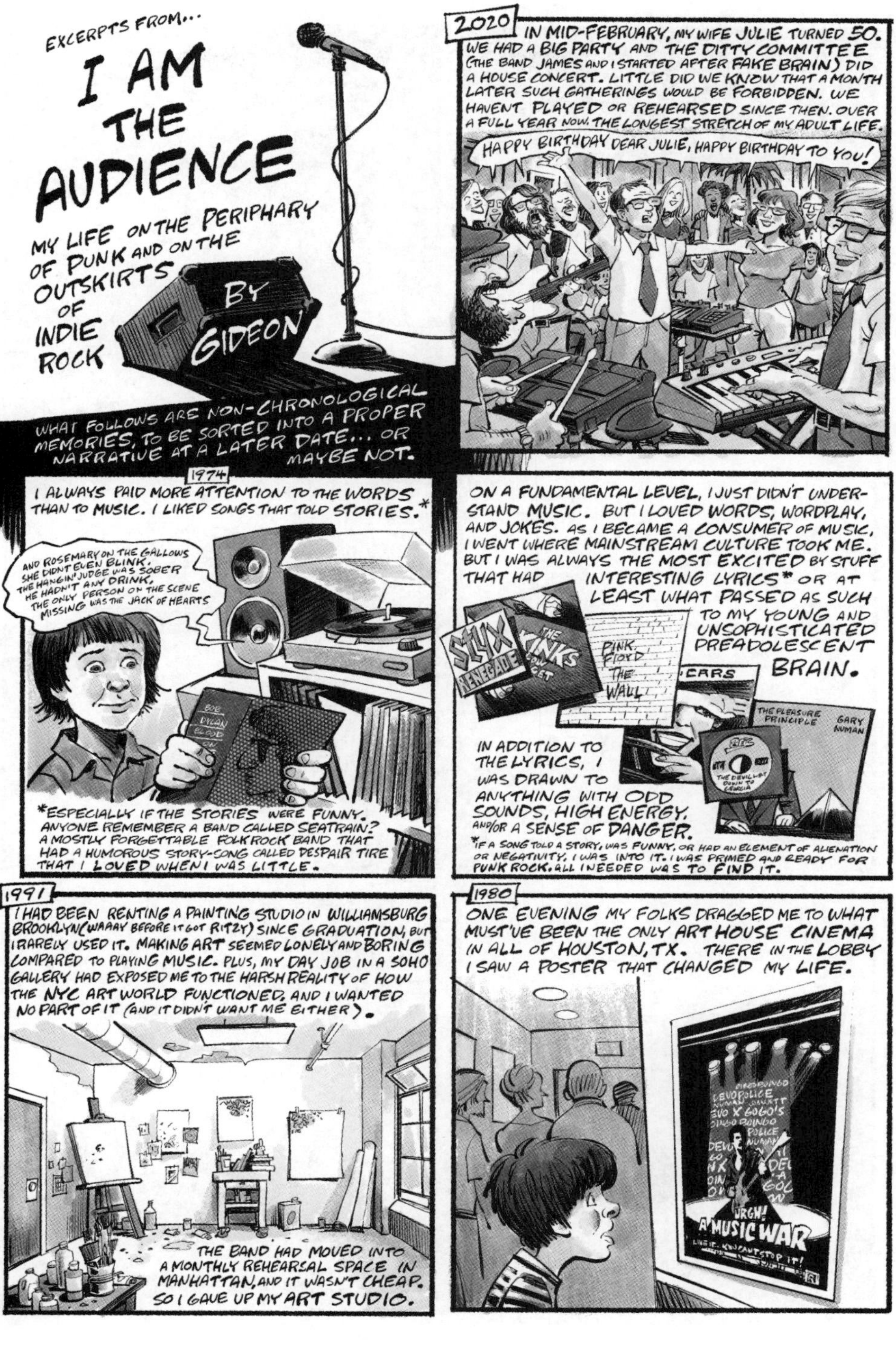
EXCERPTS FROM...
I AM THE AUDIENCE
MY LIFE ON THE PERIPHARY OF PUNK AND ON THE OUTSKIRTS OF INDIE ROCK
BY GIDEON
WHAT FOLLOWS ARE NON-CHRONOLOGICAL MEMORIES, TO BE SORTED INTO A PROPER NARRATIVE AT A LATER DATE... OR MAYBE NOT.
2020
IN MID-FEBRUARY, MY WIFE JULIE TURNED 50. WE HAD A BIG PARTY AND THE DITTY COMMITTEE (THE BAND JAMES AND I STARTED AFTER FAKE BRAIN) DID A HOUSE CONCERT. LITTLE DID WE KNOW THAT A MONTH LATER SUCH GATHERINGS WOULD BE FORBIDDEN. WE HAVEN'T PLAYED OR REHEARSED SINCE THEN. OVER A FULL YEAR NOW. THE LONGEST STRETCH OF MY ADULT LIFE.
HAPPY BIRTHDAY DEAR JULIE, HAPPY BIRTHDAY TO YOU!
1974
I ALWAYS PAID MORE ATTENTION TO THE WORDS THAN TO MUSIC. I LIKED SONGS THAT TOLD STORIES.*
AND ROSEMARY ON THE GALLOWS SHE DIDN'T EVEN BLINK. THE HANGIN' JUDGE WAS SOBER HE HADN'T HAD ANY DRINK. THE ONLY PERSON ON THE SCENE MISSING WAS THE JACK OF HEARTS
BOB DYLAN BLOOD ON
*ESPECIALLY IF THE STORIES WERE FUNNY. ANYONE REMEMBER A BAND CALLED SEATRAIN? A MOSTLY FORGETTABLE FOLK ROCK BAND THAT HAD A HUMOROUS STORY-SONG CALLED DESPAIR TIRE THAT I LOVED WHEN I WAS LITTLE.
ON A FUNDAMENTAL LEVEL, I JUST DIDN'T UNDERSTAND MUSIC. BUT I LOVED WORDS, WORDPLAY, AND JOKES. AS I BECAME A CONSUMER OF MUSIC, I WENT WHERE MAINSTREAM CULTURE TOOK ME. BUT I WAS ALWAYS THE MOST EXCITED BY STUFF THAT HAD INTERESTING LYRICS* OR AT LEAST WHAT PASSED AS SUCH TO MY YOUNG AND UNSOPHISTICATED PREADOLESCENT BRAIN.
STYX RENEGADE
THE KINKS
PINK FLOYD THE WALL
CARS
THE PLEASURE PRINCIPLE GARY NUMAN
IN ADDITION TO THE LYRICS, I WAS DRAWN TO ANYTHING WITH ODD SOUNDS, HIGH ENERGY, AND/OR A SENSE OF DANGER.
*IF A SONG TOLD A STORY, WAS FUNNY, OR HAD AN ELEMENT OF ALIENATION OR NEGATIVITY, I WAS INTO IT. I WAS PRIMED AND READY FOR PUNK ROCK. ALL I NEEDED WAS TO FIND IT.
1991
I HAD BEEN RENTING A PAINTING STUDIO IN WILLIAMSBURG BROOKLYN (WAAAY BEFORE IT GOT RITZY) SINCE GRADUATION, BUT I RARELY USED IT. MAKING ART SEEMED LONELY AND BORING COMPARED TO PLAYING MUSIC. PLUS, MY DAY JOB IN A SOHO GALLERY HAD EXPOSED ME TO THE HARSH REALITY OF HOW THE NYC ART WORLD FUNCTIONED, AND I WANTED NO PART OF IT (AND IT DIDN'T WANT ME EITHER).
THE BAND HAD MOVED INTO A MONTHLY REHEARSAL SPACE IN MANHATTAN, AND IT WASN'T CHEAP. SO I GAVE UP MY ART STUDIO.
1980
ONE EVENING MY FOLKS DRAGGED ME TO WHAT MUST'VE BEEN THE ONLY ART HOUSE CINEMA IN ALL OF HOUSTON, TX. THERE IN THE LOBBY I SAW A POSTER THAT CHANGED MY LIFE.
DEVO POLICE
URGH! A MUSIC WAR

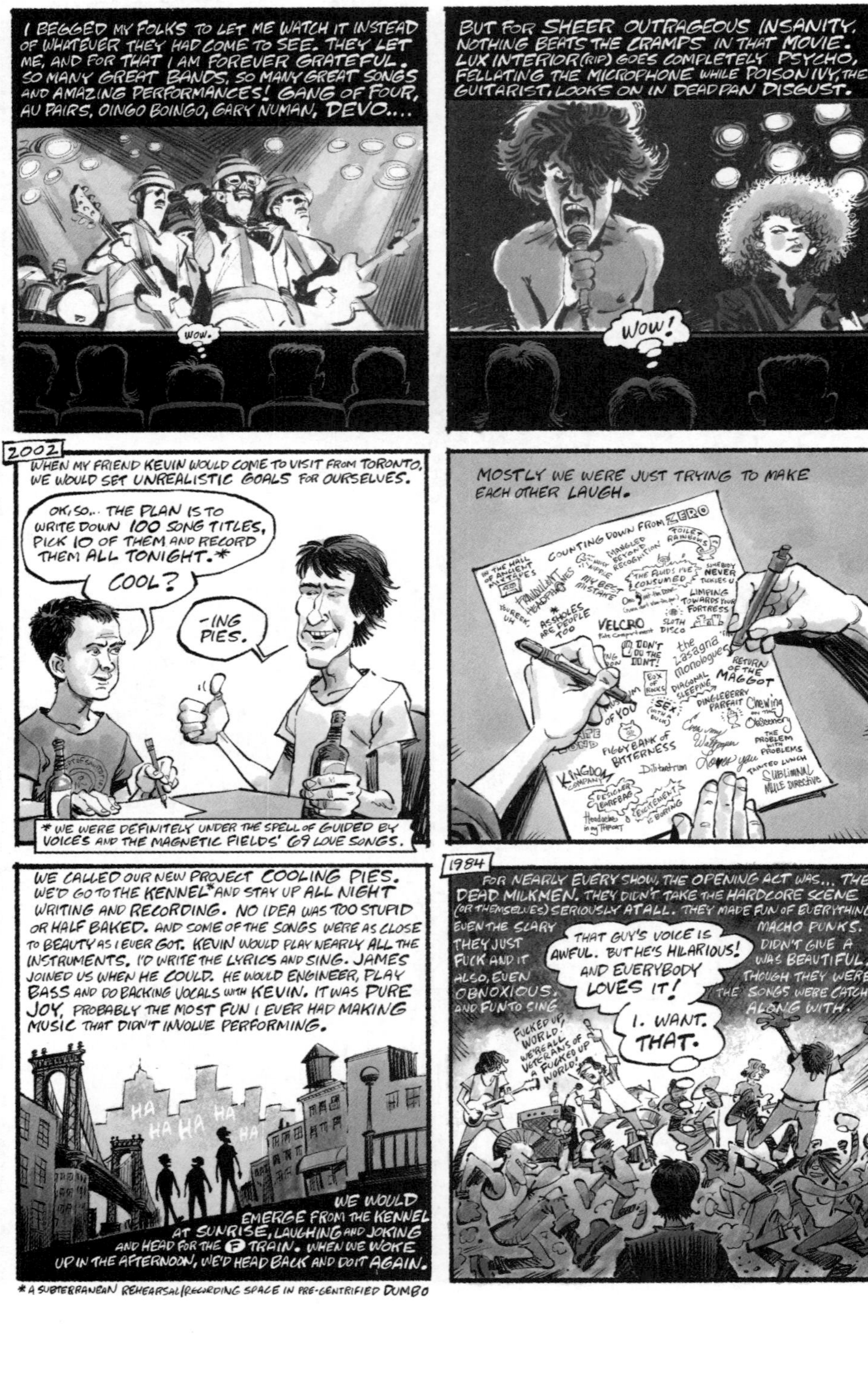
I BEGGED MY FOLKS TO LET ME WATCH IT INSTEAD OF WHATEVER THEY HAD COME TO SEE. THEY LET ME, AND FOR THAT I AM FOREVER GRATEFUL. SO MANY GREAT BANDS, SO MANY GREAT SONGS AND AMAZING PERFORMANCES! GANG OF FOUR, AU PAIRS, OINGO BOINGO, GARY NUMAN, DEVO...
WOW.
BUT FOR SHEER OUTRAGEOUS INSANITY, NOTHING BEATS THE CRAMPS IN THAT MOVIE. LUX INTERIOR (RIP) GOES COMPLETELY PSYCHO, FELLATING THE MICROPHONE WHILE POISON IVY, THE GUITARIST, LOOKS ON IN DEADPAN DISGUST.
WOW!
2002
WHEN MY FRIEND KEVIN WOULD COME TO VISIT FROM TORONTO, WE WOULD SET UNREALISTIC GOALS FOR OURSELVES.
OK, SO... THE PLAN IS TO WRITE DOWN 100 SONG TITLES, PICK 10 OF THEM AND RECORD THEM ALL TONIGHT.* COOL?
-ING PIES.
* WE WERE DEFINITELY UNDER THE SPELL OF GUIDED BY VOICES AND THE MAGNETIC FIELDS' 69 LOVE SONGS.
MOSTLY WE WERE JUST TRYING TO MAKE EACH OTHER LAUGH.
COUNTING DOWN FROM ZERO
TOILET RAINBOWS
IN THE HALL OF ANCIENT MIXTAPES
MANGLED BEYOND RECOGNITION
NOISY NIPPLE
FRAUDULENT HEADPHONES
MY BEST MISTAKE
THE FLUIDS I'VE CONSUMED
SOMEBODY NEVER TICKLES U
LIMPING TOWARDS YOUR FORTRESS
YOUREEK, UH
* ASSHOLES ARE PEOPLE TOO
VELCRO
SLOTH DISCO
DON'T DO THE DONT!
the Lasagna monologues
RETURN OF THE MAGGOT
BOX OF ROCKS
DIAGONAL SLEEPING
DINGLEBERRY PARFAIT
Chewing on the Obscenery
SEX (WITH A BULK)
OF YOU
PIGGYBANK OF BITTERNESS
Wallpaper
THE PROBLEM WITH PROBLEMS
Dilitantrum
TAINTED LUNCH
SUBLIMINAL MULE DIRECTIVE
KINGDOM COMPANY
DESIGNER BARFBAG
EXCITEMENT IS BORING
Headache in my THROAT
WE CALLED OUR NEW PROJECT COOLING PIES. WE'D GO TO THE KENNEL* AND STAY UP ALL NIGHT WRITING AND RECORDING. NO IDEA WAS TOO STUPID OR HALF BAKED. AND SOME OF THE SONGS WERE AS CLOSE TO BEAUTY AS I EVER GOT. KEVIN WOULD PLAY NEARLY ALL THE INSTRUMENTS. I'D WRITE THE LYRICS AND SING. JAMES JOINED US WHEN HE COULD. HE WOULD ENGINEER, PLAY BASS AND DO BACKING VOCALS WITH KEVIN. IT WAS PURE JOY, PROBABLY THE MOST FUN I EVER HAD MAKING MUSIC THAT DIDN'T INVOLVE PERFORMING.
HA HA HA HA HA
WE WOULD EMERGE FROM THE KENNEL AT SUNRISE, LAUGHING AND JOKING AND HEAD FOR THE F TRAIN. WHEN WE WOKE UP IN THE AFTERNOON, WE'D HEAD BACK AND DO IT AGAIN.
* A SUBTERRANEAN REHEARSAL/RECORDING SPACE IN PRE-GENTRIFIED DUMBO
1984
FOR NEARLY EVERY SHOW, THE OPENING ACT WAS... THE DEAD MILKMEN. THEY DIDN'T TAKE THE HARDCORE SCENE (OR THEMSELVES) SERIOUSLY AT ALL. THEY MADE FUN OF EVERYTHING, EVEN THE SCARY MACHO PUNKS. THEY JUST DIDN'T GIVE A FUCK AND IT WAS BEAUTIFUL. ALSO, EVEN THOUGH THEY WERE OBNOXIOUS, THE SONGS WERE CATCHY AND FUN TO SING ALONG WITH.
THAT GUY'S VOICE IS AWFUL. BUT HE'S HILARIOUS! AND EVERYBODY LOVES IT!
FUCKED UP WORLD! WE'RE ALL VETERANS OF A FUCKED UP WORLD!
I. WANT. THAT.

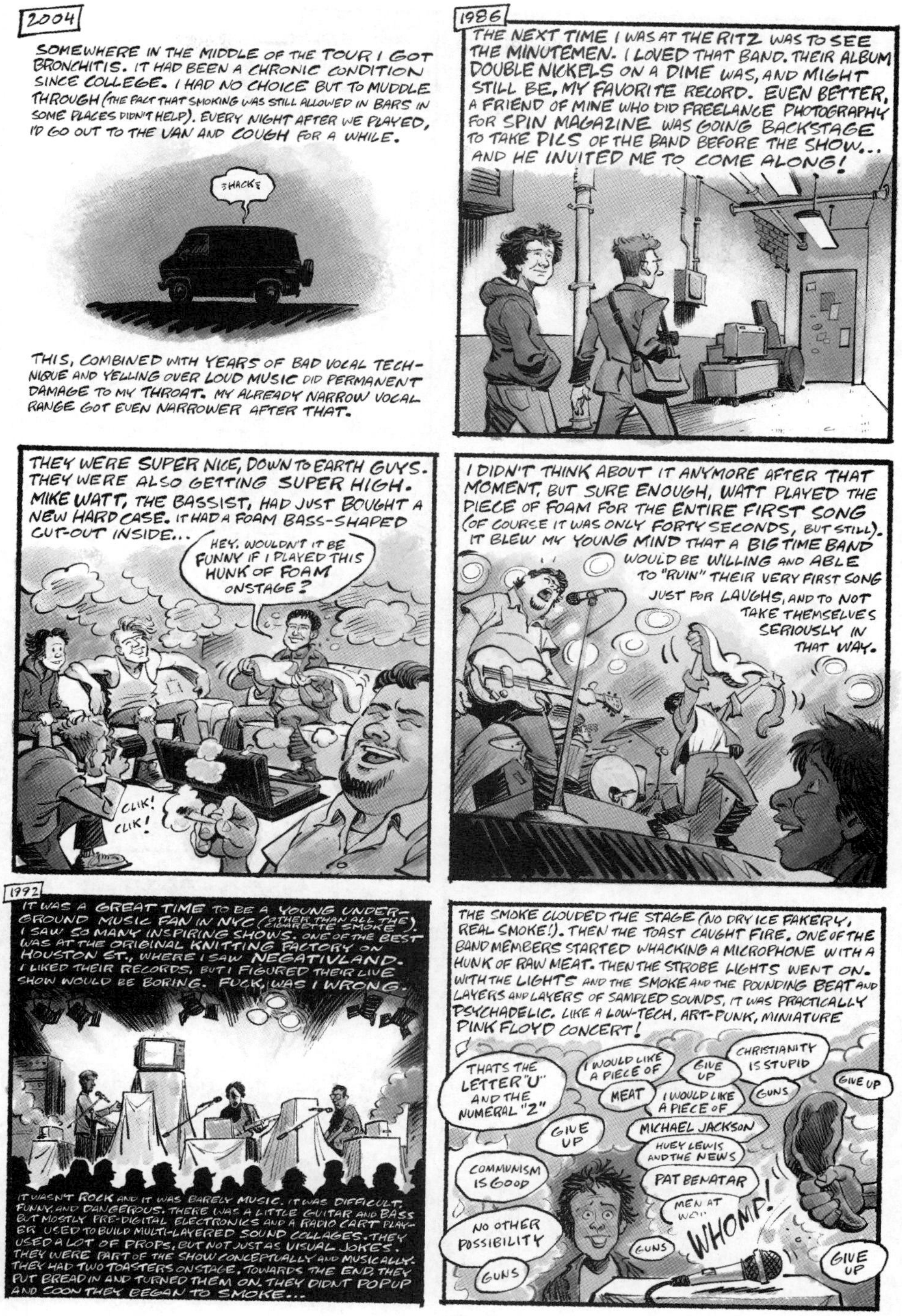
2004
SOMEWHERE IN THE MIDDLE OF THE TOUR I GOT BRONCHITIS. IT HAD BEEN A CHRONIC CONDITION SINCE COLLEGE. I HAD NO CHOICE BUT TO MUDDLE THROUGH (THE FACT THAT SMOKING WAS STILL ALLOWED IN BARS IN SOME PLACES DIDN'T HELP). EVERY NIGHT AFTER WE PLAYED, I'D GO OUT TO THE VAN AND COUGH FOR A WHILE.
HACK
THIS, COMBINED WITH YEARS OF BAD VOCAL TECHNIQUE AND YELLING OVER LOUD MUSIC DID PERMANENT DAMAGE TO MY THROAT. MY ALREADY NARROW VOCAL RANGE GOT EVEN NARROWER AFTER THAT.
1986
THE NEXT TIME I WAS AT THE RITZ WAS TO SEE THE MINUTEMEN. I LOVED THAT BAND. THEIR ALBUM DOUBLE NICKELS ON A DIME WAS, AND MIGHT STILL BE, MY FAVORITE RECORD. EVEN BETTER, A FRIEND OF MINE WHO DID FREELANCE PHOTOGRAPHY FOR SPIN MAGAZINE WAS GOING BACKSTAGE TO TAKE PICS OF THE BAND BEFORE THE SHOW... AND HE INVITED ME TO COME ALONG!
THEY WERE SUPER NICE, DOWN TO EARTH GUYS. THEY WERE ALSO GETTING SUPER HIGH. MIKE WATT, THE BASSIST, HAD JUST BOUGHT A NEW HARD CASE. IT HAD A FOAM BASS-SHAPED CUT-OUT INSIDE...
HEY. WOULDN'T IT BE FUNNY IF I PLAYED THIS HUNK OF FOAM ONSTAGE?
CLIK! CLIK!
I DIDN'T THINK ABOUT IT ANYMORE AFTER THAT MOMENT, BUT SURE ENOUGH, WATT PLAYED THE PIECE OF FOAM FOR THE ENTIRE FIRST SONG (OF COURSE IT WAS ONLY FORTY SECONDS, BUT STILL). IT BLEW MY YOUNG MIND THAT A BIG TIME BAND WOULD BE WILLING AND ABLE TO "RUIN" THEIR VERY FIRST SONG JUST FOR LAUGHS, AND TO NOT TAKE THEMSELVES SERIOUSLY IN THAT WAY.
1992
IT WAS A GREAT TIME TO BE A YOUNG UNDERGROUND MUSIC FAN IN NYC (OTHER THAN ALL THE CIGARETTE SMOKE). I SAW SO MANY INSPIRING SHOWS. ONE OF THE BEST WAS AT THE ORIGINAL KNITTING FACTORY ON HOUSTON ST., WHERE I SAW NEGATIVLAND. I LIKED THEIR RECORDS, BUT I FIGURED THEIR LIVE SHOW WOULD BE BORING. FUCK, WAS I WRONG.
IT WASN'T ROCK AND IT WAS BARELY MUSIC. IT WAS DIFFICULT, FUNNY, AND DANGEROUS. THERE WAS A LITTLE GUITAR AND BASS BUT MOSTLY PRE-DIGITAL ELECTRONICS AND A RADIO CART PLAYER USED TO BUILD MULTI-LAYERED SOUND COLLAGES. THEY USED A LOT OF PROPS, BUT NOT JUST AS VISUAL JOKES. THEY WERE PART OF THE SHOW CONCEPTUALLY AND MUSICALLY. THEY HAD TWO TOASTERS ONSTAGE. TOWARDS THE END, THEY PUT BREAD IN AND TURNED THEM ON. THEY DIDNT POPUP AND SOON THEY BEGAN TO SMOKE...
THE SMOKE CLOUDED THE STAGE (NO DRY ICE FAKERY, REAL SMOKE!). THEN THE TOAST CAUGHT FIRE. ONE OF THE BAND MEMBERS STARTED WHACKING A MICROPHONE WITH A HUNK OF RAW MEAT. THEN THE STROBE LIGHTS WENT ON. WITH THE LIGHTS AND THE SMOKE AND THE POUNDING BEAT AND LAYERS AND LAYERS OF SAMPLED SOUNDS, IT WAS PRACTICALLY PSYCHADELIC. LIKE A LOW-TECH, ART-PUNK, MINIATURE PINK FLOYD CONCERT!
THATS THE LETTER "U" AND THE NUMERAL "2"
I WOULD LIKE A PIECE OF
MEAT
GIVE UP
CHRISTIANITY IS STUPID
I WOULD LIKE A PIECE OF
GUNS
GIVE UP
MICHAEL JACKSON
GIVE UP
HUEY LEWIS AND THE NEWS
COMMUNISM IS GOOD
PAT BENATAR
MEN AT
WHOMP!
NO OTHER POSSIBILITY
GUNS
GUNS
GIVE UP

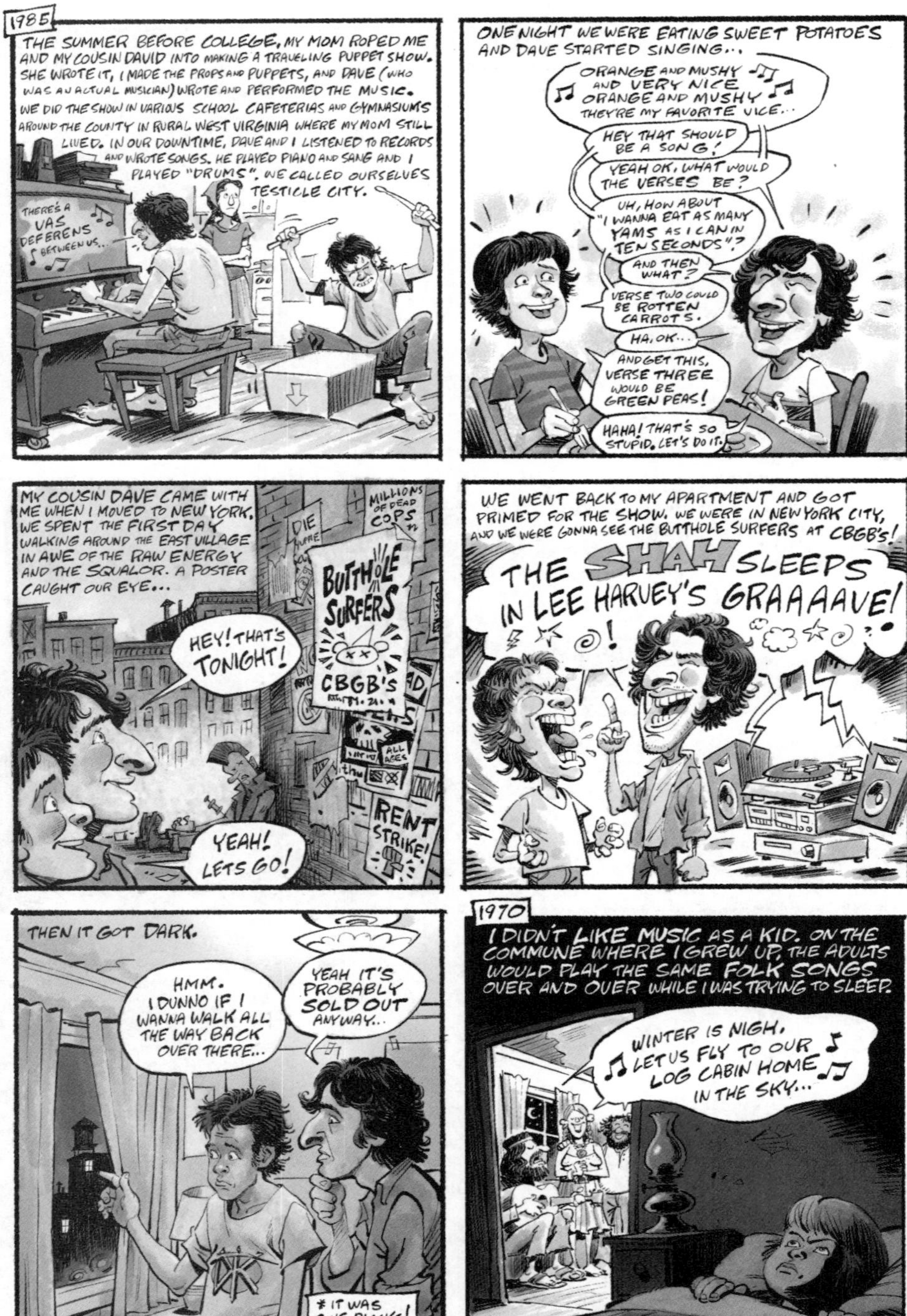
1985
THE SUMMER BEFORE COLLEGE, MY MOM ROPED ME AND MY COUSIN DAVID INTO MAKING A TRAVELING PUPPET SHOW. SHE WROTE IT, I MADE THE PROPS AND PUPPETS, AND DAVE (WHO WAS AN ACTUAL MUSICIAN) WROTE AND PERFORMED THE MUSIC. WE DID THE SHOW IN VARIOUS SCHOOL CAFETERIAS AND GYMNASIUMS AROUND THE COUNTY IN RURAL WEST VIRGINIA WHERE MY MOM STILL LIVED. IN OUR DOWNTIME, DAVE AND I LISTENED TO RECORDS AND WROTE SONGS. HE PLAYED PIANO AND SANG AND I PLAYED "DRUMS". WE CALLED OURSELVES TESTICLE CITY.
THERE'S A VAS DEFERENS BETWEEN US...
ONE NIGHT WE WERE EATING SWEET POTATOES AND DAVE STARTED SINGING...
ORANGE AND MUSHY AND VERY NICE ORANGE AND MUSHY THEY'RE MY FAVORITE VICE...
HEY THAT SHOULD BE A SONG!
YEAH OK, WHAT WOULD THE VERSES BE?
UH, HOW ABOUT "I WANNA EAT AS MANY YAMS AS I CAN IN TEN SECONDS"?
AND THEN WHAT?
VERSE TWO COULD BE ROTTEN CARROTS.
HA, OK...
AND GET THIS, VERSE THREE WOULD BE GREEN PEAS!
HAHA! THAT'S SO STUPID. LET'S DO IT.
MY COUSIN DAVE CAME WITH ME WHEN I MOVED TO NEW YORK. WE SPENT THE FIRST DAY WALKING AROUND THE EAST VILLAGE IN AWE OF THE RAW ENERGY AND THE SQUALOR. A POSTER CAUGHT OUR EYE...
MILLIONS OF DEAD COPS
BUTTHOLE SURFERS
CBGB'S
ALL AGES
RENT STRIKE!
HEY! THAT'S TONIGHT!
YEAH! LETS GO!
WE WENT BACK TO MY APARTMENT AND GOT PRIMED FOR THE SHOW. WE WERE IN NEW YORK CITY, AND WE WERE GONNA SEE THE BUTTHOLE SURFERS AT CBGB's!
THE SHAH SLEEPS IN LEE HARVEY'S GRAAAAVE!
THEN IT GOT DARK.
HMM. I DUNNO IF I WANNA WALK ALL THE WAY BACK OVER THERE...
YEAH IT'S PROBABLY SOLD OUT ANYWAY...
* IT WAS FIVE BLOCKS!
1970
I DIDN'T LIKE MUSIC AS A KID. ON THE COMMUNE WHERE I GREW UP, THE ADULTS WOULD PLAY THE SAME FOLK SONGS OVER AND OVER WHILE I WAS TRYING TO SLEEP.
WINTER IS NIGH, LET US FLY TO OUR LOG CABIN HOME IN THE SKY...

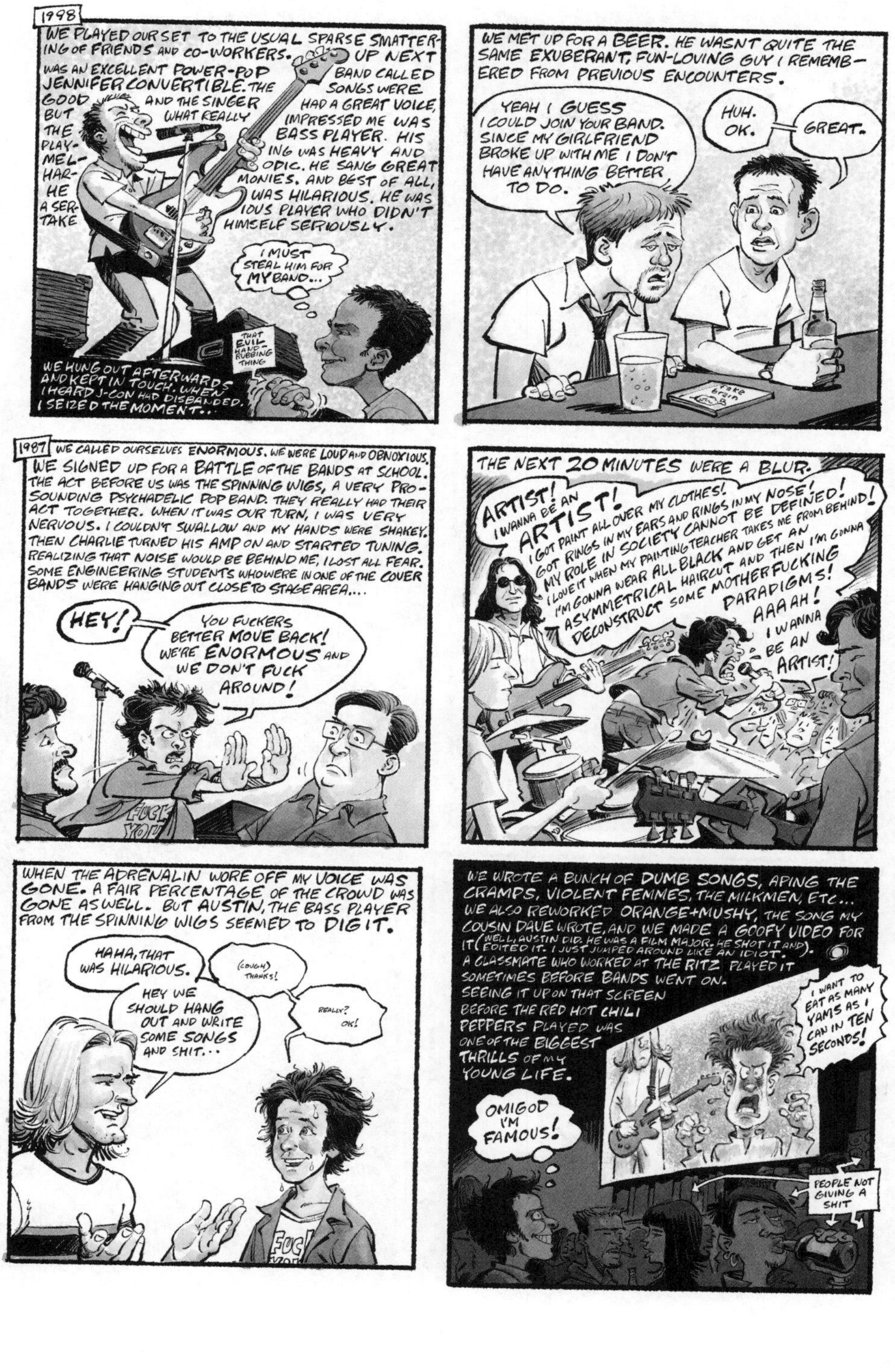
1998
WE PLAYED OUR SET TO THE USUAL SPARSE SMATTERING OF FRIENDS AND CO-WORKERS. UP NEXT WAS AN EXCELLENT POWER-POP BAND CALLED JENNIFER CONVERTIBLE. THE SONGS WERE GOOD AND THE SINGER HAD A GREAT VOICE, BUT WHAT REALLY IMPRESSED ME WAS THE BASS PLAYER. HIS PLAYING WAS HEAVY AND MELODIC. HE SANG GREAT HARMONIES. AND BEST OF ALL, HE WAS HILARIOUS. HE WAS A SERIOUS PLAYER WHO DIDN'T TAKE HIMSELF SERIOUSLY.
I MUST STEAL HIM FOR MY BAND...
THAT EVIL HAND-RUBBING THING
WE HUNG OUT AFTERWARDS AND KEPT IN TOUCH. WHEN I HEARD J-CON HAD DISBANDED, I SEIZED THE MOMENT...
WE MET UP FOR A BEER. HE WASN'T QUITE THE SAME EXUBERANT, FUN-LOVING GUY I REMEMBERED FROM PREVIOUS ENCOUNTERS.
YEAH I GUESS I COULD JOIN YOUR BAND. SINCE MY GIRLFRIEND BROKE UP WITH ME I DON'T HAVE ANYTHING BETTER TO DO.
HUH. OK.
GREAT.
1987 WE CALLED OURSELVES ENORMOUS. WE WERE LOUD AND OBNOXIOUS.
WE SIGNED UP FOR A BATTLE OF THE BANDS AT SCHOOL. THE ACT BEFORE US WAS THE SPINNING WIGS, A VERY PRO-SOUNDING PSYCHADELIC POP BAND. THEY REALLY HAD THEIR ACT TOGETHER. WHEN IT WAS OUR TURN, I WAS VERY NERVOUS. I COULDN'T SWALLOW AND MY HANDS WERE SHAKEY. THEN CHARLIE TURNED HIS AMP ON AND STARTED TUNING. REALIZING THAT NOISE WOULD BE BEHIND ME, I LOST ALL FEAR. SOME ENGINEERING STUDENTS WHO WERE IN ONE OF THE COVER BANDS WERE HANGING OUT CLOSE TO STAGE AREA....
HEY!
YOU FUCKERS BETTER MOVE BACK! WE'RE ENORMOUS AND WE DON'T FUCK AROUND!
FUCK YOU
THE NEXT 20 MINUTES WERE A BLUR.
ARTIST! I WANNA BE AN ARTIST! I GOT PAINT ALL OVER MY CLOTHES! GOT RINGS IN MY EARS AND RINGS IN MY NOSE! MY ROLE IN SOCIETY CANNOT BE DEFINED! I LOVE IT WHEN MY PAINTING TEACHER TAKES ME FROM BEHIND! I'M GONNA WEAR ALL BLACK AND GET AN ASYMMETRICAL HAIRCUT AND THEN I'M GONNA DECONSTRUCT SOME MOTHERFUCKING PARADIGMS!
AAAAH! I WANNA BE AN ARTIST!
WHEN THE ADRENALIN WORE OFF MY VOICE WAS GONE. A FAIR PERCENTAGE OF THE CROWD WAS GONE AS WELL. BUT AUSTIN, THE BASS PLAYER FROM THE SPINNING WIGS SEEMED TO DIG IT.
HAHA, THAT WAS HILARIOUS.
(COUGH) THANKS!
HEY WE SHOULD HANG OUT AND WRITE SOME SONGS AND SHIT...
REALLY? OK!
WE WROTE A BUNCH OF DUMB SONGS, APING THE CRAMPS, VIOLENT FEMMES, THE MILKMEN, ETC... WE ALSO REWORKED ORANGE+MUSHY, THE SONG MY COUSIN DAVE WROTE, AND WE MADE A GOOFY VIDEO FOR IT (WELL, AUSTIN DID. HE WAS A FILM MAJOR. HE SHOT IT AND EDITED IT. I JUST JUMPED AROUND LIKE AN IDIOT.). A CLASSMATE WHO WORKED AT THE RITZ PLAYED IT SOMETIMES BEFORE BANDS WENT ON. SEEING IT UP ON THAT SCREEN BEFORE THE RED HOT CHILI PEPPERS PLAYED WAS ONE OF THE BIGGEST THRILLS OF MY YOUNG LIFE.
I WANT TO EAT AS MANY YAMS AS I CAN IN TEN SECONDS!
OMIGOD I'M FAMOUS!
PEOPLE NOT GIVING A SHIT

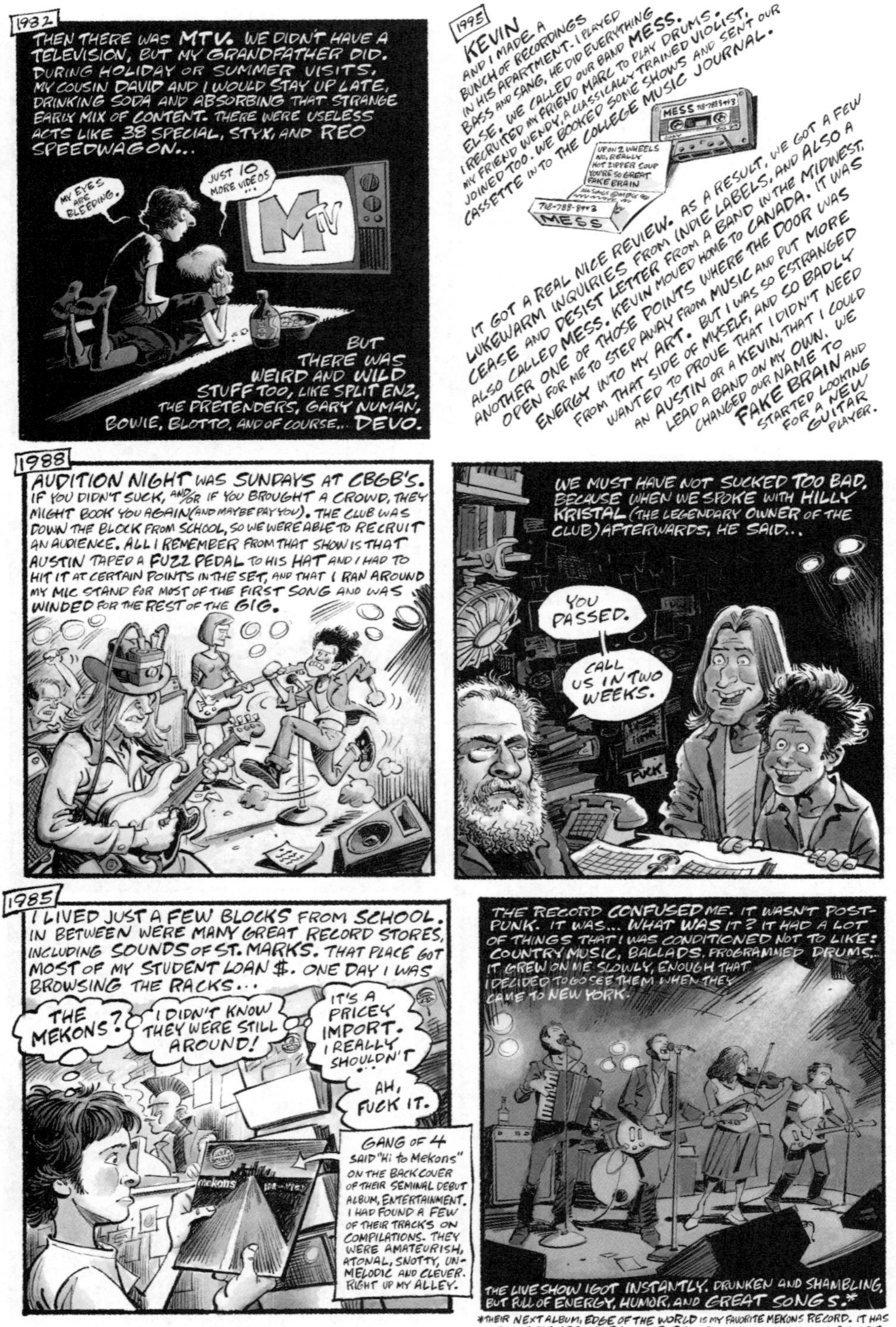
1982
THEN THERE WAS MTV. WE DIDN'T HAVE A TELEVISION, BUT MY GRANDFATHER DID. DURING HOLIDAY OR SUMMER VISITS, MY COUSIN DAVID AND I WOULD STAY UP LATE, DRINKING SODA AND ABSORBING THAT STRANGE EARLY MIX OF CONTENT. THERE WERE USELESS ACTS LIKE 38 SPECIAL, STYX, AND REO SPEEDWAGON...
MY EYES ARE BLEEDING.
JUST 10 MORE VIDEOS ...
MTV
BUT THERE WAS WEIRD AND WILD STUFF TOO, LIKE SPLIT ENZ, THE PRETENDERS, GARY NUMAN, BOWIE, BLOTTO, AND OF COURSE... DEVO.
1995
KEVIN AND I MADE A BUNCH OF RECORDINGS IN HIS APARTMENT. I PLAYED BASS AND SANG, HE DID EVERYTHING ELSE. WE CALLED OUR BAND MESS. I RECRUITED MY FRIEND MARC TO PLAY DRUMS. MY FRIEND WENDY, A CLASSICALLY TRAINED VIOLIST, JOINED TOO. WE BOOKED SOME SHOWS AND SENT OUR CASSETTE IN TO THE COLLEGE MUSIC JOURNAL.
MESS 718-788-8943
UP ON 2 WHEELS
NO, REALLY
HOT ZIPPER SOUP
YOU'RE SO GREAT
FAKE BRAIN
718-788-8943
MESS
IT GOT A REAL NICE REVIEW. AS A RESULT, WE GOT A FEW LUKEWARM INQUIRIES FROM INDIE LABELS, AND ALSO A CEASE AND DESIST LETTER FROM A BAND IN THE MIDWEST, ALSO CALLED MESS. KEVIN MOVED HOME TO CANADA. IT WAS ANOTHER ONE OF THOSE POINTS WHERE THE DOOR WAS OPEN FOR ME TO STEP AWAY FROM MUSIC AND PUT MORE ENERGY INTO MY ART. BUT I WAS SO ESTRANGED FROM THAT SIDE OF MYSELF, AND SO BADLY WANTED TO PROVE THAT I DIDN'T NEED AN AUSTIN OR A KEVIN, THAT I COULD LEAD A BAND ON MY OWN. WE CHANGED OUR NAME TO FAKE BRAIN AND STARTED LOOKING FOR A NEW GUITAR PLAYER.
1988
AUDITION NIGHT WAS SUNDAYS AT CBGB'S. IF YOU DIDN'T SUCK, AND/OR IF YOU BROUGHT A CROWD, THEY MIGHT BOOK YOU AGAIN (AND MAYBE PAY YOU). THE CLUB WAS DOWN THE BLOCK FROM SCHOOL, SO WE WERE ABLE TO RECRUIT AN AUDIENCE. ALL I REMEMBER FROM THAT SHOW IS THAT AUSTIN TAPED A FUZZ PEDAL TO HIS HAT AND I HAD TO HIT IT AT CERTAIN POINTS IN THE SET, AND THAT I RAN AROUND MY MIC STAND FOR MOST OF THE FIRST SONG AND WAS WINDED FOR THE REST OF THE GIG.
WE MUST HAVE NOT SUCKED TOO BAD, BECAUSE WHEN WE SPOKE WITH HILLY KRISTAL (THE LEGENDARY OWNER OF THE CLUB) AFTERWARDS, HE SAID...
YOU PASSED.
CALL US IN TWO WEEKS.
FUCK
1985
I LIVED JUST A FEW BLOCKS FROM SCHOOL. IN BETWEEN WERE MANY GREAT RECORD STORES, INCLUDING SOUNDS OF ST. MARKS. THAT PLACE GOT MOST OF MY STUDENT LOAN $. ONE DAY I WAS BROWSING THE RACKS...
THE MEKONS?
I DIDN'T KNOW THEY WERE STILL AROUND!
IT'S A PRICEY IMPORT. I REALLY SHOULDN'T ...
AH, FUCK IT.
mekons
GANG OF 4 SAID "Hi to Mekons" ON THE BACK COVER OF THEIR SEMINAL DEBUT ALBUM, ENTERTAINMENT. I HAD FOUND A FEW OF THEIR TRACKS ON COMPILATIONS. THEY WERE AMATEURISH, ATONAL, SNOTTY, UNMELODIC AND CLEVER. RIGHT UP MY ALLEY.
THE RECORD CONFUSED ME. IT WASN'T POST-PUNK. IT WAS... WHAT WAS IT? IT HAD A LOT OF THINGS THAT I WAS CONDITIONED NOT TO LIKE: COUNTRY MUSIC, BALLADS, PROGRAMMED DRUMS... IT GREW ON ME SLOWLY, ENOUGH THAT I DECIDED TO GO SEE THEM WHEN THEY CAME TO NEW YORK.
THE LIVE SHOW I GOT INSTANTLY. DRUNKEN AND SHAMBLING, BUT FULL OF ENERGY, HUMOR, AND GREAT SONGS.*
*THEIR NEXT ALBUM, EDGE OF THE WORLD IS MY FAVORITE MEKONS RECORD. IT HAS TWO OF THE GREATEST SONGS EVER: HELLO CRUEL WORLD AND BIG ZOMBIE.

2002

WE WERE BUMPED TO LAST IN A TOWN WHERE NO ONE KNEW US. WHEN IT WAS FINALLY OUR TURN, THE PLACE WAS DESOLATE.

YOU GUYS DON'T GOTTA PLAY IF YOU DON'T WANNA

OH, WE'RE GONNA PLAY.

SUIT YOURSELF.

WE FOUND AN "AUDIENCE": AN OLD MANNEQUIN THAT HAD BEEN LEFT IN THE DRESSING ROOM. SINCE THERE WAS ZERO CHANCE OF SELLING ANY MERCH, JAMES WRAPPED HIMSELF UP IN THE ROPE LIGHTS FROM OUR DISPLAY. HE PLAYED THE ENTIRE SHOW WITHOUT EXPLODING, BUT HE DID MELT A LITTLE.

THE STAKES WERE SO LOW AND THE SITUATION SO PATHETIC, THAT WE JUST WENT FOR IT. WE CHANNELED OUR FRUSTRATION INTO OUR ART, SUCH AS IT WAS. WAS IT OUR BEST SHOW EVER? MAYBE. AND IF NOT, NO ONE WILL EVER KNOW.

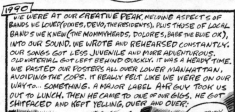

1990

WE WERE AT OUR CREATIVE PEAK, MELDING ASPECTS OF BANDS WE LOVED (PIXIES, DEVO, THE RESIDENTS), PLUS THOSE OF LOCAL BANDS WE KNEW (THE MOMMYHEADS, DOLORES, BABE THE BLUE OX), INTO OUR SOUND. WE WROTE AND REHEARSED CONSTANTLY. OUR SONGS GOT LESS JUVENILE AND MORE ADVENTUROUS. OLD MATERIAL GOT LEFT BEHIND QUICKLY. IT WAS A HEADY TIME. WE PASTED OUR POSTERS ALL OVER LOWER MANHATTAN, AVOIDING THE COPS. IT REALLY FELT LIKE WE WERE ON OUR WAY TO... SOMETHING. A MAJOR LABEL A+R GUY TOOK US OUT TO LUNCH. THEN HE CAME TO ONE OF OUR GIGS. HE GOT SHITFACED AND KEPT YELLING, OVER AND OVER:

SOMEBODY SIGN THIS FUGGIN' BAND!

BURP.

MY FOLKS CAME UP FROM PHILLY TO SEE US PLAY. MY DAD GOT IT. AFTER ALL, HE INTRODUCED ME TO SPIKE JONES, THE FUGS, AND THE MOTHERS OF INVENTION. BUT, AS ALWAYS, HE WAS BLUNT IN HIS ASSESSMENT.

THAT WAS FUN...

BUT YOU KNOW YOU'RE A MUCH BETTER ARTIST THAN YOU ARE A MUSICIAN.

YOU'RE WASTING YOUR TIME.

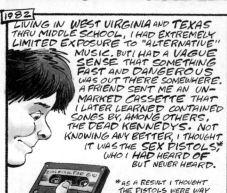

1982

LIVING IN WEST VIRGINIA AND TEXAS THRU MIDDLE SCHOOL, I HAD EXTREMELY LIMITED EXPOSURE TO "ALTERNATIVE" MUSIC. BUT I HAD A VAGUE SENSE THAT SOMETHING FAST AND DANGEROUS WAS OUT THERE SOMEWHERE. A FRIEND SENT ME AN UNMARKED CASSETTE THAT I LATER LEARNED CONTAINED SONGS BY, AMONG OTHERS, THE DEAD KENNEDYS. NOT KNOWING ANY BETTER, I THOUGHT IT WAS THE SEX PISTOLS,* WHO I HAD HEARD OF BUT NEVER HEARD.

COOL MUSIC FOR GIV

* AS A RESULT I THOUGHT THE PISTOLS WERE WAY FASTER AND MORE EXCITING THAN THEY ACTUALLY WERE. WHEN I FINALLY HEARD THEM THEY JUST SOUNDED LIKE A SLOPPY BAR BAND.

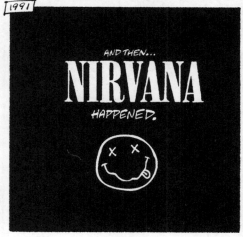

1991

AND THEN...

NIRVANA

HAPPENED.

243

I ♥ FEAR CITY

TALES OF MISSPENT YOUTH, OF HUMAN BONDAGE (AND OTHER KINKS), THE LIVABLE WAGES OF SIN, AND GIVING THE DEVIL HIS DUE IN TRAUMA, PHYSICAL AND MENTAL ILLNESS, BUT AVOIDING DEATH BY BOREDOM. IN OTHER WORDS, PUNK RAWK.

BY J. GONZALEZ-BLITZ

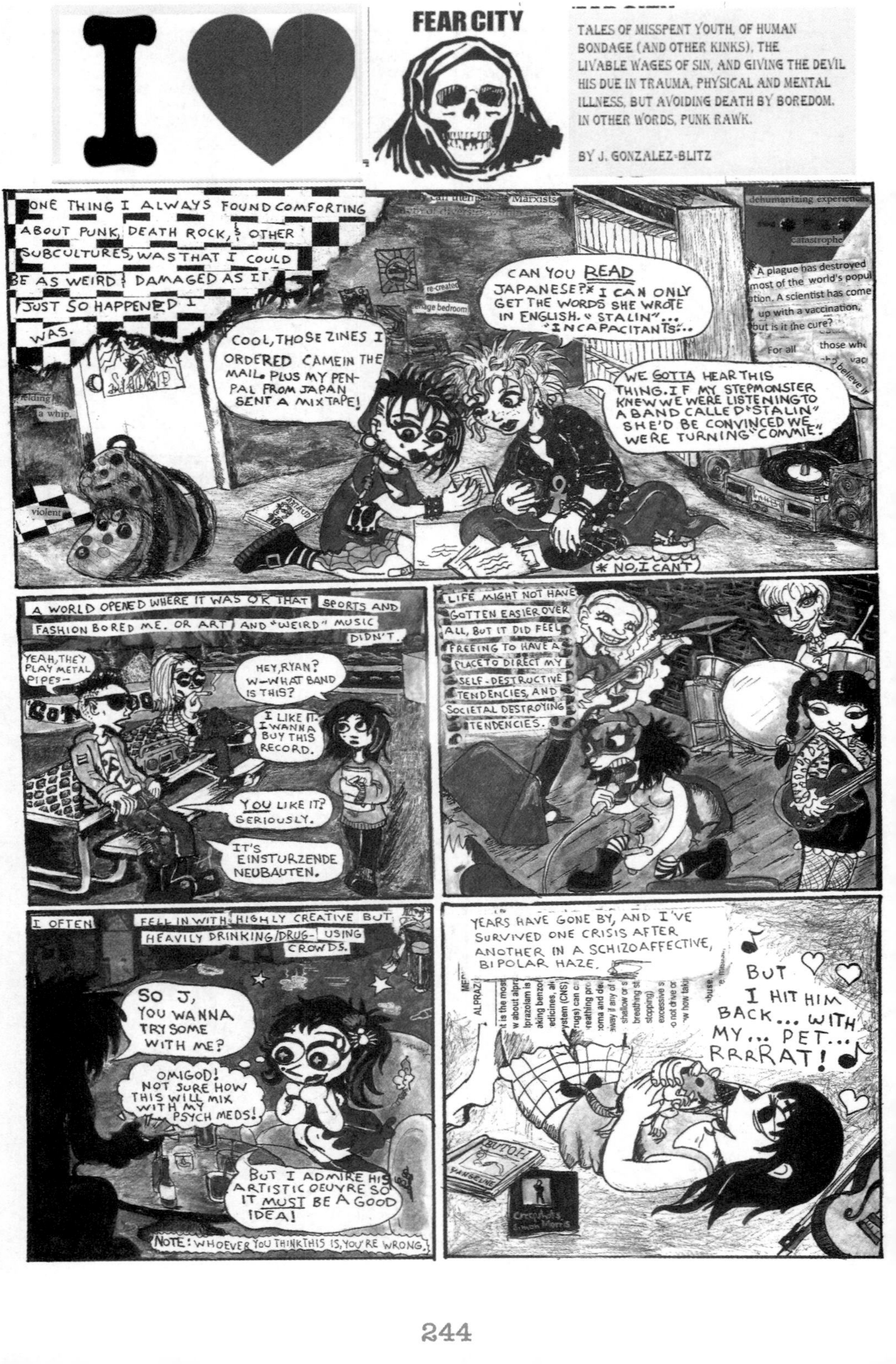

ONE THING I ALWAYS FOUND COMFORTING ABOUT PUNK, DEATH ROCK, & OTHER SUBCULTURES, WAS THAT I COULD BE AS WEIRD & DAMAGED AS IT JUST SO HAPPENED I WAS.
COOL, THOSE ZINES I ORDERED CAME IN THE MAIL. PLUS MY PEN-PAL FROM JAPAN SENT A MIXTAPE!
CAN YOU READ JAPANESE?* I CAN ONLY GET THE WORDS SHE WROTE IN ENGLISH. "STALIN"... "INCAPACITANTS"...
WE GOTTA HEAR THIS THING. IF MY STEPMONSTER KNEW WE WERE LISTENING TO A BAND CALLED "STALIN" SHE'D BE CONVINCED WE WERE TURNING "COMMIE".
* NO, I CAN'T
A plague has destroyed most of the world's population. A scientist has come up with a vaccination, but is it the cure?
A WORLD OPENED WHERE IT WAS OK THAT SPORTS AND FASHION BORED ME. OR ART AND "WEIRD" MUSIC DIDN'T.
YEAH, THEY PLAY METAL PIPES–
HEY, RYAN? W-WHAT BAND IS THIS?
I LIKE IT. I WANNA BUY THIS RECORD.
YOU LIKE IT? SERIOUSLY.
IT'S EINSTURZENDE NEUBAUTEN.
LIFE MIGHT NOT HAVE GOTTEN EASIER OVER ALL, BUT IT DID FEEL FREEING TO HAVE A PLACE TO DIRECT MY SELF-DESTRUCTIVE TENDENCIES, AND SOCIETAL DESTROYING TENDENCIES.
I OFTEN FELL IN WITH HIGHLY CREATIVE BUT HEAVILY DRINKING/DRUG-USING CROWDS.
SO J, YOU WANNA TRY SOME WITH ME?
OMIGOD! NOT SURE HOW THIS WILL MIX WITH MY PSYCH MEDS!
BUT I ADMIRE HIS ARTISTIC OEUVRE SO IT MUST BE A GOOD IDEA!
NOTE: WHOEVER YOU THINK THIS IS, YOU'RE WRONG.
YEARS HAVE GONE BY, AND I'VE SURVIVED ONE CRISIS AFTER ANOTHER IN A SCHIZOAFFECTIVE, BIPOLAR HAZE.
BUT I HIT HIM BACK... WITH MY... PET... RRRRAT!
BUTOH

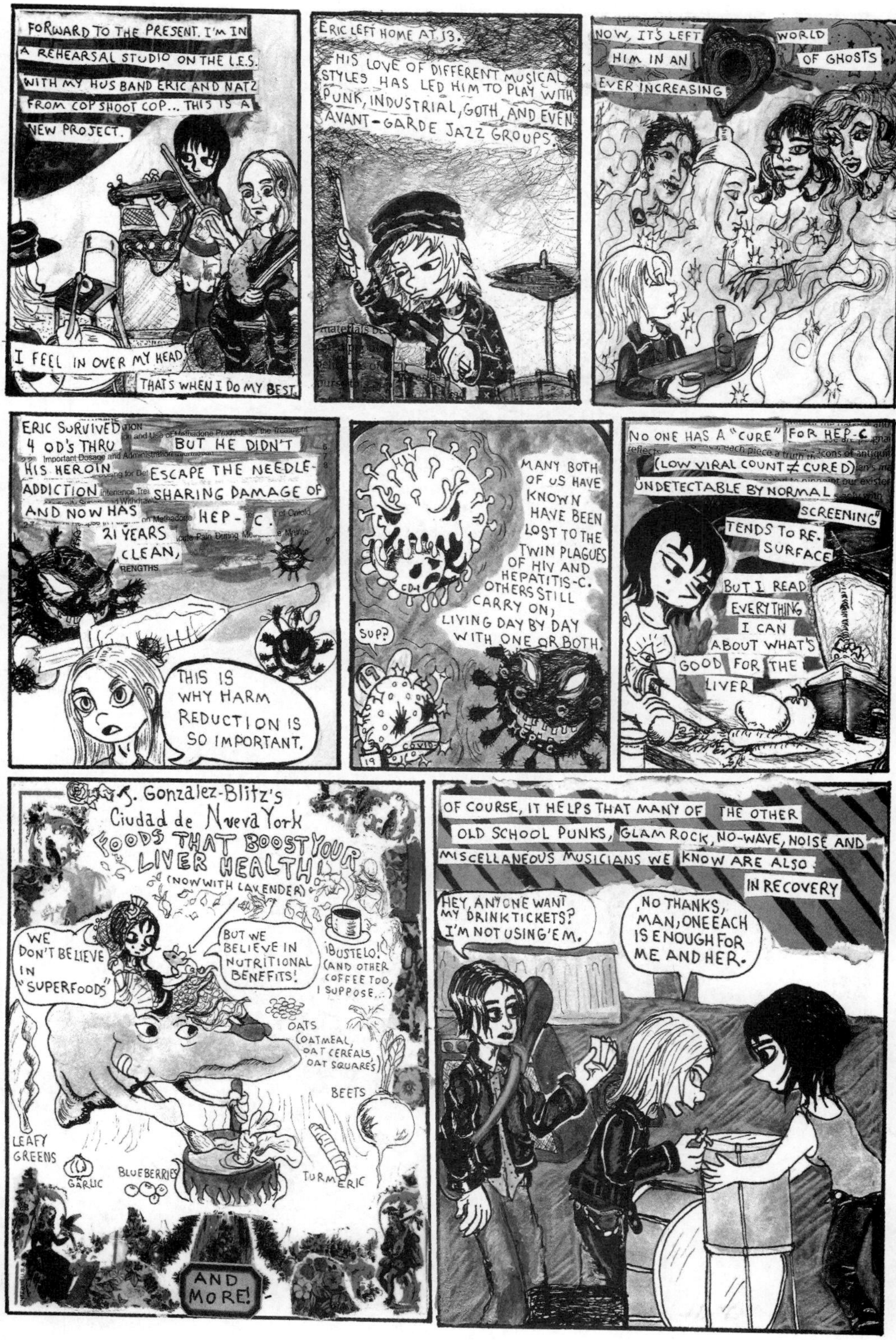
FORWARD TO THE PRESENT. I'M IN A REHEARSAL STUDIO ON THE L.E.S. WITH MY HUSBAND ERIC AND NATZ FROM COP SHOOT COP... THIS IS A NEW PROJECT.
I FEEL IN OVER MY HEAD
THAT'S WHEN I DO MY BEST.
ERIC LEFT HOME AT 13.
HIS LOVE OF DIFFERENT MUSICAL STYLES HAS LED HIM TO PLAY WITH PUNK, INDUSTRIAL, GOTH, AND EVEN AVANT-GARDE JAZZ GROUPS.
NOW, IT'S LEFT HIM IN AN EVER INCREASING WORLD OF GHOSTS
ERIC SURVIVED 4 OD'S THRU HIS HEROIN ADDICTION AND NOW HAS 21 YEARS CLEAN,
BUT HE DIDN'T ESCAPE THE NEEDLE-SHARING DAMAGE OF HEP-C.
THIS IS WHY HARM REDUCTION IS SO IMPORTANT.
HIV
CD-1
MANY BOTH OF US HAVE KNOWN HAVE BEEN LOST TO THE TWIN PLAGUES OF HIV AND HEPATITIS-C. OTHERS STILL CARRY ON, LIVING DAY BY DAY WITH ONE OR BOTH.
SUP?
COVID 19
HEP-C
NO ONE HAS A "CURE" FOR HEP-C
(LOW VIRAL COUNT ≠ CURED)
UNDETECTABLE BY NORMAL SCREENING"
TENDS TO RE-SURFACE
BUT I READ EVERYTHING I CAN ABOUT WHAT'S GOOD FOR THE LIVER
J. Gonzalez-Blitz's Ciudad de Nueva York FOODS THAT BOOST YOUR LIVER HEALTH!
(NOW WITH LAVENDER)
WE DON'T BELIEVE IN "SUPERFOODS"
BUT WE BELIEVE IN NUTRITIONAL BENEFITS!
¡BUSTELO! (AND OTHER COFFEE TOO, I SUPPOSE...)
OATS (OATMEAL, OAT CEREALS, OAT SQUARES)
BEETS
LEAFY GREENS
GARLIC
BLUEBERRIES
TURMERIC
AND MORE!
OF COURSE, IT HELPS THAT MANY OF THE OTHER OLD SCHOOL PUNKS, GLAM ROCK, NO-WAVE, NOISE AND MISCELLANEOUS MUSICIANS WE KNOW ARE ALSO IN RECOVERY
HEY, ANYONE WANT MY DRINK TICKETS? I'M NOT USING 'EM.
NO THANKS, MAN, ONE EACH IS ENOUGH FOR ME AND HER.

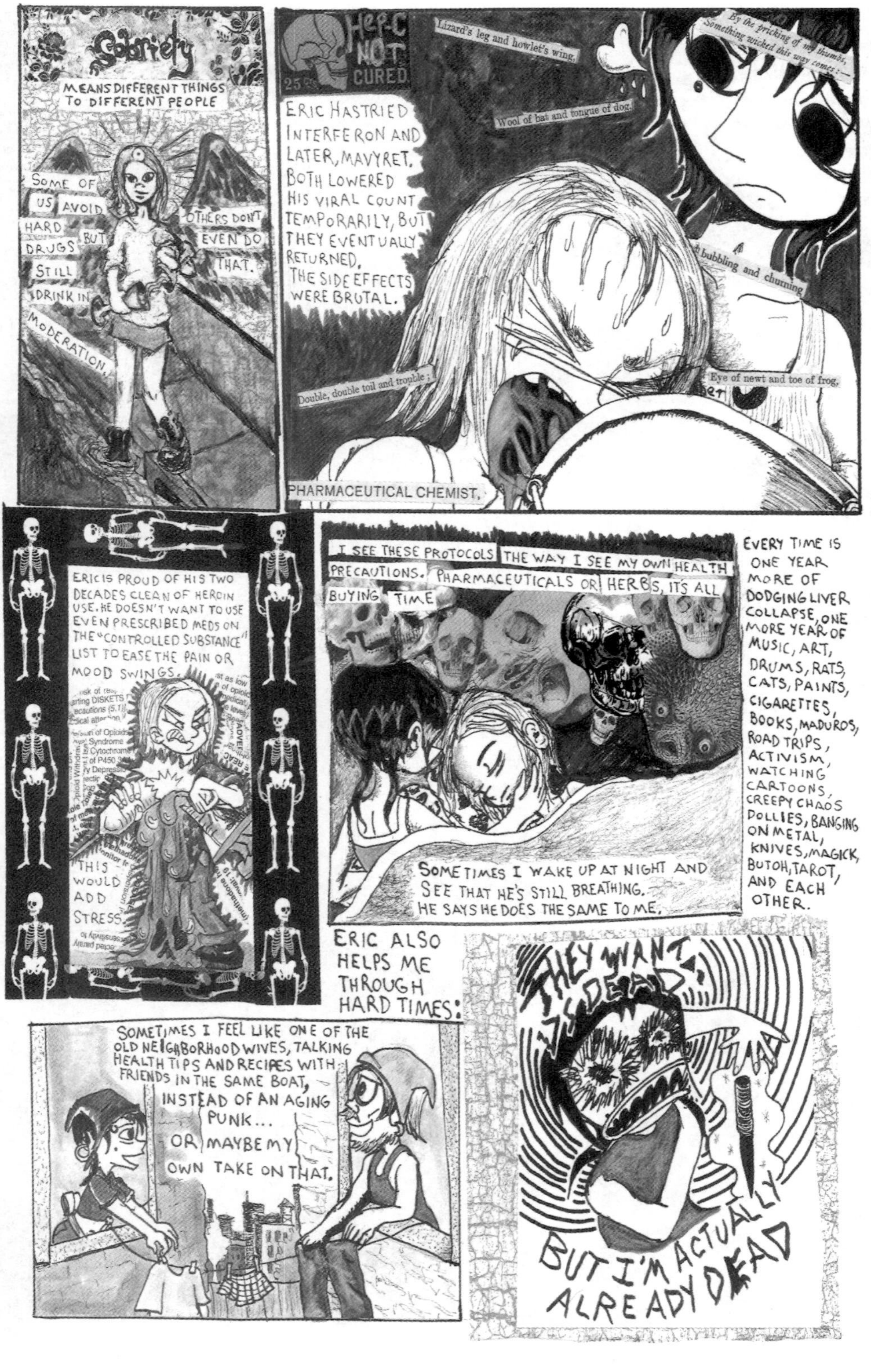
Sobriety
MEANS DIFFERENT THINGS TO DIFFERENT PEOPLE
SOME OF US AVOID HARD DRUGS BUT STILL DRINK IN MODERATION.
OTHERS DON'T EVEN DO THAT.
Hep-C NOT CURED.
25 cts
ERIC HAS TRIED INTERFERON AND LATER, MAVYRET. BOTH LOWERED HIS VIRAL COUNT TEMPORARILY, BUT THEY EVENTUALLY RETURNED. THE SIDE EFFECTS WERE BRUTAL.
Lizard's leg and howlet's wing,
By the pricking of my thumbs, Something wicked this way comes :—
Wool of bat and tongue of dog,
bubbling and churning
Double, double toil and trouble ;
Eye of newt and toe of frog,
PHARMACEUTICAL CHEMIST,
ERIC IS PROUD OF HIS TWO DECADES CLEAN OF HEROIN USE. HE DOESN'T WANT TO USE EVEN PRESCRIBED MEDS ON THE "CONTROLLED SUBSTANCE" LIST TO EASE THE PAIN OR MOOD SWINGS.
THIS WOULD ADD STRESS.
I SEE THESE PROTOCOLS THE WAY I SEE MY OWN HEALTH PRECAUTIONS. PHARMACEUTICALS OR HERBS, IT'S ALL BUYING TIME
SOMETIMES I WAKE UP AT NIGHT AND SEE THAT HE'S STILL BREATHING. HE SAYS HE DOES THE SAME TO ME.
EVERY TIME IS ONE YEAR MORE OF DODGING LIVER COLLAPSE, ONE MORE YEAR OF MUSIC, ART, DRUMS, RATS, CATS, PAINTS, CIGARETTES, BOOKS, MADUROS, ROAD TRIPS, ACTIVISM, WATCHING CARTOONS, CREEPY CHAOS DOLLIES, BANGING ON METAL, KNIVES, MAGICK, BUTOH, TAROT, AND EACH OTHER.
ERIC ALSO HELPS ME THROUGH HARD TIMES:
SOMETIMES I FEEL LIKE ONE OF THE OLD NEIGHBORHOOD WIVES, TALKING HEALTH TIPS AND RECIPES WITH FRIENDS IN THE SAME BOAT,
INSTEAD OF AN AGING PUNK...
OR MAYBE MY OWN TAKE ON THAT.
THEY WANT ME DEAD
BUT I'M ACTUALLY ALREADY DEAD

¡COÑO! WHAT DO I HAVE TO LOSE? AGAINST SO-CALLED "ANARCHISTS" WHO ABANDONED THEIR VALUES TO THE HIGHEST HIPSTER DOLLAR?

THIS IS THAT ANARCHIST PUNK LIFE

DEAD

DEAD

THEY'RE ALSO SECRETLY DEAD. CAN'T YOU SMELL IT, EVEN ALL THE WAY UP IN EL BARRIO? MULTIPLE LEVELS OF DEAD!!

OK, FINE, SO EVERYONE'S DEAD.

AND THIS IS HELL, OR ONE OF THE BARDOS, OR THE CITY OF PYRAMIDS!

IF SOME AETHYRIC FORCE LOCKED YOU AWAY FROM ME AGAIN, WHAT WOULD I DO? THE LAST TIME YOU WERE TAKEN TO BELLEVUE, THE DOCTOR TOLD ME HE MIGHT HAVE TO HOLD YOU LONGER IF IT HAPPENED AGAIN.

THEY TRIED TO FOOL YOU. ALL THE PEOPLE IN THAT BUILDING ACT LIKE FRIENDS TO YOUR FACE BUT THEY'VE BEEN POSSESSED BY THE NAZI CUNTS WHO KEEP TRYING TO KILL BUT SI HAVE N BODIES POSSESS PEOPLE OPEN CUZ A AND FUCK I GO MIN

I KNOW J., I KNOW.

*DISEMBODIED VOICES THAT THREATEN ME. THEY HAVE VAGUE FORMS.

THESE WOKE-WANNABE HIPSTERS ARE PERFECT TARGETS... POSTING SOCIAL JUSTICE MAKE BELIEVE AND CHEATING A DISABLED COUPLE WHO'S HOMELESS OUTTA LOW-INCOME HOUSING THAT'S AS BAD AS THOSE NEW LANDLORDS BRIBING THE COURT TO CHEAT ME OUT OF MY RENT CONTROL SUCCESSION RIGHTS!

HERE...

IS IT SCHIZOAFFECTIVE PARANOIA? OR NYC REAL ESTATE?

DON'T TAKE MORE THAN DR. RYBAKOV PRESCRIBED YOU...

MMM-HMM...

IT'LL BE OK.

ANYTHING YOU FEEL LIKE HEARING?

UMM — THE EX — NO... PLASMATICS— OR SATAN PANONSKI ... OR IGGY'S ALWAYS GOOD...

*INKING THIS PANEL TO ESKORBUTO

OOH I BEEN DIRT AND IT DON'T CARE OOH I BEEN DIRT BUT I DON'T CARE CUZ I'M BURNING INSIDE I'M JUST A-YEARNING INSIDE AND I'M THE FIRE OF LIFE YEAH, ALRIGHT OOH I'VE BEEN HURT AND I DON'T CARE I'VE BEEN HURT AND I DON'T CARE CUZ I'M BURNING INSIDE I'M JUST DREAMING THIS LIFE

SAID DO YOU FEEL IT WHEN YOU TOUCH ME? SAID DO YOU FEEL IT WHEN YOU TOUCH ME? THERE'S A FIRE, WELL IT'S A FIRE IT WAS JUST A BURNING, YEAH, ALRIGHT OOH, BURNING INSIDE BURNING JUST A DREAMING JUST A DREAMING IT WAS JUST A DREAMING PLAY IF FOR ME BABE WITH LOVE. —"DIRT" THE STOOGES

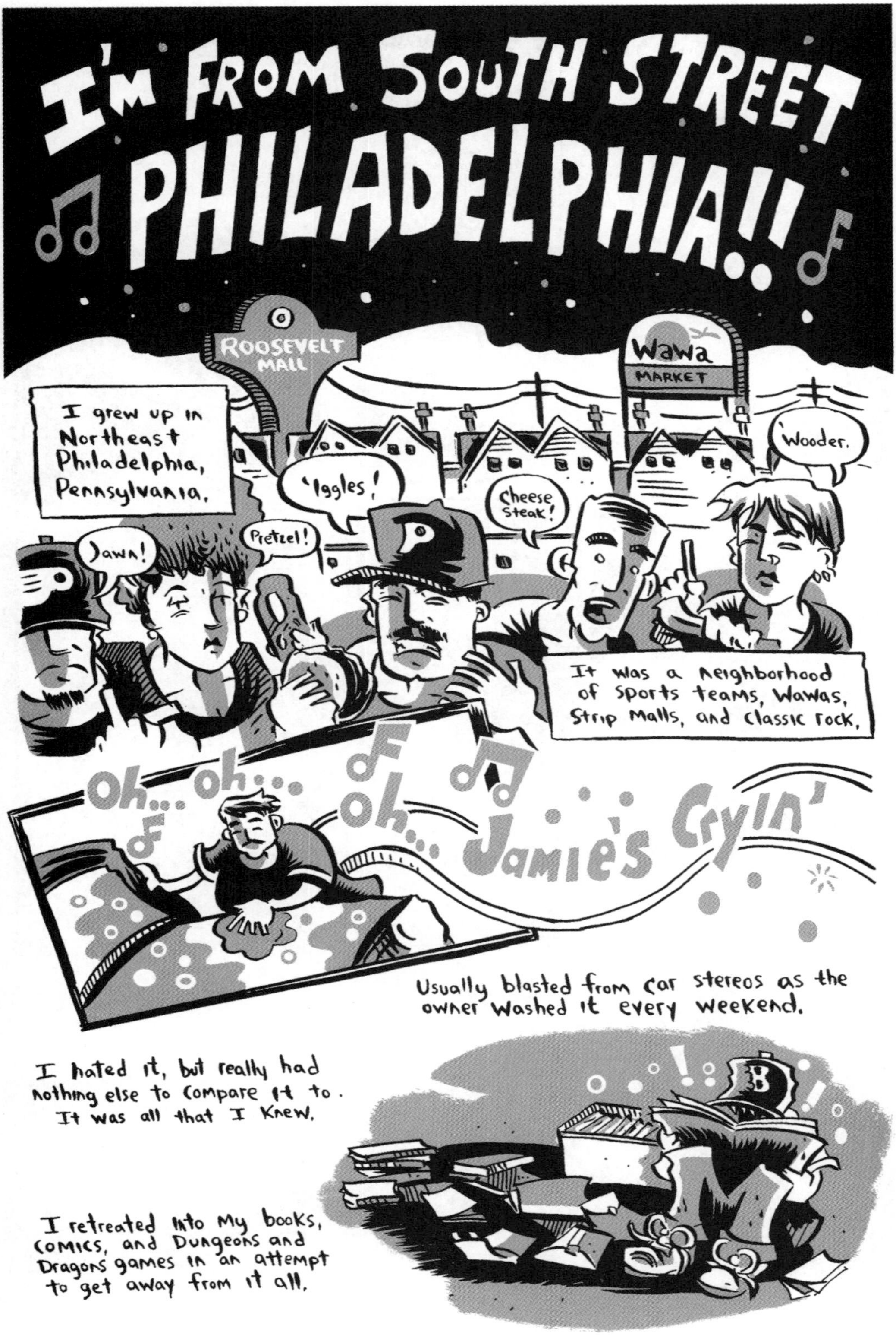
I'M FROM SOUTH STREET PHILADELPHIA!!
ROOSEVELT MALL
Wawa MARKET
I grew up in Northeast Philadelphia, Pennsylvania.
Jawn!
Pretzel!
'Iggles!
Cheese steak!
'Wooder.
It was a neighborhood of sports teams, Wawas, strip malls, and classic rock.
Oh... oh... oh... Jamie's Cryin'
Usually blasted from car stereos as the owner washed it every weekend.
I hated it, but really had nothing else to compare it to. It was all that I knew.
I retreated into my books, comics, and Dungeons and Dragons games in an attempt to get away from it all.

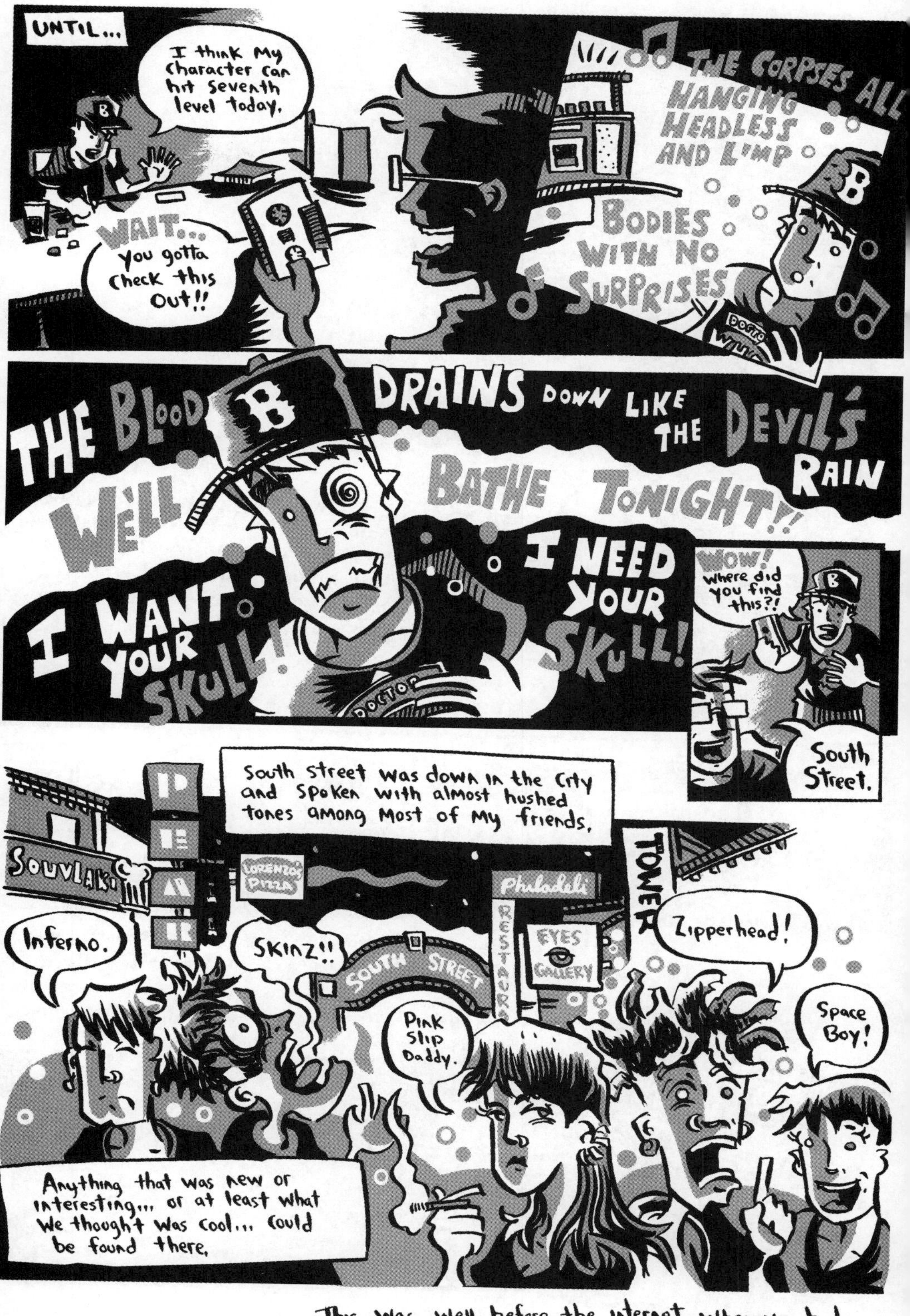

UNTIL...
I think my character can hit seventh level today.
WAIT... you gotta check this out!!
THE CORPSES ALL HANGING HEADLESS AND LIMP
BODIES WITH NO SURPRISES
THE BLOOD DRAINS DOWN LIKE THE DEVIL'S RAIN
WE'LL BATHE TONIGHT!!
I WANT YOUR SKULL!!
I NEED YOUR SKULL!
DOCTOR
WOW! Where did you find this?!
South Street.
South street was down in the city and spoken with almost hushed tones among most of my friends.
SOUVLAKI
LORENZO'S PIZZA
Philadeli
RESTAURA
TOWER
EYES GALLERY
SOUTH STREET
Inferno.
SKINZ!!
Zipperhead!
Pink Slip Daddy.
Space Boy!
Anything that was new or interesting... or at least what we thought was cool... could be found there.

This was well before the internet, when you had to go out and search for something new and brilliant.

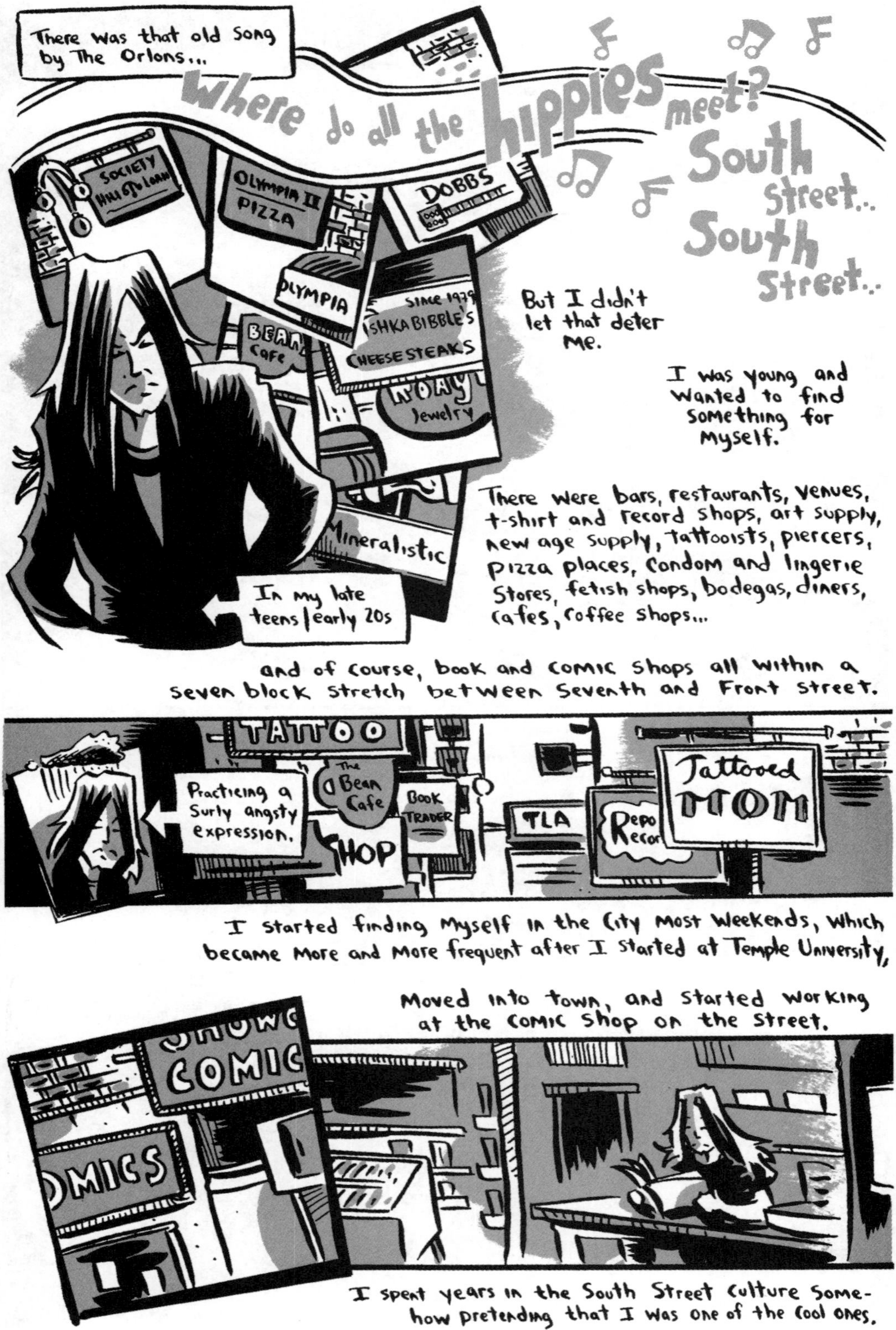

There was that old Song by The Orlons...
where do all the hippies meet? South Street... South Street...
SOCIETY
OLYMPIA II PIZZA
DOBBS
OLYMPIA
SINCE 1979 ISHKABIBBLE'S CHEESESTEAKS
BEAN Cafe
Jewelry
Mineralistic
But I didn't let that deter me.
I was young and wanted to find something for myself.
There were bars, restaurants, venues, t-shirt and record shops, art supply, new age supply, tattooists, piercers, pizza places, condom and lingerie stores, fetish shops, bodegas, diners, cafes, coffee shops...
In my late teens/early 20s
and of course, book and comic shops all within a seven block stretch between Seventh and Front street.
TATTOO
Practicing a surly angsty expression.
The Bean Cafe
BOOK TRADER
SHOP
TLA
Tattooed MOM
I started finding myself in the city most weekends, which became more and more frequent after I started at Temple University,
moved into town, and started working at the comic shop on the street.
COMIC
OMICS
I spent years in the South Street culture somehow pretending that I was one of the cool ones.

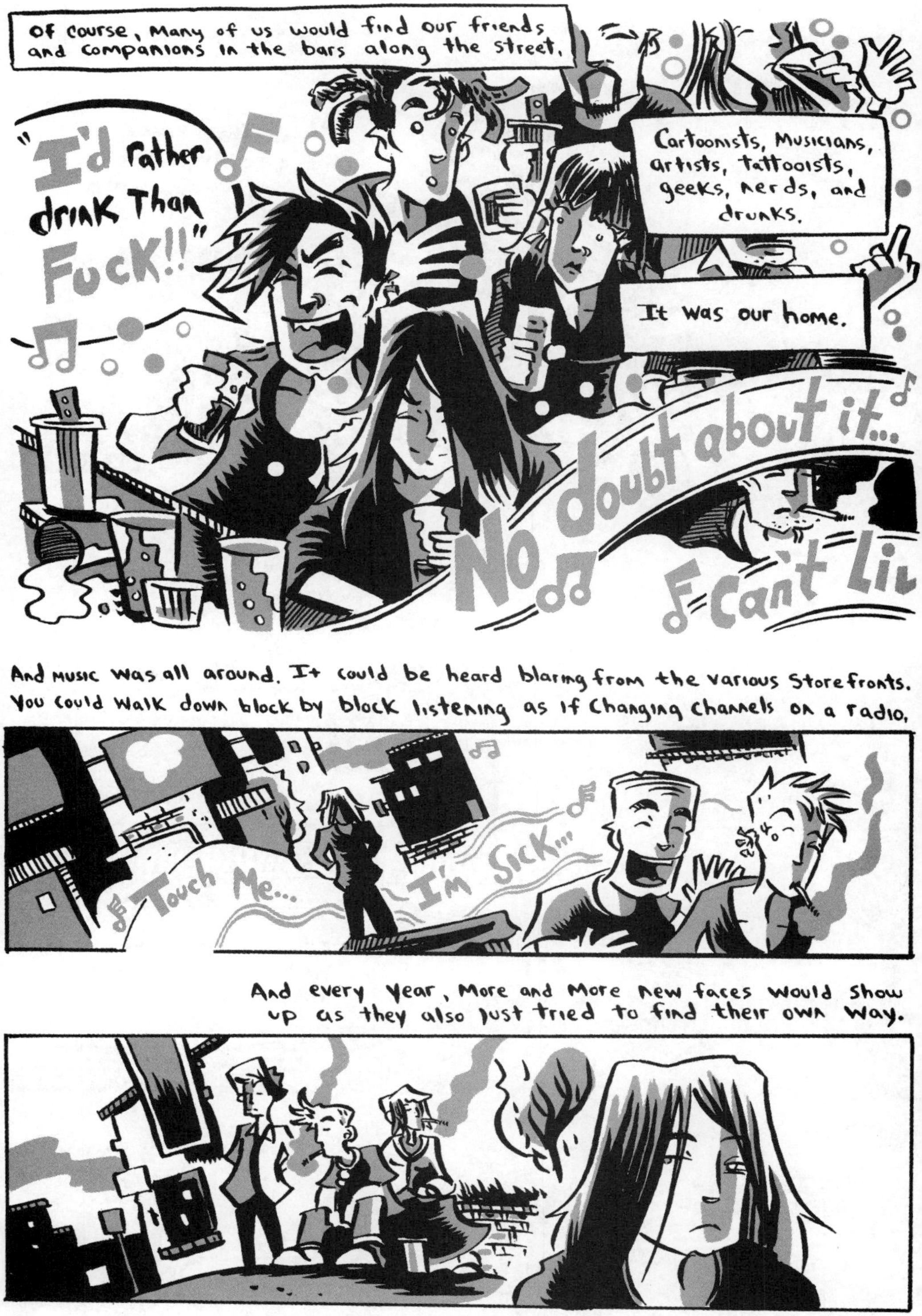
Of course, many of us would find our friends and companions in the bars along the street.
"I'd rather drink than Fuck!!"
Cartoonists, musicians, artists, tattooists, geeks, nerds, and drunks.
It was our home.
No doubt about it...
Can't Li
And music was all around. It could be heard blaring from the various storefronts. You could walk down block by block listening as if changing channels on a radio.
Touch Me...
I'm Sick...
And every year, more and more new faces would show up as they also just tried to find their own way.
This was always expected as the scene changed and evolved.

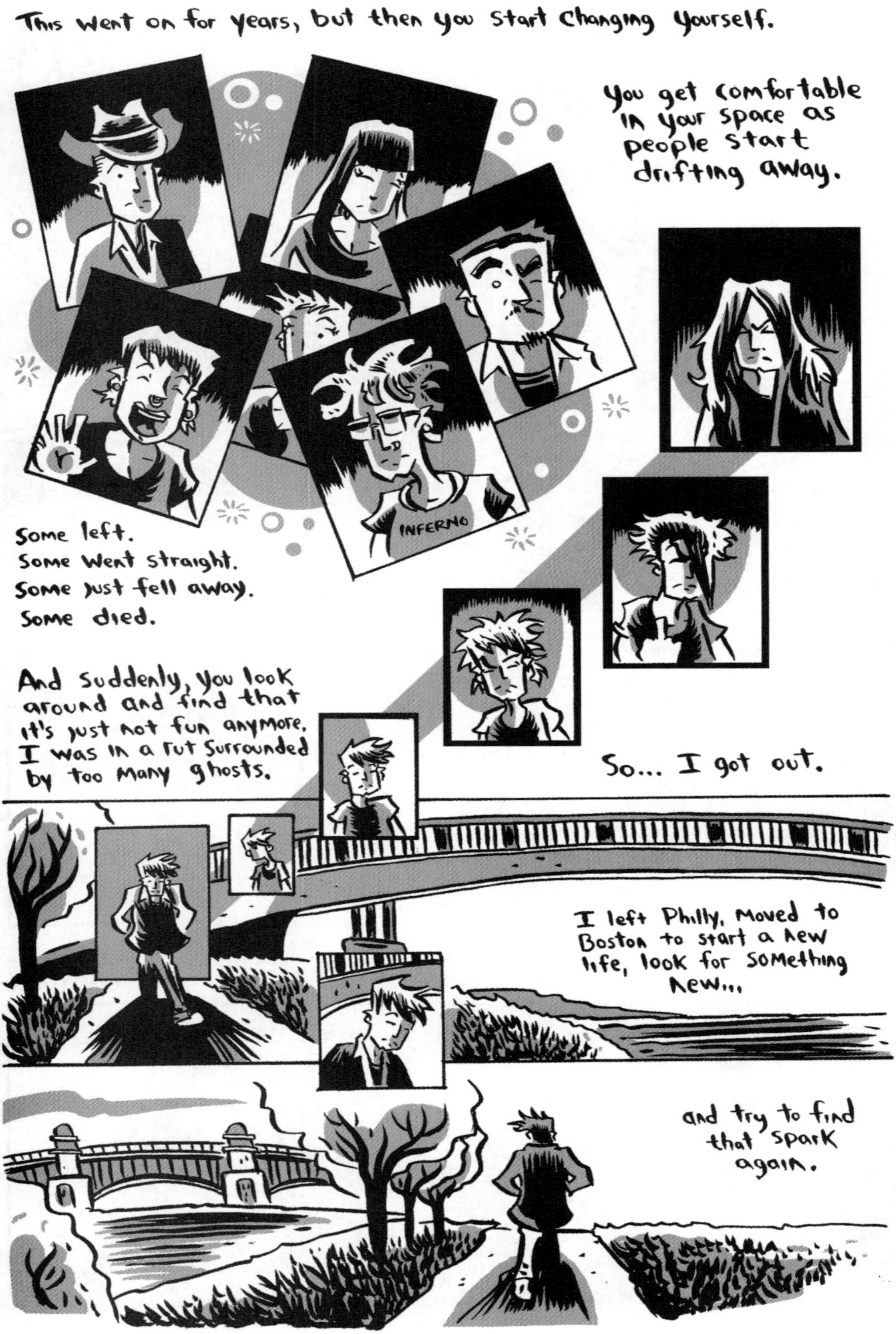
This went on for years, but then you start changing yourself.
You get comfortable in your space as people start drifting away.
INFERNO
Some left.
Some went straight.
Some just fell away.
Some died.
And suddenly, you look around and find that it's just not fun anymore. I was in a rut surrounded by too many ghosts.
So... I got out.
I left Philly, moved to Boston to start a new life, look for something new...
and try to find that spark again.

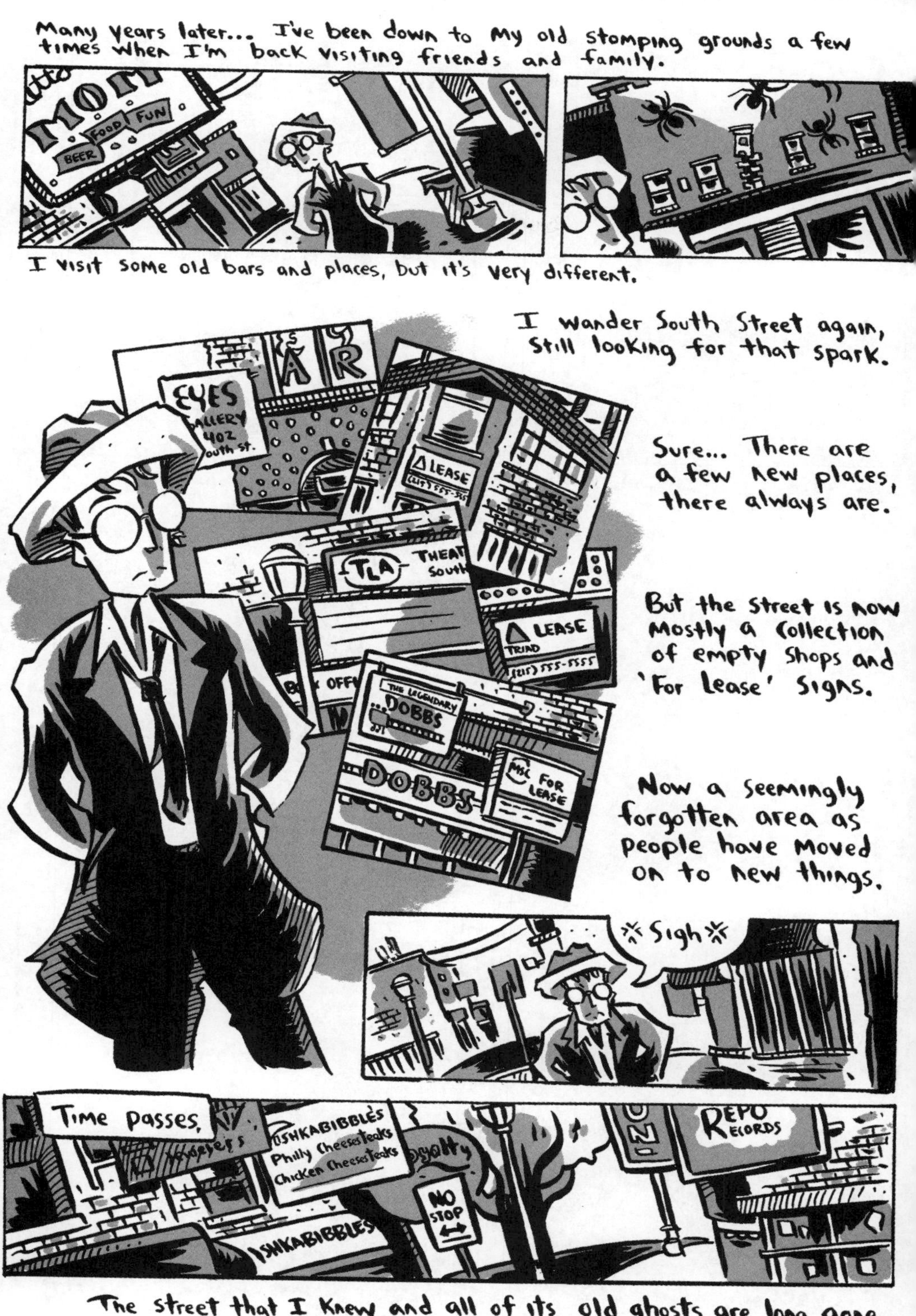
Many years later... I've been down to my old stomping grounds a few times when I'm back visiting friends and family.
BEER
FOOD
FUN
I visit some old bars and places, but it's very different.
I wander South Street again, still looking for that spark.
EYES
GALLERY
402
LEASE
TLA
LEASE
TRIAD
(215) 555-5555
THE LEGENDARY
DOBBS
DOBBS
FOR LEASE
Sure... There are a few new places, there always are.
But the street is now mostly a collection of empty shops and 'For Lease' signs.
Now a seemingly forgotten area as people have moved on to new things.
Sigh
Time passes,
Philly Cheesesteaks
Chicken Cheesesteaks
ISHKABIBBLES
NO STOP
REPO RECORDS
The street that I knew and all of its old ghosts are long gone.
—Karl Christian Krumpholz, 2021

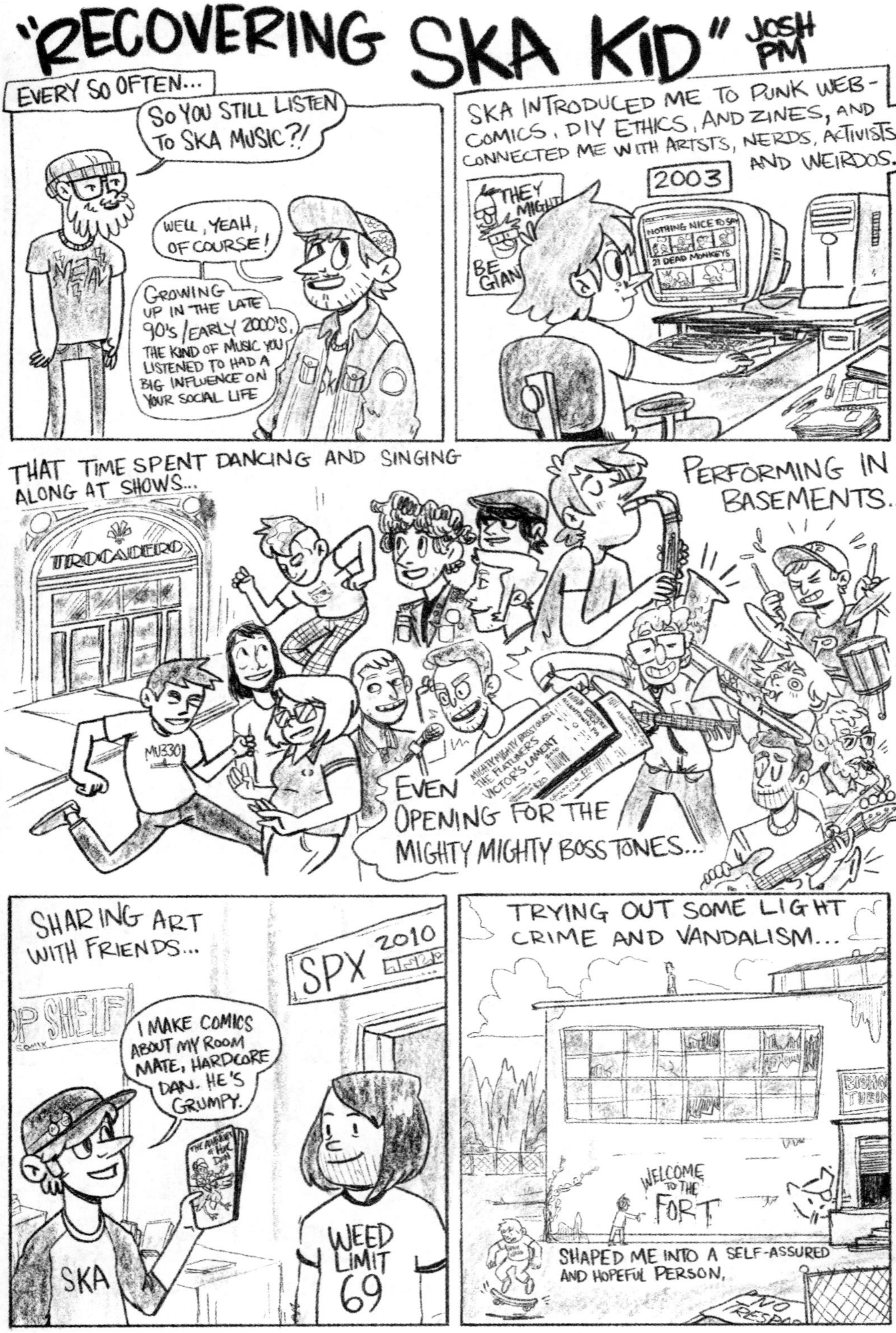
"RECOVERING SKA KID"
JOSH PM
EVERY SO OFTEN...
SO YOU STILL LISTEN TO SKA MUSIC?!
WELL, YEAH, OF COURSE!
GROWING UP IN THE LATE 90'S/EARLY 2000'S, THE KIND OF MUSIC YOU LISTENED TO HAD A BIG INFLUENCE ON YOUR SOCIAL LIFE
METAL
SKA
SKA INTRODUCED ME TO PUNK WEB-COMICS, DIY ETHICS, AND ZINES, AND CONNECTED ME WITH ARTISTS, NERDS, ACTIVISTS AND WEIRDOS.
2003
THEY MIGHT BE GIANTS
NOTHING NICE TO SAY
21 DEAD MONKEYS
THAT TIME SPENT DANCING AND SINGING ALONG AT SHOWS...
TROCADERO
PERFORMING IN BASEMENTS...
MU330
MIGHTY MIGHTY BOSSTONES
THE FLATLINERS
VICTOR'S LAMENT
EVEN OPENING FOR THE MIGHTY MIGHTY BOSSTONES...
SHARING ART WITH FRIENDS...
SPX 2010
OP SHELF
I MAKE COMICS ABOUT MY ROOMMATE, HARDCORE DAN. HE'S GRUMPY.
SKA
WEED LIMIT 69
TRYING OUT SOME LIGHT CRIME AND VANDALISM...
WELCOME TO THE FORT
SHAPED ME INTO A SELF-ASSURED AND HOPEFUL PERSON,
NO TRESPA

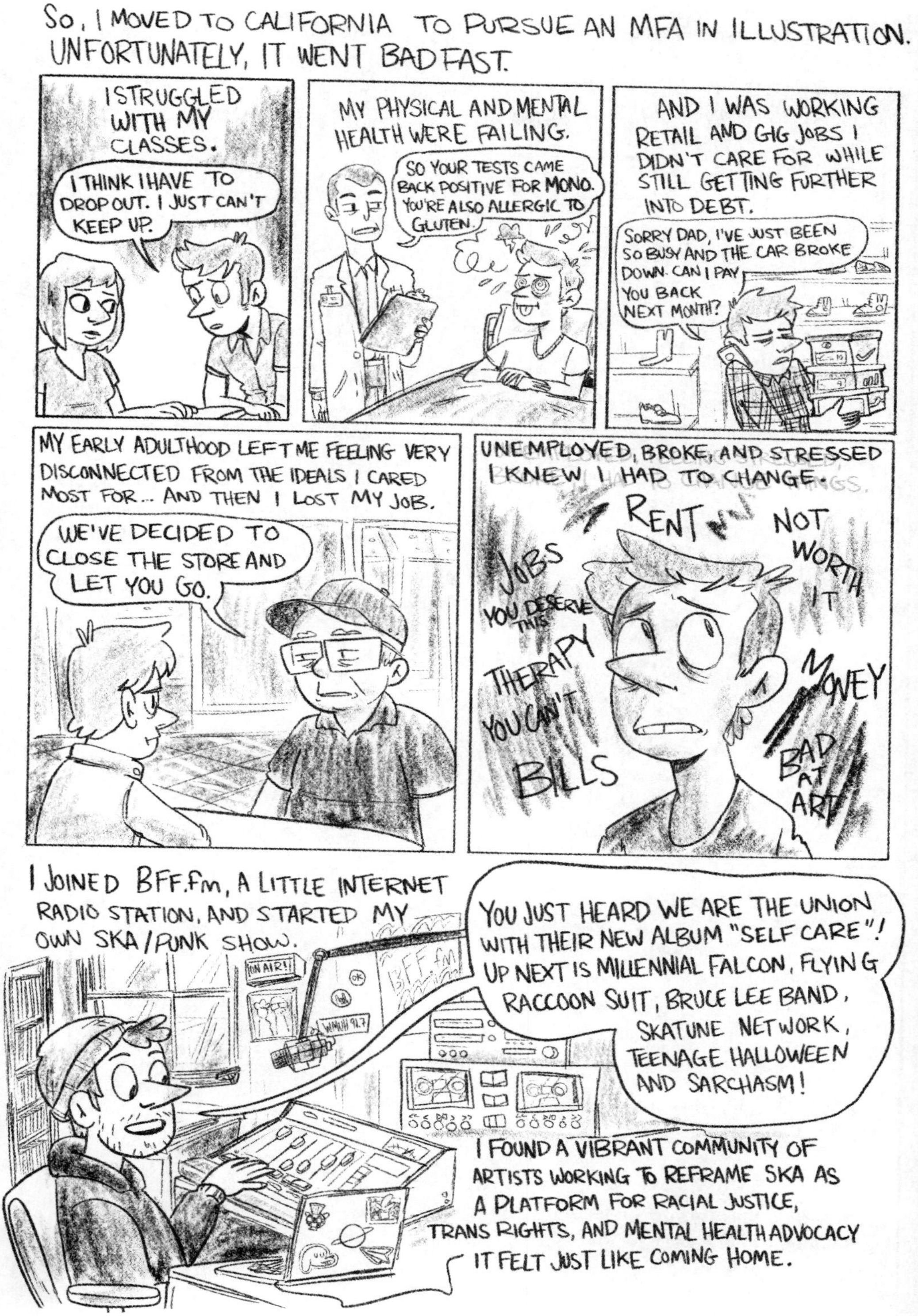

So, I moved to California to pursue an MFA in Illustration. Unfortunately, it went bad fast.
I struggled with my classes.
I think I have to drop out. I just can't keep up.
My physical and mental health were failing.
So your tests came back positive for mono. You're also allergic to gluten.
And I was working retail and gig jobs I didn't care for while still getting further into debt.
Sorry Dad, I've just been so busy and the car broke down. Can I pay you back next month!?
My early adulthood left me feeling very disconnected from the ideals I cared most for... And then I lost my job.
We've decided to close the store and let you go.
Unemployed, broke, and stressed I knew I had to change.
RENT
NOT WORTH IT
JOBS
YOU DESERVE THIS
THERAPY
YOU CAN'T
BILLS
MONEY
BAD AT ART
I joined BFF.fm, a little internet radio station, and started my own ska/punk show.
ON AIR!
BFF.fm
You just heard We Are The Union with their new album "Self Care"! Up next is Millennial Falcon, Flying Raccoon Suit, Bruce Lee Band, Skatune Network, Teenage Halloween and Sarchasm!
I found a vibrant community of artists working to reframe ska as a platform for racial justice, trans rights, and mental health advocacy
It felt just like coming home.

I FOUND A JOB WORKING FOR SILVER SPROCKET. RUNNING A COMIC SHOP INSPIRED ME TO START DRAWING AND PAINTING AGAIN.

AND I STARTED A NEW BAND, SCHLUB, MAKING FRESH JAMS AND MEETING NEW FRIENDS!

IN MY ADOLESENCE, SKA AND PUNK TAUGHT ME OPTIMISM AND CONFIDENCE. NOW I SEE THAT THEY CAN BE A LANGUAGE TO USE TO FIGHT OPRESSION, TO EMPOWER WEIRDNESS, QUEERNESS, AND UPLIFT AND UNIFY OUR VOICES

BLACK LIVES MATTER

I CAN'T BREATH

ACAB!

SAY HER NAME

VOTE OR PEG?

AT A TIME WHEN WE DESPERATELY NEED IT.

SKADULTHOOD IS STILL FULL OF NEVER-ENDING CHALLENGES, BUT EMBRACING THE STRANGE AND FUN MAKES RECOVERING FROM THE HARD TIMES MUCH EASIER.

SO BASICALLY THIS CATBITE ALBUM WILL CHANGE YOUR LIFE! DID YOU SEE THAT JEFF ROSENSTOCK IS SCORING THAT CARTOON? OH I'VE GOT TO PLAY YOU THAT SKATUNE NETWORK SKA

HELP...

EPILOGUE:

.ıll Verizon 🛜   6:53 PM   19% 🔋

Hardcore Dan ›

Wed, Dec 23, 8:31 AM

Did you tell me like 12 years ago to play Cave Story

Yes

I'm playing the remaster and wondering what else I should have listened to you about

have listened to you about

Ohh didn't know there was a remaster! Neat!

Probably not much else tbh but we can never be sure because I've definitely forgotten 67% of most things

What if I was right about ska

Let's not get carried away

iMessage

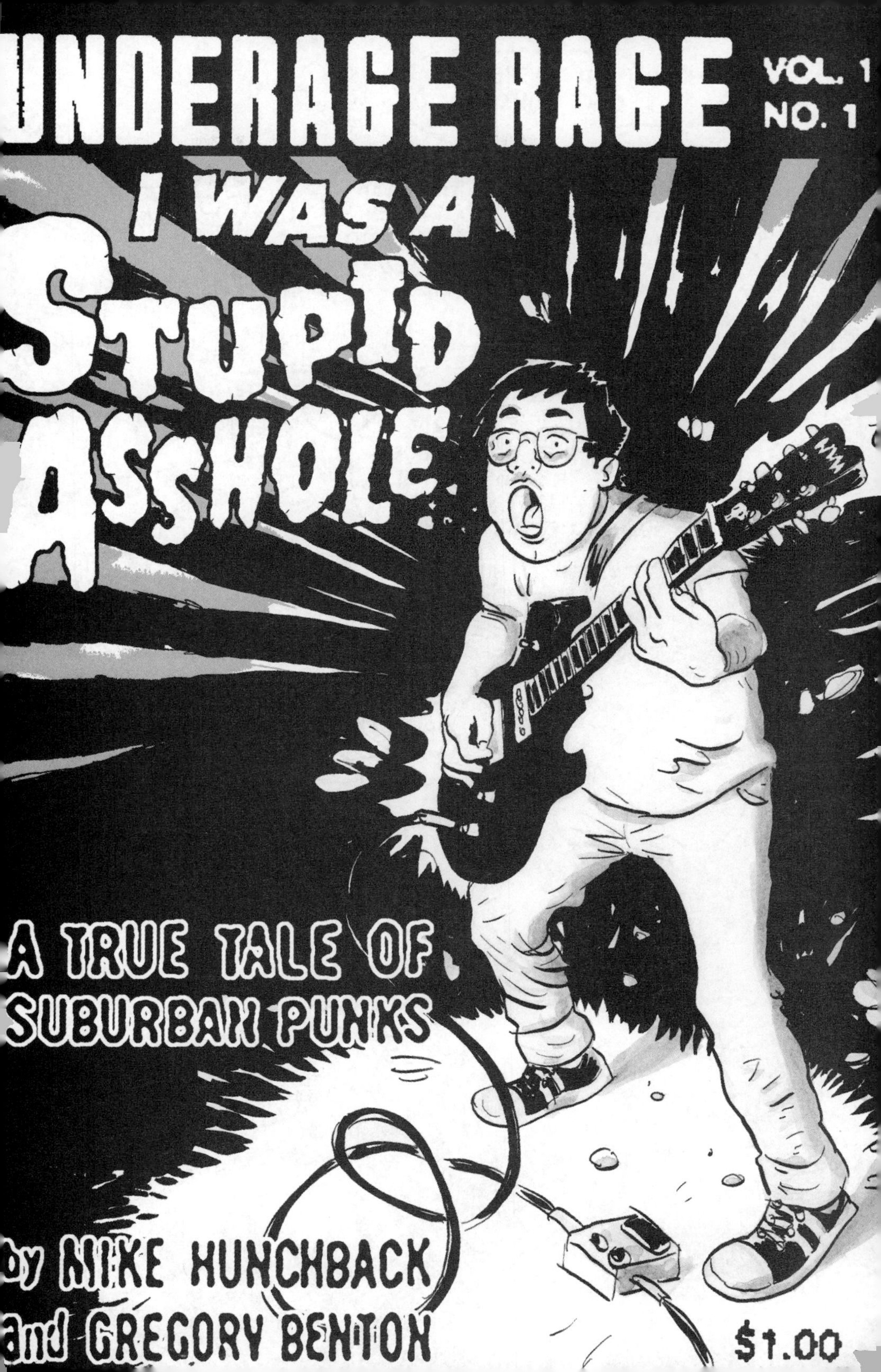
UNDERAGE RAGE
VOL. 1
NO. 1
I WAS A STUPID ASSHOLE
A TRUE TALE OF SUBURBAN PUNKS
by MIKE HUNCHBACK
and GREGORY BENTON
$1.00

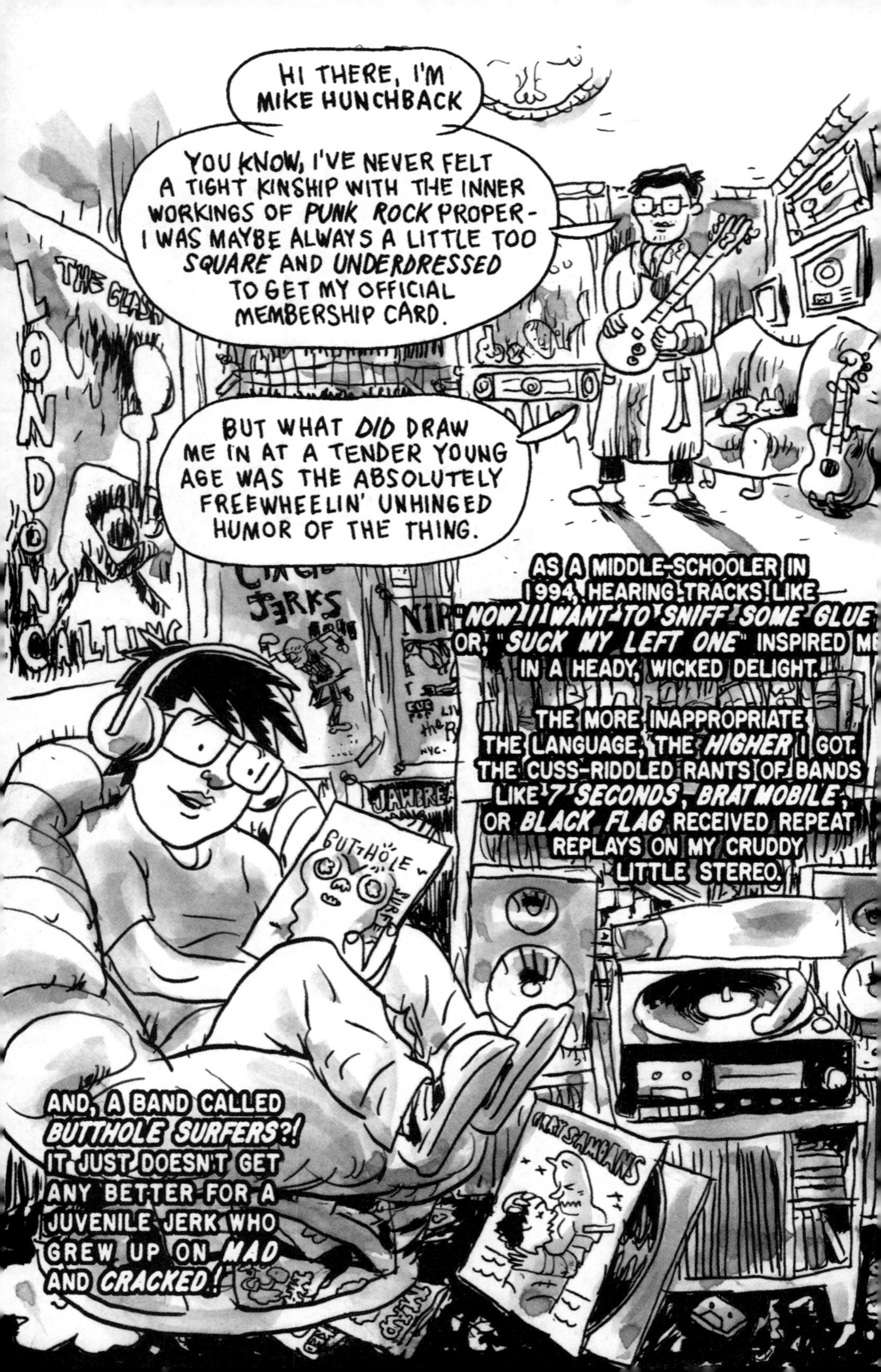
HI THERE, I'M MIKE HUNCHBACK
YOU KNOW, I'VE NEVER FELT A TIGHT KINSHIP WITH THE INNER WORKINGS OF PUNK ROCK PROPER- I WAS MAYBE ALWAYS A LITTLE TOO SQUARE AND UNDERDRESSED TO GET MY OFFICIAL MEMBERSHIP CARD.
BUT WHAT DID DRAW ME IN AT A TENDER YOUNG AGE WAS THE ABSOLUTELY FREEWHEELIN' UNHINGED HUMOR OF THE THING.
AS A MIDDLE-SCHOOLER IN 1994, HEARING TRACKS LIKE "NOW I WANT TO SNIFF SOME GLUE" OR, "SUCK MY LEFT ONE" INSPIRED ME IN A HEADY, WICKED DELIGHT.
THE MORE INAPPROPRIATE THE LANGUAGE, THE HIGHER I GOT. THE CUSS-RIDDLED RANTS OF BANDS LIKE 7 SECONDS, BRATMOBILE, OR BLACK FLAG RECEIVED REPEAT REPLAYS ON MY CRUDDY LITTLE STEREO.
AND, A BAND CALLED BUTTHOLE SURFERS?! IT JUST DOESN'T GET ANY BETTER FOR A JUVENILE JERK WHO GREW UP ON MAD AND CRACKED!
THE CLASH
LONDON CALLING
JERKS
BUTTHOLE SURFERS
GRAY SAMBANS

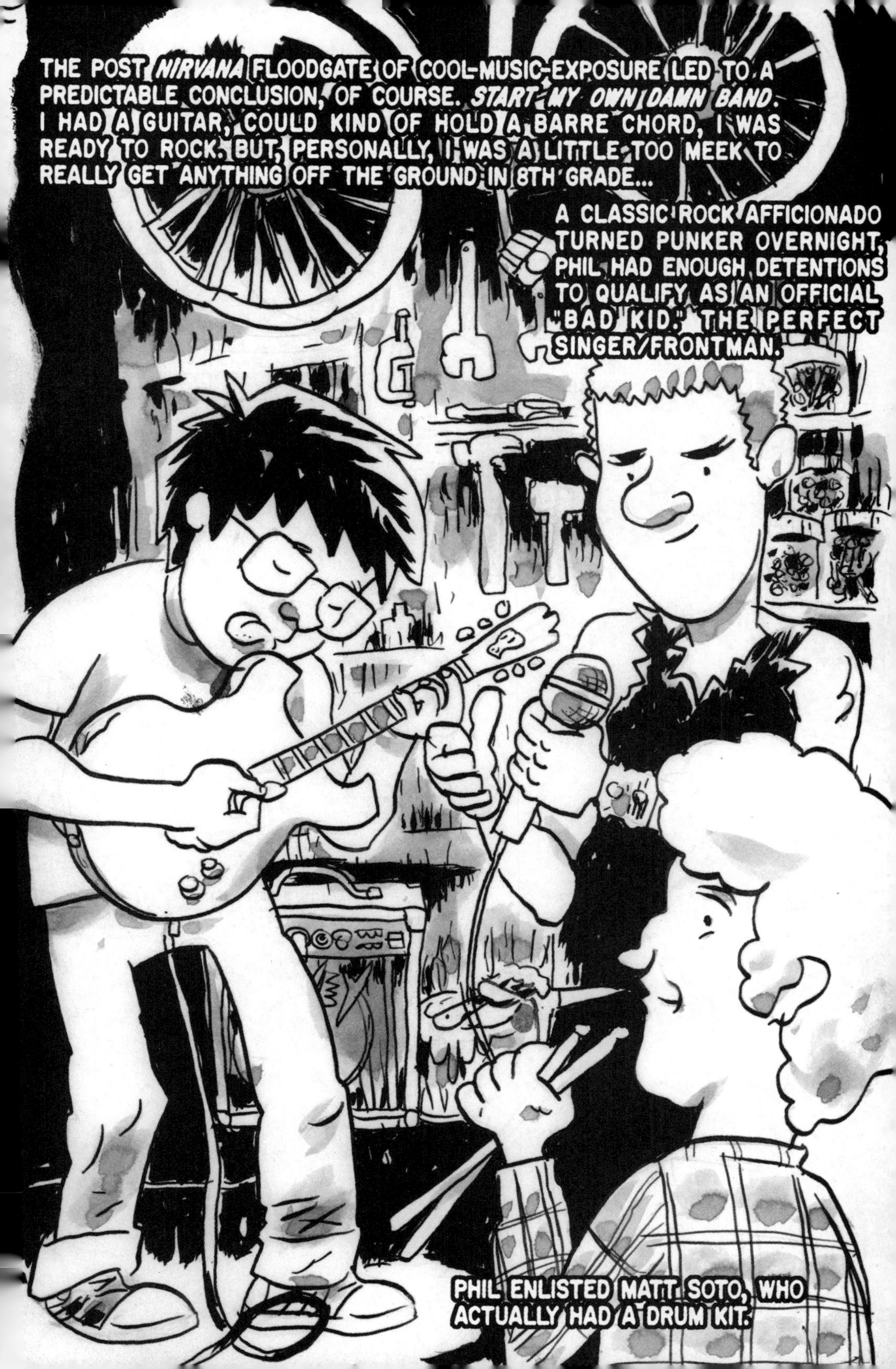
THE POST *NIRVANA* FLOODGATE OF COOL-MUSIC-EXPOSURE LED TO A PREDICTABLE CONCLUSION, OF COURSE. *START MY OWN DAMN BAND.* I HAD A GUITAR, COULD KIND OF HOLD A BARRE CHORD, I WAS READY TO ROCK. BUT, PERSONALLY, I WAS A LITTLE TOO MEEK TO REALLY GET ANYTHING OFF THE GROUND IN 8TH GRADE...
A CLASSIC ROCK AFFICIONADO TURNED PUNKER OVERNIGHT, PHIL HAD ENOUGH DETENTIONS TO QUALIFY AS AN OFFICIAL "BAD KID." THE PERFECT SINGER/FRONTMAN.
PHIL ENLISTED MATT SOTO, WHO ACTUALLY HAD A DRUM KIT.

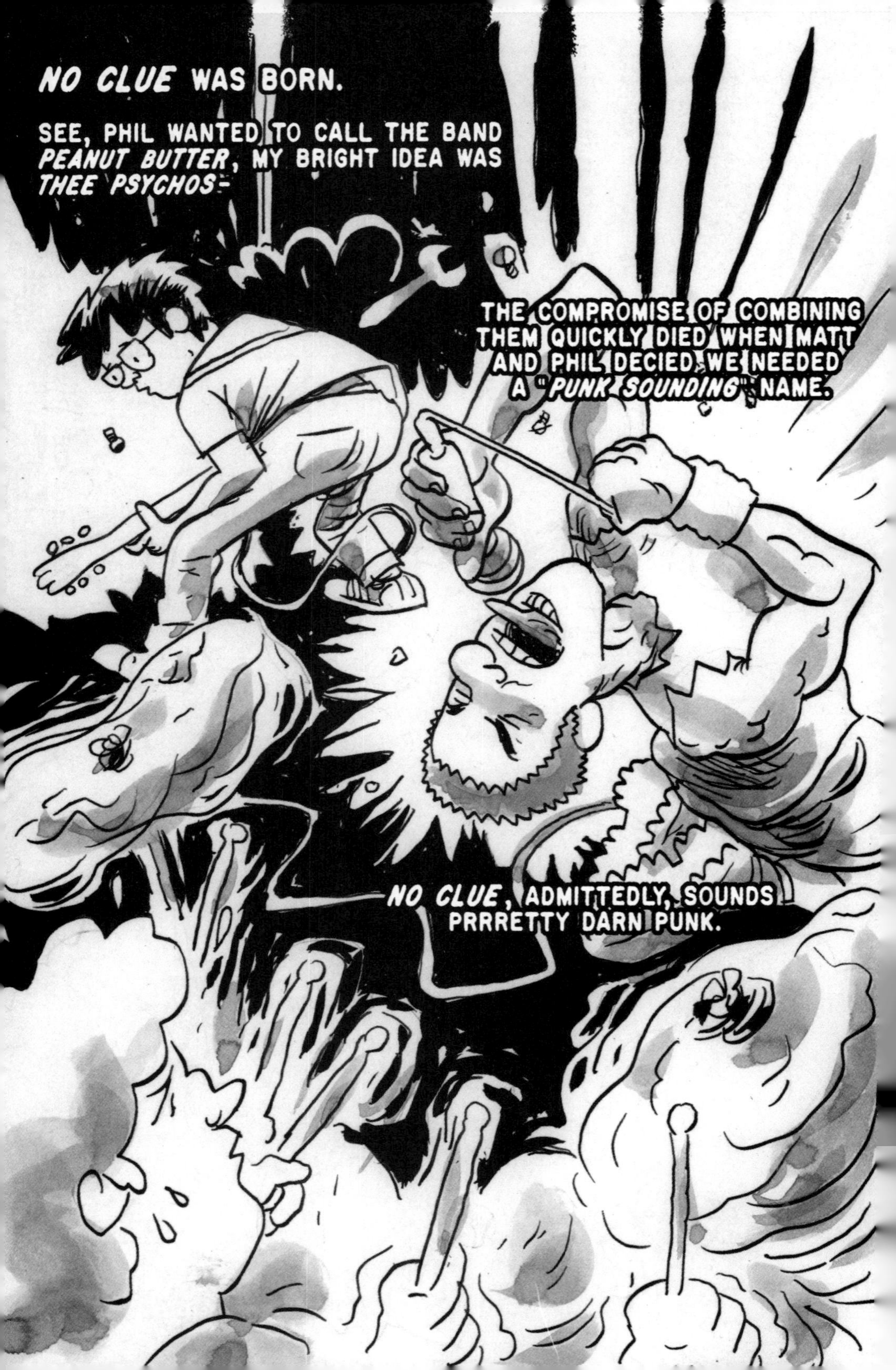
NO CLUE WAS BORN.
SEE, PHIL WANTED TO CALL THE BAND PEANUT BUTTER, MY BRIGHT IDEA WAS THEE PSYCHOS-
THE COMPROMISE OF COMBINING THEM QUICKLY DIED WHEN MATT AND PHIL DECIED WE NEEDED A "PUNK SOUNDING" NAME.
NO CLUE, ADMITTEDLY, SOUNDS PRRRETTY DARN PUNK.

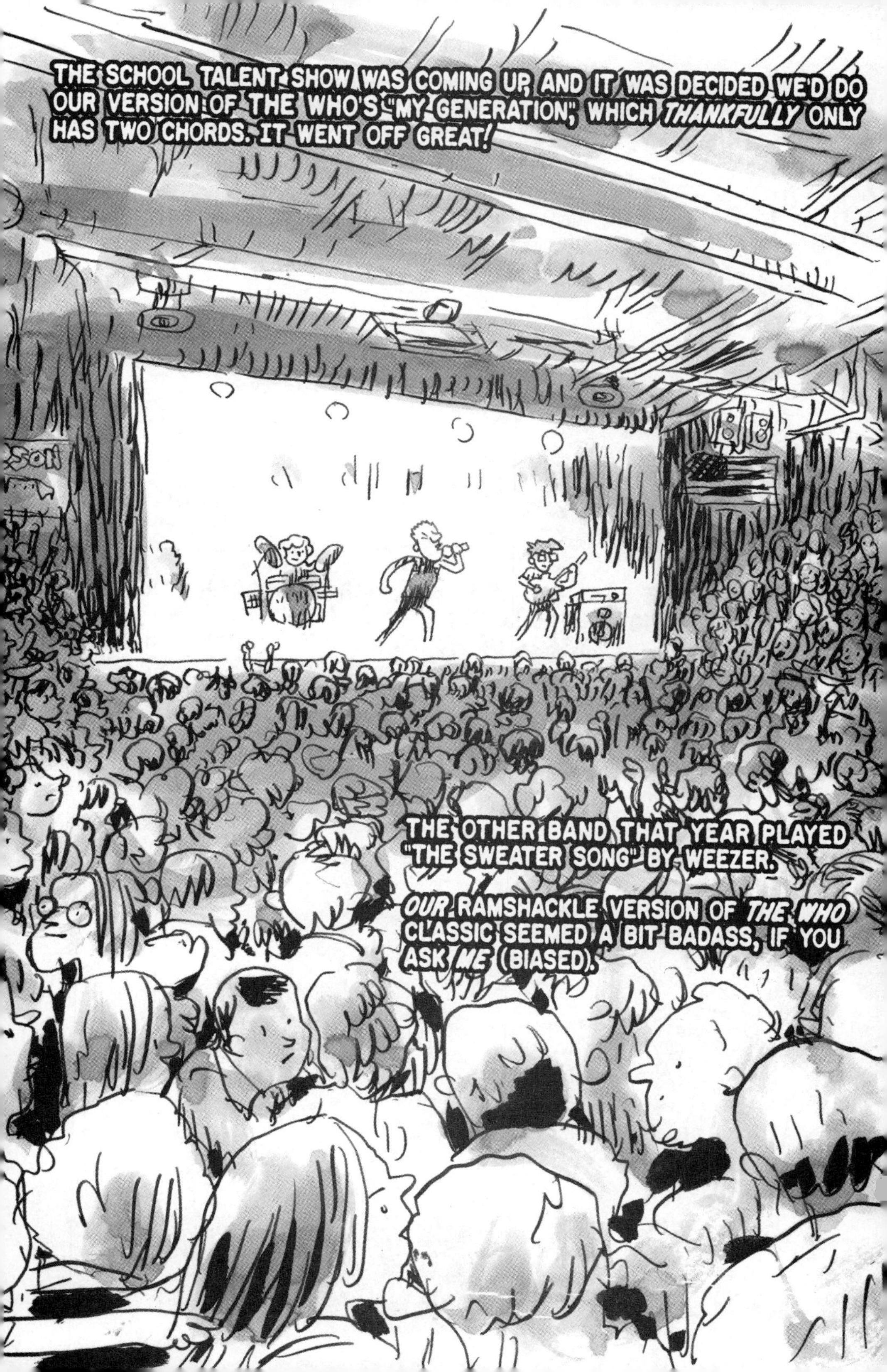
THE SCHOOL TALENT SHOW WAS COMING UP, AND IT WAS DECIDED WE'D DO OUR VERSION OF THE WHO'S "MY GENERATION", WHICH *THANKFULLY* ONLY HAS TWO CHORDS. IT WENT OFF GREAT!
THE OTHER BAND THAT YEAR PLAYED "THE SWEATER SONG" BY WEEZER.
OUR RAMSHACKLE VERSION OF *THE WHO* CLASSIC SEEMED A BIT BADASS, IF YOU ASK *ME* (BIASED).

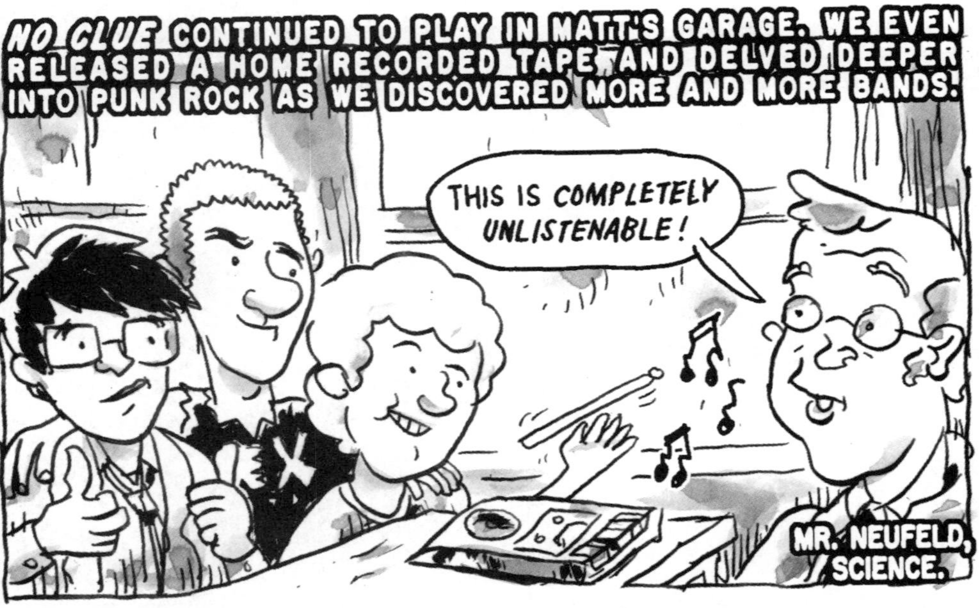
NO CLUE CONTINUED TO PLAY IN MATT'S GARAGE. WE EVEN RELEASED A HOME RECORDED TAPE AND DELVED DEEPER INTO PUNK ROCK AS WE DISCOVERED MORE AND MORE BANDS!
THIS IS COMPLETELY UNLISTENABLE!
MR. NEUFELD, SCIENCE.

UNTIL FINALLY, THE LAST DAY OF SCHOOL WAS APPROACHING. OUR MIDDLE SCHOOL WAS DOING A GRADUATION CEREMONY IN THE GYM, WHICH AS 8TH GRADERS, ALL MEMBERS OF *NO CLUE* WERE A PART OF. AT SOME POINT IT WAS DECIDED THAT THE EVENT NEEDED A BOOST, SO SOMEONE CAME UP WITH THE IDEA OF HAVING THE MUSIC ACTS FROM THE TALENT SHOW TACKED ON TO THE END OF THE PROCEEDINGS.

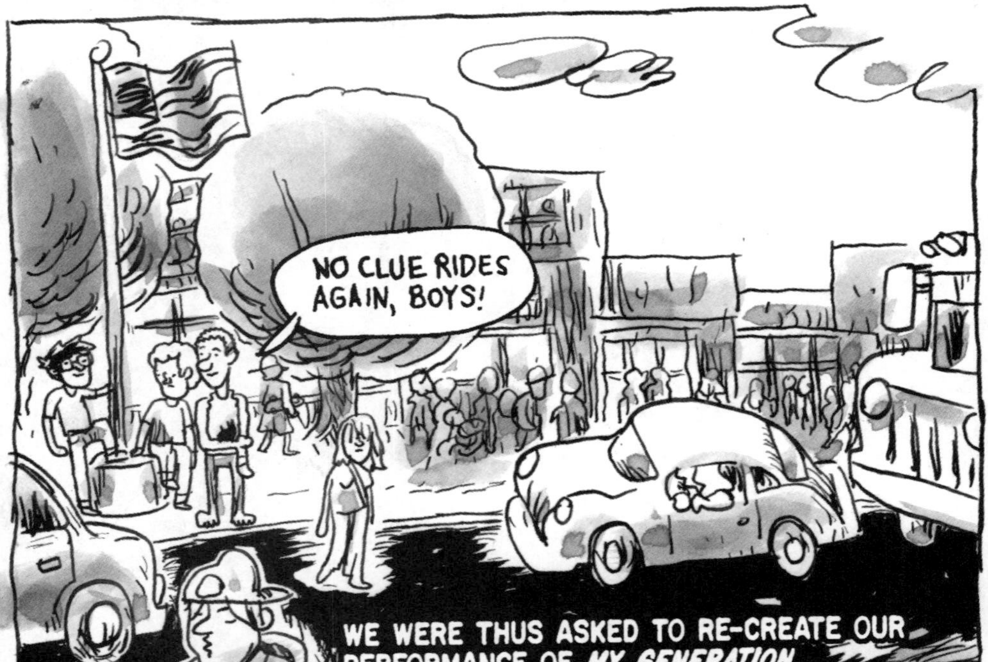
NO CLUE RIDES AGAIN, BOYS!
WE WERE THUS ASKED TO RE-CREATE OUR PERFORMANCE OF MY GENERATION...

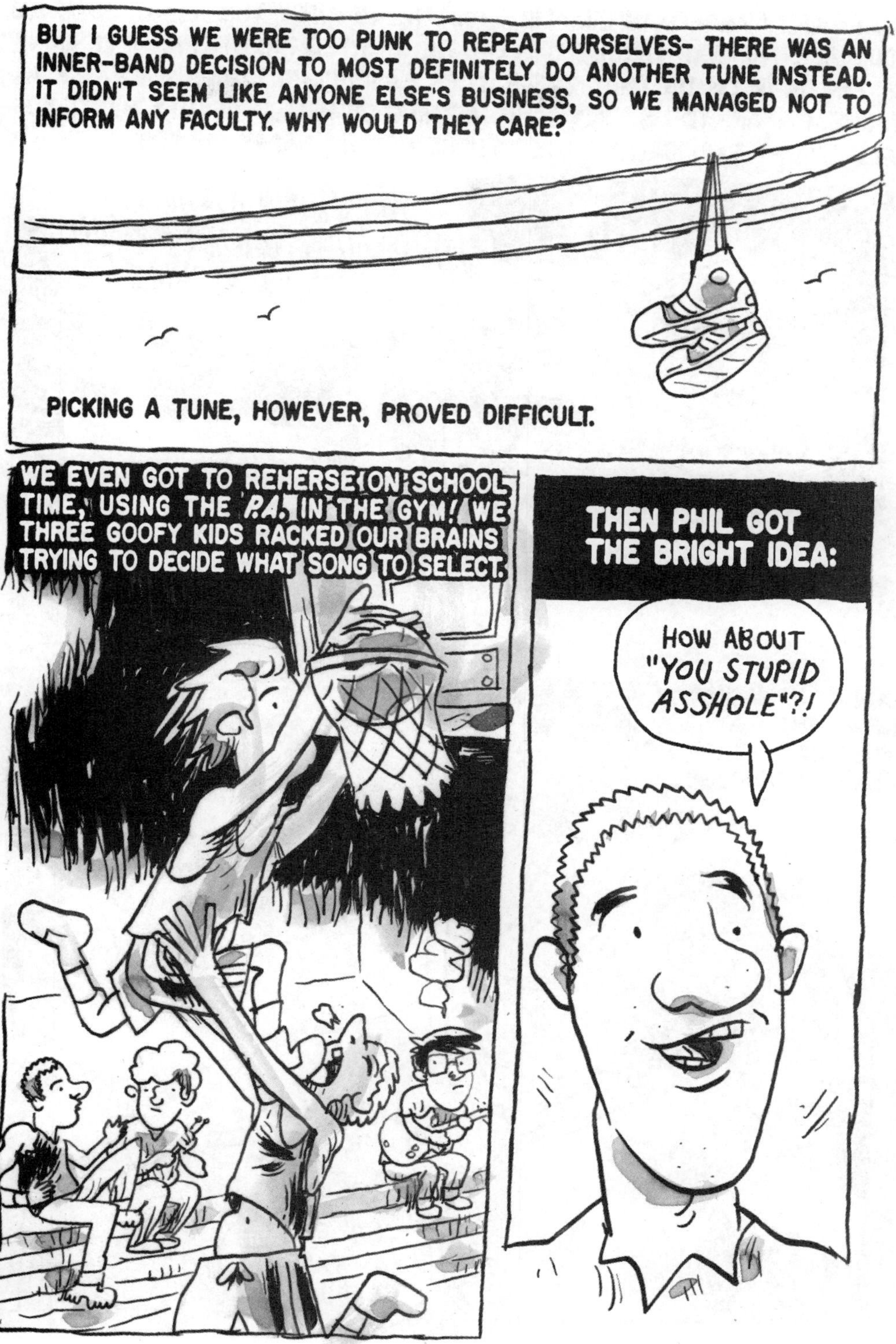
BUT I GUESS WE WERE TOO PUNK TO REPEAT OURSELVES- THERE WAS AN INNER-BAND DECISION TO MOST DEFINITELY DO ANOTHER TUNE INSTEAD. IT DIDN'T SEEM LIKE ANYONE ELSE'S BUSINESS, SO WE MANAGED NOT TO INFORM ANY FACULTY. WHY WOULD THEY CARE?
PICKING A TUNE, HOWEVER, PROVED DIFFICULT.
WE EVEN GOT TO REHERSE ON SCHOOL TIME, USING THE P.A. IN THE GYM! WE THREE GOOFY KIDS RACKED OUR BRAINS TRYING TO DECIDE WHAT SONG TO SELECT.
THEN PHIL GOT THE BRIGHT IDEA:
HOW ABOUT "YOU STUPID ASSHOLE"?!

MATT AND I AGREED IMMEDIATELY. I MEAN, WE KNEW THE *ANGRY SAMOANS* CUT ALL THE WAY THROUGH, EVEN! WE STARTED PRACTICING IT. IT DIDN'T EVEN DAWN ON US THAT THE RATHER LASCIVIOUS LYRICS *MIGHT* BE AN ISSUE. I MEAN, TO US THEY WERE A THING OF RIBALD BEAUTY. HYSTERICALLY FUNNY EXPLICATIVES OVER THOSE CATCHY, HAPPY CHORDS.

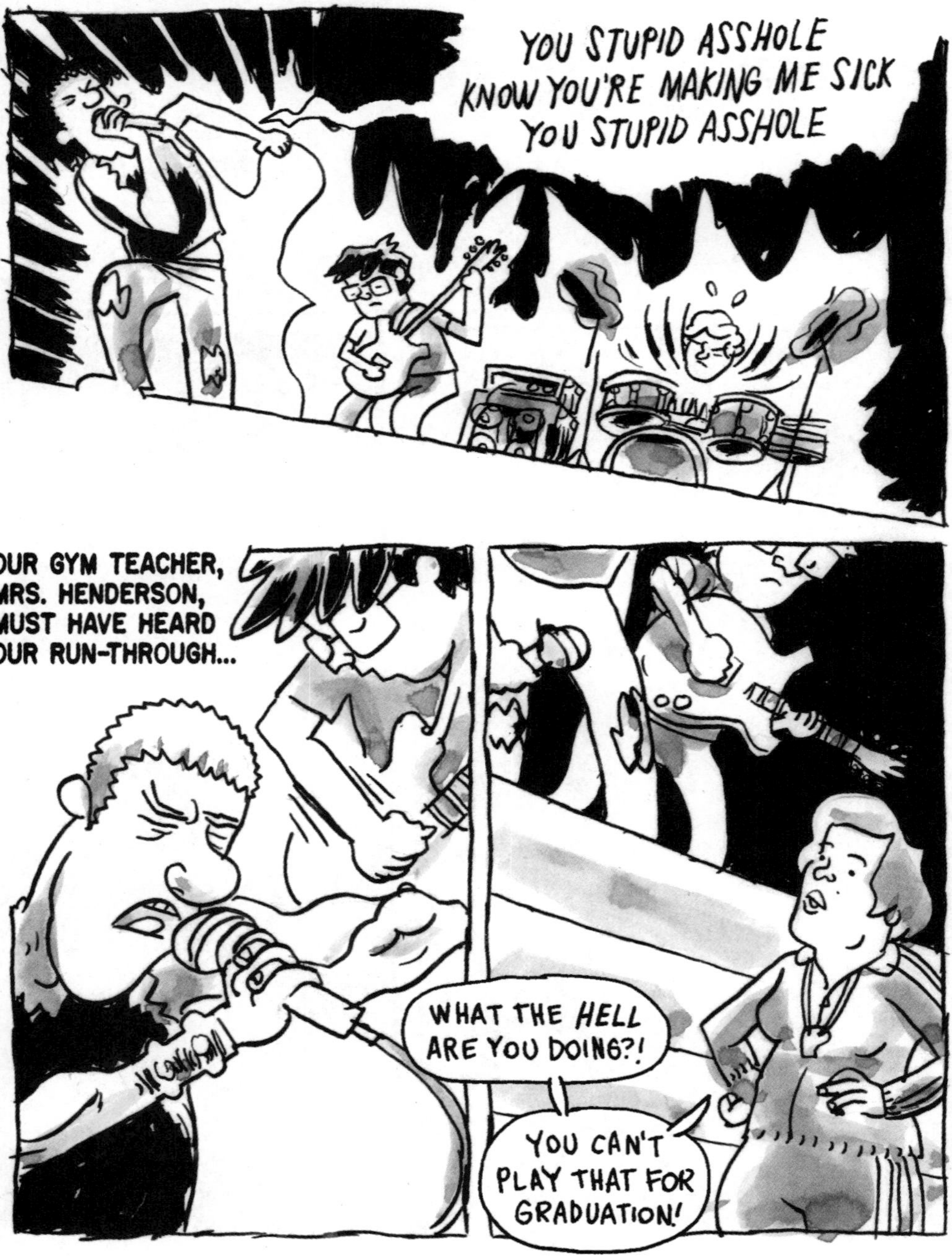
YOU STUPID ASSHOLE
KNOW YOU'RE MAKING ME SICK
YOU STUPID ASSHOLE
OUR GYM TEACHER, MRS. HENDERSON, MUST HAVE HEARD OUR RUN-THROUGH...
WHAT THE *HELL* ARE YOU DOING?!
YOU CAN'T PLAY THAT FOR GRADUATION!

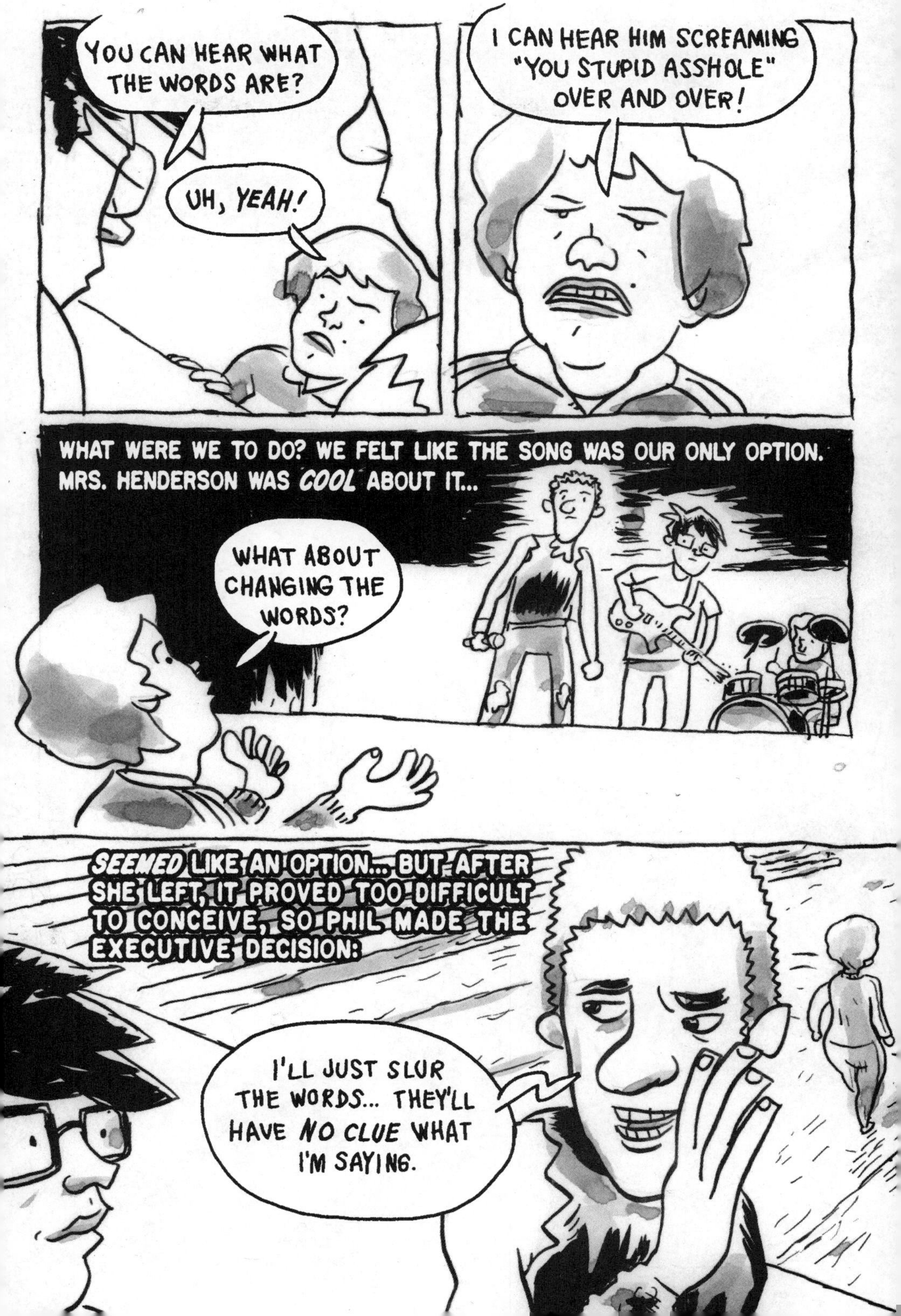
YOU CAN HEAR WHAT THE WORDS ARE?
UH, YEAH!
I CAN HEAR HIM SCREAMING "YOU STUPID ASSHOLE" OVER AND OVER!
WHAT WERE WE TO DO? WE FELT LIKE THE SONG WAS OUR ONLY OPTION. MRS. HENDERSON WAS COOL ABOUT IT...
WHAT ABOUT CHANGING THE WORDS?
SEEMED LIKE AN OPTION... BUT AFTER SHE LEFT, IT PROVED TOO DIFFICULT TO CONCEIVE, SO PHIL MADE THE EXECUTIVE DECISION:
I'LL JUST SLUR THE WORDS... THEY'LL HAVE NO CLUE WHAT I'M SAYING.

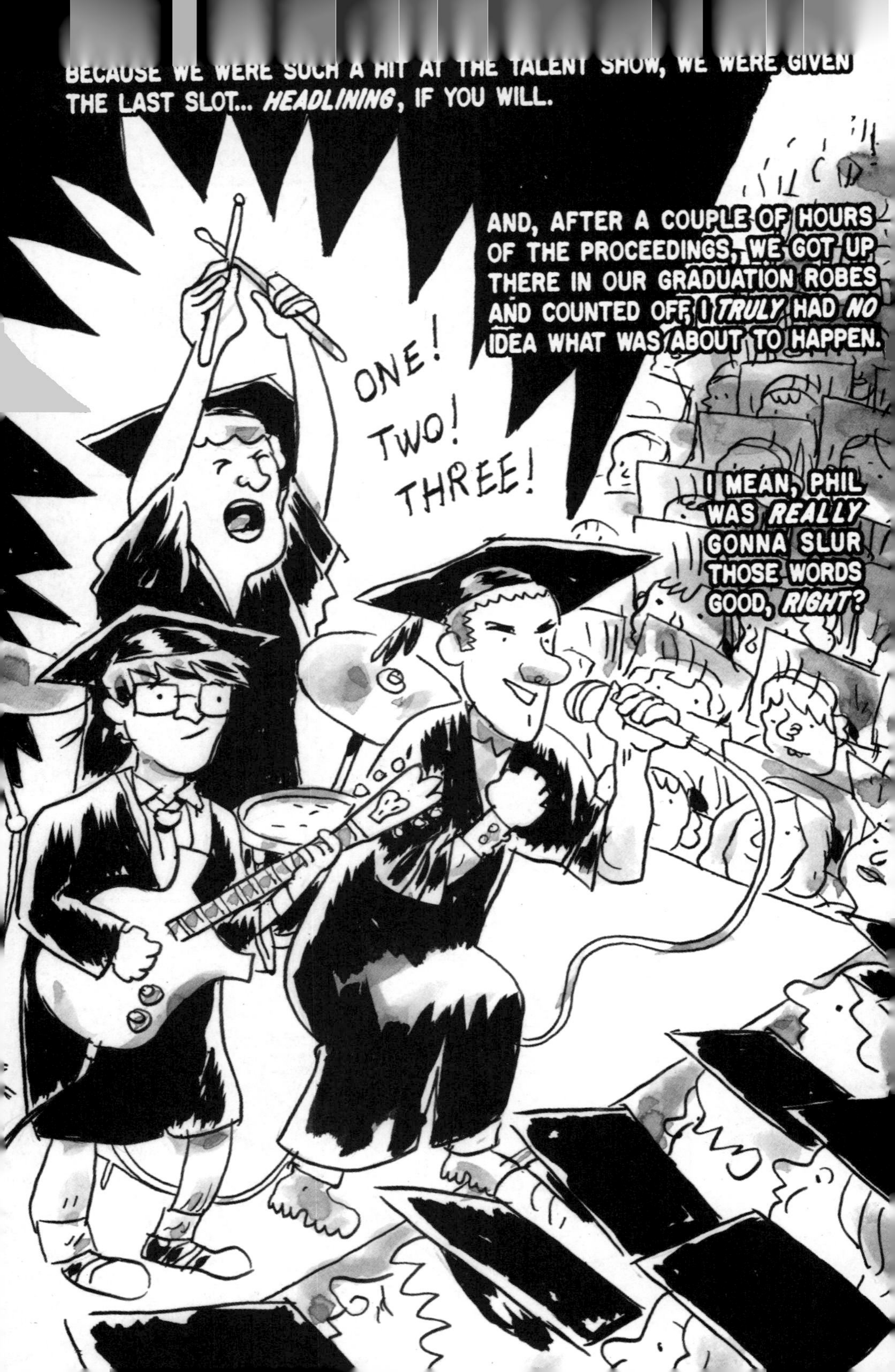

BECAUSE WE WERE SUCH A HIT AT THE TALENT SHOW, WE WERE GIVEN THE LAST SLOT... *HEADLINING*, IF YOU WILL.
AND, AFTER A COUPLE OF HOURS OF THE PROCEEDINGS, WE GOT UP THERE IN OUR GRADUATION ROBES AND COUNTED OFF. I *TRULY* HAD *NO* IDEA WHAT WAS ABOUT TO HAPPEN.
ONE! TWO! THREE!
I MEAN, PHIL WAS *REALLY* GONNA SLUR THOSE WORDS GOOD, *RIGHT*?

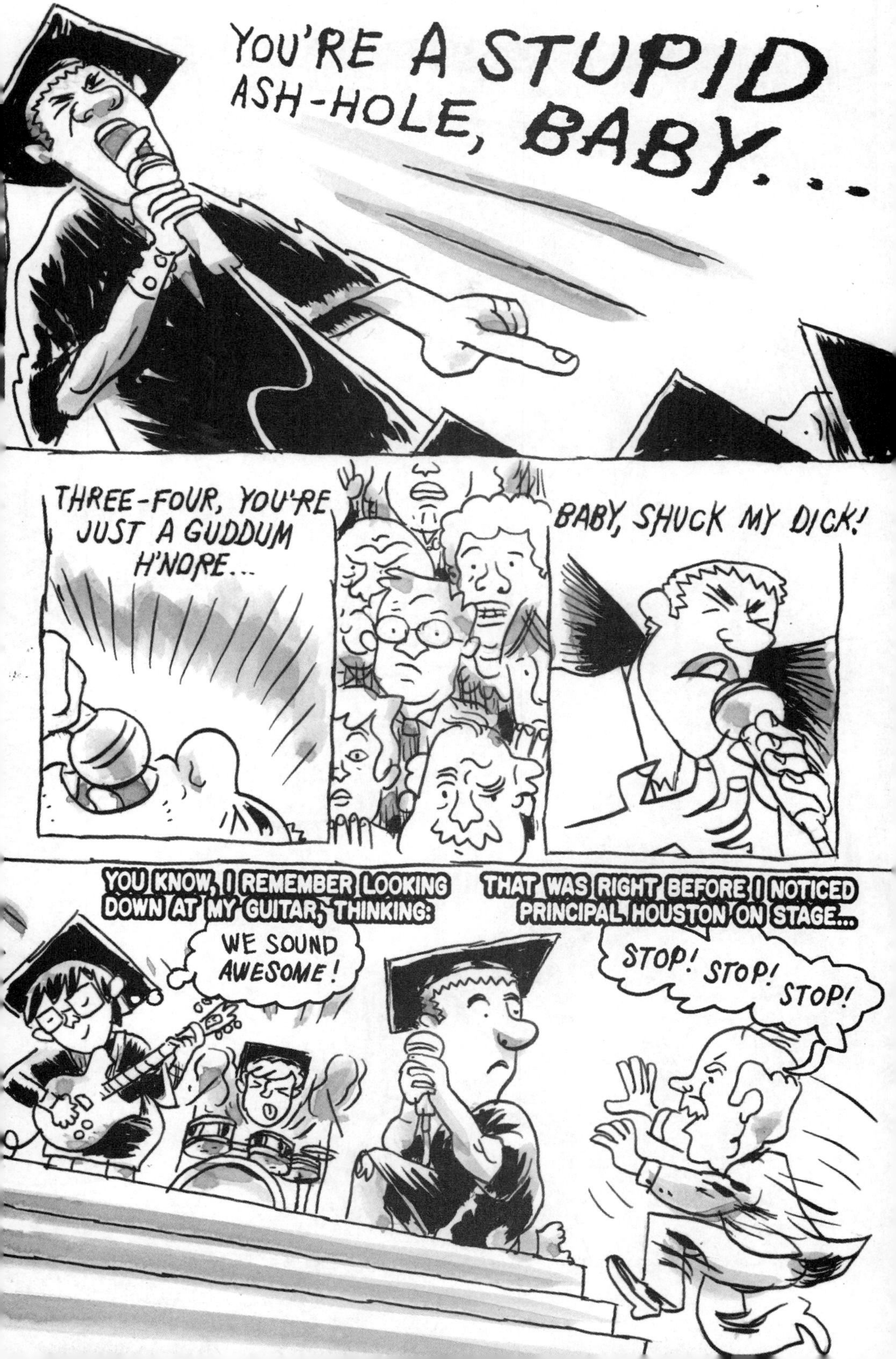

YOU'RE A STUPID ASH-HOLE, BABY...
THREE-FOUR, YOU'RE JUST A GUDDUM H'NORE...
BABY, SHUCK MY DICK!
YOU KNOW, I REMEMBER LOOKING DOWN AT MY GUITAR, THINKING:
WE SOUND AWESOME!
THAT WAS RIGHT BEFORE I NOTICED PRINCIPAL HOUSTON ON STAGE...
STOP! STOP! STOP!

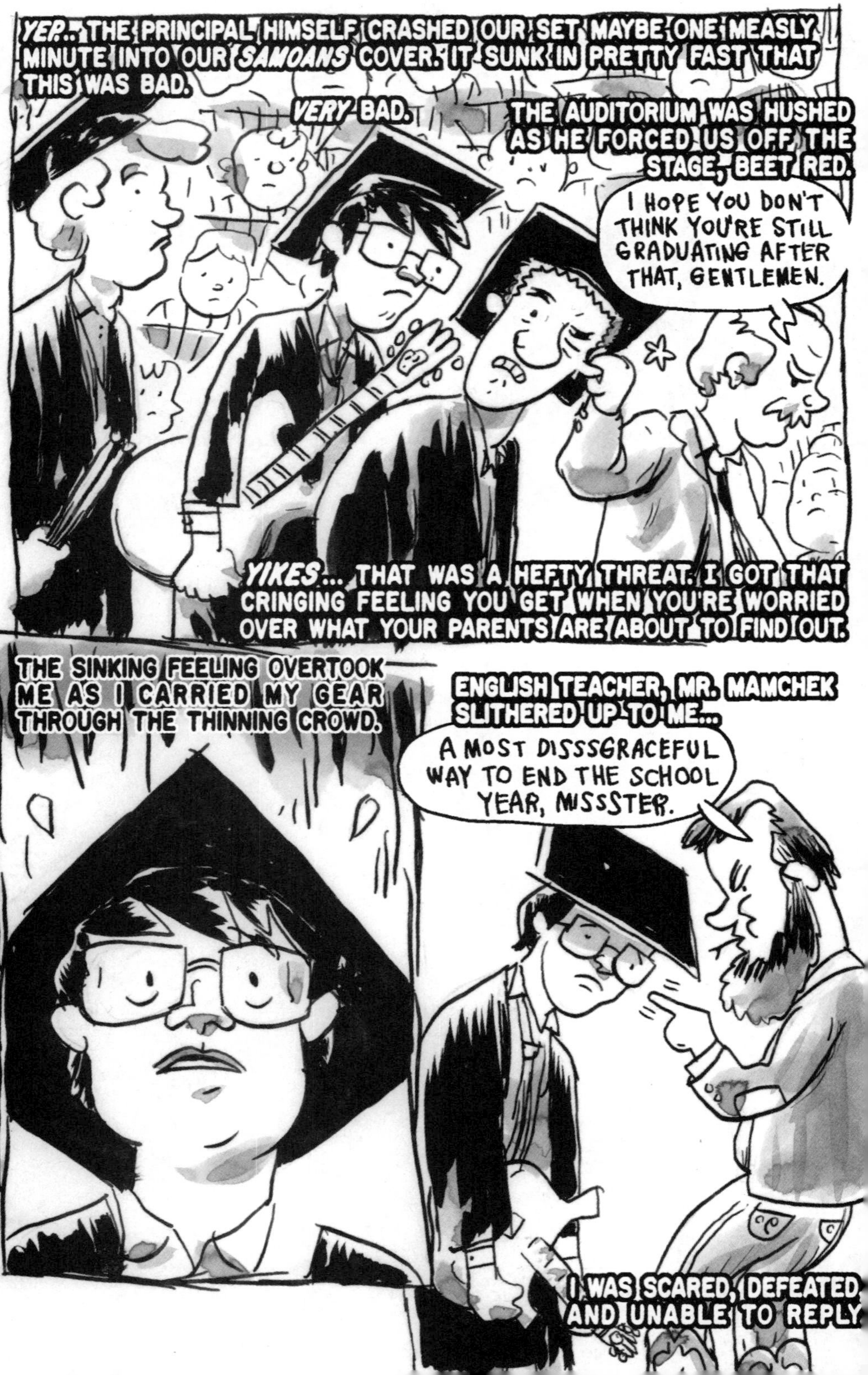
YEP.. THE PRINCIPAL HIMSELF CRASHED OUR SET MAYBE ONE MEASLY MINUTE INTO OUR SAMOANS COVER. IT SUNK IN PRETTY FAST THAT THIS WAS BAD.
VERY BAD.
THE AUDITORIUM WAS HUSHED AS HE FORCED US OFF THE STAGE, BEET RED.
I HOPE YOU DON'T THINK YOU'RE STILL GRADUATING AFTER THAT, GENTLEMEN.
YIKES... THAT WAS A HEFTY THREAT. I GOT THAT CRINGING FEELING YOU GET WHEN YOU'RE WORRIED OVER WHAT YOUR PARENTS ARE ABOUT TO FIND OUT.
THE SINKING FEELING OVERTOOK ME AS I CARRIED MY GEAR THROUGH THE THINNING CROWD.
ENGLISH TEACHER, MR. MAMCHEK SLITHERED UP TO ME...
A MOST DISSSGRACEFUL WAY TO END THE SCHOOL YEAR, MISSSTER.
I WAS SCARED, DEFEATED AND UNABLE TO REPLY

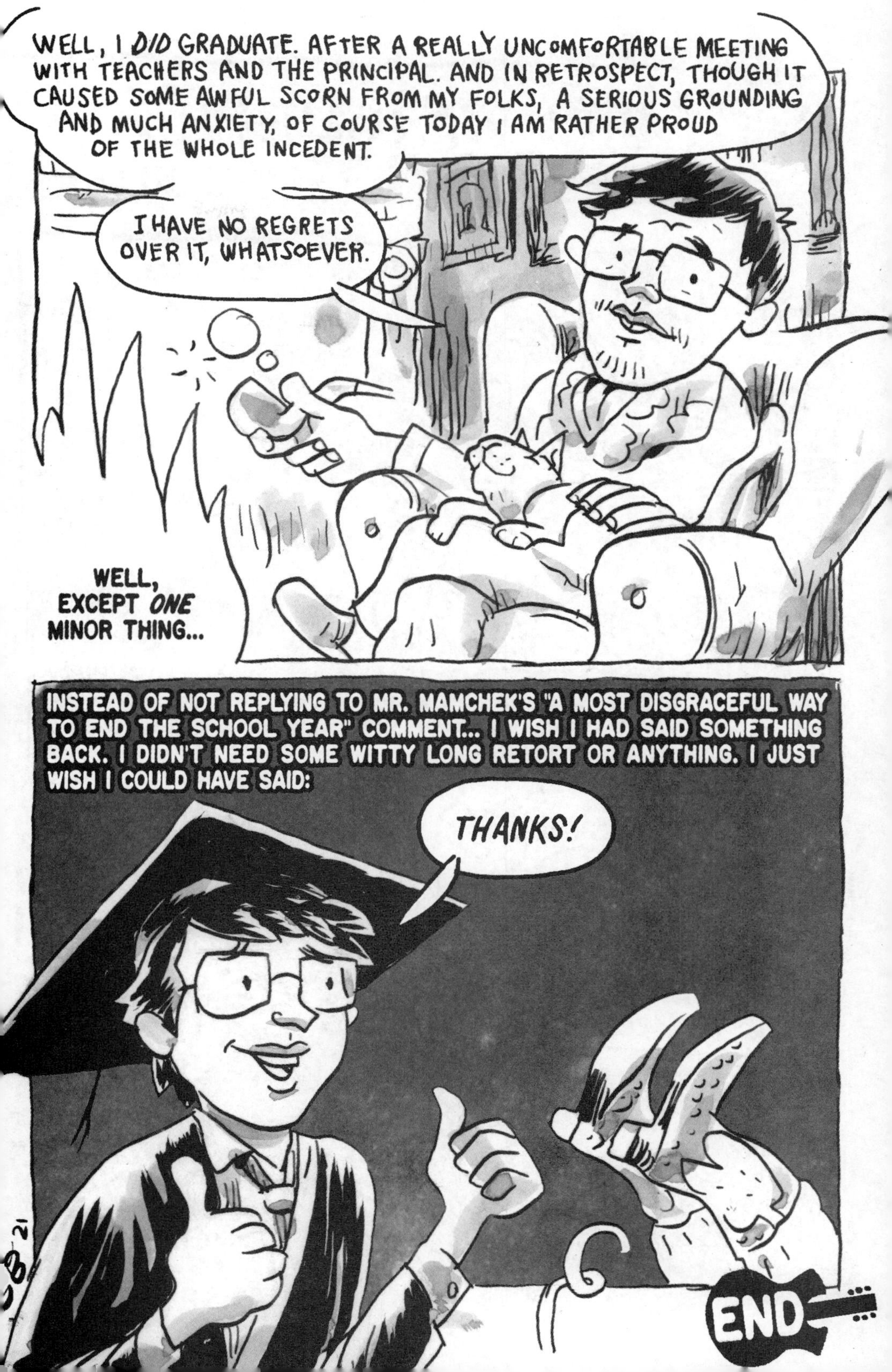
WELL, I *DID* GRADUATE. AFTER A REALLY UNCOMFORTABLE MEETING WITH TEACHERS AND THE PRINCIPAL. AND IN RETROSPECT, THOUGH IT CAUSED SOME AWFUL SCORN FROM MY FOLKS, A SERIOUS GROUNDING AND MUCH ANXIETY, OF COURSE TODAY I AM RATHER PROUD OF THE WHOLE INCEDENT.
I HAVE NO REGRETS OVER IT, WHATSOEVER.
WELL, EXCEPT *ONE* MINOR THING...
INSTEAD OF NOT REPLYING TO MR. MAMCHEK'S "A MOST DISGRACEFUL WAY TO END THE SCHOOL YEAR" COMMENT... I WISH I HAD SAID SOMETHING BACK. I DIDN'T NEED SOME WITTY LONG RETORT OR ANYTHING. I JUST WISH I COULD HAVE SAID:
THANKS!
END

THE MARK WAHLBERG STORY

BAYER *HYENA HELL*

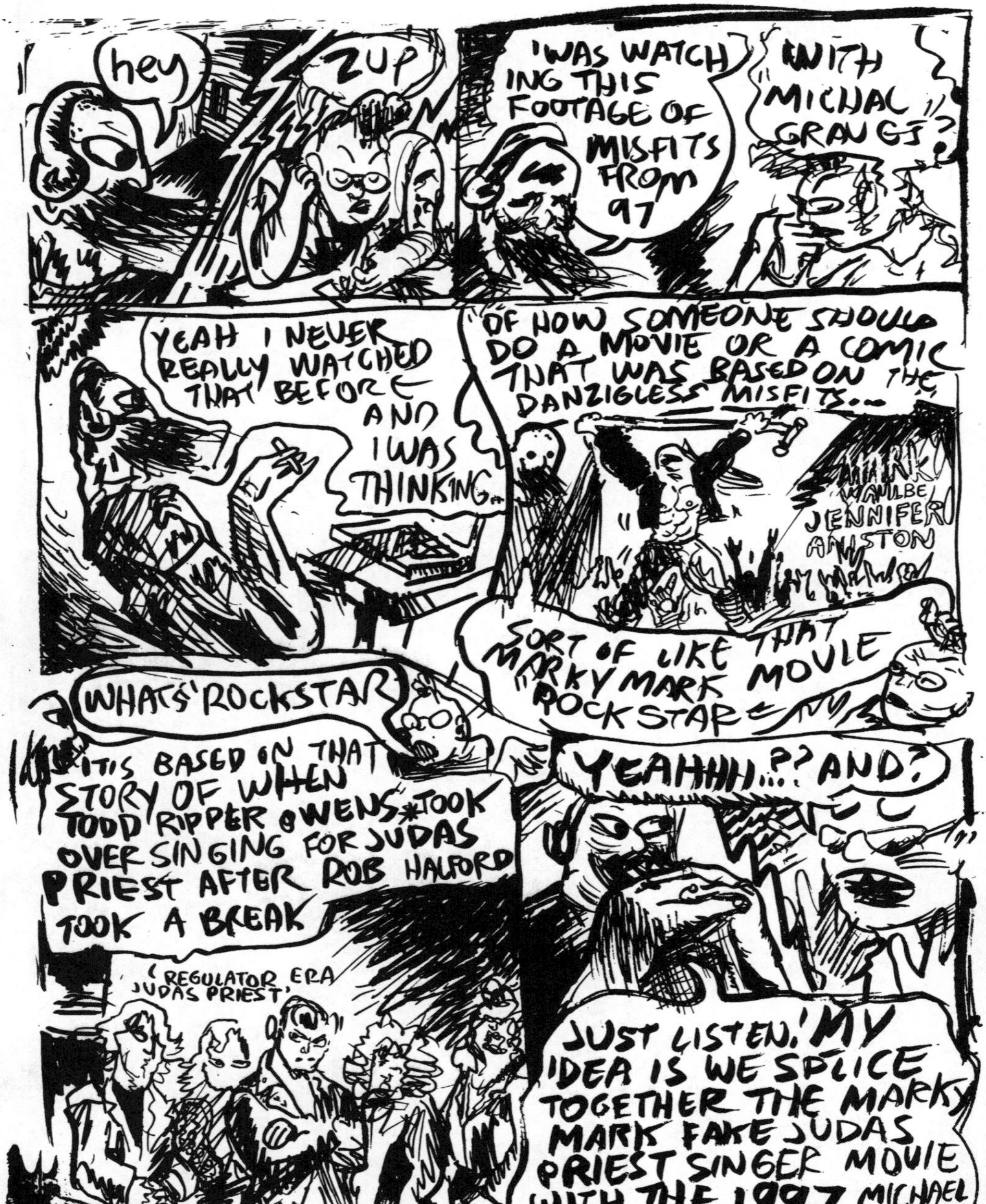
hey
ZUP
'WAS WATCHING THIS FOOTAGE OF MISFITS FROM 97
WITH MICHAL GRAVES'?
YEAH I NEVER REALLY WATCHED THAT BEFORE AND I WAS THINKING..
OF HOW SOMEONE SHOULD DO A MOVIE OR A COMIC THAT WAS BASED ON THE DANZIGLESS MISFITS..
JENNIFER ANISTON
SORT OF LIKE THAT MARKY MARK MOVIE "ROCKSTAR"
WHAT'S 'ROCKSTAR'?
IT IS BASED ON THAT STORY OF WHEN TODD RIPPER OWENS* TOOK OVER SINGING FOR JUDAS PRIEST AFTER ROB HALFORD TOOK A BREAK
YEAHHH...?? AND?
(REGULATOR ERA JUDAS PRIEST)
JUST LISTEN. MY IDEA IS WE SPLICE TOGETHER THE MARKY MARK FAKE JUDAS PRIEST SINGER MOVIE WITH THE 1997 MICHAEL GRAVES MISFITS STORY
*TIM, ACTUALLY -OOPS

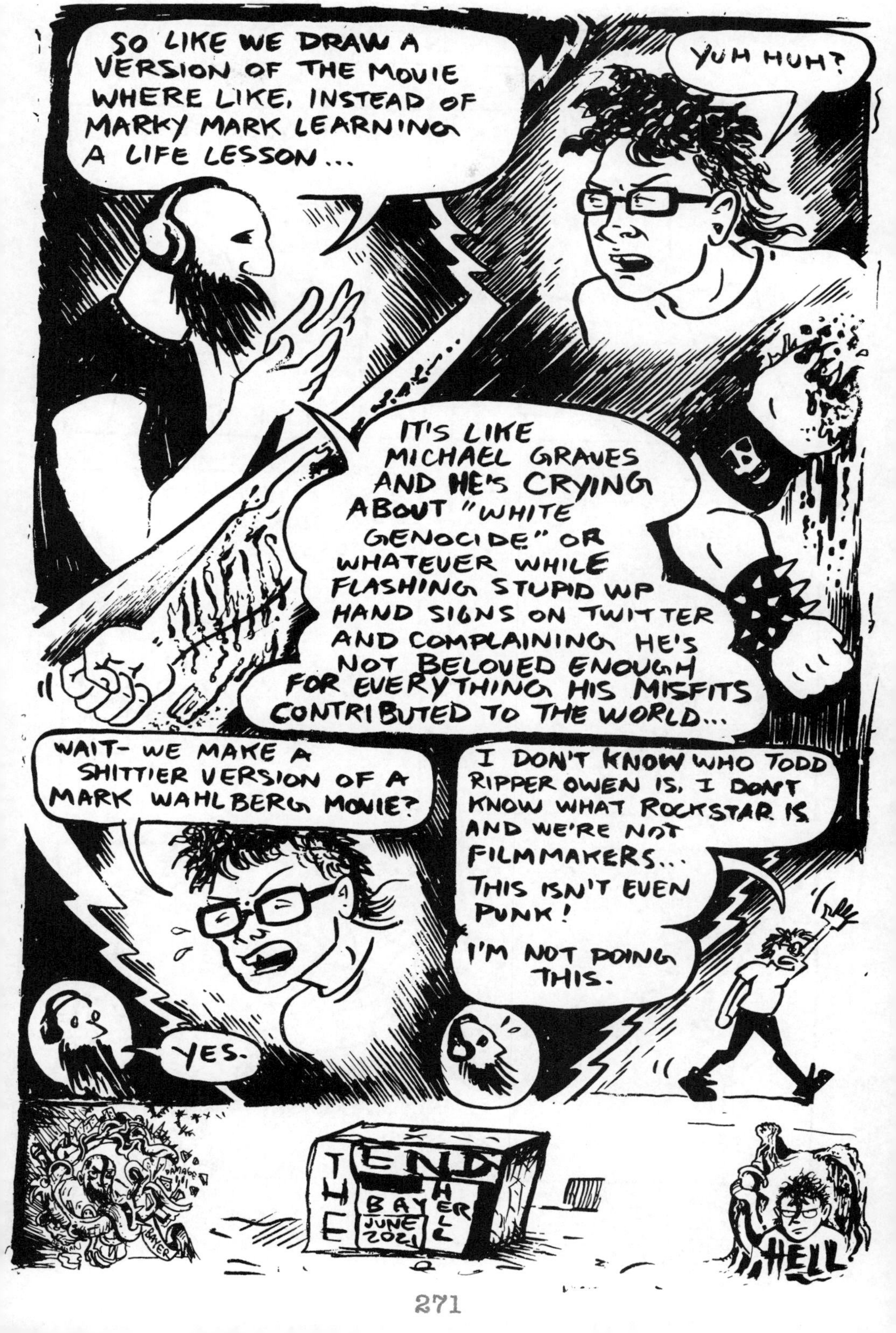
SO LIKE WE DRAW A VERSION OF THE MOVIE WHERE LIKE, INSTEAD OF MARKY MARK LEARNING A LIFE LESSON...
YUH HUH?
IT'S LIKE MICHAEL GRAVES AND HE'S CRYING ABOUT "WHITE GENOCIDE" OR WHATEVER WHILE FLASHING STUPID WP HAND SIGNS ON TWITTER AND COMPLAINING HE'S NOT BELOVED ENOUGH FOR EVERYTHING HIS MISFITS CONTRIBUTED TO THE WORLD...
WAIT- WE MAKE A SHITTIER VERSION OF A MARK WAHLBERG MOVIE?
I DON'T KNOW WHO TODD RIPPER OWEN IS, I DON'T KNOW WHAT ROCKSTAR IS AND WE'RE NOT FILMMAKERS...
THIS ISN'T EVEN PUNK!
I'M NOT DOING THIS.
YES.
THE END
BAYER
JUNE 2021
HELL

TO the AGING PUNK COUPLE at the ORCHID FARM

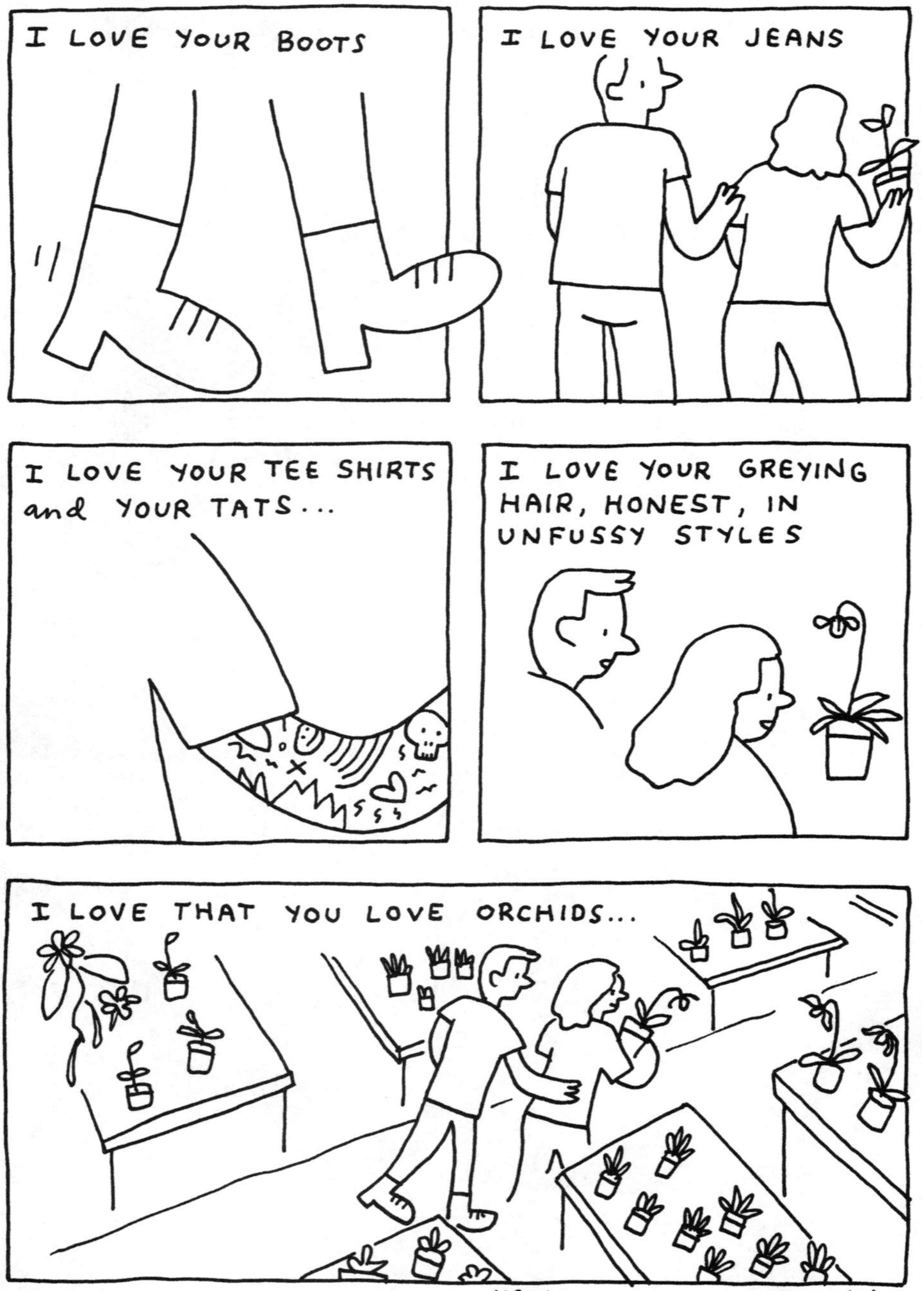
I LOVE YOUR BOOTS
I LOVE YOUR JEANS
I LOVE YOUR TEE SHIRTS and YOUR TATS...
I LOVE YOUR GREYING HAIR, HONEST, IN UNFUSSY STYLES
I LOVE THAT YOU LOVE ORCHIDS...

HAPPENED IN VILLA PARK, 6/5/21
DRAWN IN BELOIT, 6/13 - JOHN P.

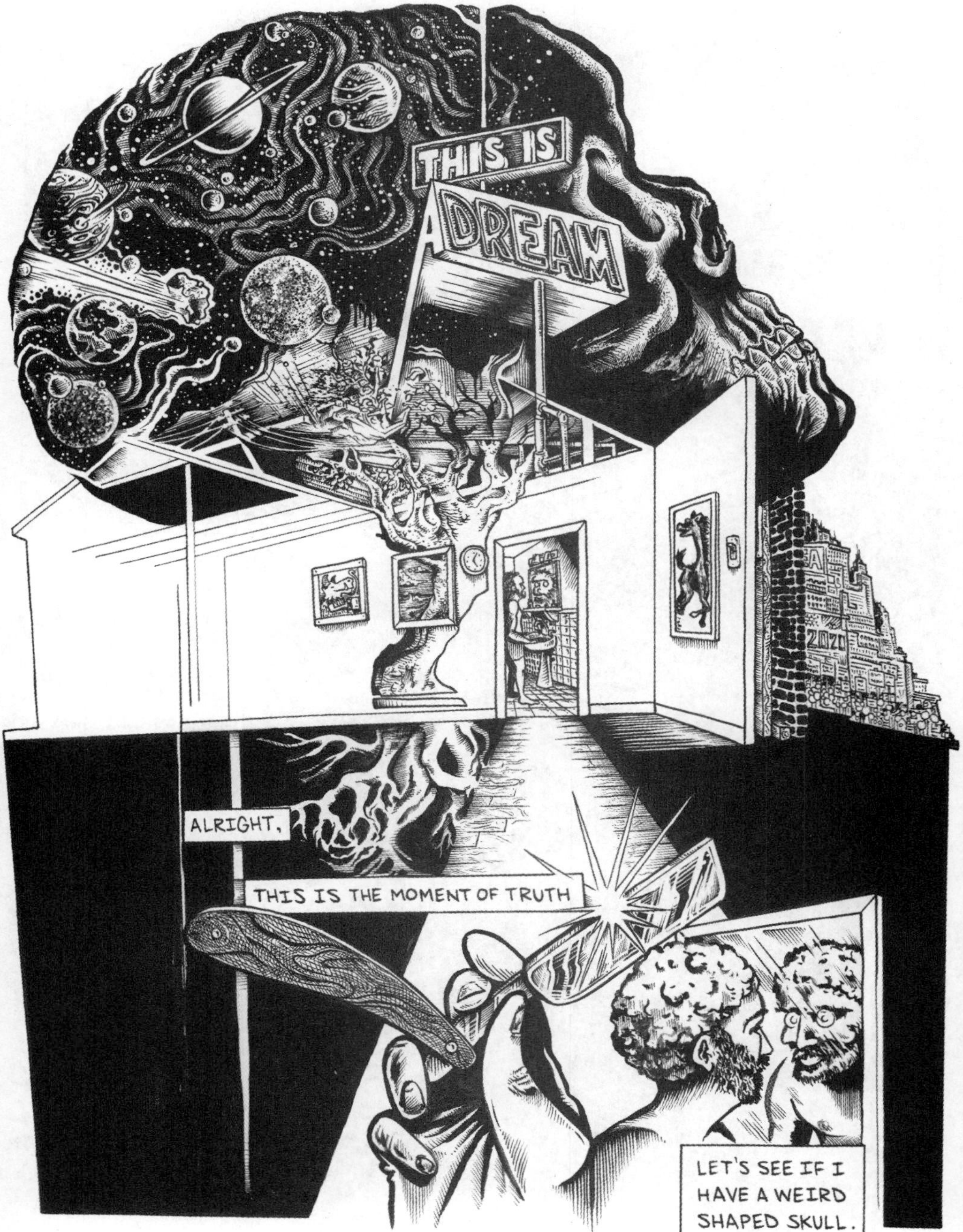
THIS IS
A DREAM
2020
ALRIGHT,
THIS IS THE MOMENT OF TRUTH
LET'S SEE IF I HAVE A WEIRD SHAPED SKULL.

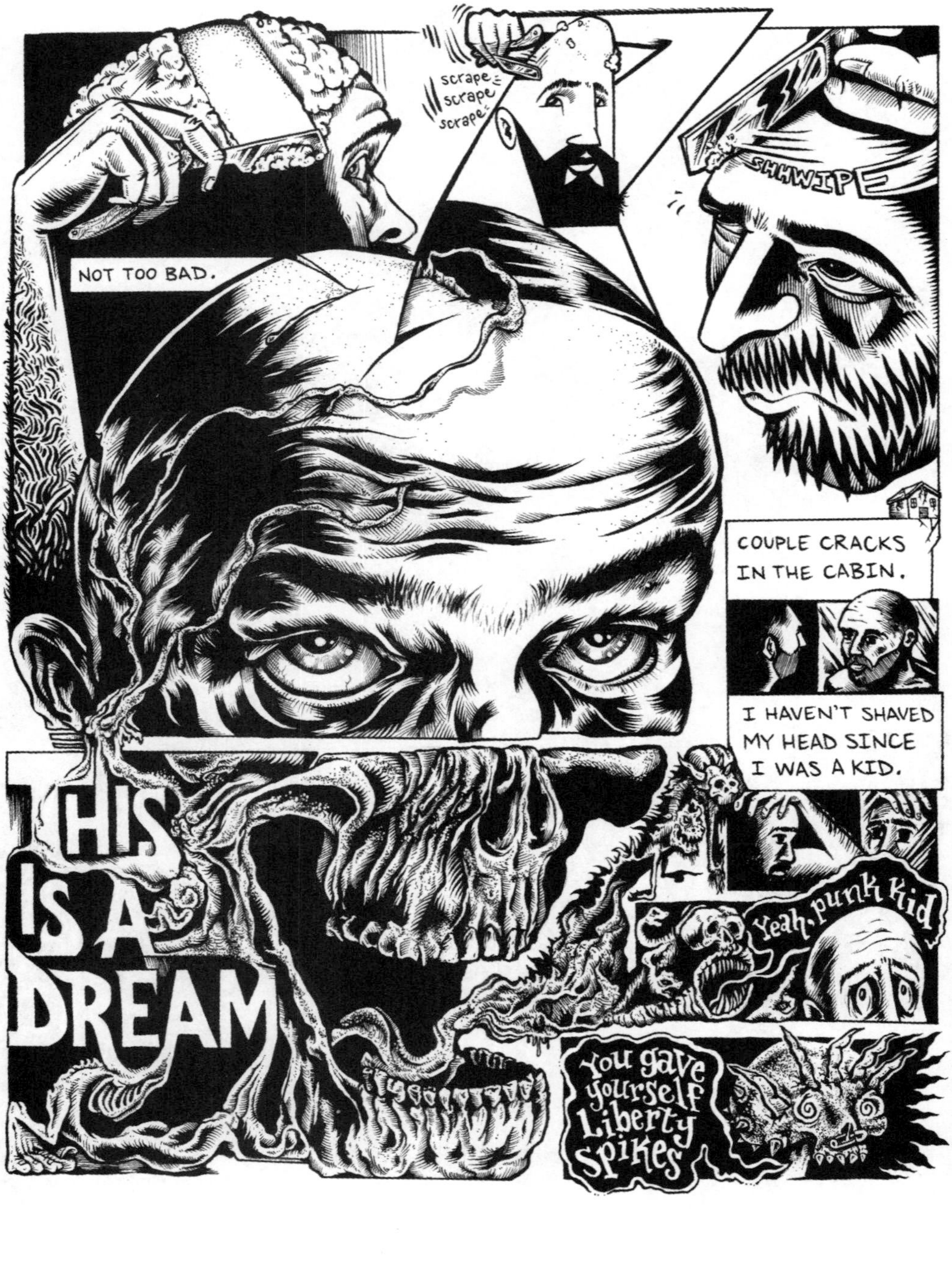

scrape
scrape
scrape
SHHWIPE
NOT TOO BAD.
COUPLE CRACKS IN THE CABIN.
I HAVEN'T SHAVED MY HEAD SINCE I WAS A KID.
THIS IS A DREAM
Yeah. punk kid
You gave yourself Liberty spikes

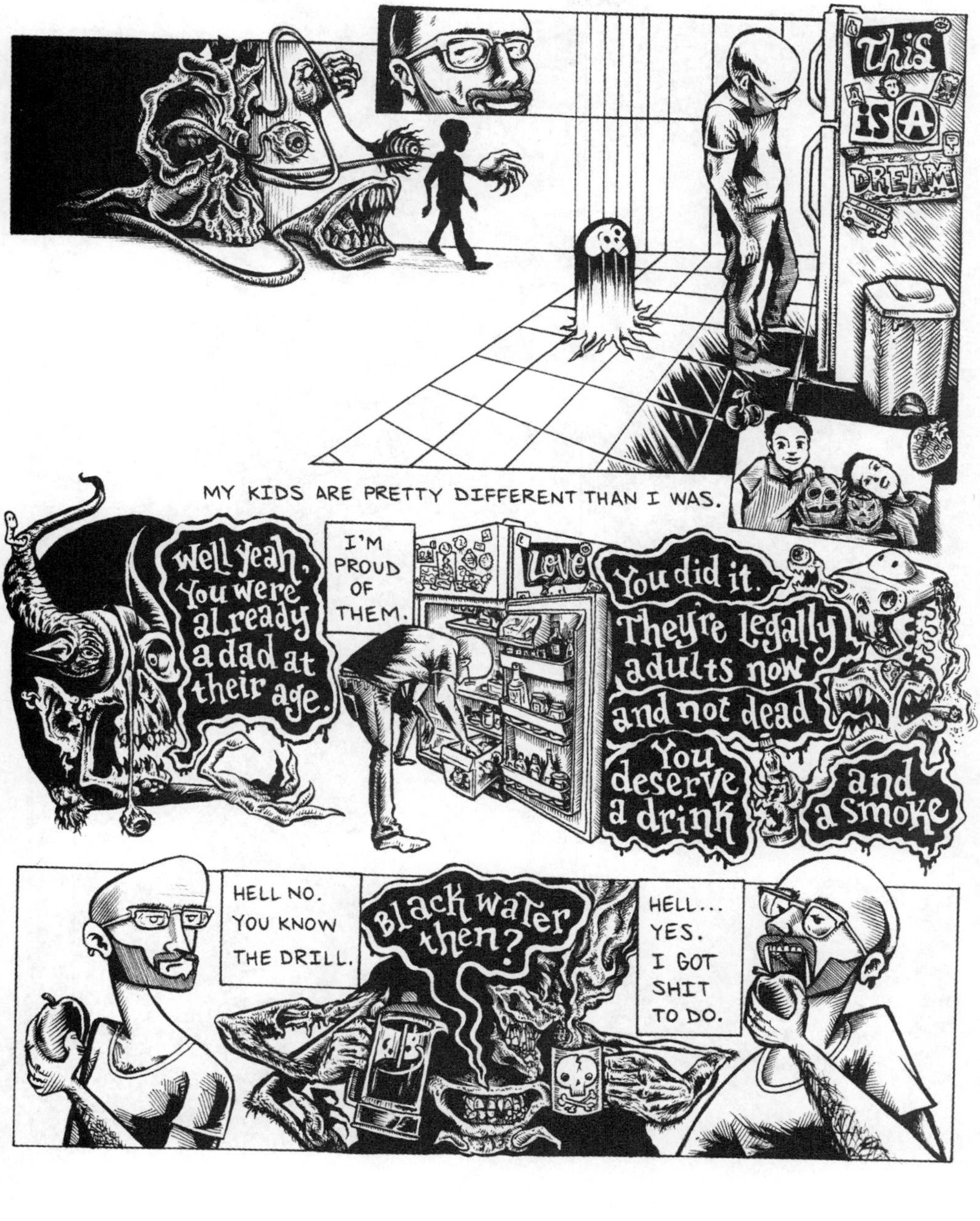
This is A DREAM
MY KIDS ARE PRETTY DIFFERENT THAN I WAS.
Well yeah, You were already a dad at their age.
I'M PROUD OF THEM.
LOVE
You did it. They're legally adults now and not dead
You deserve a drink
and a smoke
HELL NO. YOU KNOW THE DRILL.
Black water then?
HELL... YES. I GOT SHIT TO DO.

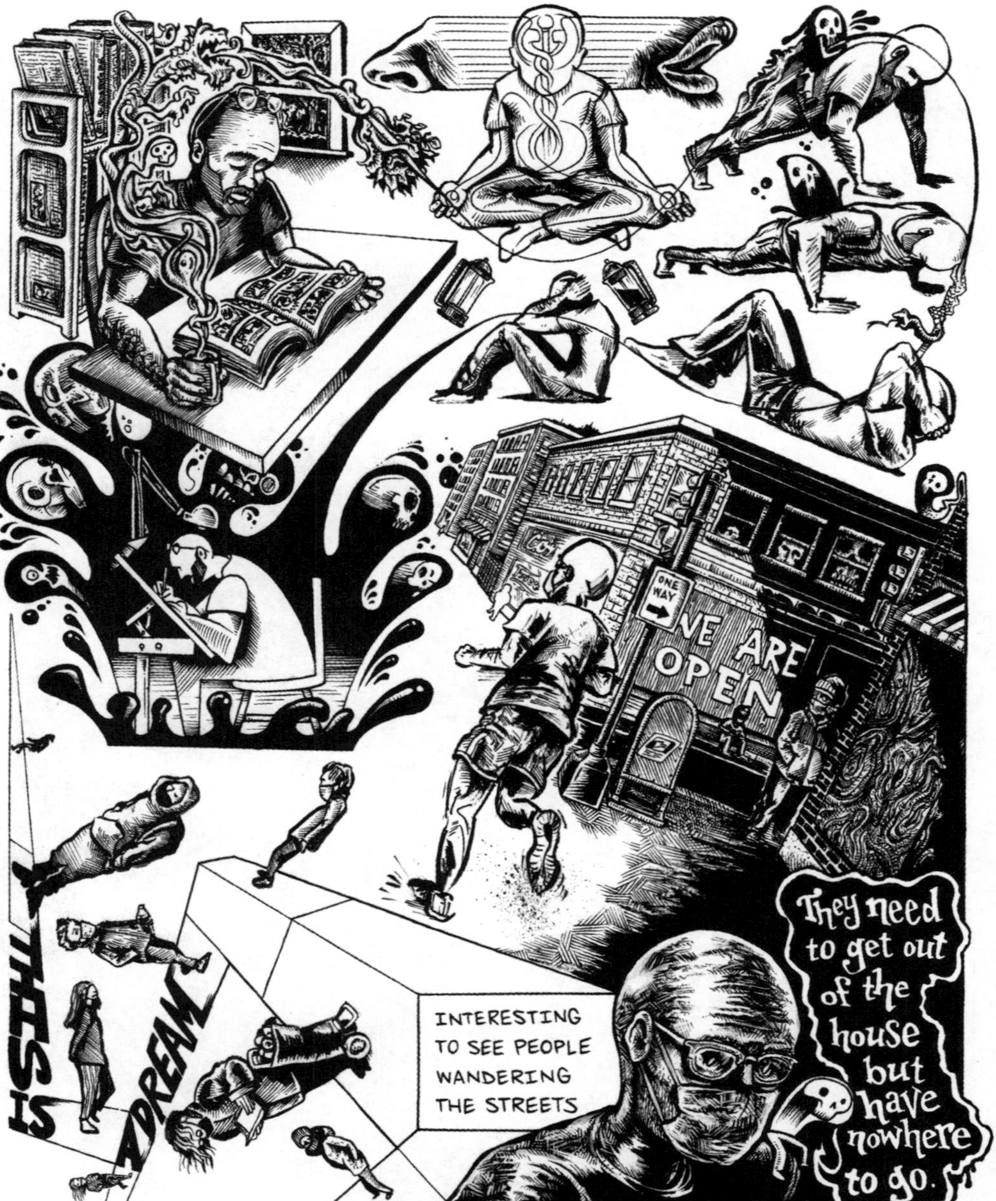
ONE WAY
ARE OPEN
THIS IS A DREAM
INTERESTING TO SEE PEOPLE WANDERING THE STREETS
They need to get out of the house but have nowhere to go.

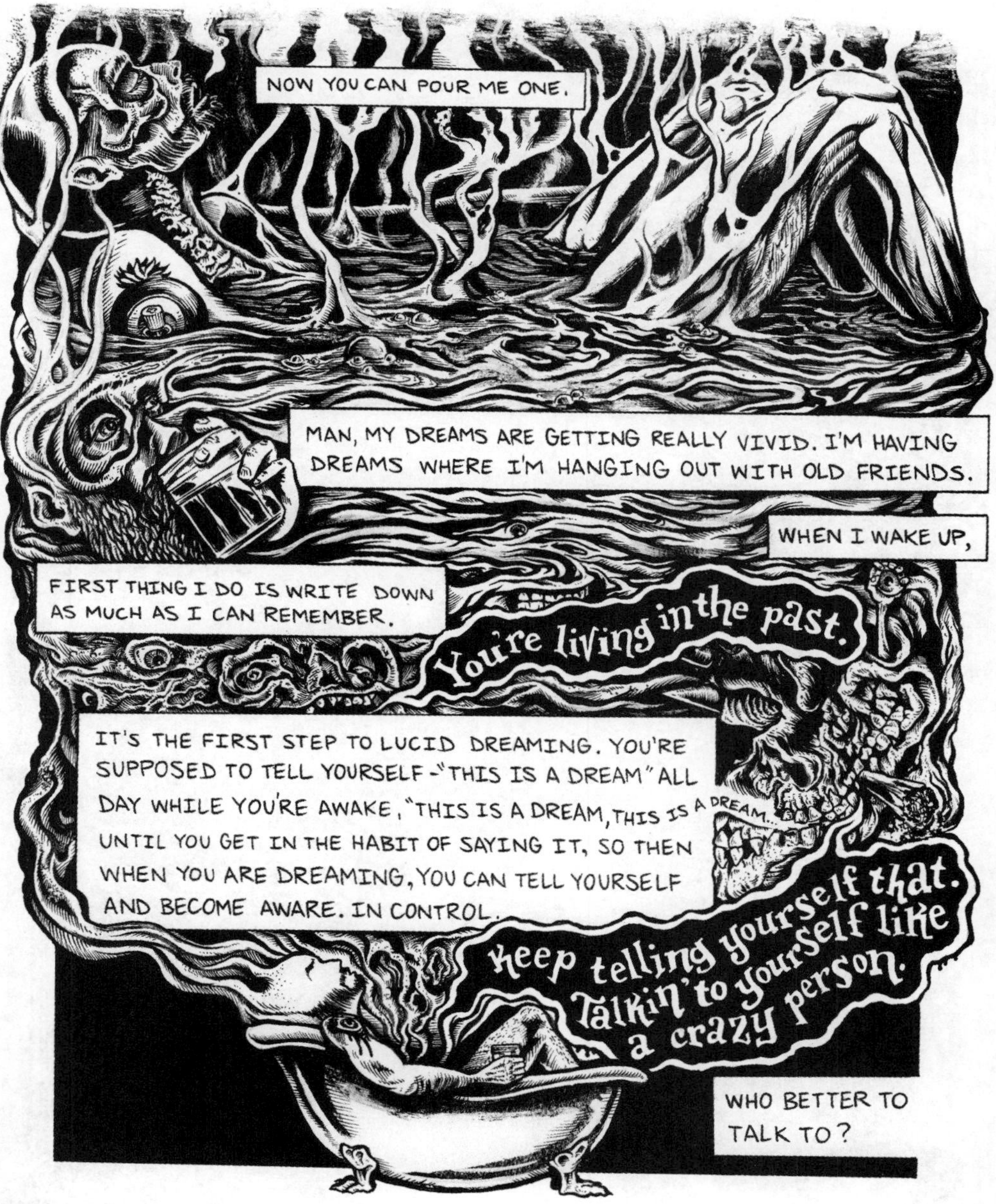
NOW YOU CAN POUR ME ONE.
MAN, MY DREAMS ARE GETTING REALLY VIVID. I'M HAVING DREAMS WHERE I'M HANGING OUT WITH OLD FRIENDS.
WHEN I WAKE UP,
FIRST THING I DO IS WRITE DOWN AS MUCH AS I CAN REMEMBER.
You're living in the past.
IT'S THE FIRST STEP TO LUCID DREAMING. YOU'RE SUPPOSED TO TELL YOURSELF -"THIS IS A DREAM" ALL DAY WHILE YOU'RE AWAKE, "THIS IS A DREAM, THIS IS A DREAM..." UNTIL YOU GET IN THE HABIT OF SAYING IT, SO THEN WHEN YOU ARE DREAMING, YOU CAN TELL YOURSELF AND BECOME AWARE. IN CONTROL.
Keep telling yourself that. Talkin' to yourself like a crazy person.
WHO BETTER TO TALK TO?

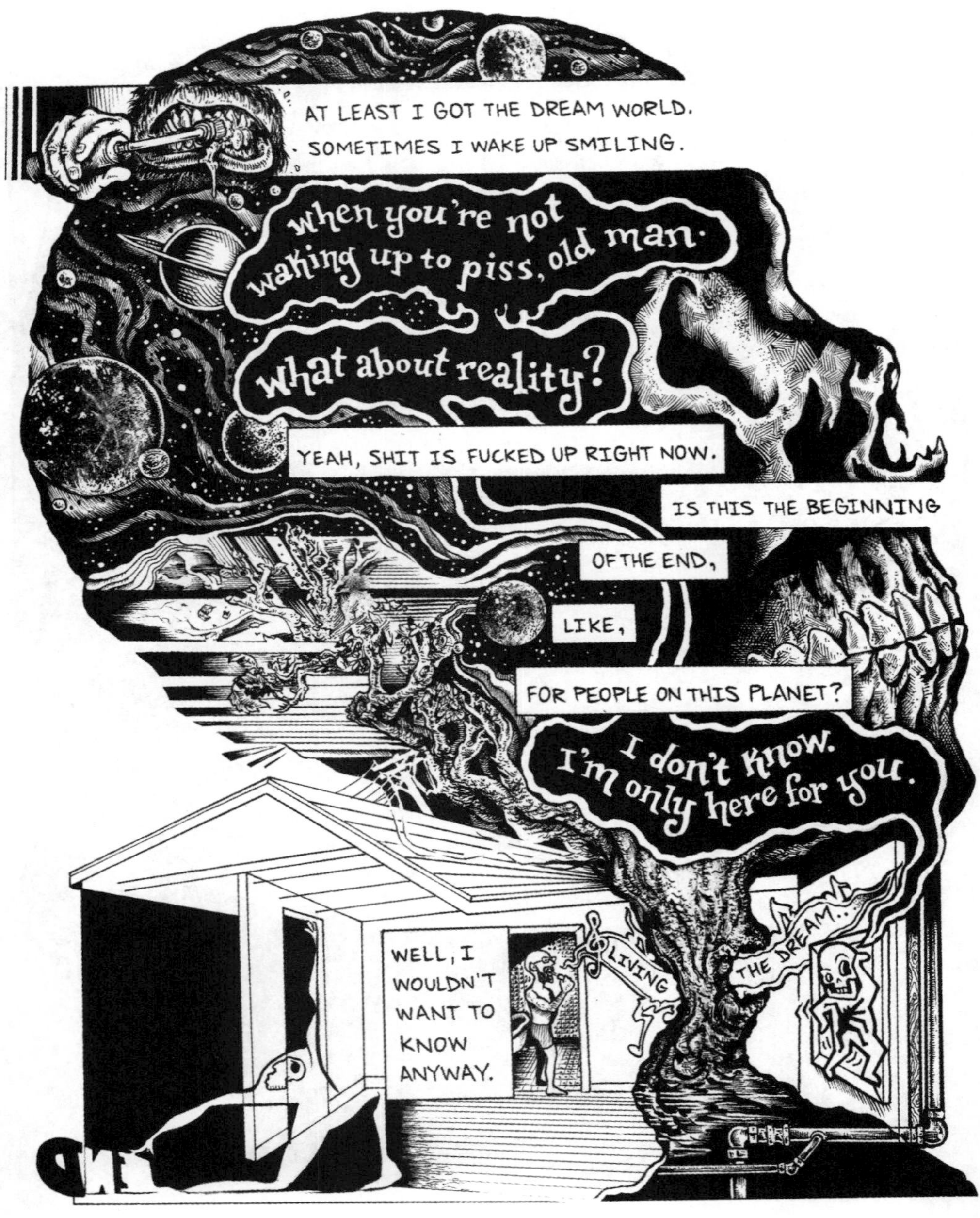
AT LEAST I GOT THE DREAM WORLD.
SOMETIMES I WAKE UP SMILING.
when you're not waking up to piss, old man.
what about reality?
YEAH, SHIT IS FUCKED UP RIGHT NOW.
IS THIS THE BEGINNING
OF THE END,
LIKE,
FOR PEOPLE ON THIS PLANET?
I don't know. I'm only here for you.
WELL, I WOULDN'T WANT TO KNOW ANYWAY.
LIVING
THE DREAM..

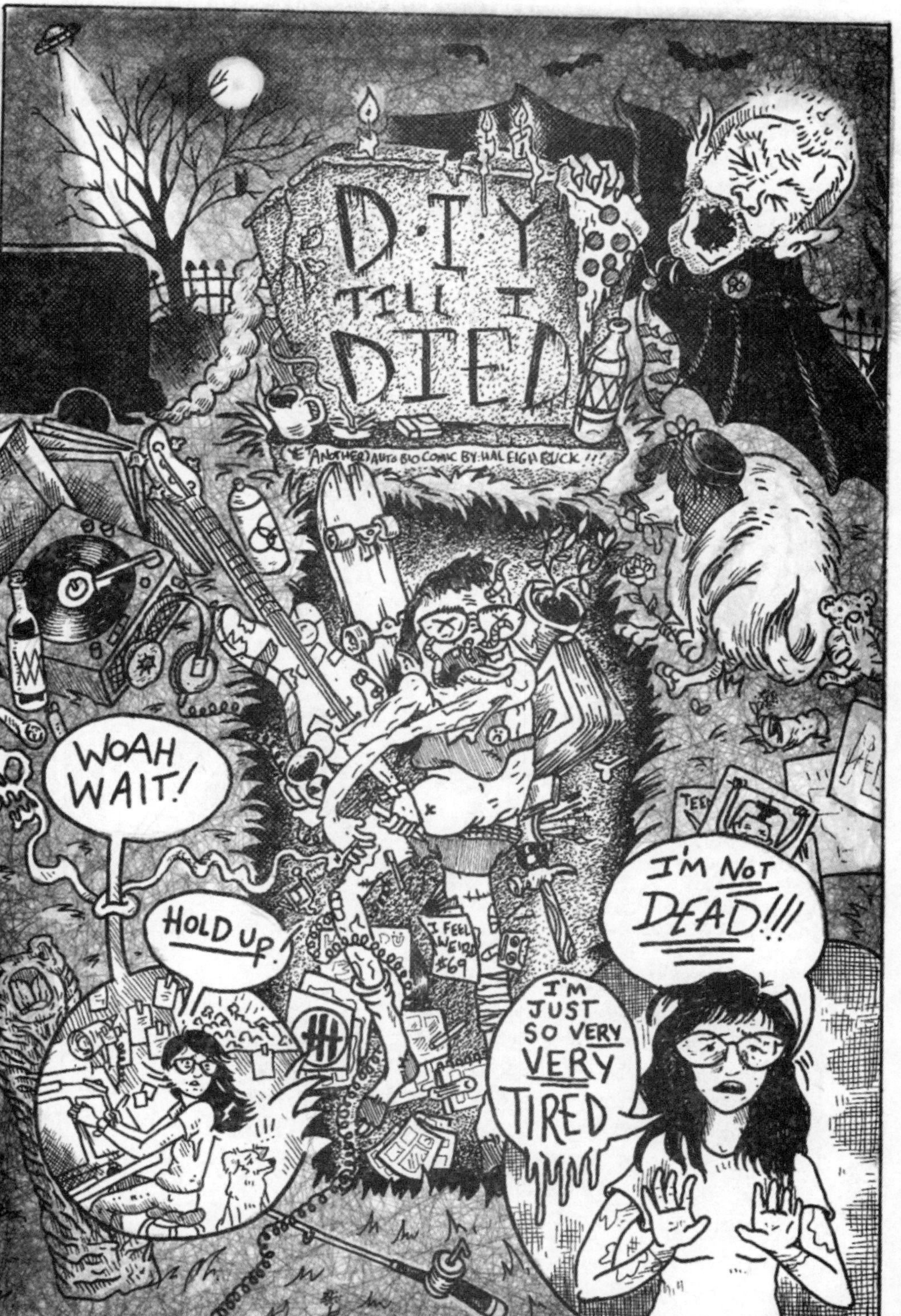
D·I·Y
TILL I
DIED
YE ANOTHER) AUTO BIO COMIC BY: HALEIGH BUCK !!!
WOAH WAIT!
HOLD UP.
I FEEL WEIRD $69
I'M NOT DEAD!!!
I'M JUST SO VERY VERY TIRED

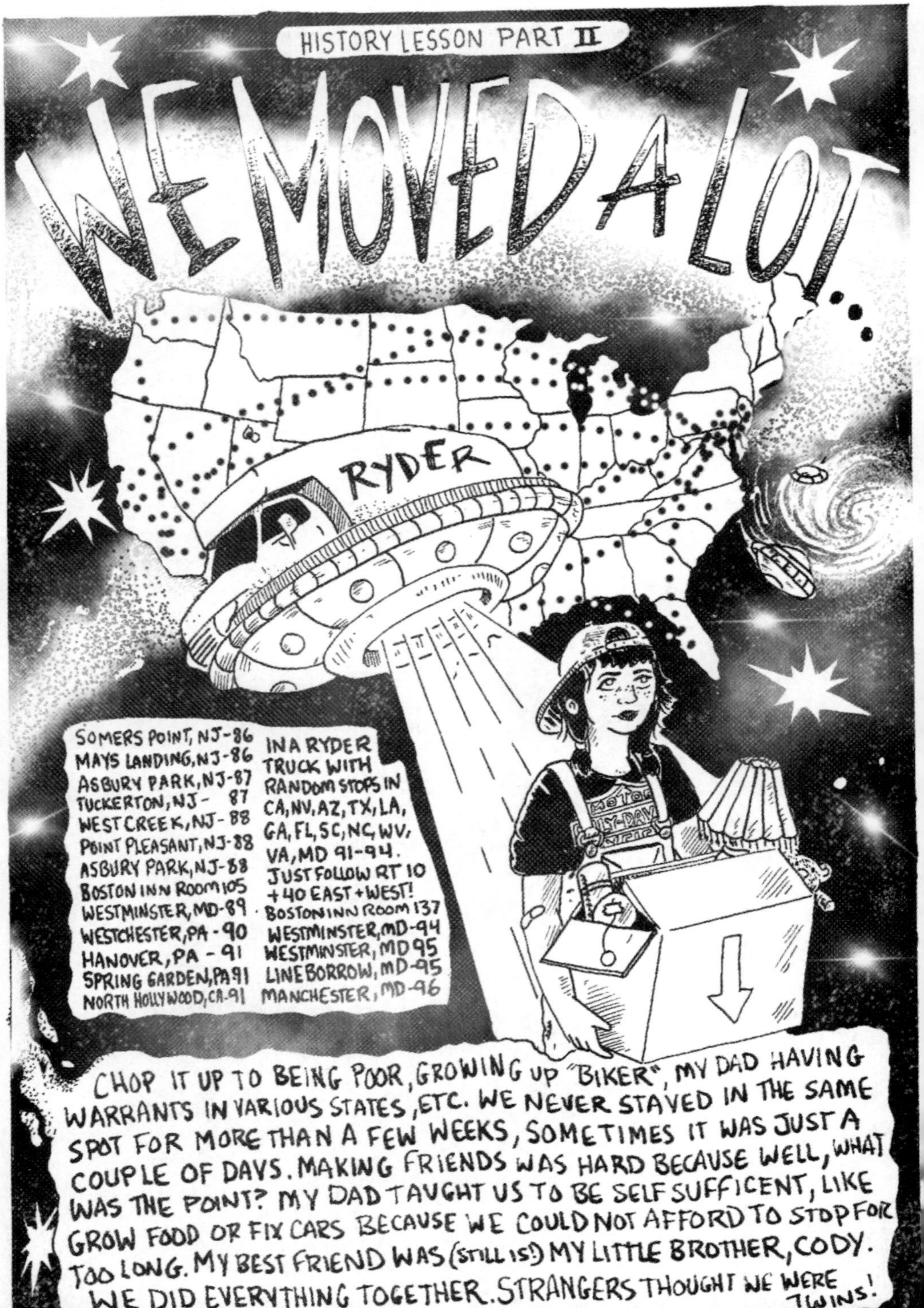
HISTORY LESSON PART II
WE MOVED A LOT...
RYDER
SOMERS POINT, NJ-86
MAYS LANDING, NJ-86
ASBURY PARK, NJ-87
TUCKERTON, NJ- 87
WEST CREEK, NJ- 88
POINT PLEASANT, NJ-88
ASBURY PARK, NJ-88
BOSTON INN ROOM 105
WESTMINSTER, MD-89
WESTCHESTER, PA - 90
HANOVER, PA - 91
SPRING GARDEN, PA 91
NORTH HOLLYWOOD, CA-91
IN A RYDER TRUCK WITH RANDOM STOPS IN CA, NV, AZ, TX, LA, GA, FL, SC, NC, WV, VA, MD 91-94. JUST FOLLOW RT 10 + 40 EAST + WEST!
BOSTON INN ROOM 137
WESTMINSTER, MD-94
WESTMINSTER, MD 95
LINEBORROW, MD-95
MANCHESTER, MD-96
CHOP IT UP TO BEING POOR, GROWING UP "BIKER", MY DAD HAVING WARRANTS IN VARIOUS STATES, ETC. WE NEVER STAYED IN THE SAME SPOT FOR MORE THAN A FEW WEEKS, SOMETIMES IT WAS JUST A COUPLE OF DAYS. MAKING FRIENDS WAS HARD BECAUSE WELL, WHAT WAS THE POINT? MY DAD TAUGHT US TO BE SELF SUFFICENT, LIKE GROW FOOD OR FIX CARS BECAUSE WE COULD NOT AFFORD TO STOP FOR TOO LONG. MY BEST FRIEND WAS (STILL IS!) MY LITTLE BROTHER, CODY. WE DID EVERYTHING TOGETHER. STRANGERS THOUGHT WE WERE TWINS!

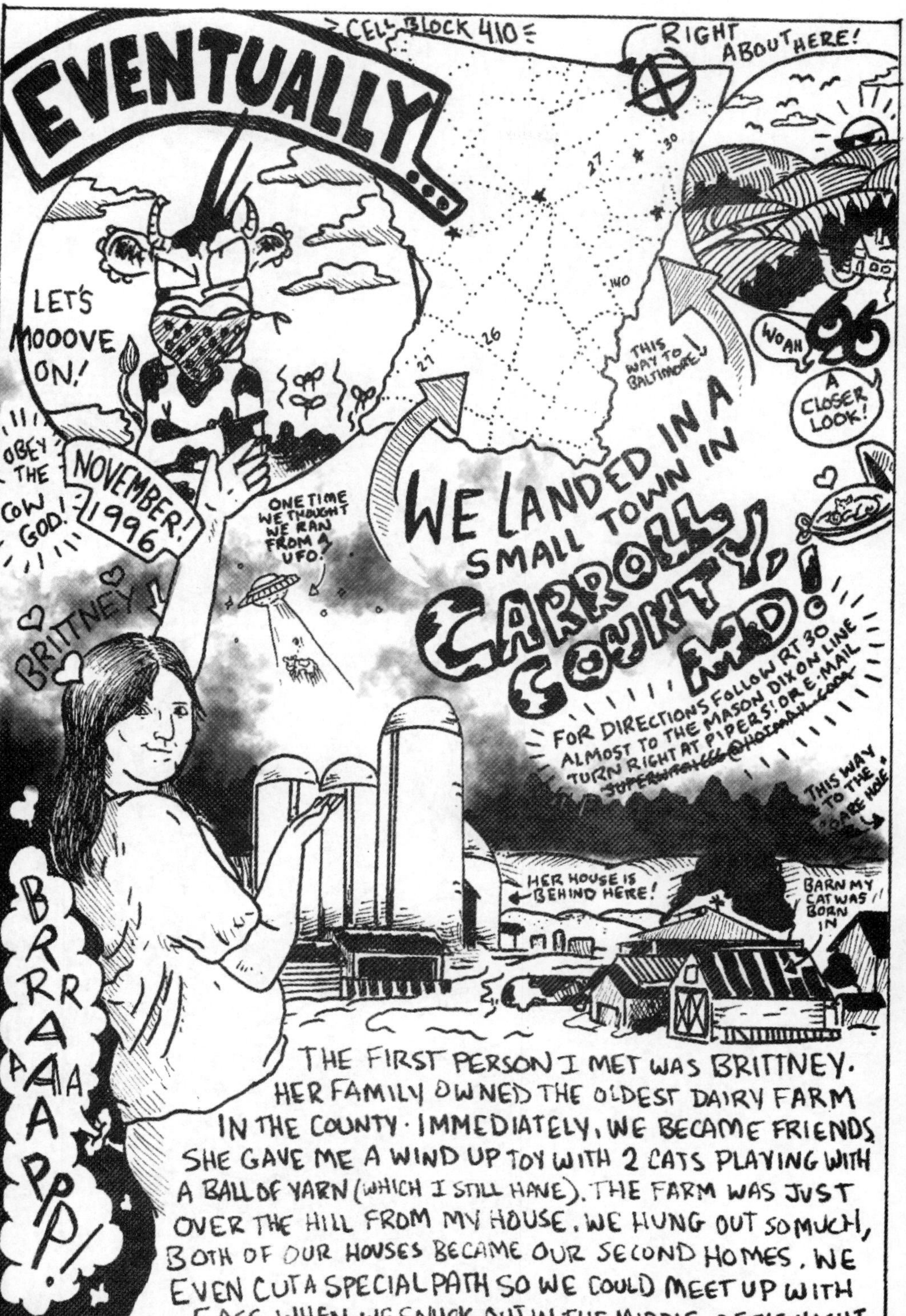

EVENTUALLY...
CELL BLOCK 410
RIGHT ABOUT HERE!
27
30
140
26
27
THIS WAY TO BALTIMORE!
LET'S MOOOVE ON!
OBEY THE COW GOD!
NOVEMBER! 1996
WOAH
A CLOSER LOOK!
WE LANDED IN A SMALL TOWN IN CARROLL COUNTY, MD!
ONE TIME WE THOUGHT WE RAN FROM A UFO!
BRITTNEY
FOR DIRECTIONS FOLLOW RT 30 ALMOST TO THE MASON DIXON LINE TURN RIGHT AT PIPERS! OR E-MAIL
THIS WAY TO THE
HER HOUSE IS BEHIND HERE!
BARN MY CAT WAS BORN IN
BRRRAAAAAPPP!
THE FIRST PERSON I MET WAS BRITTNEY. HER FAMILY OWNED THE OLDEST DAIRY FARM IN THE COUNTY. IMMEDIATELY, WE BECAME FRIENDS. SHE GAVE ME A WIND UP TOY WITH 2 CATS PLAYING WITH A BALL OF YARN (WHICH I STILL HAVE). THE FARM WAS JUST OVER THE HILL FROM MY HOUSE. WE HUNG OUT SO MUCH, BOTH OF OUR HOUSES BECAME OUR SECOND HOMES. WE EVEN CUT A SPECIAL PATH SO WE COULD MEET UP WITH EASE WHEN WE SNUCK OUT IN THE MIDDLE OF THE NIGHT.

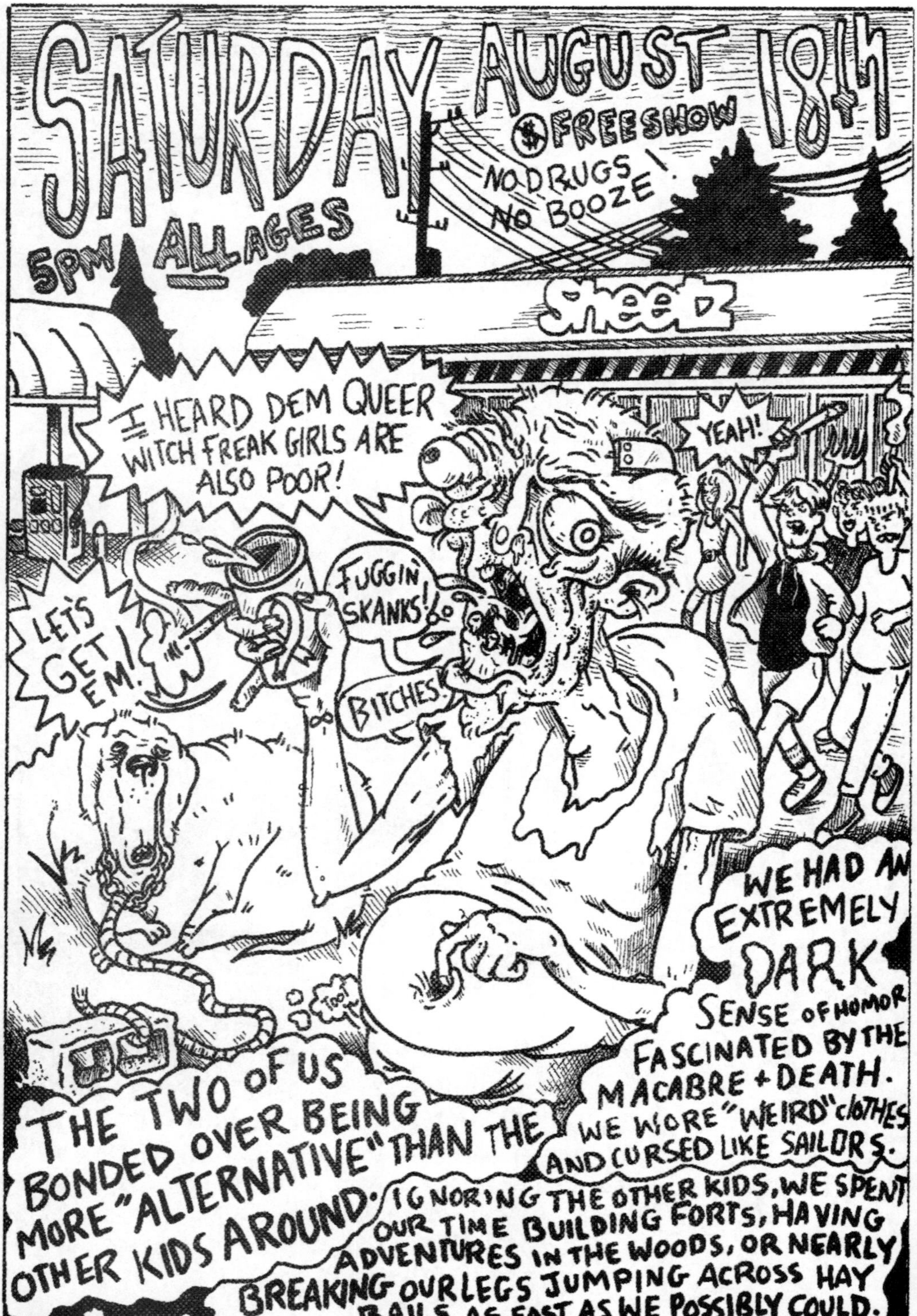
SATURDAY AUGUST 18th
FREE SHOW
NO DRUGS NO BOOZE!
5PM ALL AGES
Sheetz
I HEARD DEM QUEER WITCH FREAK GIRLS ARE ALSO POOR!
YEAH!
LET'S GET EM!
FUGGIN' SKANKS!
BITCHES!
TOOT
WE HAD AN EXTREMELY DARK SENSE OF HOMOR FASCINATED BY THE MACABRE + DEATH. WE WORE "WEIRD" CLOTHES AND CURSED LIKE SAILORS.
THE TWO OF US BONDED OVER BEING MORE "ALTERNATIVE" THAN THE OTHER KIDS AROUND.
IGNORING THE OTHER KIDS, WE SPENT OUR TIME BUILDING FORTS, HAVING ADVENTURES IN THE WOODS, OR NEARLY BREAKING OUR LEGS JUMPING ACROSS HAY BAILS AS FAST AS WE POSSIBLY COULD.

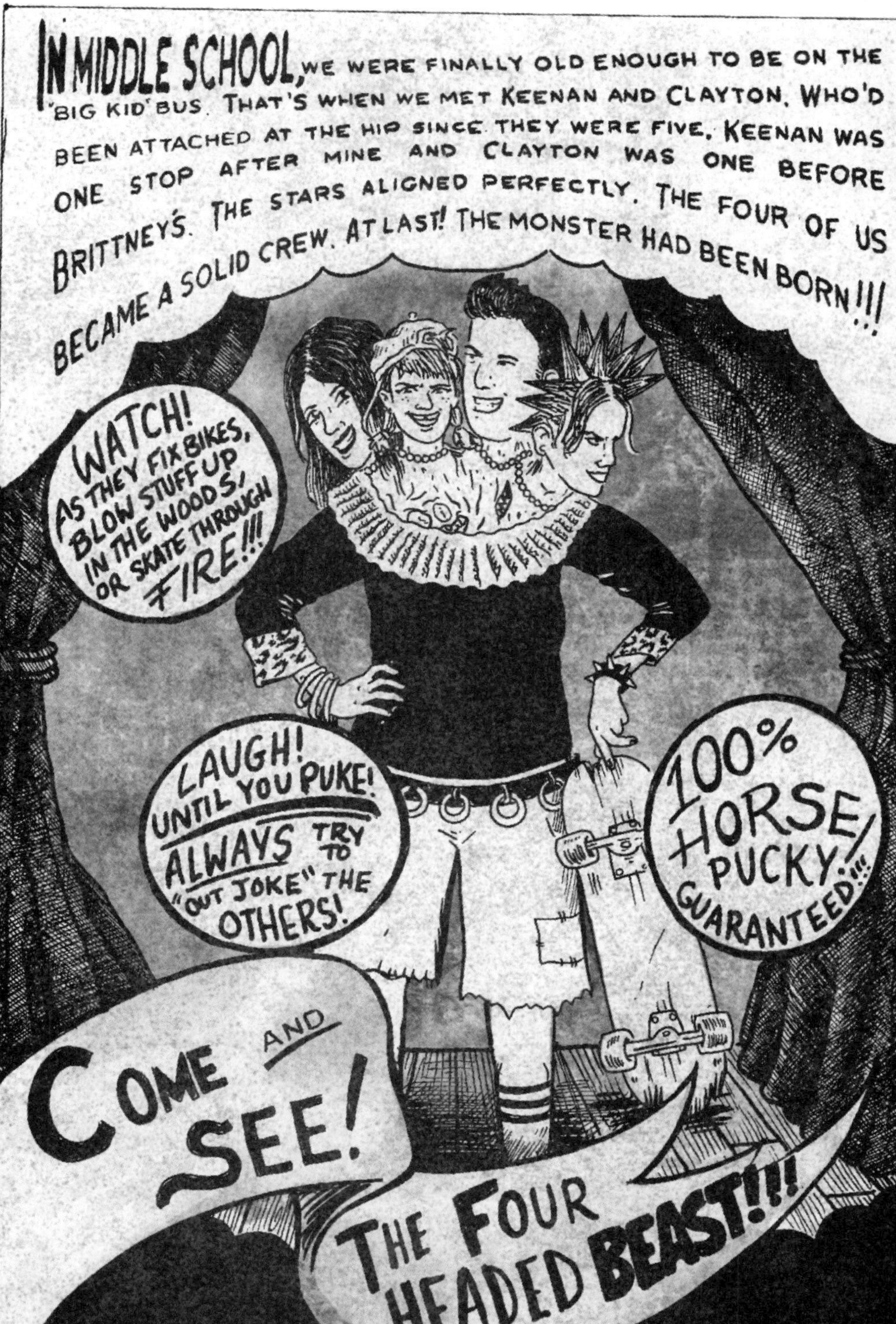

IN MIDDLE SCHOOL, WE WERE FINALLY OLD ENOUGH TO BE ON THE "BIG KID" BUS. THAT'S WHEN WE MET KEENAN AND CLAYTON, WHO'D BEEN ATTACHED AT THE HIP SINCE THEY WERE FIVE. KEENAN WAS ONE STOP AFTER MINE AND CLAYTON WAS ONE BEFORE BRITTNEY'S. THE STARS ALIGNED PERFECTLY. THE FOUR OF US BECAME A SOLID CREW. AT LAST! THE MONSTER HAD BEEN BORN!!!
WATCH! AS THEY FIX BIKES, BLOW STUFF UP IN THE WOODS, OR SKATE THROUGH FIRE!!!
LAUGH! UNTIL YOU PUKE! ALWAYS TRY TO "OUT JOKE" THE OTHERS!
100% HORSE PUCKY! GUARANTEED!!!
COME AND SEE!
THE FOUR HEADED BEAST!!!

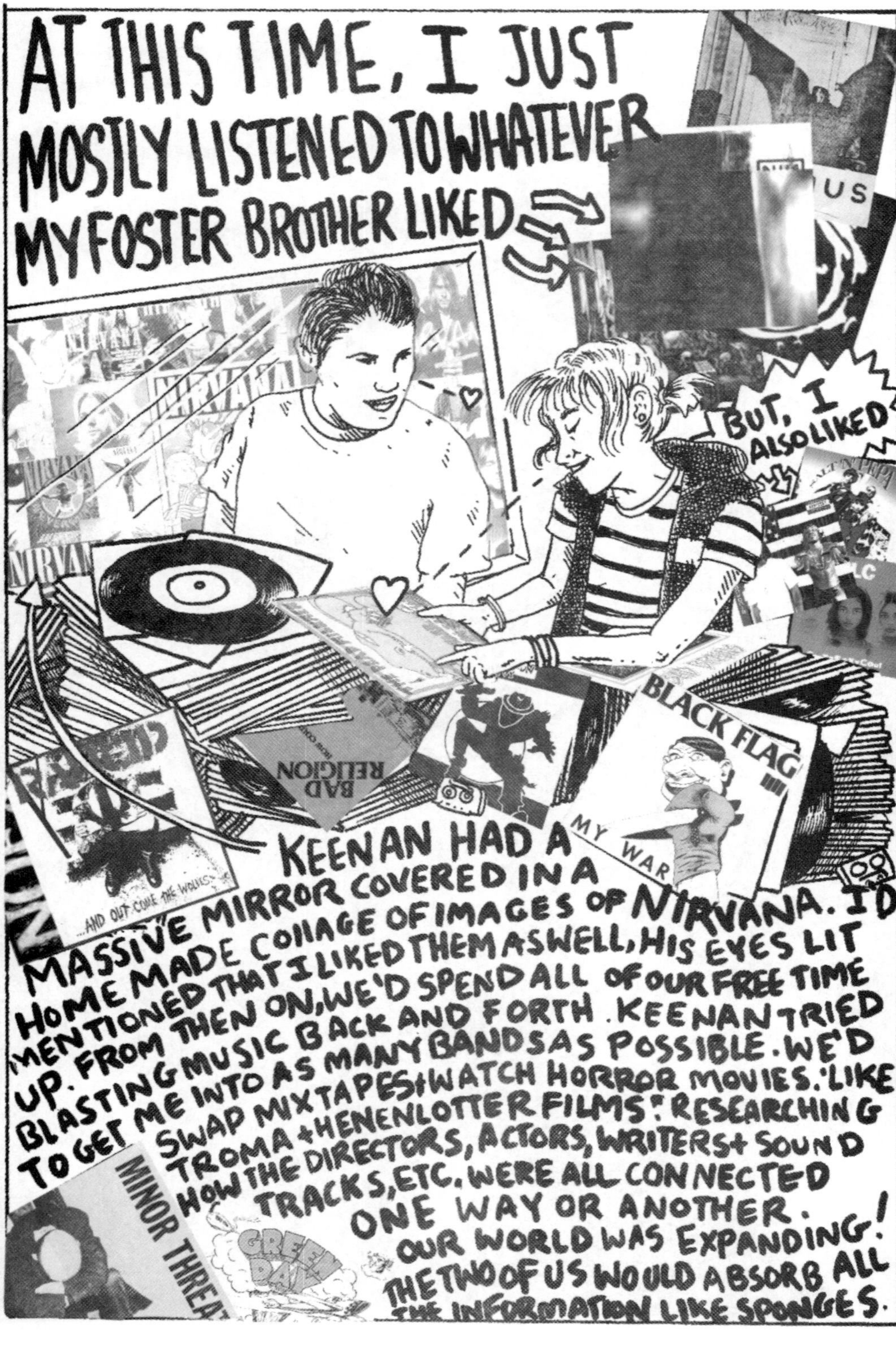
AT THIS TIME, I JUST MOSTLY LISTENED TO WHATEVER MY FOSTER BROTHER LIKED
BUT, I ALSO LIKED
BLACK FLAG
MY WAR
BAD RELIGION
MINOR THREAT
GREEN DAY
...AND OUT COME THE WOLVES
KEENAN HAD A MASSIVE MIRROR COVERED IN A HOMEMADE COLLAGE OF IMAGES OF NIRVANA. I'D MENTIONED THAT I LIKED THEM AS WELL, HIS EYES LIT UP. FROM THEN ON, WE'D SPEND ALL OF OUR FREE TIME BLASTING MUSIC BACK AND FORTH. KEENAN TRIED TO GET ME INTO AS MANY BANDS AS POSSIBLE. WE'D SWAP MIXTAPES & WATCH HORROR MOVIES. "LIKE TROMA & HENENLOTTER FILMS" RESEARCHING HOW THE DIRECTORS, ACTORS, WRITERS & SOUNDTRACKS, ETC. WERE ALL CONNECTED ONE WAY OR ANOTHER.
OUR WORLD WAS EXPANDING! THE TWO OF US WOULD ABSORB ALL THE INFORMATION LIKE SPONGES.

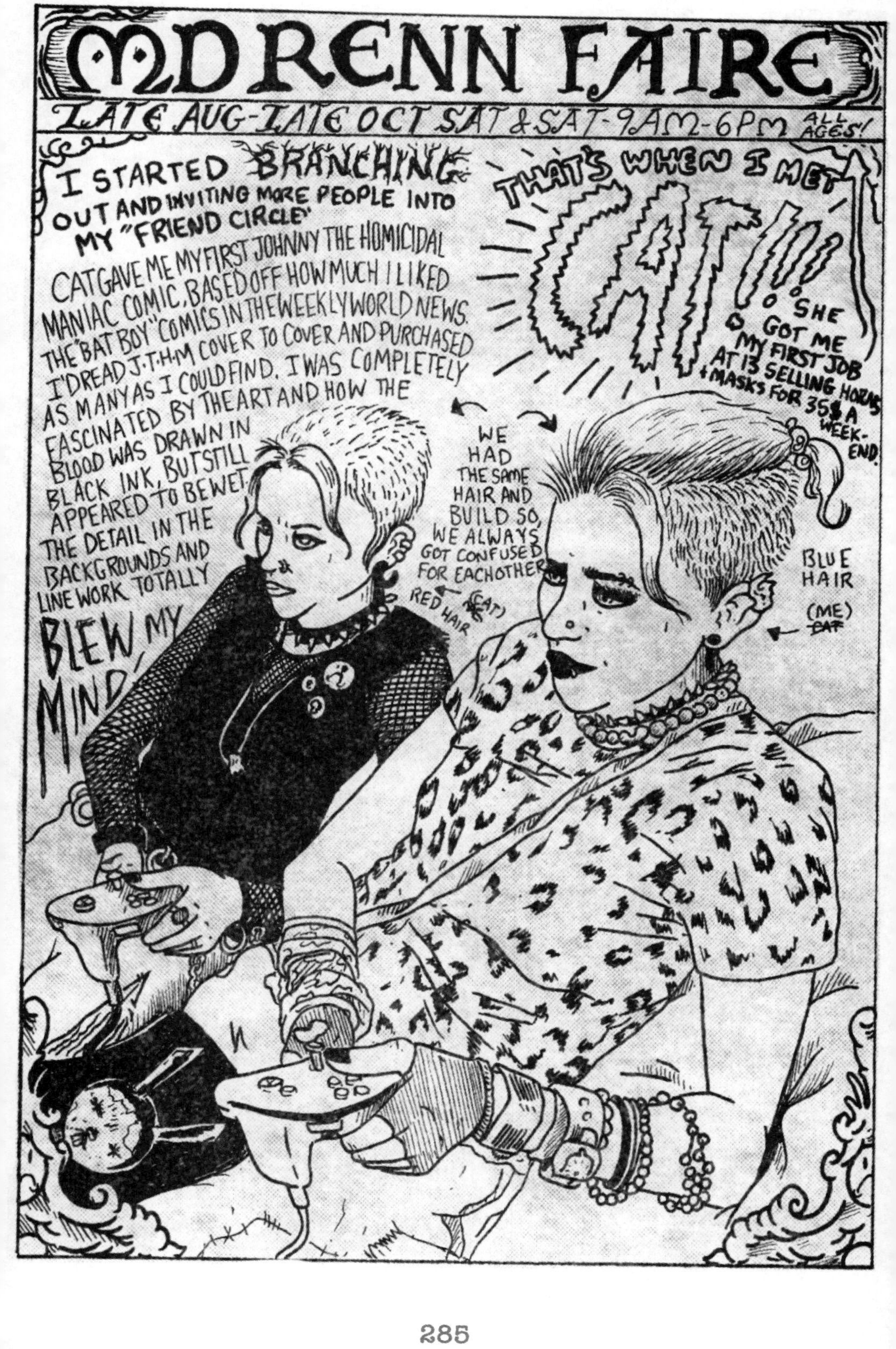
MDRENN FAIRE
LATE AUG-LATE OCT SAT & SAT-9AM-6PM ALL AGES!
I STARTED BRANCHING OUT AND INVITING MORE PEOPLE INTO MY "FRIEND CIRCLE"
CAT GAVE ME MY FIRST JOHNNY THE HOMICIDAL MANIAC COMIC, BASED OFF HOW MUCH I LIKED THE "BAT BOY" COMICS IN THE WEEKLY WORLD NEWS. I'D READ J.T.H.M COVER TO COVER AND PURCHASED AS MANY AS I COULD FIND. I WAS COMPLETELY FASCINATED BY THE ART AND HOW THE BLOOD WAS DRAWN IN BLACK INK, BUT STILL APPEARED TO BE WET. THE DETAIL IN THE BACKGROUNDS AND LINE WORK TOTALLY BLEW MY MIND.
THAT'S WHEN I MET CAT!!
SHE GOT ME MY FIRST JOB AT 13 SELLING HORNS + MASKS FOR 35$ A WEEK-END.
WE HAD THE SAME HAIR AND BUILD SO, WE ALWAYS GOT CONFUSED FOR EACHOTHER
RED HAIR (CAT)
BLUE HAIR (ME) BAT

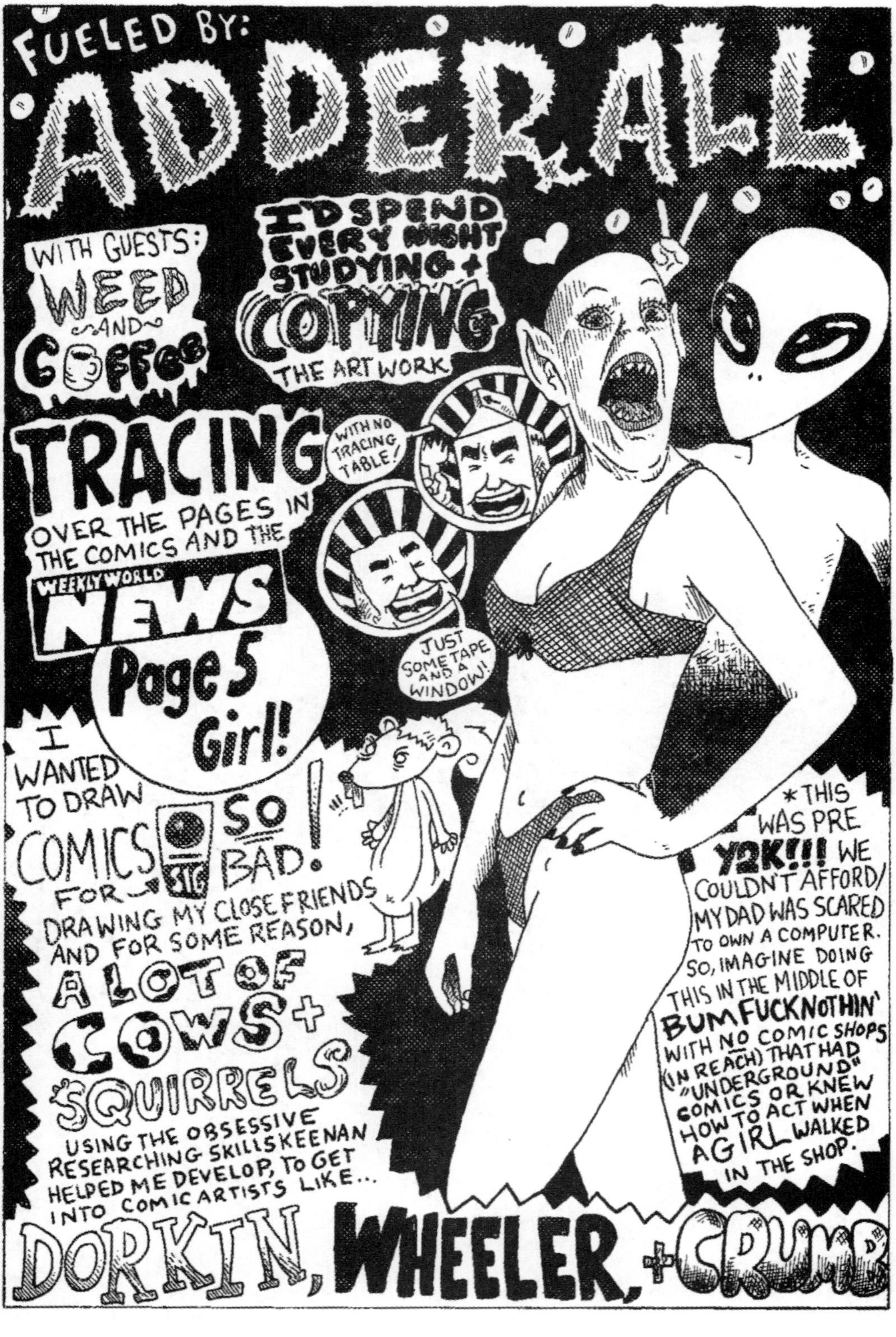
FUELED BY:
ADDERALL
WITH GUESTS: WEED AND COFFEE
I'D SPEND EVERY NIGHT STUDYING + COPYING THE ART WORK
TRACING OVER THE PAGES IN THE COMICS AND THE WEEKLY WORLD NEWS Page 5 Girl!
WITH NO TRACING TABLE!
JUST SOME TAPE AND A WINDOW!
I WANTED TO DRAW COMICS SO BAD! FOR → DRAWING MY CLOSE FRIENDS AND FOR SOME REASON, A LOT OF COWS + SQUIRRELS
USING THE OBSESSIVE RESEARCHING SKILLS KEENAN HELPED ME DEVELOP, TO GET INTO COMIC ARTISTS LIKE...
* THIS WAS PRE Y2K!!! WE COULDN'T AFFORD/ MY DAD WAS SCARED TO OWN A COMPUTER. SO, IMAGINE DOING THIS IN THE MIDDLE OF BUMFUCKNOTHIN' WITH NO COMIC SHOPS (IN REACH) THAT HAD "UNDERGROUND" COMICS OR KNEW HOW TO ACT WHEN A GIRL WALKED IN THE SHOP.
DORKIN, WHEELER, + CRUMB

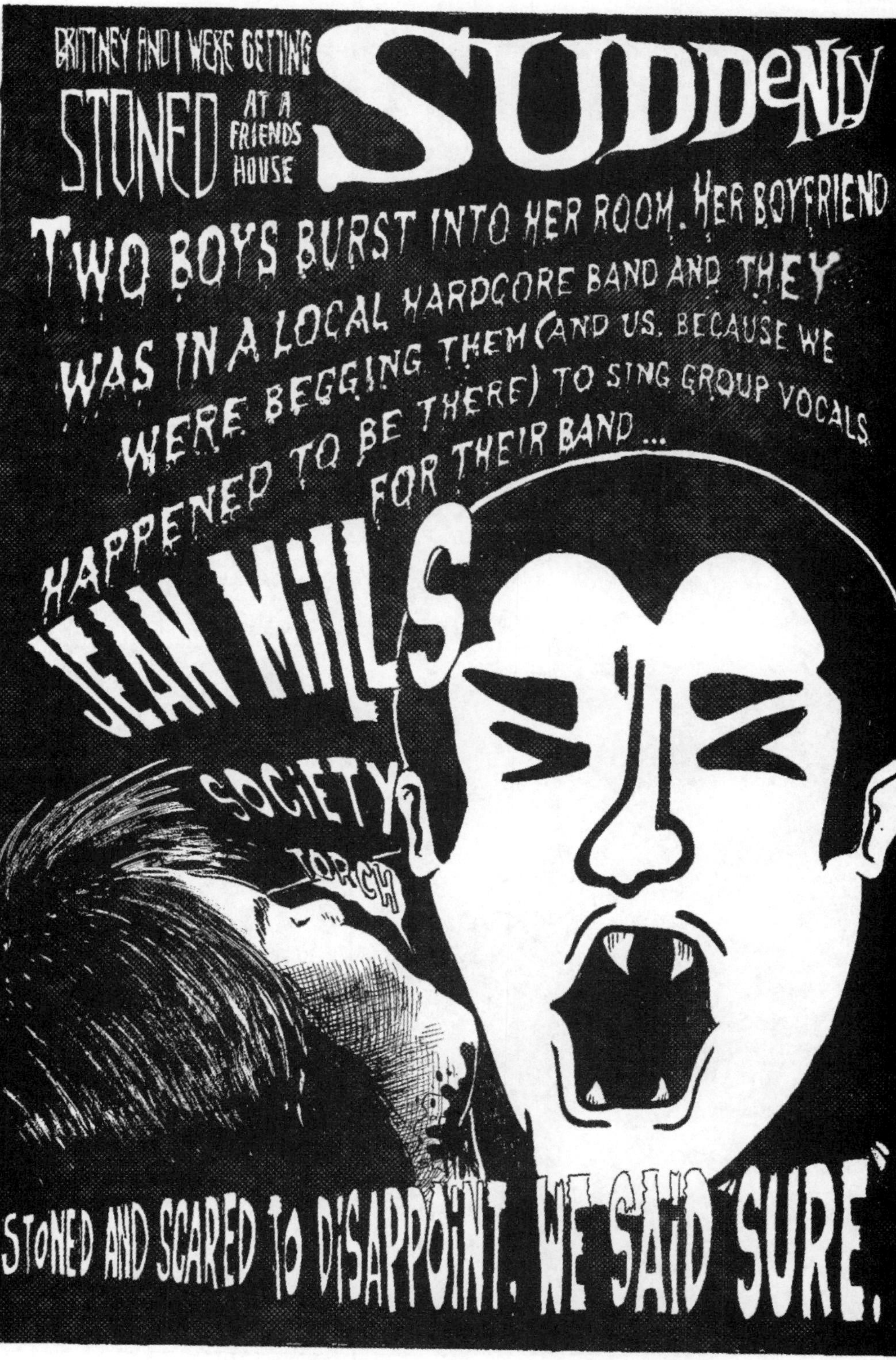
BRITTNEY AND I WERE GETTING STONED AT A FRIENDS HOUSE
SUDDENLY
TWO BOYS BURST INTO HER ROOM. HER BOYFRIEND WAS IN A LOCAL HARDCORE BAND AND THEY WERE BEGGING THEM (AND US, BECAUSE WE HAPPENED TO BE THERE) TO SING GROUP VOCALS FOR THEIR BAND...
JEAN MILLS SOCIETY
TORCH
STONED AND SCARED TO DISAPPOINT. WE SAID "SURE."

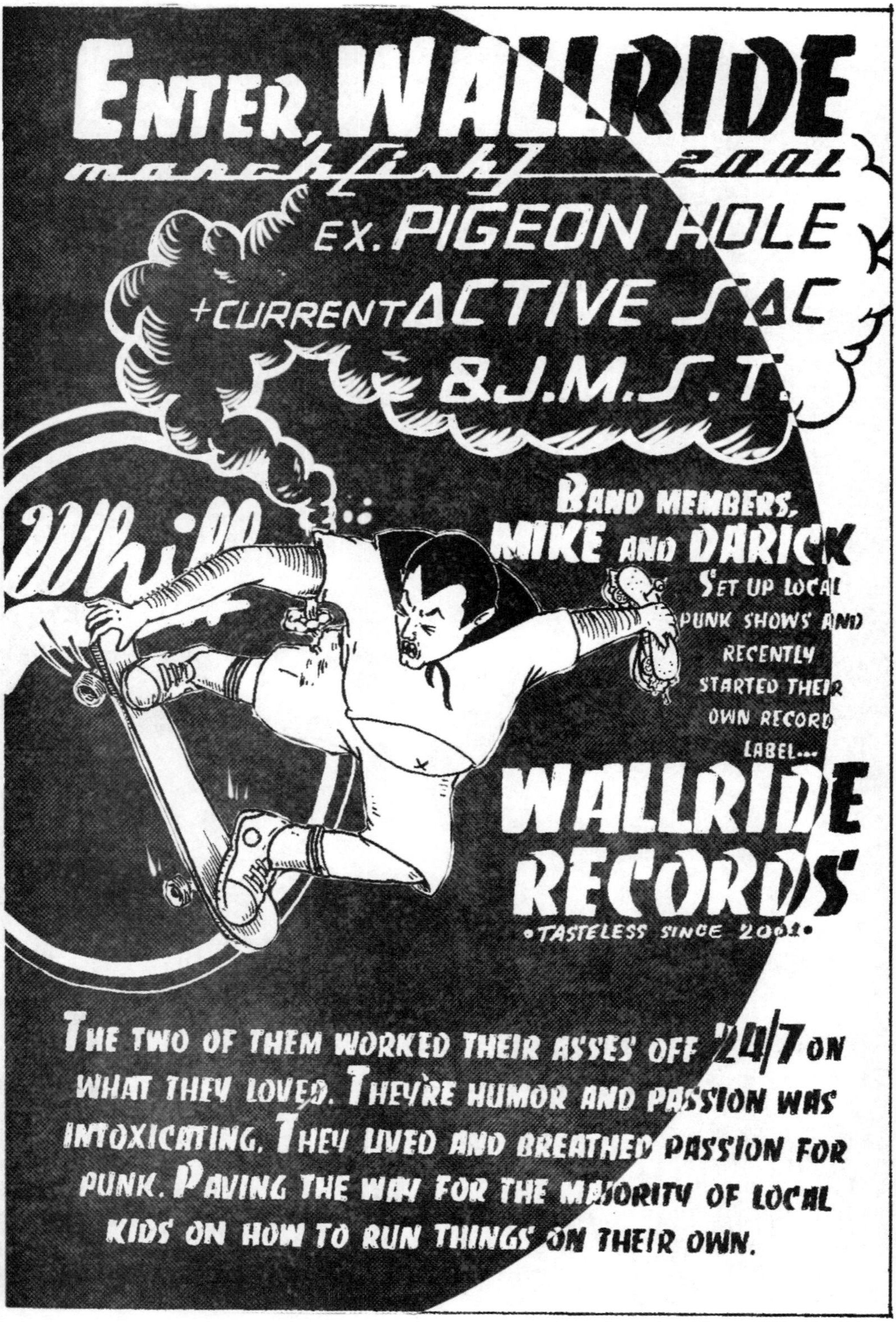
ENTER, WALLRIDE
march[ish] 2001
EX. PIGEON HOLE
+CURRENT ACTIVE SAC
&J.M.S.T.
BAND MEMBERS, MIKE AND DARICK SET UP LOCAL PUNK SHOWS AND RECENTLY STARTED THEIR OWN RECORD LABEL...
WALLRIDE RECORDS
•TASTELESS SINCE 2001•
THE TWO OF THEM WORKED THEIR ASSES OFF 24/7 ON WHAT THEY LOVED. THEY'RE HUMOR AND PASSION WAS INTOXICATING. THEY LIVED AND BREATHED PASSION FOR PUNK. PAVING THE WAY FOR THE MAJORITY OF LOCAL KIDS ON HOW TO RUN THINGS ON THEIR OWN.

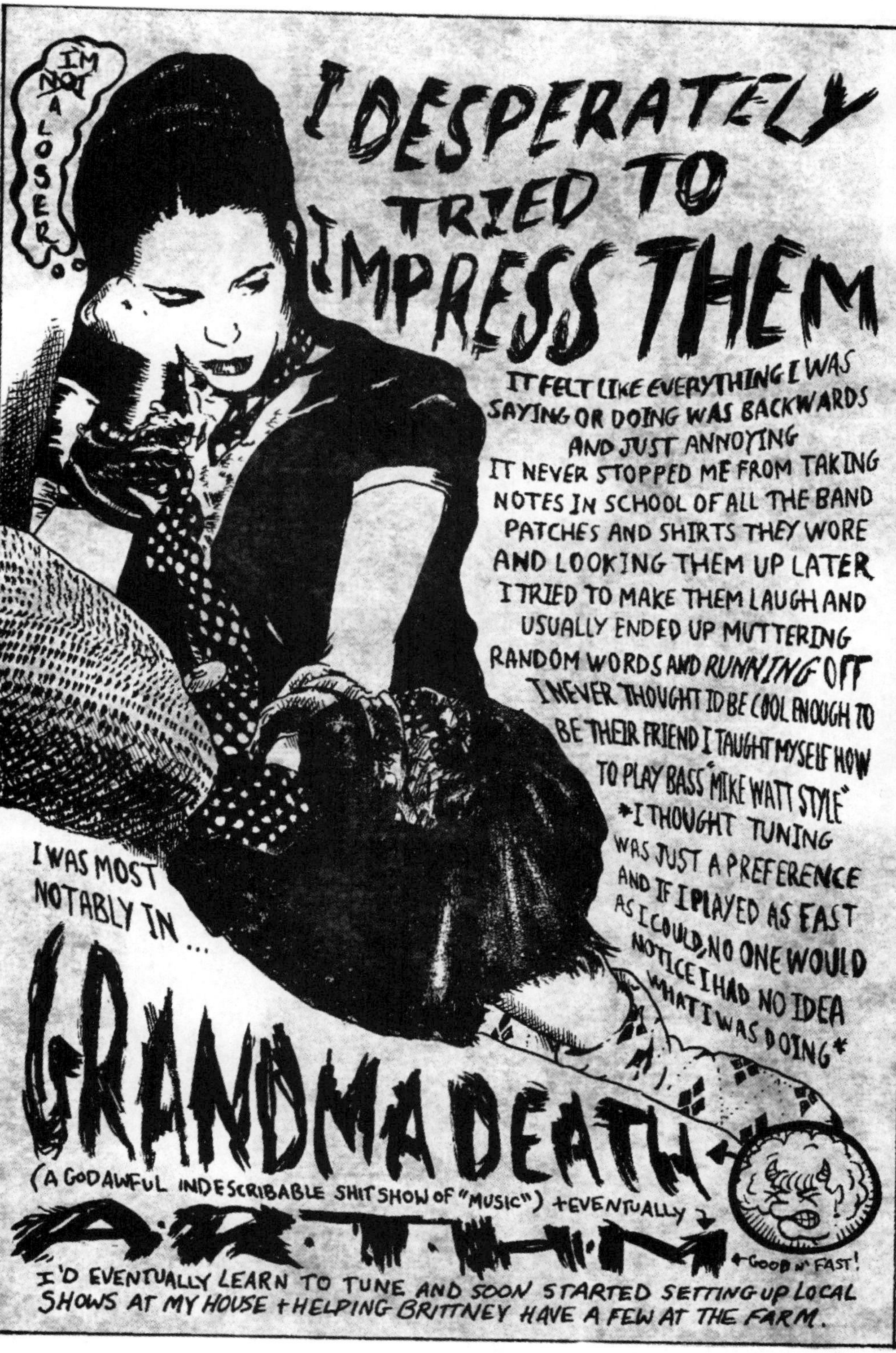
I'M NOT A LOSER
I DESPERATELY TRIED TO IMPRESS THEM
IT FELT LIKE EVERYTHING I WAS SAYING OR DOING WAS BACKWARDS AND JUST ANNOYING
IT NEVER STOPPED ME FROM TAKING NOTES IN SCHOOL OF ALL THE BAND PATCHES AND SHIRTS THEY WORE AND LOOKING THEM UP LATER
I TRIED TO MAKE THEM LAUGH AND USUALLY ENDED UP MUTTERING RANDOM WORDS AND RUNNING OFF
I NEVER THOUGHT ID BE COOL ENOUGH TO BE THEIR FRIEND I TAUGHT MYSELF HOW TO PLAY BASS "MIKE WATT STYLE"
I THOUGHT TUNING WAS JUST A PREFERENCE AND IF I PLAYED AS FAST AS I COULD, NO ONE WOULD NOTICE I HAD NO IDEA WHAT I WAS DOING
I WAS MOST NOTABLY IN...
GRANDMA DEATH
(A GODAWFUL INDESCRIBABLE SHIT SHOW OF "MUSIC") +EVENTUALLY
A.R.T.H.M
←GOOD N' FAST!
I'D EVENTUALLY LEARN TO TUNE AND SOON STARTED SETTING UP LOCAL SHOWS AT MY HOUSE + HELPING BRITTNEY HAVE A FEW AT THE FARM.

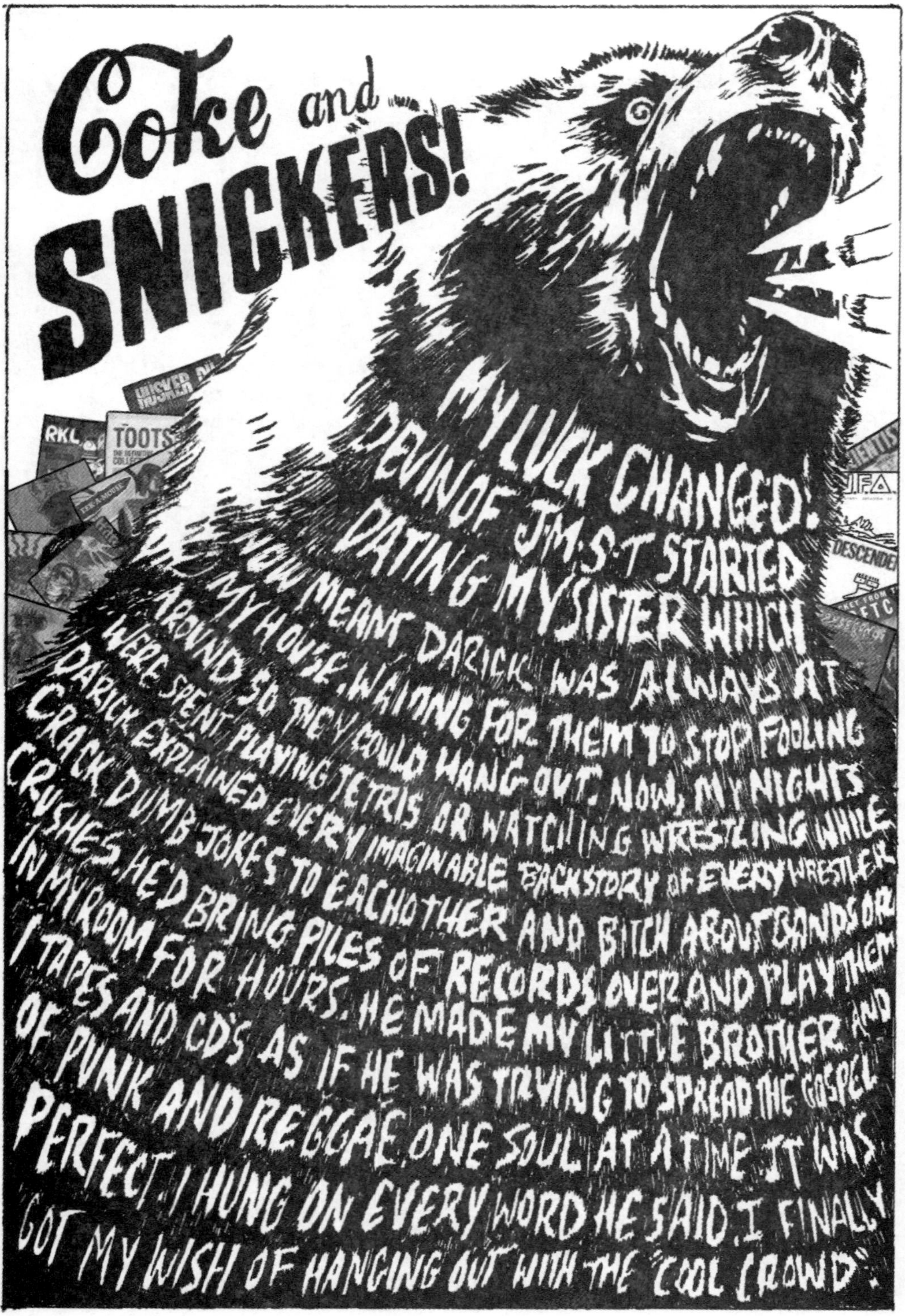
Coke and SNICKERS!
MY LUCK CHANGED!
DEVIN OF J.M.S.T STARTED
DATING MY SISTER WHICH
NOW MEANT DARICK WAS ALWAYS AT
MY HOUSE, WAITING FOR THEM TO STOP FOOLING
AROUND SO THEY COULD HANG OUT. NOW, MY NIGHTS
WERE SPENT PLAYING TETRIS OR WATCHING WRESTLING WHILE
DARICK EXPLAINED EVERY IMAGINABLE BACKSTORY OF EVERY WRESTLER.
CRACK DUMB JOKES TO EACH OTHER AND BITCH ABOUT BANDS OR
CRUSHES. HE'D BRING PILES OF RECORDS OVER AND PLAY THEM
IN MY ROOM FOR HOURS. HE MADE MY LITTLE BROTHER AND
I TAPES AND CD'S AS IF HE WAS TRYING TO SPREAD THE GOSPEL
OF PUNK AND REGGAE ONE SOUL AT A TIME. IT WAS
PERFECT. I HUNG ON EVERY WORD HE SAID. I FINALLY
GOT MY WISH OF HANGING OUT WITH THE "COOL CROWD".
RKL
TOOTS

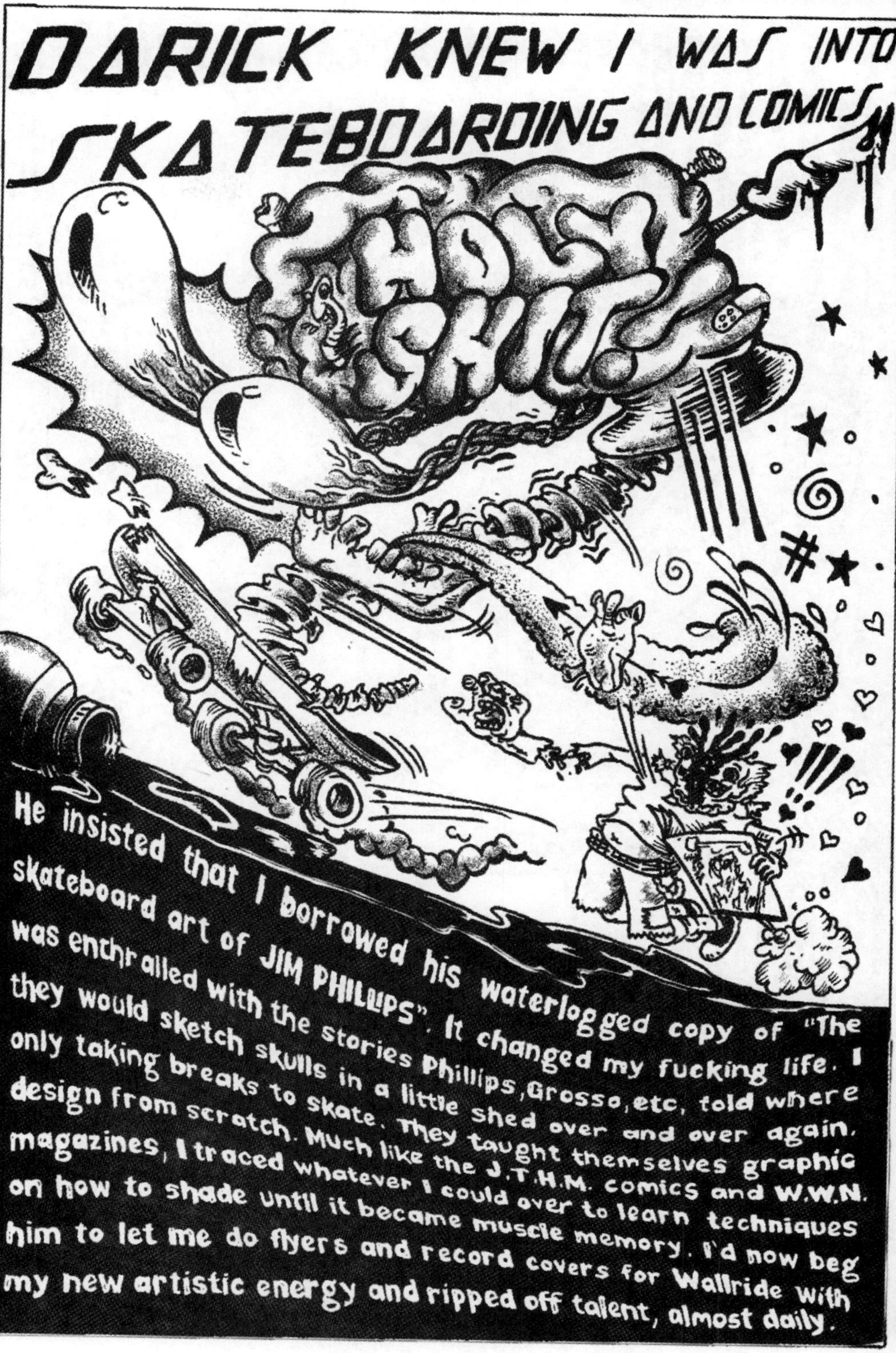
DARICK KNEW I WAS INTO SKATEBOARDING AND COMICS
HOLY SHIT.
He insisted that I borrowed his waterlogged copy of "The
skateboard art of JIM PHILLIPS". It changed my fucking life. I
was enthralled with the stories Phillips, Grosso, etc, told where
they would sketch skulls in a little shed over and over again,
only taking breaks to skate. They taught themselves graphic
design from scratch. Much like the J.T.H.M. comics and W.W.N.
magazines, I traced whatever I could over to learn techniques
on how to shade until it became muscle memory. I'd now beg
him to let me do flyers and record covers for Wallride with
my new artistic energy and ripped off talent, almost daily.

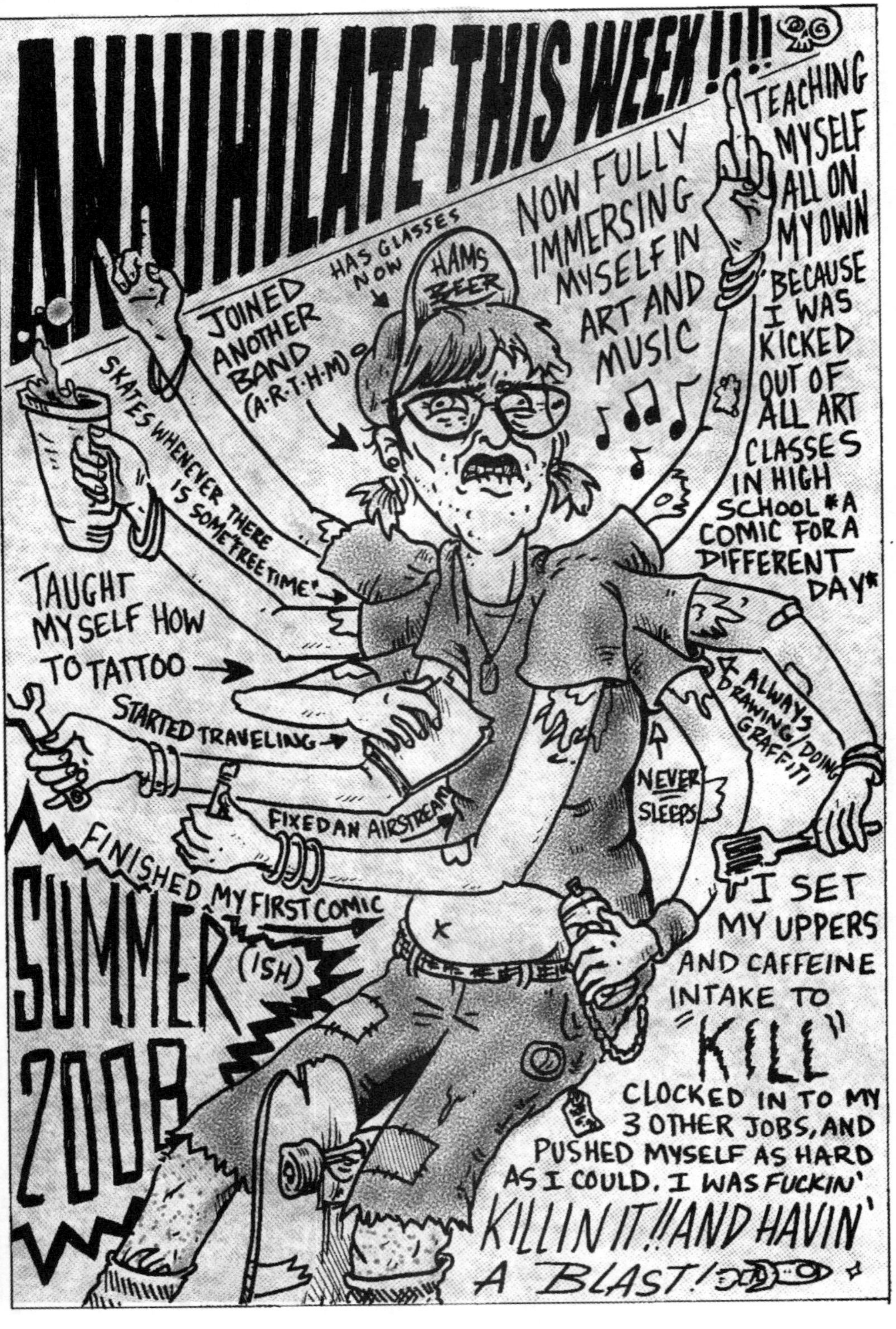
ANNIHILATE THIS WEEK!!!!
HAS GLASSES NOW
HAMS BEER
JOINED ANOTHER BAND (A·R·T·H·M)
NOW FULLY IMMERSING MYSELF IN ART AND MUSIC
TEACHING MYSELF ALL ON MY OWN "BECAUSE I WAS KICKED OUT OF ALL ART CLASSES IN HIGH SCHOOL *A COMIC FOR A DIFFERENT DAY*
SKATES WHENEVER THERE IS SOME "FREE TIME"
TAUGHT MYSELF HOW TO TATTOO
STARTED TRAVELING
ALWAYS DRAWING/DOING GRAFFITI
NEVER SLEEPS
FIXED AN AIRSTREAM
FINISHED MY FIRST COMIC
SUMMER (ISH) 2008
I SET MY UPPERS AND CAFFEINE INTAKE TO "KILL"
CLOCKED IN TO MY 3 OTHER JOBS, AND PUSHED MYSELF AS HARD AS I COULD. I WAS FUCKIN' KILLIN IT!! AND HAVIN' A BLAST!

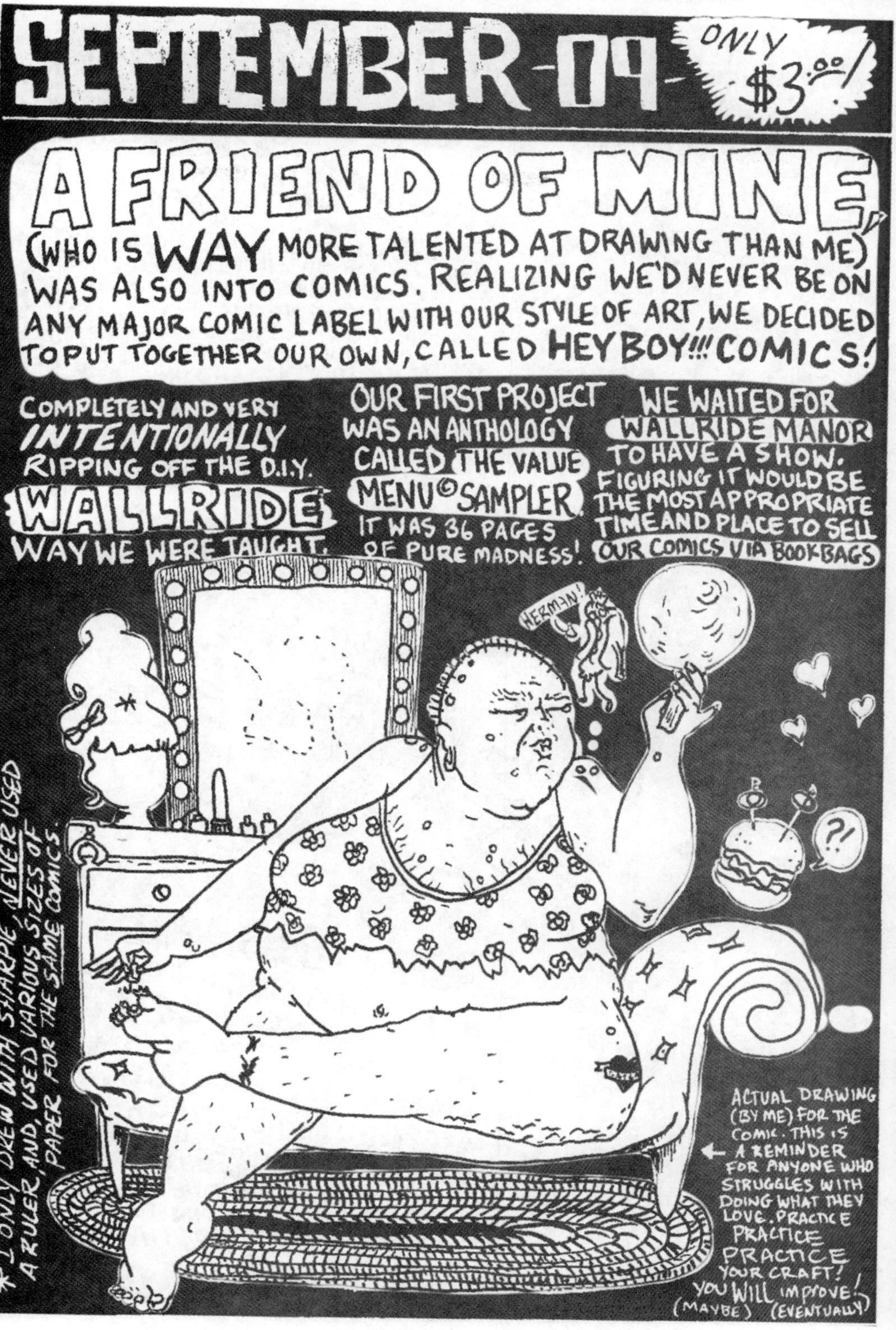
SEPTEMBER -09-
ONLY $3.00!
A FRIEND OF MINE, (WHO IS WAY MORE TALENTED AT DRAWING THAN ME) WAS ALSO INTO COMICS. REALIZING WE'D NEVER BE ON ANY MAJOR COMIC LABEL WITH OUR STYLE OF ART, WE DECIDED TO PUT TOGETHER OUR OWN, CALLED HEY BOY!!! COMICS!
COMPLETELY AND VERY INTENTIONALLY RIPPING OFF THE D.I.Y. WALLRIDE WAY WE WERE TAUGHT.
OUR FIRST PROJECT WAS AN ANTHOLOGY CALLED THE VALUE MENU© SAMPLER. IT WAS 36 PAGES OF PURE MADNESS!
WE WAITED FOR WALLRIDE MANOR TO HAVE A SHOW. FIGURING IT WOULD BE THE MOST APPROPRIATE TIME AND PLACE TO SELL OUR COMICS VIA BOOKBAGS
HERMAN!
?!
* I ONLY DREW WITH SHARPIE, NEVER USED A RULER, AND, USED VARIOUS SIZES OF PAPER FOR THE SAME COMICS.
ACTUAL DRAWING (BY ME) FOR THE COMIC. THIS IS A REMINDER FOR ANYONE WHO STRUGGLES WITH DOING WHAT THEY LOVE. PRACTICE PRACTICE PRACTICE YOUR CRAFT! YOU WILL improve! (MAYBE) (EVENTUALLY)

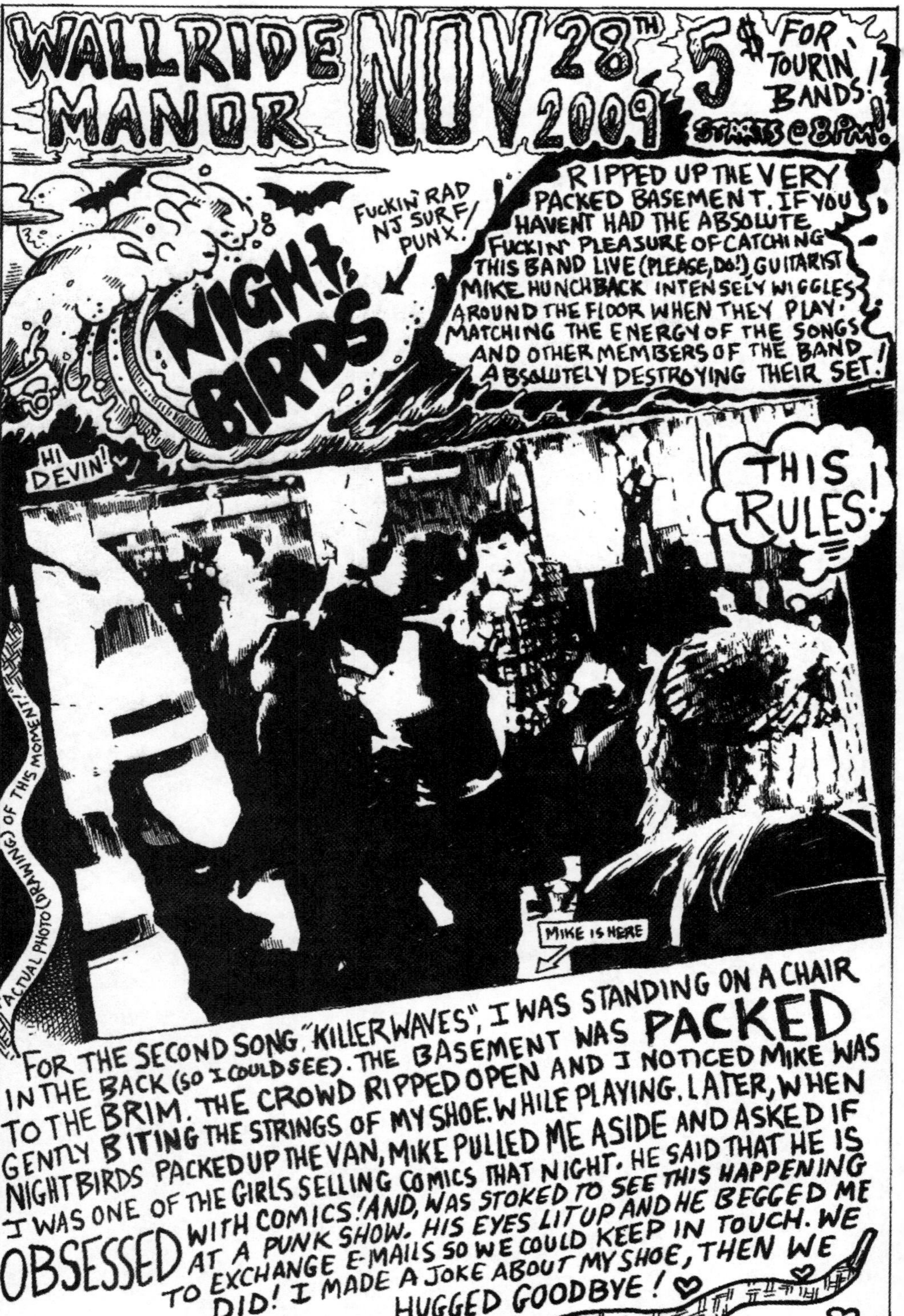

WALLRIDE MANOR
NOV 28TH 2009
5$ FOR TOURIN' BANDS!
STARTS @ 8PM!
FUCKIN' RAD NJ SURF/PUNX!
NIGHT BIRDS
RIPPED UP THE VERY PACKED BASEMENT. IF YOU HAVENT HAD THE ABSOLUTE FUCKIN' PLEASURE OF CATCHING THIS BAND LIVE (PLEASE, DO!), GUITARIST MIKE HUNCHBACK INTENSELY WIGGLES AROUND THE FLOOR WHEN THEY PLAY. MATCHING THE ENERGY OF THE SONGS AND OTHER MEMBERS OF THE BAND ABSOLUTELY DESTROYING THEIR SET!
HI DEVIN!
THIS RULES!
ACTUAL PHOTO (DRAWING) OF THIS MOMENT!
MIKE IS HERE
FOR THE SECOND SONG "KILLER WAVES", I WAS STANDING ON A CHAIR IN THE BACK (SO I COULD SEE). THE BASEMENT WAS PACKED TO THE BRIM. THE CROWD RIPPED OPEN AND I NOTICED MIKE WAS GENTLY BITING THE STRINGS OF MY SHOE WHILE PLAYING. LATER, WHEN NIGHT BIRDS PACKED UP THE VAN, MIKE PULLED ME ASIDE AND ASKED IF I WAS ONE OF THE GIRLS SELLING COMICS THAT NIGHT. HE SAID THAT HE IS OBSESSED WITH COMICS! AND, WAS STOKED TO SEE THIS HAPPENING AT A PUNK SHOW. HIS EYES LIT UP AND HE BEGGED ME TO EXCHANGE E-MAILS SO WE COULD KEEP IN TOUCH. WE DID! I MADE A JOKE ABOUT MY SHOE, THEN WE HUGGED GOODBYE!

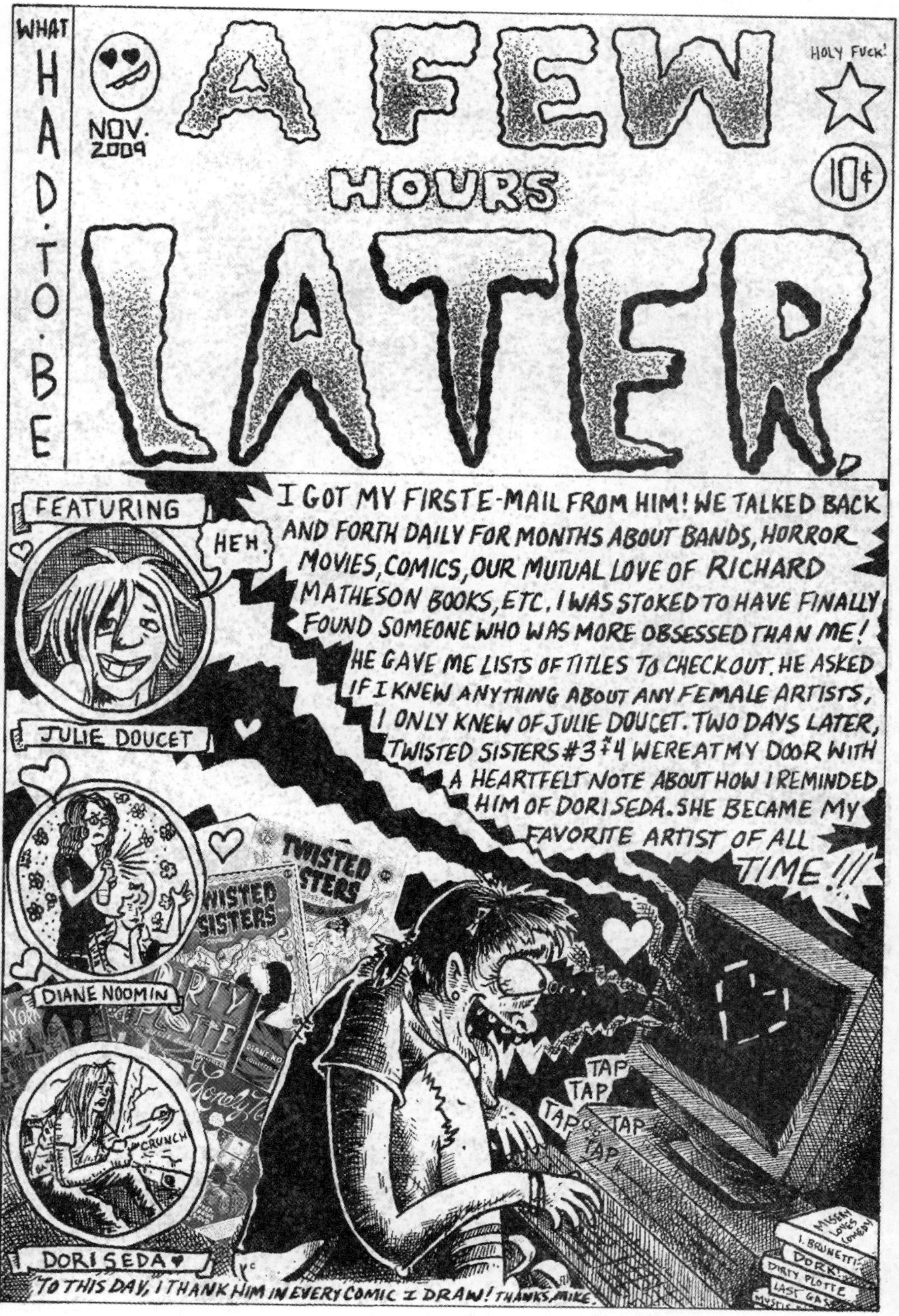
WHAT HAD TO BE
NOV. 2009
A FEW HOURS LATER,
HOLY FUCK!
10¢
FEATURING
JULIE DOUCET
HEH.
I GOT MY FIRST E-MAIL FROM HIM! WE TALKED BACK AND FORTH DAILY FOR MONTHS ABOUT BANDS, HORROR MOVIES, COMICS, OUR MUTUAL LOVE OF RICHARD MATHESON BOOKS, ETC. I WAS STOKED TO HAVE FINALLY FOUND SOMEONE WHO WAS MORE OBSESSED THAN ME! HE GAVE ME LISTS OF TITLES TO CHECK OUT. HE ASKED IF I KNEW ANYTHING ABOUT ANY FEMALE ARTISTS, I ONLY KNEW OF JULIE DOUCET. TWO DAYS LATER, TWISTED SISTERS #3 & 4 WERE AT MY DOOR WITH A HEARTFELT NOTE ABOUT HOW I REMINDED HIM OF DORI SEDA. SHE BECAME MY FAVORITE ARTIST OF ALL TIME!!!
TWISTED SISTERS
TWISTED SISTERS
DIANE NOOMIN
CRUNCH
DORI SEDA
TAP TAP TAP TAP TAP
MISERY LOVES COMEDY
I. BRUNETTI
DORK
DIRTY PLOTTE
TO THIS DAY, I THANK HIM IN EVERY COMIC I DRAW! THANKS, MIKE.

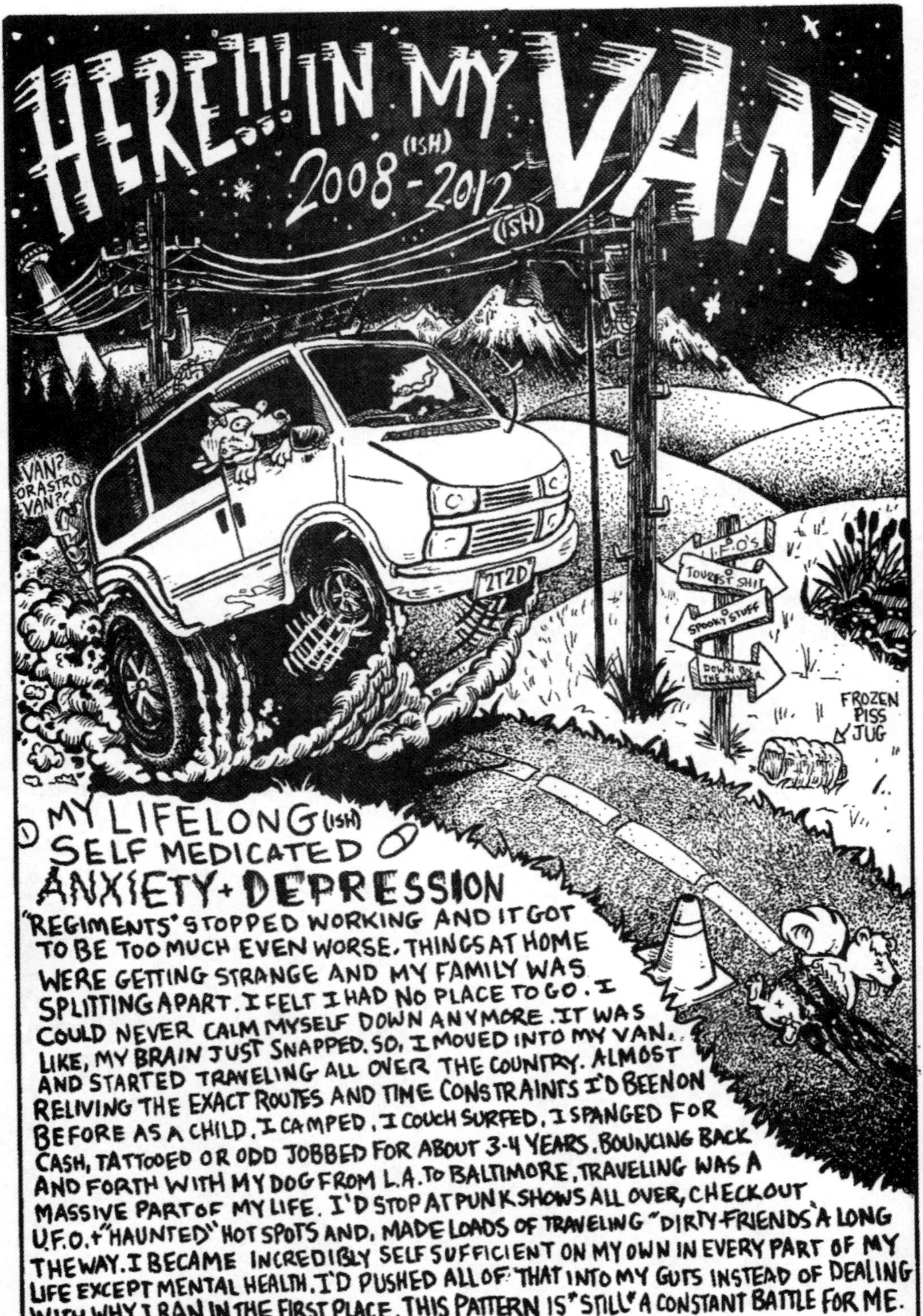
HERE!!! IN MY VAN!
2008 (ISH) - 2012 (ISH)
VAN? OR ASTRO VAN?!
2T2D
U.F.O'S
TOURIST SHIT
SPOOKY STUFF
FROZEN PISS JUG
① MY LIFELONG (ISH) SELF MEDICATED ANXIETY + DEPRESSION
"REGIMENTS" STOPPED WORKING AND IT GOT
TO BE TOO MUCH EVEN WORSE. THINGS AT HOME
WERE GETTING STRANGE AND MY FAMILY WAS
SPLITTING APART. I FELT I HAD NO PLACE TO GO. I
COULD NEVER CALM MYSELF DOWN ANYMORE. IT WAS
LIKE, MY BRAIN JUST SNAPPED. SO, I MOVED INTO MY VAN.
AND STARTED TRAVELING ALL OVER THE COUNTRY. ALMOST
RELIVING THE EXACT ROUTES AND TIME CONSTRAINTS I'D BEEN ON
BEFORE AS A CHILD. I CAMPED, I COUCH SURFED, I SPANGED FOR
CASH, TATTOOED OR ODD JOBBED FOR ABOUT 3-4 YEARS. BOUNCING BACK
AND FORTH WITH MY DOG FROM L.A. TO BALTIMORE, TRAVELING WAS A
MASSIVE PART OF MY LIFE. I'D STOP AT PUNK SHOWS ALL OVER, CHECK OUT
U.F.O. + "HAUNTED" HOT SPOTS AND, MADE LOADS OF TRAVELING "DIRTY FRIENDS" A LONG
THE WAY. I BECAME INCREDIBLY SELF SUFFICIENT ON MY OWN IN EVERY PART OF MY
LIFE EXCEPT MENTAL HEALTH. I'D PUSHED ALL OF THAT INTO MY GUTS INSTEAD OF DEALING
WITH WHY I RAN IN THE FIRST PLACE. THIS PATTERN IS "STILL" A CONSTANT BATTLE FOR ME.

15th of August 2012 BALTIMORE

I'd finally crash landed in a place that felt like my true home. I fell in love with Baltimore immediately. It was close enough to the local scene I grew up around that I had instant connections for work and a place to live. A friend that had lived in a diy venue hooked me up with a job doing dishes and learning to bartend at a dive bar, Club Charles. After getting reacquainted with the Baltimore scene, I started to draw for bands and venues again.

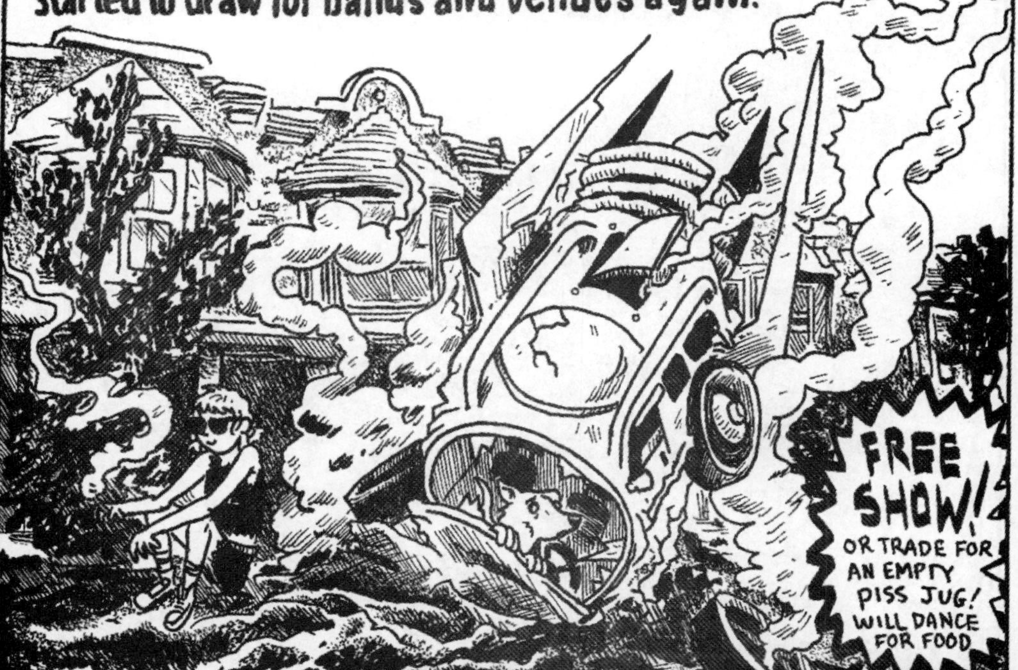
FREE SHOW!
OR TRADE FOR AN EMPTY PISS JUG! WILL DANCE FOR FOOD

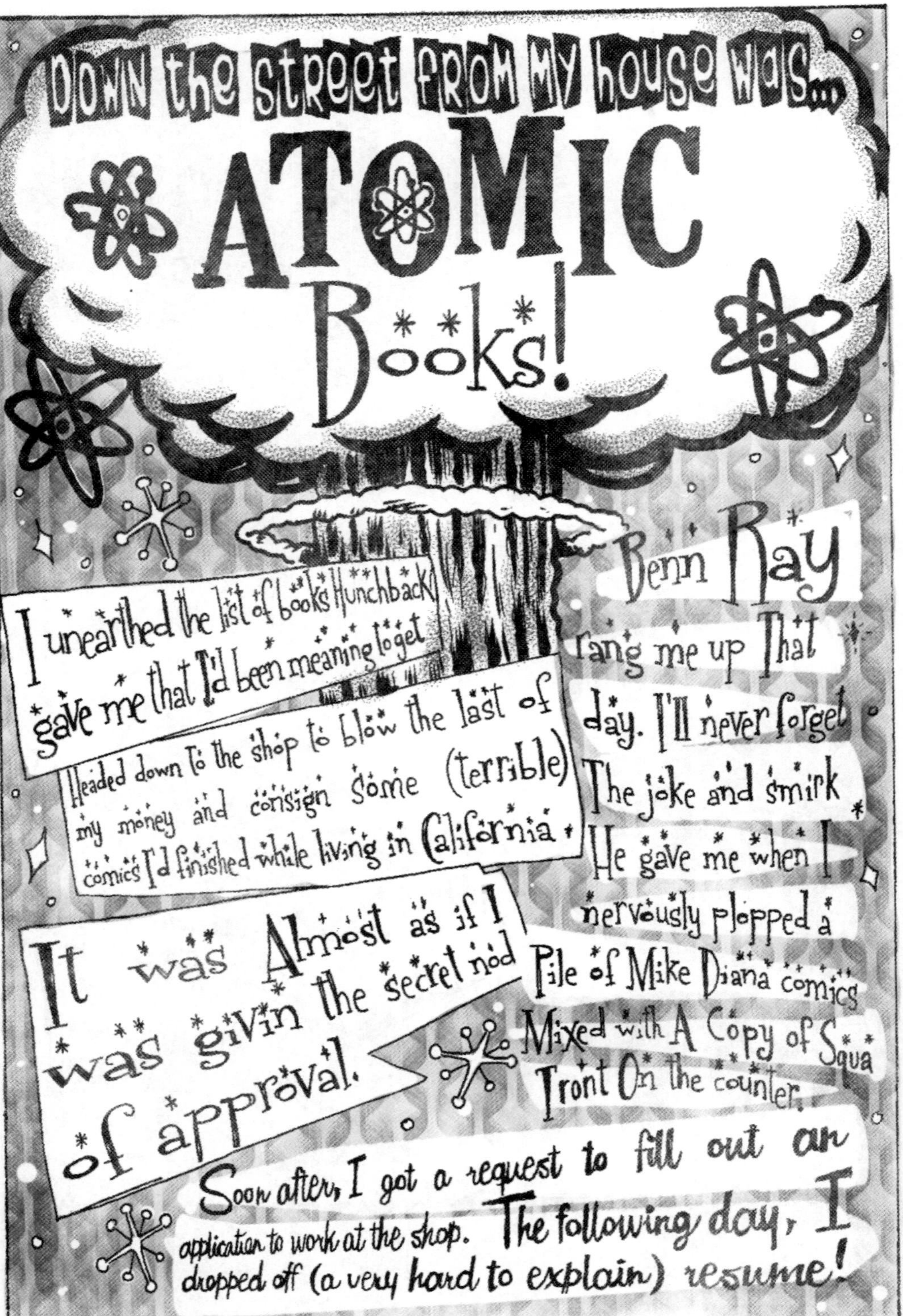

Down the street from my house was...
ATOMIC Books!
I unearthed the list of books Hunchback gave me that I'd been meaning to get.
Headed down to the shop to blow the last of my money and consign some (terrible) comics I'd finished while living in California.
Benn Ray rang me up that day. I'll never forget the joke and smirk he gave me when I nervously plopped a pile of Mike Diana comics mixed with a copy of Squa Tront on the counter.
It was almost as if I was givin the secret nod of approval.
Soon after, I got a request to fill out an application to work at the shop. The following day, I dropped off (a very hard to explain) resume!

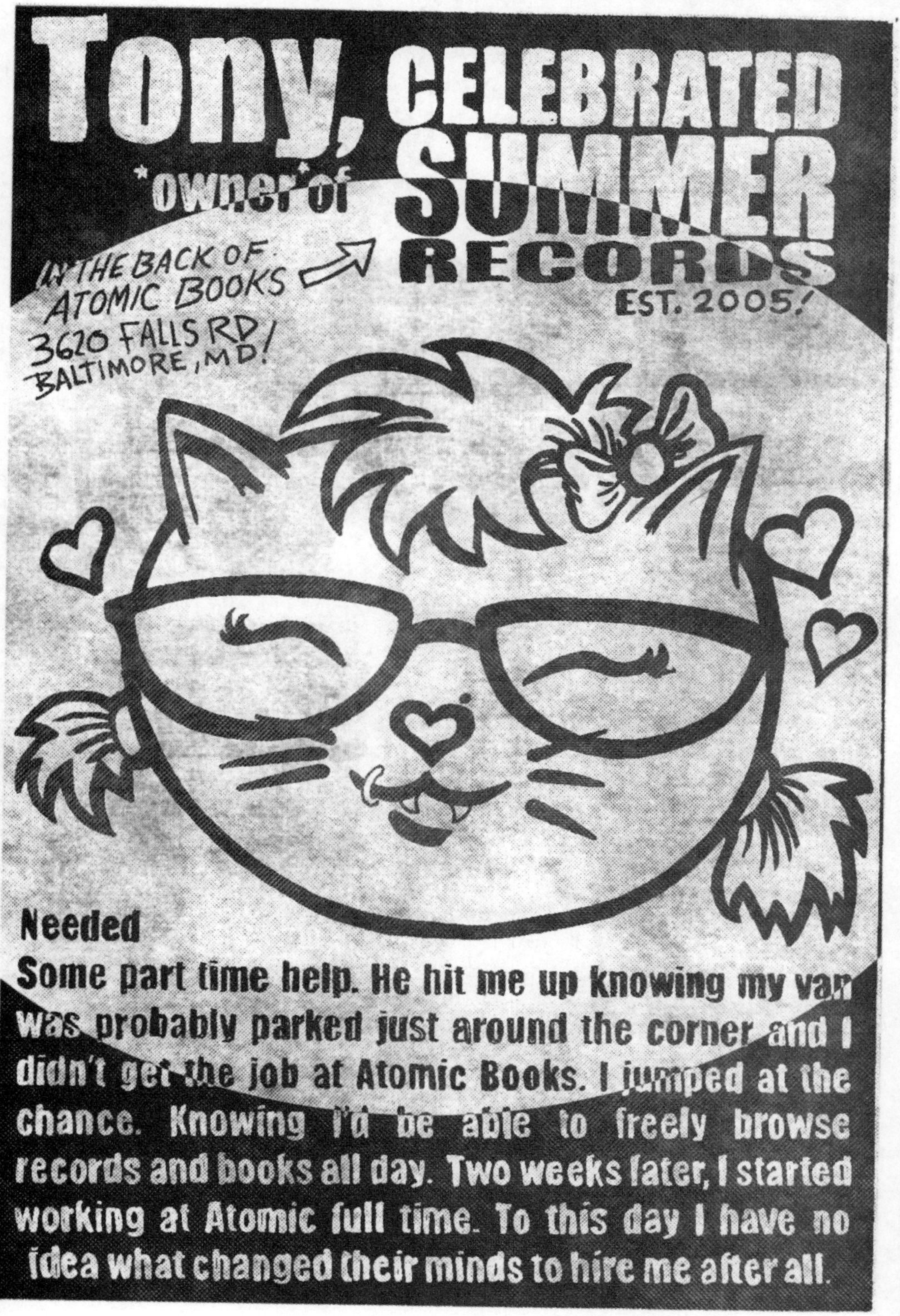
Tony, *owner* of
CELEBRATED SUMMER RECORDS
EST. 2005!
IN THE BACK OF ATOMIC BOOKS 3620 FALLS RD! BALTIMORE, MD!
Needed
Some part time help. He hit me up knowing my van was probably parked just around the corner and I didn't get the job at Atomic Books. I jumped at the chance. Knowing I'd be able to freely browse records and books all day. Two weeks later, I started working at Atomic full time. To this day I have no idea what changed their minds to hire me after all.

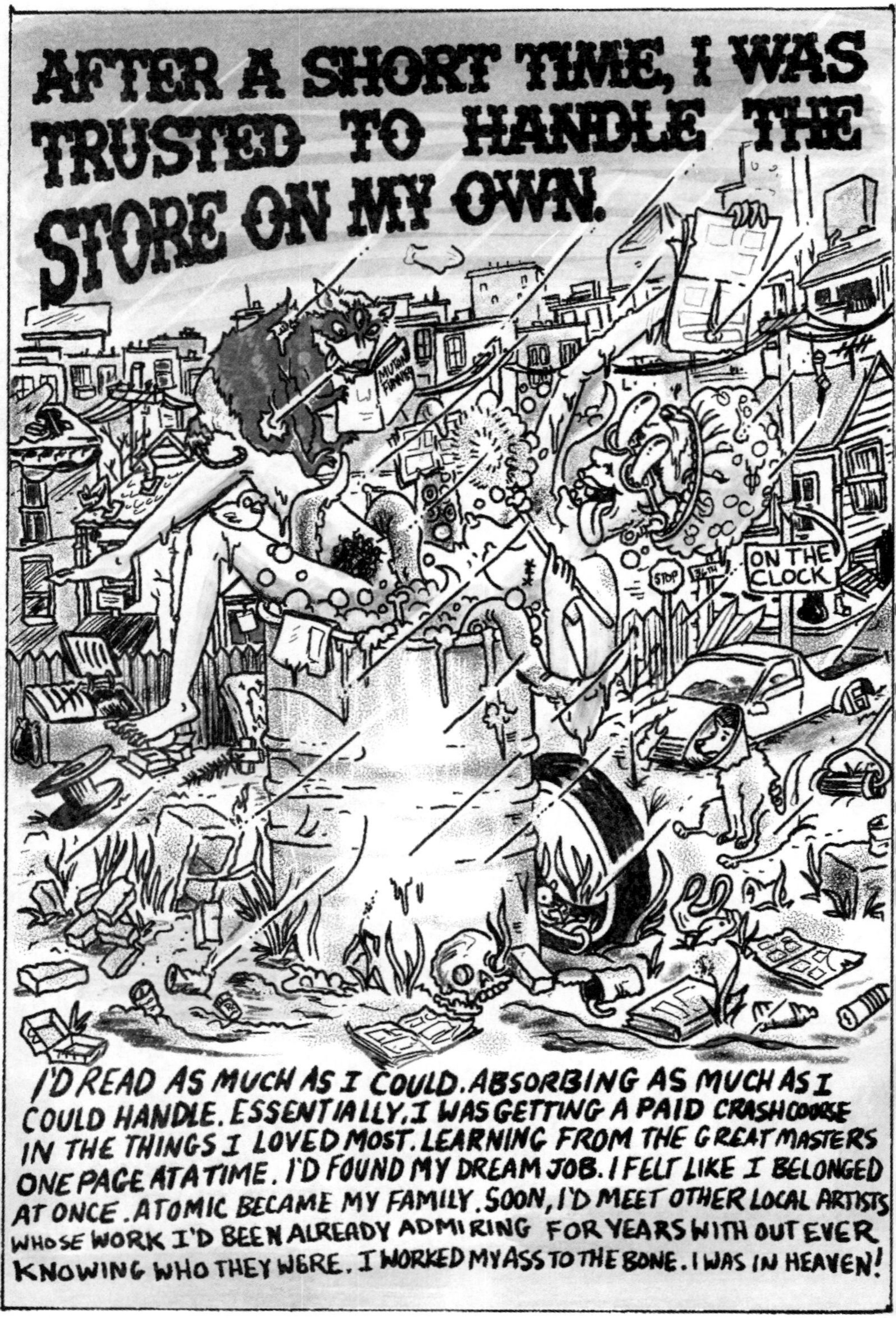
AFTER A SHORT TIME, I WAS TRUSTED TO HANDLE THE STORE ON MY OWN.
STOP
ON THE CLOCK
I'D READ AS MUCH AS I COULD. ABSORBING AS MUCH AS I COULD HANDLE. ESSENTIALLY, I WAS GETTING A PAID CRASH COURSE IN THE THINGS I LOVED MOST. LEARNING FROM THE GREAT MASTERS ONE PAGE AT A TIME. I'D FOUND MY DREAM JOB. I FELT LIKE I BELONGED AT ONCE. ATOMIC BECAME MY FAMILY. SOON, I'D MEET OTHER LOCAL ARTISTS WHOSE WORK I'D BEEN ALREADY ADMIRING FOR YEARS WITH OUT EVER KNOWING WHO THEY WERE. I WORKED MY ASS TO THE BONE. I WAS IN HEAVEN!

ATOMIC SUPER CHARGED MY DRIVE TO DRAW COMICS FULL TIME. BUT THEY HAD TO BE BETTER. I HAD TO MAKE ATOMIC PROUD, AND GO TO CONVENTIONS LIKE A TOURING BAND!

I GOT PROMOTED TO CONSIGNMENT MANAGER WHICH INTRODUCED ME TO MORE ARTISTS LIKE, NOAH VAN SCIVER, JOSH BAYER, SARA LAUTMAN AND SO ON...

THE MAIN PROBLEM I HAD WAS THE ONLY COMIC IDEA I HAD WAS FOR A DISGUSTING HOT DOG NAMED HERMAN. I HAD YET TO TAP INTO WHAT I FELT WERE "REAL" COMICS. I STARTED DABBLING INTO AUTO BIO COMICS AND POSTING THEM ONLINE ONCE A WEEK. IT WAS MOSTLY SHIT ABOUT HOW LONELY I FELT OR STUFF FROM WORK. TRYING MY BEST TO NOT RIP OFF TONY'S THEN GIRLFRIEND, LIZ PRINCE.

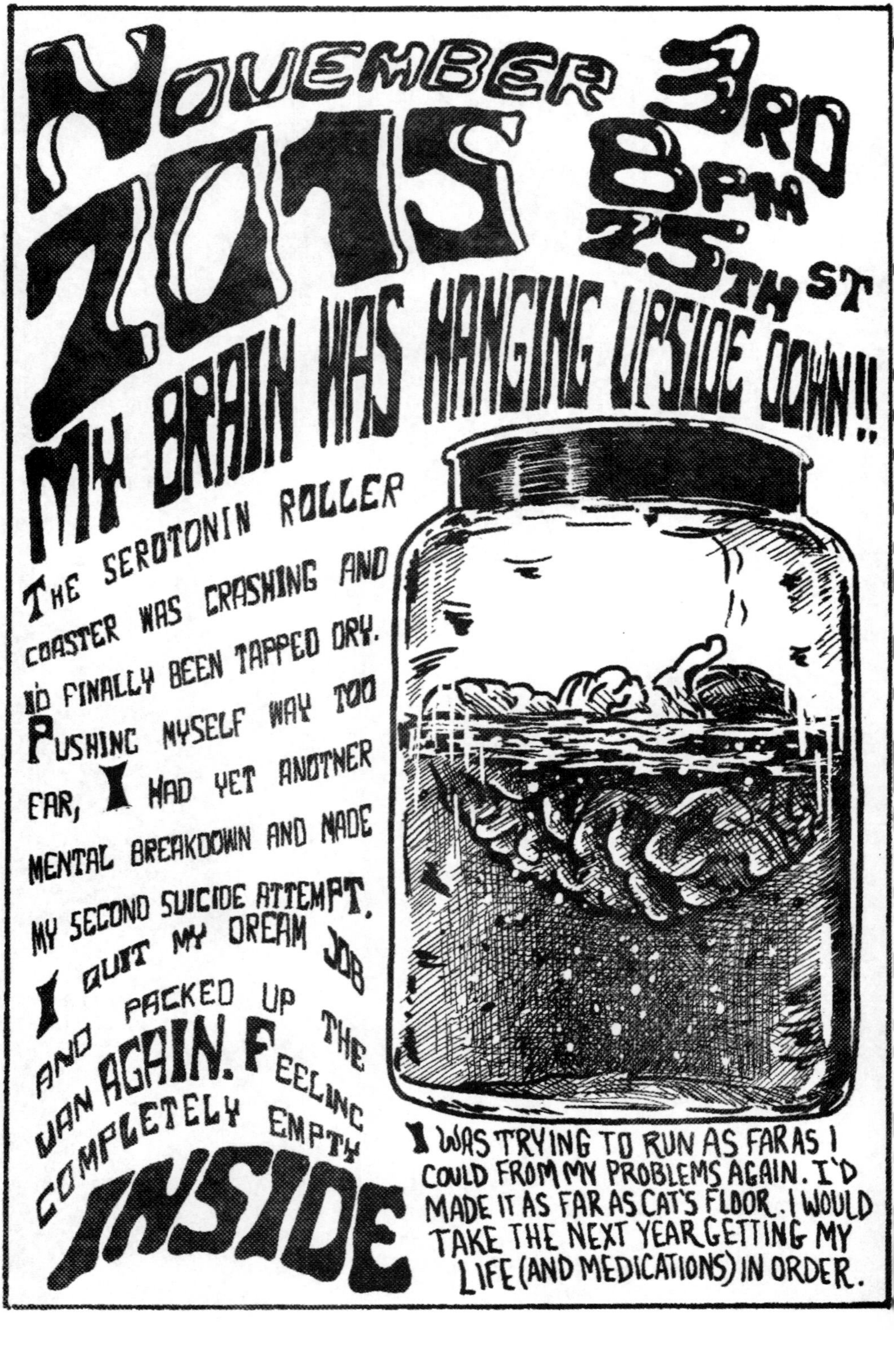
NOVEMBER 3RD 2015
8PM 25TH ST
MY BRAIN WAS HANGING UPSIDE DOWN!!
THE SEROTONIN ROLLER COASTER WAS CRASHING AND I'D FINALLY BEEN TAPPED DRY. PUSHING MYSELF WAY TOO FAR, I HAD YET ANOTHER MENTAL BREAKDOWN AND MADE MY SECOND SUICIDE ATTEMPT. I QUIT MY DREAM JOB AND PACKED UP THE VAN AGAIN. FEELING COMPLETELY EMPTY
INSIDE
I WAS TRYING TO RUN AS FAR AS I COULD FROM MY PROBLEMS AGAIN. I'D MADE IT AS FAR AS CAT'S FLOOR. I WOULD TAKE THE NEXT YEAR GETTING MY LIFE (AND MEDICATIONS) IN ORDER.

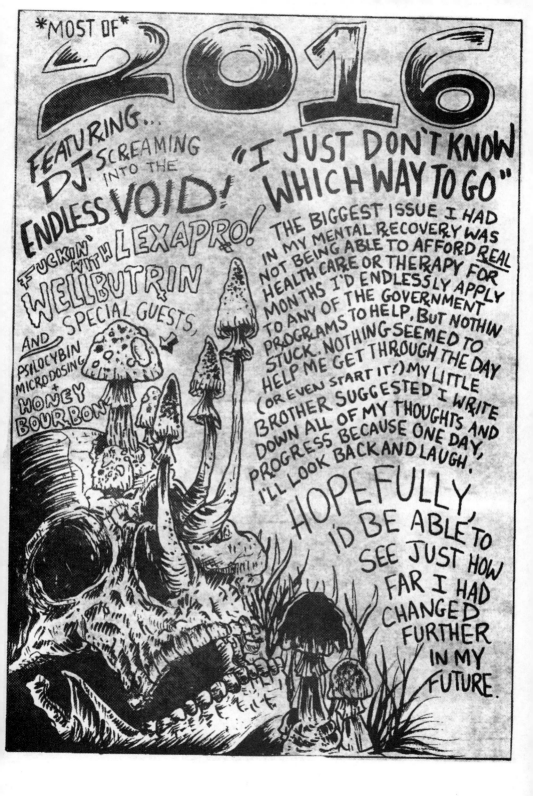

MOST OF 2016

FEATURING... DJ SCREAMING INTO THE ENDLESS VOID!

"I JUST DON'T KNOW WHICH WAY TO GO"

FUCKIN' WITH LEXAPRO! WELLBUTRIN AND SPECIAL GUESTS, PSILOCYBIN MICRODOSING + HONEY BOURBON

THE BIGGEST ISSUE I HAD IN MY MENTAL RECOVERY WAS NOT BEING ABLE TO AFFORD REAL HEALTH CARE OR THERAPY FOR MONTHS I'D ENDLESSLY APPLY TO ANY OF THE GOVERNMENT PROGRAMS TO HELP, BUT NOTHIN STUCK. NOTHING SEEMED TO HELP ME GET THROUGH THE DAY (OR EVEN START IT!) MY LITTLE BROTHER SUGGESTED I WRITE DOWN ALL OF MY THOUGHTS AND PROGRESS BECAUSE ONE DAY, I'LL LOOK BACK AND LAUGH.

HOPEFULLY, I'D BE ABLE TO SEE JUST HOW FAR I HAD CHANGED FURTHER IN MY FUTURE.

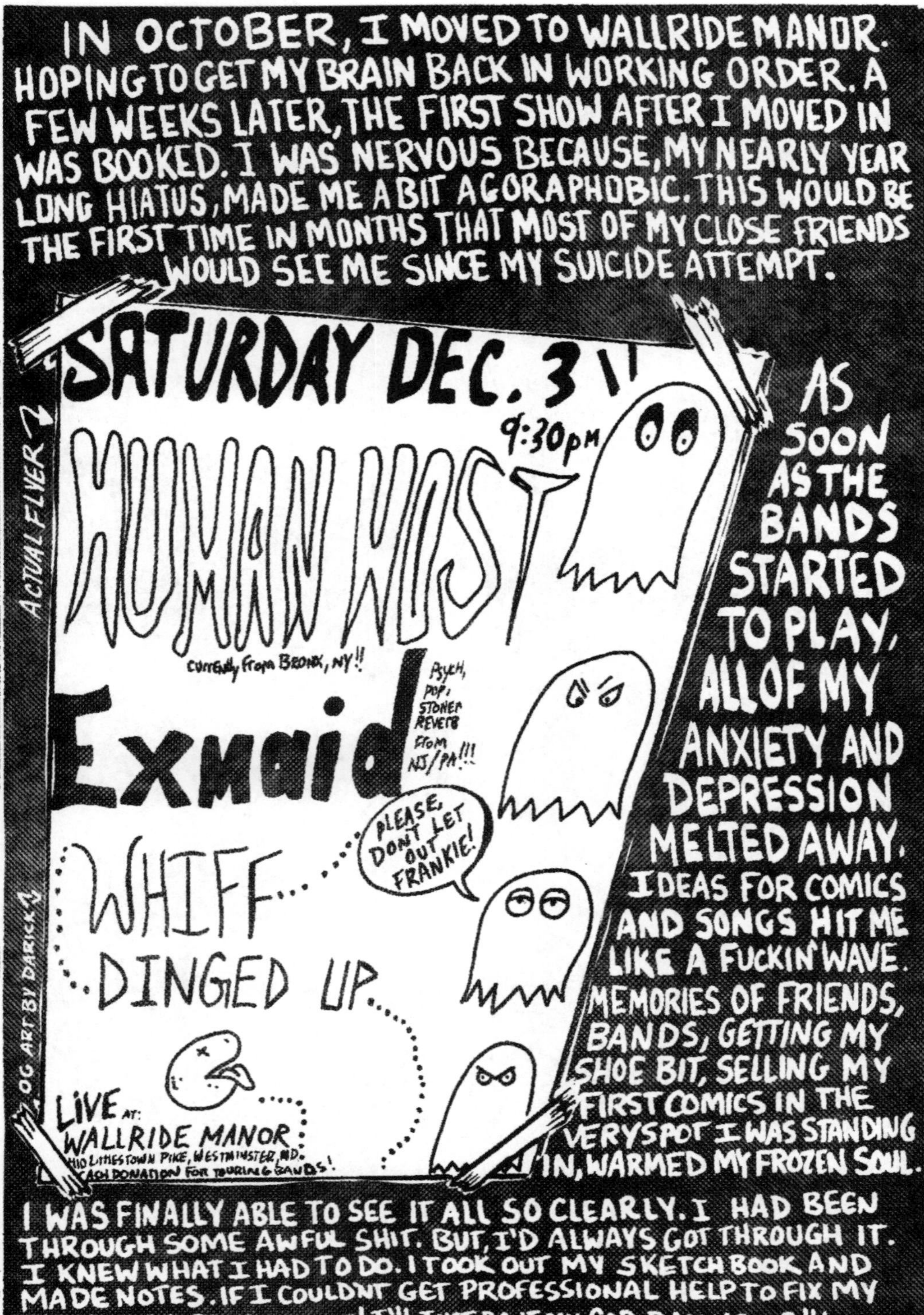
IN OCTOBER, I MOVED TO WALLRIDE MANOR. HOPING TO GET MY BRAIN BACK IN WORKING ORDER. A FEW WEEKS LATER, THE FIRST SHOW AFTER I MOVED IN WAS BOOKED. I WAS NERVOUS BECAUSE, MY NEARLY YEAR LONG HIATUS, MADE ME A BIT AGORAPHOBIC. THIS WOULD BE THE FIRST TIME IN MONTHS THAT MOST OF MY CLOSE FRIENDS WOULD SEE ME SINCE MY SUICIDE ATTEMPT.
ACTUAL FLYER
SATURDAY DEC. 3!!
9:30pm
HUMAN HOST
currently from BRONX, NY!!
Exmaid
Psych, pop, stoner reverb from NJ/PA!!!
WHIFF
DINGED UP
PLEASE, DON'T LET OUT FRANKIE!
LIVE AT: WALLRIDE MANOR
LITTLESTOWN PIKE, WESTMINSTER, MD.
CASH DONATION FOR TOURING BANDS!
OG ART BY DARICK
AS SOON AS THE BANDS STARTED TO PLAY, ALL OF MY ANXIETY AND DEPRESSION MELTED AWAY. IDEAS FOR COMICS AND SONGS HIT ME LIKE A FUCKIN' WAVE. MEMORIES OF FRIENDS, BANDS, GETTING MY SHOE BIT, SELLING MY FIRST COMICS IN THE VERY SPOT I WAS STANDING IN, WARMED MY FROZEN SOUL.
I WAS FINALLY ABLE TO SEE IT ALL SO CLEARLY. I HAD BEEN THROUGH SOME AWFUL SHIT. BUT, I'D ALWAYS GOT THROUGH IT. I KNEW WHAT I HAD TO DO. I TOOK OUT MY SKETCHBOOK AND MADE NOTES. IF I COULDN'T GET PROFESSIONAL HELP TO FIX MY HEAD, WELL THEN, FUCK IT! I'LL JUST DO IT MY GOD DAMN SELF!!!

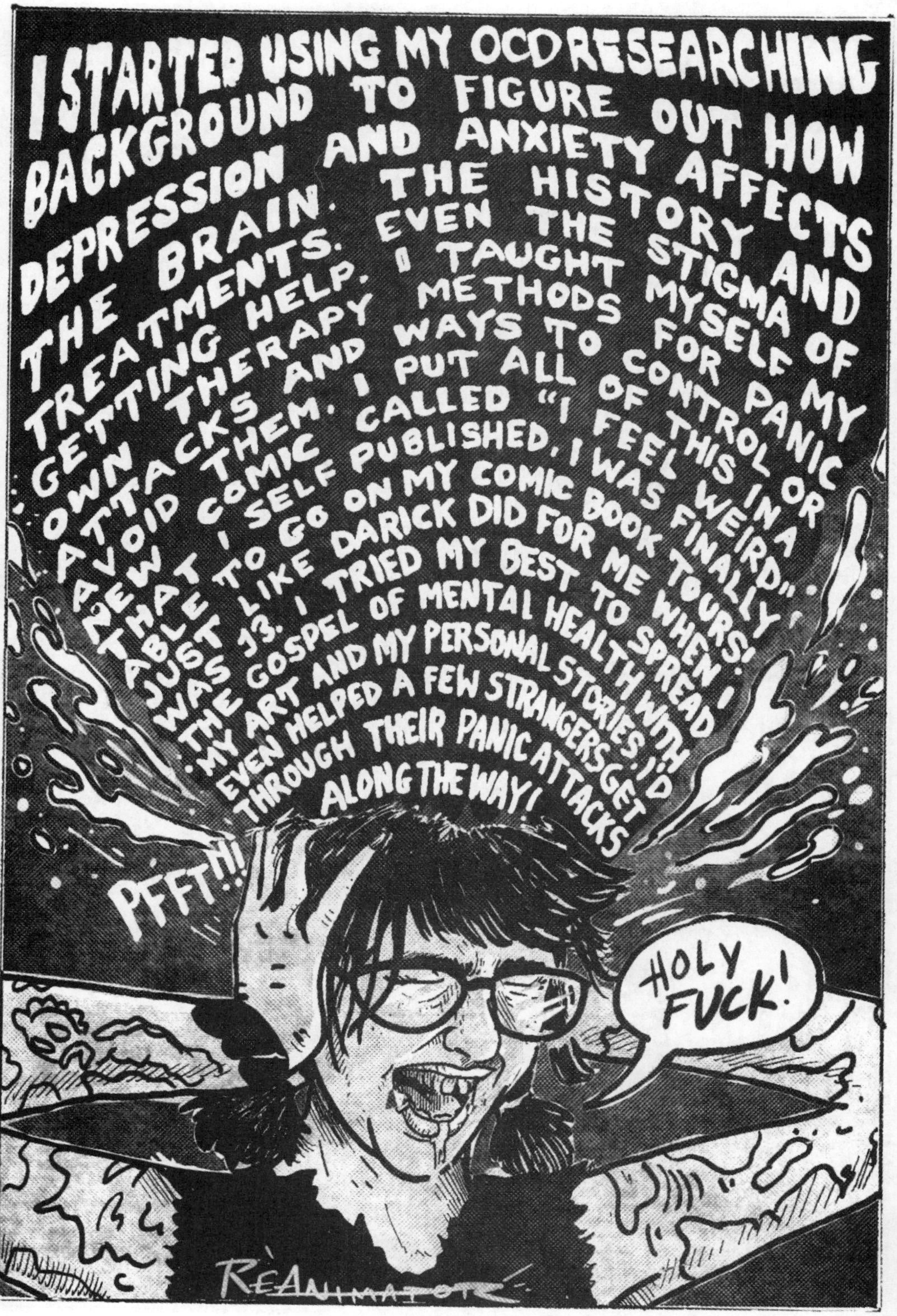
I STARTED USING MY OCD RESEARCHING BACKGROUND TO FIGURE OUT HOW DEPRESSION AND ANXIETY AFFECTS THE BRAIN. THE HISTORY AND TREATMENTS. EVEN THE STIGMA OF GETTING HELP. I TAUGHT MYSELF MY OWN THERAPY METHODS FOR PANIC ATTACKS AND WAYS TO CONTROL OR AVOID THEM. I PUT ALL OF THIS IN A NEW COMIC CALLED "I FEEL WEIRD" THAT I SELF PUBLISHED. I WAS FINALLY ABLE TO GO ON MY COMIC BOOK TOURS! JUST LIKE DARICK DID FOR ME WHEN I WAS 13. I TRIED MY BEST TO SPREAD THE GOSPEL OF MENTAL HEALTH WITH MY ART AND MY PERSONAL STORIES. I'D EVEN HELPED A FEW STRANGERS GET THROUGH THEIR PANIC ATTACKS ALONG THE WAY!
PFFTH!!
HOLY FUCK!
REANIMATOR

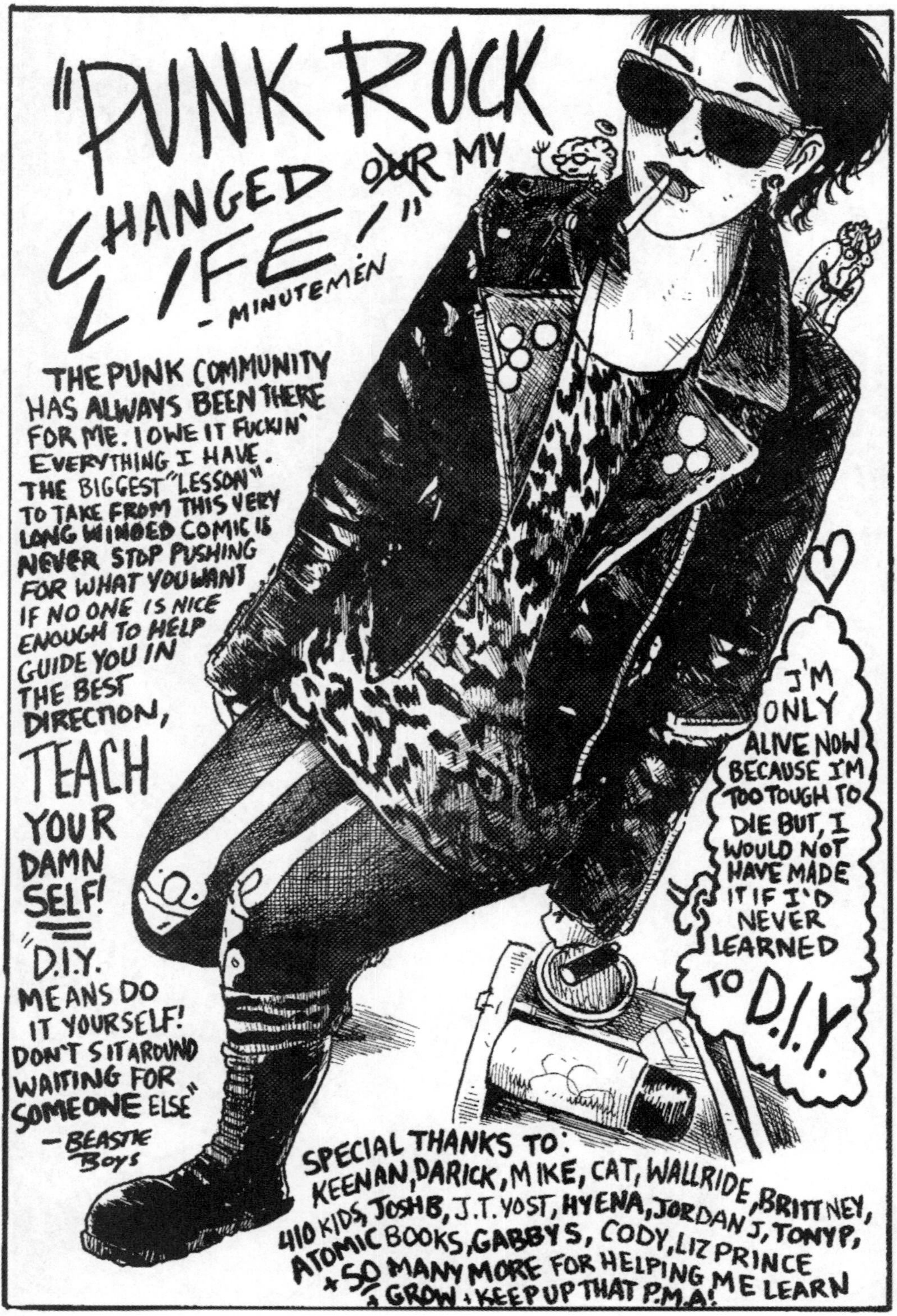
"PUNK ROCK CHANGED OUR MY LIFE!"
- MINUTEMEN
THE PUNK COMMUNITY HAS ALWAYS BEEN THERE FOR ME. I OWE IT FUCKIN' EVERYTHING I HAVE. THE BIGGEST "LESSON" TO TAKE FROM THIS VERY LONG WINDED COMIC IS NEVER STOP PUSHING FOR WHAT YOU WANT IF NO ONE IS NICE ENOUGH TO HELP GUIDE YOU IN THE BEST DIRECTION, TEACH YOUR DAMN SELF!
"D.I.Y. MEANS DO IT YOURSELF! DON'T SIT AROUND WAITING FOR SOMEONE ELSE"
- BEASTIE BOYS
I'M ONLY ALIVE NOW BECAUSE I'M TOO TOUGH TO DIE BUT, I WOULD NOT HAVE MADE IT IF I'D NEVER LEARNED TO D.I.Y.
SPECIAL THANKS TO: KEENAN, DARICK, MIKE, CAT, WALLRIDE, BRITTNEY, 410 KIDS, JOSH B, J.T. YOST, HYENA, JORDAN J, TONY P, ATOMIC BOOKS, GABBY S, CODY, LIZ PRINCE + SO MANY MORE FOR HELPING ME LEARN + GROW + KEEP UP THAT P.M.A.!

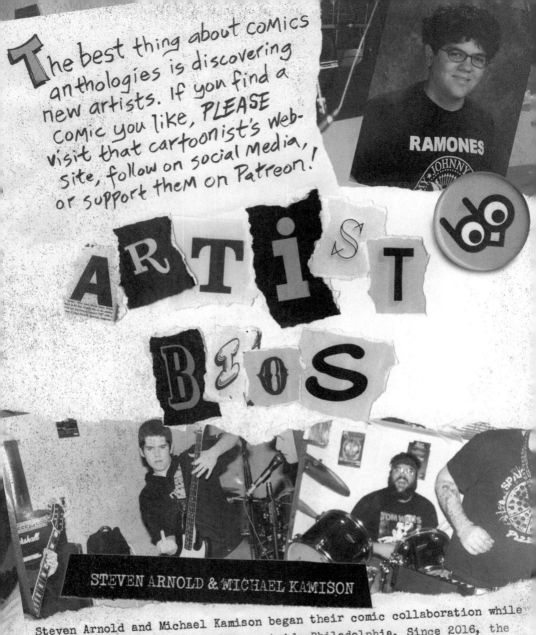

The best thing about comics anthologies is discovering new artists. If you find a comic you like, PLEASE visit that cartoonist's web-site, follow on social media, or support them on Patreon!

ARTIST BIOS

STEVEN ARNOLD & MICHAEL KAMISON

Steven Arnold and Michael Kamison began their comic collaboration while co-managing an arthouse theater outside Philadelphia. Since 2016, the dopey duo has published five comics under the moniker Heel on the Press Comics. Combining their useless knowledge of film, music, and art, Heel on the Press publishes comix with nods to body horror, American literature, and punk rock. Steven & Michael live in the swamps of South Philly and endlessly fawn over their dogs Penny, Zooey, and Sacco. Write them, please! They're begging you.

hotpresscomics@gmail.com

@hotpresscomics

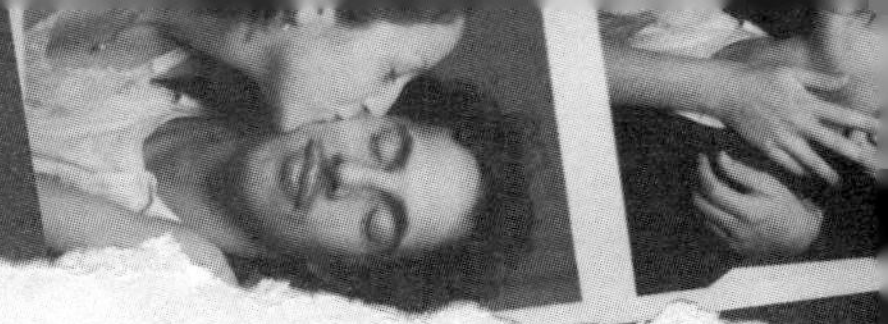

JOSH BAYER

Josh Bayer lives in Harlem and has worked as a graphic novelist, fine artist and illustrator for 20 years. Josh is the editor of the anthology Suspect Device and the author of Raw Power, RM, Black Star, Theth and its sequel Theth: Tomorrow Forever, an Ignatz award nominee for Outstanding Graphic Novel of 2020. Additionally, he is the editor and writer of All Time Comics imprint from Floating World Comics. He teaches extensively all over New York and on the internet. In 2021, he was nominated for a Distinguished Teaching Award at Parsons University. The best live show he ever saw was The Laughing Hyenas in Columbus, OH 1990.

joshbayer.com
@joshmbayer

GREGORY BENTON

Gregory Benton spent the late '80s to early '90s terrorizing eardrums from Boston to NYC playing guitar & kazoo in The Inflatable Children.

gregorybenton.com
@gregorybenton

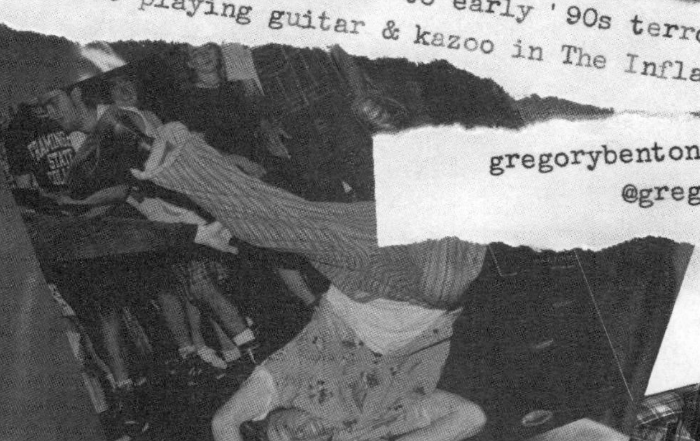

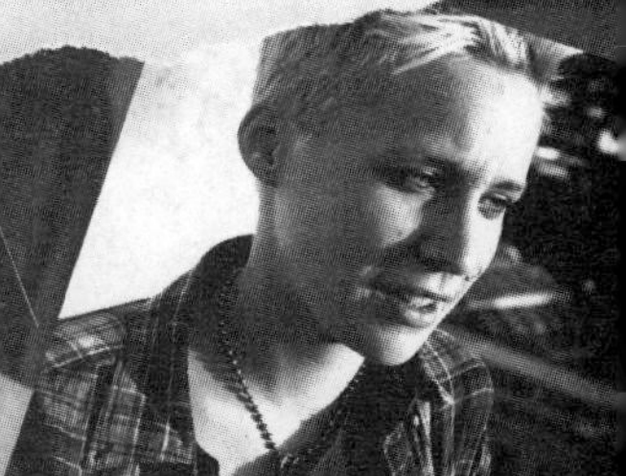

JANELLE BLARG

Janelle Blarg (otherwise known as Janelle Hessig) is a Bay Area writer and cartoonist. While other bad kids were making secret bongs in her high school arts & crafts class, she made her first punk fanzine, Tales of Blarg. That was one billion years ago (1990, if you're bad at math) and she's been creating comics, illustrations, and writing ever since

janelleblarg.com
PATREON: /Janelleblarg
@janelleblarg

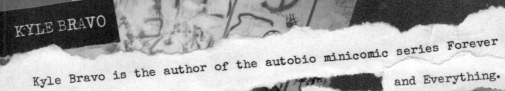

KYLE BRAVO

Kyle Bravo is the author of the autobio minicomic series Forever and Everything.

PATREON: /kylebravo
@kyle_bravo_
@KyleBravo

HALEIGH BUCK

Haleigh Buck is a 35-year-old poser/square goin' nowhere living mostly out her van somewhere between Baltimore and the Catoctin mountains with her dog/life coach, Professor Frankenstein. You might know her from her comic series I Feel Weird, a comic about anxiety and depressio or Herman the Hotdog *which she apologizes for*. She's also a tattoo artist, environmentalist, and a #1 fan of anything Wallride records distributes.

@haleighcouchsurfer

SOPHIE CRUMB

Born in Cali, 1981, moved to France in 1991. Sketchbooks, watercolors, illustrations, embroidering, tattooing and old music! Lives in the wood in France with kids and animals.

@sophcrumb

EMILY FLAKE

mily Flake is a cartoonist, writer, illustrator and performer living n Brooklyn, NY. Her work appears regularly in the New Yorker, McSweeney's, he Nib, and many other publications. She is the author, most recently, f That Was Awkward: The Art and Etiquette of the Awkward Hug and the proprietress of St. Nell's, a humor writing residence for ladies in Williamsport, PA. She grew up in the mid-90s central CT punk scene and has a stack of old flyers she'd love to show you.

emilyflake.com
@emilyflake
@eflakeagogo

CN "PINKY" FRANKENSTEIN

Born into this hellscape in 1967, Pinky Frankenstein was, and remains an observer. Pinky is an avatar that has learned to thrive in the strang limbo of the in-between, encompassing either/or-neither/nor-Black/White, Male/Female, Old/Young. And as such, is able to gain access to the disparate-experiences and speak truth to what has become us.

@pinkyfrankenstein

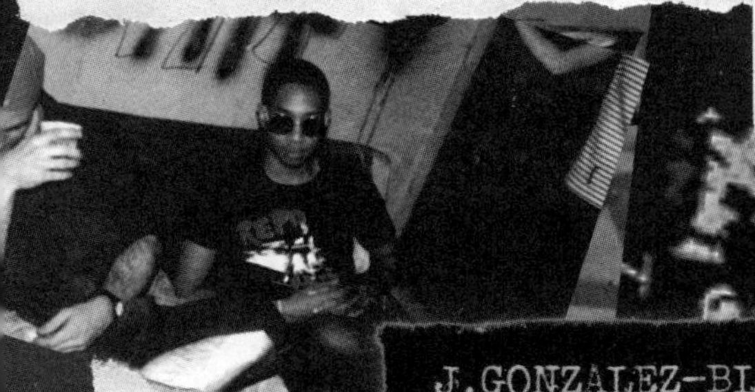

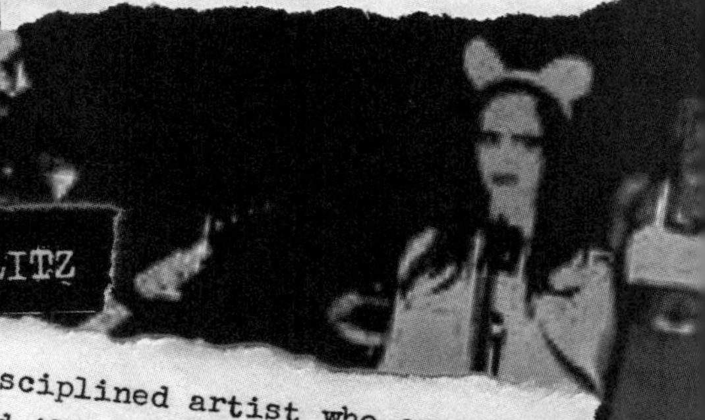

J. GONZALEZ-BLITZ

J. Gonzalez-Blitz is a multi-disciplined artist who creates paintings, drawings, comics and illustrations. She also does experimental music as part of Astral Knife, soundbeds for a new project called N. Alias, and for video shorts she makes. She is trying to teach herself violin. She practices butoh and incorporates it into her performances. J. was born in Hell's Kitchen, NYC to Cuban and Irish parents who grew up onthe same block. Diagnosed with schizo-affective disorder, she says it's her drummer husband, rats, knives, Bustelo and malta that keep her fired up to fight.

jgonzalezblitz.com

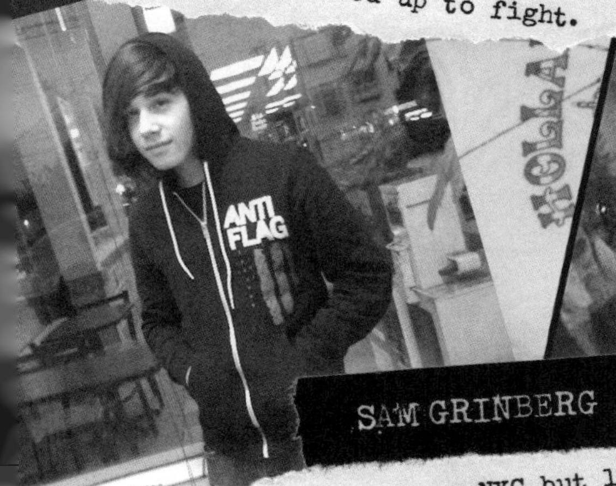
ANTI
FLAG

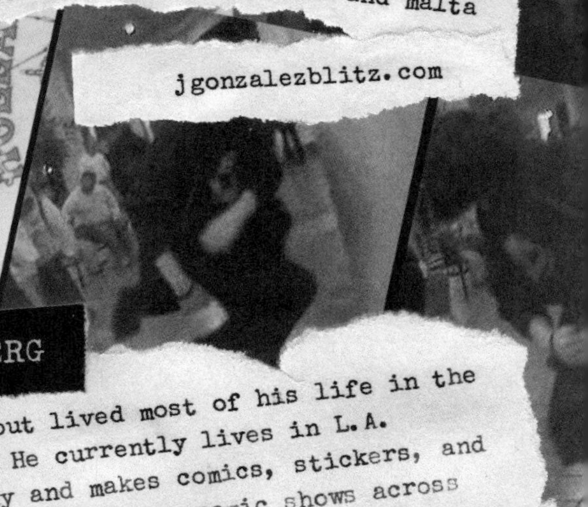

SAM GRINBERG

Sam Grinberg was born in NYC but lived most of his life in the woodsy suburbs of New Jersey. He currently lives in L.A. working on The Simpsons by day and makes comics, stickers, and band flyers by night. You can find him at comic shows across the country.

samgrinberg.com
@samgrinberg

HYENA HELL

Hyena Hell is a cartoonist, illustrator, and sometimes printmaker Her work also appears in books published by Silver Sprocket, Tinto Press, and her own DIY imprint Horror Vacui Press. She is best known as that person talking to themselves and rummaging aimlessly through a series of disheveled bags containing items of indiscern- ible purpose or value, who you avoid sitting next to on the train.

@hyenahell

DANNY HELLMAN

Danny Hellman's drawings have appeared in countless publications since 1988, including Time, the Village Voice, New York Press and SCREW Magazine. Hellman edited and published the critically acclaimed comics anthologies LEGAL ACTION COMICS Volumes 1 & 2, and TYPHON Volume 1. He lives in Brooklyn, NY with his wife and daughter.

dannyhellman.com
@dannyhellmanillustration

JOAKIMA HILLYARD

Joakima Hillyard (Jo) resides in Reno with Eddie the dog who is the amazing age of 17.

@its_my_life_studios

MIKE HUNCHBACK

Mike Hunchback is currently a guitar player in Screeching Weasel and Night Birds. He co-authored PULP MACABRE, a book containing the last decade's worth of art from weird fiction, pulp, and fanzine artist Lee Brown Coye, and is a current contributor to the relaunched Deep Red Magazine. Hunchback also co-produced the recent BOILED ANGELS: THE TRIAL OF MIKE DIANA, a feature documentary on the 1990s arrest and obscenity trial of comix artist Mike Diana.

JORDAN JEFFRIES

Jordan Jeffries is a cartoonist currently living in the Hudson Valley with his wife and their two cats. His books include The Complete Matinee Junkie, Complex Machines, So Young, and more.

jordanjeffries.com
@snackaddict

GIDEON KENDALL

Gideon Kendall is the Eisner-winning artist of Harvey Kurtzman's Marley's Ghost (ComiXology) and the Reuben Award-nominated MegaGhost (Albatross Funnybooks). He is also the creator of the sci-fi comic WHATZIT (Heavy Metal/Virus), and a member of the MAD Magazine gang of idiots, R.I.P. Gideon teaches drawing, illustration, and anatomy for artists at CUNY City Tech and SVA. He was also the lead singer in several bands you've never heard of, including Very Pleasant Neighbor, Fake Brain, Cooling Pies, and The Ditty Committee.

gideon.kendall.com
@gideonkendall

VICTOR KERLOW

Victor Kerlow is a commercial artist, hobby cartoonist, professor at The School of Visual Arts, and generally a pretty cool guy.

victorkerlow.com
@victorkerlow

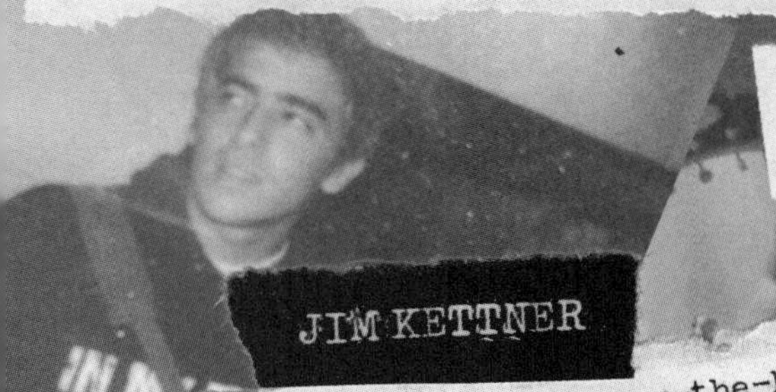

JIM KETTNER

Jim Kettner is just another over-the-hill hardcore kid witnessing the collapse of the environment and late-stage capitalism. He also makes comics about his messy life in these messy times and teaches for the MFA is Comics program at California College of the Arts. He lives and works in a van down by the river with his doggo/muppet Tortellini.

kettnerd.com
@xkettnerdx

AYTI KRALI

Ayti Krali spent a good bit of the early 90s as a roadie for Four Walls Falling and later screamed his head off in Ipecac (RVA). He has worked as a gardener for 15 years and has made comics off and on for 30 years. I'm honored to share book space with these talented folks.

@aytikrali

KARL CHRISTIAN KRUMPHOLZ

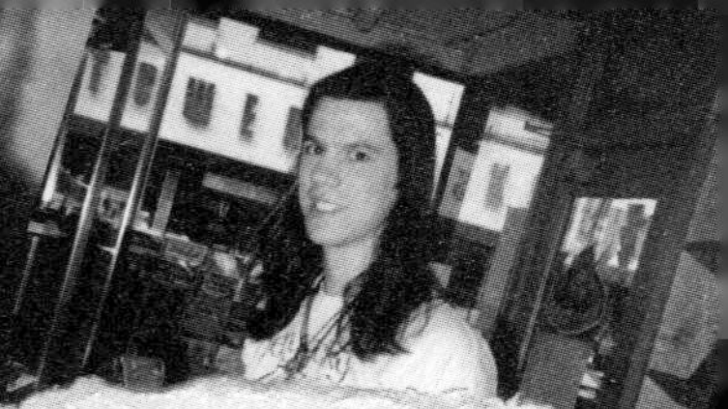

Originally from a city on the East Coast, Karl's work has appeared in many different formats, publications, and even animated in a documentary. He is currently working on several projects including the daily autobiographical comic The Lighthouse in The City since January 2020; Queen City, a collection of architectural illustrations, comics, and history from around Denver, CO from Tinto Press; and the continuing series of short stories and slice of life comics set in The City: 30 Miles of Crazy! Karl continues to live in a City, though a different one now, and he still thinks Nomeansno's 'Live + Cuddly' is one of the best live albums ever made.

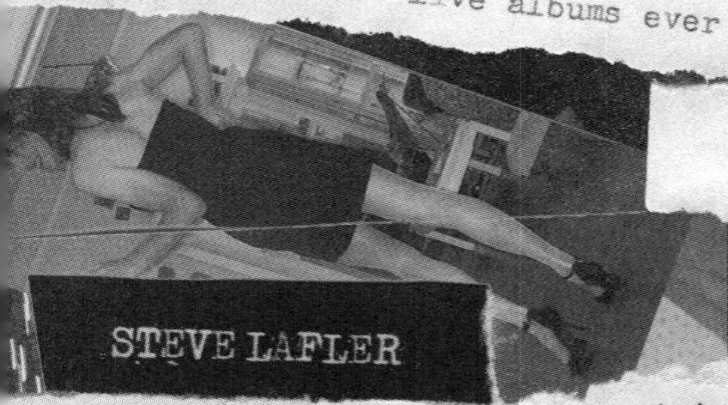

karlchristiankrumpholz.com
@karlchristiankrumpholz

STEVE LAFLER

Steve Lafler has maintained his status as a loose cannon on the deck of Alt/Underground movement of comics for decades.

Ever the maverick marching to his own beat, Lafler enjoyed long runs of his improvised Dog Boy comic books as well as the jaunty, unhinged Buzzard anthology. From there the self-styled maestro settled into the BugHouse trilogy of graphic novels, a history of Bebop jazz realized with an all-insect cast.

Subsequently, the artist decamped to Ozxaca, Mexico with his family for a decade. There, he started a country punk band, "Radio Insecto", with Nacho Desorden, the legendary bass player for Mexico City's

stevelafler.com
@stevelafler

WILL LAREN

ll Laren is an artist and printmaker living and working in Philadelphia ince graduating from MICA in 2012 with a degree in Illustration Will has ad his work featured on skateboards, album covers, and card games. His omics have been published on the websites of Vice UK and Adult Swim. He as been a member of the Philadelphia art collective Space 1026 for the ast 9 years.

@willlaren

BROTHER MALCOLM

Brother Malcolm lives and works on the Gulf Coast of Florida, drawing cartoons to amuse his wife, daughter and two cats. When the dream of becoming a pop-punk superstar died after high school, Brother Malcolm became a Florida State Park Ranger. Help Turtles Cross!

@1989am.comix

LYNNE MARGEAUX

Lynne Margeaux is a fine artist and illustrator who has endeavored to convey the beauty and magic of the natural world since 2007. Be it animal or in this case, plant.

lynnemargeaux.com
@lynnemargeaux

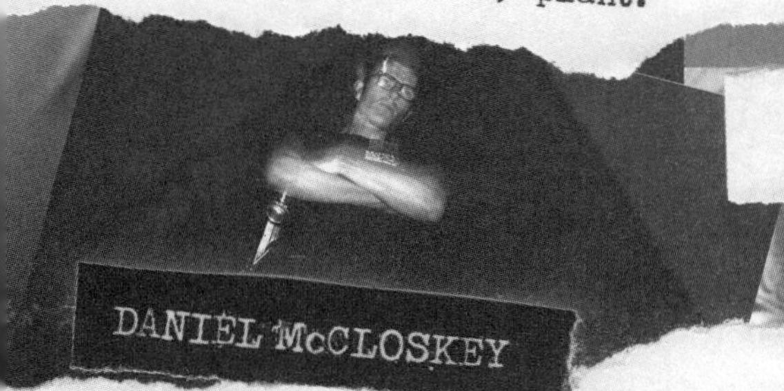

DANIEL McCLOSKEY

Daniel McCloskey has traveled all over the U.S. drawing comics. He currently lives in Oakland, CA. You can get some of his first comics ever by joining the email list on his website.

danielmccloskey.com
@beancandan

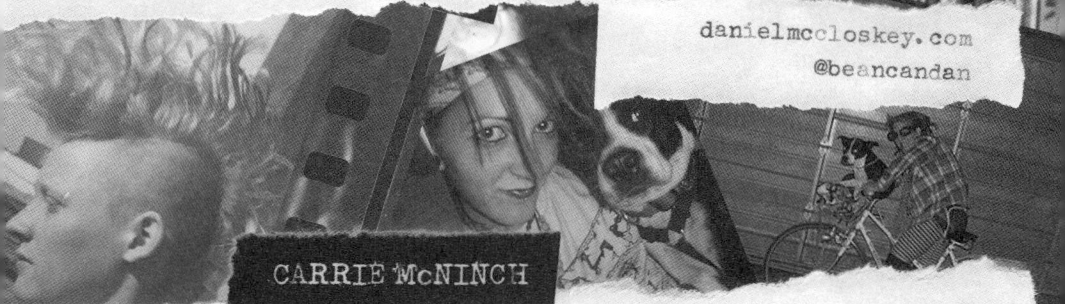

CARRIE McNINCH

Carrie McNinch hangs out with a lot of cats and dogs and does a diary comic called You Don't Get There From Here.

PATREON: /carriemcninch

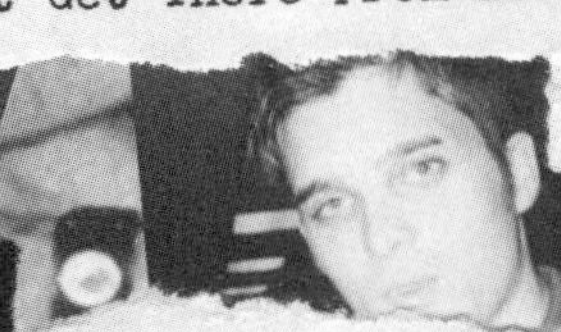

ADAM MEUSE

Adam Meuse is the author of the mini comic Sad Animals among others. In 2017 Birdcage Bottom Books released a collection of his post-Trump election sketchbook pages. He lives in Raleigh, NC with his wife and daughters and some animals.

meusetrap.etsy.com
@meusetrap

ROBB MIRSKY

Robb Mirsky is a cartoonist in Toronto, Canada. He spends his days parenting his two small kids and spends his nights drawing weirdo comics and illustrations. Robb has been self-publishing comics for the better part of two decades. He grew up on a steady diet of newspaper strips, Rat Fink and Looney Tunes, which have then informed his creative path since. Currently, Robb has been bouncing back and forth between his ongoing comic about a sludge-monster with a heart of gold (Sludgy), and his 1930s oddball comic strip (Dingus & Dum-Dum) making work inspired by his different loves of the medium. He also runs a small t-shirt company with his wife called 'My Moving Parts'.

robbmirsky.com
mymovingparts.com
@mirsktoons

EVA MULLER

Eva Muller is an old punk who studied illustraion at the HAW in Hamburg, Germany. She has dedicated her artistic life to drawing comics. Eva's comics and graphic novels have been published in magazines, newspapers and anthologies worldwide.

evamueller.org
@evazeichnet

FRED NOLAND

Fred Noland is an Oakland-based artist. In his civilian life he bikes and teaches his son the important things - be a good person and always listen to your mother and The Ramones. Drawn & Quarterly will release his biography about champion Black cyclist Major Taylor in 2023.

frednoland.com
@frednoland

ANDREA PEARSON

Andrea Pearson is a comics artist from Chicago, IL. She writes and draws an autobiographical comic zine series titled No Pants Revolution.

@saturn2169

JOSH PM

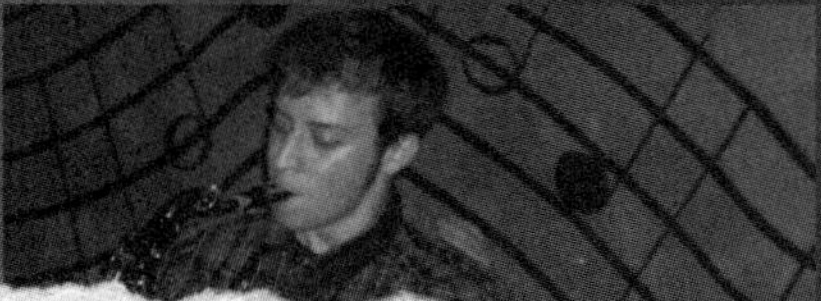

Josh PM is a hectic ska fiend picking it up in San Francisco, CA. They make music about good butts, art about cool stuff, and do their best to help keep the gears running at Silver Sprocket!

joshpmfrees.com
@joshpm

JOHN PORCELLINO

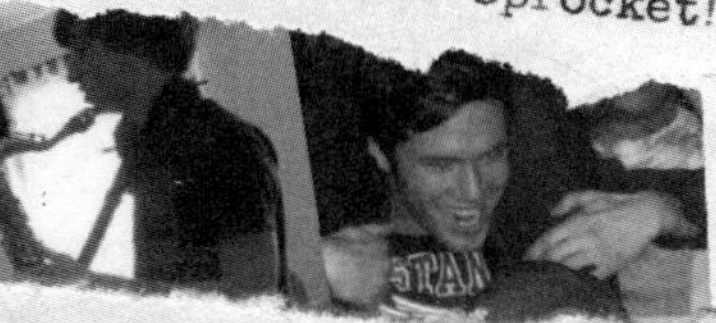

John Porcellino has been self-publishing his zine, King-Cat Comics, since 1989.

HALEY SIMONE POTTER

Haley Simone is an illustrator from New Jersey. her work revolves around music, often including gig posters, merch, and her specialty - live performance drawing. She graduated from Pratt Institute in 2017 and has been drawing Jersey music ever since.

haleydrawsmusic.com
@haleydrawsmusic

LIZ PRINCE

Liz Prince was on the cover of MRR and a few issues later they ceased publication. Coincidence? Wethinks not.

lizprincecomics.com
@lizprincecomics
@comicnrrd

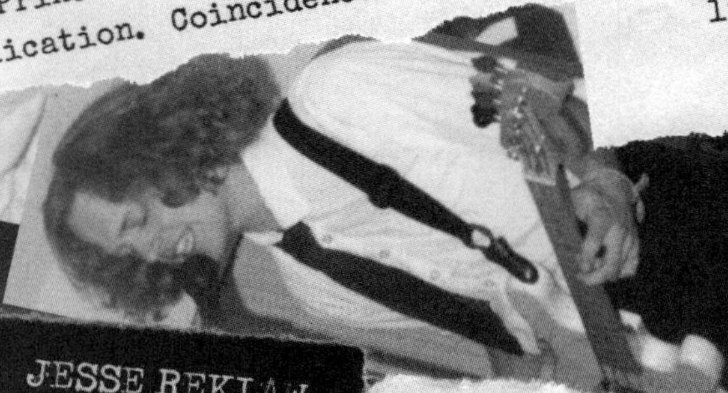

JESSE REKLAW

Jesse began drawing comics during the DIY frenzy of the late '80s and '90s and has designed and self-published over 75 books, comics and zines. His (non-self-)published books include Dreamtoons (Shambhala, 2000), Applicant (Microcosm, 2006), The Night of Your Life (Dark Horse Books, 2008), Couch Tag (Fantagraphics Books, 2012), and LOVF (Fantagraphics Books, 2016).

jessereklaw.com

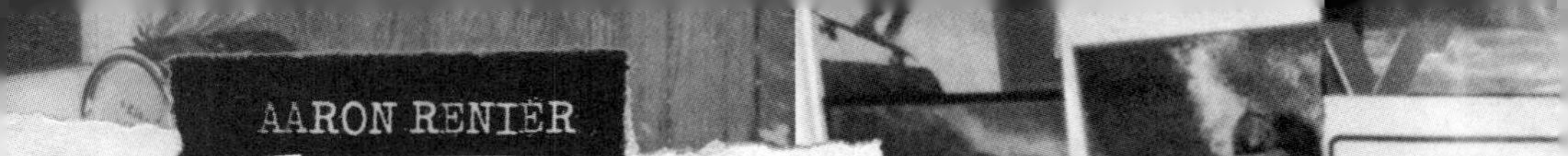

AARON RENIER

Aaron Renier has created three graphic novels for younger readers: Spiral-Bound, The Unsinkable Walker Bean and the sequel The Unsinkable Walker Bean and the Knights of the Waxing Moon. He also illustrates picture books and teaches drawing and comics. He started the online collaborative comic project infinitecorpse.com (contribute if you haven't!) with his art collective Trubble Club and has a periodically updated comic on Instagram called @unchained_melanie.

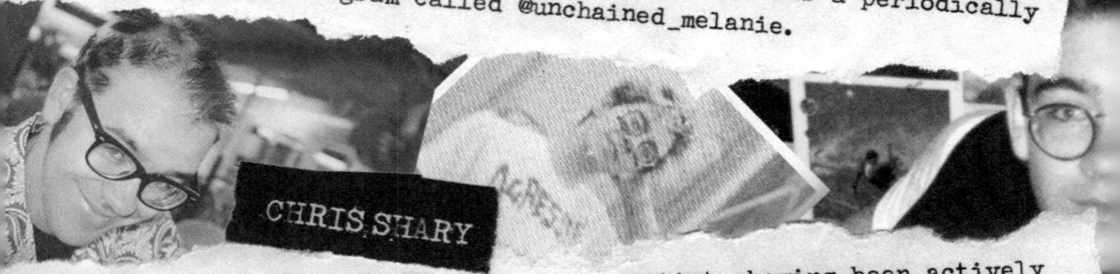

CHRIS SHARY

Chris Shary is a world-renowned punk rock artist, having been actively involved since the late '80s. Chris began as a teenager designing shirts for The Stupids, Hard-Ons, Libido Boys, and eventually Chemical People, Big Drill Car and ALL. In 2011, Chris' idea for DESCENDENTS fake ugly Christmas sweater kicked off a genuine craze which has, oddly, continued to gain momentum. His Sharpie sketches have graced the covers of records as well as the movie poster for Descendents' FILMAGE documentary. While Chris is primarily known for his work with DESCENDENTS/ALL, he has worked with Rancid, NOFX, FLAG, The Damned, TSOL, Channel 3, The Dickies, Agent Orange, Cock Sparrer, BLINK-182, Good Riddance, Turbonegro, Lagwagon, 7SECONDS, Masked Intruder, Night Birds, Teenage Bottlerocket, Bad Cop Bad Cop, The Muffs, Adolescents, Gorilla Biscuits, The Aquabats, The Interrupters, PEARS...you get the idea. Chris is also a high school drama teacher in Northern California where he lives with his amazingly talented artist wife Lori Herbst & his eighteen-year-old son Sam.

@chrisshary

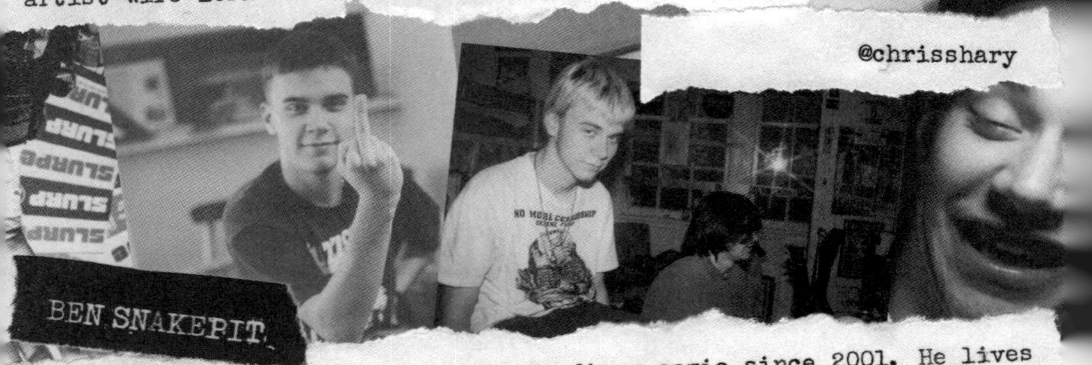

BEN SNAKEPIT

Ben Snakepit has been drawing a daily diary comic since 2001. He lives in San Francisco with his wife and their dog.

bensnakepit.com

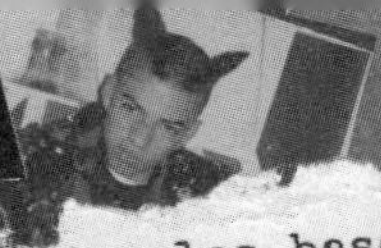

JAMES SPOONER

James Spooner is a Los Angeles based tattoo artist, illustrator, and
filmmaker. He directed the seminal documentary AFRO-PUNK which enjoyed
its premieres at both national & international film festivals, including
Toronto International and The American Black Film Festival, and garnered
various awards. James is also the co-founder of the Afropunk Festival
which now boasts attendance in the hundreds of thousands but parted ways
with the company due to ideological differences.

Spooner is also a contributor to RazorCake Punk Magazine. His graphic
memoir The HIGH DESERT willbbe published by Houghton Mifflin Harcourt
in spring 2022.

spoonersnofun.com
@spoonersnofun
@monocletattoo

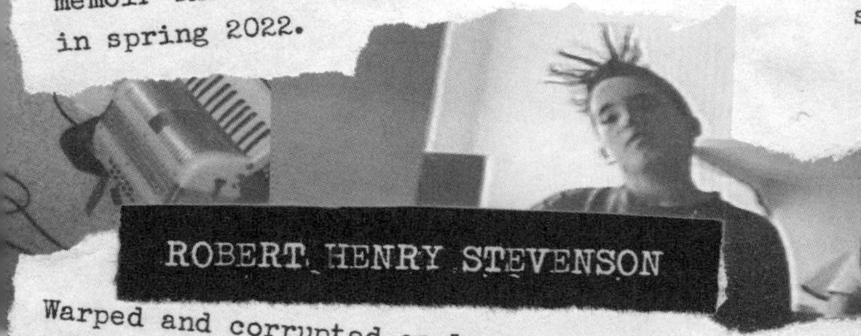

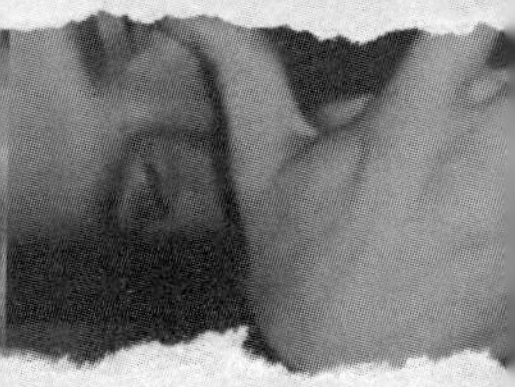

ROBERT HENRY STEVENSON

Warped and corrupted early in life by a multitude of destructive forces
growing from rebel mutations like the punk/industrial phase of the 1980
in Chicago, RHS continues to absorb and contribute to a variety of polluted & delinquent arts in a professional and craftsman-like manner.
Currently working on a sci-fi comic and a collection of illustrated
rhymes & creatures.

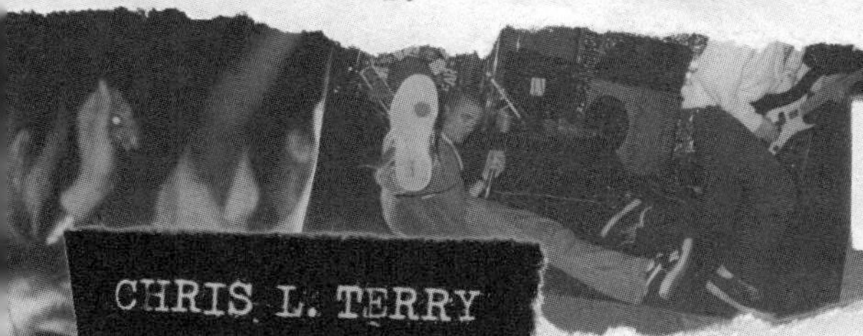

simpleheady.com
@simpleheady

CHRIS L. TERRY

Chris L. Terry is the author of the novel Black Card, about a mixed-race
punk bassist with a black imaginary friend. NPR called Black Card,
"hilariously searing" and listed it as one of the best books of 2019.
Terry's debut novel Zero Fade was on Best of 2013 lists by Slate and
Kirkus Reviews, who called it, "Original, hilarious, thought-provoking,
and wicked smart...not to be missed" in a starred review.

Terry was born in 1979 to a black father and white mother. He lives in
Los Angeles, where he teaches creative writing and works as a screen-
writer. His work has appeared in Razorcake, Very Smart Brothas/The Root
Stereogum, theLAnd, Apogee, Best Small Fictions 2015, PANK, and more.

@chrislterry

STEVE THUESON

Steve Thueson is a cartoonist from Salt Lake City living in Philadelphia.
Their favorite restaurant is Subway.

stevethueson.com
@steve_thueson

LANCE WARD

Lance Ward is an award-winning cartoonist and the author of over 40 books
including Blood and Drugs and the Flop Sweat series from Birdcage Bottom
Books.

tatertotdiaperman.wordpress.com
@lanceward1328

ADAM YEATER

Adam Yeater was a grindcore singer many years ago. Now he is an artist
and self-publisher. He is infamous for his underground comic strip called
One Last Day. Adam is also the creator and publisher of the World of Knom
series. He is currently working on his extreme horror comic book series
called Blood Desert.

onelastday.storenvy.com
blooddesert.bigcartel.com
@blooddesertcomix

J.T. YOST

J.T. Yost founded the Birdcage Bottom Books comics press & distro in
2008 thanks to a Xeric grant. He has edited four anthologies including
DIGESTATE: A Food & Eating Themed Anthology, CRINGE: An Anthology of
Embarrassment, BOTTOMS UP: True Tales of Hitting Rock-Bottom and the
one you're currently reading. His work has most recently appeared in
AMERICAN CULT and WILLIE NELSON: A Graphic History.

jtyost.com
birdcagebottombooks.com
@birdcage_bottom_books